W9-DAT-985

DAN DIDIO Senior VP-Executive Editor | MICHAEL MARTS Editor-original series | JEANINE SCHAEFER Associate Editor-original series
BOB HARRAS Editor-collected edition | ROBBIN BROSTERMAN Senior Art Director | PAUL LEVITZ President & Publisher
GEORG BREWER VP-Design & DC Direct Creative | RICHARD BRUNING Senior VP-Creative Director | PATRICK CALDON Executive VP-Finance & Operations
CHRIS CARAMALIS VP-Finance | JOHN CUNNINGHAM VP-Marketing | TERRI CUNNINGHAM VP-Managing Editor
ALISON GILL VP-Manufacturing | DAVID HYDE VP-Publicity | HANK KANALZ VP-General Manager, WildStorm
JIM LEE Editorial Director, WildStorm | PAULA LOWITT Senior VP-Business & Legal Affairs | MARYELLEN MCLAUGHLIN VP-Advertising & Custom Publishing
JOHN NEE Senior VP-Business Development | GREGORY NOVECK Senior VP-Creative Affairs | SUE POHJA VP-Book Trade Sales
STEVE ROTTERDAM Senior VP-Sales & Marketing | CHERYL RUBIN Senior VP-Brand Management
JEFF TROJAN VP-Business Development, DC Direct | BOB WAYNE VP-Sales

Cover by Andy Kubert. Cover colored by Laura Martin. Publication design by Amelia Grohman.

BATMAN: THE RESURRECTION OF RA'S AL GHUL
Published by DC Comics. Cover, text and compilation Copyright © 2008 DC Comics. All Rights Reserved.
Originally published in single magazine form in BATMAN ANNUAL 26, ROBIN ANNUAL 7, BATMAN 670-671, ROBIN 168-169,
NIGHTWING 138-139, DETECTIVE COMICS 838-839 Copyright © 2007, 2008 DC Comics. All Rights Reserved.
All characters, their distinctive likenesses and related elements featured in this publication are trademarks
of DC Comics. The stories, characters and incidents featured in this publication are entirely fictional.
DC Comics does not read or accept unsolicited submissions of ideas, stories or artwork.

DC Comics, 1700 Broadway, New York, NY 10019 | A Warner Bros. Entertainment Company
Printed in USA. First Printing. HC ISBN: 978-1-4012-1785-3 SC ISBN: 978-1-4012-2032-7

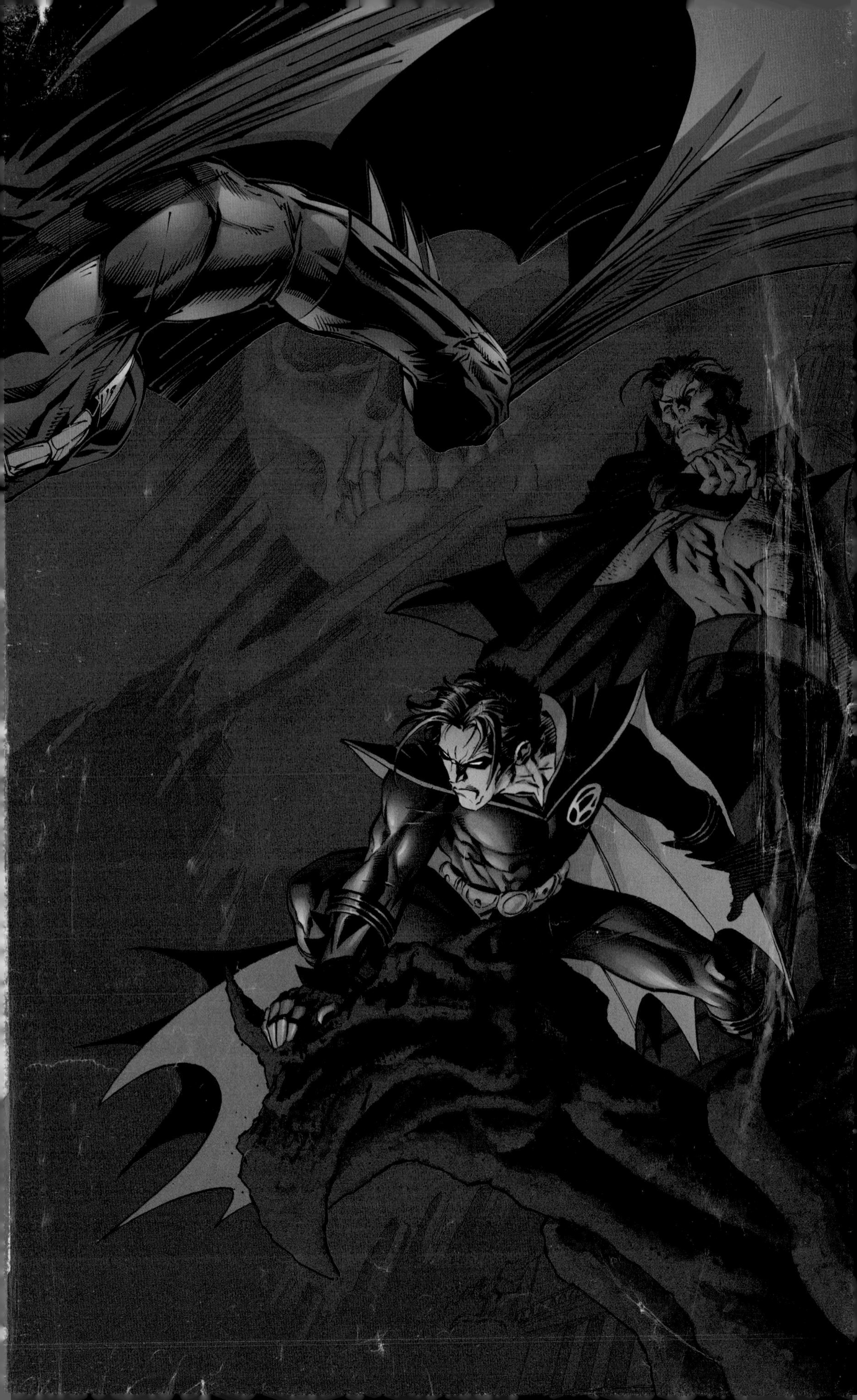

B A T M A N

THE RESURRECTION OF RA'S AL GHUL

**Paul Dini   Grant Morrison   Peter Milligan
Fabian Nicieza   Keith Champagne**
Writers

**David López   Jason Pearson   Tony S. Daniel
Freddie E. Williams II   Don Kramer** with **Carlos Rodriguez
Ryan Benjamin   David Baldeón**
Pencillers

Álvaro López   Jonathan Glapion   Wayne Faucher with **Bit
Saleem Crawford   Steve Bird**
Inkers

**Phil Balsman   John J. Hill   Travis Lanham
Steve Wands**
Letterers

Trish Mulvihill   Guy Major   Studio F   John Kalisz
Colorists

BATMAN created by **Bob Kane**

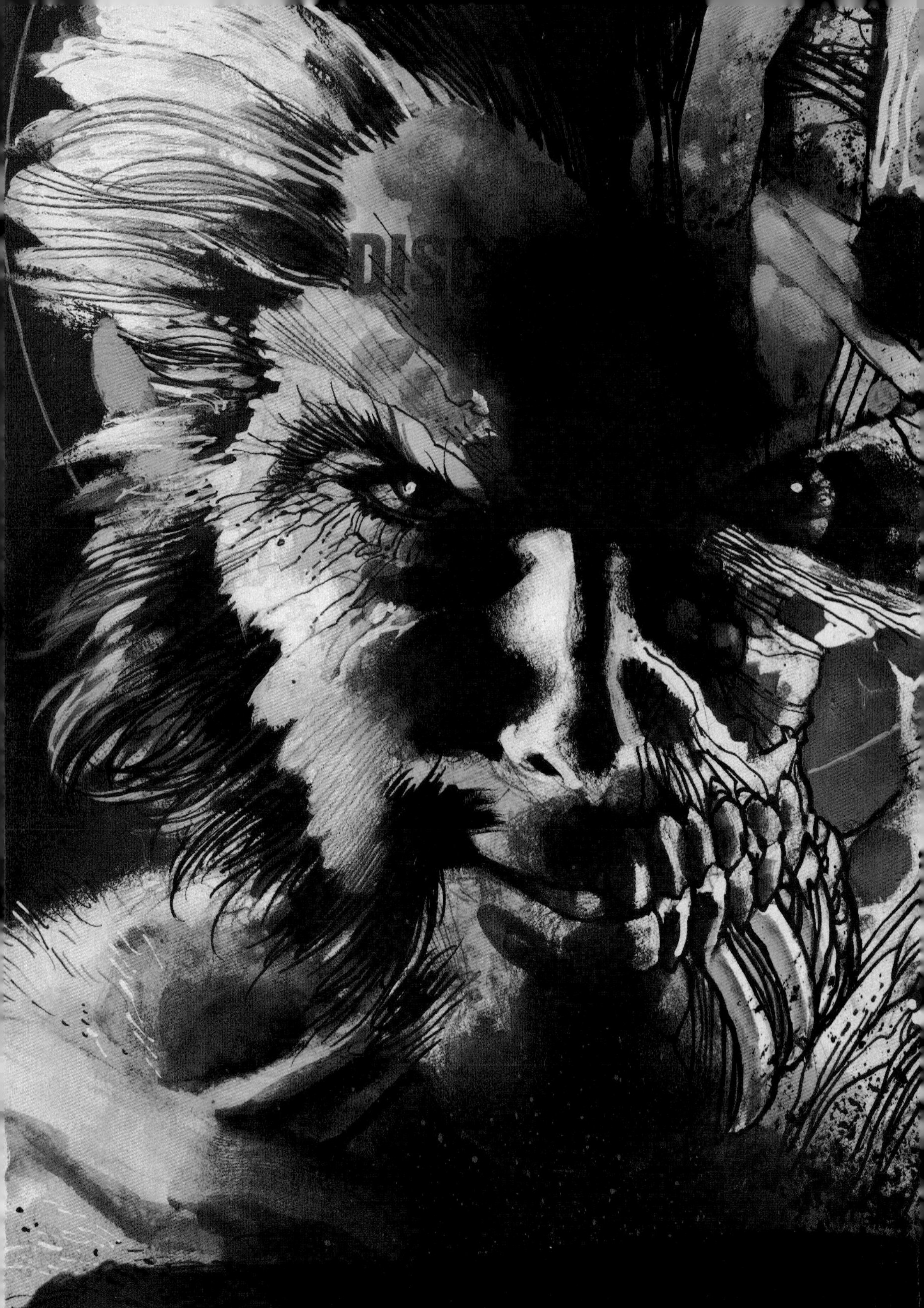

B A T M A N

THE RESURRECTION OF RA'S AL GHUL

B A T M A N

After his parents were gunned down before his eyes, young Bruce Wayne vowed to protect the innocents of Gotham City. Traveling the world, Bruce trained his mind and body to the peak of human perfection before returning home to become a fearsome creature of the night – the Batman.

N I G H T W I N G

Dick Grayson watched as his circus aerialist parents plummeted to their deaths in a mob hit. The young orphan was taken in by Bruce Wayne and became Robin, the Boy Wonder, fighting crime alongside the Dark Knight detective. Now an adult, the acrobatic hero currently patrols the streets of New York as Nightwing.

R O B I N

Tim Drake grew up fascinated by the life of a circus acrobat named Dick Grayson. His curiosity led to linking Grayson to Robin and discovering the secret identity of Batman. Although resistant at first, the Dark Knight eventually took Tim under his wing and trained him to become the new Robin.

RA'S AL GHUL

His real name has been lost to time; the near-immortal believed human civilization would thrive only if its population was drastically culled. After centuries of social machinations, the "Demon's Head" met his match in the Batman – and his own twisted family dynamics. He was prevented from bathing in his life-restoring Lazarus Pit and his body was destroyed. Ra's al Ghul is finally dead… or is he…?

TALIA

Daughter of Ra's al Ghul, Talia is both a brilliant businesswoman and physical force to be reckoned with. She has been at odds with her father as often as she has schemed alongside him. Currently, Talia operates the League of Assassins and seeks to protect her young son from both *her* father and *his* father.

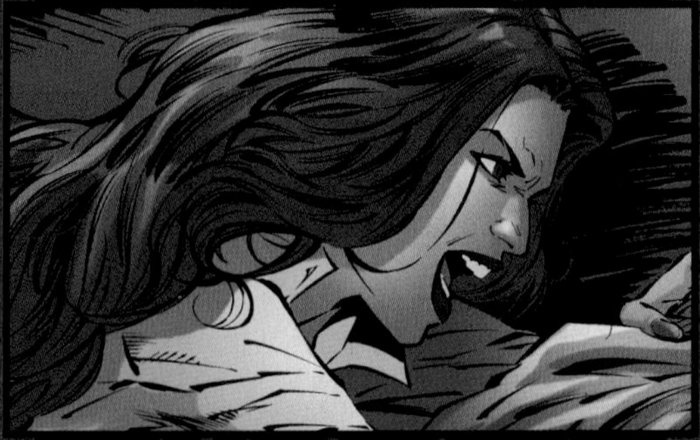

DAMIAN

Conceived after a brief liaison between the Batman and Talia, Daughter of the Demon, the young Damian was raised in secret. The boy is socially maladjusted and perpetually irritating. Questions abound regarding the true nature of his birth and upbringing, leaving Damian an unfortunate pawn in the games of very powerful people.

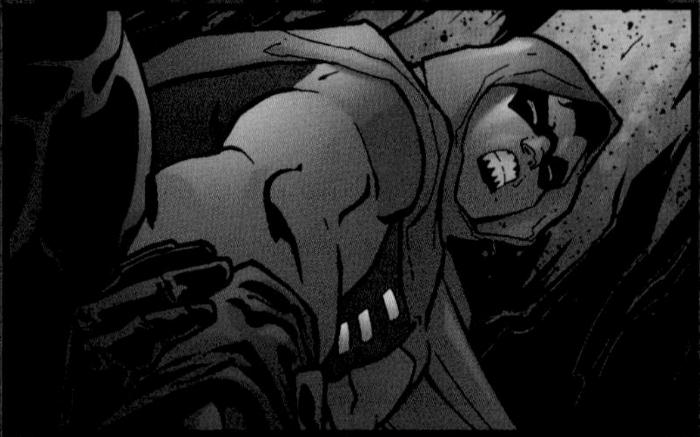

SENSEI

He is an implacable assassin, rumored to have killed for profit or honor over many centuries. No one knows the old man's name, only that he is the world's preeminent master of martial arts. To Sensei, killing is more than art, it is his reason for being. Currently, he is using the elite assassins of the Seven Men of Death to investigate rumors of al Ghul's return.

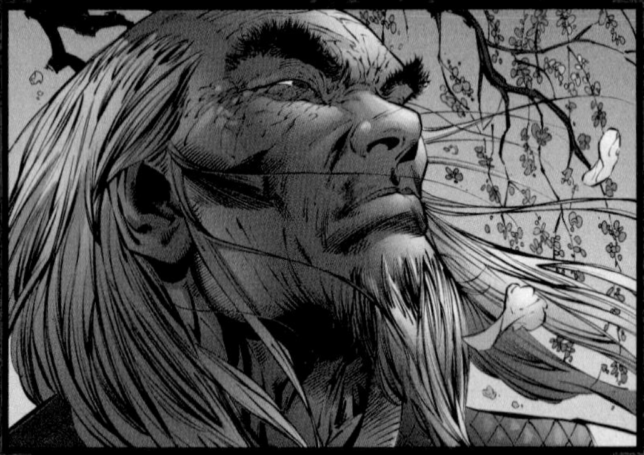

WHITE GHOST

Devoted servant to Ra's al Ghul, the albino has long kept to the shadows of his master's organization, content to write the Demon Head's historical narrative. Now, he has been granted an unprecedented honor – to prepare for his master's resurrection. He will serve, no matter the personal cost…

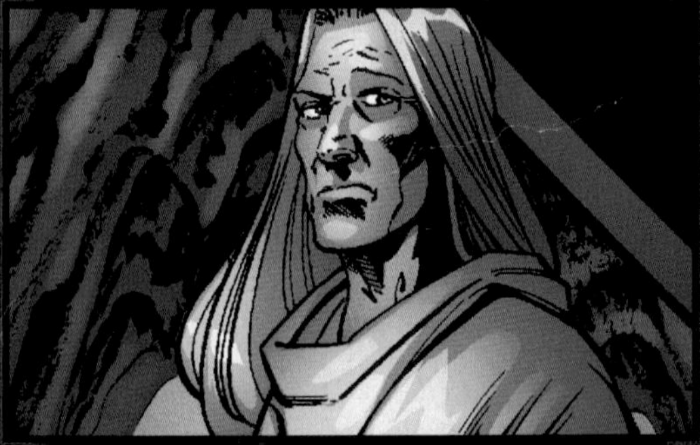

I-CHING

Mystic monk, secret agent, unstoppable fighting force of one, the mysterious I-Ching has been all that and more in his long life. Now, he comes out of serene retirement to help the Dark Knight detective combat an immortal force of nature.

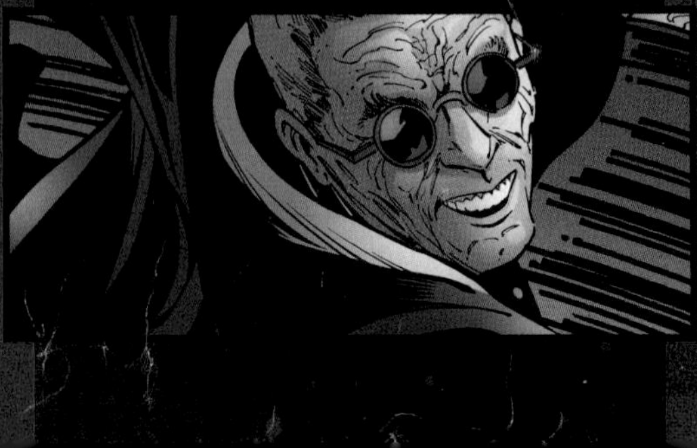

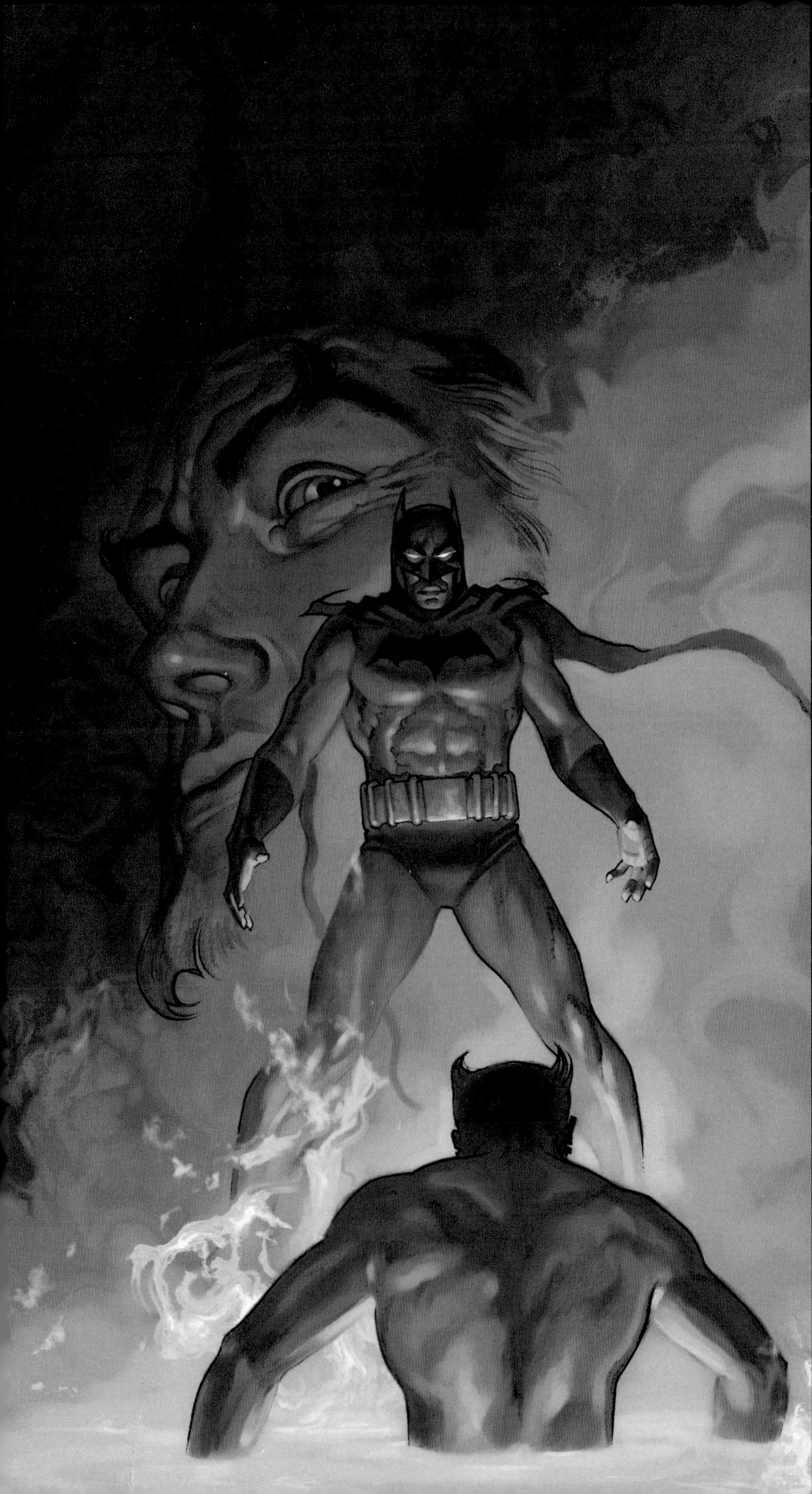

PRELUDE RESURRECTION SHUFFLE

Cover art by Brian Stelfreeze | Chapter written by Peter Milligan | Chapter pencilled by David López | Chapter inked by Álvaro López

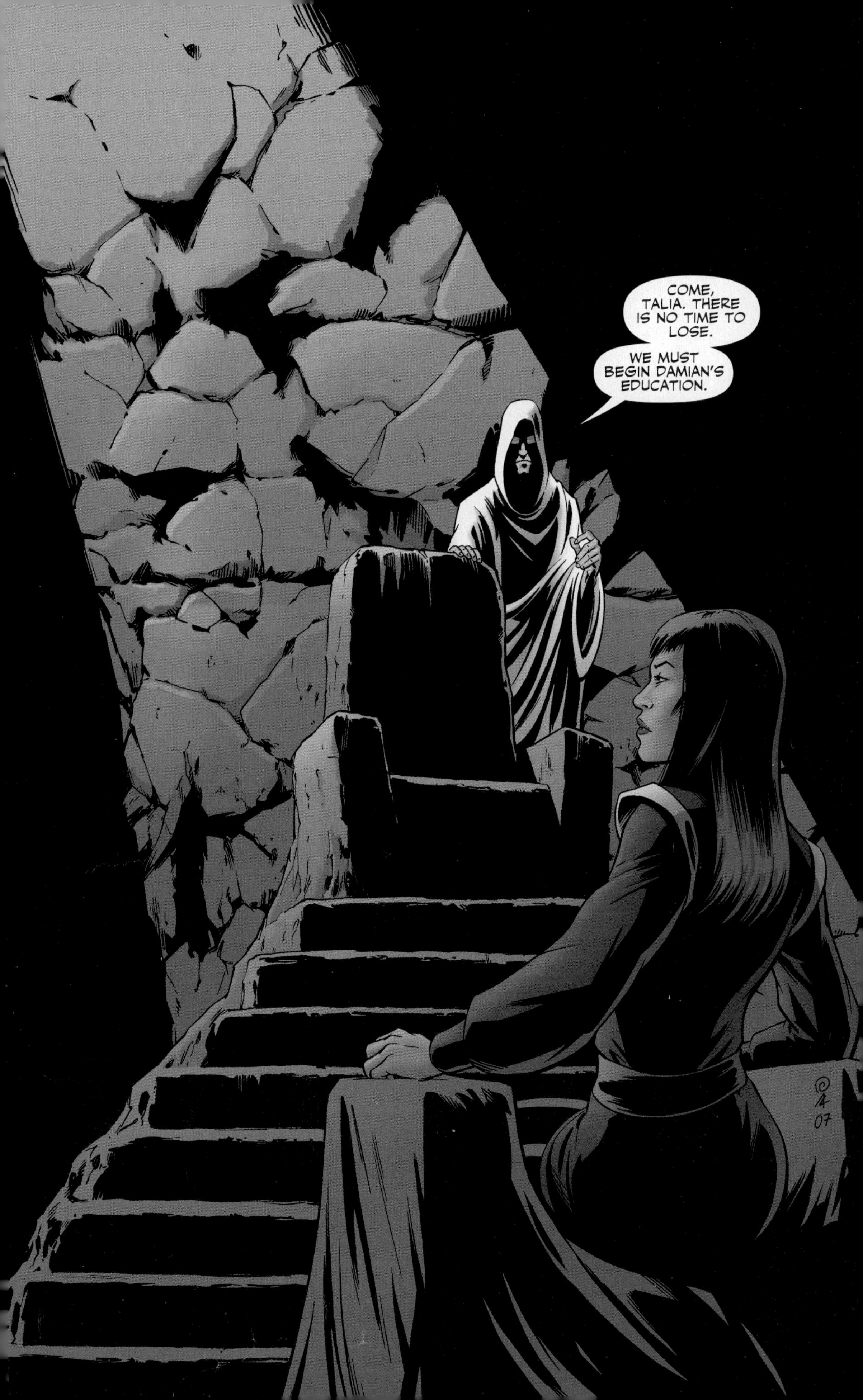
COME, TALIA. THERE IS NO TIME TO LOSE.
WE MUST BEGIN DAMIAN'S EDUCATION.

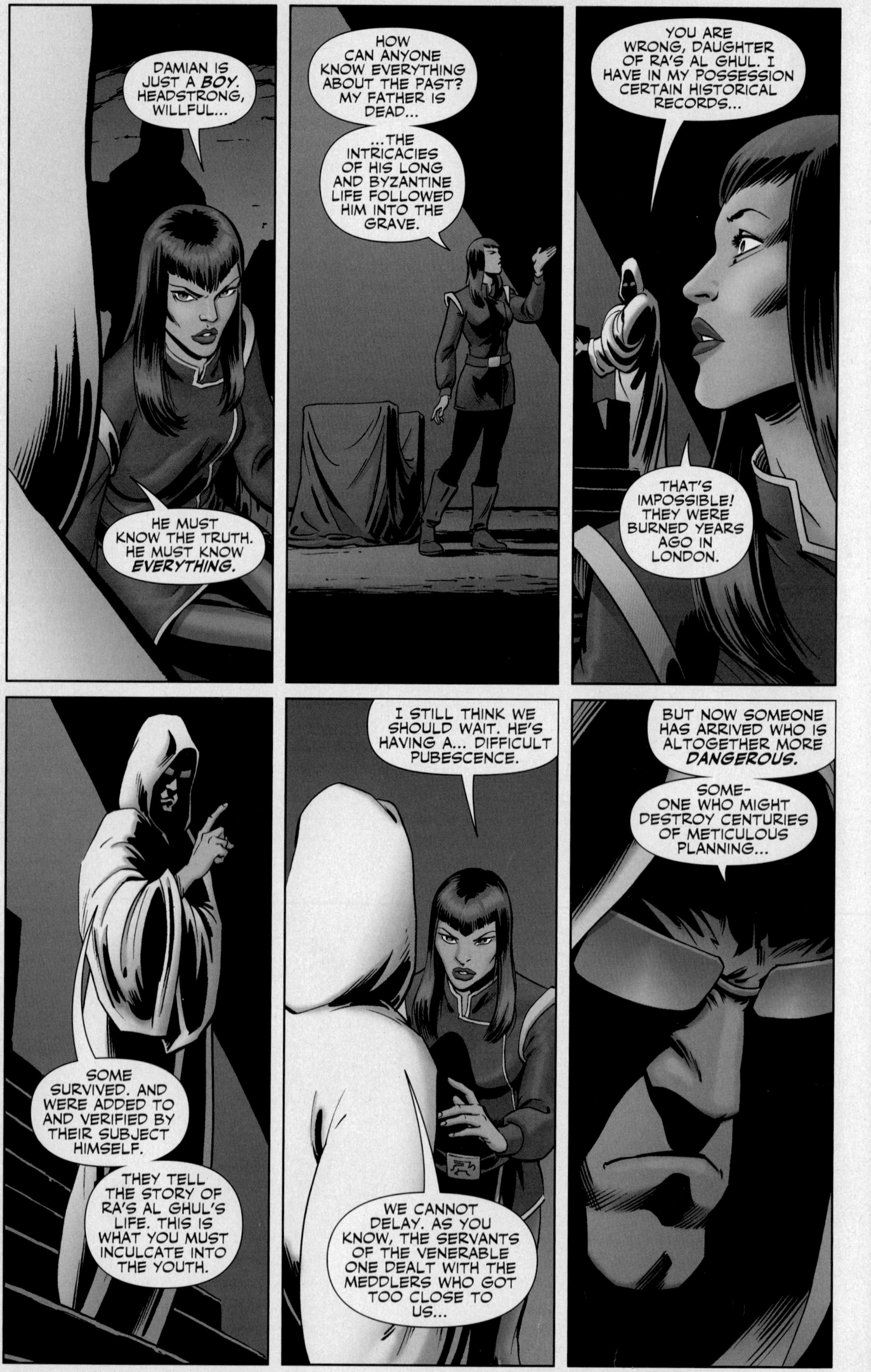
DAMIAN IS JUST A BOY. HEADSTRONG, WILLFUL...
HE MUST KNOW THE TRUTH. HE MUST KNOW EVERYTHING.
HOW CAN ANYONE KNOW EVERYTHING ABOUT THE PAST? MY FATHER IS DEAD...
...THE INTRICACIES OF HIS LONG AND BYZANTINE LIFE FOLLOWED HIM INTO THE GRAVE.
YOU ARE WRONG, DAUGHTER OF RA'S AL GHUL. I HAVE IN MY POSSESSION CERTAIN HISTORICAL RECORDS...
THAT'S IMPOSSIBLE! THEY WERE BURNED YEARS AGO IN LONDON.
SOME SURVIVED. AND WERE ADDED TO AND VERIFIED BY THEIR SUBJECT HIMSELF.
THEY TELL THE STORY OF RA'S AL GHUL'S LIFE. THIS IS WHAT YOU MUST INCULCATE INTO THE YOUTH.
I STILL THINK WE SHOULD WAIT. HE'S HAVING A... DIFFICULT PUBESCENCE.
WE CANNOT DELAY. AS YOU KNOW, THE SERVANTS OF THE VENERABLE ONE DEALT WITH THE MEDDLERS WHO GOT TOO CLOSE TO US...
BUT NOW SOMEONE HAS ARRIVED WHO IS ALTOGETHER MORE DANGEROUS.
SOME-ONE WHO MIGHT DESTROY CENTURIES OF METICULOUS PLANNING...

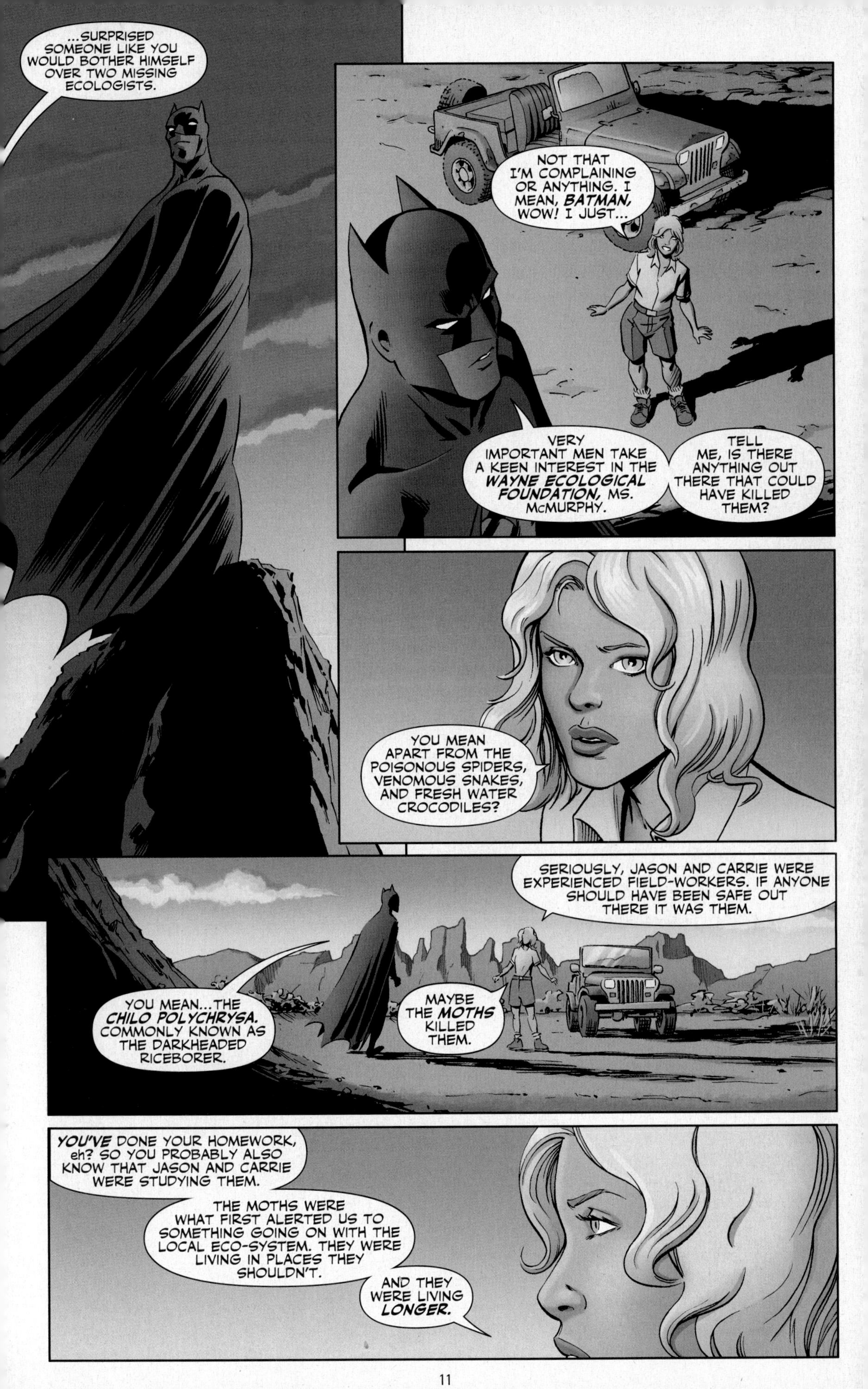
...SURPRISED SOMEONE LIKE YOU WOULD BOTHER HIMSELF OVER TWO MISSING ECOLOGISTS.
NOT THAT I'M COMPLAINING OR ANYTHING. I MEAN, BATMAN, WOW! I JUST...
VERY IMPORTANT MEN TAKE A KEEN INTEREST IN THE WAYNE ECOLOGICAL FOUNDATION, MS. McMURPHY.
TELL ME, IS THERE ANYTHING OUT THERE THAT COULD HAVE KILLED THEM?
YOU MEAN APART FROM THE POISONOUS SPIDERS, VENOMOUS SNAKES, AND FRESH WATER CROCODILES?
SERIOUSLY, JASON AND CARRIE WERE EXPERIENCED FIELD-WORKERS. IF ANYONE SHOULD HAVE BEEN SAFE OUT THERE IT WAS THEM.
MAYBE THE MOTHS KILLED THEM.
YOU MEAN...THE CHILO POLYCHRYSA. COMMONLY KNOWN AS THE DARKHEADED RICEBORER.
YOU'VE DONE YOUR HOMEWORK, eh? SO YOU PROBABLY ALSO KNOW THAT JASON AND CARRIE WERE STUDYING THEM.
THE MOTHS WERE WHAT FIRST ALERTED US TO SOMETHING GOING ON WITH THE LOCAL ECO-SYSTEM. THEY WERE LIVING IN PLACES THEY SHOULDN'T.
AND THEY WERE LIVING LONGER.

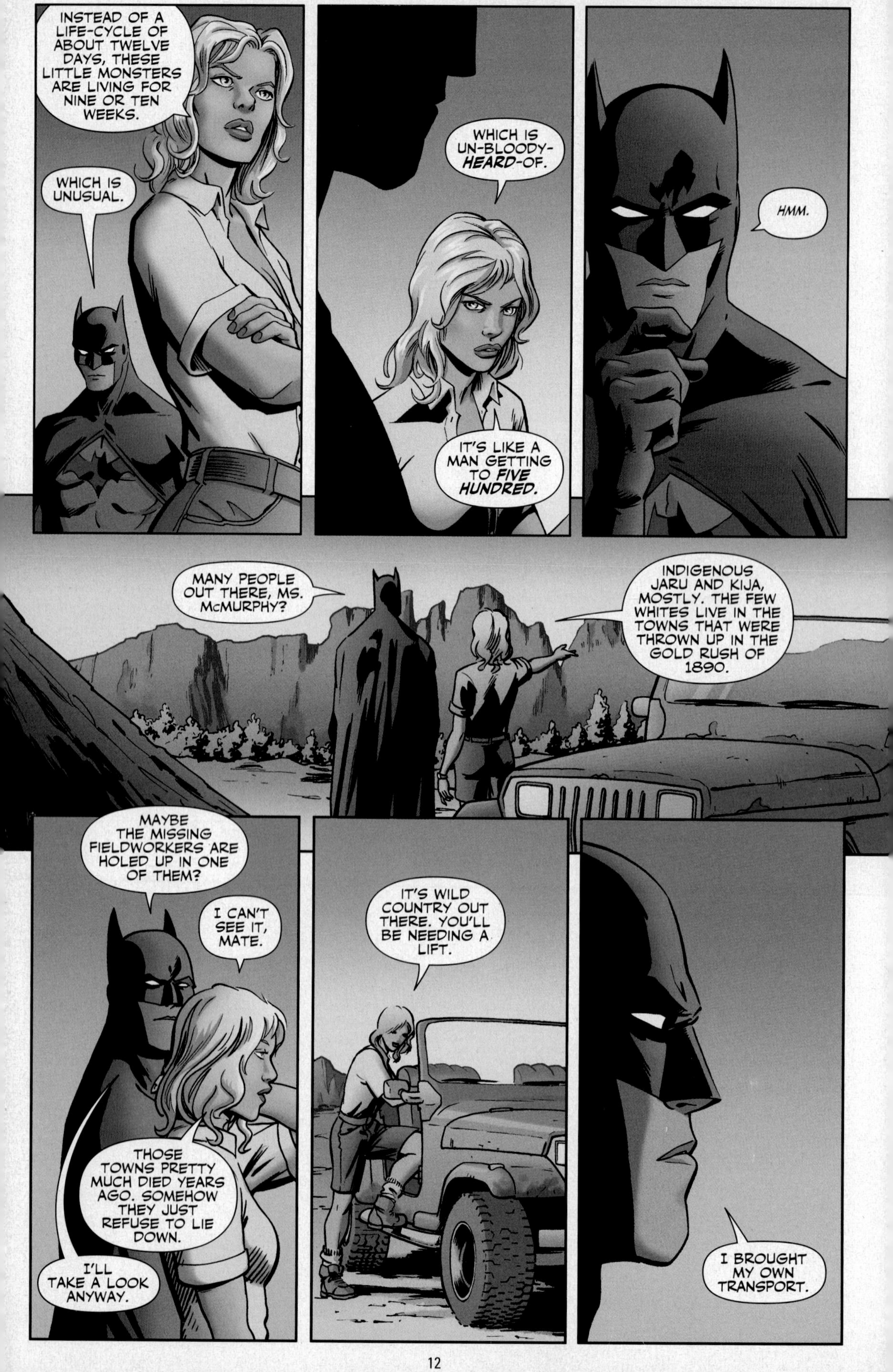
INSTEAD OF A LIFE-CYCLE OF ABOUT TWELVE DAYS, THESE LITTLE MONSTERS ARE LIVING FOR NINE OR TEN WEEKS.
WHICH IS UNUSUAL.
WHICH IS UN-BLOODY-HEARD-OF.
IT'S LIKE A MAN GETTING TO FIVE HUNDRED.
HMM.
MANY PEOPLE OUT THERE, MS. McMURPHY?
INDIGENOUS JARU AND KIJA, MOSTLY. THE FEW WHITES LIVE IN THE TOWNS THAT WERE THROWN UP IN THE GOLD RUSH OF 1890.
MAYBE THE MISSING FIELDWORKERS ARE HOLED UP IN ONE OF THEM?
I CAN'T SEE IT, MATE.
THOSE TOWNS PRETTY MUCH DIED YEARS AGO. SOMEHOW THEY JUST REFUSE TO LIE DOWN.
I'LL TAKE A LOOK ANYWAY.
IT'S WILD COUNTRY OUT THERE. YOU'LL BE NEEDING A LIFT.
I BROUGHT MY OWN TRANSPORT.

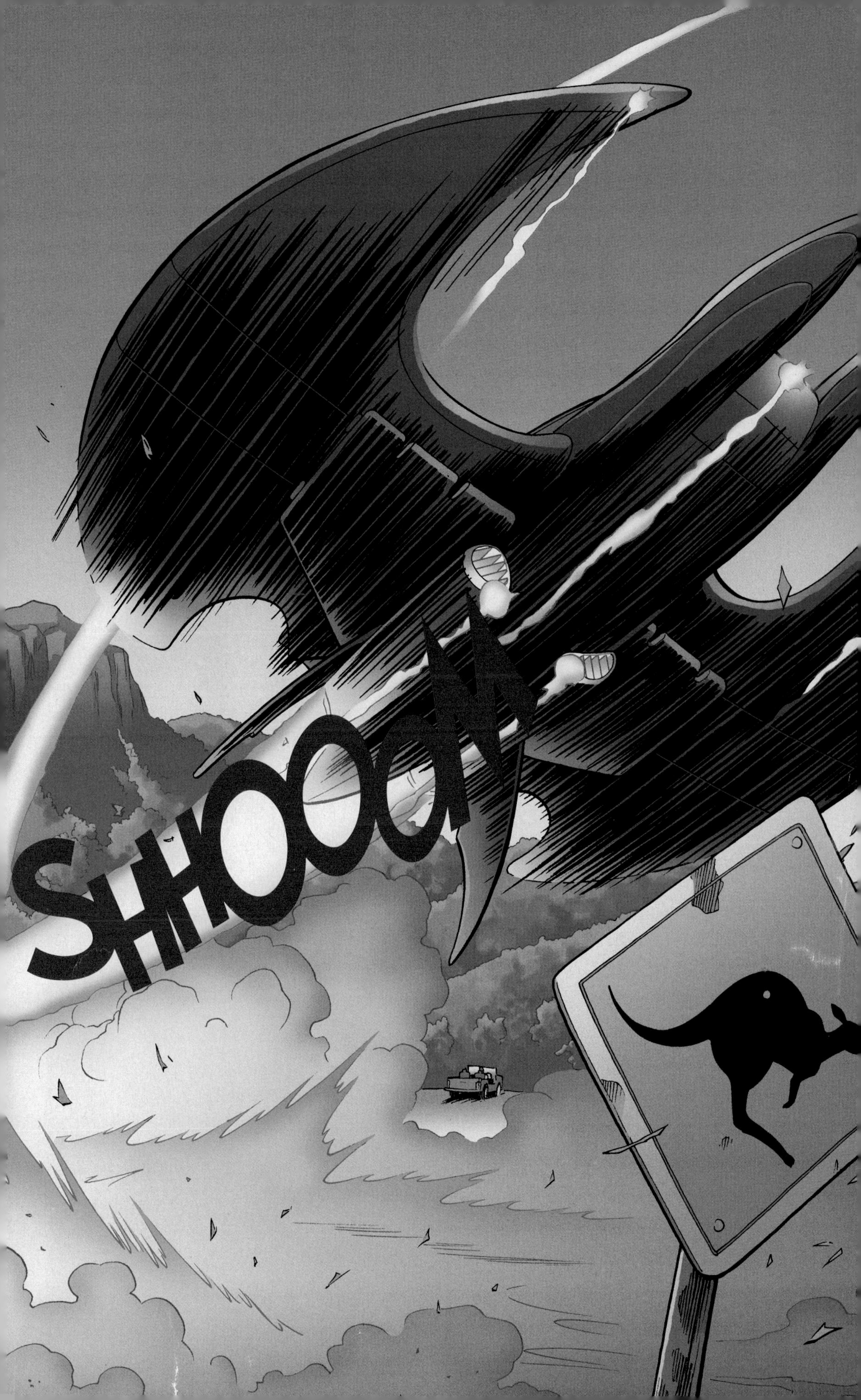
SHOOOM

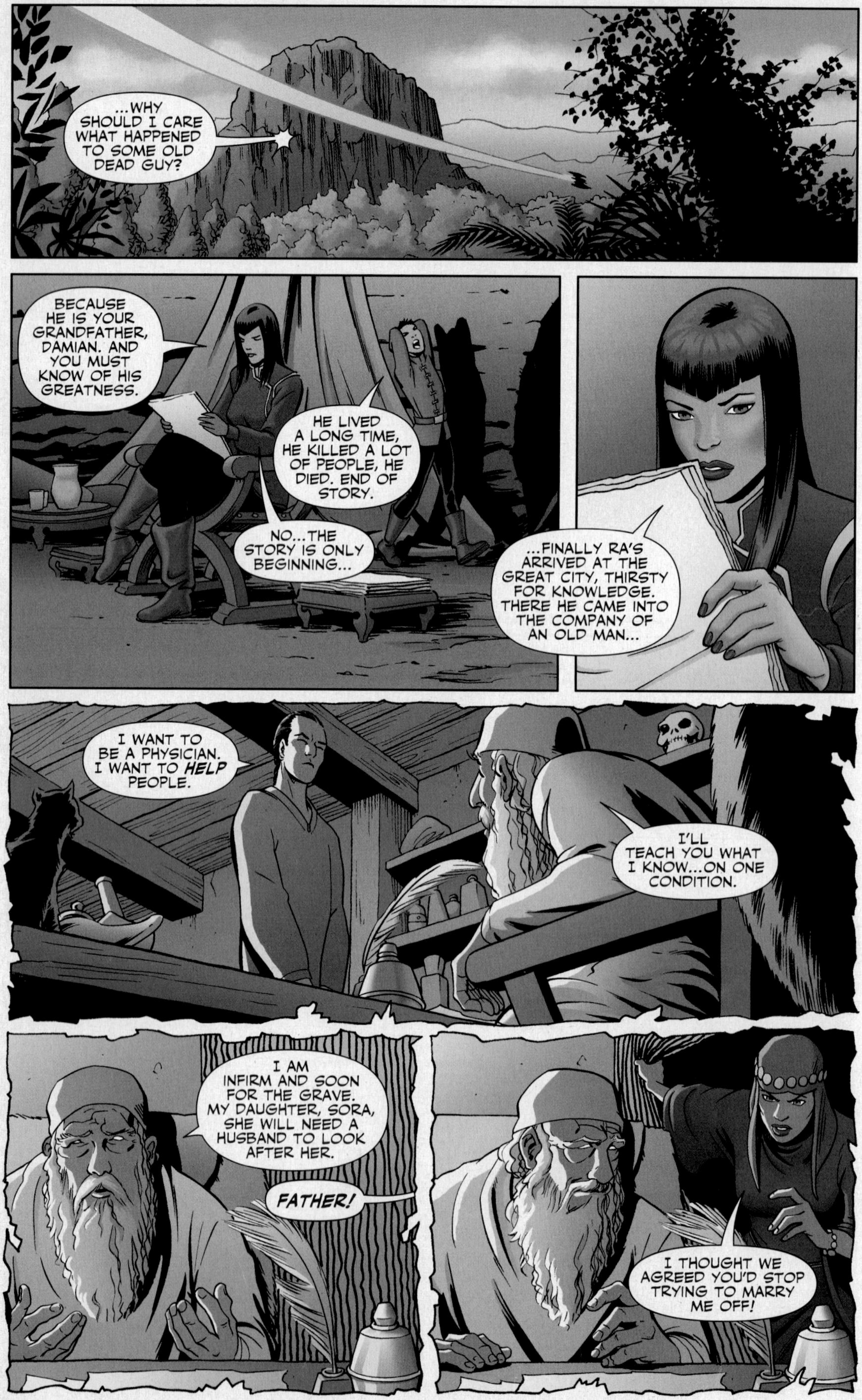
...WHY SHOULD I CARE WHAT HAPPENED TO SOME OLD DEAD GUY?
BECAUSE HE IS YOUR GRANDFATHER, DAMIAN. AND YOU MUST KNOW OF HIS GREATNESS.
HE LIVED A LONG TIME, HE KILLED A LOT OF PEOPLE, HE DIED. END OF STORY.
NO...THE STORY IS ONLY BEGINNING...
...FINALLY RA'S ARRIVED AT THE GREAT CITY, THIRSTY FOR KNOWLEDGE. THERE HE CAME INTO THE COMPANY OF AN OLD MAN...
I WANT TO BE A PHYSICIAN. I WANT TO HELP PEOPLE.
I'LL TEACH YOU WHAT I KNOW...ON ONE CONDITION.
I AM INFIRM AND SOON FOR THE GRAVE. MY DAUGHTER, SORA, SHE WILL NEED A HUSBAND TO LOOK AFTER HER.
FATHER!
I THOUGHT WE AGREED YOU'D STOP TRYING TO MARRY ME OFF!

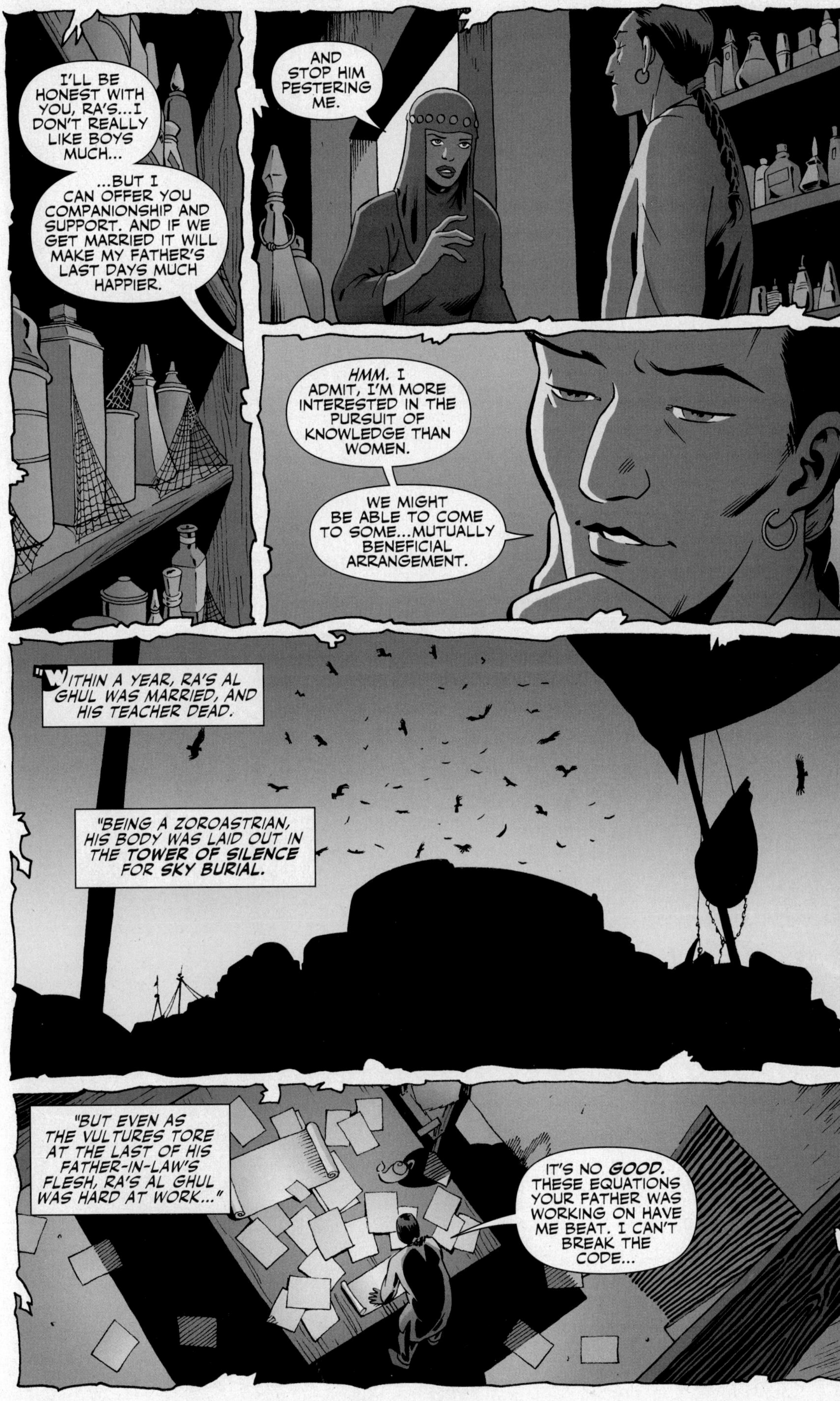
I'LL BE HONEST WITH YOU, RA'S...I DON'T REALLY LIKE BOYS MUCH...
...BUT I CAN OFFER YOU COMPANIONSHIP AND SUPPORT. AND IF WE GET MARRIED IT WILL MAKE MY FATHER'S LAST DAYS MUCH HAPPIER.
AND STOP HIM PESTERING ME.
HMM. I ADMIT, I'M MORE INTERESTED IN THE PURSUIT OF KNOWLEDGE THAN WOMEN.
WE MIGHT BE ABLE TO COME TO SOME...MUTUALLY BENEFICIAL ARRANGEMENT.
"WITHIN A YEAR, RA'S AL GHUL WAS MARRIED, AND HIS TEACHER DEAD.
"BEING A ZOROASTRIAN, HIS BODY WAS LAID OUT IN THE TOWER OF SILENCE FOR SKY BURIAL.
"BUT EVEN AS THE VULTURES TORE AT THE LAST OF HIS FATHER-IN-LAW'S FLESH, RA'S AL GHUL WAS HARD AT WORK..."
IT'S NO GOOD. THESE EQUATIONS YOUR FATHER WAS WORKING ON HAVE ME BEAT. I CAN'T BREAK THE CODE...

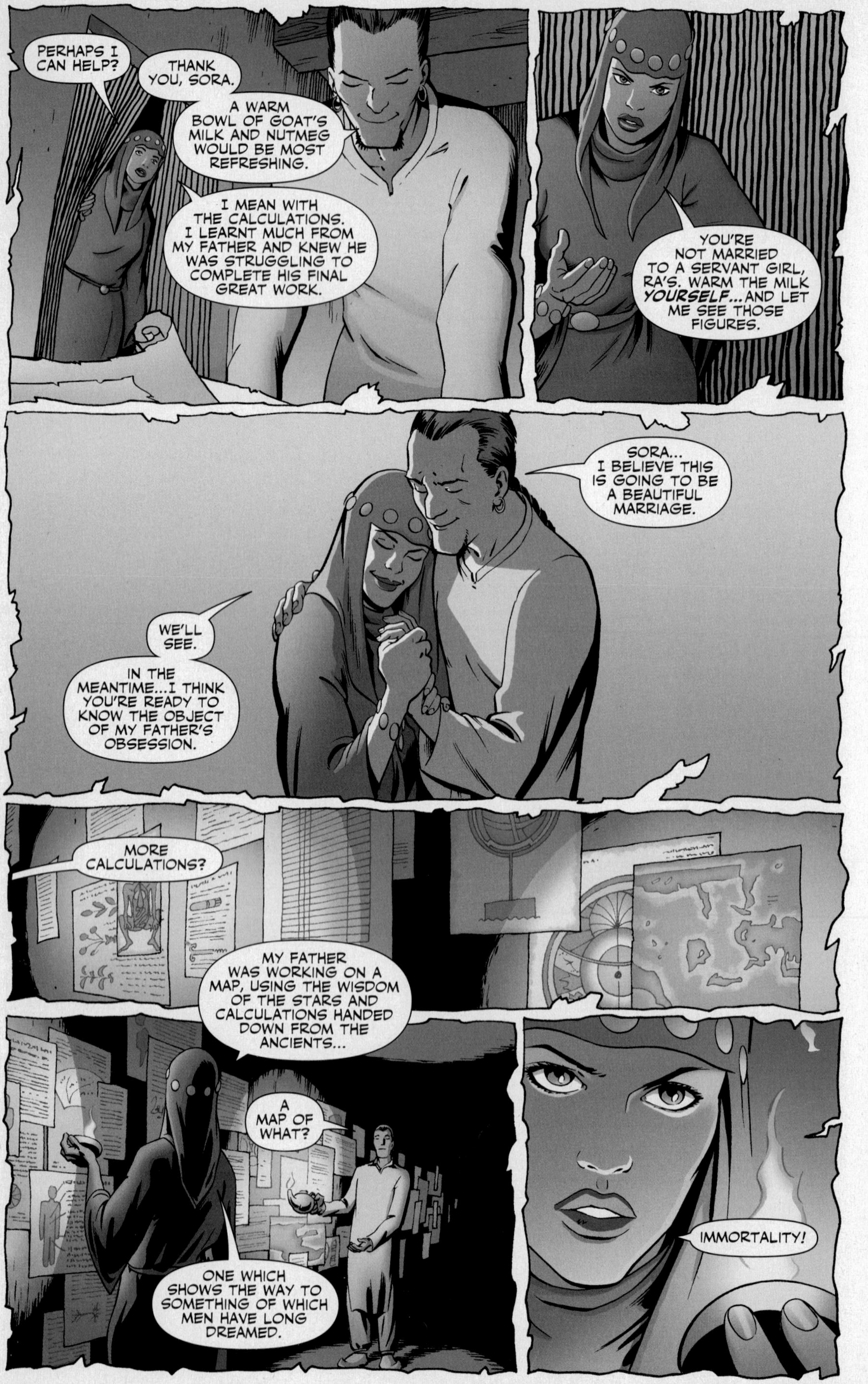
PERHAPS I CAN HELP?
THANK YOU, SORA.
A WARM BOWL OF GOAT'S MILK AND NUTMEG WOULD BE MOST REFRESHING.
I MEAN WITH THE CALCULATIONS. I LEARNT MUCH FROM MY FATHER AND KNEW HE WAS STRUGGLING TO COMPLETE HIS FINAL GREAT WORK.
YOU'RE NOT MARRIED TO A SERVANT GIRL, RA'S. WARM THE MILK *YOURSELF*...AND LET ME SEE THOSE FIGURES.
SORA... I BELIEVE THIS IS GOING TO BE A BEAUTIFUL MARRIAGE.
WE'LL SEE.
IN THE MEANTIME...I THINK YOU'RE READY TO KNOW THE OBJECT OF MY FATHER'S OBSESSION.
MORE CALCULATIONS?
MY FATHER WAS WORKING ON A MAP, USING THE WISDOM OF THE STARS AND CALCULATIONS HANDED DOWN FROM THE ANCIENTS...
A MAP OF WHAT?
ONE WHICH SHOWS THE WAY TO SOMETHING OF WHICH MEN HAVE LONG DREAMED.
IMMORTALITY!

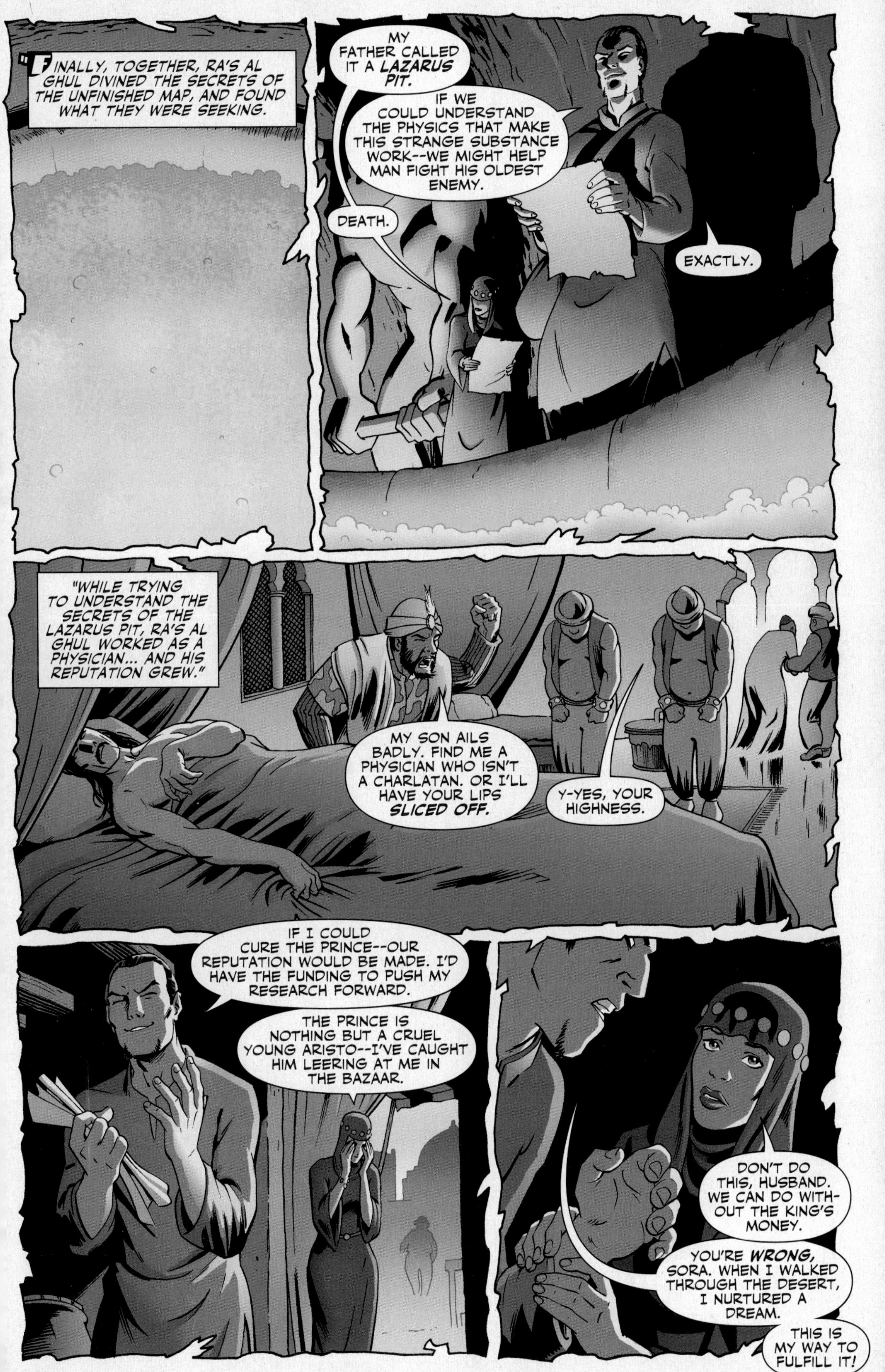
"FINALLY, TOGETHER, RA'S AL GHUL DIVINED THE SECRETS OF THE UNFINISHED MAP, AND FOUND WHAT THEY WERE SEEKING.
MY FATHER CALLED IT A LAZARUS PIT.
IF WE COULD UNDERSTAND THE PHYSICS THAT MAKE THIS STRANGE SUBSTANCE WORK--WE MIGHT HELP MAN FIGHT HIS OLDEST ENEMY.
DEATH.
EXACTLY.
"WHILE TRYING TO UNDERSTAND THE SECRETS OF THE LAZARUS PIT, RA'S AL GHUL WORKED AS A PHYSICIAN... AND HIS REPUTATION GREW."
MY SON AILS BADLY. FIND ME A PHYSICIAN WHO ISN'T A CHARLATAN. OR I'LL HAVE YOUR LIPS SLICED OFF.
Y-YES, YOUR HIGHNESS.
IF I COULD CURE THE PRINCE--OUR REPUTATION WOULD BE MADE. I'D HAVE THE FUNDING TO PUSH MY RESEARCH FORWARD.
THE PRINCE IS NOTHING BUT A CRUEL YOUNG ARISTO--I'VE CAUGHT HIM LEERING AT ME IN THE BAZAAR.
DON'T DO THIS, HUSBAND. WE CAN DO WITH-OUT THE KING'S MONEY.
YOU'RE WRONG, SORA. WHEN I WALKED THROUGH THE DESERT, I NURTURED A DREAM.
THIS IS MY WAY TO FULFILL IT!

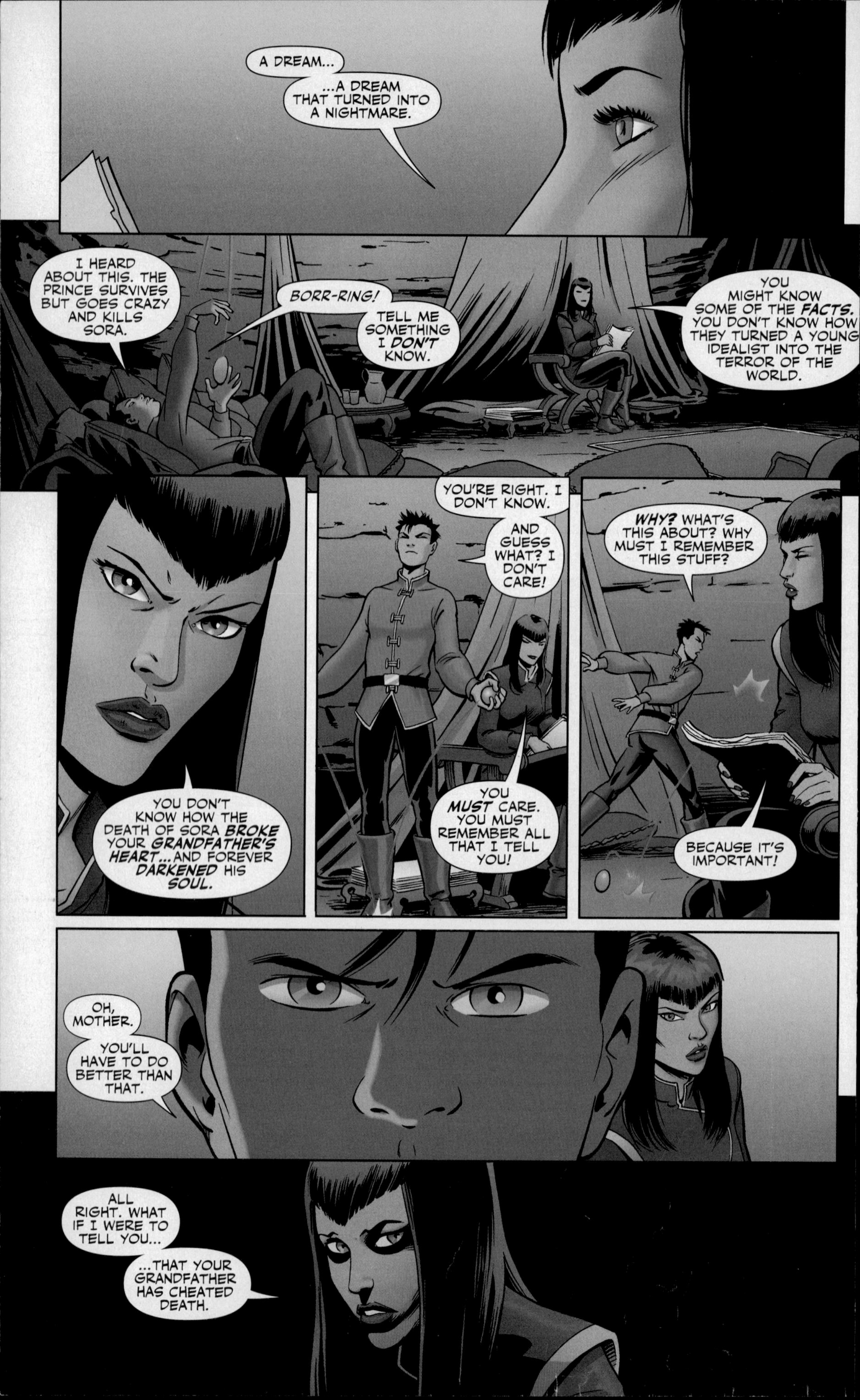
A DREAM...
...A DREAM THAT TURNED INTO A NIGHTMARE.
I HEARD ABOUT THIS. THE PRINCE SURVIVES BUT GOES CRAZY AND KILLS SORA.
BORR-RING!
TELL ME SOMETHING I DON'T KNOW.
YOU MIGHT KNOW SOME OF THE FACTS. YOU DON'T KNOW HOW THEY TURNED A YOUNG IDEALIST INTO THE TERROR OF THE WORLD.
YOU DON'T KNOW HOW THE DEATH OF SORA BROKE YOUR GRANDFATHER'S HEART...AND FOREVER DARKENED HIS SOUL.
YOU'RE RIGHT. I DON'T KNOW.
AND GUESS WHAT? I DON'T CARE!
YOU MUST CARE. YOU MUST REMEMBER ALL THAT I TELL YOU!
WHY? WHAT'S THIS ABOUT? WHY MUST I REMEMBER THIS STUFF?
BECAUSE IT'S IMPORTANT!
OH, MOTHER.
YOU'LL HAVE TO DO BETTER THAN THAT.
ALL RIGHT. WHAT IF I WERE TO TELL YOU...
...THAT YOUR GRANDFATHER HAS CHEATED DEATH.

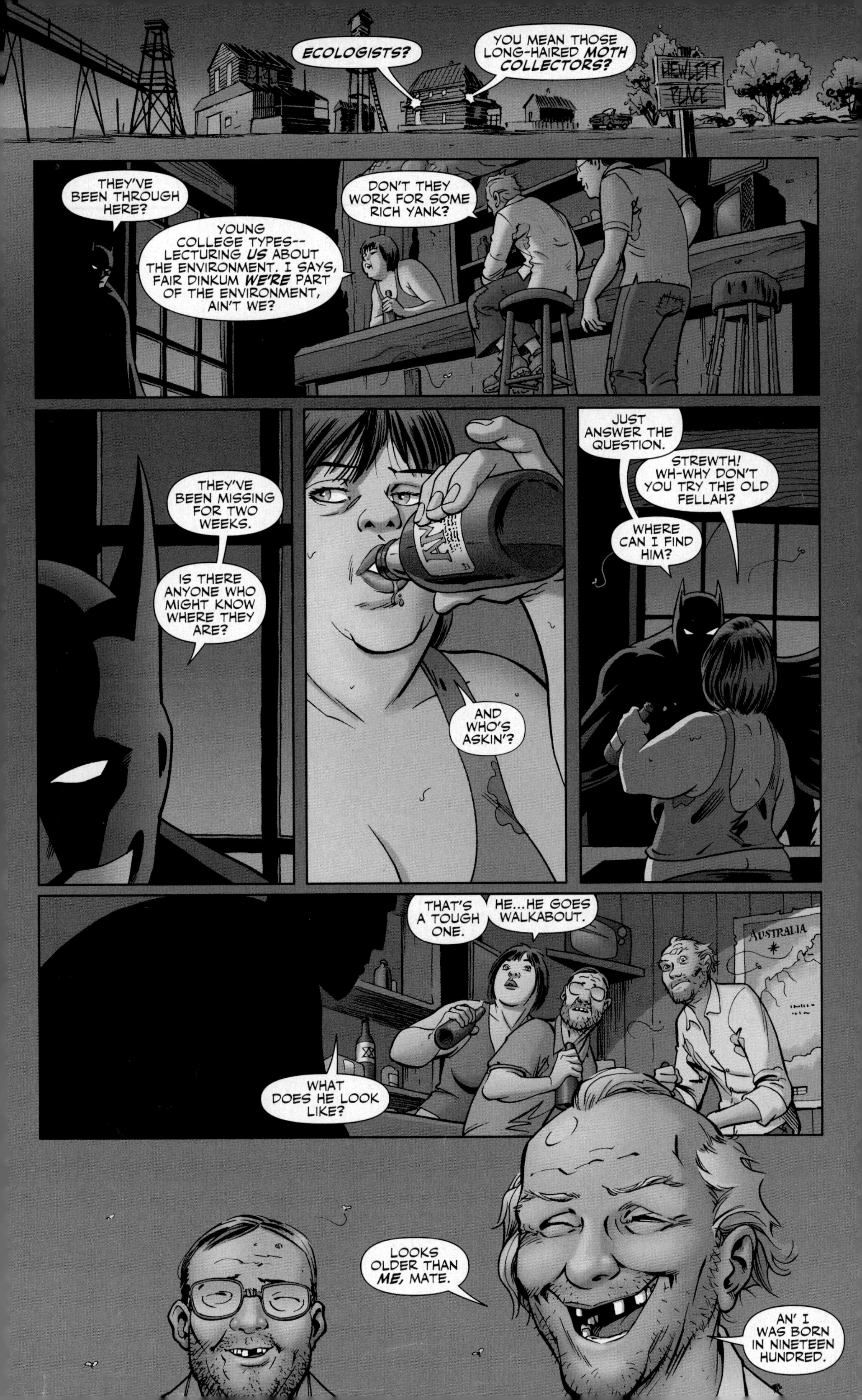
ECOLOGISTS?
YOU MEAN THOSE LONG-HAIRED MOTH COLLECTORS?
HEWLETT PLACE
THEY'VE BEEN THROUGH HERE?
DON'T THEY WORK FOR SOME RICH YANK?
YOUNG COLLEGE TYPES-- LECTURING US ABOUT THE ENVIRONMENT. I SAYS, FAIR DINKUM WE'RE PART OF THE ENVIRONMENT, AIN'T WE?
THEY'VE BEEN MISSING FOR TWO WEEKS.
IS THERE ANYONE WHO MIGHT KNOW WHERE THEY ARE?
AND WHO'S ASKIN'?
JUST ANSWER THE QUESTION.
STREWTH! WH-WHY DON'T YOU TRY THE OLD FELLAH?
WHERE CAN I FIND HIM?
THAT'S A TOUGH ONE.
HE...HE GOES WALKABOUT.
AUSTRALIA
WHAT DOES HE LOOK LIKE?
LOOKS OLDER THAN ME, MATE.
AN' I WAS BORN IN NINETEEN HUNDRED.

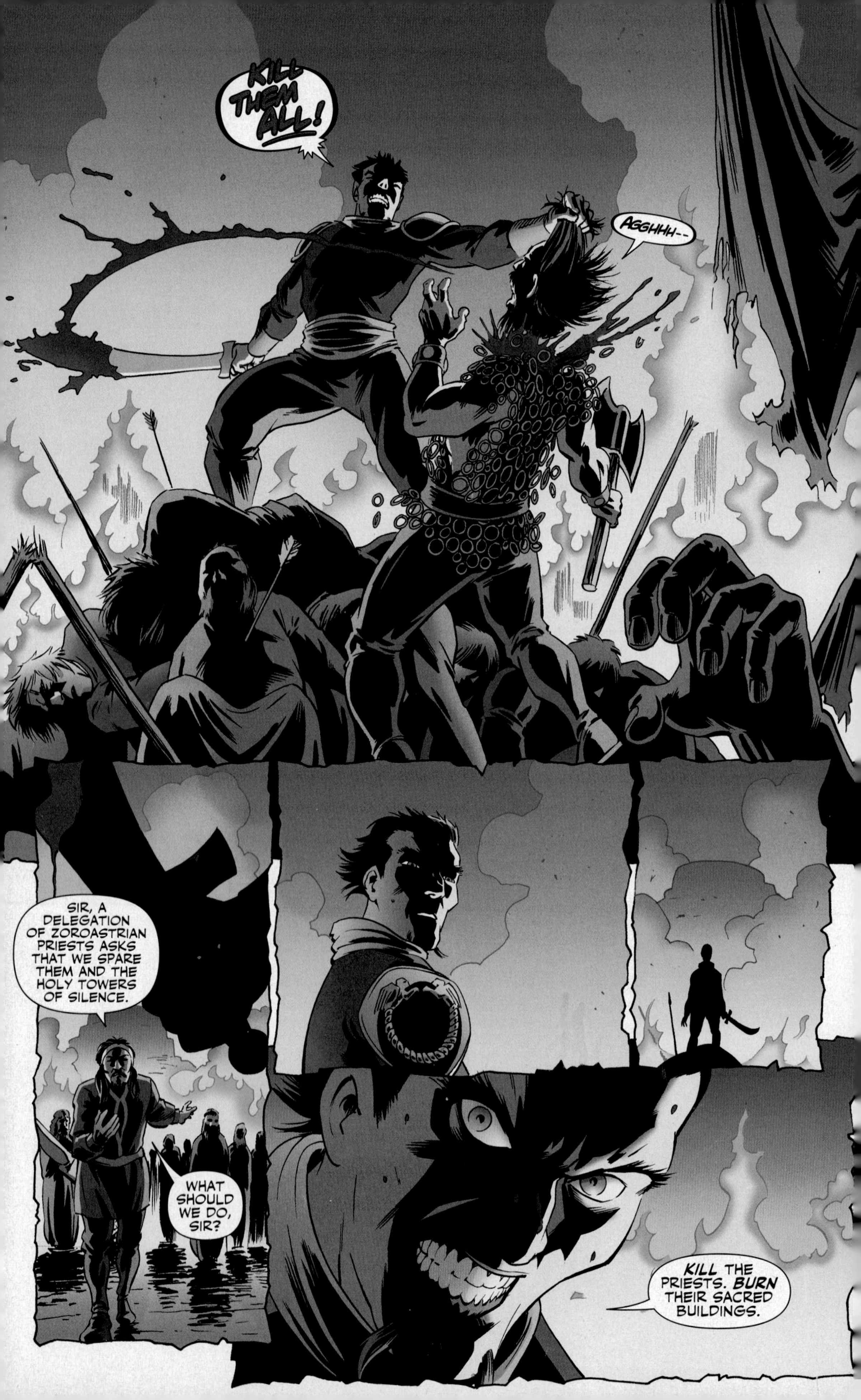
KILL THEM ALL!
AGGHHH--
SIR, A DELEGATION OF ZOROASTRIAN PRIESTS ASKS THAT WE SPARE THEM AND THE HOLY TOWERS OF SILENCE.
WHAT SHOULD WE DO, SIR?
KILL THE PRIESTS. BURN THEIR SACRED BUILDINGS.

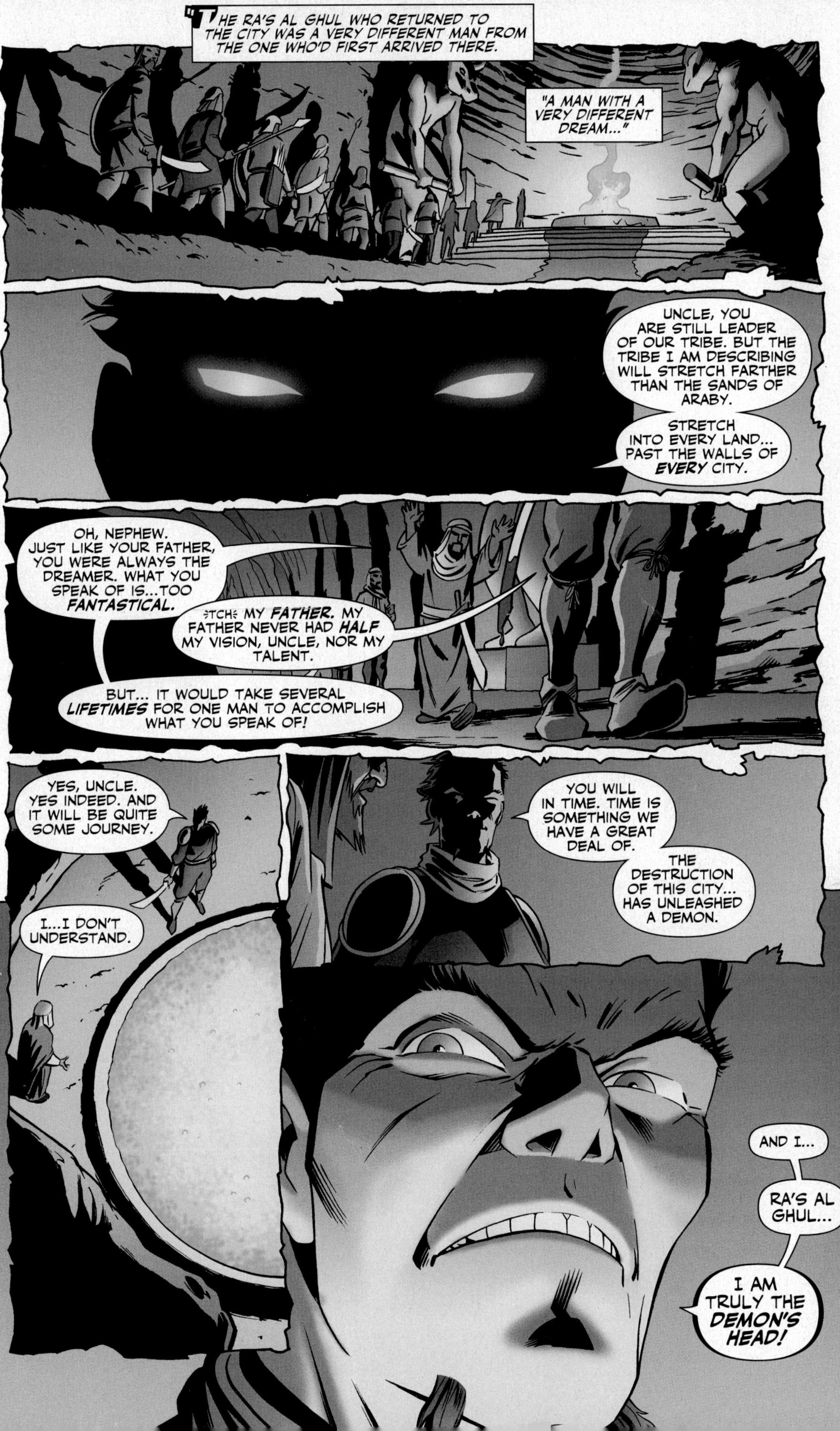
"THE RA'S AL GHUL WHO RETURNED TO THE CITY WAS A VERY DIFFERENT MAN FROM THE ONE WHO'D FIRST ARRIVED THERE.
"A MAN WITH A VERY DIFFERENT DREAM..."
UNCLE, YOU ARE STILL LEADER OF OUR TRIBE. BUT THE TRIBE I AM DESCRIBING WILL STRETCH FARTHER THAN THE SANDS OF ARABY.
STRETCH INTO EVERY LAND... PAST THE WALLS OF EVERY CITY.
OH, NEPHEW. JUST LIKE YOUR FATHER, YOU WERE ALWAYS THE DREAMER. WHAT YOU SPEAK OF IS...TOO FANTASTICAL.
TCH MY FATHER. MY FATHER NEVER HAD HALF MY VISION, UNCLE, NOR MY TALENT.
BUT... IT WOULD TAKE SEVERAL LIFETIMES FOR ONE MAN TO ACCOMPLISH WHAT YOU SPEAK OF!
YES, UNCLE. YES INDEED. AND IT WILL BE QUITE SOME JOURNEY.
YOU WILL IN TIME. TIME IS SOMETHING WE HAVE A GREAT DEAL OF.
THE DESTRUCTION OF THIS CITY... HAS UNLEASHED A DEMON.
I...I DON'T UNDERSTAND.
AND I...
RA'S AL GHUL...
I AM TRULY THE DEMON'S HEAD!

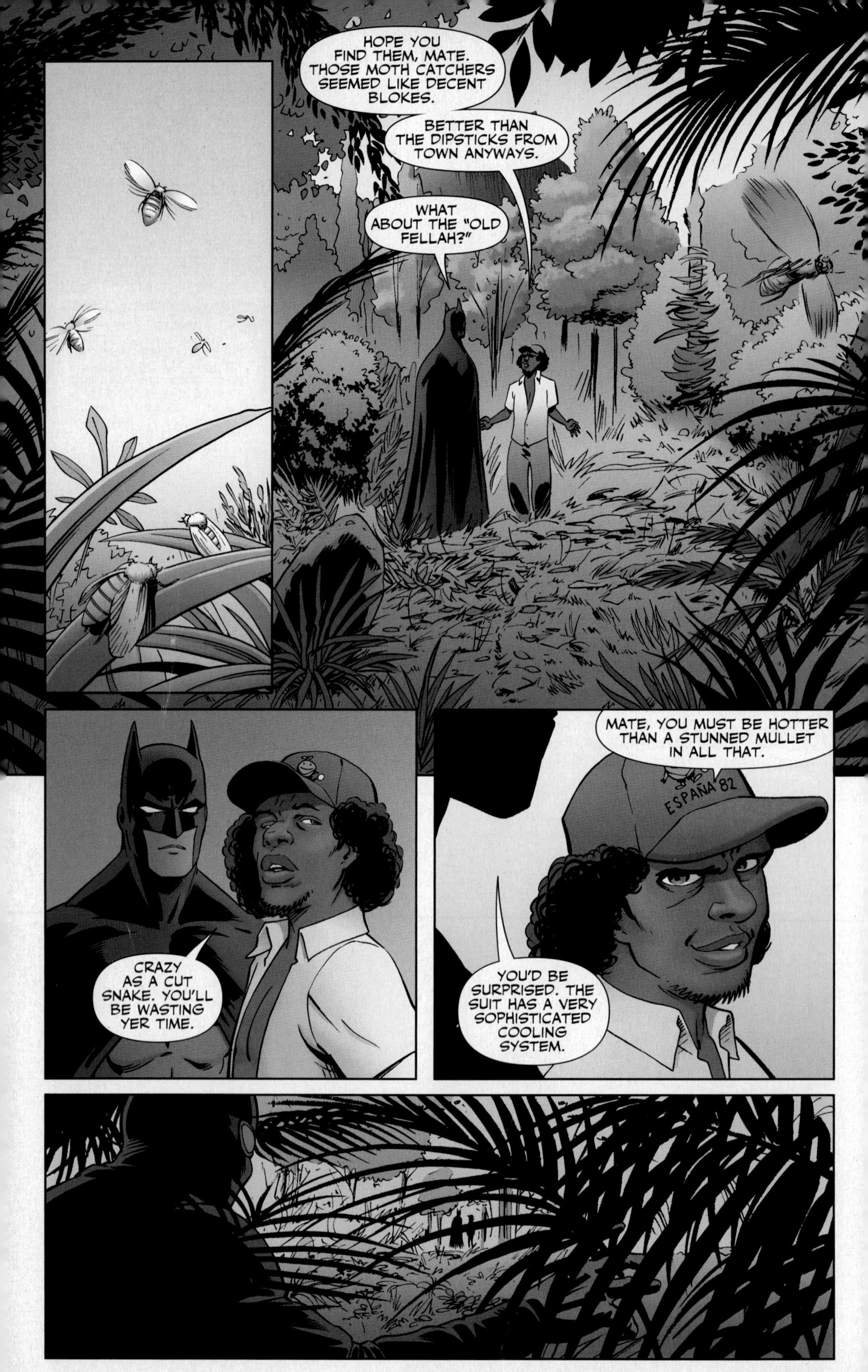
HOPE YOU FIND THEM, MATE. THOSE MOTH CATCHERS SEEMED LIKE DECENT BLOKES.
BETTER THAN THE DIPSTICKS FROM TOWN ANYWAYS.
WHAT ABOUT THE "OLD FELLAH?"
CRAZY AS A CUT SNAKE. YOU'LL BE WASTING YER TIME.
MATE, YOU MUST BE HOTTER THAN A STUNNED MULLET IN ALL THAT.
ESPAÑA '82
YOU'D BE SURPRISED. THE SUIT HAS A VERY SOPHISTICATED COOLING SYSTEM.

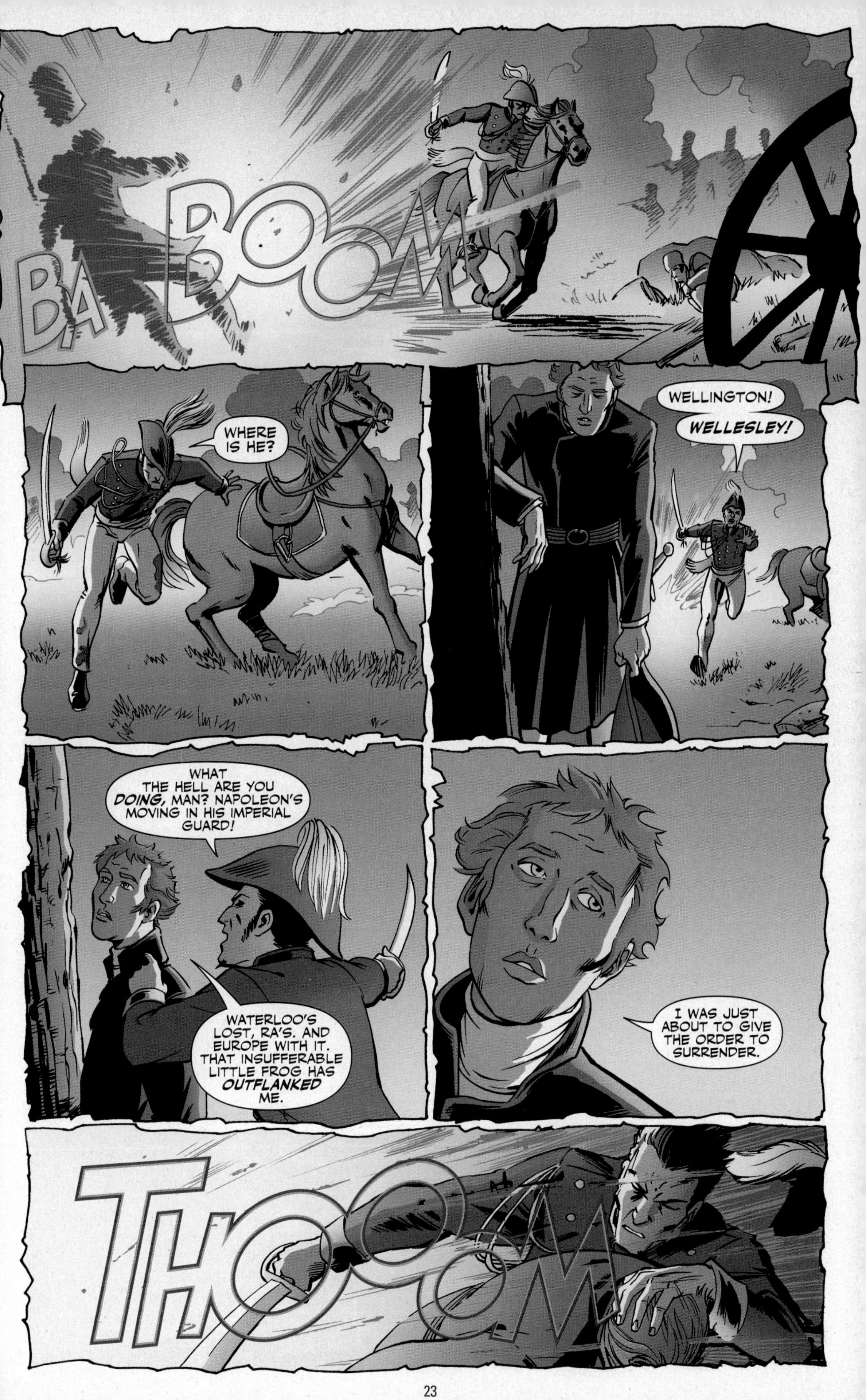
BA-BOOM
WHERE IS HE?
WELLINGTON! WELLESLEY!
WHAT THE HELL ARE YOU DOING, MAN? NAPOLEON'S MOVING IN HIS IMPERIAL GUARD!
WATERLOO'S LOST, RA'S. AND EUROPE WITH IT. THAT INSUFFERABLE LITTLE FROG HAS OUTFLANKED ME.
I WAS JUST ABOUT TO GIVE THE ORDER TO SURRENDER.
THOOOM

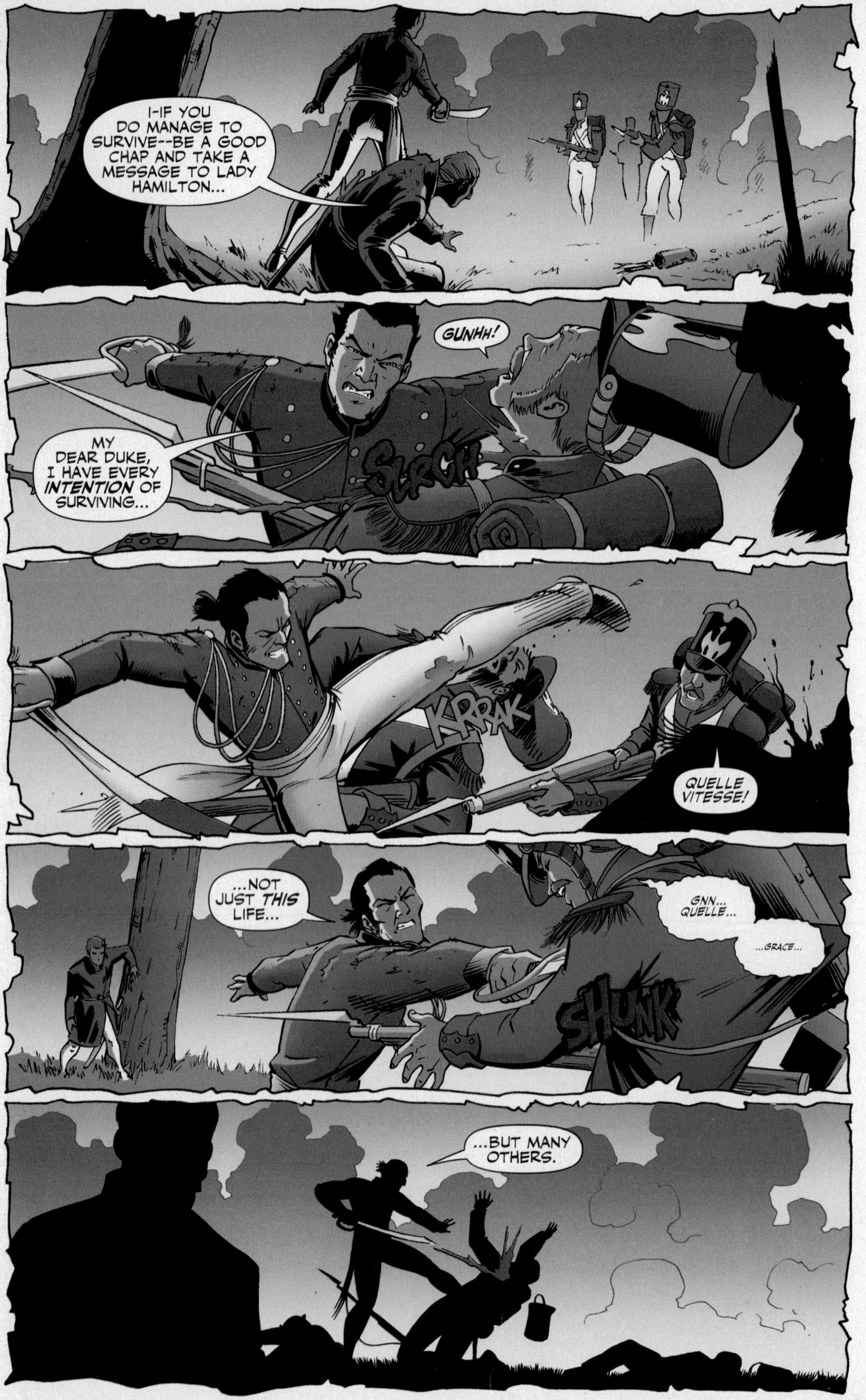
I-IF YOU DO MANAGE TO SURVIVE--BE A GOOD CHAP AND TAKE A MESSAGE TO LADY HAMILTON...
GUNHH!
MY DEAR DUKE, I HAVE EVERY *INTENTION* OF SURVIVING...
SLRCH
KRRAK
QUELLE VITESSE!
...NOT JUST *THIS* LIFE...
GNN... QUELLE...
...GRACE...
SHUNK
...BUT MANY OTHERS.

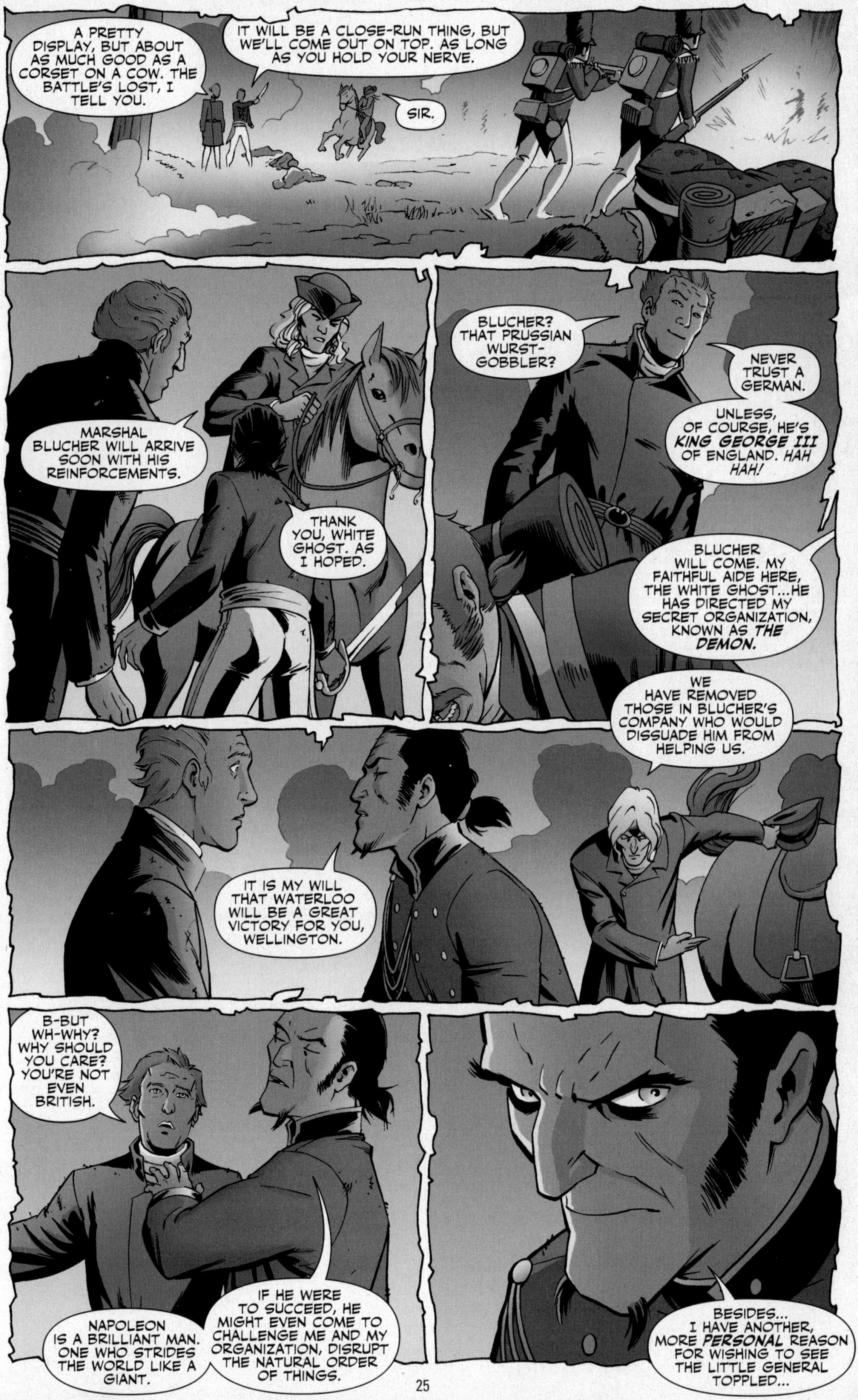
A PRETTY DISPLAY, BUT ABOUT AS MUCH GOOD AS A CORSET ON A COW. THE BATTLE'S LOST, I TELL YOU.
IT WILL BE A CLOSE-RUN THING, BUT WE'LL COME OUT ON TOP. AS LONG AS YOU HOLD YOUR NERVE.
SIR.
MARSHAL BLUCHER WILL ARRIVE SOON WITH HIS REINFORCEMENTS.
THANK YOU, WHITE GHOST. AS I HOPED.
BLUCHER? THAT PRUSSIAN WURST-GOBBLER?
NEVER TRUST A GERMAN.
UNLESS, OF COURSE, HE'S ***KING GEORGE III*** OF ENGLAND. *HAH HAH!*
BLUCHER WILL COME. MY FAITHFUL AIDE HERE, THE WHITE GHOST...HE HAS DIRECTED MY SECRET ORGANIZATION, KNOWN AS ***THE DEMON.***
WE HAVE REMOVED THOSE IN BLUCHER'S COMPANY WHO WOULD DISSUADE HIM FROM HELPING US.
IT IS MY WILL THAT WATERLOO WILL BE A GREAT VICTORY FOR YOU, WELLINGTON.
B-BUT WH-WHY? WHY SHOULD YOU CARE? YOU'RE NOT EVEN BRITISH.
NAPOLEON IS A BRILLIANT MAN. ONE WHO STRIDES THE WORLD LIKE A GIANT.
IF HE WERE TO SUCCEED, HE MIGHT EVEN COME TO CHALLENGE ME AND MY ORGANIZATION, DISRUPT THE NATURAL ORDER OF THINGS.
BESIDES... I HAVE ANOTHER, MORE ***PERSONAL*** REASON FOR WISHING TO SEE THE LITTLE GENERAL TOPPLED...

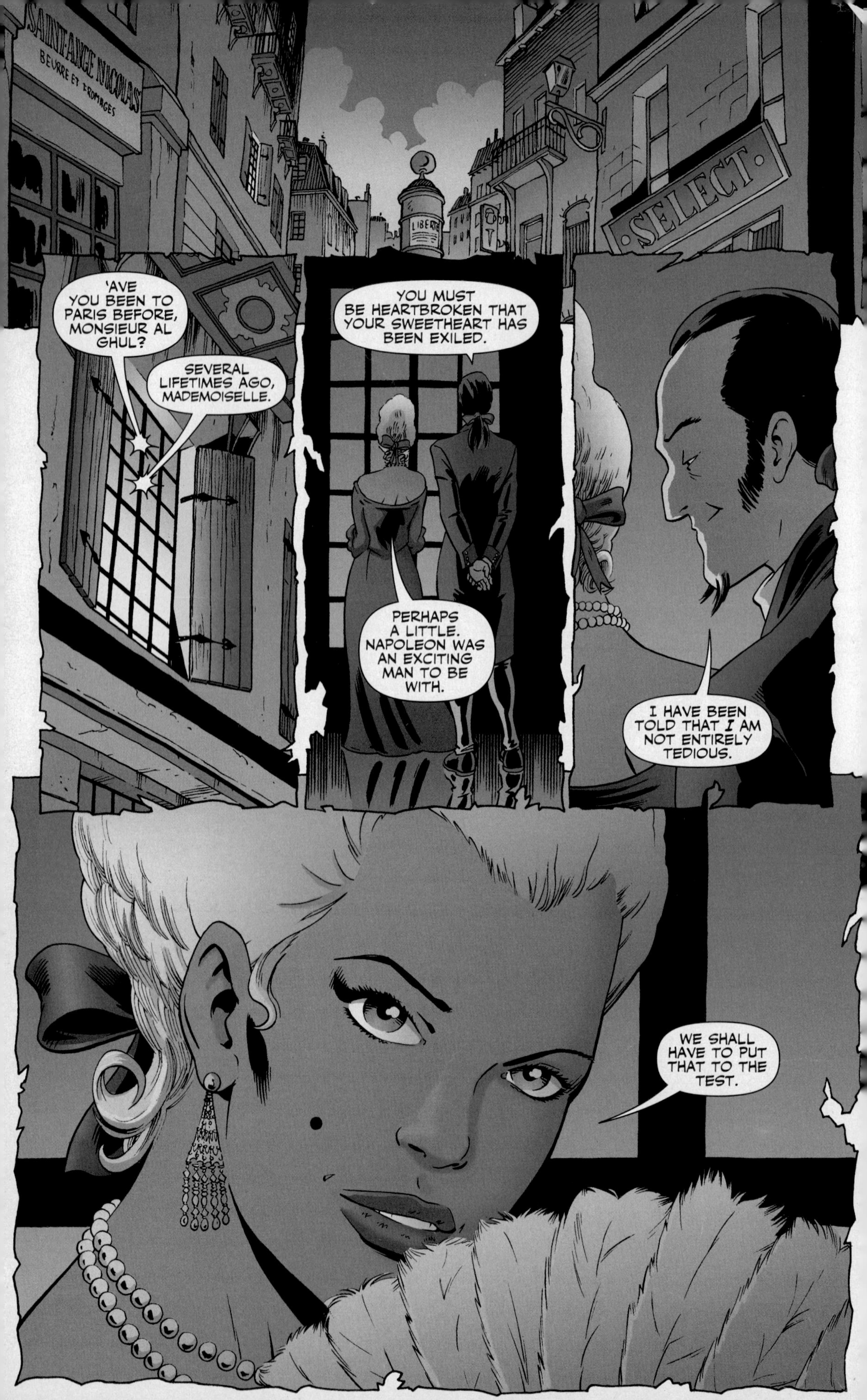
SAINT-ANGE NICOLAS
BEURRE ET FROMAGES
LIBERTÉ
SELECT
'AVE YOU BEEN TO PARIS BEFORE, MONSIEUR AL GHUL?
SEVERAL LIFETIMES AGO, MADEMOISELLE.
YOU MUST BE HEARTBROKEN THAT YOUR SWEETHEART HAS BEEN EXILED.
PERHAPS A LITTLE. NAPOLEON WAS AN EXCITING MAN TO BE WITH.
I HAVE BEEN TOLD THAT *I* AM NOT ENTIRELY TEDIOUS.
WE SHALL HAVE TO PUT THAT TO THE TEST.

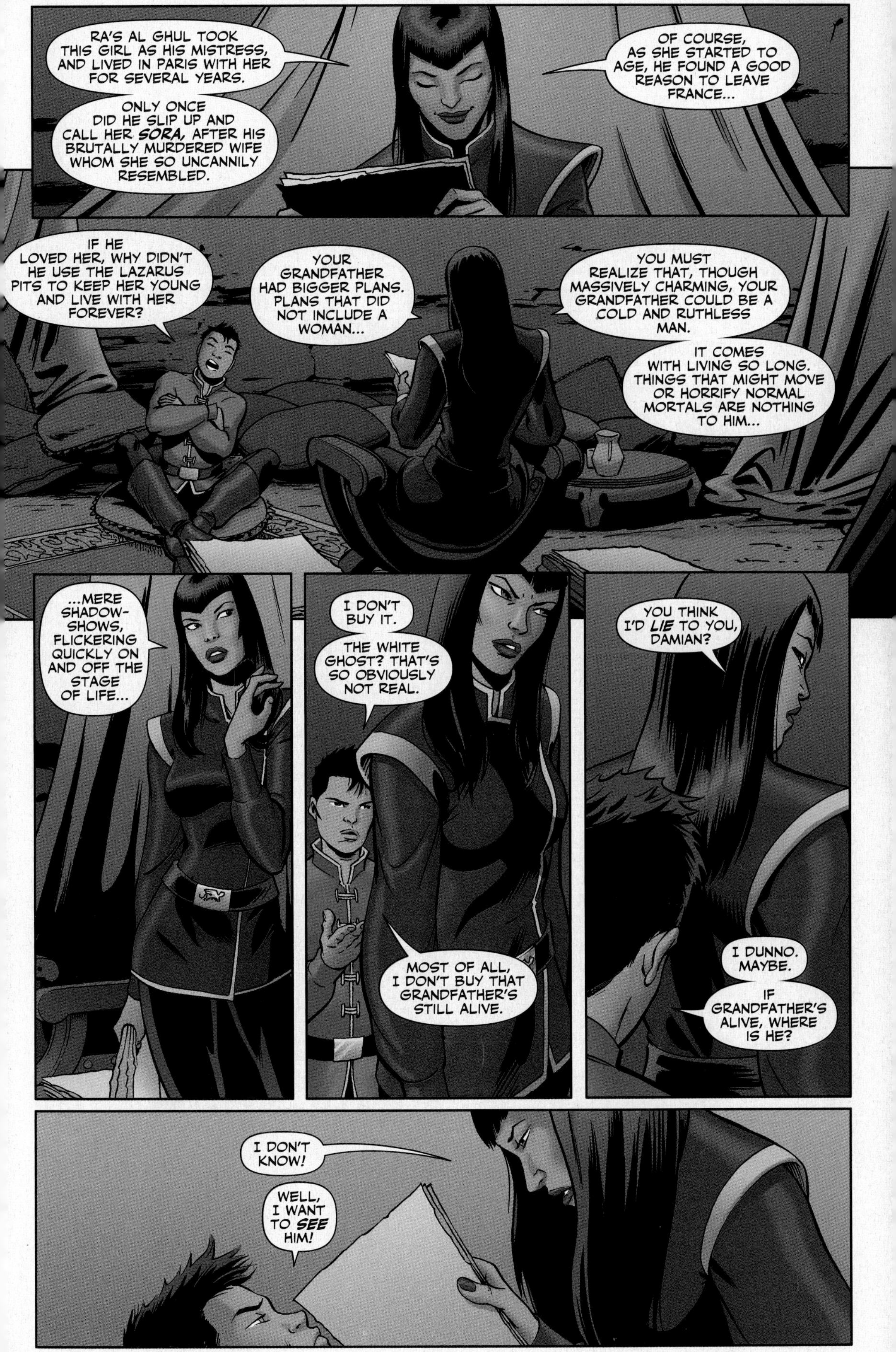
RA'S AL GHUL TOOK THIS GIRL AS HIS MISTRESS, AND LIVED IN PARIS WITH HER FOR SEVERAL YEARS.
ONLY ONCE DID HE SLIP UP AND CALL HER SORA, AFTER HIS BRUTALLY MURDERED WIFE WHOM SHE SO UNCANNILY RESEMBLED.
OF COURSE, AS SHE STARTED TO AGE, HE FOUND A GOOD REASON TO LEAVE FRANCE...
IF HE LOVED HER, WHY DIDN'T HE USE THE LAZARUS PITS TO KEEP HER YOUNG AND LIVE WITH HER FOREVER?
YOUR GRANDFATHER HAD BIGGER PLANS. PLANS THAT DID NOT INCLUDE A WOMAN...
YOU MUST REALIZE THAT, THOUGH MASSIVELY CHARMING, YOUR GRANDFATHER COULD BE A COLD AND RUTHLESS MAN.
IT COMES WITH LIVING SO LONG. THINGS THAT MIGHT MOVE OR HORRIFY NORMAL MORTALS ARE NOTHING TO HIM...
...MERE SHADOW-SHOWS, FLICKERING QUICKLY ON AND OFF THE STAGE OF LIFE...
I DON'T BUY IT.
THE WHITE GHOST? THAT'S SO OBVIOUSLY NOT REAL.
MOST OF ALL, I DON'T BUY THAT GRANDFATHER'S STILL ALIVE.
YOU THINK I'D LIE TO YOU, DAMIAN?
I DUNNO. MAYBE.
IF GRANDFATHER'S ALIVE, WHERE IS HE?
I DON'T KNOW!
WELL, I WANT TO SEE HIM!

HERE IS THE NEXT INSTALLMENT OF THE HISTORICAL RECORDS.

WHY CAN'T YOU GIVE ME ALL OF THEM AT ONCE?

WE DON'T WANT YOU SKIPPING AHEAD TO THE END!

NOW, JUST BE SURE YOU DON'T STRAY FROM THE TEXT, TALIA. DON'T LET THAT WOMAN'S IMAGINATION OF YOURS EMBROIDER THE TRUTH.

ARE YOU SAYING YOU NEVER DO A LITTLE EMBROIDERY YOURSELF?

I AM A SLAVE TO YOUR FATHER--AND TO THE TRUTH.

JUST REMEMBER TO KEEP YOURSELF AND THE BOY AWAY FROM THIS CHAMBER.

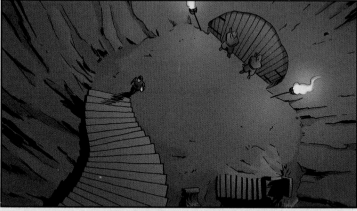

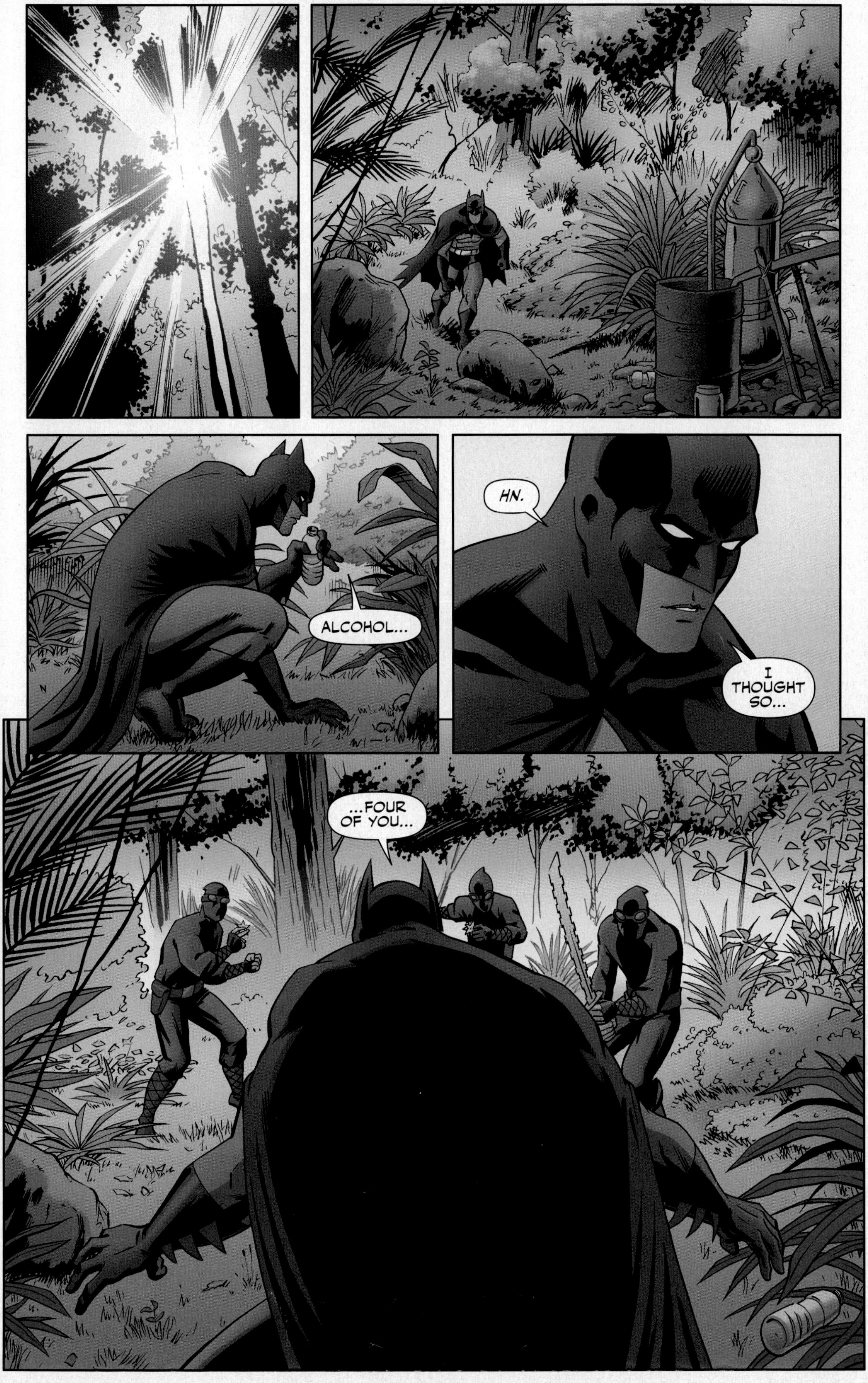
ALCOHOL...
HN.
I THOUGHT SO...
...FOUR OF YOU...

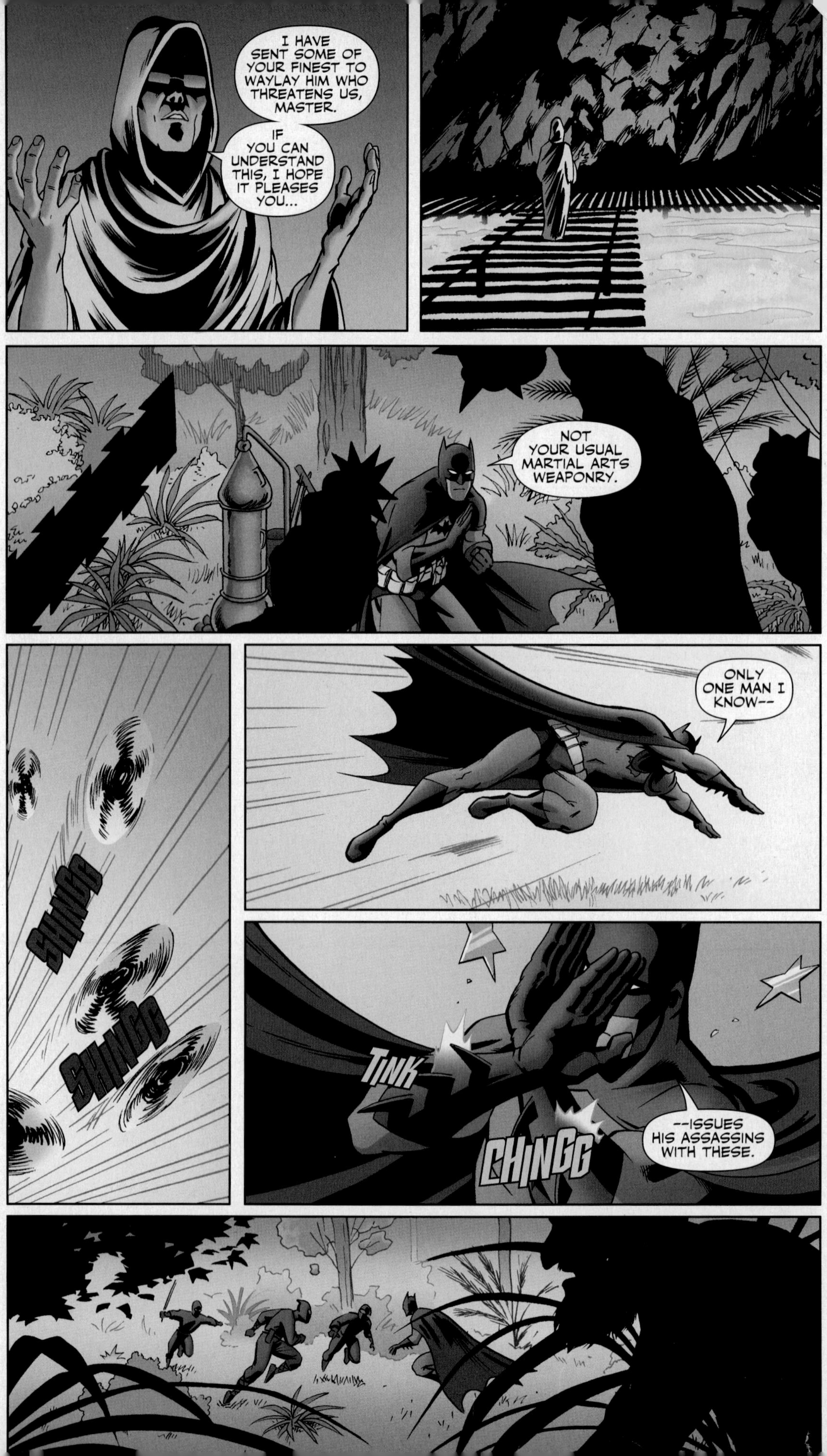
I HAVE SENT SOME OF YOUR FINEST TO WAYLAY HIM WHO THREATENS US, MASTER.
IF YOU CAN UNDERSTAND THIS, I HOPE IT PLEASES YOU...
NOT YOUR USUAL MARTIAL ARTS WEAPONRY.
SHINGG
SHINGG
ONLY ONE MAN I KNOW--
TINK
CHINGG
--ISSUES HIS ASSASSINS WITH THESE.

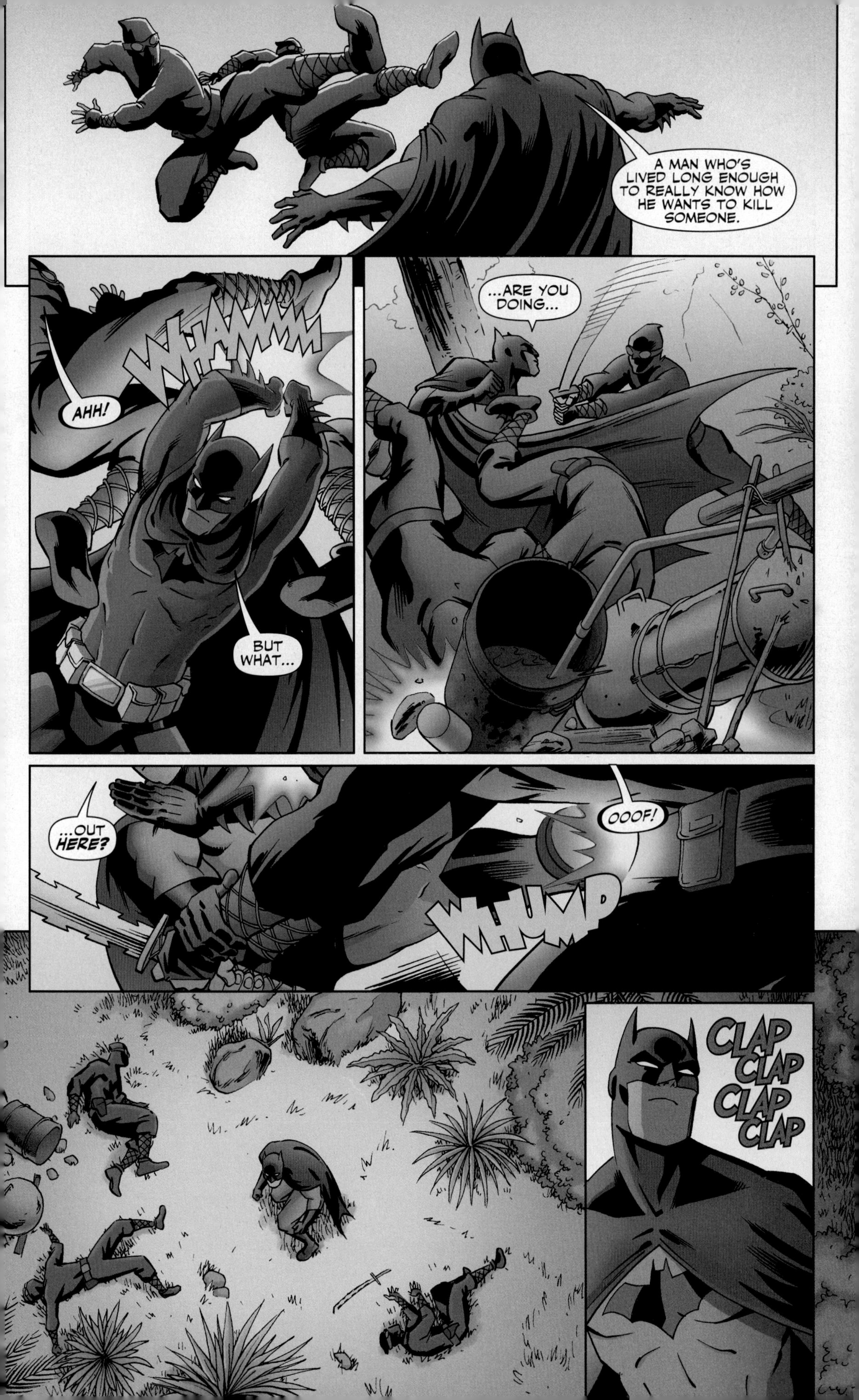
A MAN WHO'S LIVED LONG ENOUGH TO REALLY KNOW HOW HE WANTS TO KILL SOMEONE.
WHAMMM
AHH!
BUT WHAT...
...ARE YOU DOING...
...OUT HERE?
OOOF!
WHUMP
CLAP CLAP CLAP CLAP

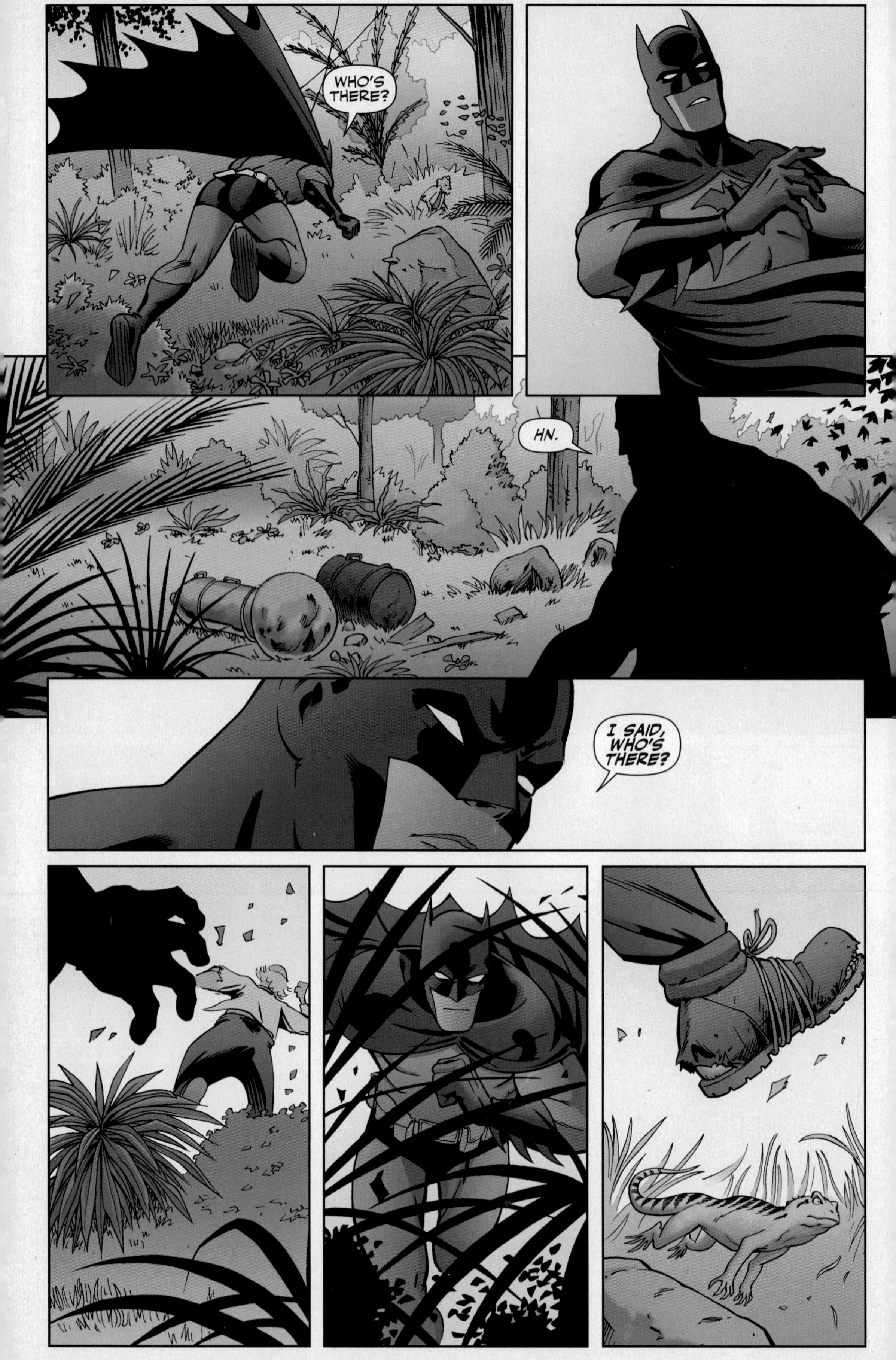
WHO'S THERE?
HN.
I SAID, WHO'S THERE?

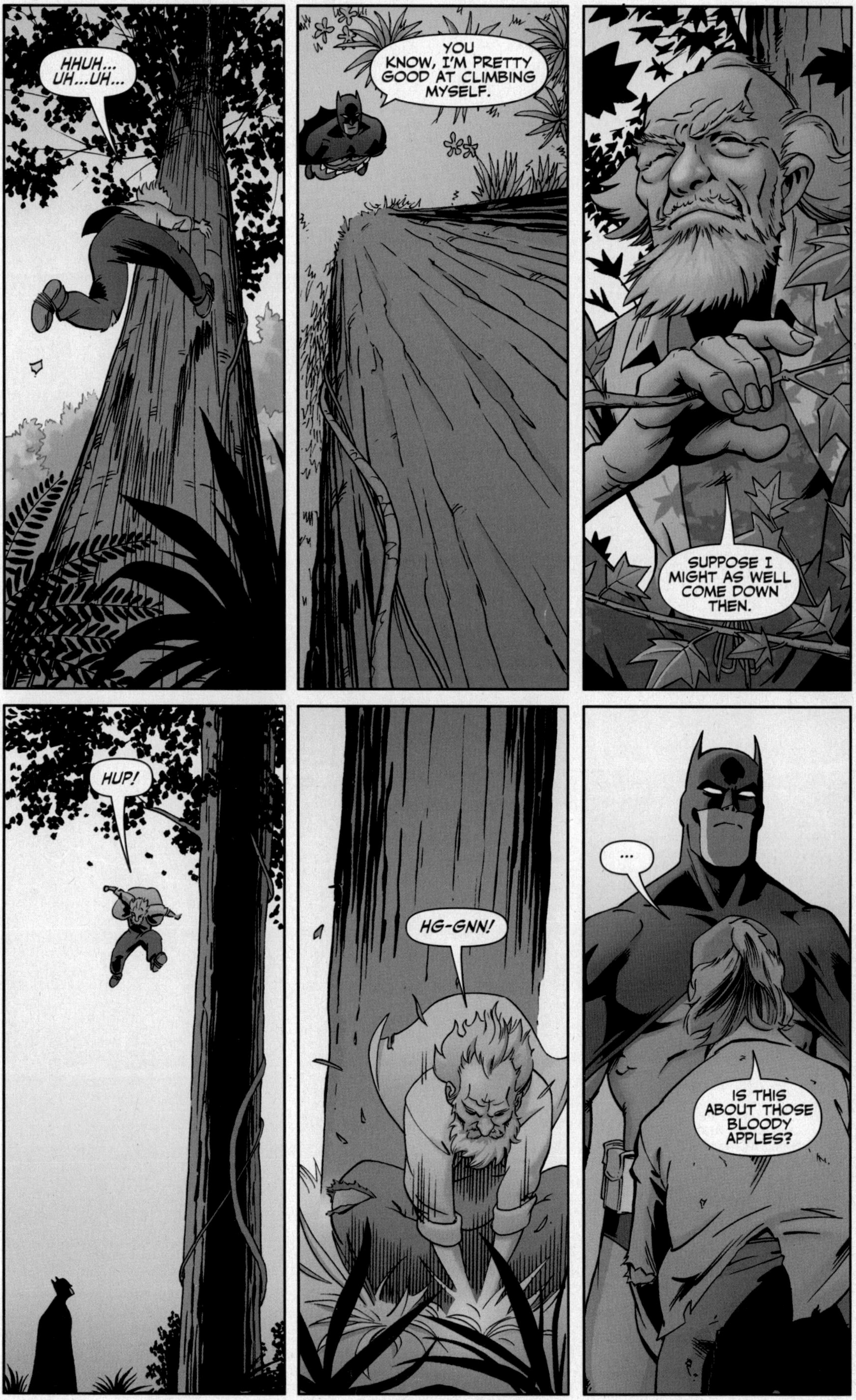
HHUH... UH...UH...
YOU KNOW, I'M PRETTY GOOD AT CLIMBING MYSELF.
SUPPOSE I MIGHT AS WELL COME DOWN THEN.
HUP!
HG-GNN!
...
IS THIS ABOUT THOSE BLOODY APPLES?

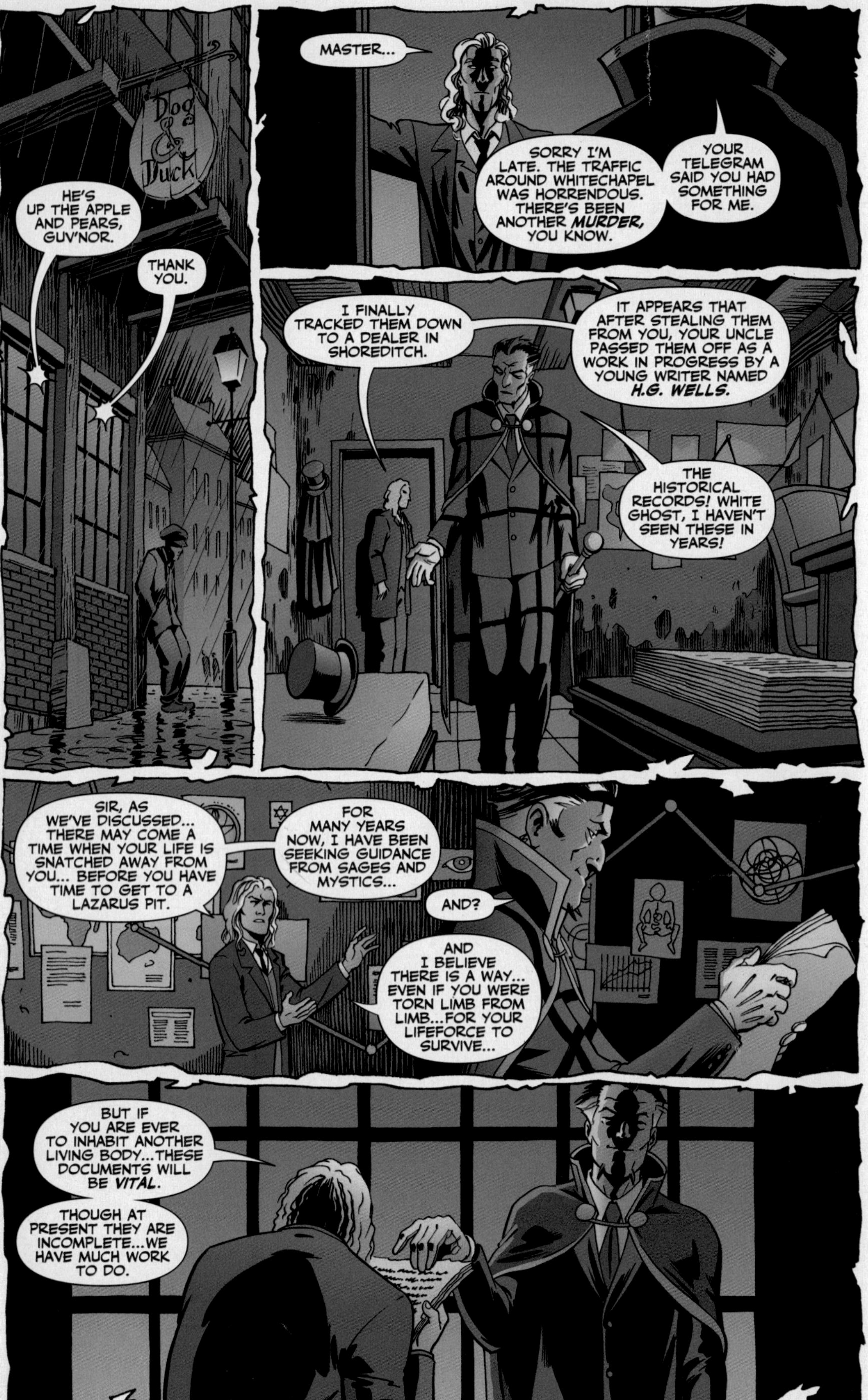
Dog & Duck
HE'S UP THE APPLE AND PEARS, GUV'NOR.
THANK YOU.
MASTER...
SORRY I'M LATE. THE TRAFFIC AROUND WHITECHAPEL WAS HORRENDOUS. THERE'S BEEN ANOTHER MURDER, YOU KNOW.
YOUR TELEGRAM SAID YOU HAD SOMETHING FOR ME.
I FINALLY TRACKED THEM DOWN TO A DEALER IN SHOREDITCH.
IT APPEARS THAT AFTER STEALING THEM FROM YOU, YOUR UNCLE PASSED THEM OFF AS A WORK IN PROGRESS BY A YOUNG WRITER NAMED H.G. WELLS.
THE HISTORICAL RECORDS! WHITE GHOST, I HAVEN'T SEEN THESE IN YEARS!
SIR, AS WE'VE DISCUSSED... THERE MAY COME A TIME WHEN YOUR LIFE IS SNATCHED AWAY FROM YOU... BEFORE YOU HAVE TIME TO GET TO A LAZARUS PIT.
FOR MANY YEARS NOW, I HAVE BEEN SEEKING GUIDANCE FROM SAGES AND MYSTICS...
AND?
AND I BELIEVE THERE IS A WAY... EVEN IF YOU WERE TORN LIMB FROM LIMB...FOR YOUR LIFEFORCE TO SURVIVE...
BUT IF YOU ARE EVER TO INHABIT ANOTHER LIVING BODY...THESE DOCUMENTS WILL BE VITAL.
THOUGH AT PRESENT THEY ARE INCOMPLETE...WE HAVE MUCH WORK TO DO.

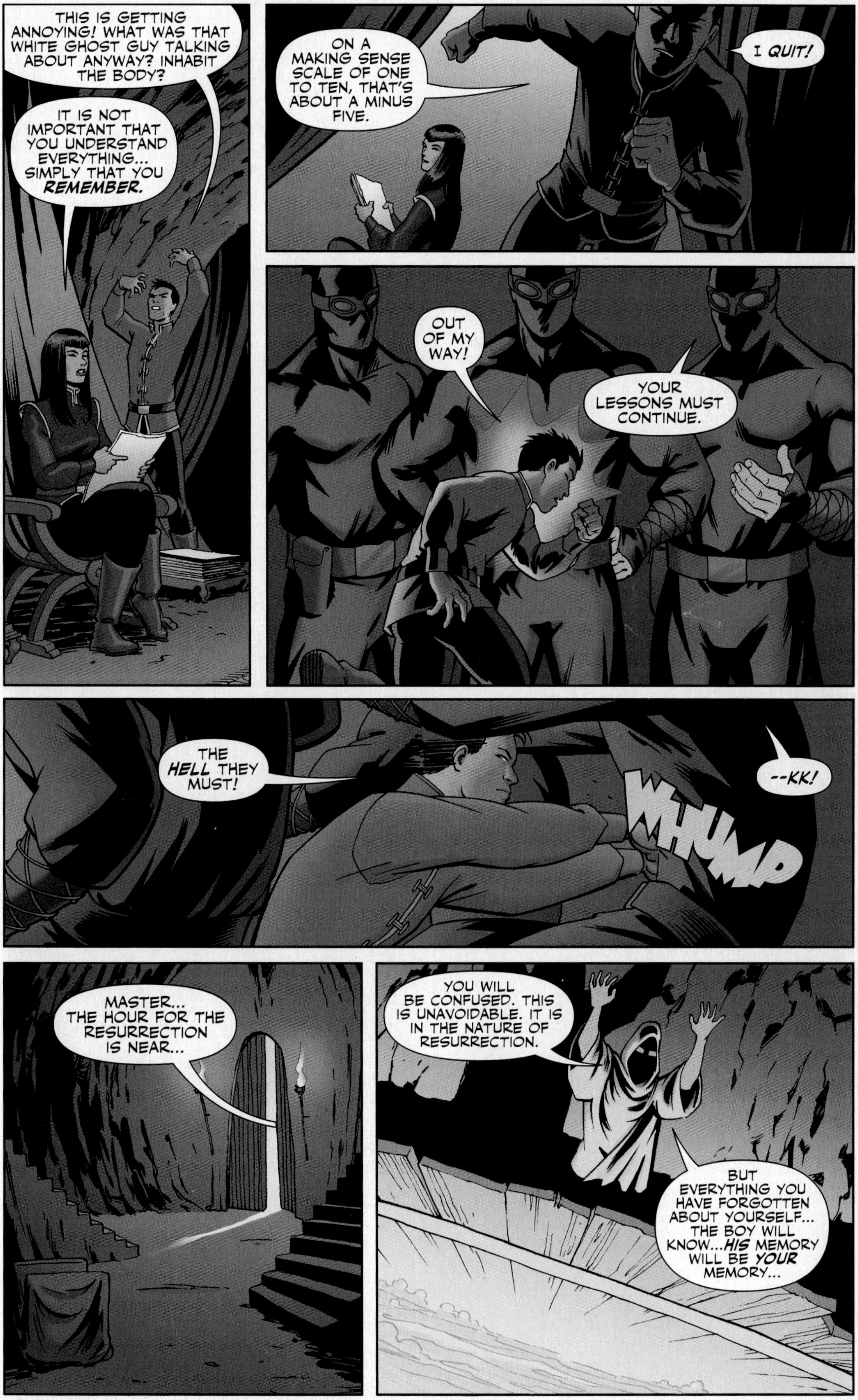
THIS IS GETTING ANNOYING! WHAT WAS THAT WHITE GHOST GUY TALKING ABOUT ANYWAY? INHABIT THE BODY?
IT IS NOT IMPORTANT THAT YOU UNDERSTAND EVERYTHING... SIMPLY THAT YOU REMEMBER.
ON A MAKING SENSE SCALE OF ONE TO TEN, THAT'S ABOUT A MINUS FIVE.
I QUIT!
OUT OF MY WAY!
YOUR LESSONS MUST CONTINUE.
THE HELL THEY MUST!
WHUMP
--KK!
MASTER... THE HOUR FOR THE RESURRECTION IS NEAR...
YOU WILL BE CONFUSED. THIS IS UNAVOIDABLE. IT IS IN THE NATURE OF RESURRECTION.
BUT EVERYTHING YOU HAVE FORGOTTEN ABOUT YOURSELF... THE BOY WILL KNOW...HIS MEMORY WILL BE YOUR MEMORY...

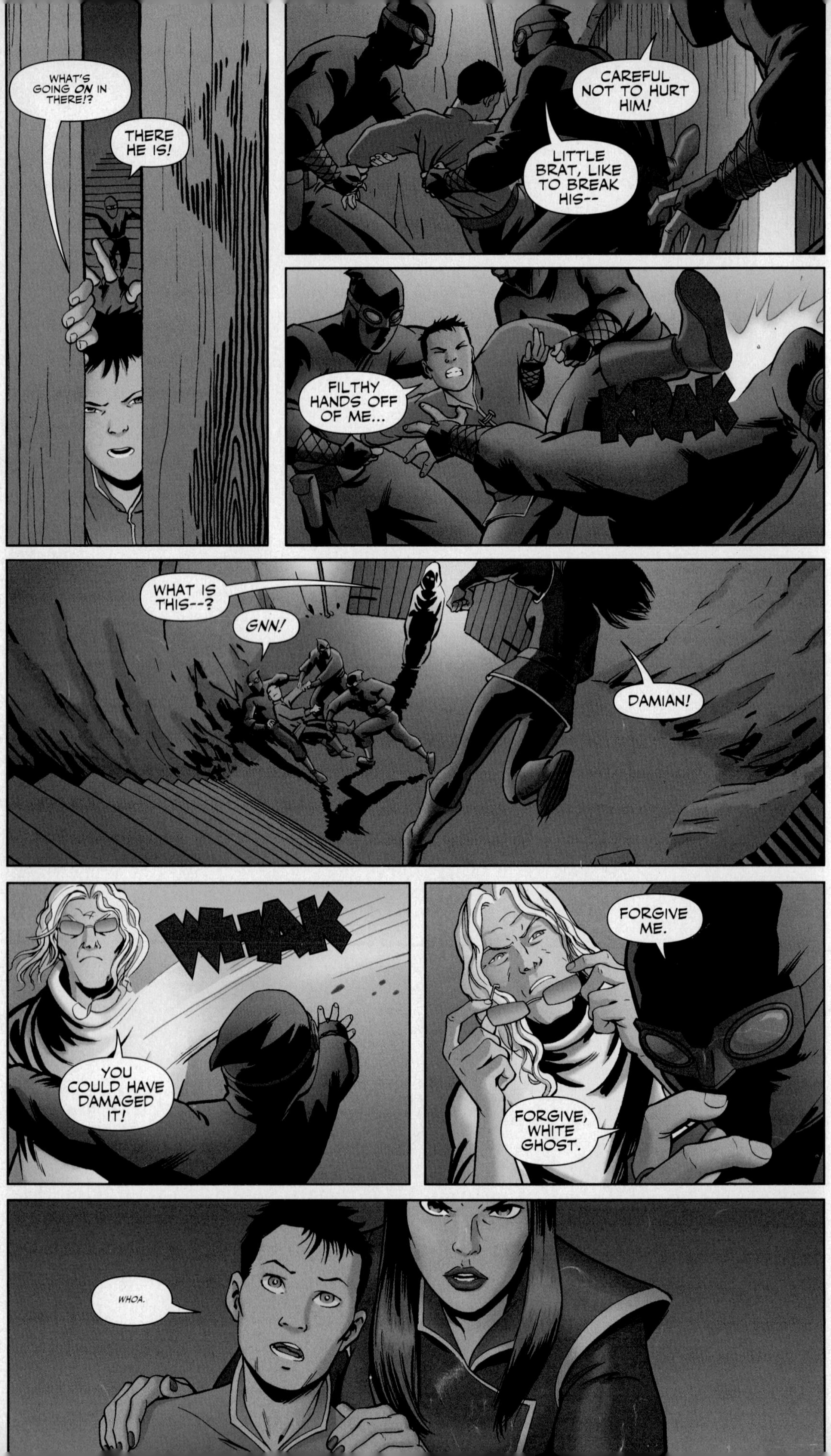
WHAT'S GOING ON IN THERE!?
THERE HE IS!
CAREFUL NOT TO HURT HIM!
LITTLE BRAT, LIKE TO BREAK HIS--
FILTHY HANDS OFF OF ME...
KRAK
WHAT IS THIS--?
GNN!
DAMIAN!
WHAK
YOU COULD HAVE DAMAGED IT!
FORGIVE ME.
FORGIVE, WHITE GHOST.
WHOA.

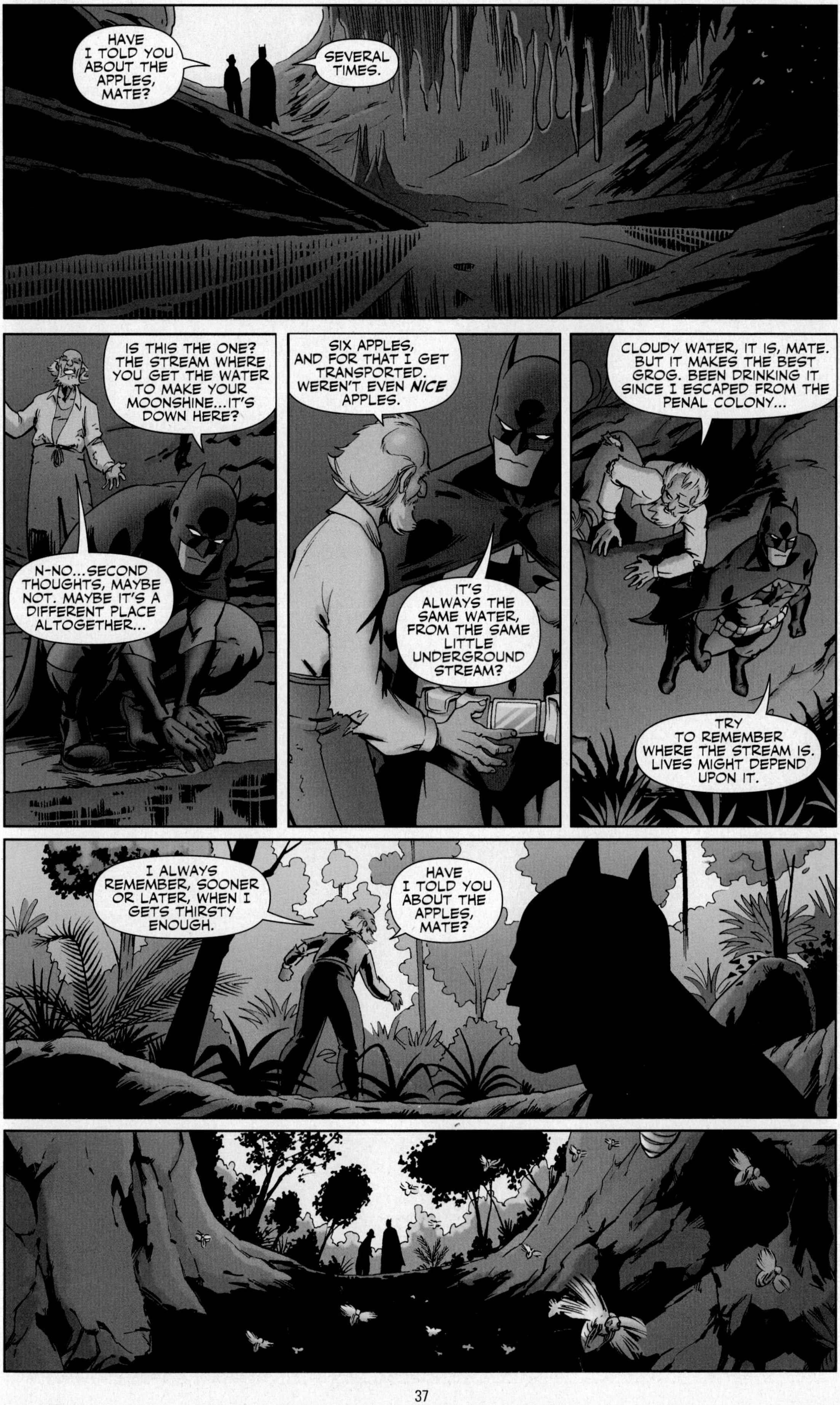
HAVE I TOLD YOU ABOUT THE APPLES, MATE?
SEVERAL TIMES.
IS THIS THE ONE? THE STREAM WHERE YOU GET THE WATER TO MAKE YOUR MOONSHINE...IT'S DOWN HERE?
N-NO...SECOND THOUGHTS, MAYBE NOT. MAYBE IT'S A DIFFERENT PLACE ALTOGETHER...
SIX APPLES, AND FOR THAT I GET TRANSPORTED. WEREN'T EVEN *NICE* APPLES.
IT'S ALWAYS THE SAME WATER, FROM THE SAME LITTLE UNDERGROUND STREAM?
CLOUDY WATER, IT IS, MATE. BUT IT MAKES THE BEST GROG. BEEN DRINKING IT SINCE I ESCAPED FROM THE PENAL COLONY...
TRY TO REMEMBER WHERE THE STREAM IS. LIVES MIGHT DEPEND UPON IT.
I ALWAYS REMEMBER, SOONER OR LATER, WHEN I GETS THIRSTY ENOUGH.
HAVE I TOLD YOU ABOUT THE APPLES, MATE?

RA'S AL GHUL IS YOUR FATHER. YOU CANNOT STAND IN THE WAY OF WHAT HAS BEEN PLANNED FOR CENTURIES.

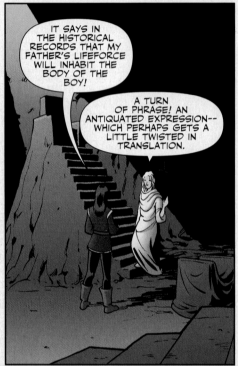

IT SAYS IN THE HISTORICAL RECORDS THAT MY FATHER'S LIFEFORCE WILL INHABIT THE BODY OF THE BOY!

A TURN OF PHRASE! AN ANTIQUATED EXPRESSION-- WHICH PERHAPS GETS A LITTLE TWISTED IN TRANSLATION.

HERE'S WHAT WILL HAPPEN. YOUR FATHER WILL BE SUMMONED... HIS LIFEFORCE WILL FORM INTO A NEW BODY, THANKS TO THE WONDROUS PROPERTIES OF THE LAZARUS PIT.

BUT HE WILL BE CONFUSED... HE WILL HAVE QUESTIONS ABOUT HIMSELF, ABOUT WHO HE IS...

YOU COULD SURELY ANSWER THOSE...

QUESTIONS THAT ONLY A MALE BLOOD RELATIVE CAN ANSWER. IT HAS TO BE DAMIAN, TALIA. THE RULES OF THIS GAME WERE SET IN MOTION LONG BEFORE ANY OF US WERE ALIVE.

I PROMISE YOU, ON EVERYTHING I HOLD DEAR...

...YOUR SON WILL COME TO NO HARM.

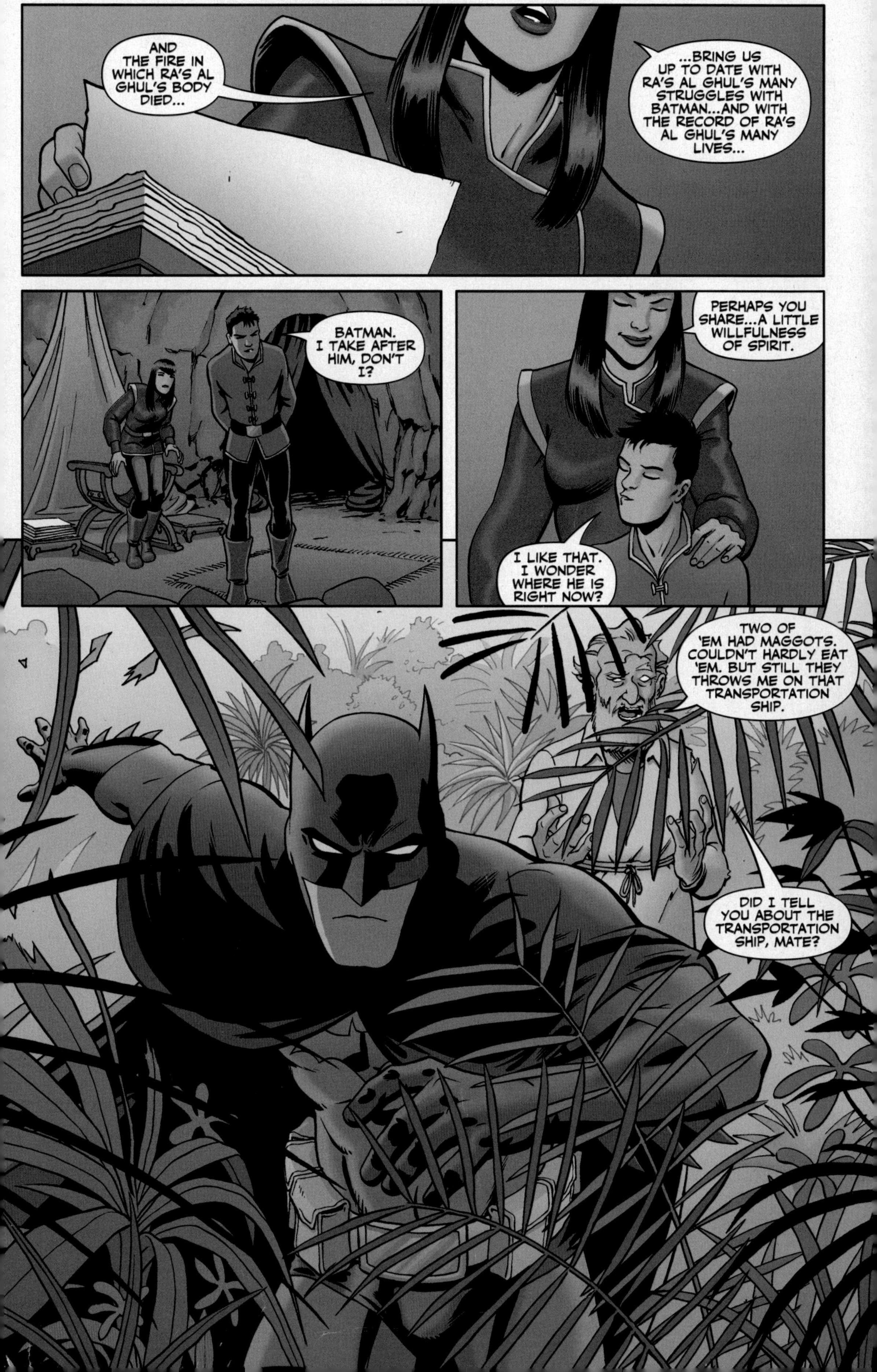
AND THE FIRE IN WHICH RA'S AL GHUL'S BODY DIED...
...BRING US UP TO DATE WITH RA'S AL GHUL'S MANY STRUGGLES WITH BATMAN...AND WITH THE RECORD OF RA'S AL GHUL'S MANY LIVES...
BATMAN. I TAKE AFTER HIM, DON'T I?
PERHAPS YOU SHARE...A LITTLE WILLFULNESS OF SPIRIT.
I LIKE THAT. I WONDER WHERE HE IS RIGHT NOW?
TWO OF 'EM HAD MAGGOTS. COULDN'T HARDLY EAT 'EM. BUT STILL THEY THROWS ME ON THAT TRANSPORTATION SHIP.
DID I TELL YOU ABOUT THE TRANSPORTATION SHIP, MATE?

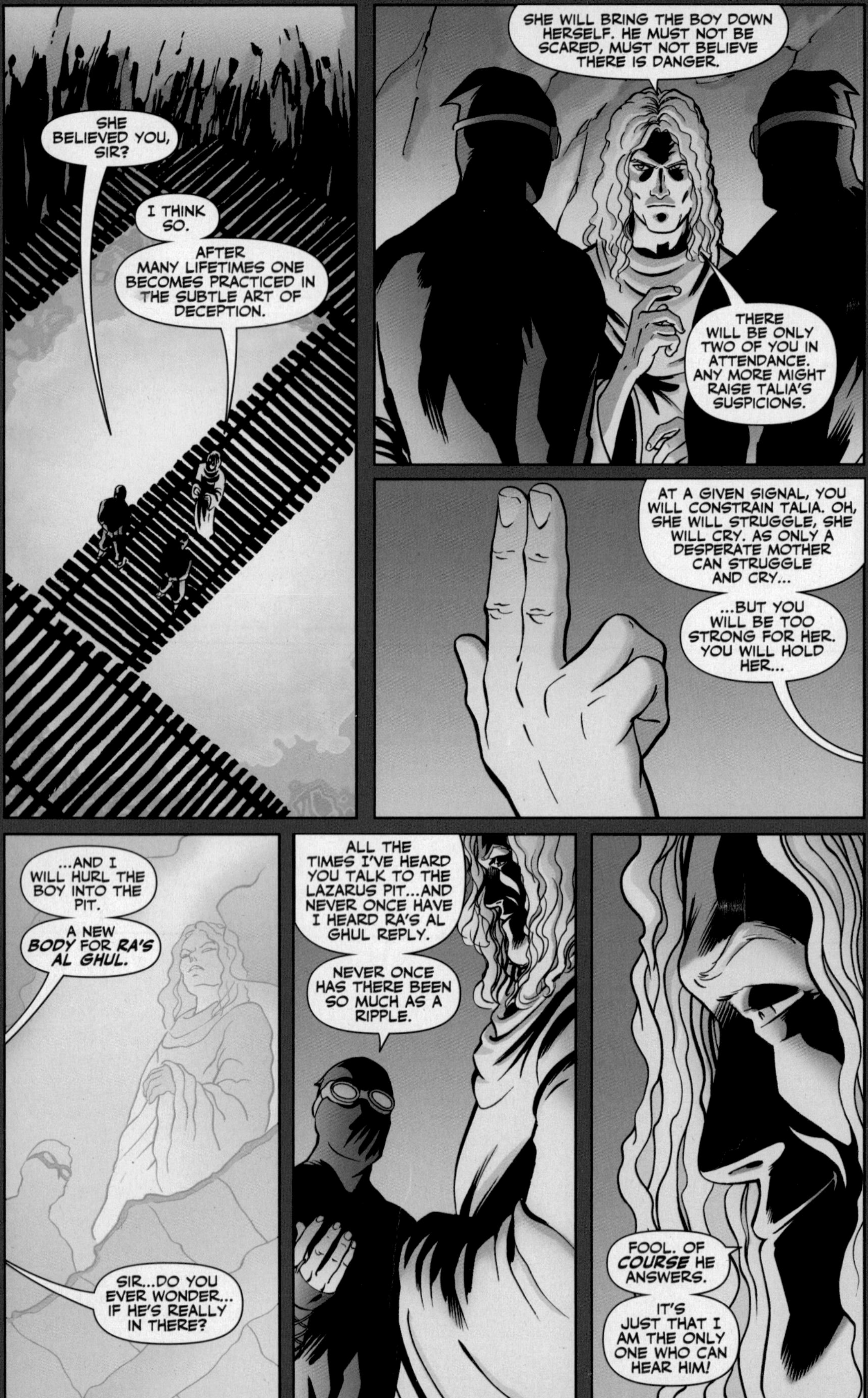
SHE BELIEVED YOU, SIR?
I THINK SO.
AFTER MANY LIFETIMES ONE BECOMES PRACTICED IN THE SUBTLE ART OF DECEPTION.
SHE WILL BRING THE BOY DOWN HERSELF. HE MUST NOT BE SCARED, MUST NOT BELIEVE THERE IS DANGER.
THERE WILL BE ONLY TWO OF YOU IN ATTENDANCE. ANY MORE MIGHT RAISE TALIA'S SUSPICIONS.
AT A GIVEN SIGNAL, YOU WILL CONSTRAIN TALIA. OH, SHE WILL STRUGGLE, SHE WILL CRY. AS ONLY A DESPERATE MOTHER CAN STRUGGLE AND CRY...
...BUT YOU WILL BE TOO STRONG FOR HER. YOU WILL HOLD HER...
...AND I WILL HURL THE BOY INTO THE PIT.
A NEW *BODY* FOR *RA'S AL GHUL.*
SIR...DO YOU EVER WONDER... IF HE'S REALLY IN THERE?
ALL THE TIMES I'VE HEARD YOU TALK TO THE LAZARUS PIT...AND NEVER ONCE HAVE I HEARD RA'S AL GHUL REPLY.
NEVER ONCE HAS THERE BEEN SO MUCH AS A RIPPLE.
FOOL. OF *COURSE* HE ANSWERS.
IT'S JUST THAT I AM THE ONLY ONE WHO CAN HEAR HIM!

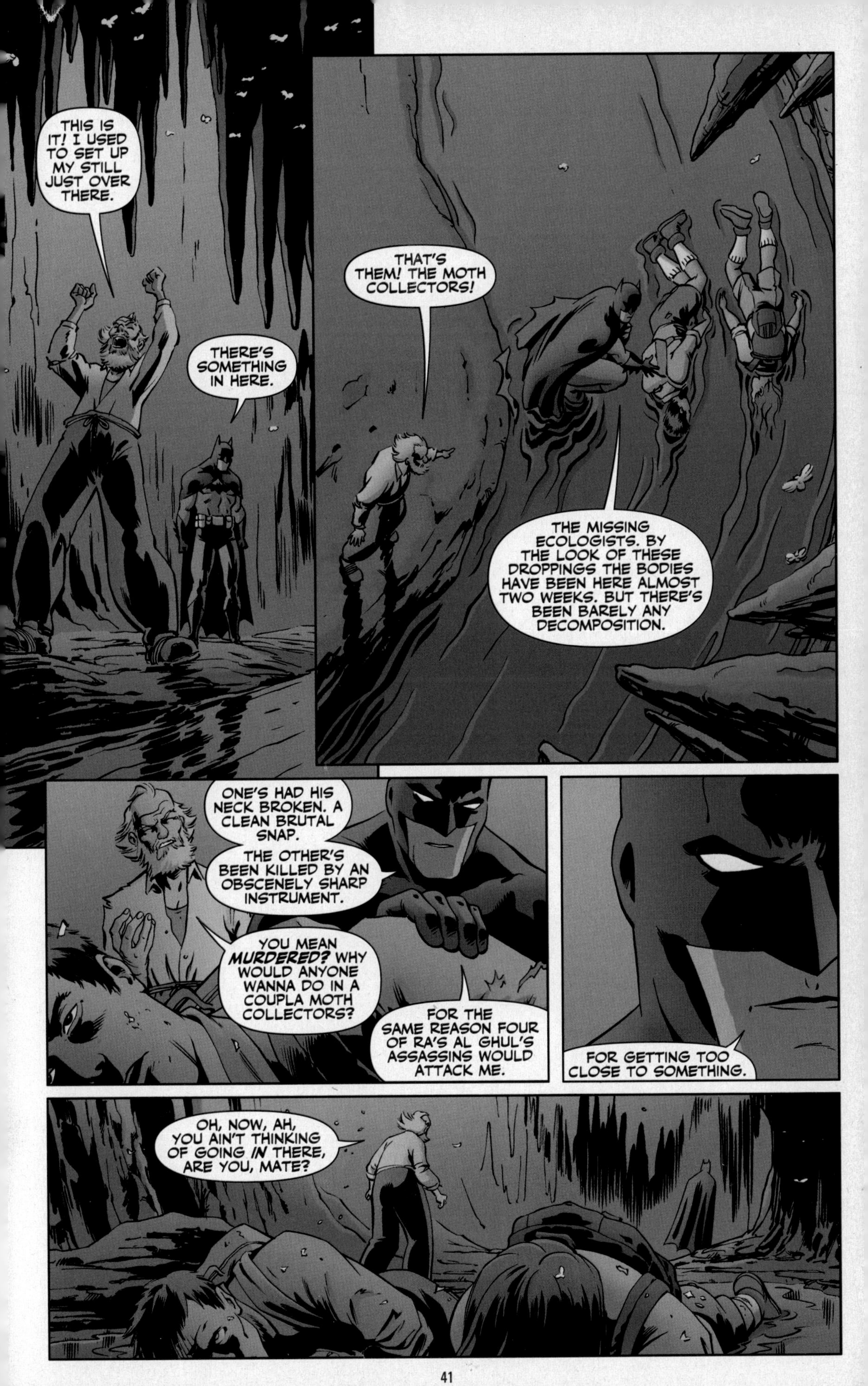
THIS IS IT! I USED TO SET UP MY STILL JUST OVER THERE.
THERE'S SOMETHING IN HERE.
THAT'S THEM! THE MOTH COLLECTORS!
THE MISSING ECOLOGISTS. BY THE LOOK OF THESE DROPPINGS THE BODIES HAVE BEEN HERE ALMOST TWO WEEKS. BUT THERE'S BEEN BARELY ANY DECOMPOSITION.
ONE'S HAD HIS NECK BROKEN. A CLEAN BRUTAL SNAP.
THE OTHER'S BEEN KILLED BY AN OBSCENELY SHARP INSTRUMENT.
YOU MEAN MURDERED? WHY WOULD ANYONE WANNA DO IN A COUPLA MOTH COLLECTORS?
FOR THE SAME REASON FOUR OF RA'S AL GHUL'S ASSASSINS WOULD ATTACK ME.
FOR GETTING TOO CLOSE TO SOMETHING.
OH, NOW, AH, YOU AIN'T THINKING OF GOING IN THERE, ARE YOU, MATE?

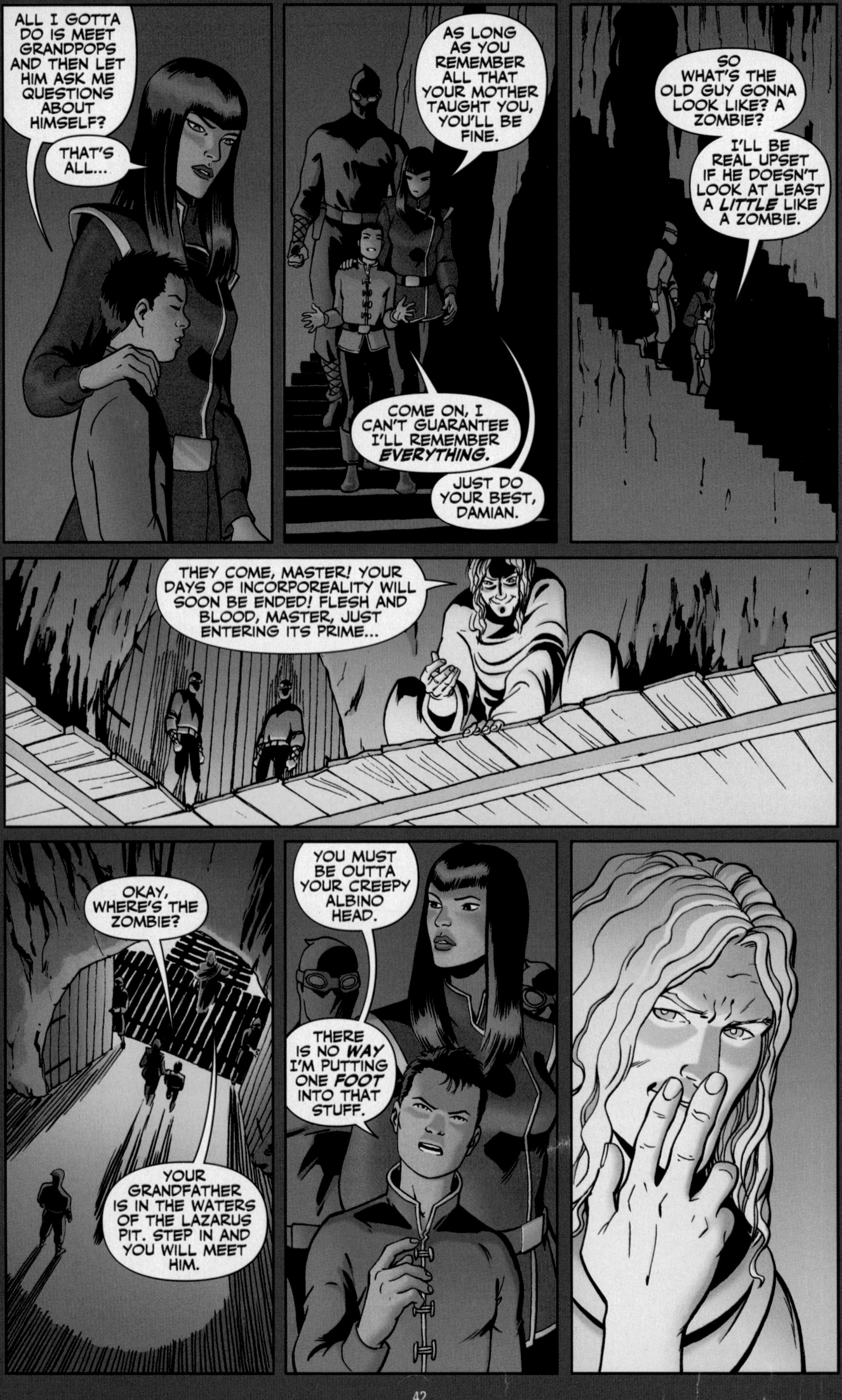
ALL I GOTTA DO IS MEET GRANDPOPS AND THEN LET HIM ASK ME QUESTIONS ABOUT HIMSELF?
THAT'S ALL...
AS LONG AS YOU REMEMBER ALL THAT YOUR MOTHER TAUGHT YOU, YOU'LL BE FINE.
COME ON, I CAN'T GUARANTEE I'LL REMEMBER *EVERYTHING.*
JUST DO YOUR BEST, DAMIAN.
SO WHAT'S THE OLD GUY GONNA LOOK LIKE? A ZOMBIE?
I'LL BE REAL UPSET IF HE DOESN'T LOOK AT LEAST A *LITTLE* LIKE A ZOMBIE.
THEY COME, MASTER! YOUR DAYS OF INCORPOREALITY WILL SOON BE ENDED! FLESH AND BLOOD, MASTER, JUST ENTERING ITS PRIME...
OKAY, WHERE'S THE ZOMBIE?
YOUR GRANDFATHER IS IN THE WATERS OF THE LAZARUS PIT. STEP IN AND YOU WILL MEET HIM.
YOU MUST BE OUTTA YOUR CREEPY ALBINO HEAD.
THERE IS NO *WAY* I'M PUTTING ONE *FOOT* INTO THAT STUFF.

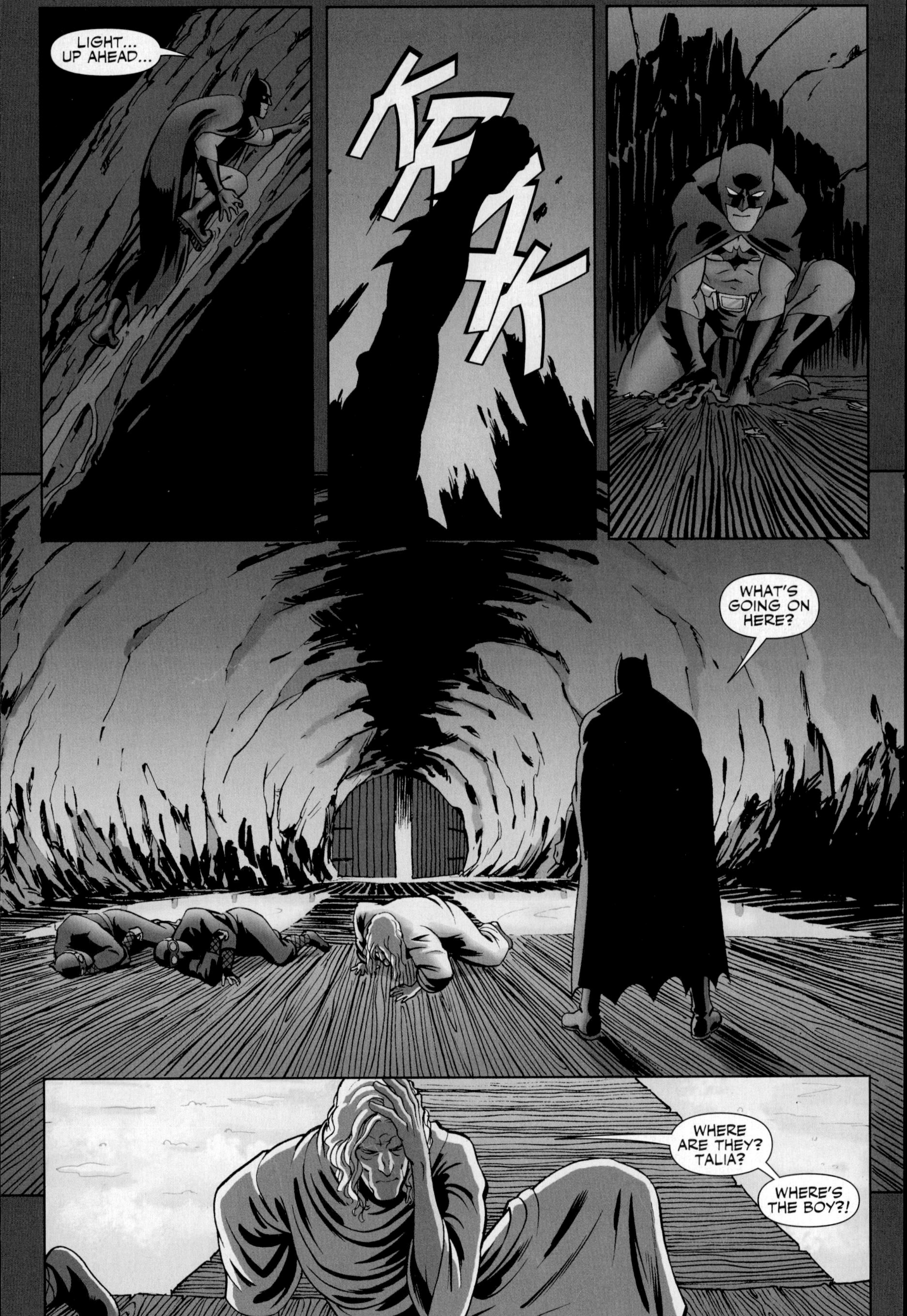
LIGHT... UP AHEAD...
KRAK
WHAT'S GOING ON HERE?
WHERE ARE THEY? TALIA?
WHERE'S THE BOY?!

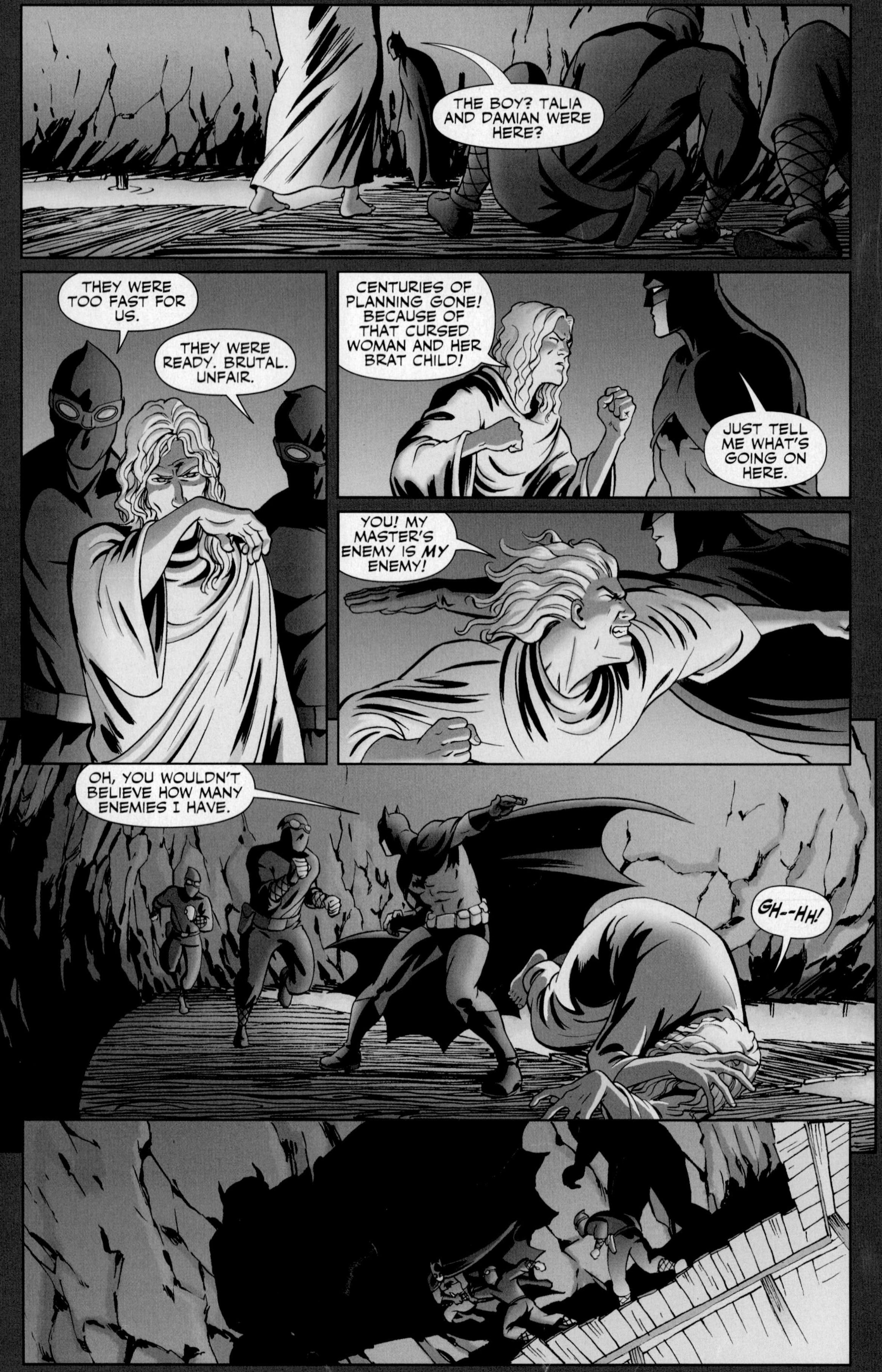
THE BOY? TALIA AND DAMIAN WERE HERE?
THEY WERE TOO FAST FOR US.
THEY WERE READY. BRUTAL. UNFAIR.
CENTURIES OF PLANNING GONE! BECAUSE OF THAT CURSED WOMAN AND HER BRAT CHILD!
JUST TELL ME WHAT'S GOING ON HERE.
YOU! MY MASTER'S ENEMY IS *MY* ENEMY!
OH, YOU WOULDN'T BELIEVE HOW MANY ENEMIES I HAVE.
GH--HH!

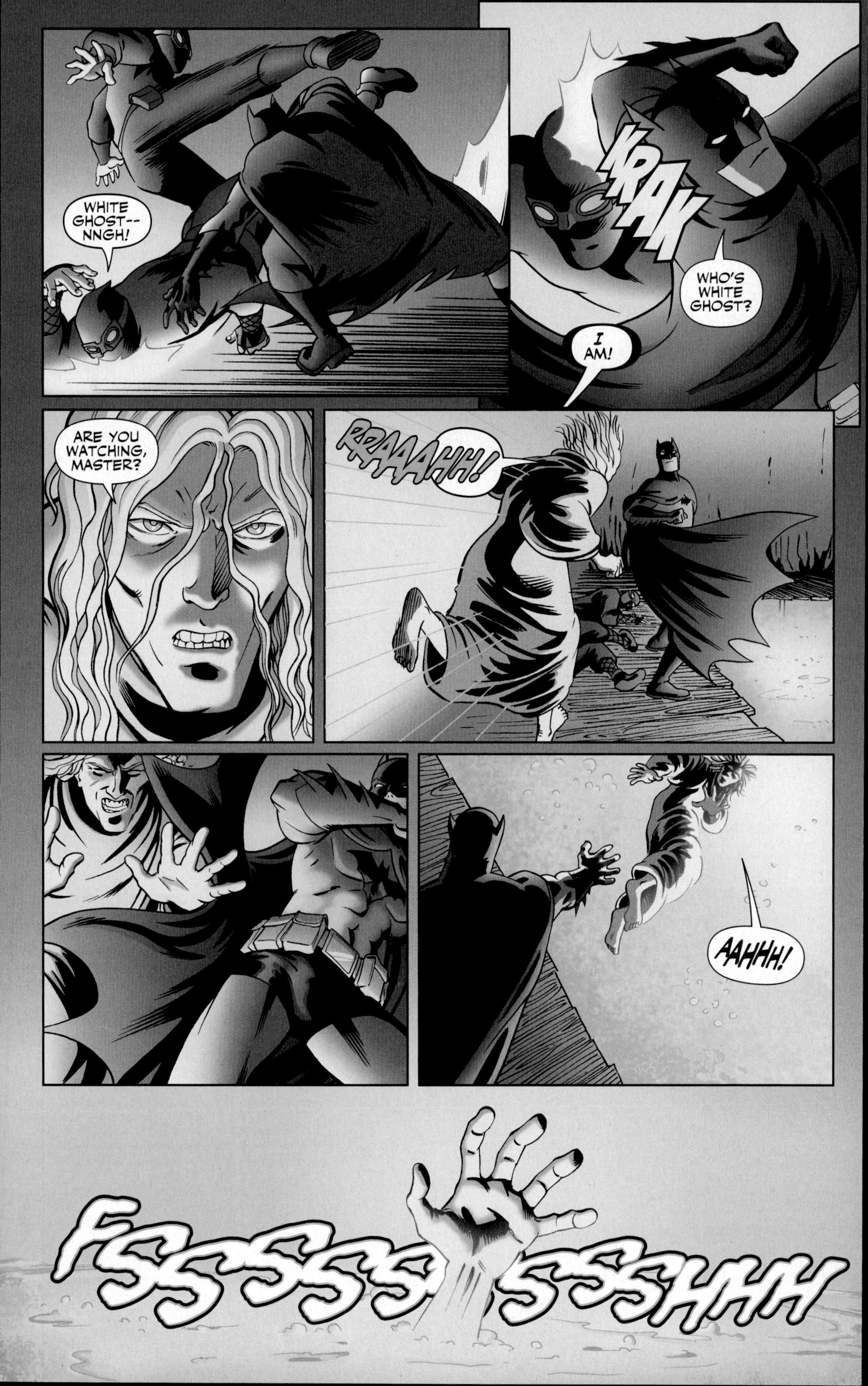
WHITE GHOST-- NNGH!
KRAK
WHO'S WHITE GHOST?
I AM!
ARE YOU WATCHING, MASTER?
RRAAAHH!
AAHHH!
FSSSSSSSSSHHH

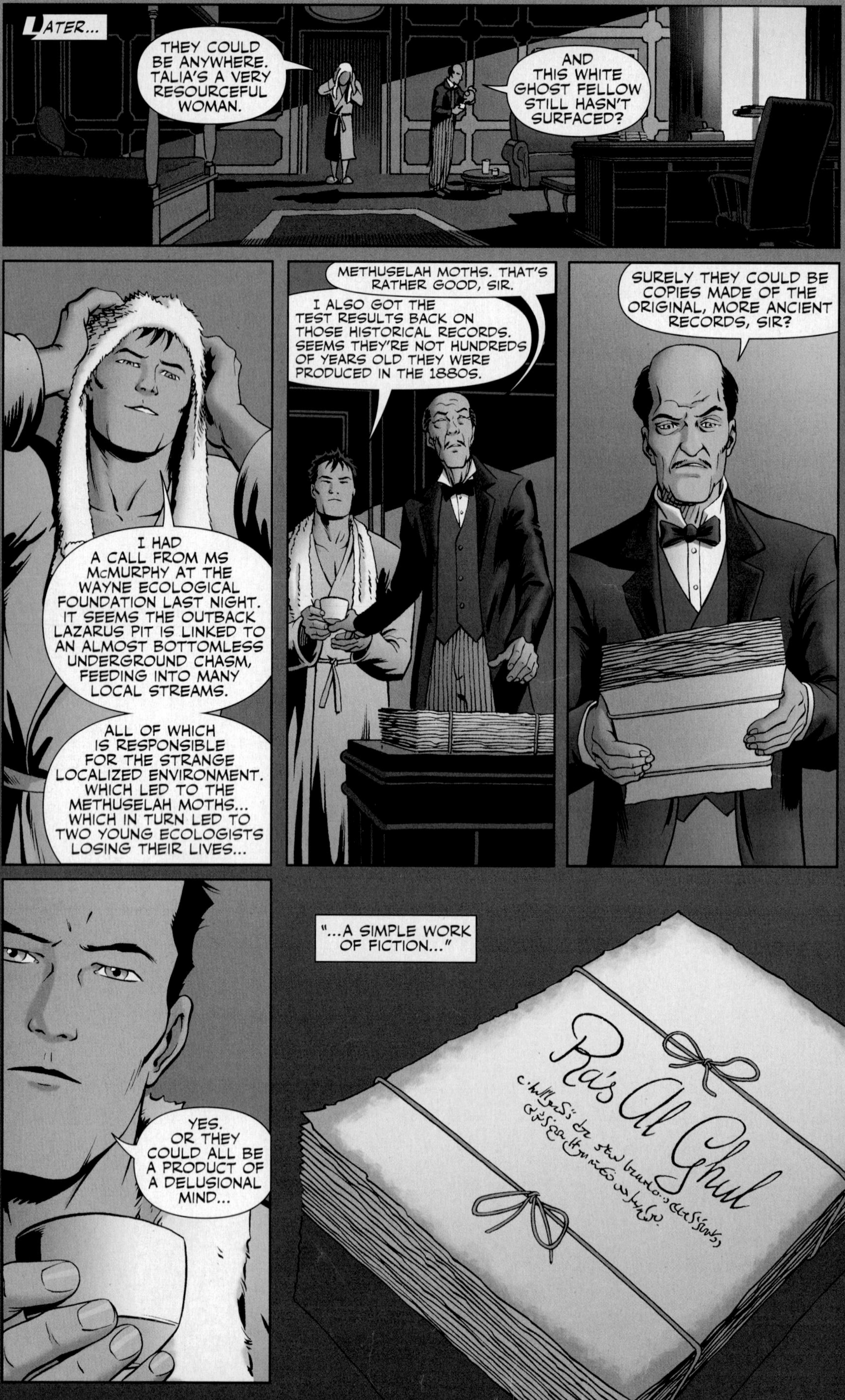
LATER...
THEY COULD BE ANYWHERE. TALIA'S A VERY RESOURCEFUL WOMAN.
AND THIS WHITE GHOST FELLOW STILL HASN'T SURFACED?
I HAD A CALL FROM MS McMURPHY AT THE WAYNE ECOLOGICAL FOUNDATION LAST NIGHT. IT SEEMS THE OUTBACK LAZARUS PIT IS LINKED TO AN ALMOST BOTTOMLESS UNDERGROUND CHASM, FEEDING INTO MANY LOCAL STREAMS.
ALL OF WHICH IS RESPONSIBLE FOR THE STRANGE LOCALIZED ENVIRONMENT. WHICH LED TO THE METHUSELAH MOTHS... WHICH IN TURN LED TO TWO YOUNG ECOLOGISTS LOSING THEIR LIVES...
METHUSELAH MOTHS. THAT'S RATHER GOOD, SIR.
I ALSO GOT THE TEST RESULTS BACK ON THOSE HISTORICAL RECORDS. SEEMS THEY'RE NOT HUNDREDS OF YEARS OLD THEY WERE PRODUCED IN THE 1880S.
SURELY THEY COULD BE COPIES MADE OF THE ORIGINAL, MORE ANCIENT RECORDS, SIR?
YES. OR THEY COULD ALL BE A PRODUCT OF A DELUSIONAL MIND...
"...A SIMPLE WORK OF FICTION..."
Ra's Al Ghul

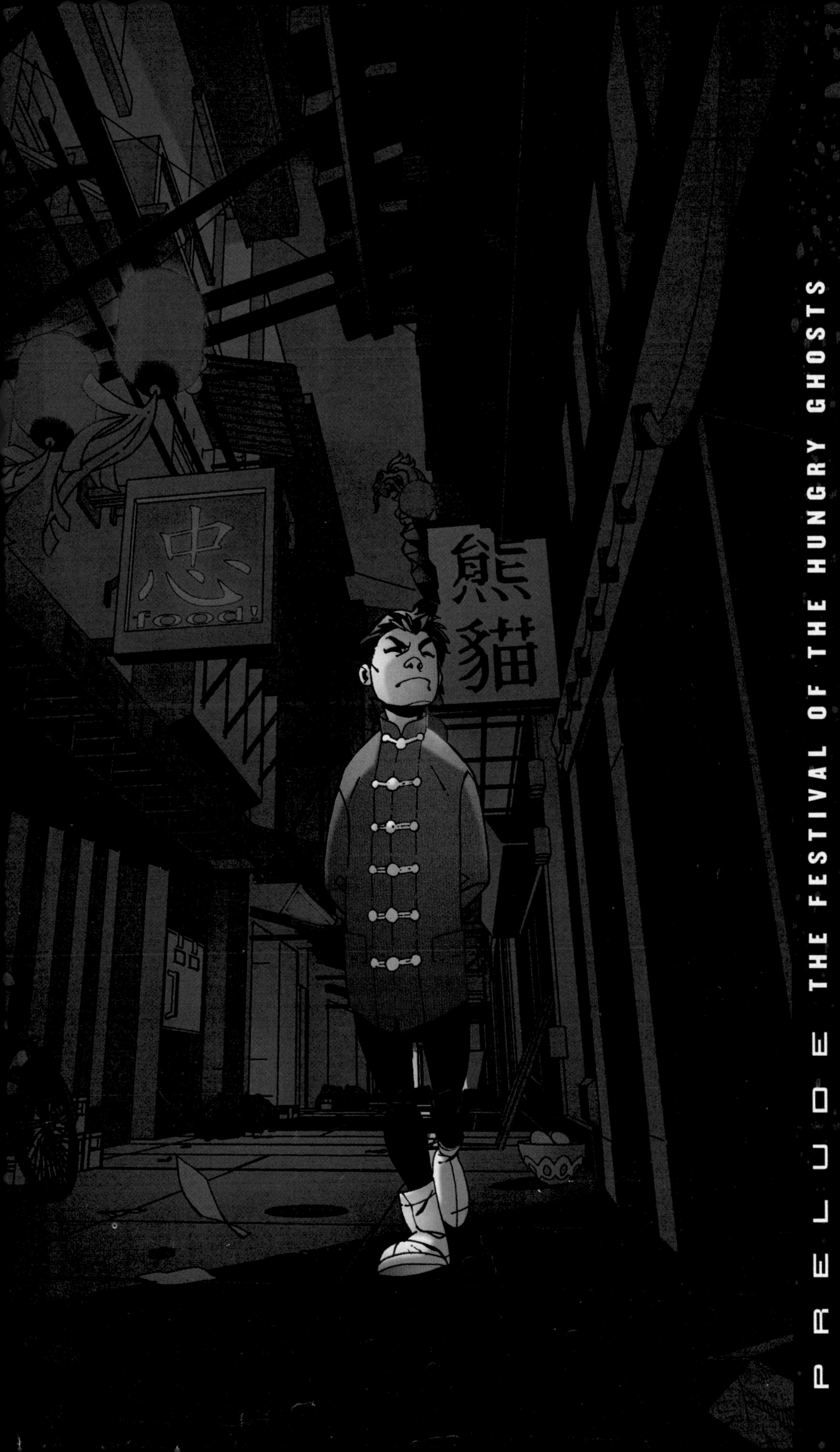
忠
food!
熊貓

PRELUDE THE FESTIVAL OF THE HUNGRY GHOSTS

Chapter written by Keith Champagne | Chapter art by Jason Pearson

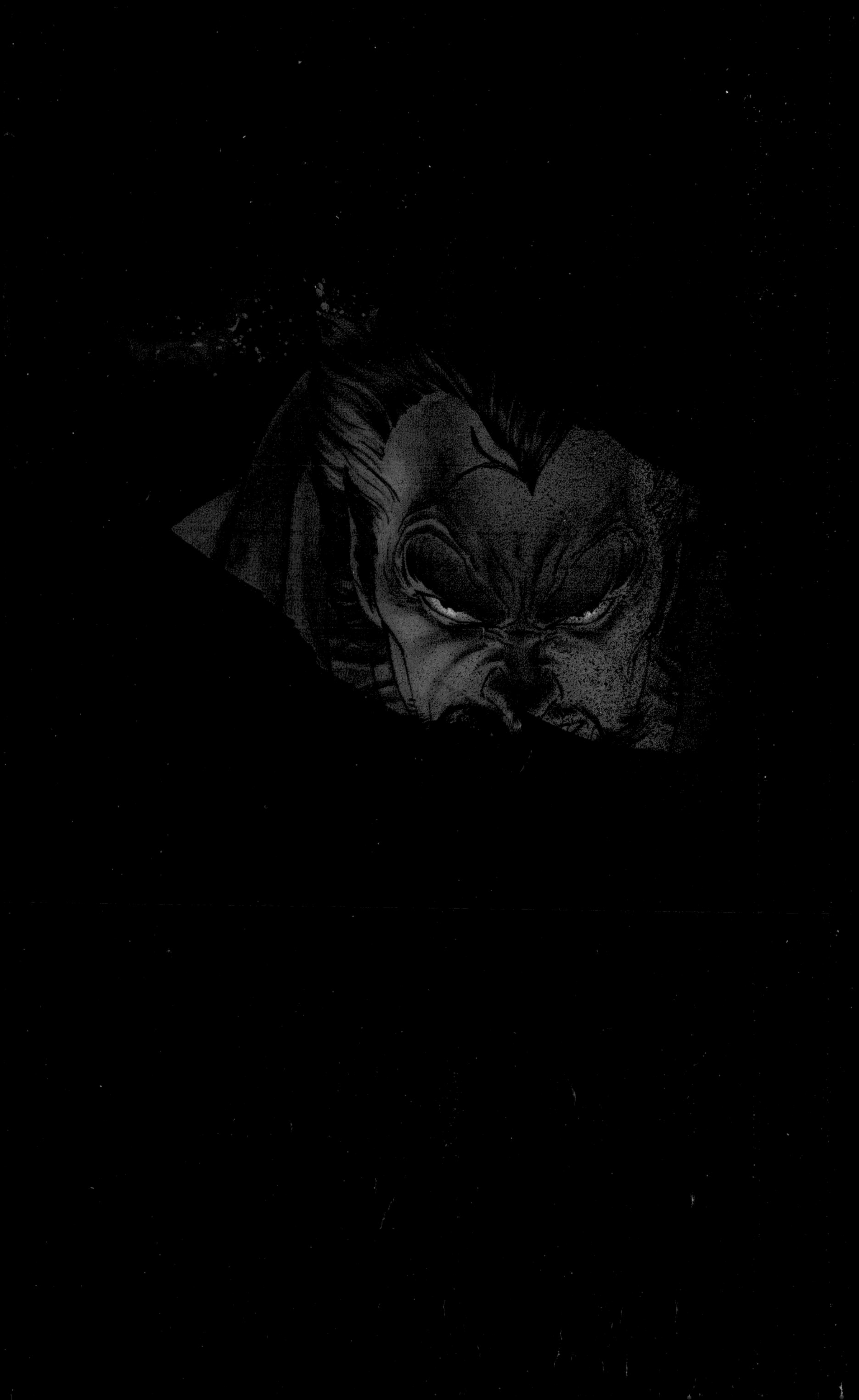

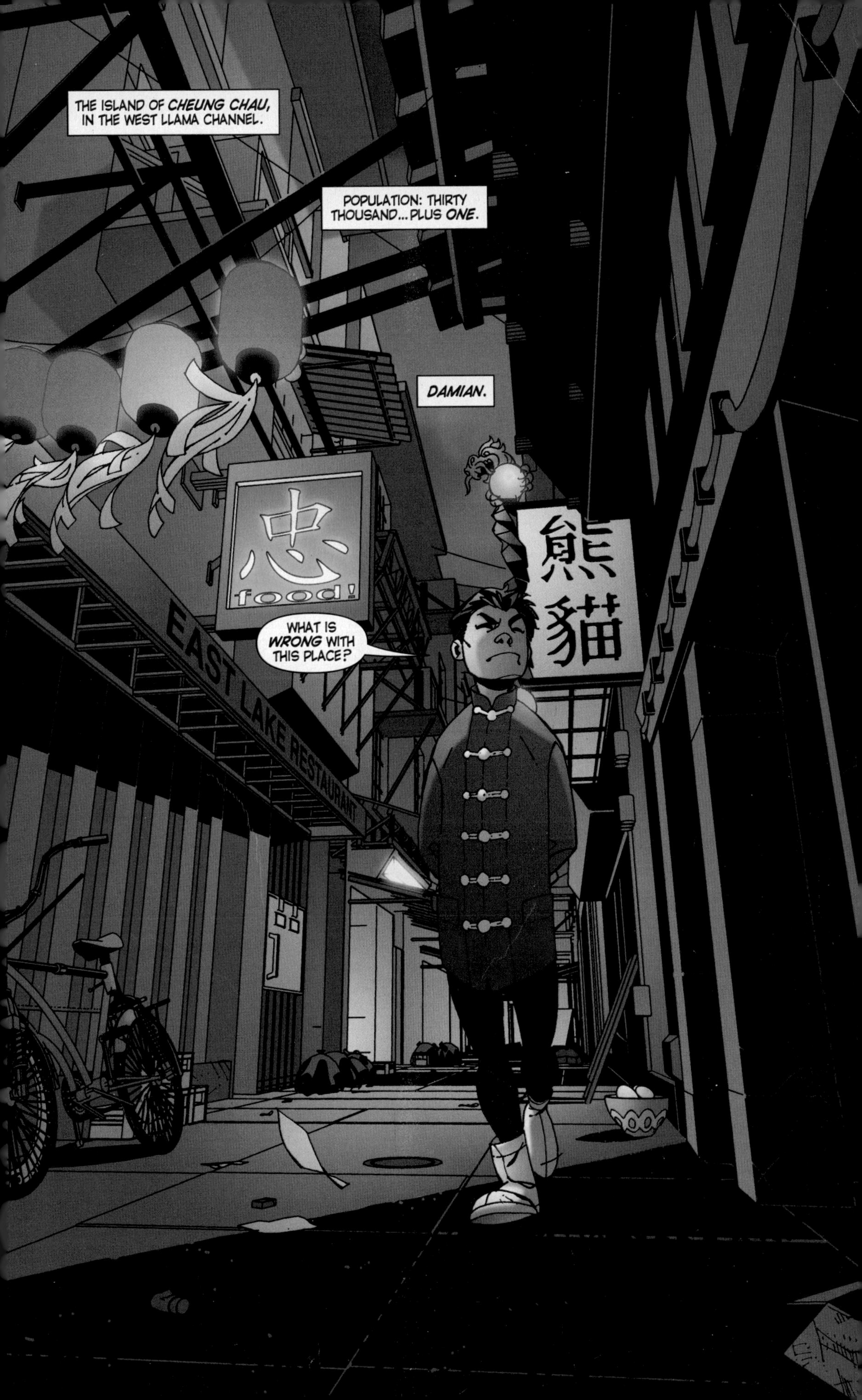
THE ISLAND OF CHEUNG CHAU, IN THE WEST LLAMA CHANNEL.
POPULATION: THIRTY THOUSAND...PLUS ONE.
DAMIAN.
忠
food!
EAST LAKE RESTAURANT
熊貓
WHAT IS WRONG WITH THIS PLACE?

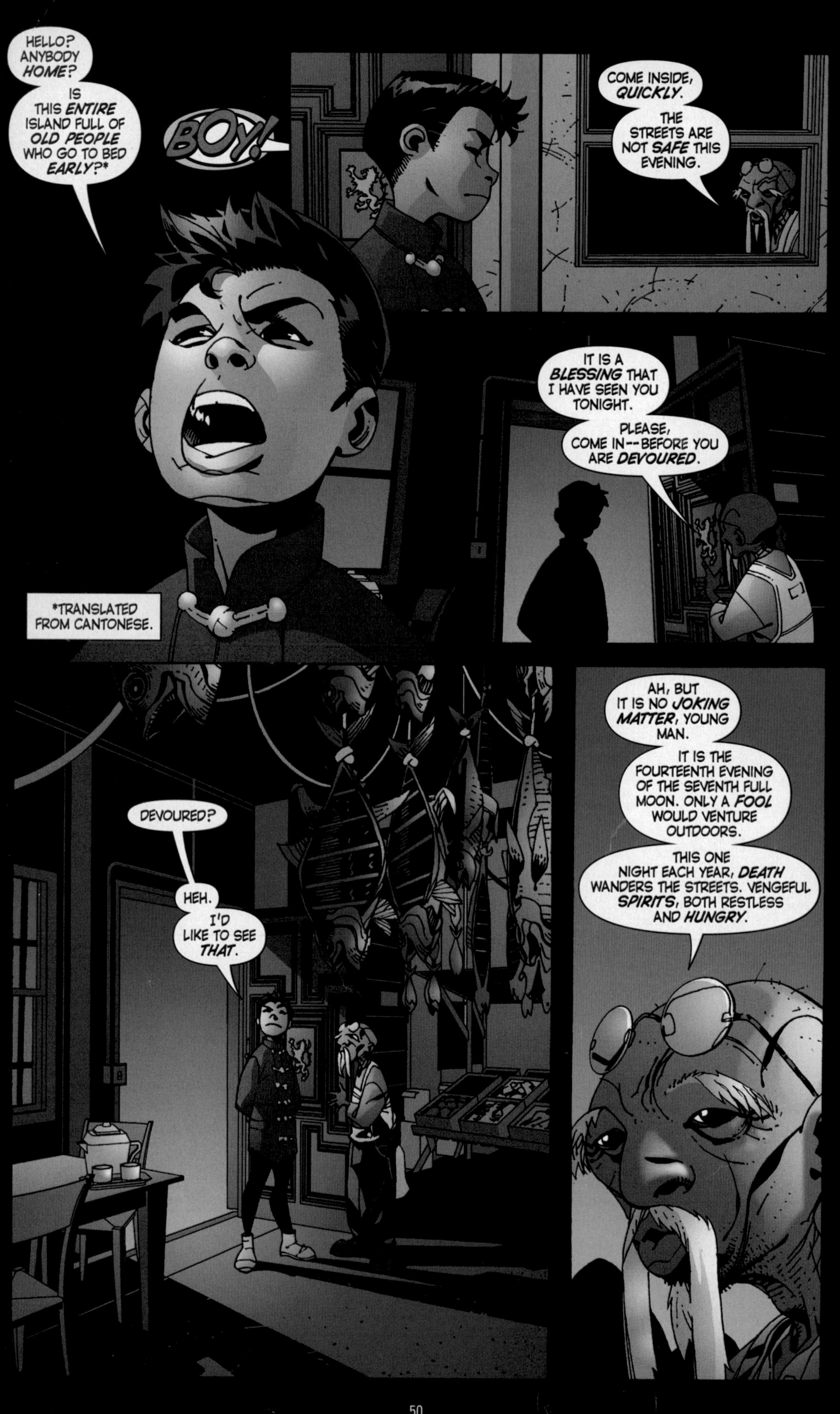

HELLO? ANYBODY HOME?
IS THIS ENTIRE ISLAND FULL OF OLD PEOPLE WHO GO TO BED EARLY?*
BOY!
COME INSIDE, QUICKLY.
THE STREETS ARE NOT SAFE THIS EVENING.
*TRANSLATED FROM CANTONESE.
IT IS A BLESSING THAT I HAVE SEEN YOU TONIGHT.
PLEASE, COME IN--BEFORE YOU ARE DEVOURED.
DEVOURED?
HEH.
I'D LIKE TO SEE THAT.
AH, BUT IT IS NO JOKING MATTER, YOUNG MAN.
IT IS THE FOURTEENTH EVENING OF THE SEVENTH FULL MOON. ONLY A FOOL WOULD VENTURE OUTDOORS.
THIS ONE NIGHT EACH YEAR, DEATH WANDERS THE STREETS. VENGEFUL SPIRITS, BOTH RESTLESS AND HUNGRY.

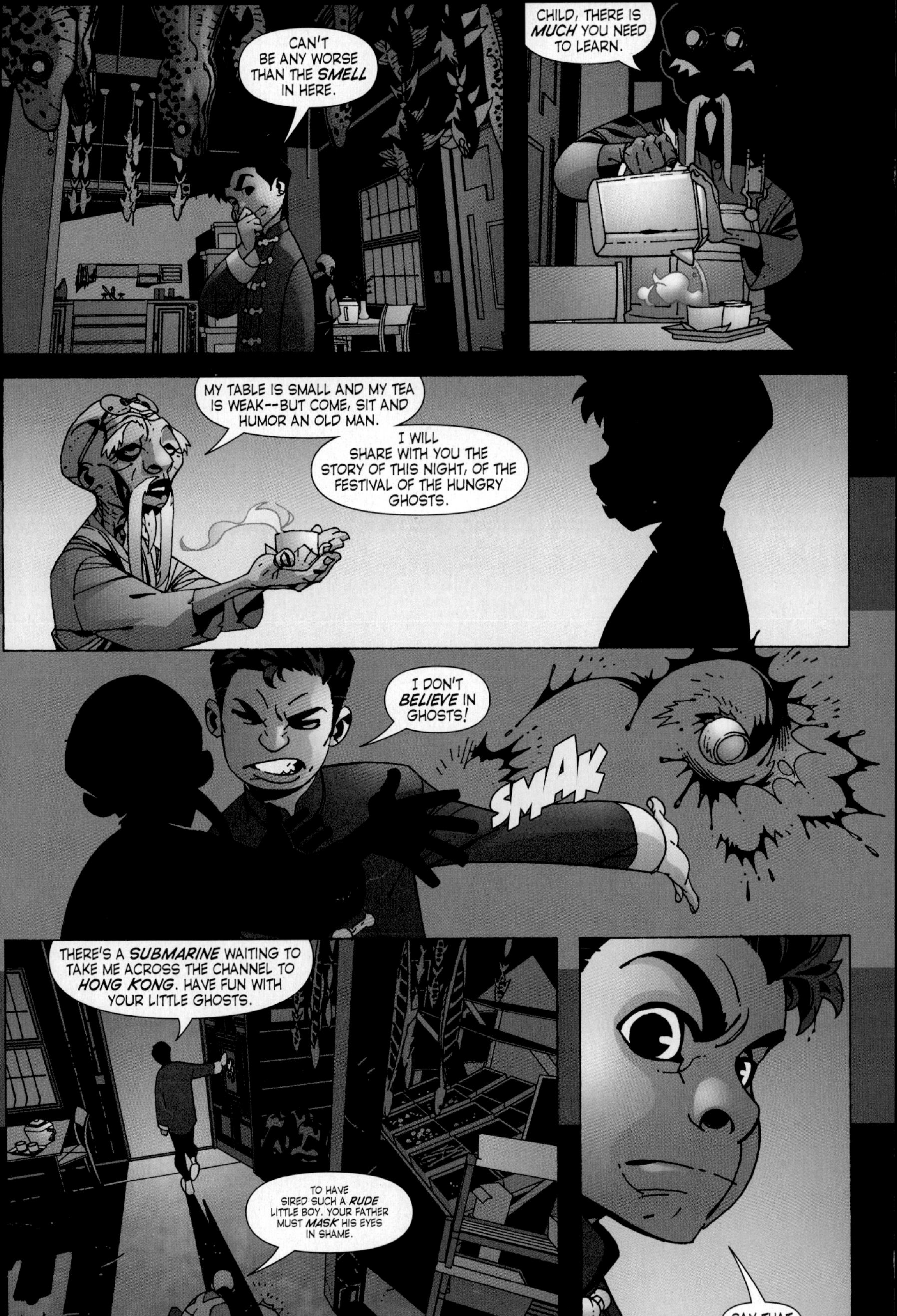
CAN'T BE ANY WORSE THAN THE SMELL IN HERE.
CHILD, THERE IS MUCH YOU NEED TO LEARN.
MY TABLE IS SMALL AND MY TEA IS WEAK--BUT COME, SIT AND HUMOR AN OLD MAN.
I WILL SHARE WITH YOU THE STORY OF THIS NIGHT, OF THE FESTIVAL OF THE HUNGRY GHOSTS.
I DON'T BELIEVE IN GHOSTS!
SMAK
THERE'S A SUBMARINE WAITING TO TAKE ME ACROSS THE CHANNEL TO HONG KONG. HAVE FUN WITH YOUR LITTLE GHOSTS.
TO HAVE SIRED SUCH A RUDE LITTLE BOY. YOUR FATHER MUST MASK HIS EYES IN SHAME.
SAY THAT AGAIN?

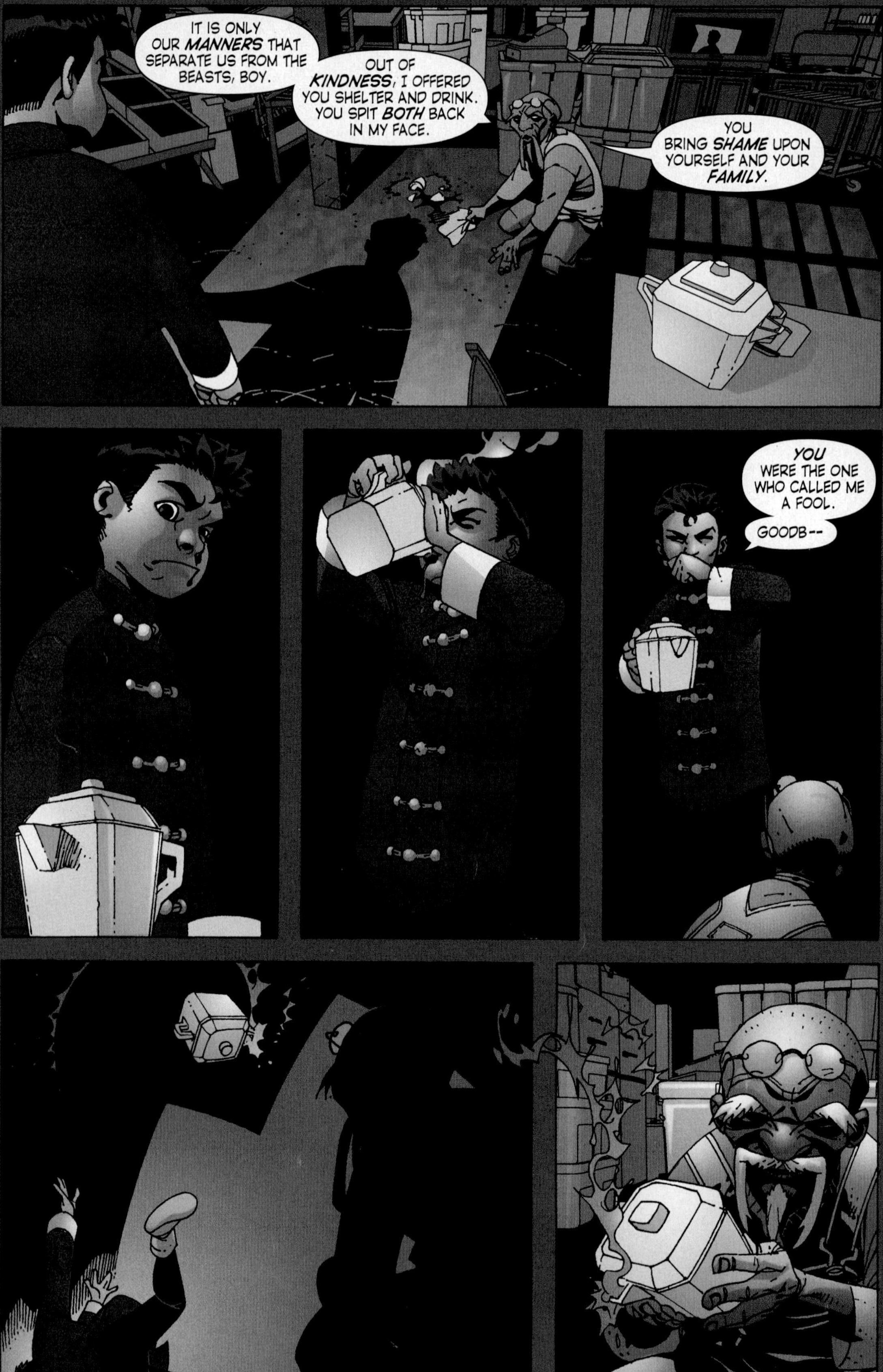
IT IS ONLY OUR MANNERS THAT SEPARATE US FROM THE BEASTS, BOY.
OUT OF KINDNESS, I OFFERED YOU SHELTER AND DRINK. YOU SPIT BOTH BACK IN MY FACE.
YOU BRING SHAME UPON YOURSELF AND YOUR FAMILY.
YOU WERE THE ONE WHO CALLED ME A FOOL.
GOODB--

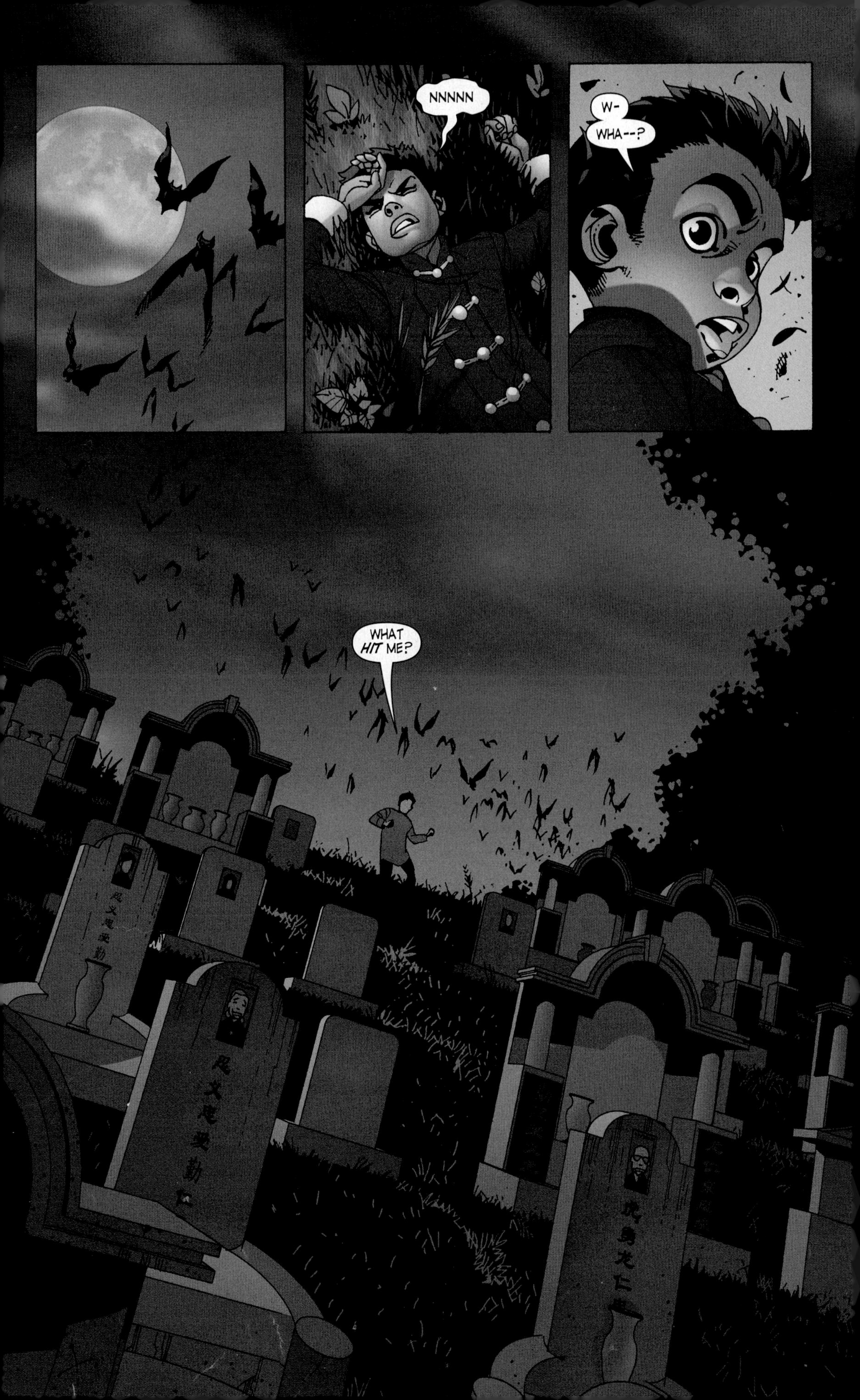
NNNNN
W-
WHA--?
WHAT HIT ME?

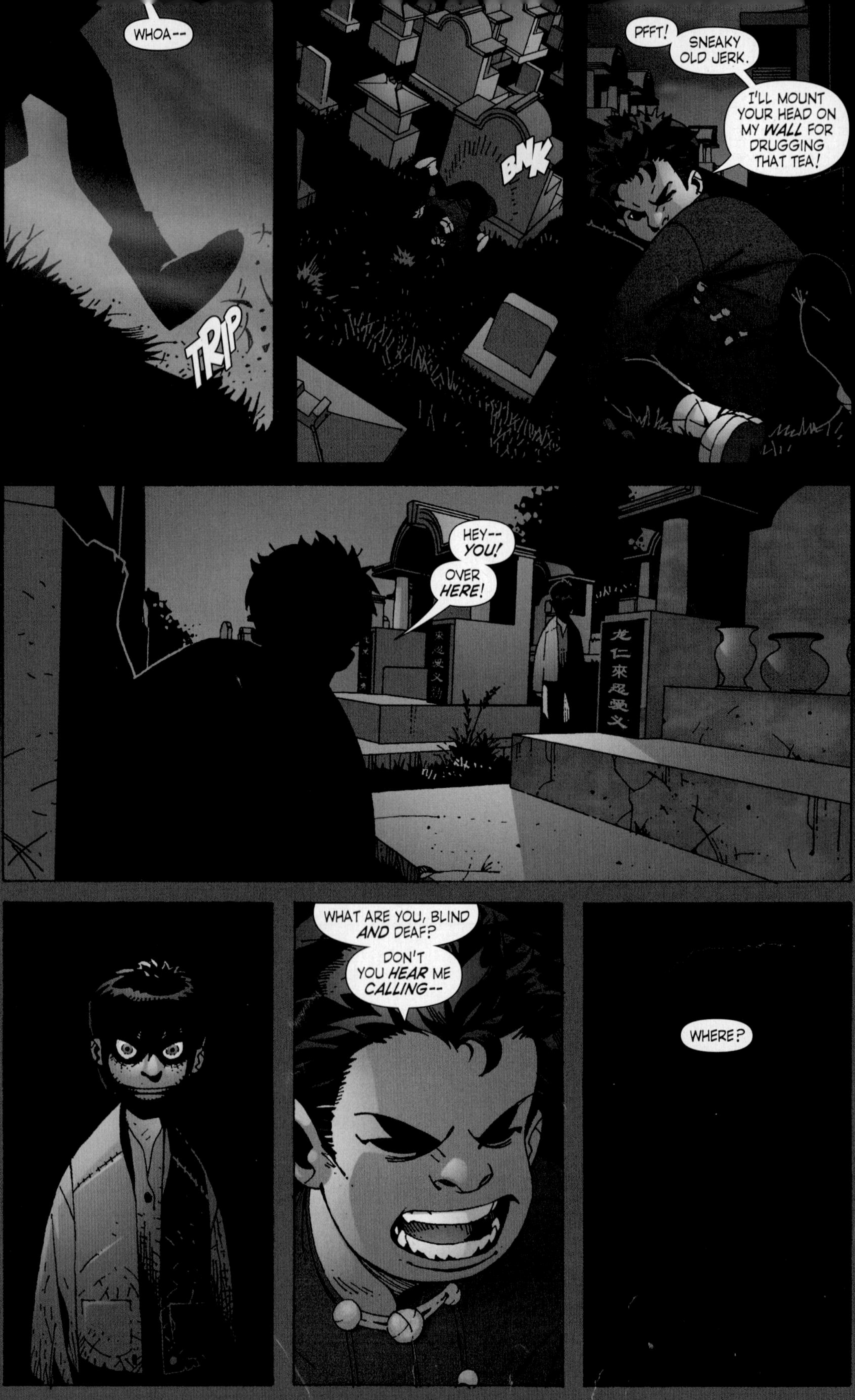
WHOA--
TRIP
BNK
PFFT!
SNEAKY OLD JERK.
I'LL MOUNT YOUR HEAD ON MY WALL FOR DRUGGING THAT TEA!
HEY-- YOU!
OVER HERE!
WHAT ARE YOU, BLIND AND DEAF?
DON'T YOU HEAR ME CALLING--
WHERE?

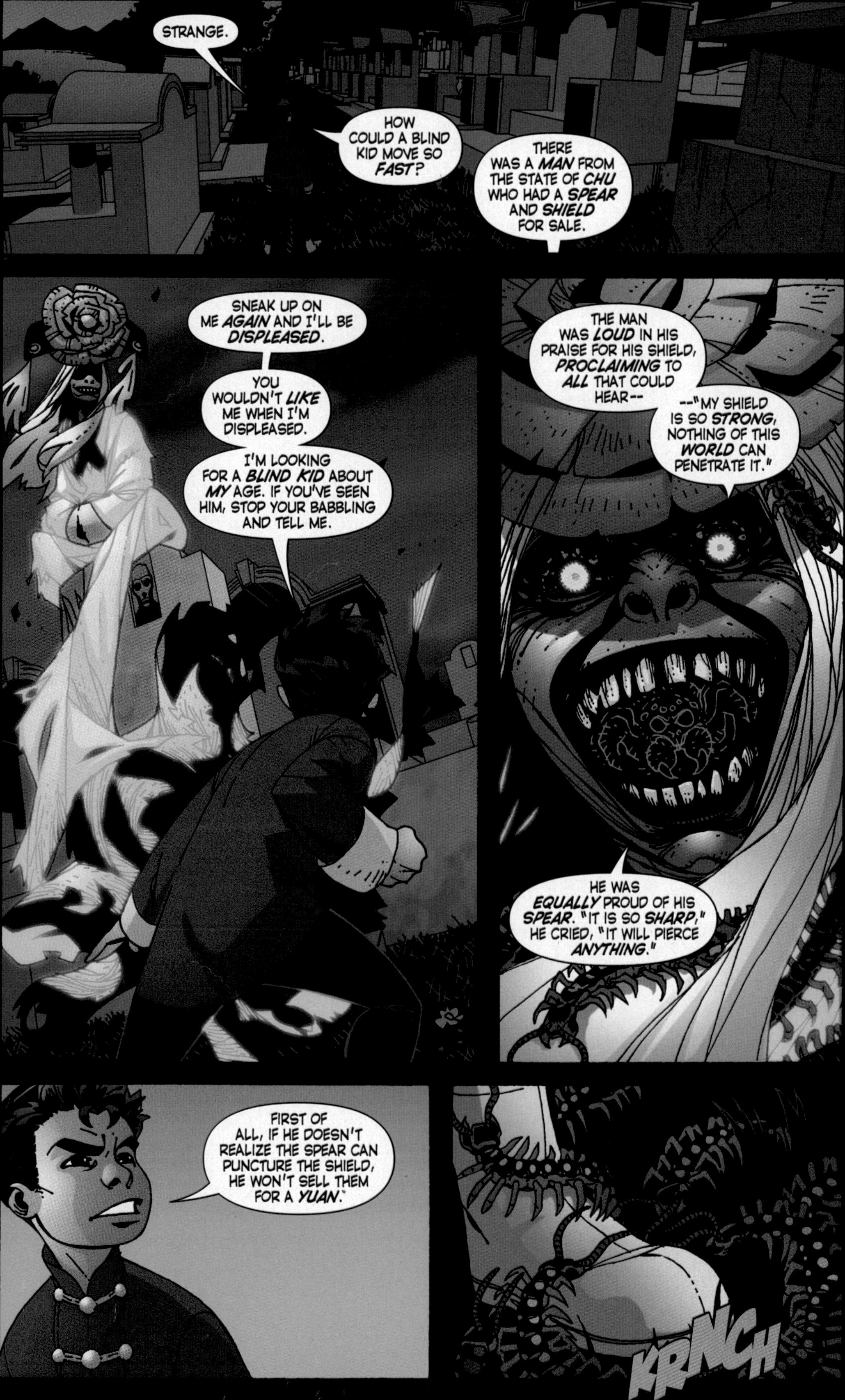
STRANGE.
HOW COULD A BLIND KID MOVE SO FAST?
THERE WAS A MAN FROM THE STATE OF CHU WHO HAD A SPEAR AND SHIELD FOR SALE.
SNEAK UP ON ME AGAIN AND I'LL BE DISPLEASED.
YOU WOULDN'T LIKE ME WHEN I'M DISPLEASED.
I'M LOOKING FOR A BLIND KID ABOUT MY AGE. IF YOU'VE SEEN HIM, STOP YOUR BABBLING AND TELL ME.
THE MAN WAS LOUD IN HIS PRAISE FOR HIS SHIELD, PROCLAIMING TO ALL THAT COULD HEAR--
--"MY SHIELD IS SO STRONG, NOTHING OF THIS WORLD CAN PENETRATE IT."
HE WAS EQUALLY PROUD OF HIS SPEAR. "IT IS SO SHARP," HE CRIED, "IT WILL PIERCE ANYTHING."
FIRST OF ALL, IF HE DOESN'T REALIZE THE SPEAR CAN PUNCTURE THE SHIELD, HE WON'T SELL THEM FOR A YUAN.
KRNCH

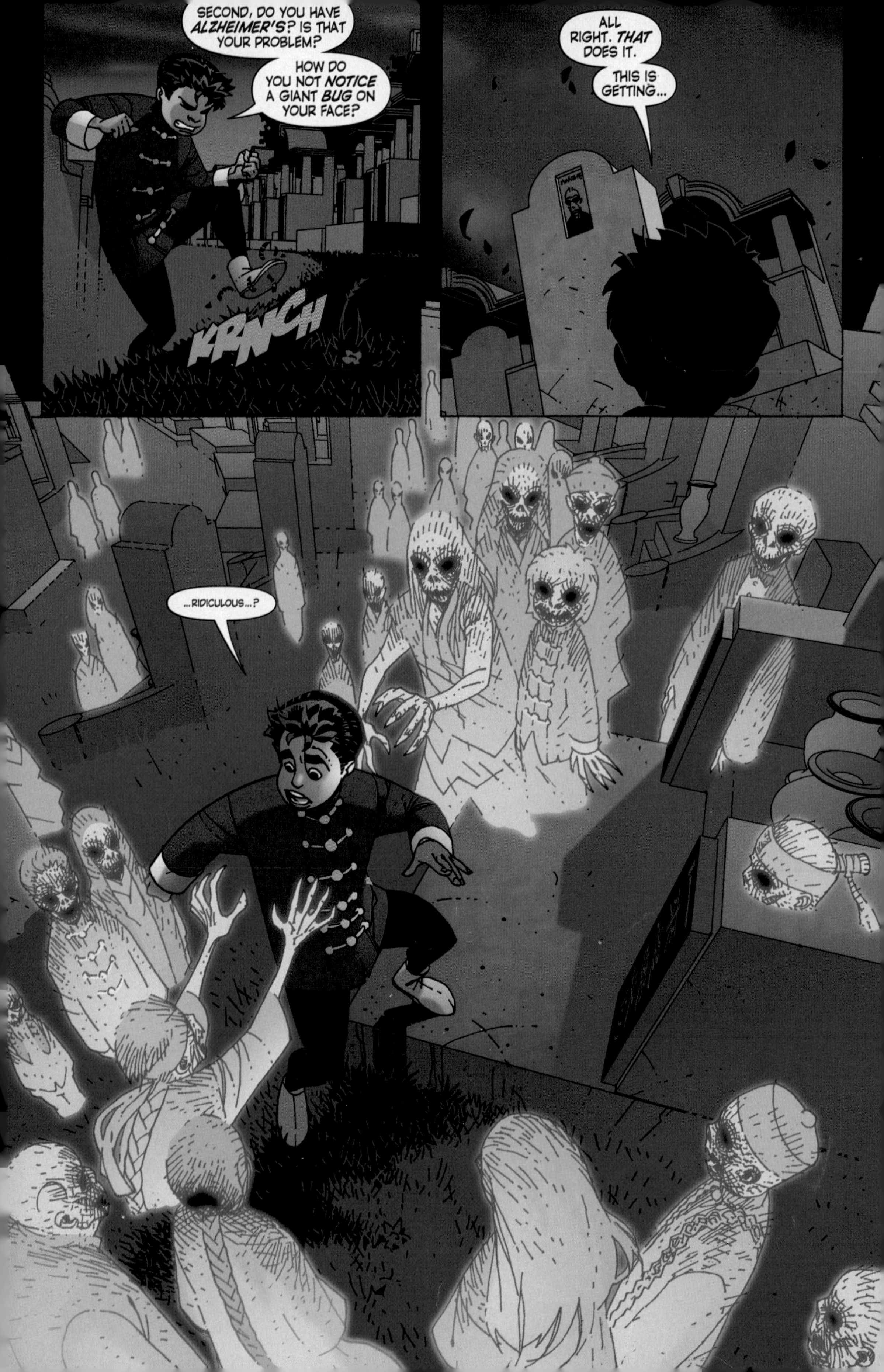
SECOND, DO YOU HAVE ALZHEIMER'S? IS THAT YOUR PROBLEM?
HOW DO YOU NOT NOTICE A GIANT BUG ON YOUR FACE?
KRNCH
ALL RIGHT. THAT DOES IT.
THIS IS GETTING...
...RIDICULOUS...?

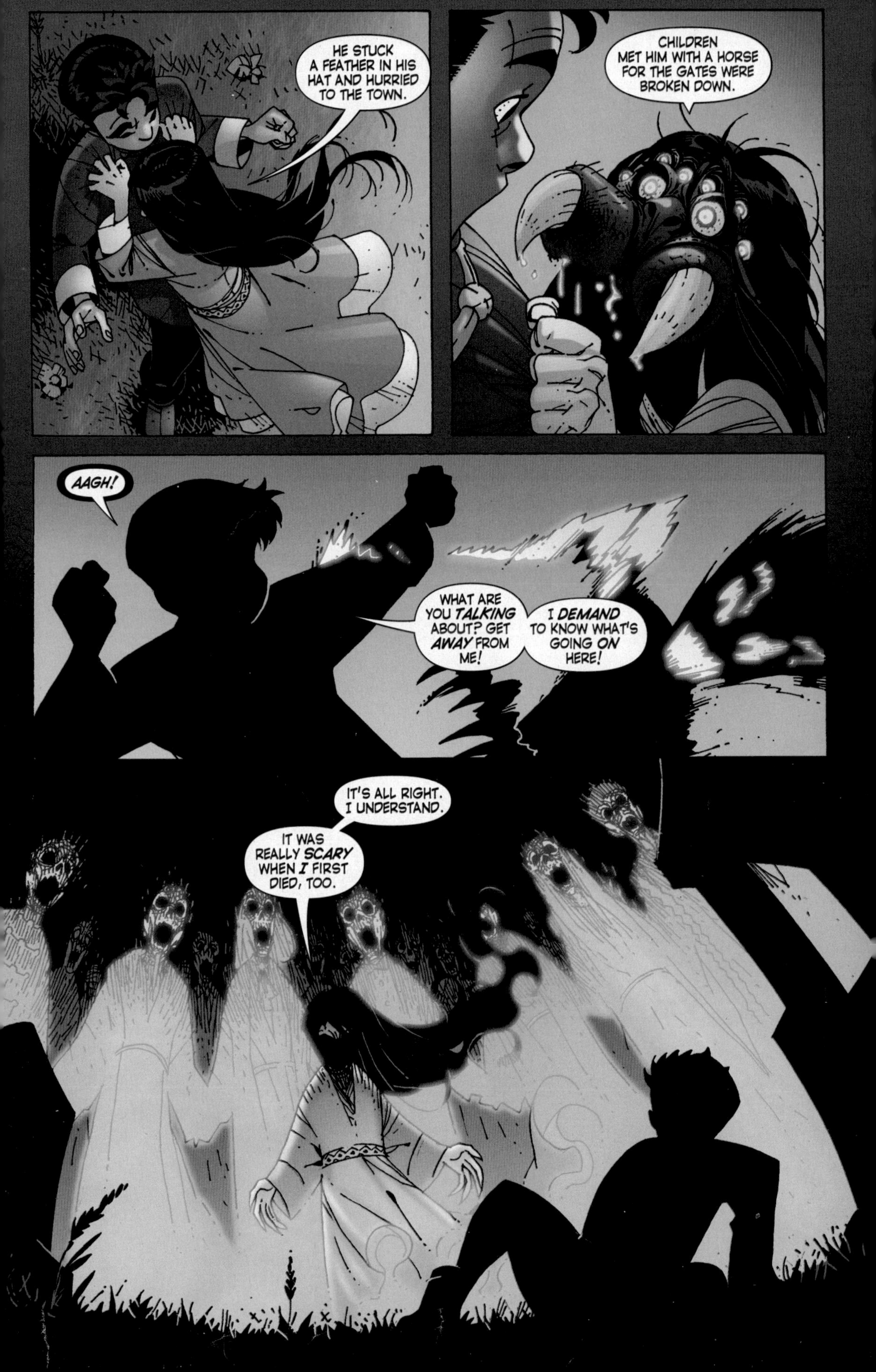
HE STUCK A FEATHER IN HIS HAT AND HURRIED TO THE TOWN.
CHILDREN MET HIM WITH A HORSE FOR THE GATES WERE BROKEN DOWN.
AAGH!
WHAT ARE YOU TALKING ABOUT? GET AWAY FROM ME!
I DEMAND TO KNOW WHAT'S GOING ON HERE!
IT'S ALL RIGHT. I UNDERSTAND.
IT WAS REALLY SCARY WHEN I FIRST DIED, TOO.

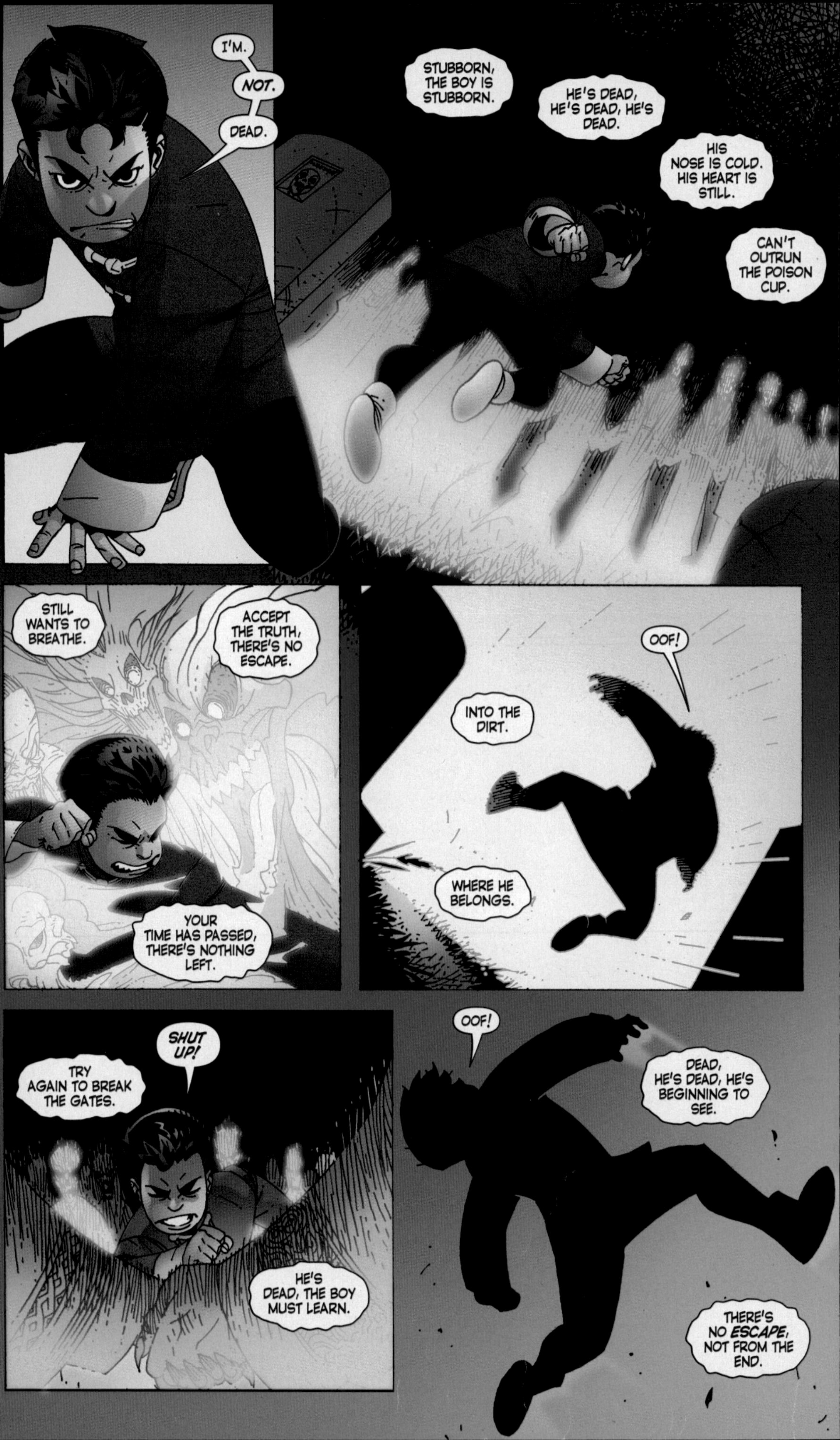
I'M.
NOT.
DEAD.
STUBBORN, THE BOY IS STUBBORN.
HE'S DEAD, HE'S DEAD, HE'S DEAD.
HIS NOSE IS COLD. HIS HEART IS STILL.
CAN'T OUTRUN THE POISON CUP.
STILL WANTS TO BREATHE.
ACCEPT THE TRUTH, THERE'S NO ESCAPE.
YOUR TIME HAS PASSED, THERE'S NOTHING LEFT.
OOF!
INTO THE DIRT.
WHERE HE BELONGS.
TRY AGAIN TO BREAK THE GATES.
SHUT UP!
HE'S DEAD, THE BOY MUST LEARN.
OOF!
DEAD, HE'S DEAD, HE'S BEGINNING TO SEE.
THERE'S NO ESCAPE, NOT FROM THE END.

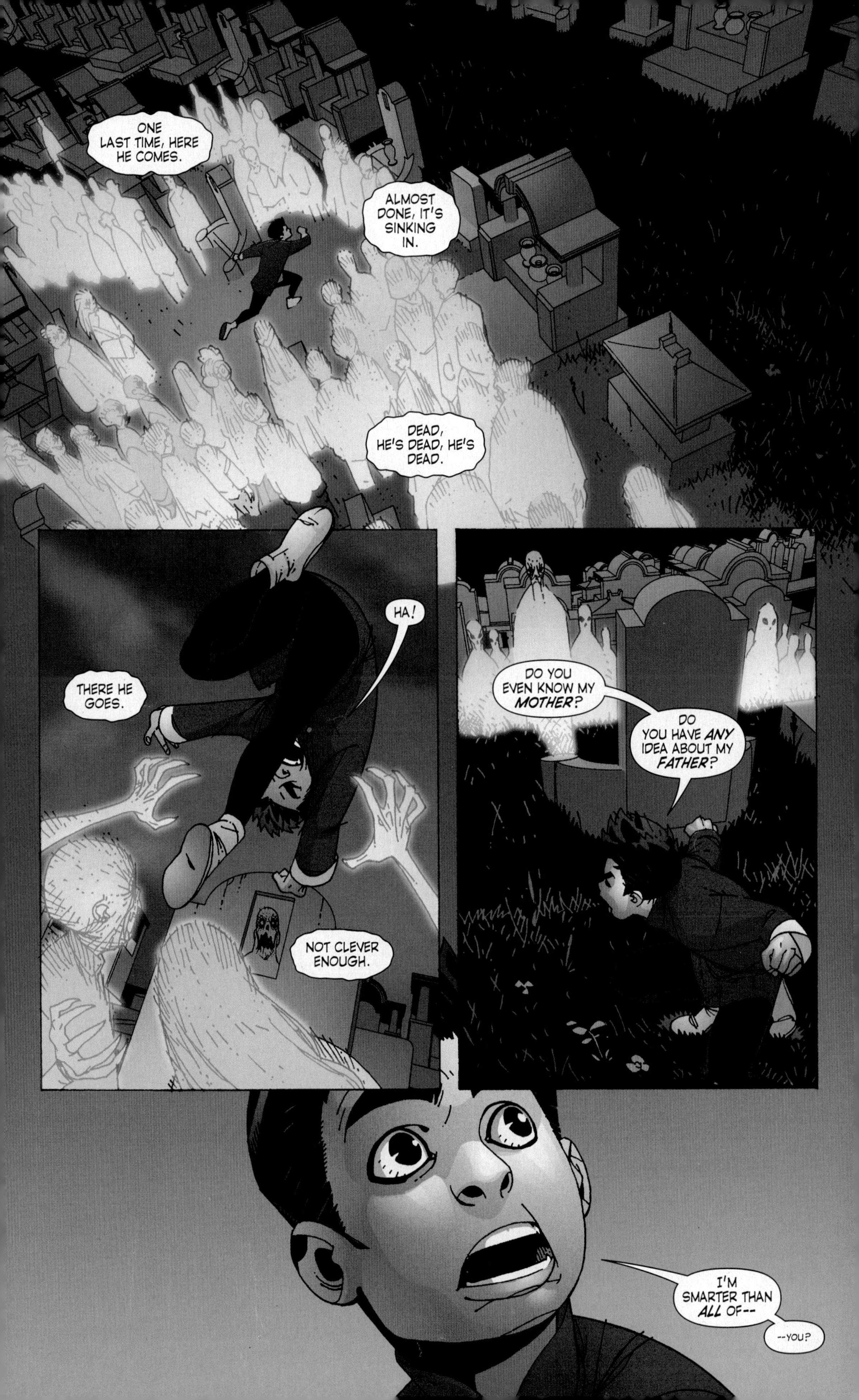
ONE LAST TIME, HERE HE COMES.
ALMOST DONE, IT'S SINKING IN.
DEAD, HE'S DEAD, HE'S DEAD.
HA!
THERE HE GOES.
NOT CLEVER ENOUGH.
DO YOU EVEN KNOW MY *MOTHER*?
DO YOU HAVE *ANY* IDEA ABOUT MY *FATHER*?
I'M SMARTER THAN *ALL* OF--
--YOU?

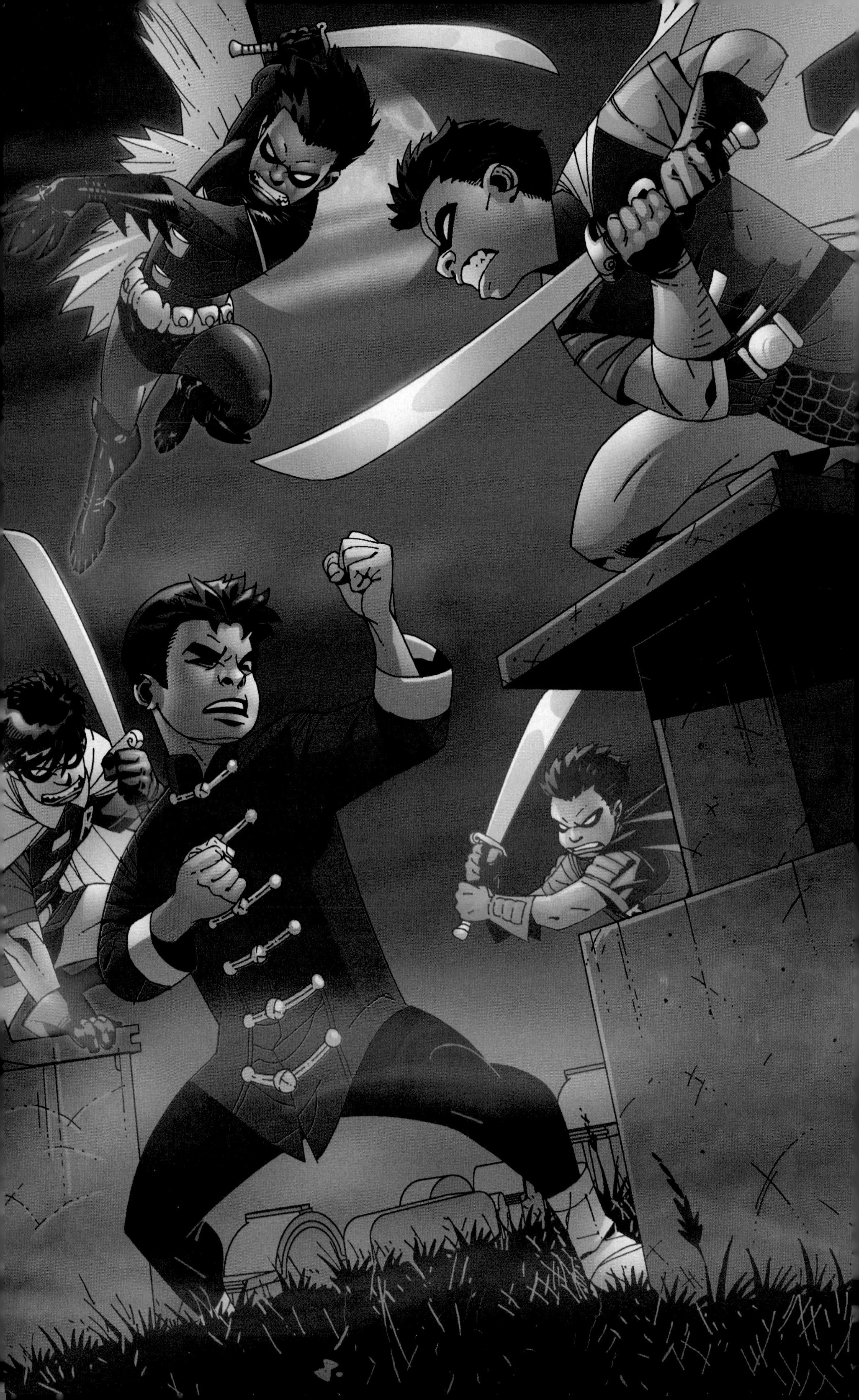

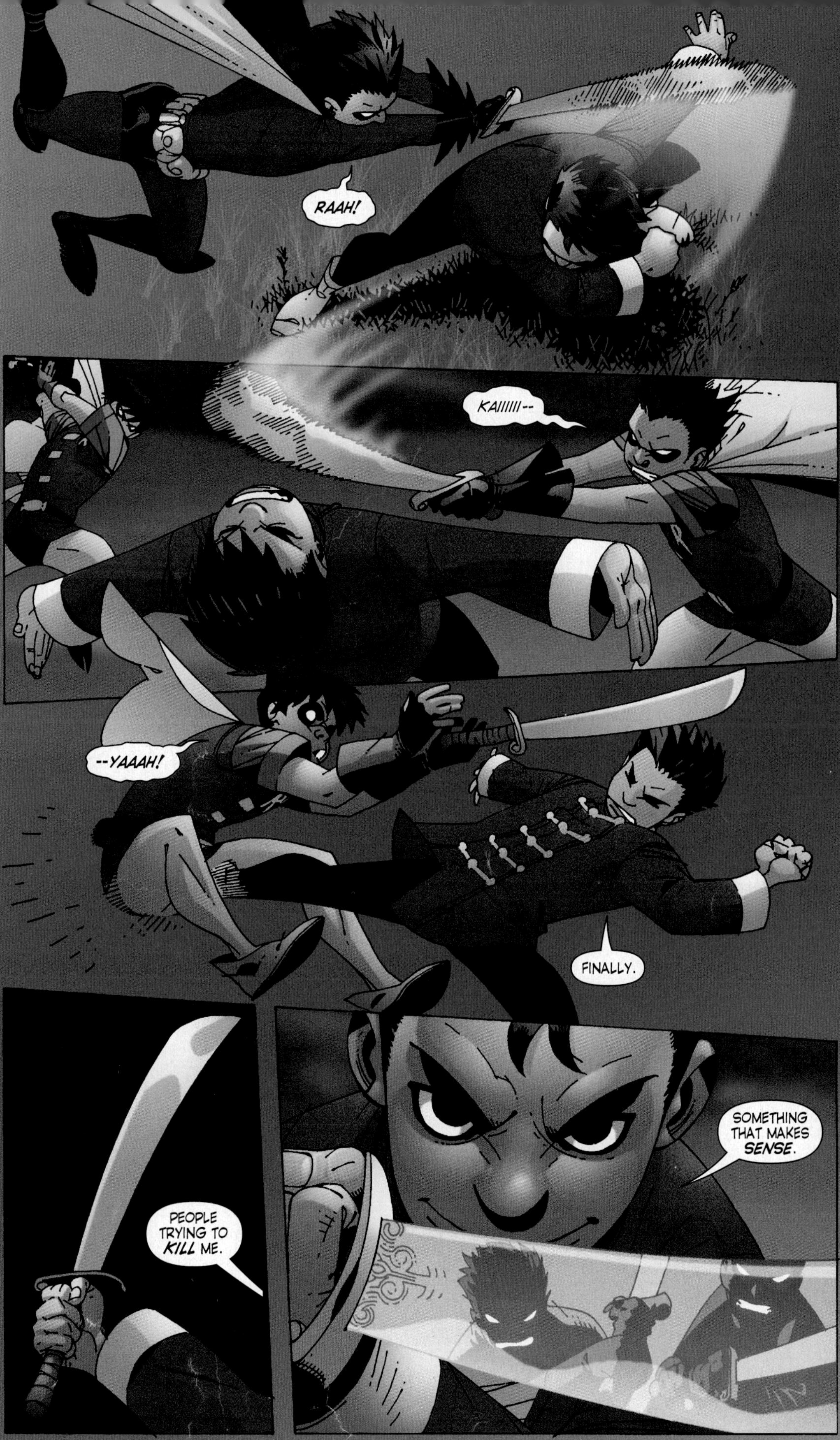
RAAH!
KAIIIIII--
--YAAAH!
FINALLY.
PEOPLE TRYING TO KILL ME.
SOMETHING THAT MAKES SENSE.

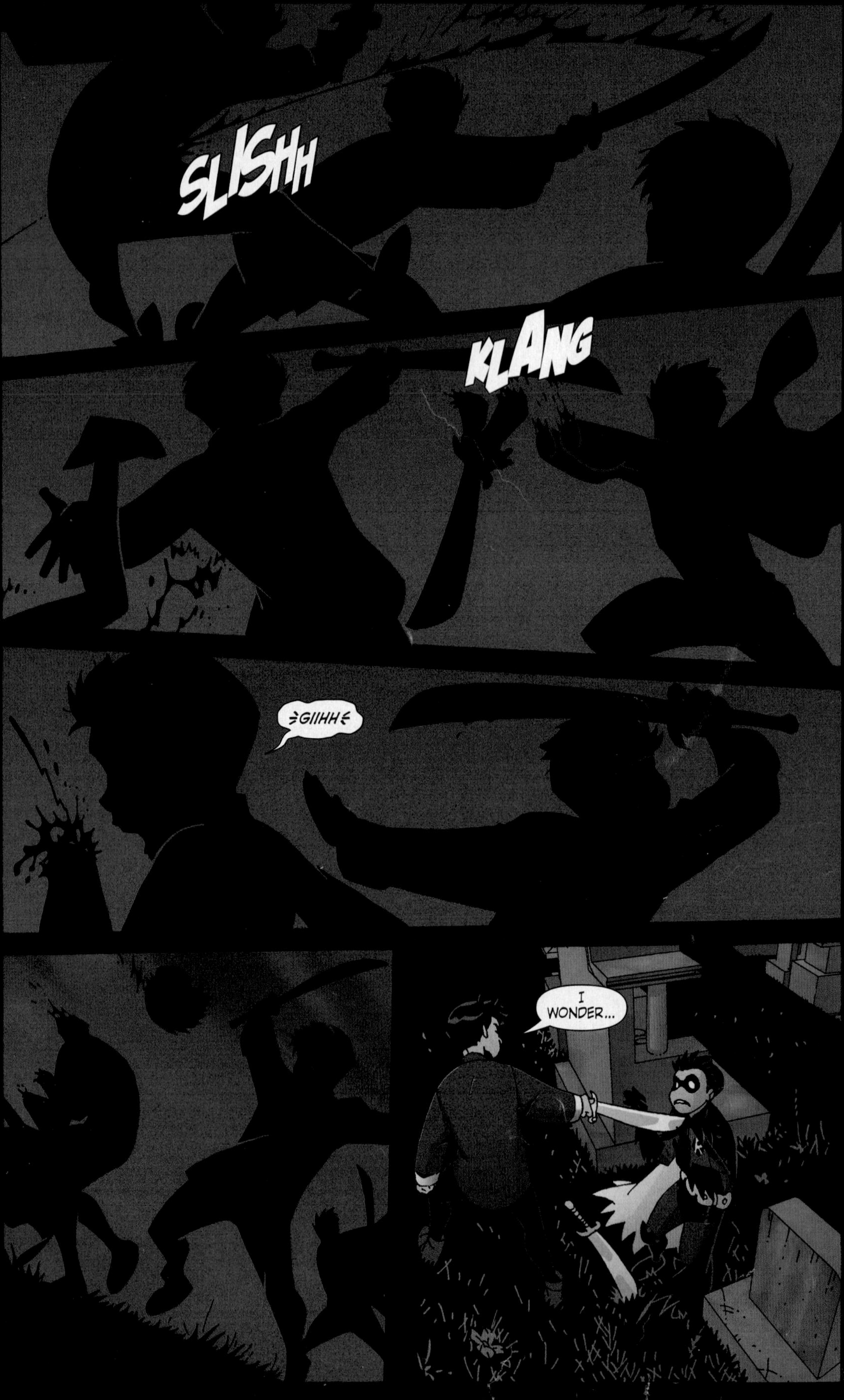
SLISHH
KLANG
GIIHH
I WONDER...

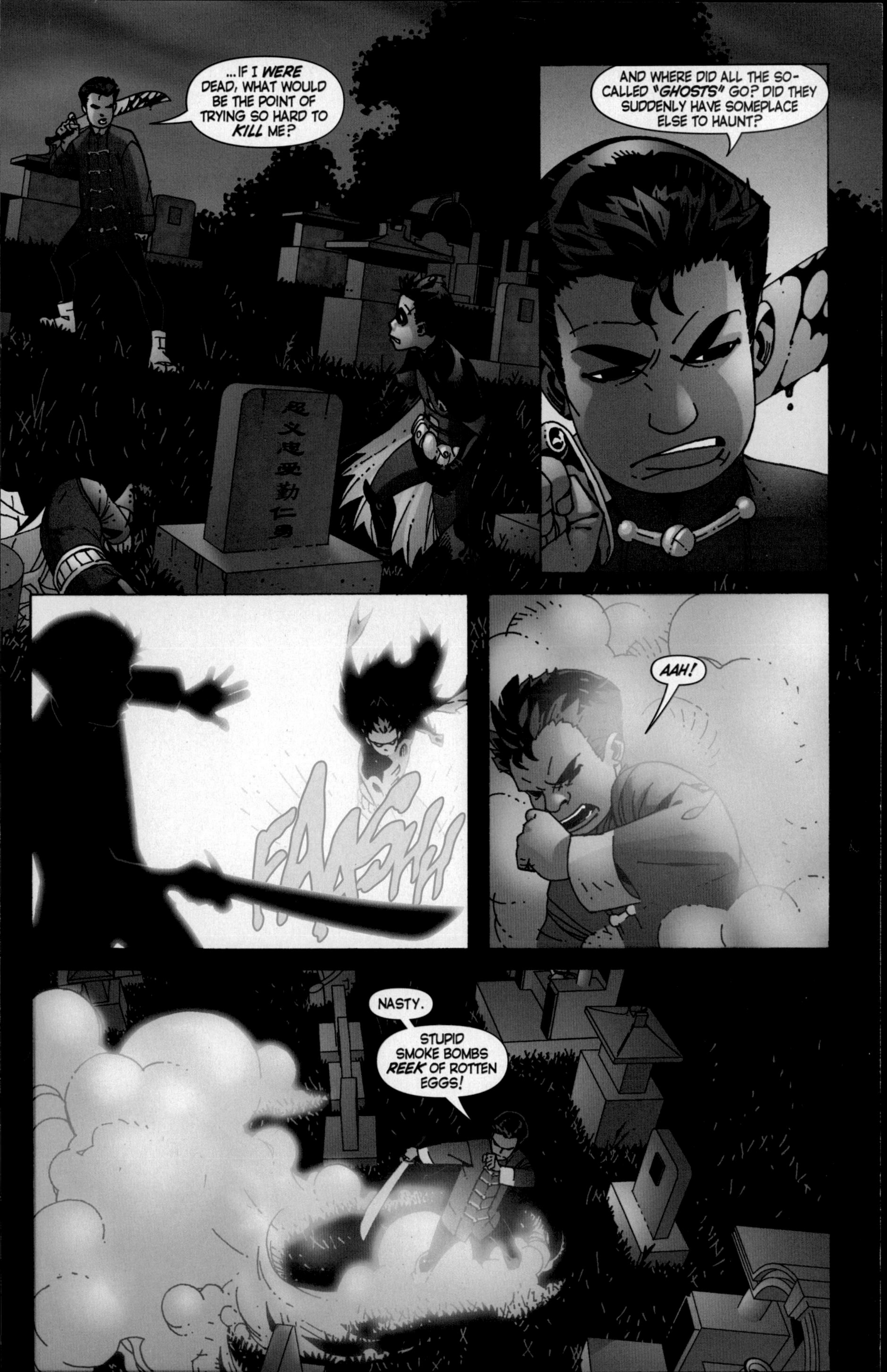

...IF I WERE DEAD, WHAT WOULD BE THE POINT OF TRYING SO HARD TO KILL ME?
AND WHERE DID ALL THE SO-CALLED "GHOSTS" GO? DID THEY SUDDENLY HAVE SOMEPLACE ELSE TO HAUNT?
FAASHH
AAH!
NASTY.
STUPID SMOKE BOMBS REEK OF ROTTEN EGGS!

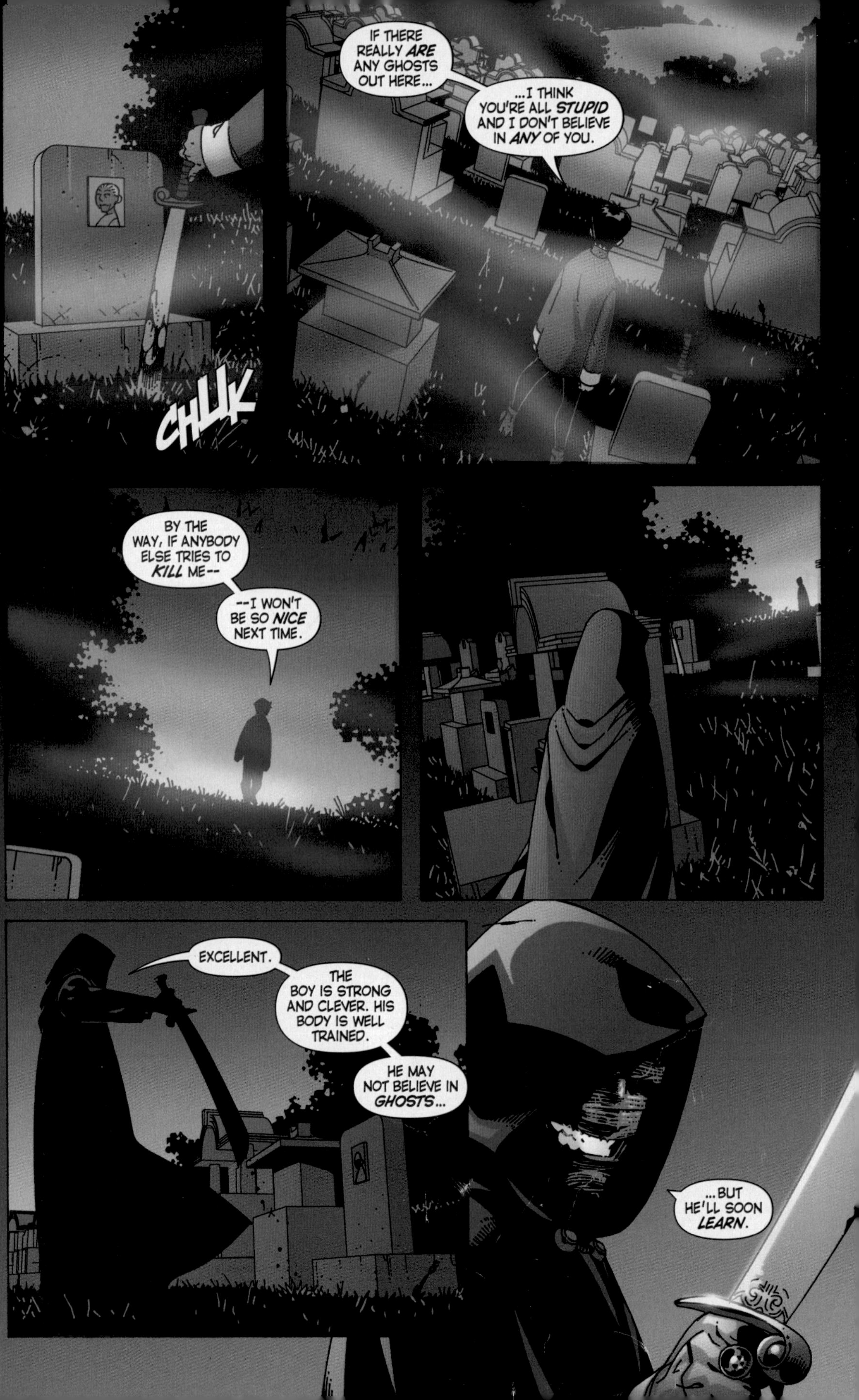
CHUK
IF THERE REALLY *ARE* ANY GHOSTS OUT HERE...
...I THINK YOU'RE ALL *STUPID* AND I DON'T BELIEVE IN *ANY* OF YOU.
BY THE WAY, IF ANYBODY ELSE TRIES TO *KILL* ME--
--I WON'T BE SO *NICE* NEXT TIME.
EXCELLENT.
THE BOY IS STRONG AND CLEVER. HIS BODY IS WELL TRAINED.
HE MAY NOT BELIEVE IN *GHOSTS*...
...BUT HE'LL SOON *LEARN*.

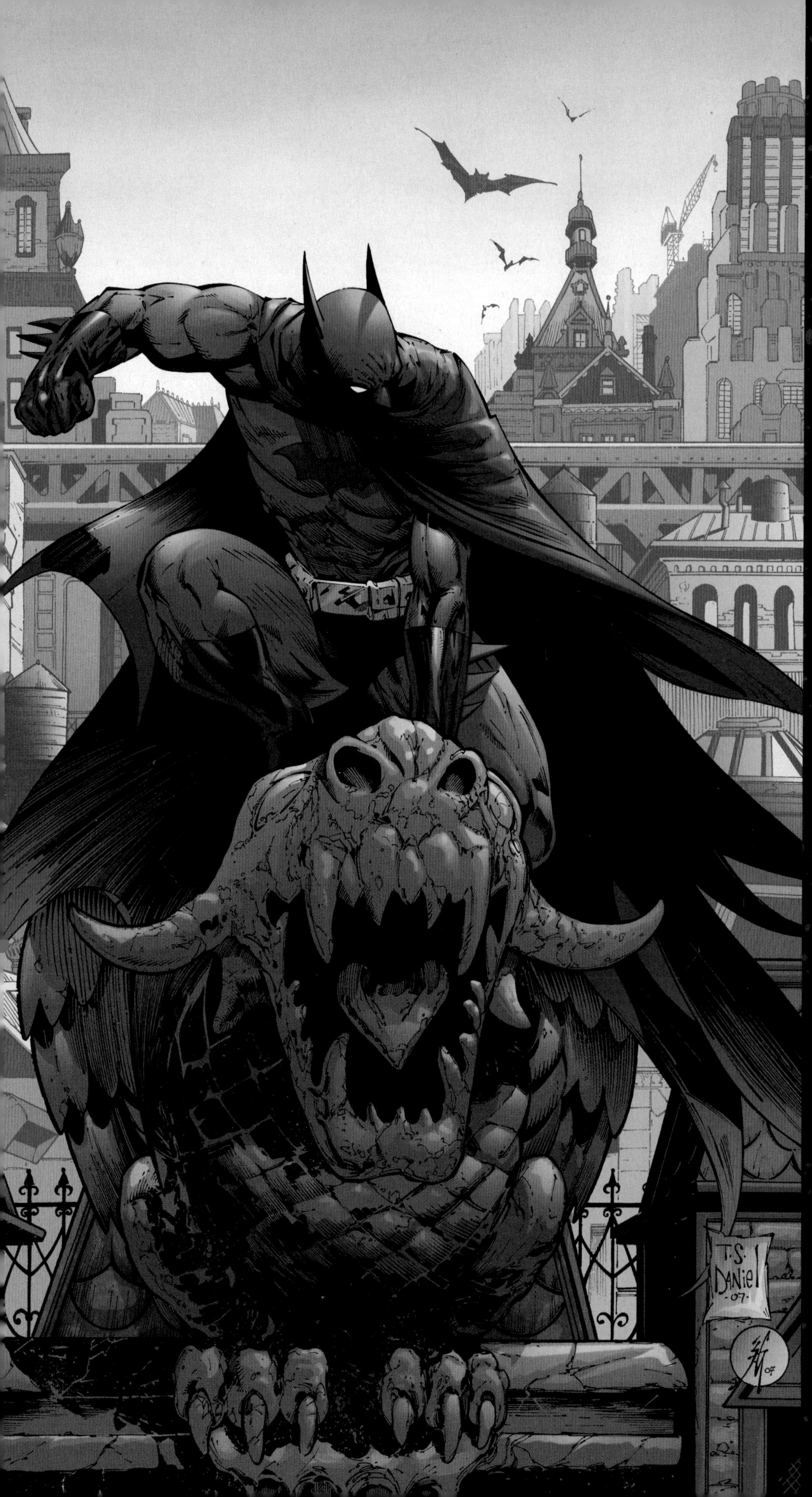
T.S. DANIEL ·07·

PRELUDE LAZARUS RISING

Cover art by Tony S. Daniel and Jonathan Glapion | Chapter written by Grant Morrison | Chapter penciled by Tony S. Daniel | Chapter inked by Jonathan Glapion

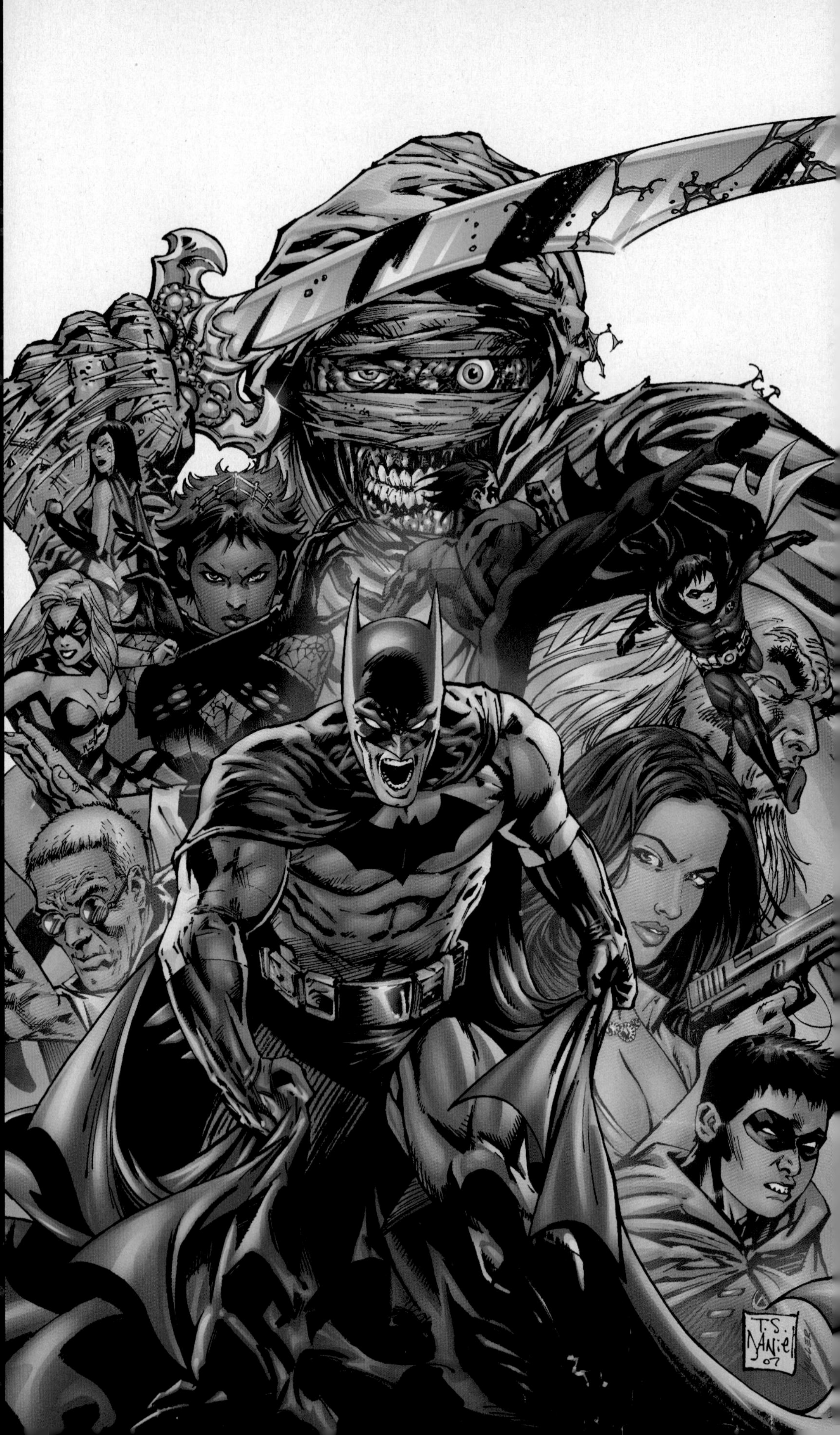

Variant cover by Tony S. Daniel

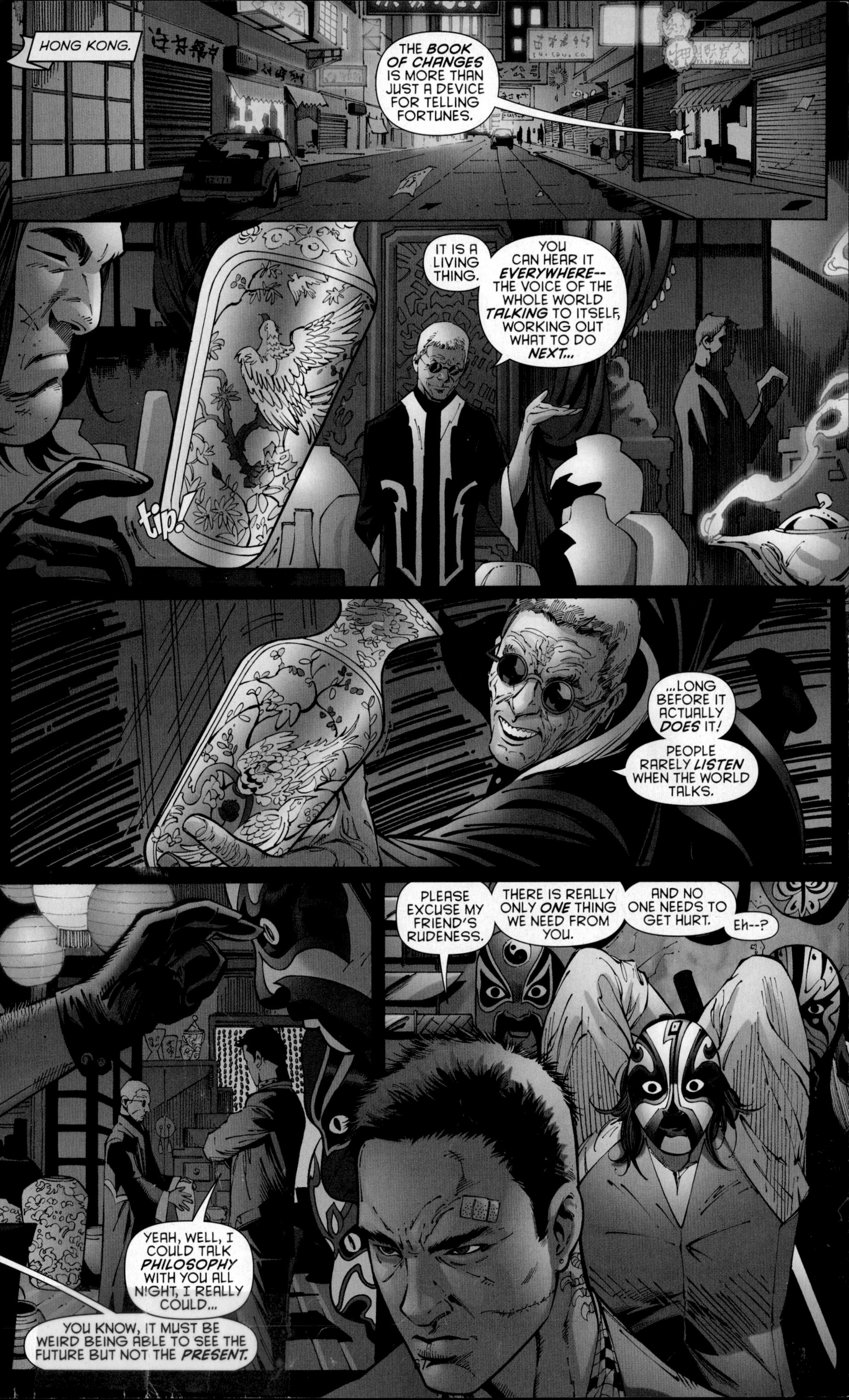
HONG KONG.
THE BOOK OF CHANGES IS MORE THAN JUST A DEVICE FOR TELLING FORTUNES.
IT IS A LIVING THING.
YOU CAN HEAR IT EVERYWHERE-- THE VOICE OF THE WHOLE WORLD TALKING TO ITSELF, WORKING OUT WHAT TO DO NEXT...
tip!
...LONG BEFORE IT ACTUALLY DOES IT!
PEOPLE RARELY LISTEN WHEN THE WORLD TALKS.
PLEASE EXCUSE MY FRIEND'S RUDENESS.
THERE IS REALLY ONLY ONE THING WE NEED FROM YOU.
AND NO ONE NEEDS TO GET HURT.
Eh--?
YEAH, WELL, I COULD TALK PHILOSOPHY WITH YOU ALL NIGHT, I REALLY COULD...
YOU KNOW, IT MUST BE WEIRD BEING ABLE TO SEE THE FUTURE BUT NOT THE PRESENT.

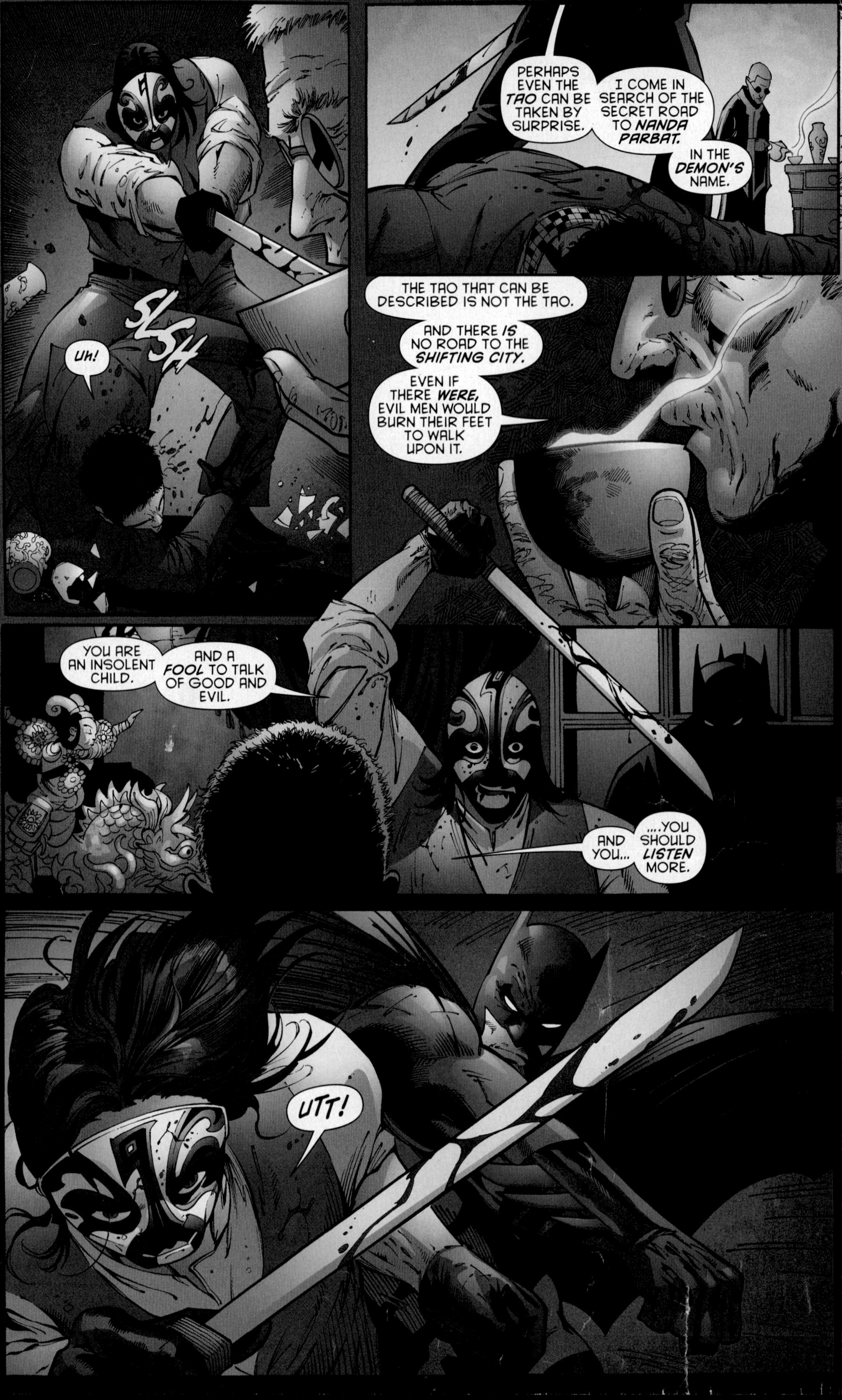
SLSH
Uh!
PERHAPS EVEN THE TAO CAN BE TAKEN BY SURPRISE.
I COME IN SEARCH OF THE SECRET ROAD TO NANDA PARBAT.
IN THE DEMON'S NAME.
THE TAO THAT CAN BE DESCRIBED IS NOT THE TAO.
AND THERE IS NO ROAD TO THE SHIFTING CITY.
EVEN IF THERE WERE, EVIL MEN WOULD BURN THEIR FEET TO WALK UPON IT.
YOU ARE AN INSOLENT CHILD.
AND A FOOL TO TALK OF GOOD AND EVIL.
AND YOU...
....YOU SHOULD LISTEN MORE.
UTT!

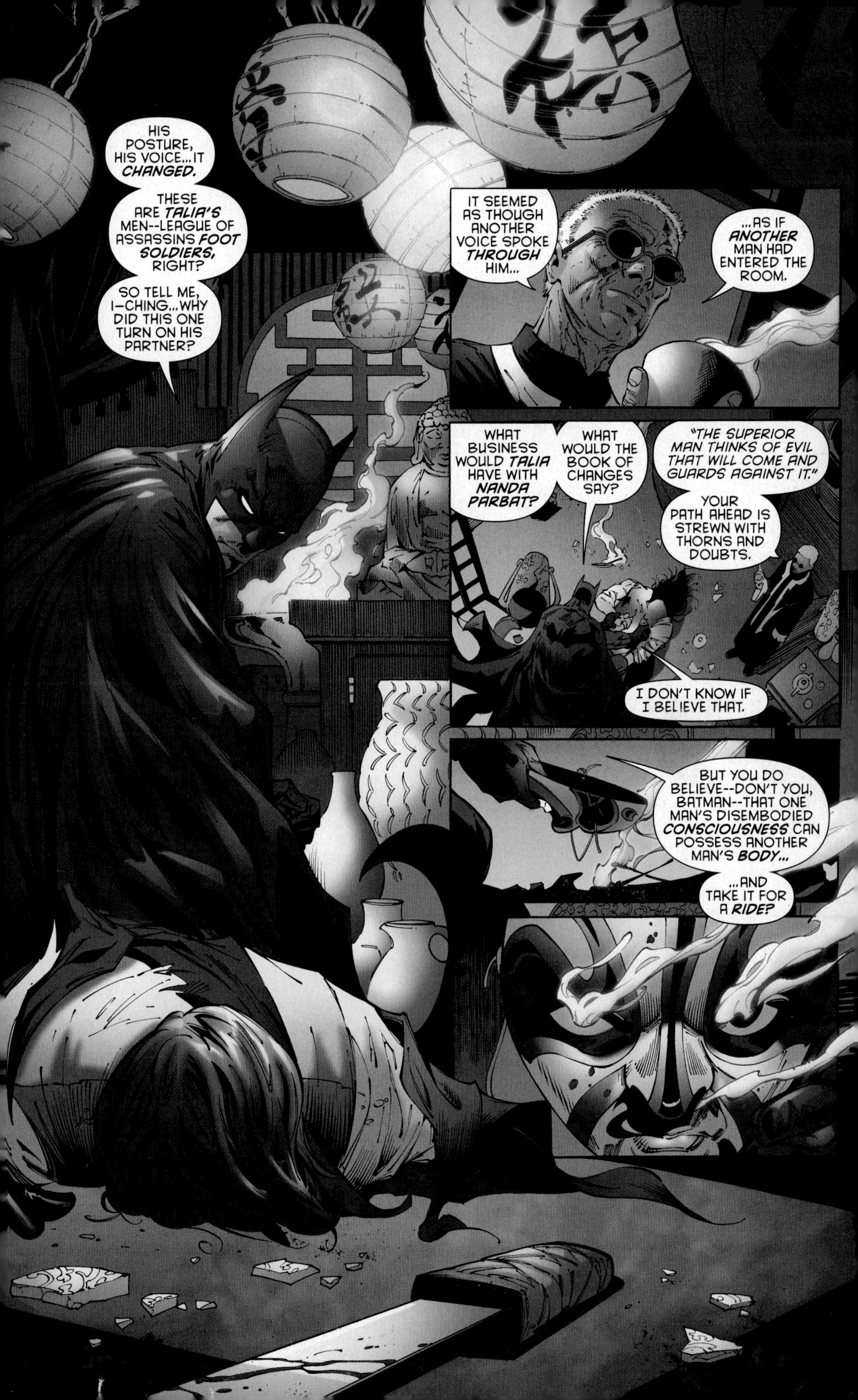
HIS POSTURE, HIS VOICE...IT CHANGED.
THESE ARE TALIA'S MEN--LEAGUE OF ASSASSINS FOOT SOLDIERS, RIGHT?
SO TELL ME, I-CHING...WHY DID THIS ONE TURN ON HIS PARTNER?
IT SEEMED AS THOUGH ANOTHER VOICE SPOKE THROUGH HIM...
...AS IF ANOTHER MAN HAD ENTERED THE ROOM.
WHAT BUSINESS WOULD TALIA HAVE WITH NANDA PARBAT?
WHAT WOULD THE BOOK OF CHANGES SAY?
"THE SUPERIOR MAN THINKS OF EVIL THAT WILL COME AND GUARDS AGAINST IT."
YOUR PATH AHEAD IS STREWN WITH THORNS AND DOUBTS.
I DON'T KNOW IF I BELIEVE THAT.
BUT YOU DO BELIEVE--DON'T YOU, BATMAN--THAT ONE MAN'S DISEMBODIED CONSCIOUSNESS CAN POSSESS ANOTHER MAN'S BODY...
...AND TAKE IT FOR A RIDE?

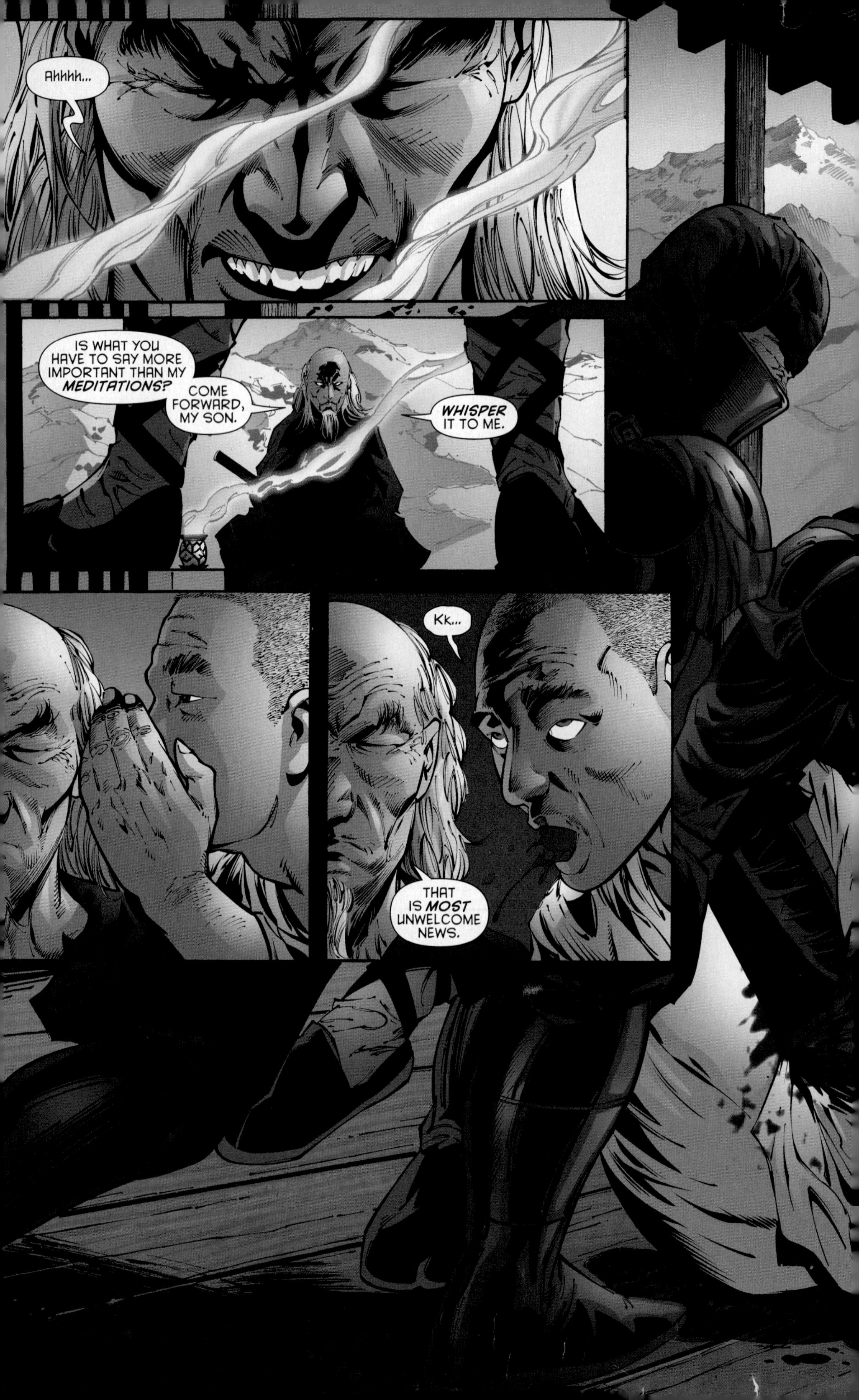
Ahhhh...
IS WHAT YOU HAVE TO SAY MORE IMPORTANT THAN MY *MEDITATIONS?*
COME FORWARD, MY SON.
WHISPER IT TO ME.
Kk...
THAT IS *MOST* UNWELCOME NEWS.

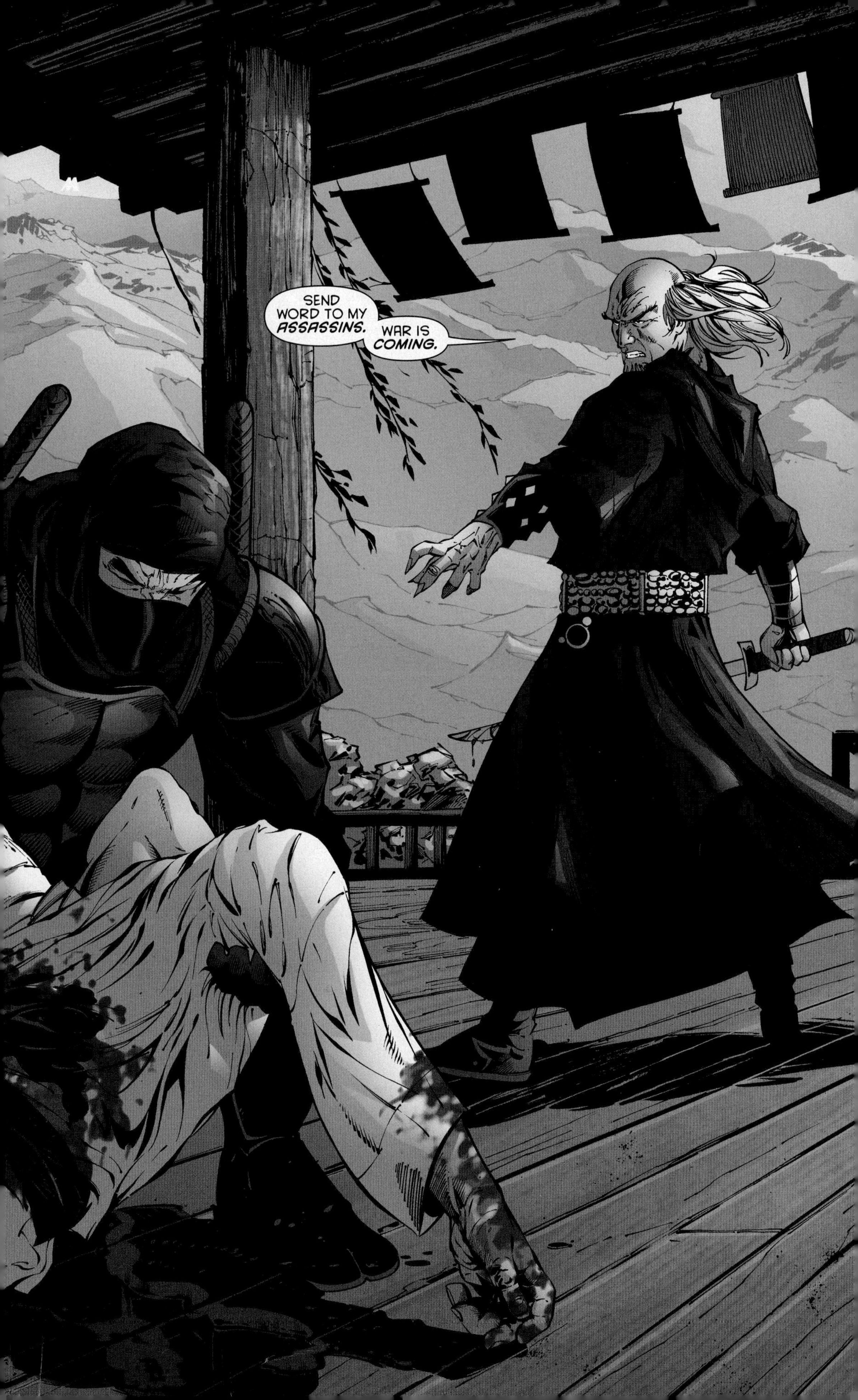
SEND WORD TO MY ASSASSINS.
WAR IS COMING.

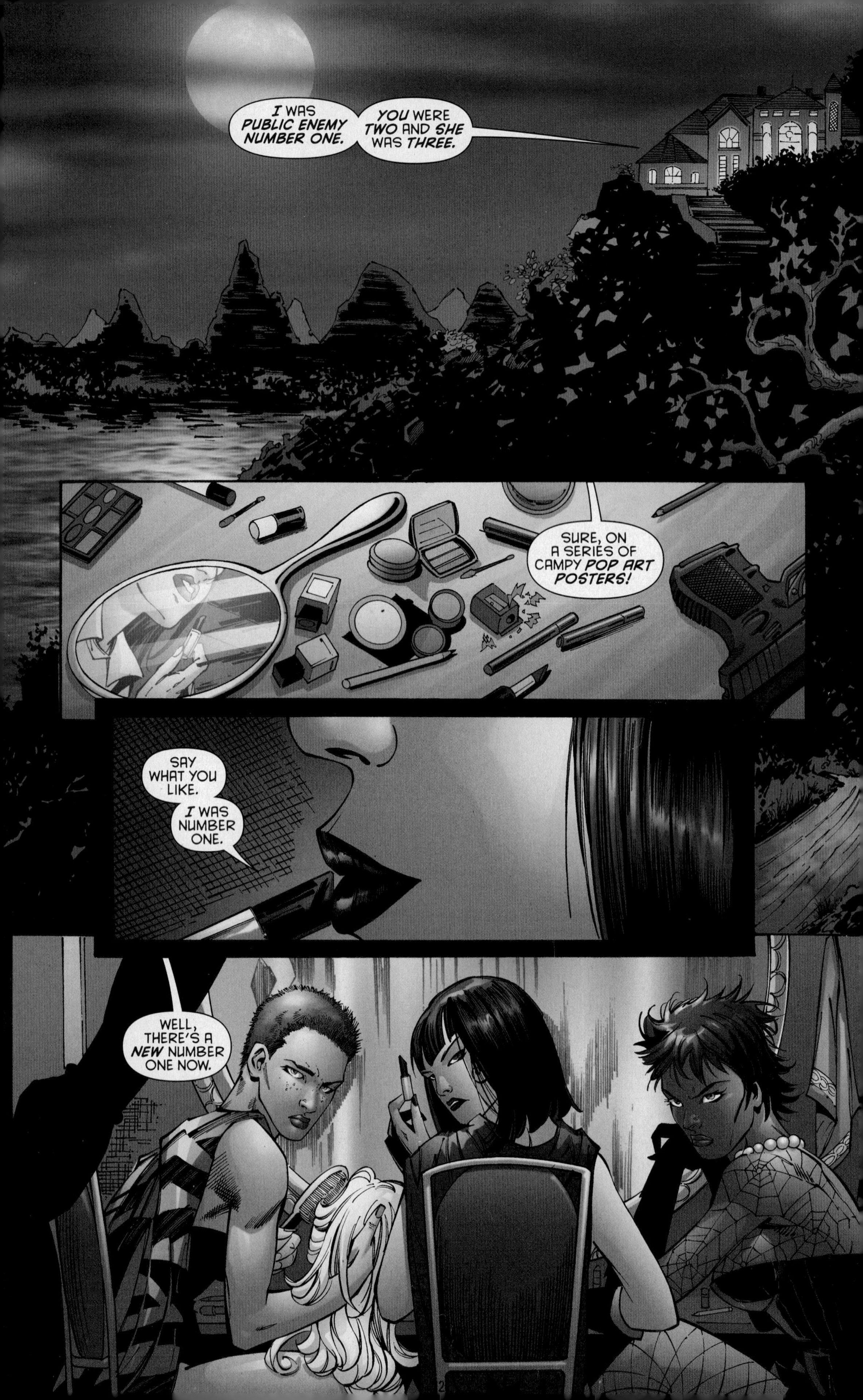
I WAS PUBLIC ENEMY NUMBER ONE.
YOU WERE TWO AND SHE WAS THREE.
SURE, ON A SERIES OF CAMPY POP ART POSTERS!
SAY WHAT YOU LIKE.
I WAS NUMBER ONE.
WELL, THERE'S A NEW NUMBER ONE NOW.

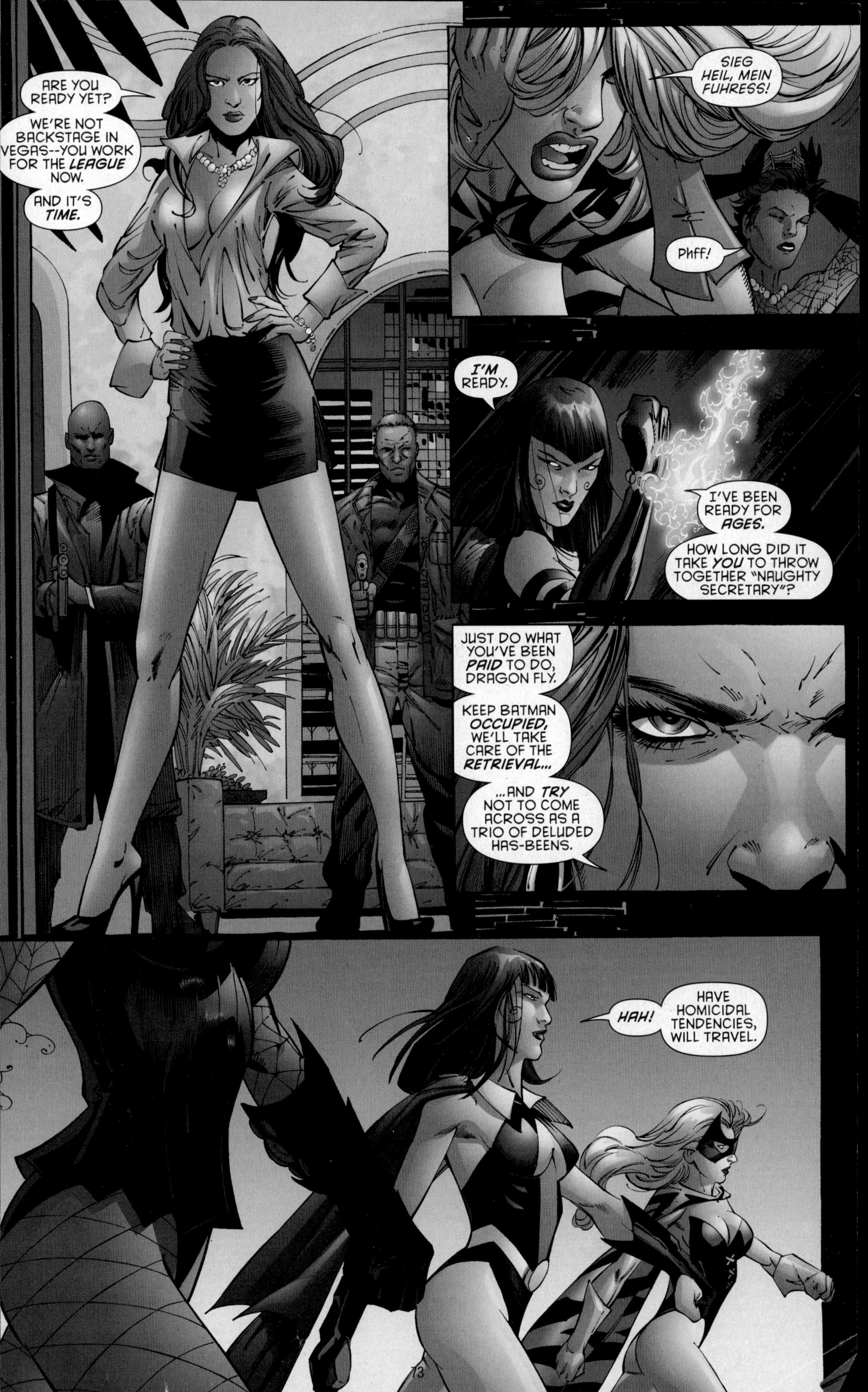
ARE YOU READY YET?
WE'RE NOT BACKSTAGE IN VEGAS--YOU WORK FOR THE LEAGUE NOW.
AND IT'S TIME.
SIEG HEIL, MEIN FUHRESS!
Phff!
I'M READY.
I'VE BEEN READY FOR AGES.
HOW LONG DID IT TAKE YOU TO THROW TOGETHER "NAUGHTY SECRETARY"?
JUST DO WHAT YOU'VE BEEN PAID TO DO, DRAGON FLY.
KEEP BATMAN OCCUPIED, WE'LL TAKE CARE OF THE RETRIEVAL...
...AND TRY NOT TO COME ACROSS AS A TRIO OF DELUDED HAS-BEENS.
HAH!
HAVE HOMICIDAL TENDENCIES, WILL TRAVEL.

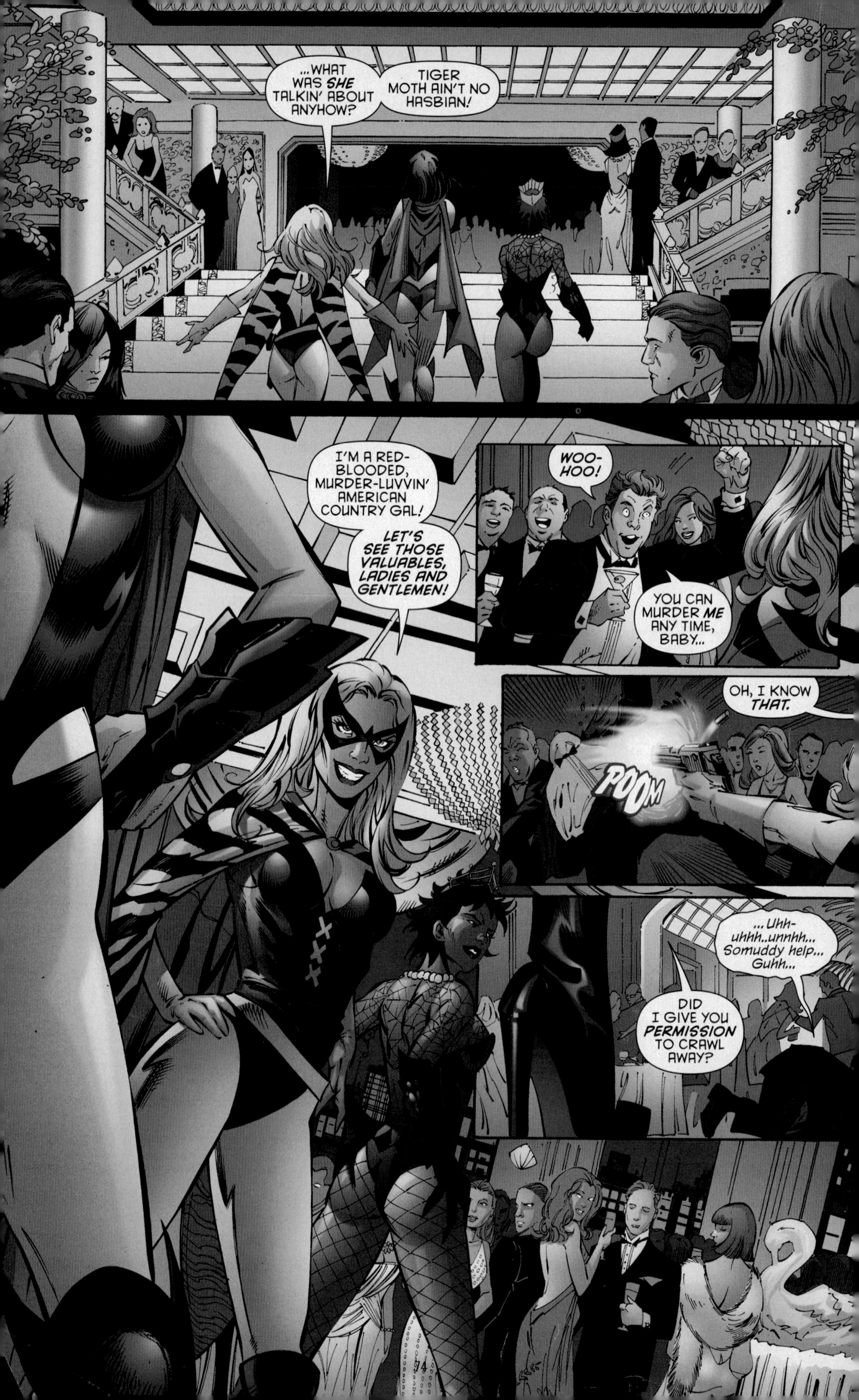

...WHAT WAS *SHE* TALKIN' ABOUT ANYHOW?
TIGER MOTH AIN'T NO HASBIAN!
I'M A RED-BLOODED, MURDER-LUVVIN' AMERICAN COUNTRY GAL!
LET'S SEE THOSE VALUABLES, LADIES AND GENTLEMEN!
WOO-HOO!
YOU CAN MURDER *ME* ANY TIME, BABY...
OH, I KNOW *THAT.*
POOM
...Uhh-uhhh..unnhh... Somuddy help... Guhh...
DID I GIVE YOU *PERMISSION* TO CRAWL AWAY?

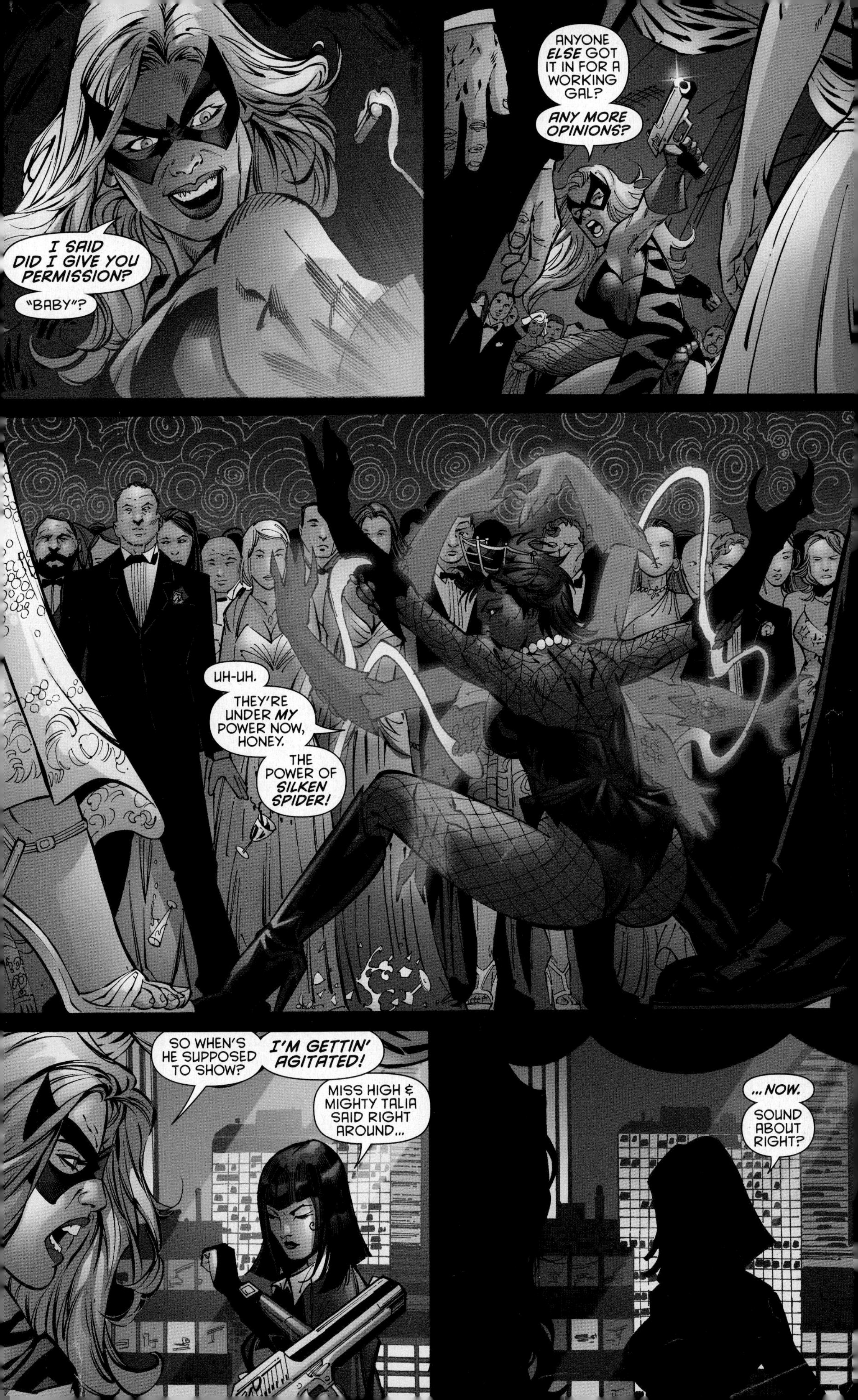
I SAID DID I GIVE YOU PERMISSION?
"BABY"?
ANYONE ELSE GOT IT IN FOR A WORKING GAL?
ANY MORE OPINIONS?
UH-UH.
THEY'RE UNDER MY POWER NOW, HONEY.
THE POWER OF SILKEN SPIDER!
SO WHEN'S HE SUPPOSED TO SHOW?
I'M GETTIN' AGITATED!
MISS HIGH & MIGHTY TALIA SAID RIGHT AROUND...
...NOW.
SOUND ABOUT RIGHT?

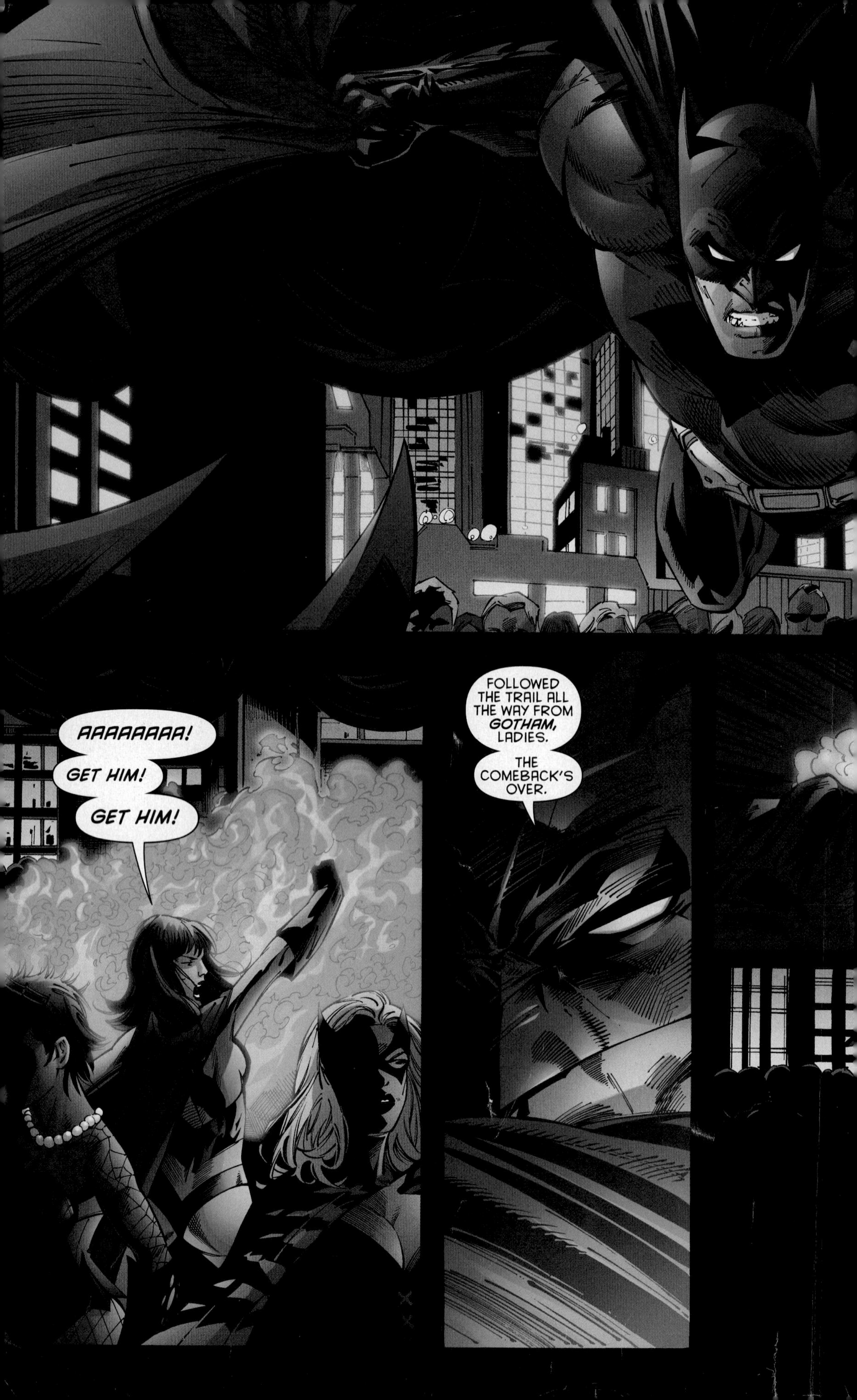
AAAAAAAA!
GET HIM!
GET HIM!
FOLLOWED THE TRAIL ALL THE WAY FROM GOTHAM, LADIES.
THE COMEBACK'S OVER.

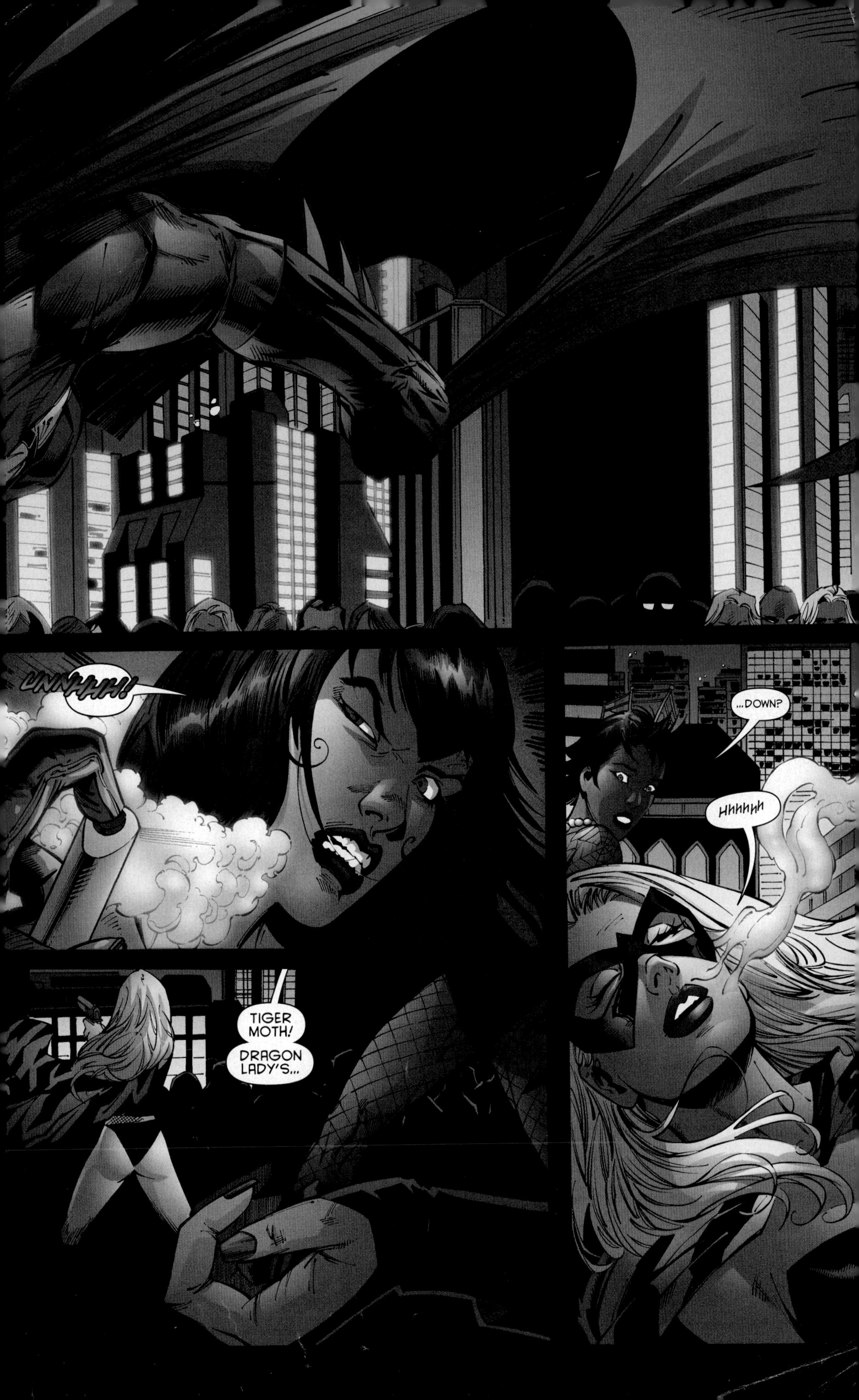
UNHHH!
...DOWN?
HHHHHH
TIGER MOTH! DRAGON LADY'S...

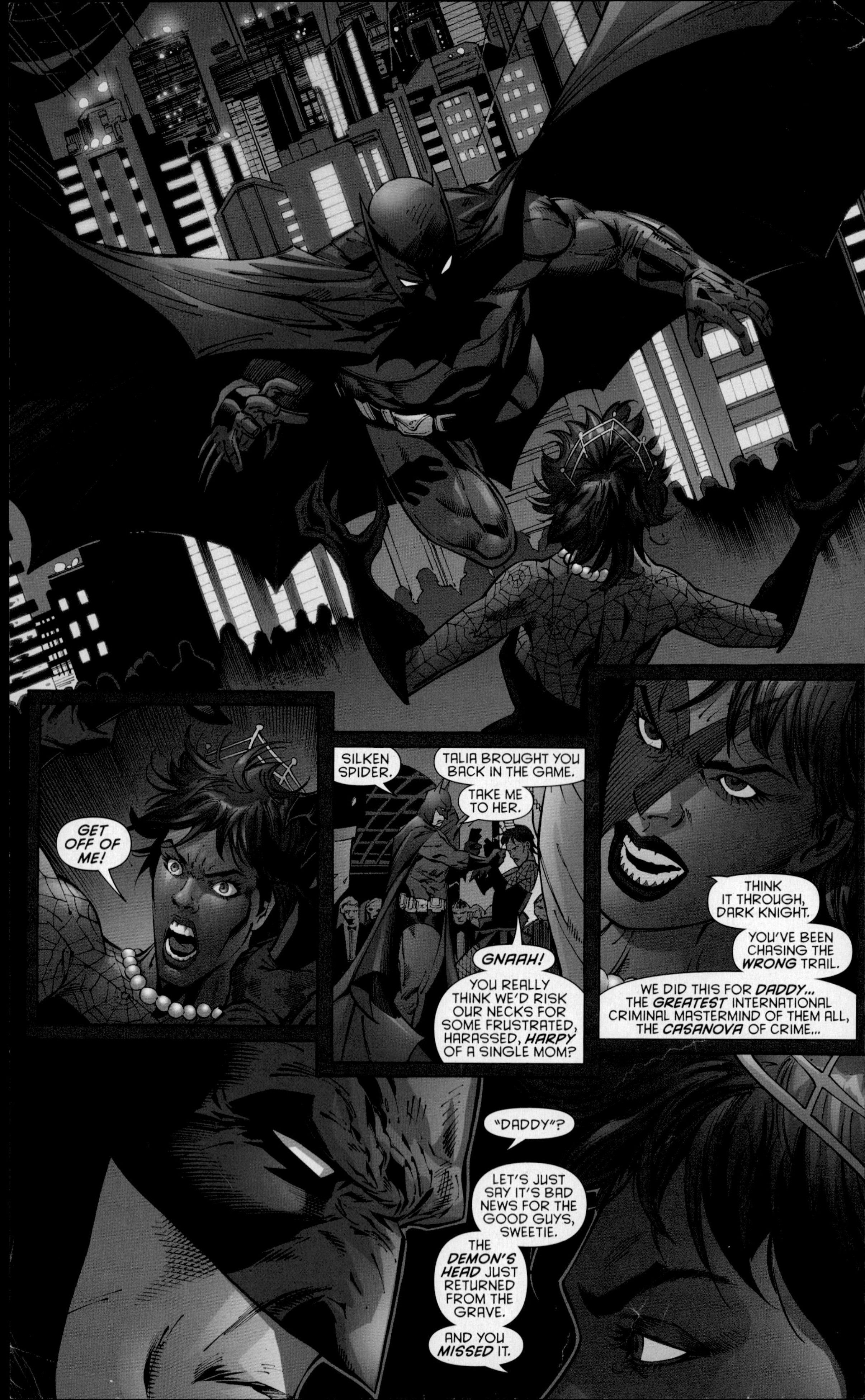
GET OFF OF ME!
SILKEN SPIDER.
TALIA BROUGHT YOU BACK IN THE GAME.
TAKE ME TO HER.
GNAAH!
YOU REALLY THINK WE'D RISK OUR NECKS FOR SOME FRUSTRATED, HARASSED, HARPY OF A SINGLE MOM?
THINK IT THROUGH, DARK KNIGHT.
YOU'VE BEEN CHASING THE WRONG TRAIL.
WE DID THIS FOR DADDY... THE GREATEST INTERNATIONAL CRIMINAL MASTERMIND OF THEM ALL, THE CASANOVA OF CRIME...
"DADDY"?
LET'S JUST SAY IT'S BAD NEWS FOR THE GOOD GUYS, SWEETIE.
THE DEMON'S HEAD JUST RETURNED FROM THE GRAVE.
AND YOU MISSED IT.

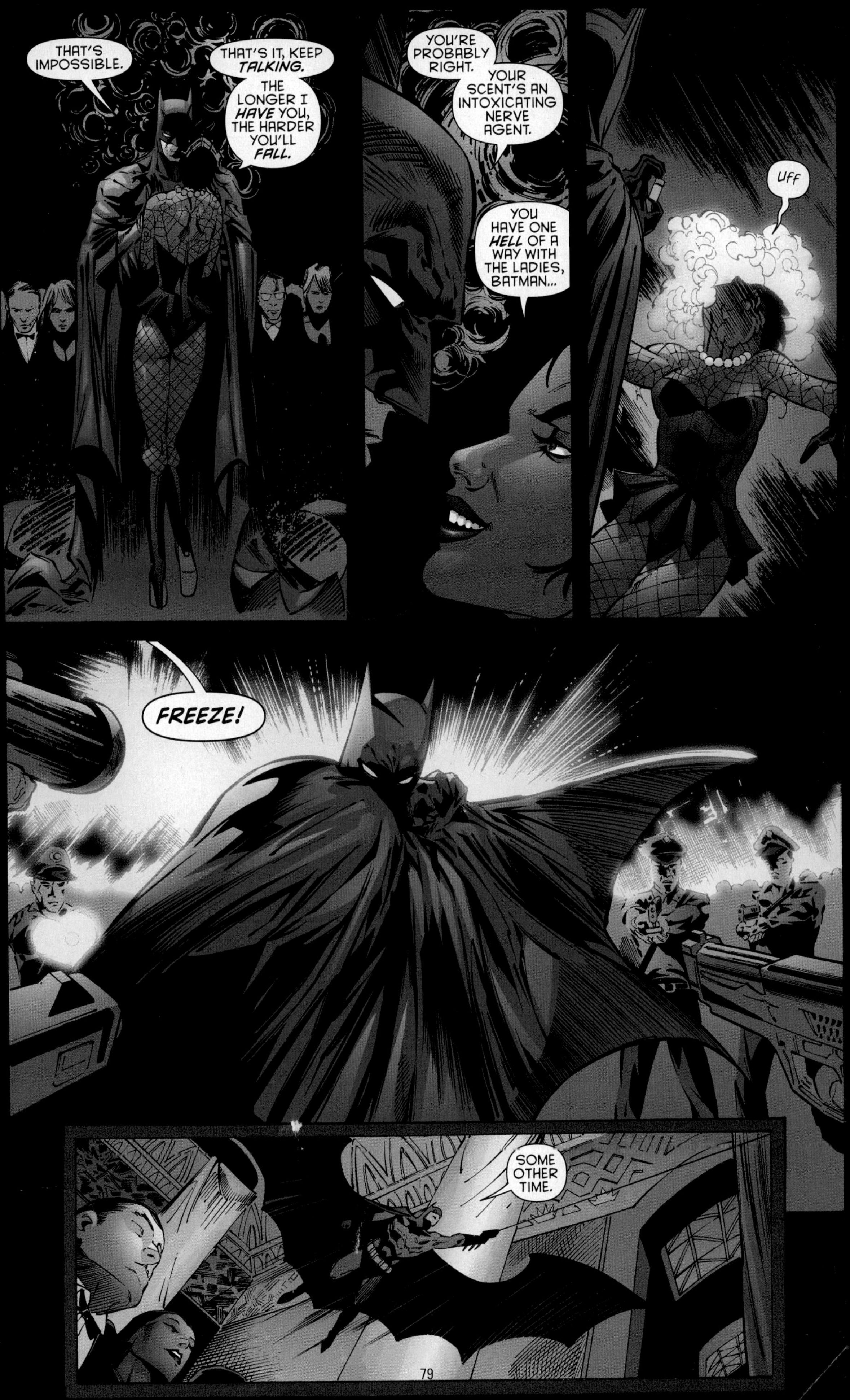
THAT'S IMPOSSIBLE.
THAT'S IT, KEEP TALKING.
THE LONGER I HAVE YOU, THE HARDER YOU'LL FALL.
YOU'RE PROBABLY RIGHT.
YOUR SCENT'S AN INTOXICATING NERVE AGENT.
YOU HAVE ONE HELL OF A WAY WITH THE LADIES, BATMAN...
UFF
FREEZE!
SOME OTHER TIME.

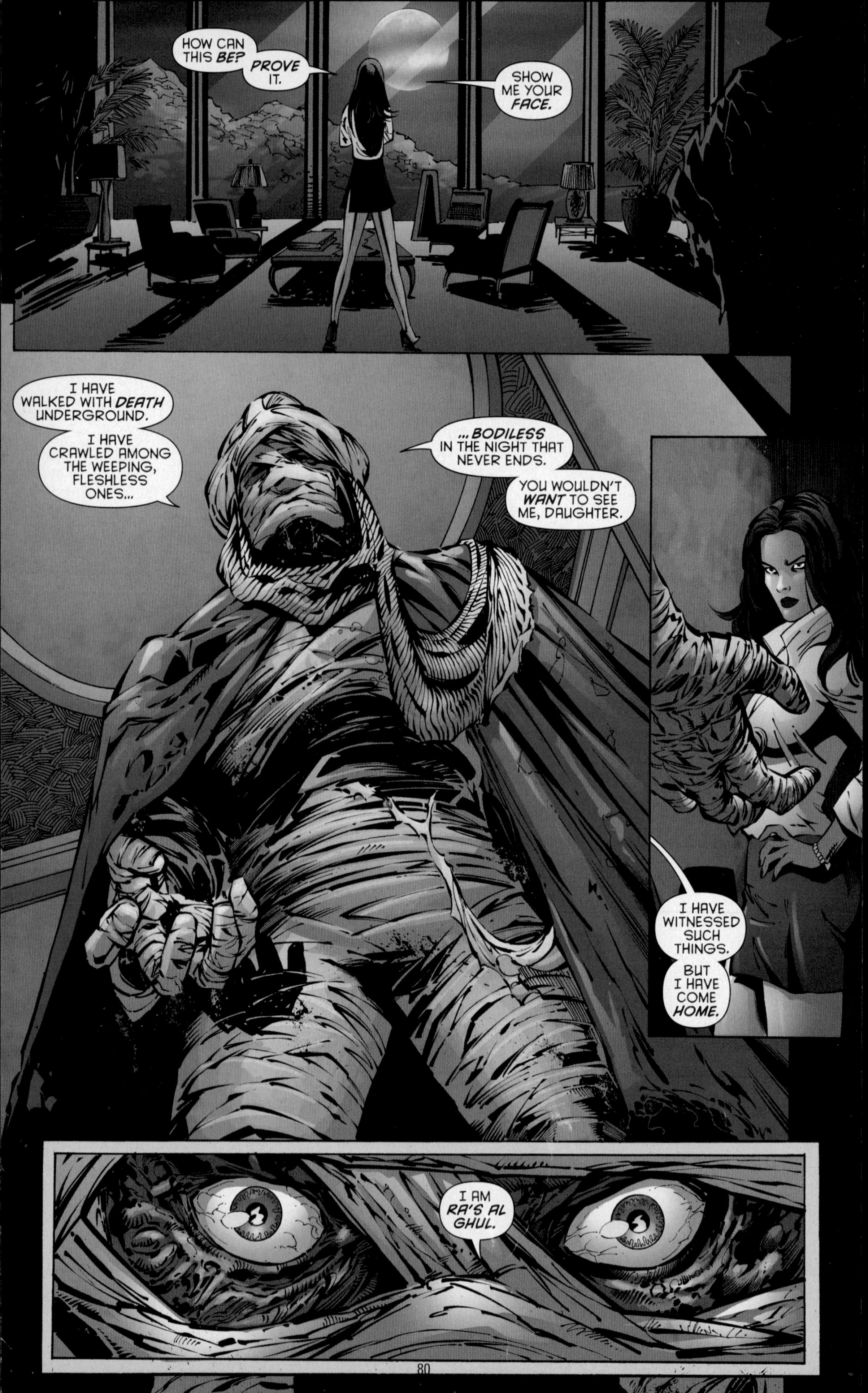
HOW CAN THIS BE? PROVE IT.
SHOW ME YOUR FACE.
I HAVE WALKED WITH DEATH UNDERGROUND.
I HAVE CRAWLED AMONG THE WEEPING, FLESHLESS ONES...
...BODILESS IN THE NIGHT THAT NEVER ENDS.
YOU WOULDN'T WANT TO SEE ME, DAUGHTER.
I HAVE WITNESSED SUCH THINGS.
BUT I HAVE COME HOME.
I AM RA'S AL GHUL.

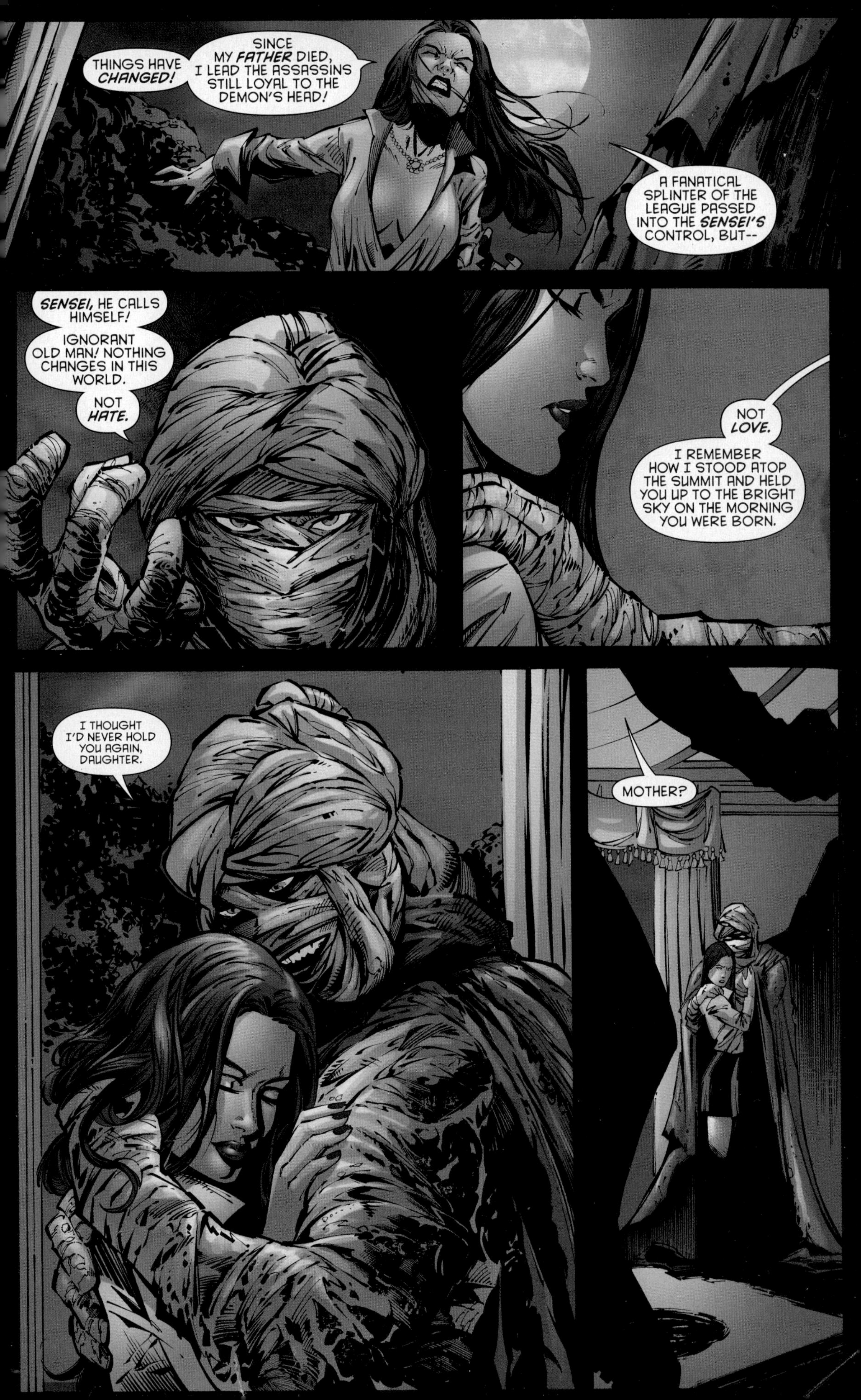
THINGS HAVE CHANGED!
SINCE MY FATHER DIED, I LEAD THE ASSASSINS STILL LOYAL TO THE DEMON'S HEAD!
A FANATICAL SPLINTER OF THE LEAGUE PASSED INTO THE SENSEI'S CONTROL, BUT--
SENSEI, HE CALLS HIMSELF!
IGNORANT OLD MAN! NOTHING CHANGES IN THIS WORLD.
NOT HATE.
NOT LOVE.
I REMEMBER HOW I STOOD ATOP THE SUMMIT AND HELD YOU UP TO THE BRIGHT SKY ON THE MORNING YOU WERE BORN.
I THOUGHT I'D NEVER HOLD YOU AGAIN, DAUGHTER.
MOTHER?

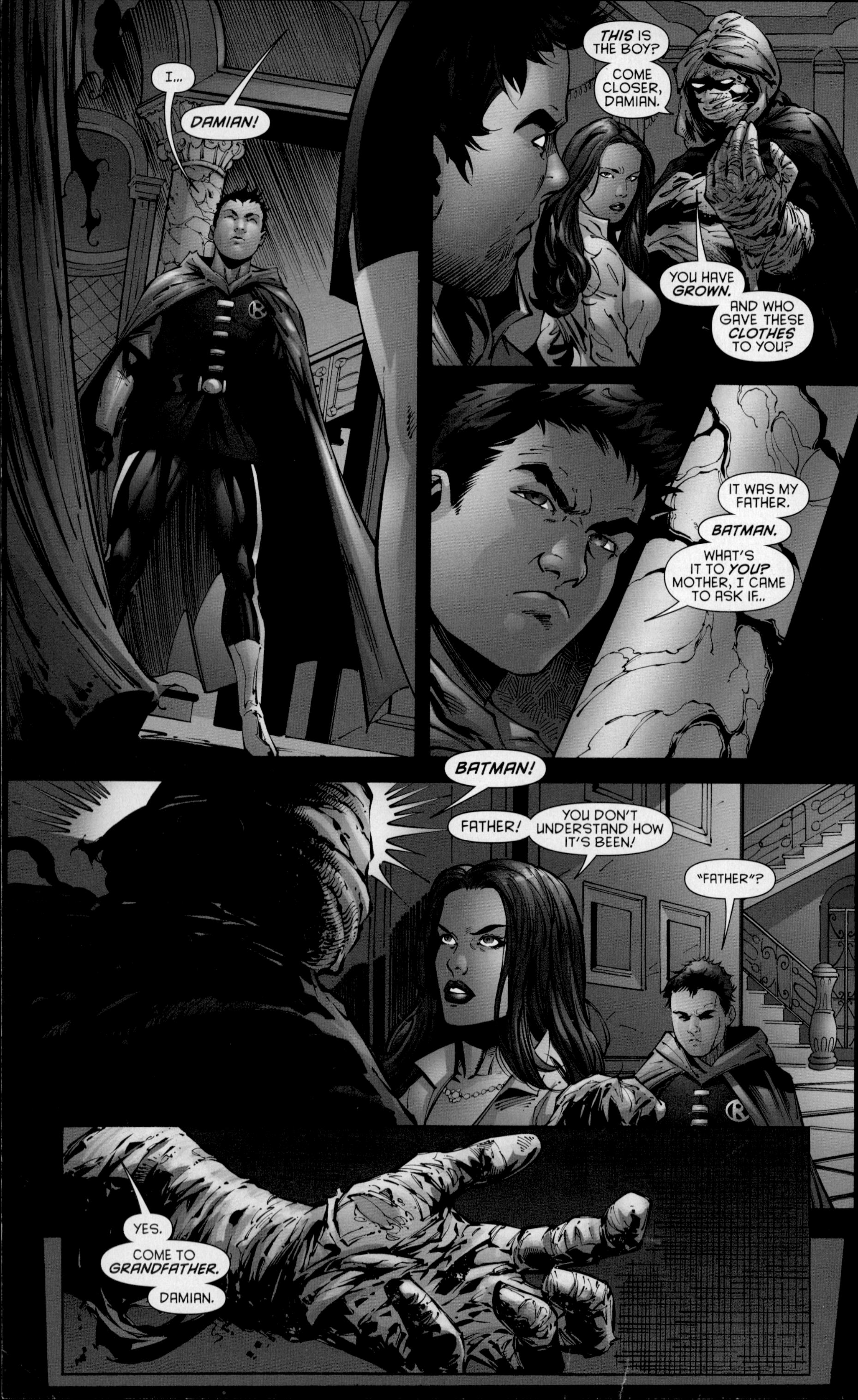
I...
DAMIAN!
THIS IS THE BOY?
COME CLOSER, DAMIAN.
YOU HAVE GROWN.
AND WHO GAVE THESE CLOTHES TO YOU?
IT WAS MY FATHER.
BATMAN.
WHAT'S IT TO YOU? MOTHER, I CAME TO ASK IF...
BATMAN!
FATHER!
YOU DON'T UNDERSTAND HOW IT'S BEEN!
"FATHER"?
YES.
COME TO GRANDFATHER.
DAMIAN.

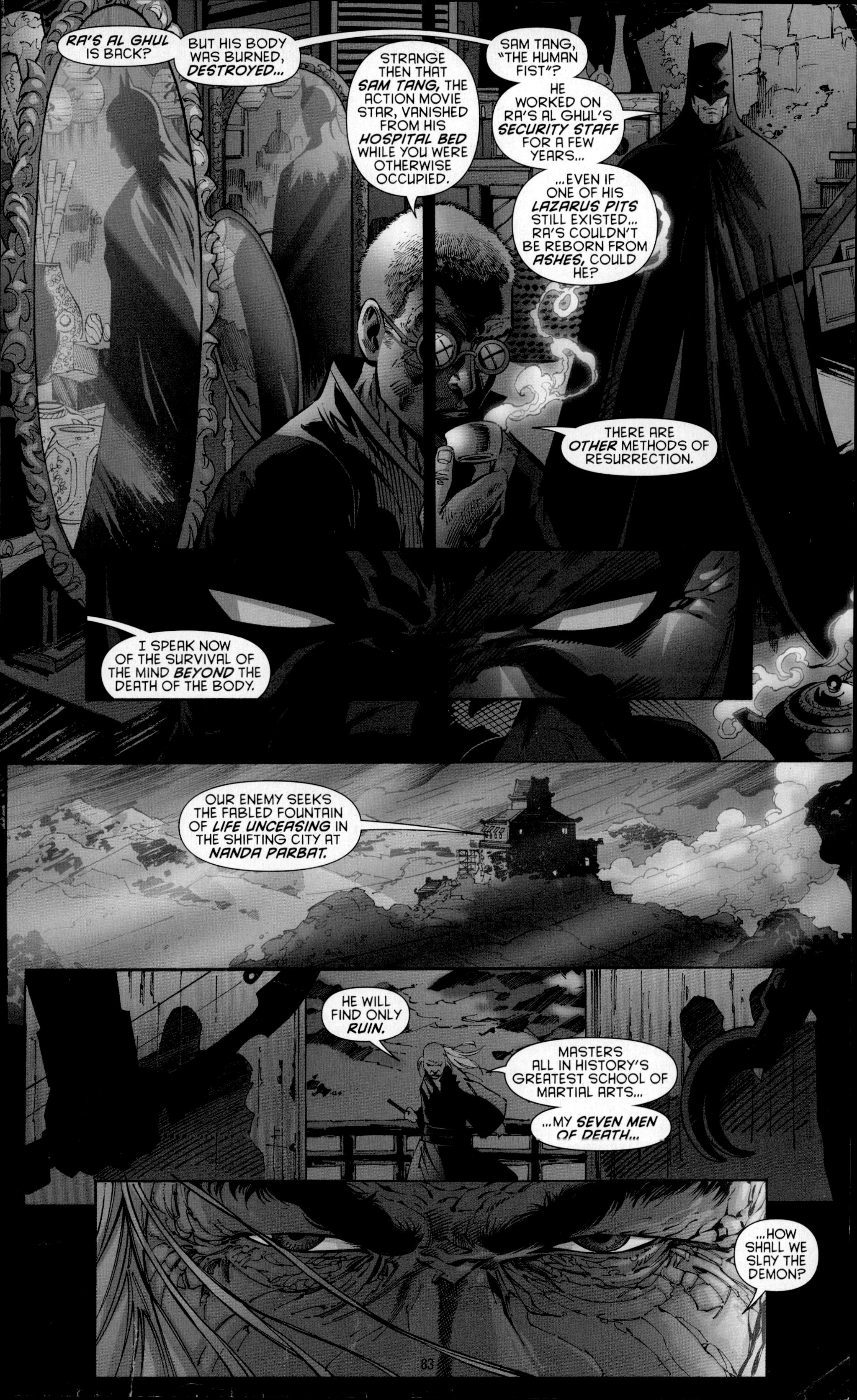
RA'S AL GHUL IS BACK?
BUT HIS BODY WAS BURNED, DESTROYED...
SAM TANG, "THE HUMAN FIST"?
HE WORKED ON RA'S AL GHUL'S SECURITY STAFF FOR A FEW YEARS...
STRANGE THEN THAT SAM TANG, THE ACTION MOVIE STAR, VANISHED FROM HIS HOSPITAL BED WHILE YOU WERE OTHERWISE OCCUPIED.
...EVEN IF ONE OF HIS LAZARUS PITS STILL EXISTED... RA'S COULDN'T BE REBORN FROM ASHES, COULD HE?
THERE ARE OTHER METHODS OF RESURRECTION.
I SPEAK NOW OF THE SURVIVAL OF THE MIND BEYOND THE DEATH OF THE BODY.
OUR ENEMY SEEKS THE FABLED FOUNTAIN OF LIFE UNCEASING IN THE SHIFTING CITY AT NANDA PARBAT.
HE WILL FIND ONLY RUIN.
MASTERS ALL IN HISTORY'S GREATEST SCHOOL OF MARTIAL ARTS...
...MY SEVEN MEN OF DEATH...
...HOW SHALL WE SLAY THE DEMON?

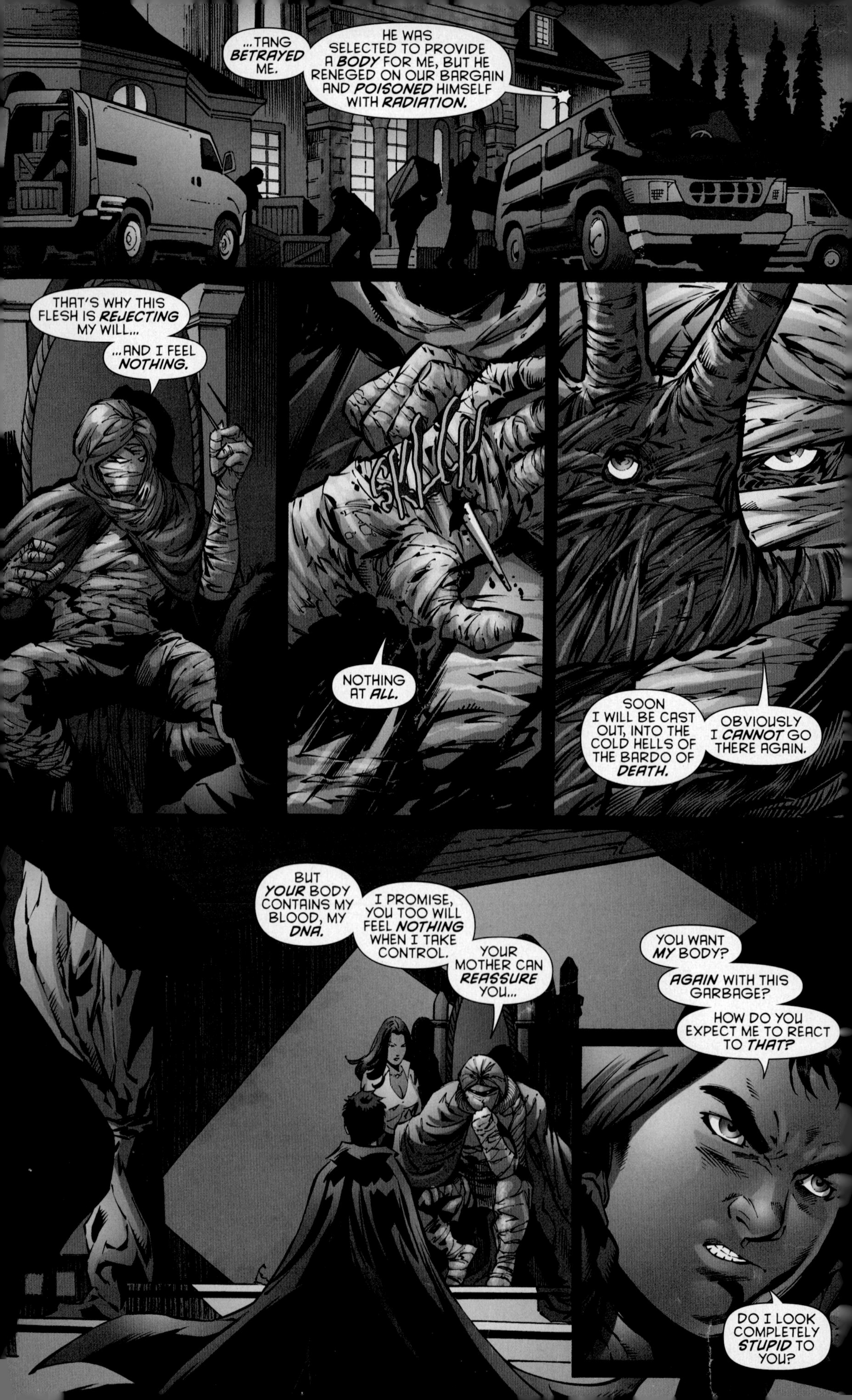
...TANG BETRAYED ME.
HE WAS SELECTED TO PROVIDE A BODY FOR ME, BUT HE RENEGED ON OUR BARGAIN AND POISONED HIMSELF WITH RADIATION.
THAT'S WHY THIS FLESH IS REJECTING MY WILL...
...AND I FEEL NOTHING.
NOTHING AT ALL.
SOON I WILL BE CAST OUT, INTO THE COLD HELLS OF THE BARDO OF DEATH.
OBVIOUSLY I CANNOT GO THERE AGAIN.
BUT YOUR BODY CONTAINS MY BLOOD, MY DNA.
I PROMISE, YOU TOO WILL FEEL NOTHING WHEN I TAKE CONTROL.
YOUR MOTHER CAN REASSURE YOU...
YOU WANT MY BODY?
AGAIN WITH THIS GARBAGE?
HOW DO YOU EXPECT ME TO REACT TO THAT?
DO I LOOK COMPLETELY STUPID TO YOU?

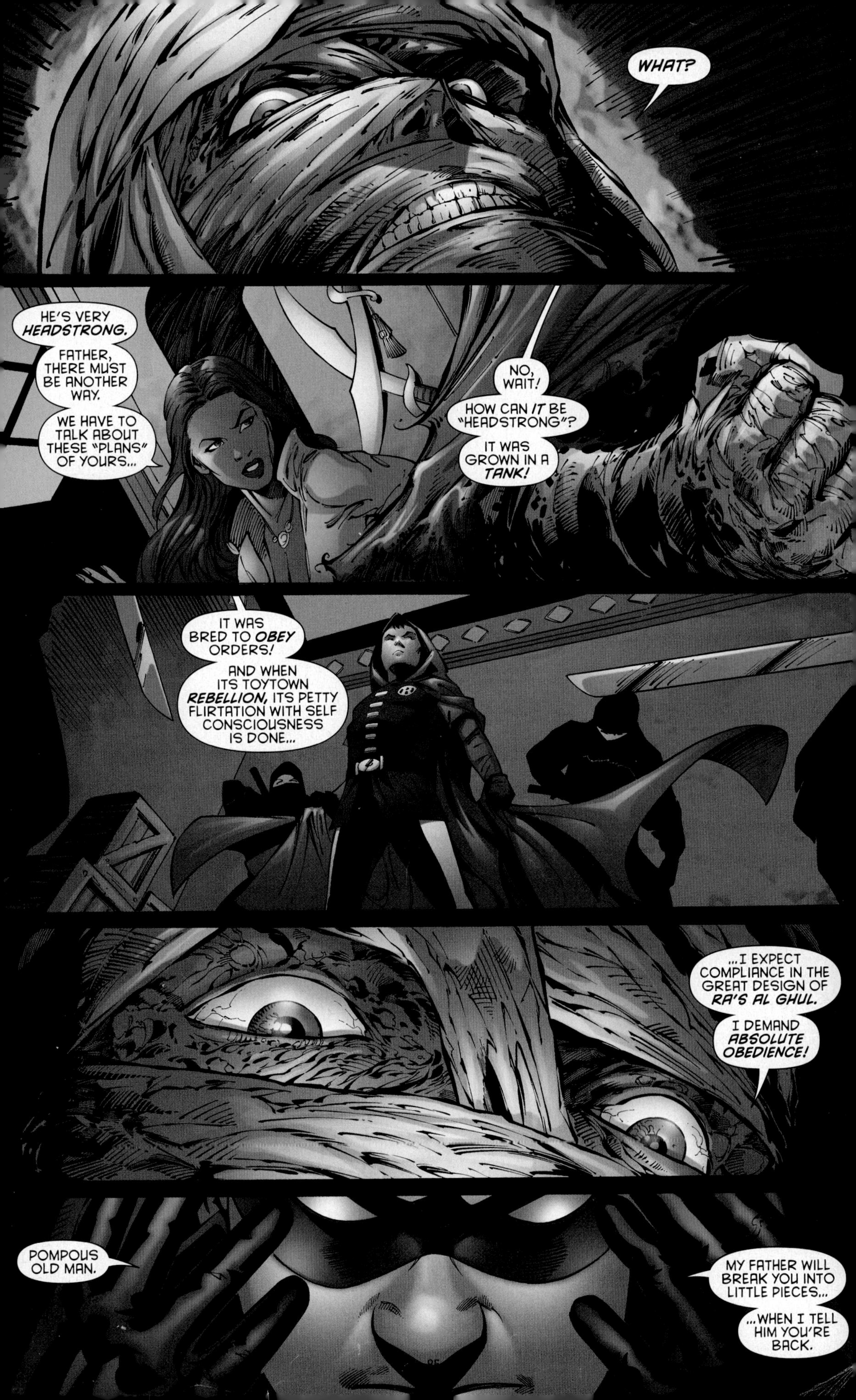
WHAT?
HE'S VERY HEADSTRONG.
FATHER, THERE MUST BE ANOTHER WAY.
WE HAVE TO TALK ABOUT THESE "PLANS" OF YOURS...
NO, WAIT!
HOW CAN IT BE "HEADSTRONG"?
IT WAS GROWN IN A TANK!
IT WAS BRED TO OBEY ORDERS!
AND WHEN ITS TOYTOWN REBELLION, ITS PETTY FLIRTATION WITH SELF CONSCIOUSNESS IS DONE...
...I EXPECT COMPLIANCE IN THE GREAT DESIGN OF RA'S AL GHUL.
I DEMAND ABSOLUTE OBEDIENCE!
POMPOUS OLD MAN.
MY FATHER WILL BREAK YOU INTO LITTLE PIECES...
...WHEN I TELL HIM YOU'RE BACK.

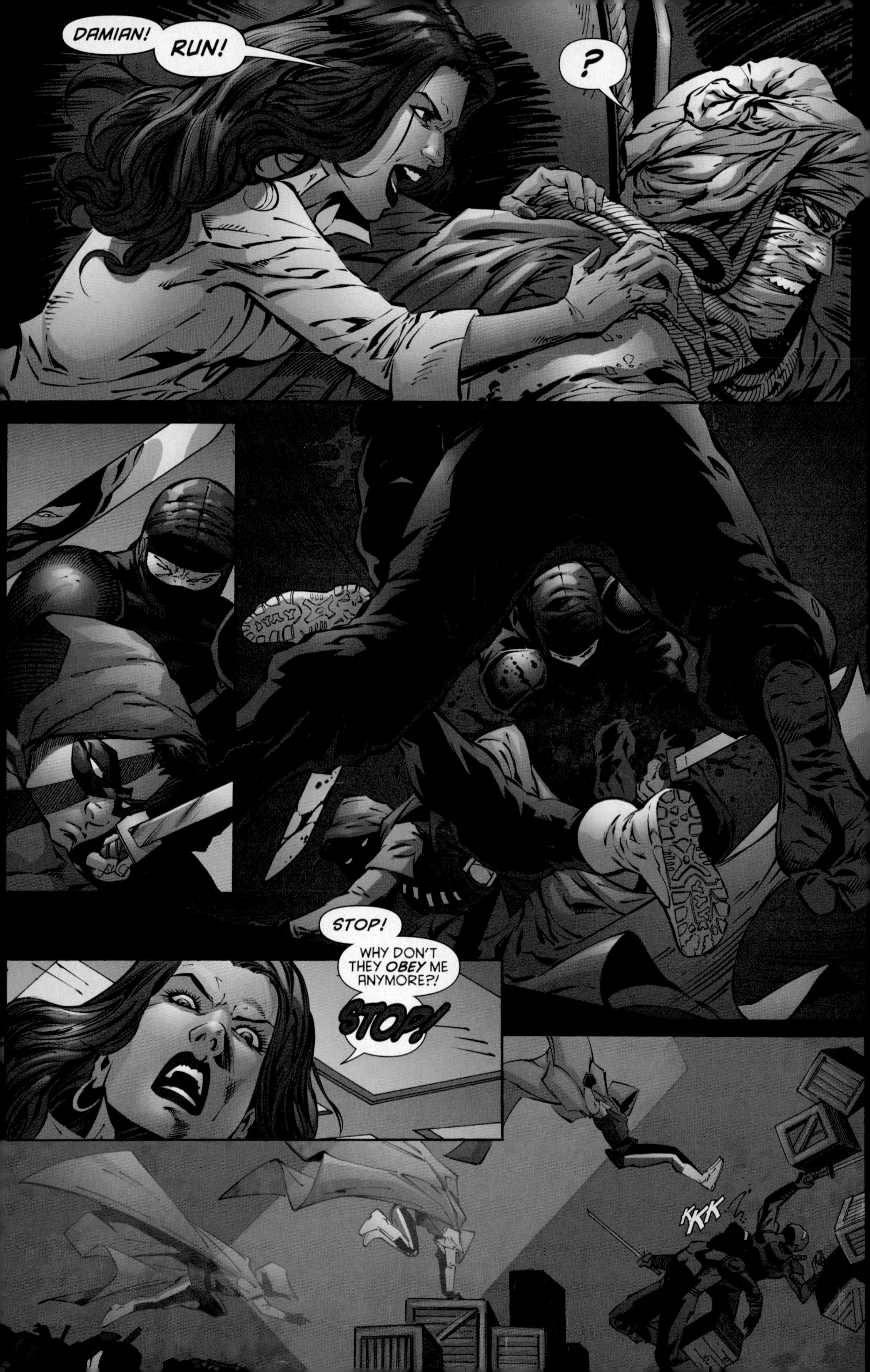
DAMIAN!
RUN!
?
STOP!
WHY DON'T THEY OBEY ME ANYMORE?!
STOP!
KKK

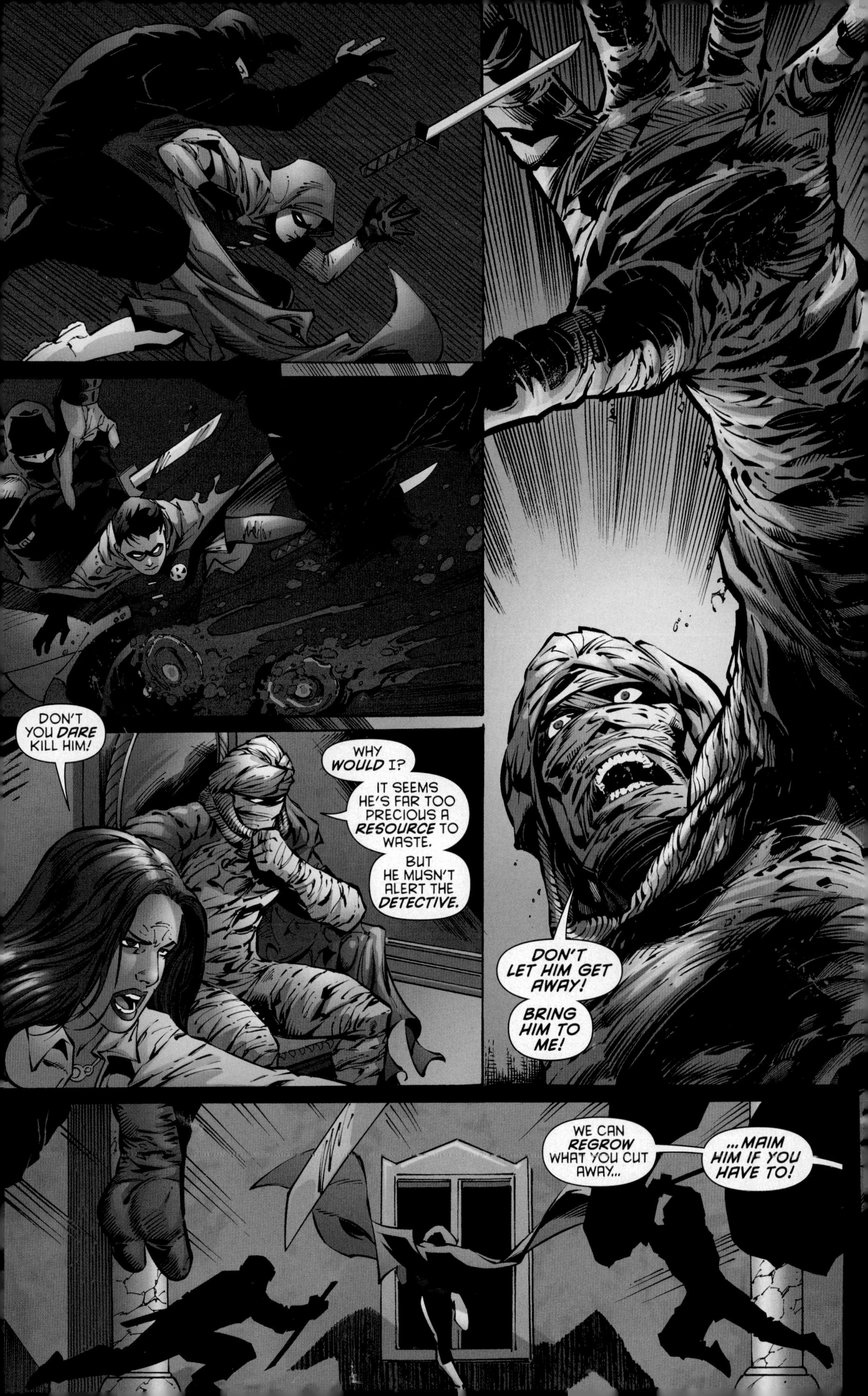
DON'T YOU DARE KILL HIM!
WHY WOULD I?
IT SEEMS HE'S FAR TOO PRECIOUS A RESOURCE TO WASTE.
BUT HE MUSN'T ALERT THE DETECTIVE.
DON'T LET HIM GET AWAY!
BRING HIM TO ME!
WE CAN REGROW WHAT YOU CUT AWAY...
...MAIM HIM IF YOU HAVE TO!

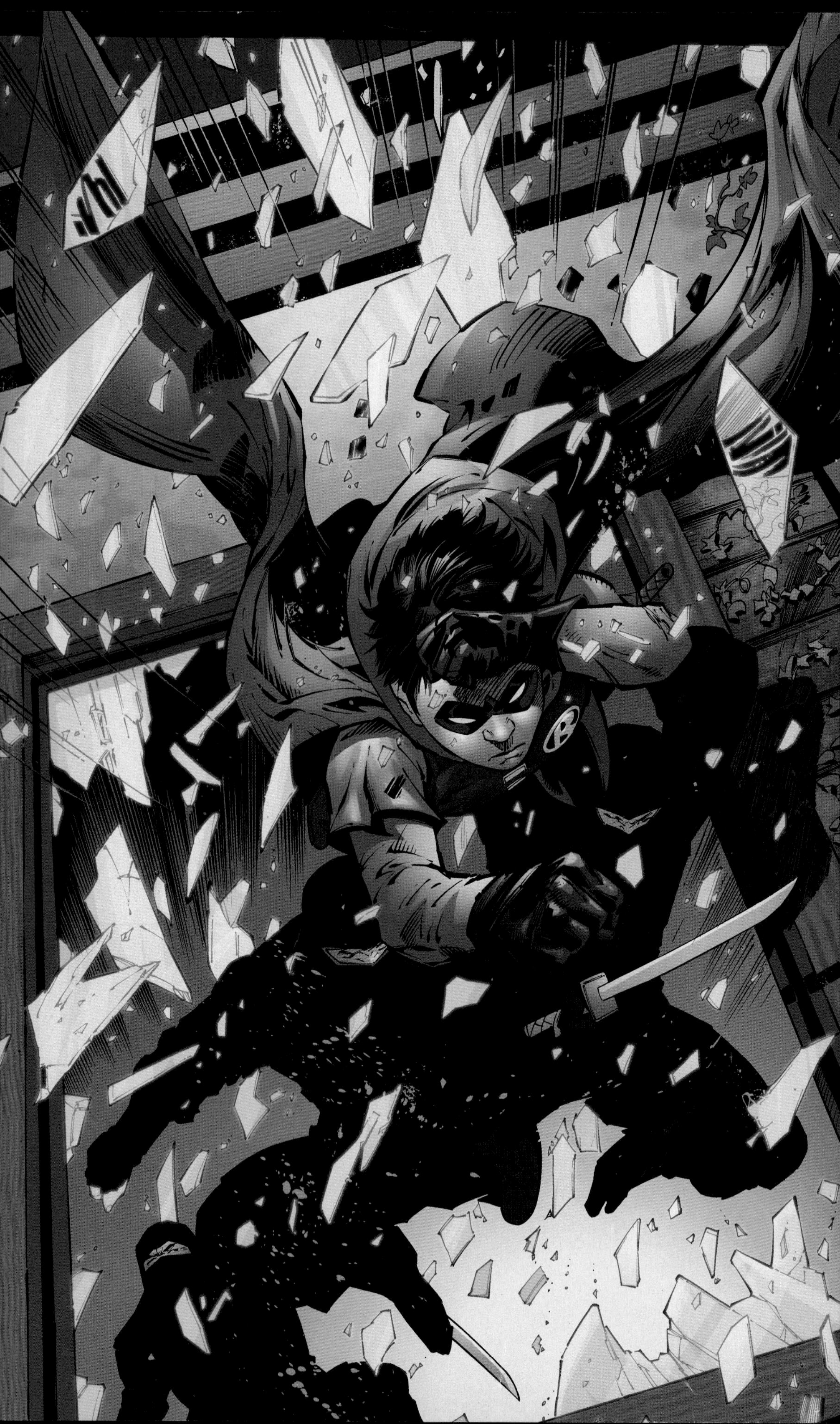

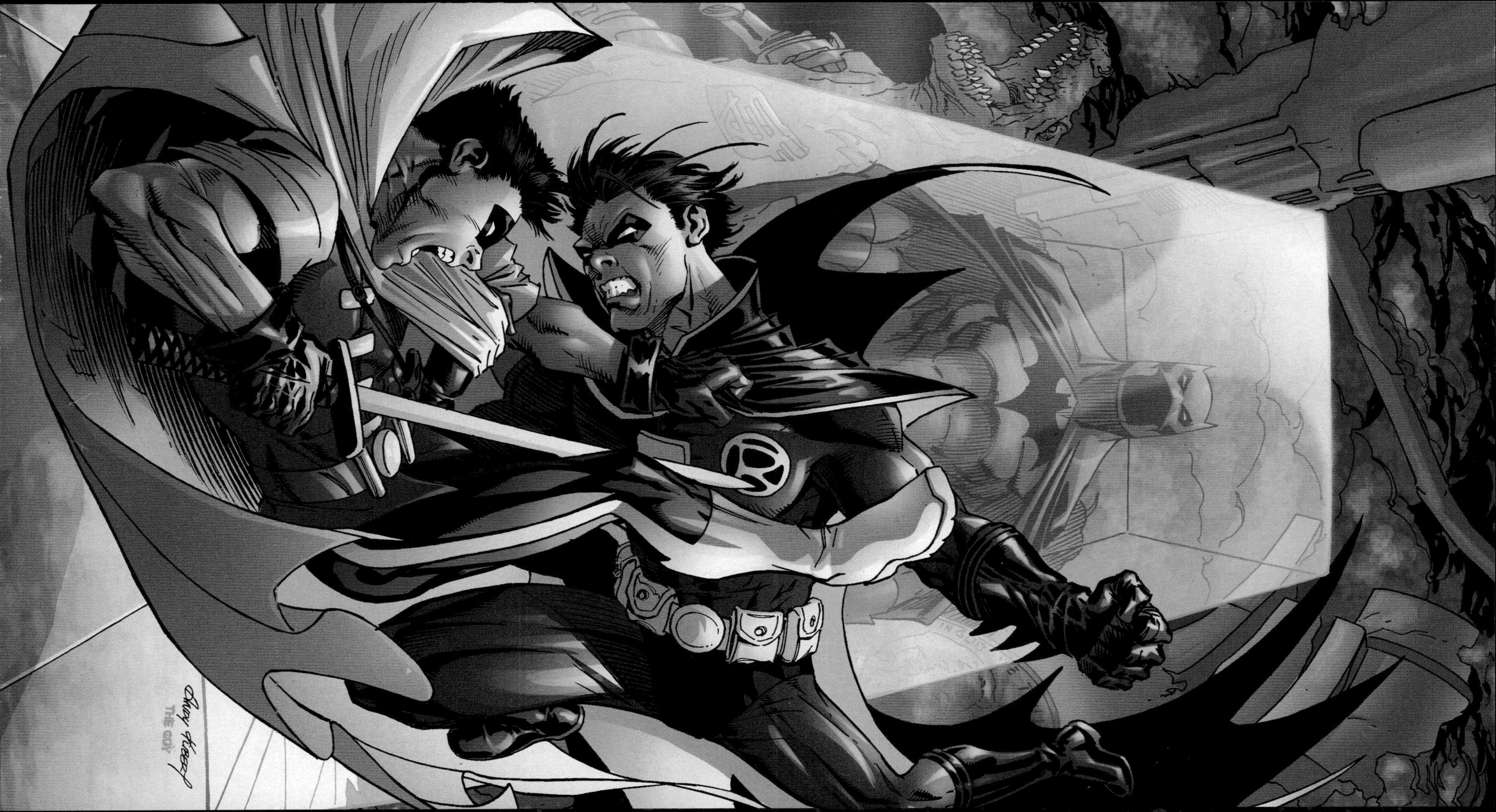
ANDY KUBERT
THE GUY

CHAPTER ONE A BOY FOR THE DEMON

Cover art by Andy Kubert | Chapter written by Peter Milligan | Chapter art by Freddie E. Williams II

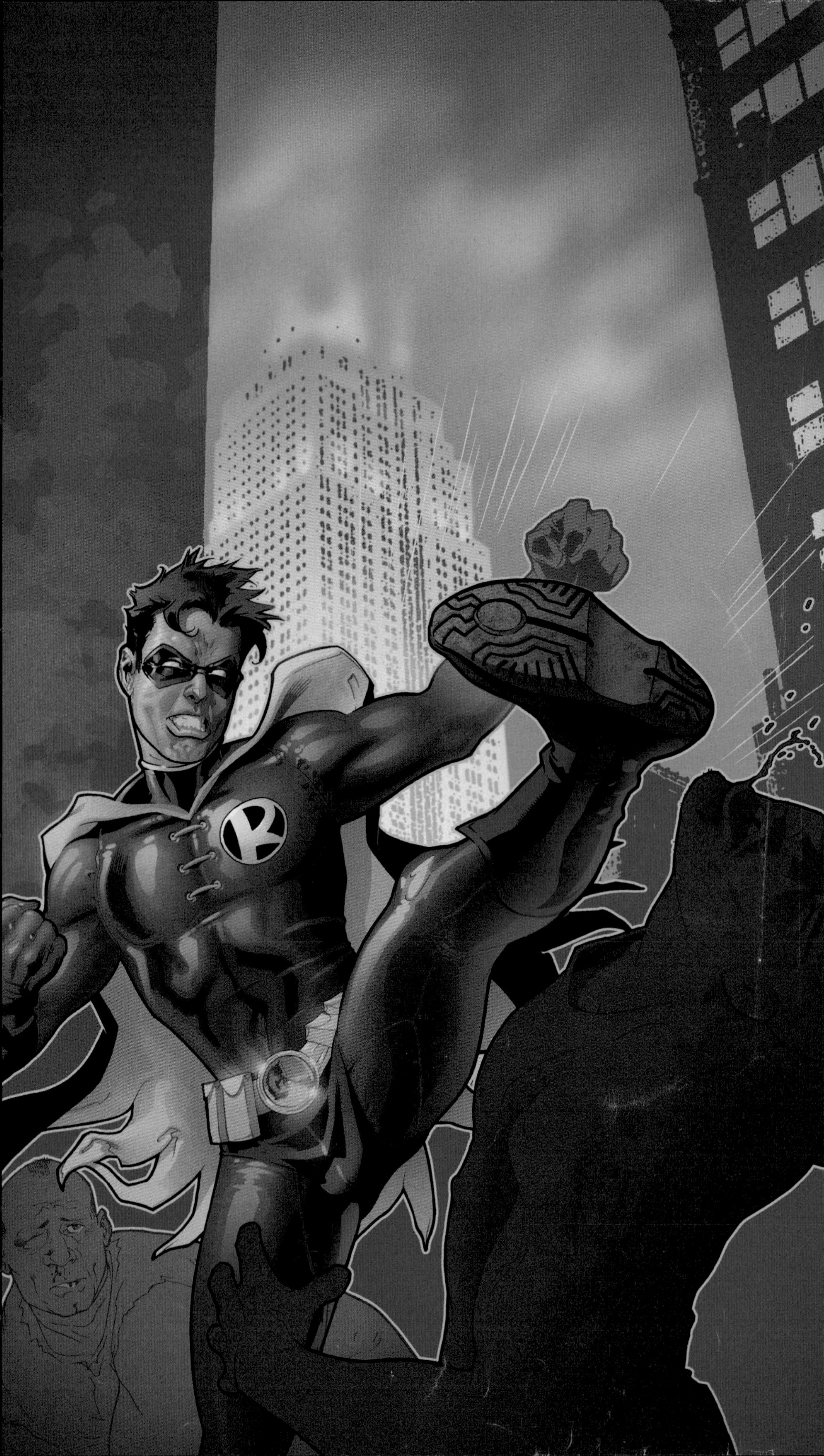

Variant cover by Stephane Roux

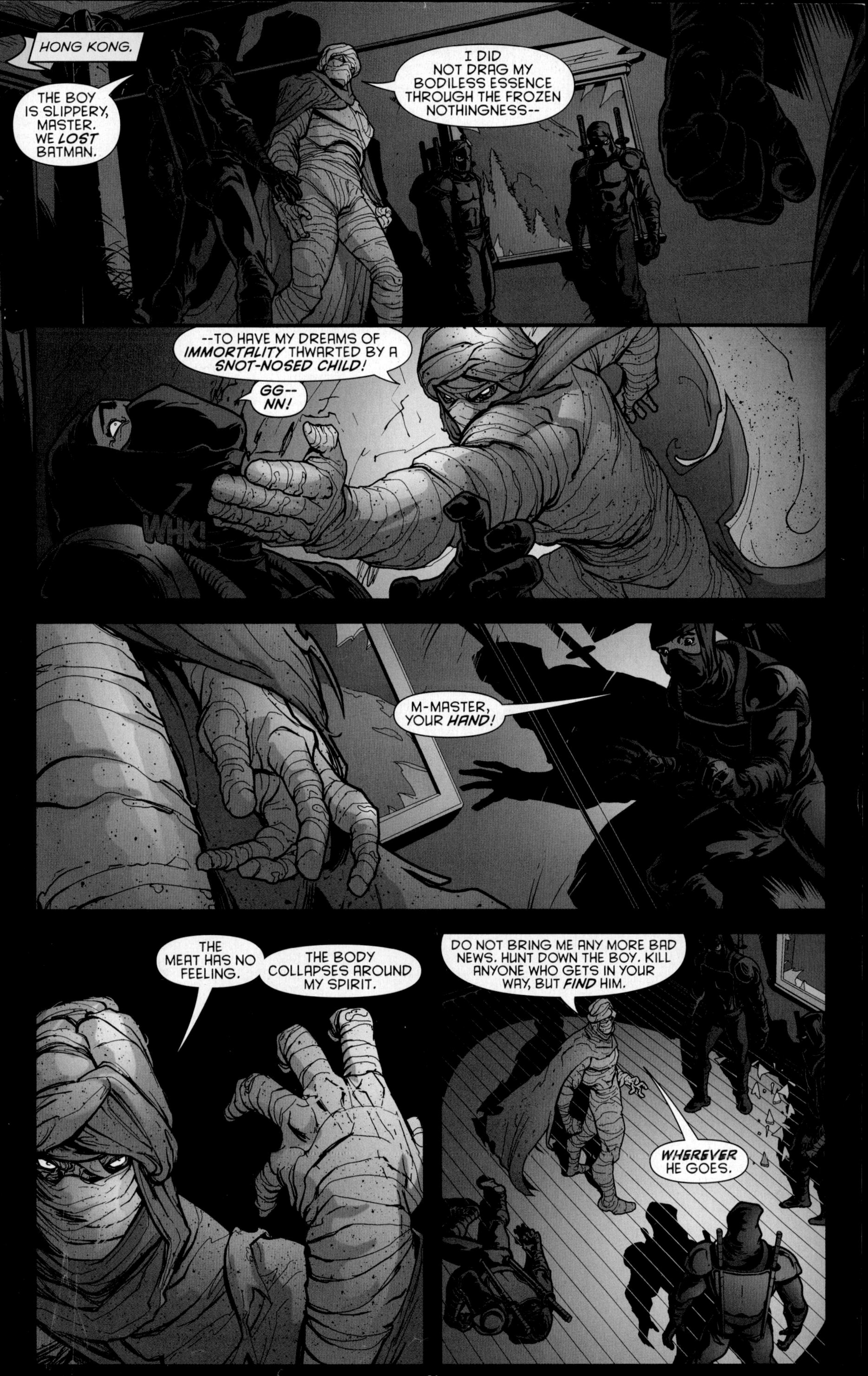
HONG KONG.
THE BOY IS SLIPPERY, MASTER. WE *LOST* BATMAN.
I DID NOT DRAG MY BODILESS ESSENCE THROUGH THE FROZEN NOTHINGNESS--
--TO HAVE MY DREAMS OF *IMMORTALITY* THWARTED BY A *SNOT-NOSED CHILD!*
GG--NN!
WHK!
M-MASTER, YOUR *HAND!*
THE MEAT HAS NO FEELING.
THE BODY COLLAPSES AROUND MY SPIRIT.
DO NOT BRING ME ANY MORE BAD NEWS. HUNT DOWN THE BOY. KILL ANYONE WHO GETS IN YOUR WAY, BUT *FIND* HIM.
WHEREVER HE GOES.

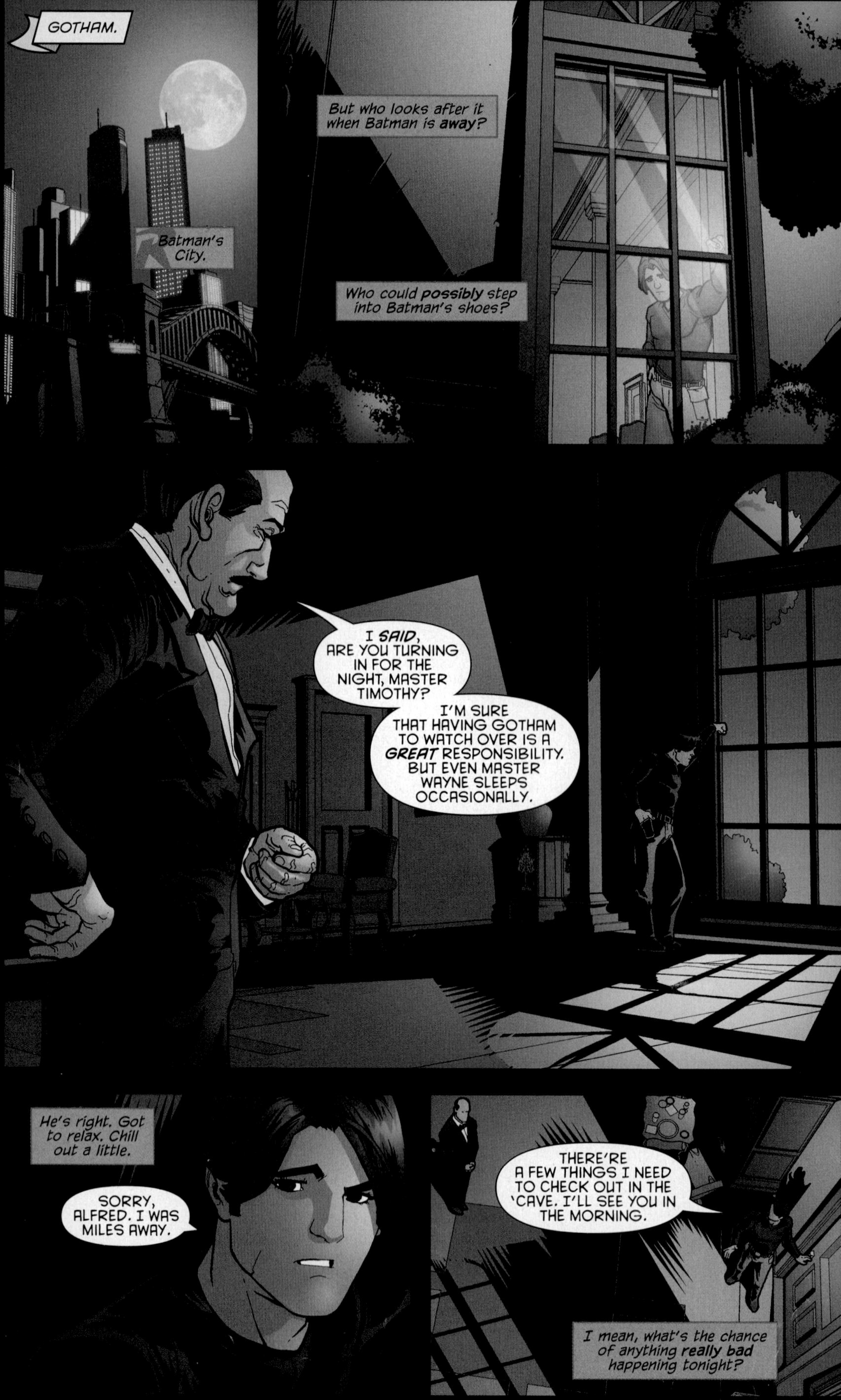

GOTHAM.
Batman's City.
But who looks after it when Batman is **away**?
Who could **possibly** step into Batman's shoes?
I *SAID*, ARE YOU TURNING IN FOR THE NIGHT, MASTER TIMOTHY?
I'M SURE THAT HAVING GOTHAM TO WATCH OVER IS A *GREAT* RESPONSIBILITY. BUT EVEN MASTER WAYNE SLEEPS OCCASIONALLY.
He's right. Got to relax. Chill out a little.
SORRY, ALFRED. I WAS MILES AWAY.
THERE'RE A FEW THINGS I NEED TO CHECK OUT IN THE 'CAVE. I'LL SEE YOU IN THE MORNING.
I mean, what's the chance of anything **really bad** happening tonight?

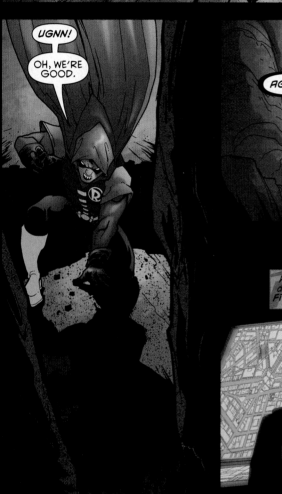

UGNN!

OH, WE'RE GOOD.

AGGHH!

SKREE! SKREE!

High criminal activity in the downtown Saint Paul's area. Five murders tonight already.

Five murders. Someone's loved ones.

GOTHAM CITY i-MAP: TOP VIEW

Maybe someone's father.

Or son.

Don't go there.

GOTHAM CITY i-MAP: TOP VIEW

Give yourself nightmares.

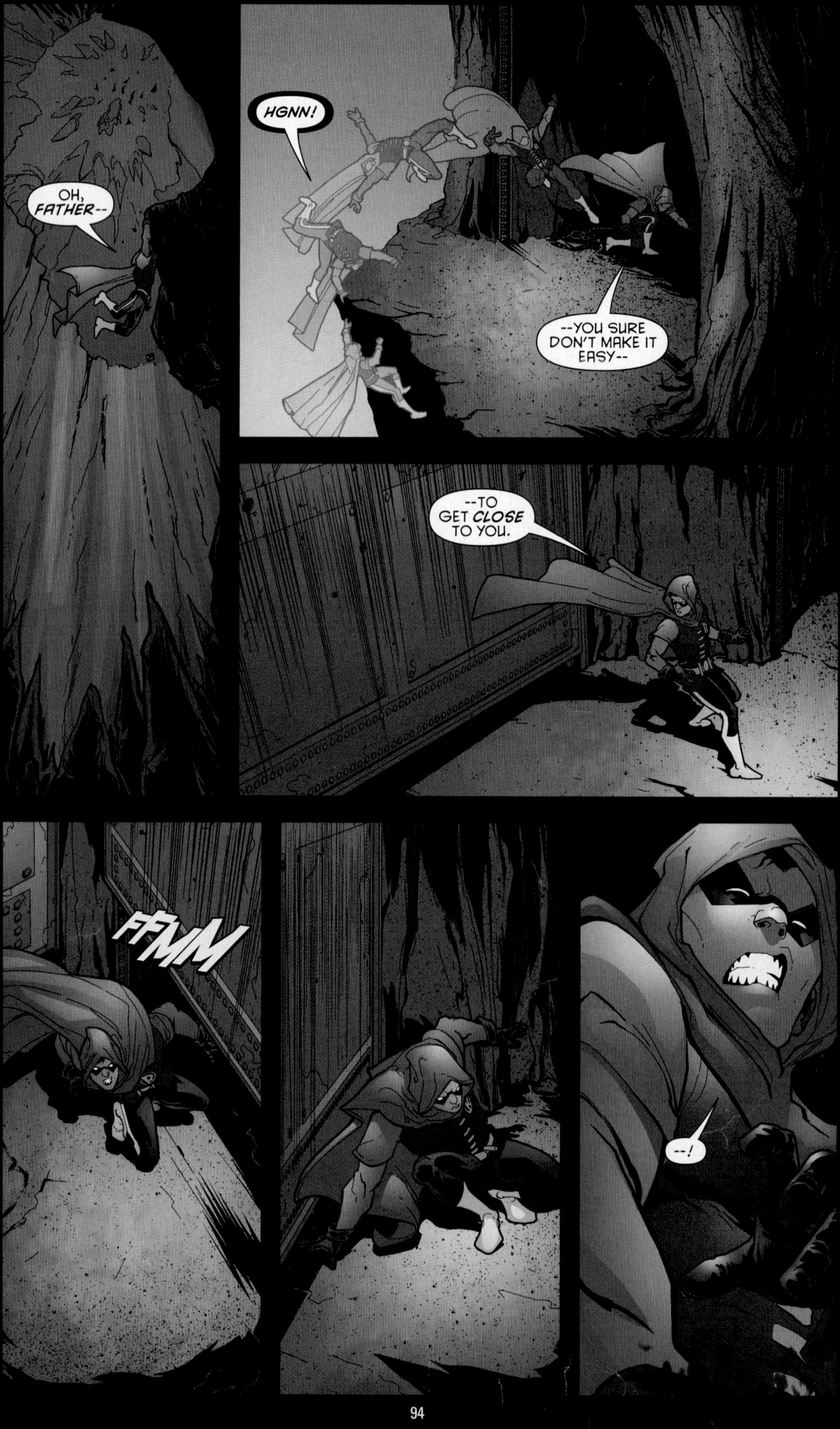
OH, FATHER--
HGNN!
--YOU SURE DON'T MAKE IT EASY--
--TO GET CLOSE TO YOU.
FFMM
--!

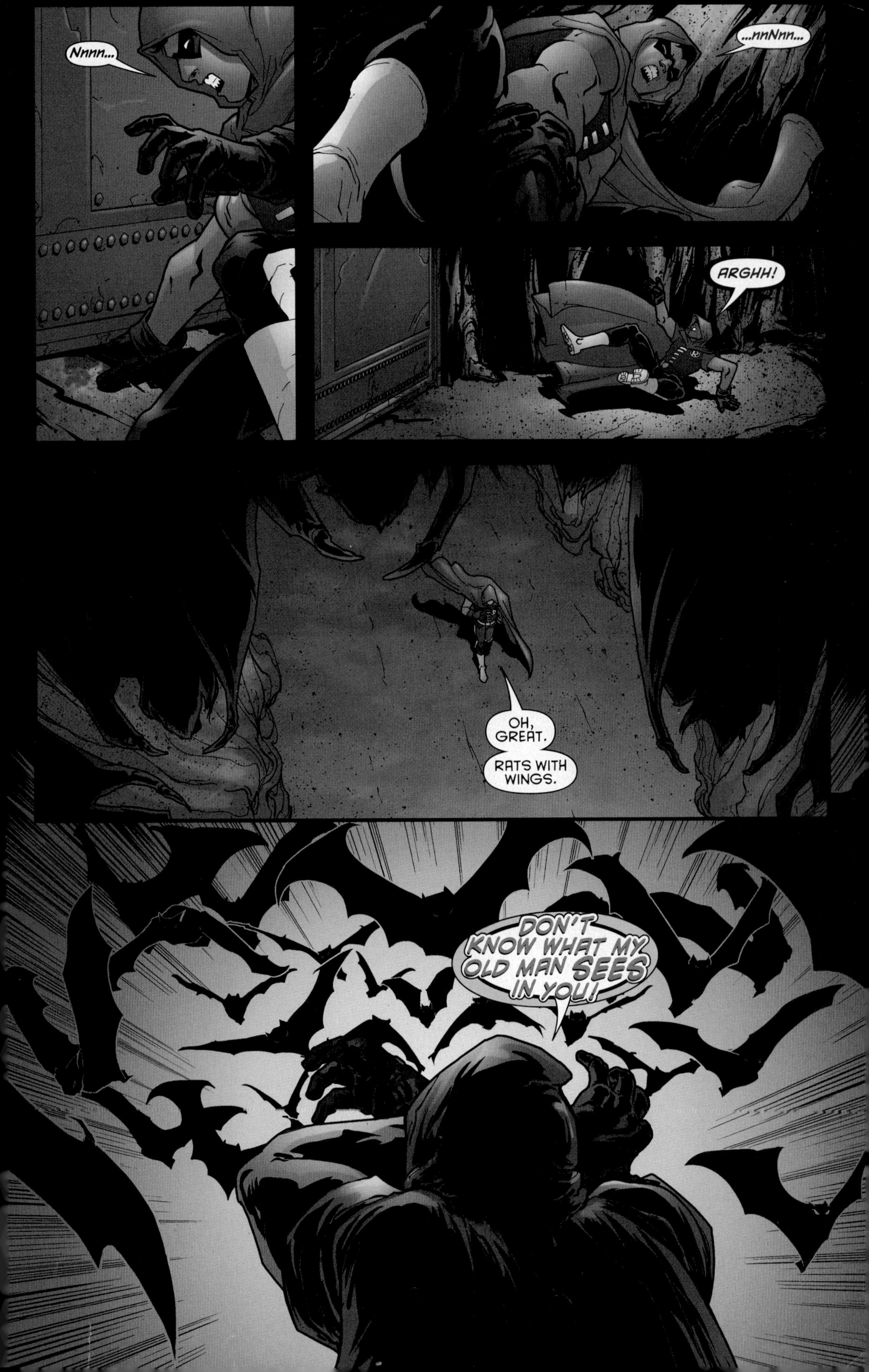
Nnnn...
...nnNnn...
ARGHH!
OH, GREAT.
RATS WITH WINGS.
DON'T KNOW WHAT MY OLD MAN SEES IN YOU!

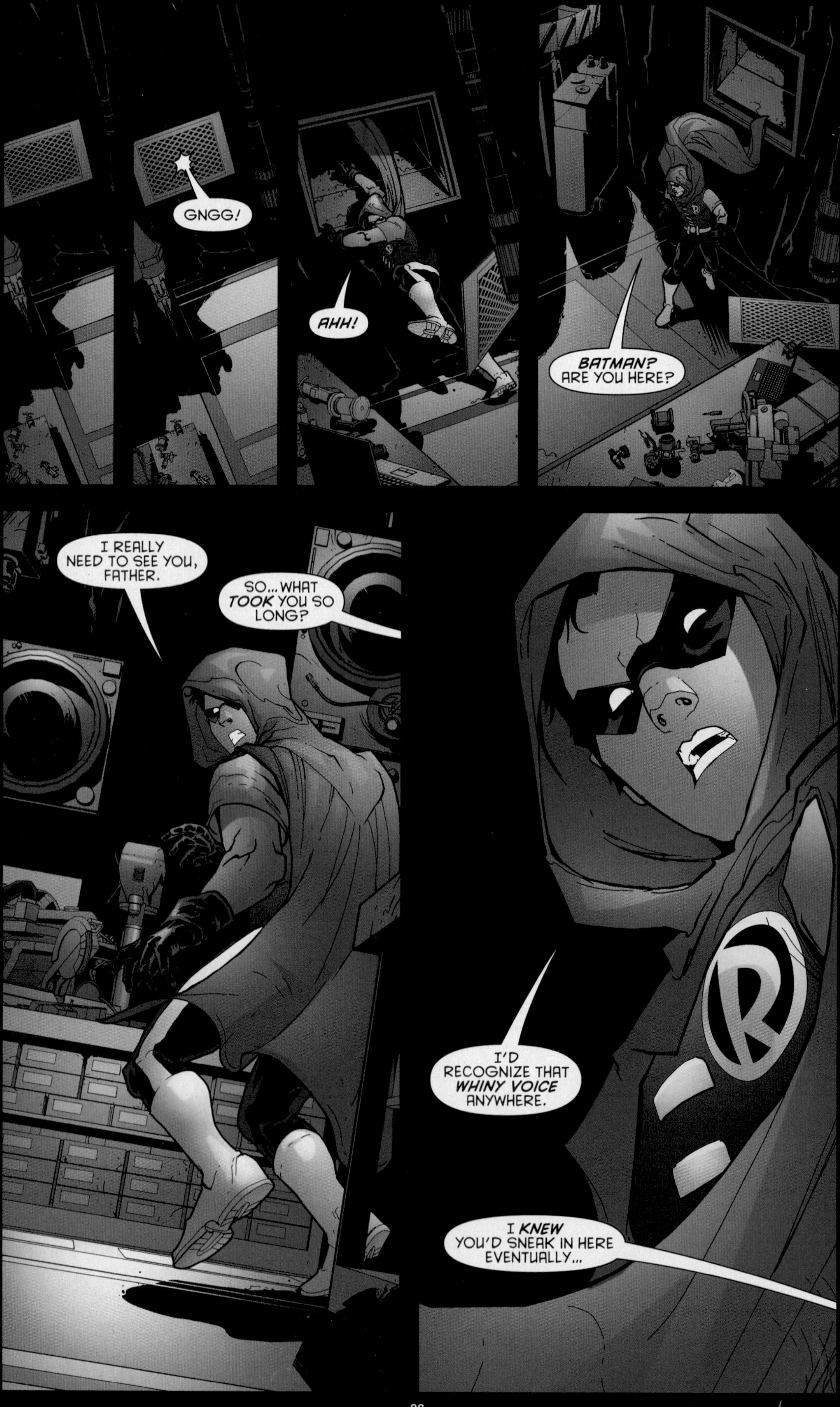

GNGG!
AHH!
BATMAN? ARE YOU HERE?
I REALLY NEED TO SEE YOU, FATHER.
SO... WHAT TOOK YOU SO LONG?
I'D RECOGNIZE THAT WHINY VOICE ANYWHERE.
I KNEW YOU'D SNEAK IN HERE EVENTUALLY...

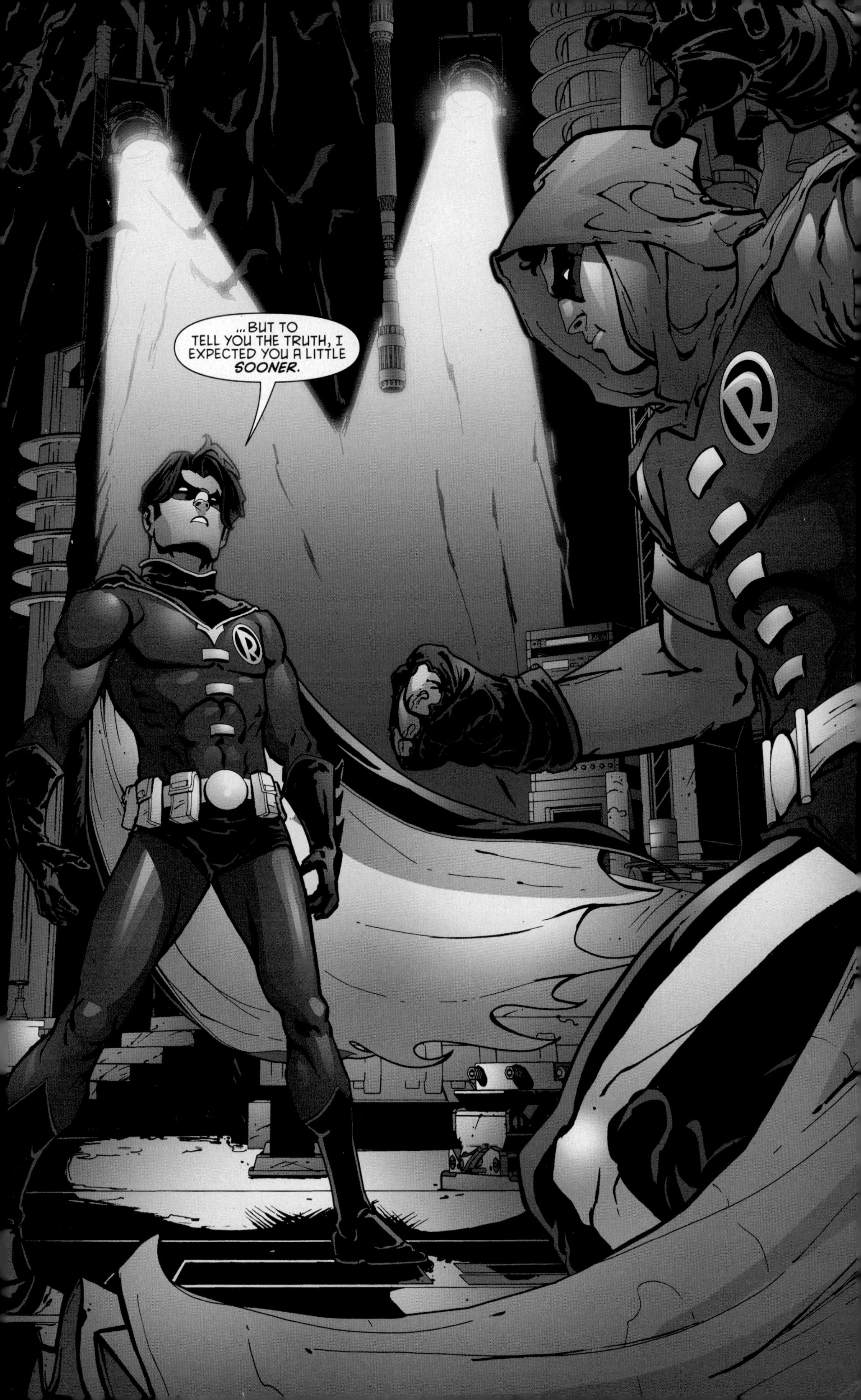
...BUT TO TELL YOU THE TRUTH, I EXPECTED YOU A LITTLE SOONER.

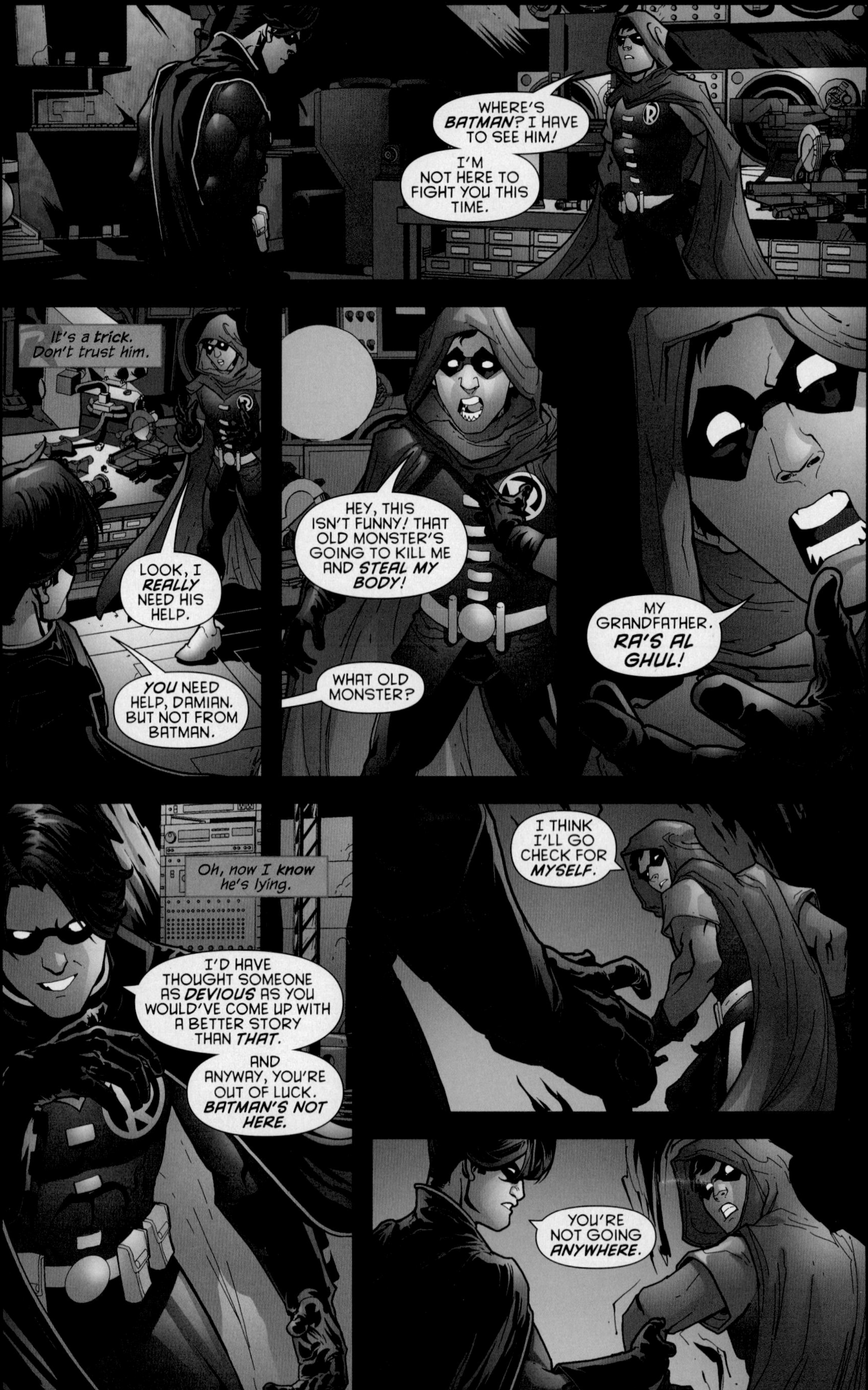
WHERE'S BATMAN? I HAVE TO SEE HIM!
I'M NOT HERE TO FIGHT YOU THIS TIME.
It's a trick. Don't trust him.
LOOK, I REALLY NEED HIS HELP.
YOU NEED HELP, DAMIAN. BUT NOT FROM BATMAN.
HEY, THIS ISN'T FUNNY! THAT OLD MONSTER'S GOING TO KILL ME AND STEAL MY BODY!
WHAT OLD MONSTER?
MY GRANDFATHER. RA'S AL GHUL!
Oh, now I know he's lying.
I'D HAVE THOUGHT SOMEONE AS DEVIOUS AS YOU WOULD'VE COME UP WITH A BETTER STORY THAN THAT.
AND ANYWAY, YOU'RE OUT OF LUCK. BATMAN'S NOT HERE.
I THINK I'LL GO CHECK FOR MYSELF.
YOU'RE NOT GOING ANYWHERE.

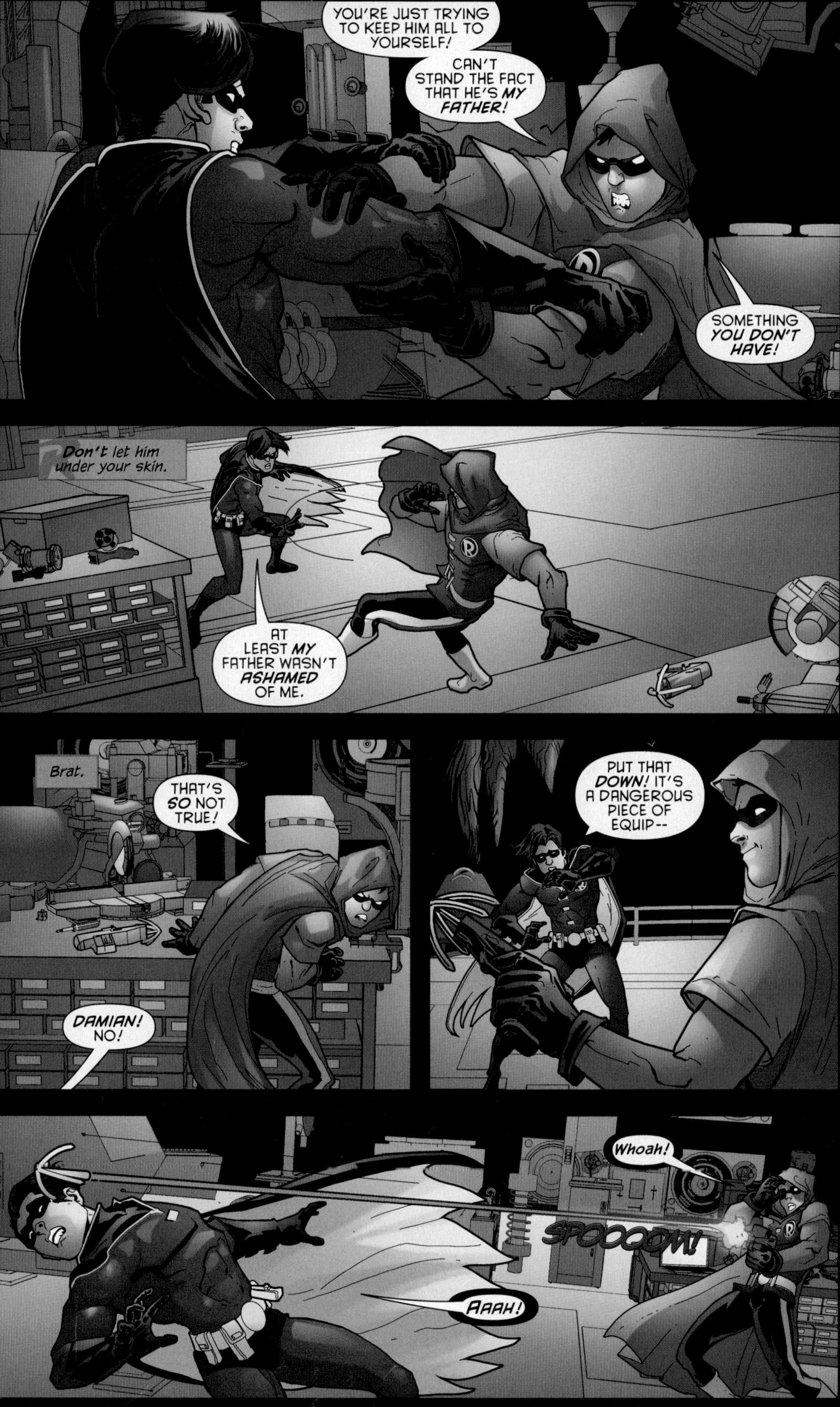

YOU'RE JUST TRYING TO KEEP HIM ALL TO YOURSELF!
CAN'T STAND THE FACT THAT HE'S MY FATHER!
SOMETHING YOU DON'T HAVE!
Don't let him under your skin.
AT LEAST MY FATHER WASN'T ASHAMED OF ME.
Brat.
THAT'S SO NOT TRUE!
DAMIAN! NO!
PUT THAT DOWN! IT'S A DANGEROUS PIECE OF EQUIP--
Whoah!
SPOOOOM!
AAAH!

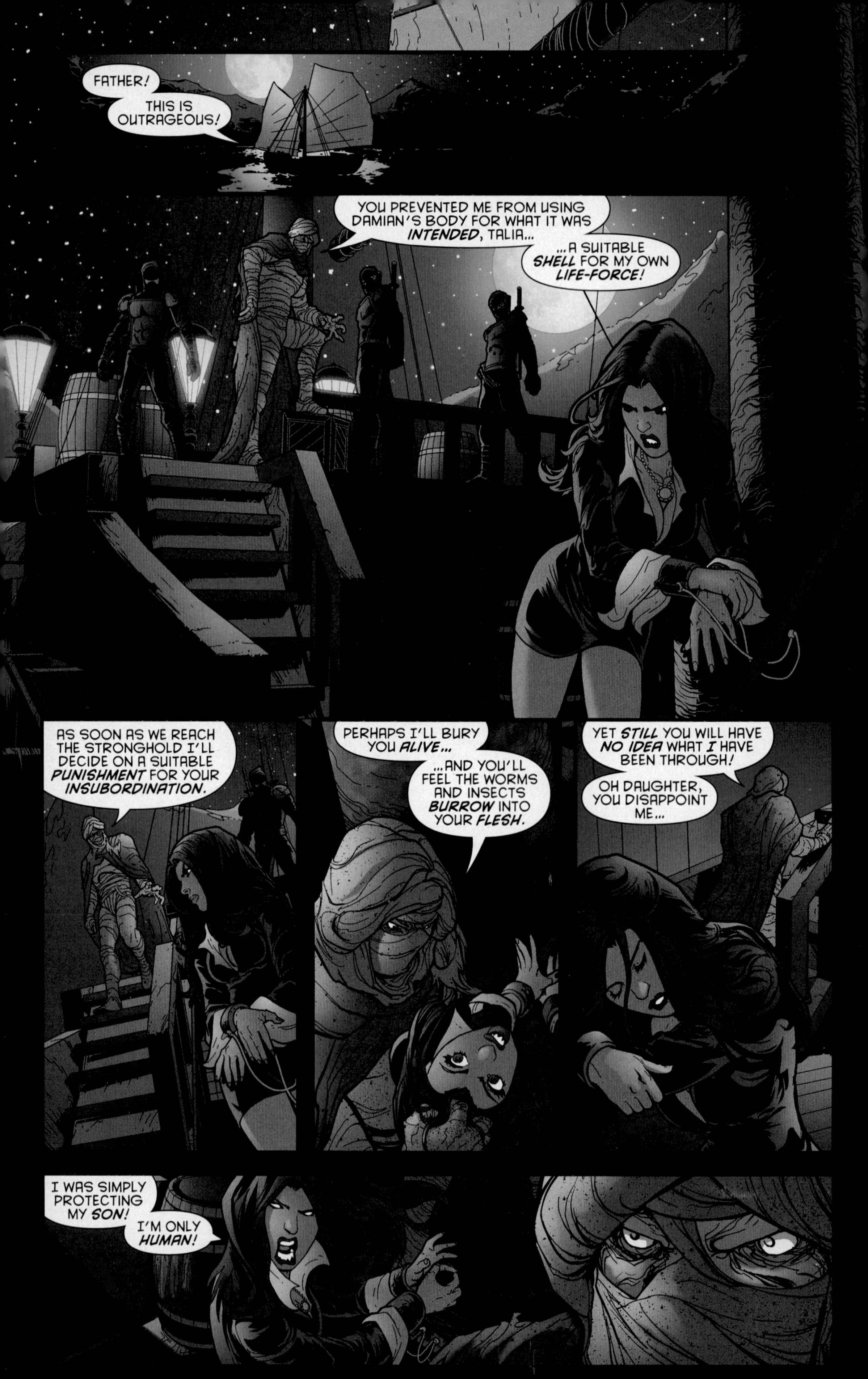
FATHER!
THIS IS OUTRAGEOUS!
YOU PREVENTED ME FROM USING DAMIAN'S BODY FOR WHAT IT WAS INTENDED, TALIA...
...A SUITABLE SHELL FOR MY OWN LIFE-FORCE!
AS SOON AS WE REACH THE STRONGHOLD I'LL DECIDE ON A SUITABLE PUNISHMENT FOR YOUR INSUBORDINATION.
PERHAPS I'LL BURY YOU ALIVE...
...AND YOU'LL FEEL THE WORMS AND INSECTS BURROW INTO YOUR FLESH.
YET STILL YOU WILL HAVE NO IDEA WHAT I HAVE BEEN THROUGH!
OH DAUGHTER, YOU DISAPPOINT ME...
I WAS SIMPLY PROTECTING MY SON!
I'M ONLY HUMAN!

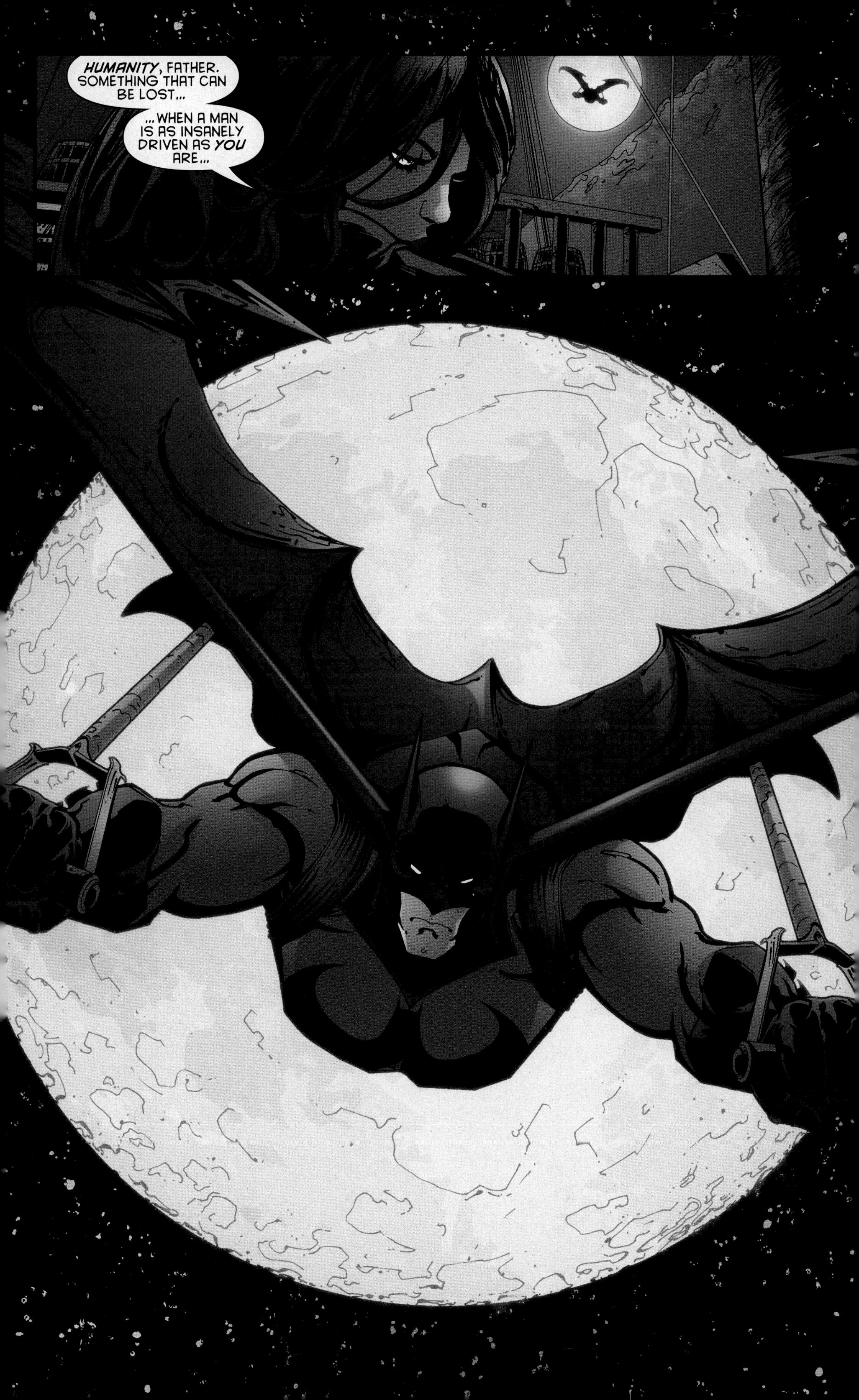
HUMANITY, FATHER. SOMETHING THAT CAN BE LOST...
...WHEN A MAN IS AS INSANELY DRIVEN AS YOU ARE...

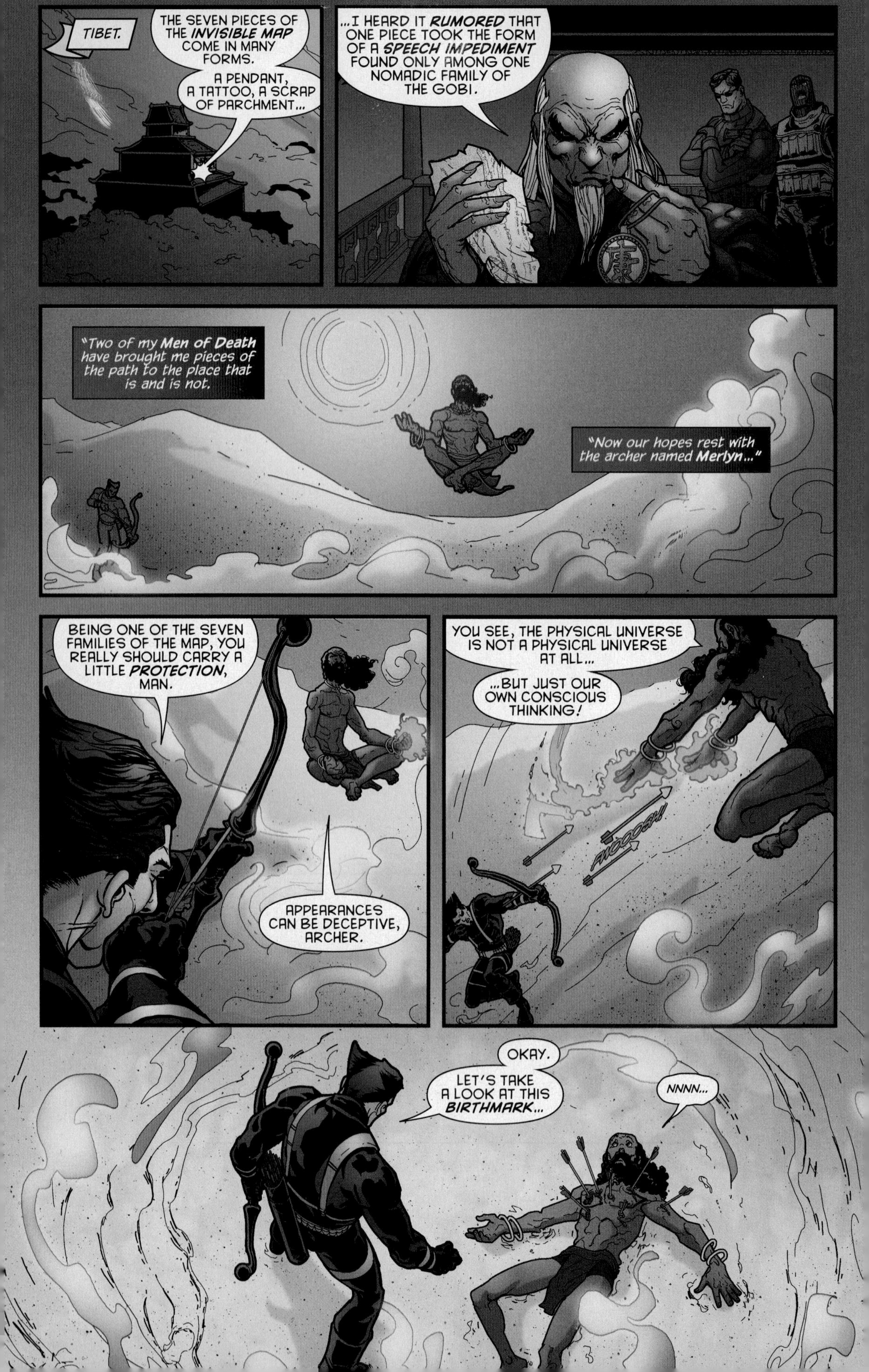
TIBET.
THE SEVEN PIECES OF THE INVISIBLE MAP COME IN MANY FORMS.
A PENDANT, A TATTOO, A SCRAP OF PARCHMENT...
...I HEARD IT RUMORED THAT ONE PIECE TOOK THE FORM OF A SPEECH IMPEDIMENT FOUND ONLY AMONG ONE NOMADIC FAMILY OF THE GOBI.
"Two of my Men of Death have brought me pieces of the path to the place that is and is not.
"Now our hopes rest with the archer named Merlyn..."
BEING ONE OF THE SEVEN FAMILIES OF THE MAP, YOU REALLY SHOULD CARRY A LITTLE PROTECTION, MAN.
APPEARANCES CAN BE DECEPTIVE, ARCHER.
YOU SEE, THE PHYSICAL UNIVERSE IS NOT A PHYSICAL UNIVERSE AT ALL...
...BUT JUST OUR OWN CONSCIOUS THINKING!
FWOOOSH!!
OKAY.
LET'S TAKE A LOOK AT THIS BIRTHMARK...
NNNN...

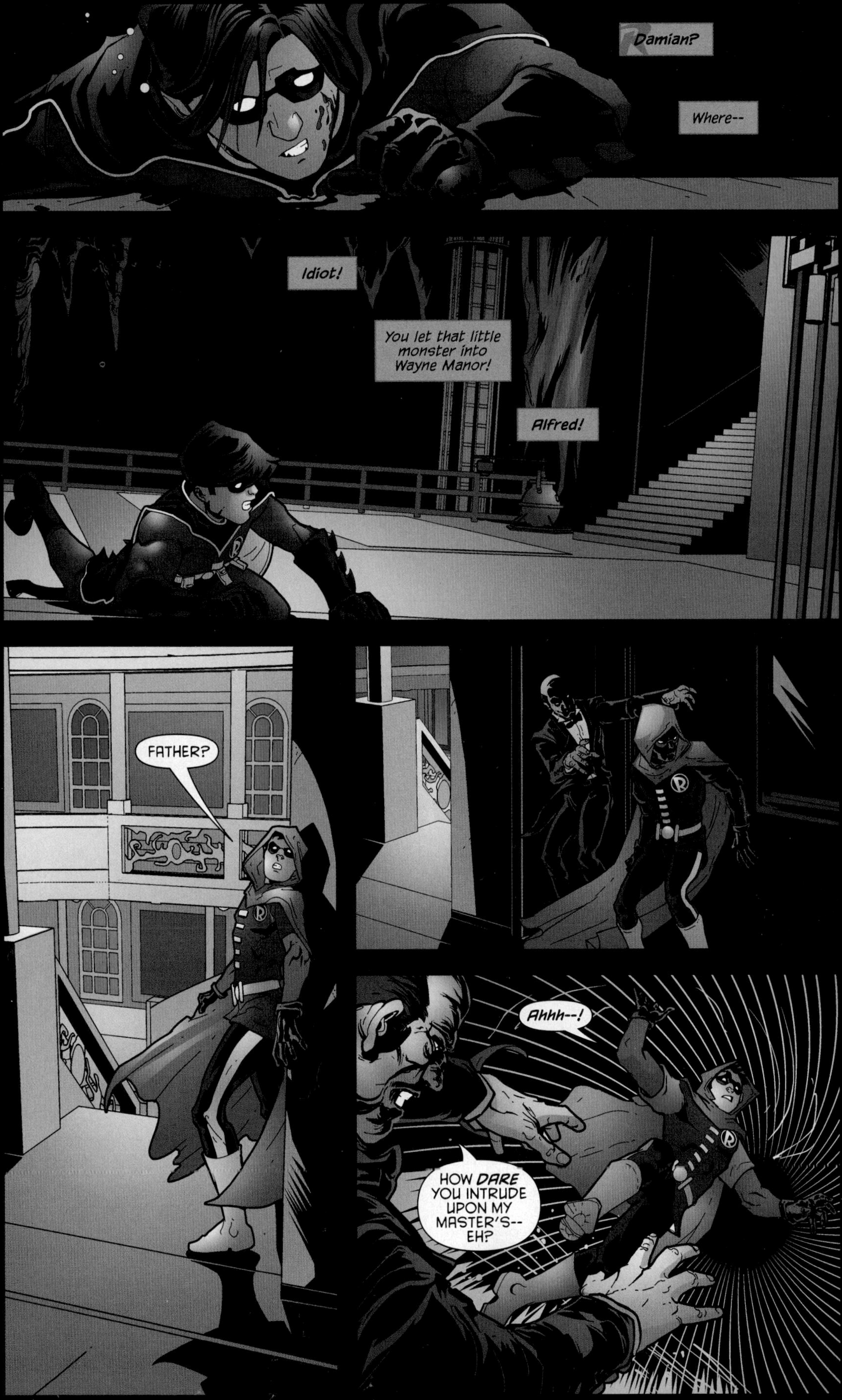
Damian?
Where--
Idiot!
You let that little monster into Wayne Manor!
Alfred!
FATHER?
Ahhh--!
HOW DARE YOU INTRUDE UPON MY MASTER'S-- EH?

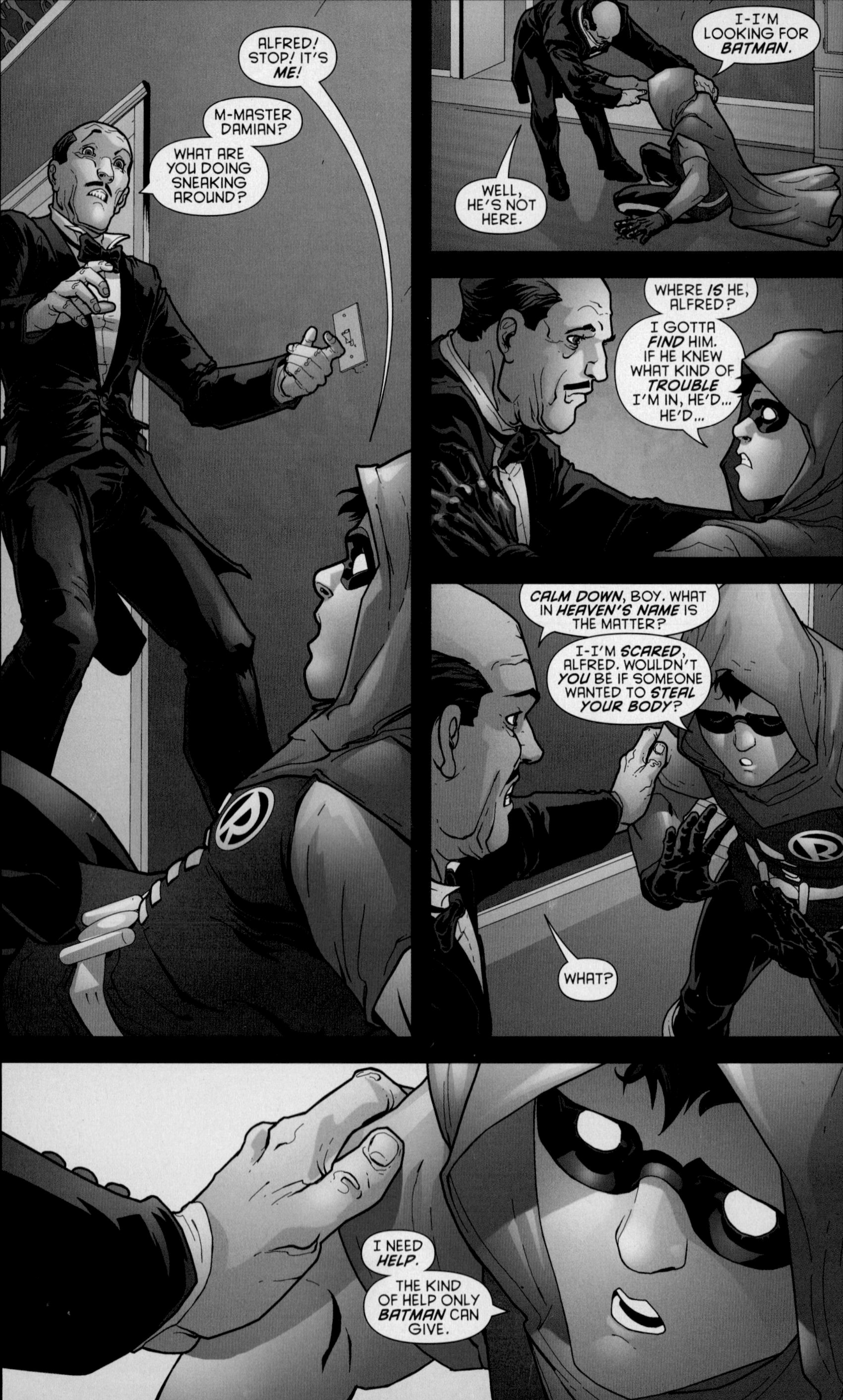
ALFRED! STOP! IT'S ME!
M-MASTER DAMIAN?
WHAT ARE YOU DOING SNEAKING AROUND?
I-I'M LOOKING FOR BATMAN.
WELL, HE'S NOT HERE.
WHERE IS HE, ALFRED?
I GOTTA FIND HIM. IF HE KNEW WHAT KIND OF TROUBLE I'M IN, HE'D... HE'D...
CALM DOWN, BOY. WHAT IN HEAVEN'S NAME IS THE MATTER?
I-I'M SCARED, ALFRED. WOULDN'T YOU BE IF SOMEONE WANTED TO STEAL YOUR BODY?
WHAT?
I NEED HELP.
THE KIND OF HELP ONLY BATMAN CAN GIVE.

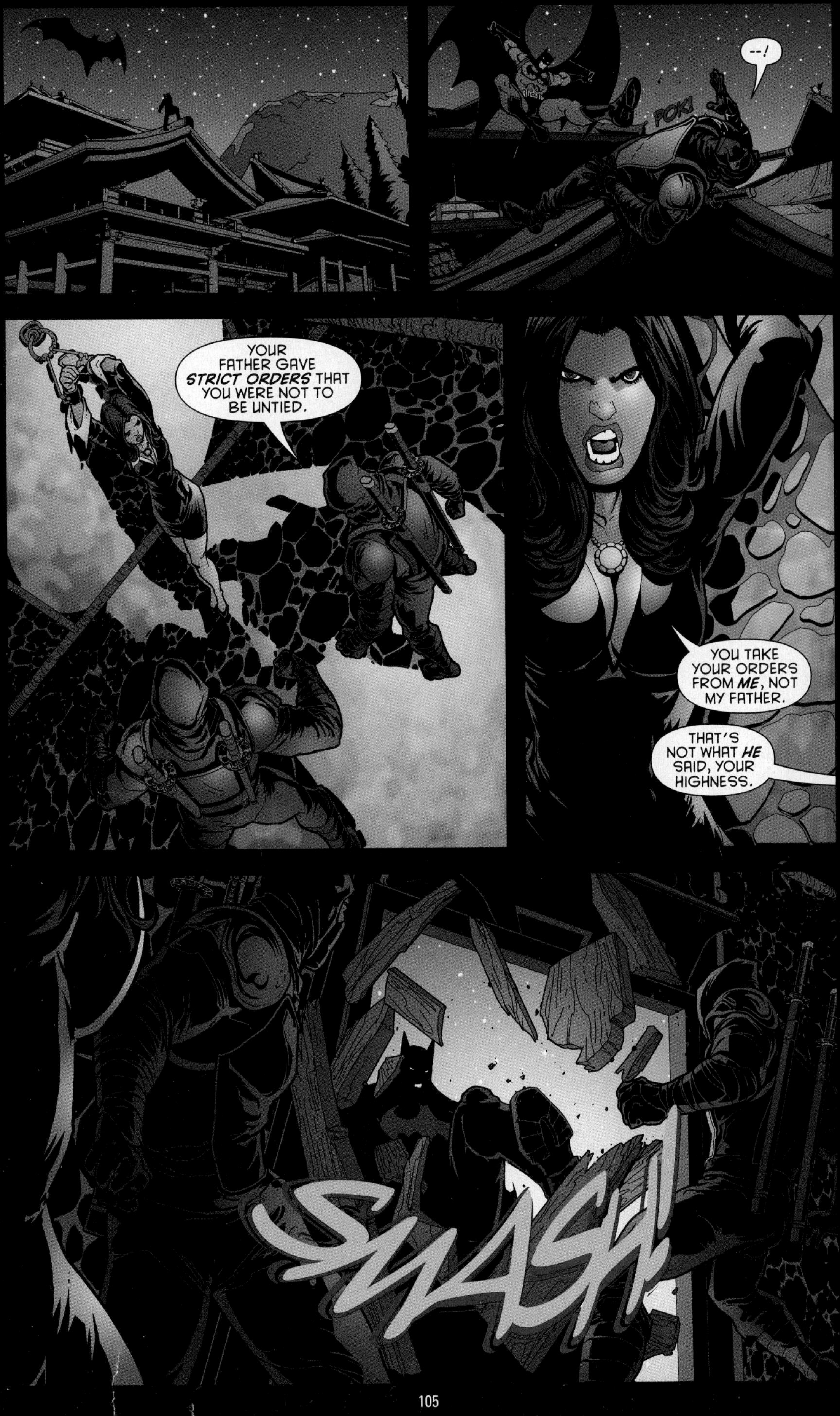
--!
POK!
YOUR FATHER GAVE STRICT ORDERS THAT YOU WERE NOT TO BE UNTIED.
YOU TAKE YOUR ORDERS FROM ME, NOT MY FATHER.
THAT'S NOT WHAT HE SAID, YOUR HIGHNESS.
SMASH!

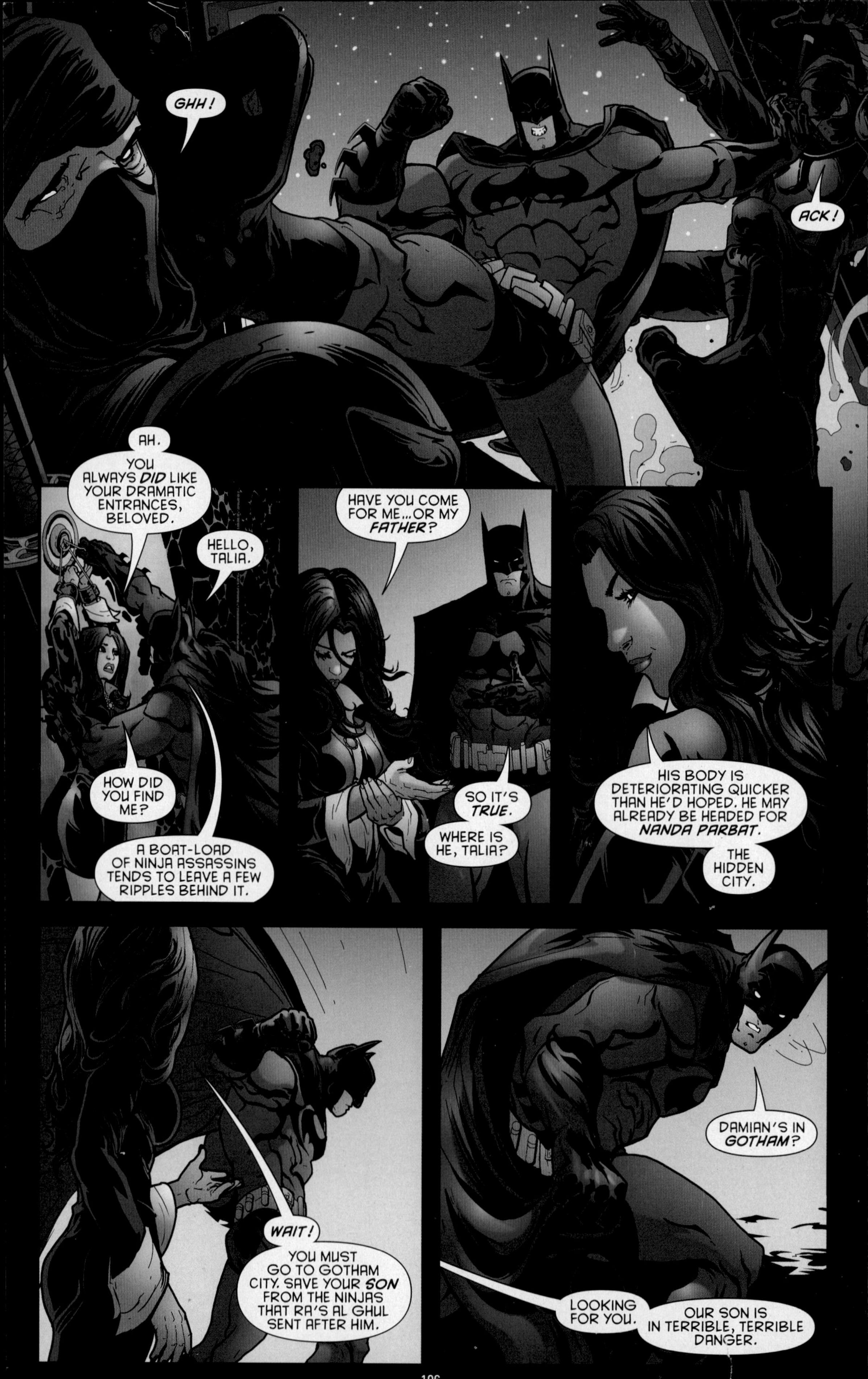
GHH!
ACK!
AH.
YOU ALWAYS DID LIKE YOUR DRAMATIC ENTRANCES, BELOVED.
HELLO, TALIA.
HOW DID YOU FIND ME?
A BOAT-LOAD OF NINJA ASSASSINS TENDS TO LEAVE A FEW RIPPLES BEHIND IT.
HAVE YOU COME FOR ME...OR MY FATHER?
SO IT'S TRUE.
WHERE IS HE, TALIA?
HIS BODY IS DETERIORATING QUICKER THAN HE'D HOPED. HE MAY ALREADY BE HEADED FOR NANDA PARBAT.
THE HIDDEN CITY.
WAIT!
YOU MUST GO TO GOTHAM CITY. SAVE YOUR SON FROM THE NINJAS THAT RA'S AL GHUL SENT AFTER HIM.
DAMIAN'S IN GOTHAM?
LOOKING FOR YOU.
OUR SON IS IN TERRIBLE, TERRIBLE DANGER.

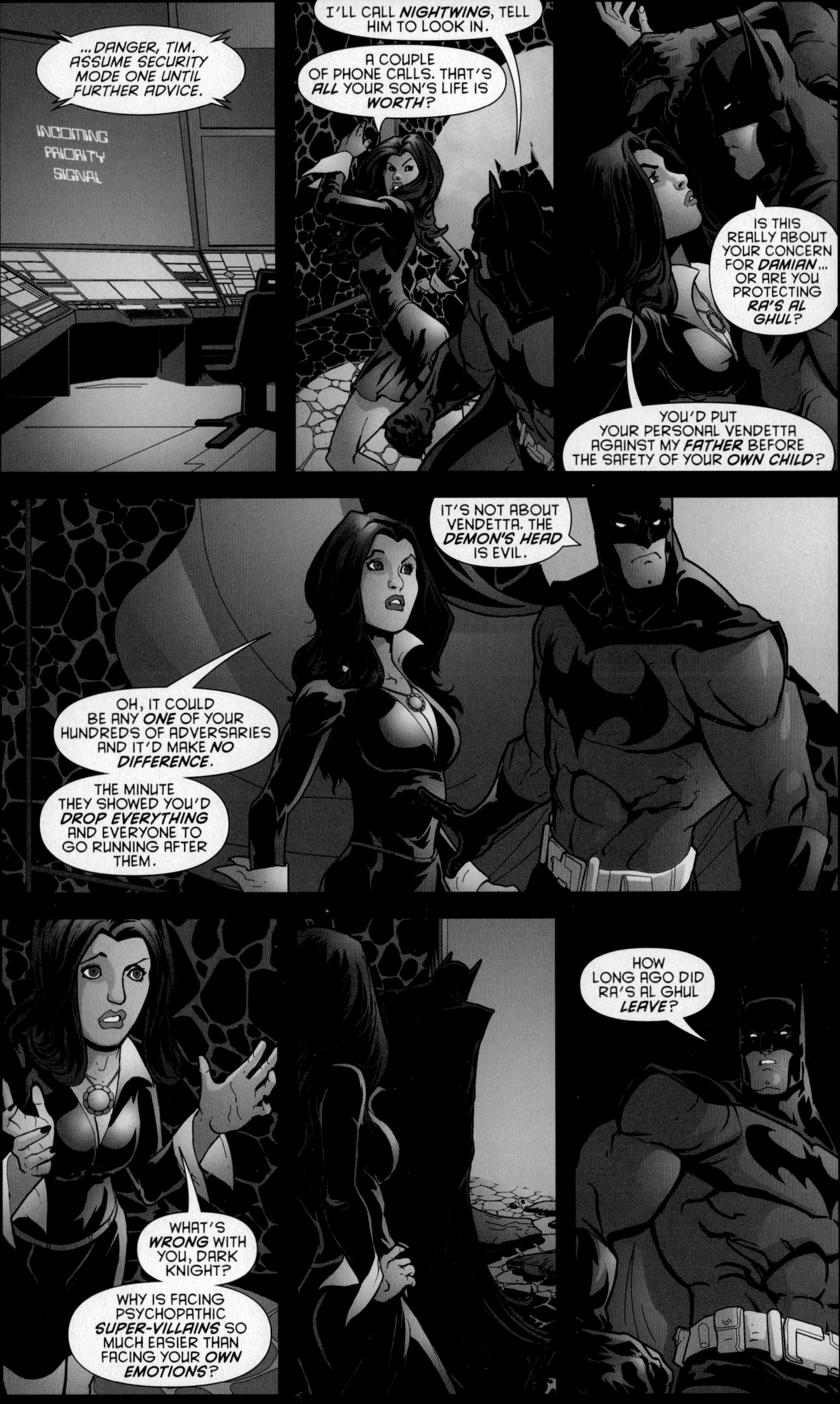
...DANGER, TIM. ASSUME SECURITY MODE ONE UNTIL FURTHER ADVICE.
INCOMING PRIORITY SIGNAL
I'LL CALL NIGHTWING, TELL HIM TO LOOK IN.
A COUPLE OF PHONE CALLS. THAT'S ALL YOUR SON'S LIFE IS WORTH?
IS THIS REALLY ABOUT YOUR CONCERN FOR DAMIAN... OR ARE YOU PROTECTING RA'S AL GHUL?
YOU'D PUT YOUR PERSONAL VENDETTA AGAINST MY FATHER BEFORE THE SAFETY OF YOUR OWN CHILD?
IT'S NOT ABOUT VENDETTA. THE DEMON'S HEAD IS EVIL.
OH, IT COULD BE ANY ONE OF YOUR HUNDREDS OF ADVERSARIES AND IT'D MAKE NO DIFFERENCE.
THE MINUTE THEY SHOWED YOU'D DROP EVERYTHING AND EVERYONE TO GO RUNNING AFTER THEM.
WHAT'S WRONG WITH YOU, DARK KNIGHT?
WHY IS FACING PSYCHOPATHIC SUPER-VILLAINS SO MUCH EASIER THAN FACING YOUR OWN EMOTIONS?
HOW LONG AGO DID RA'S AL GHUL LEAVE?

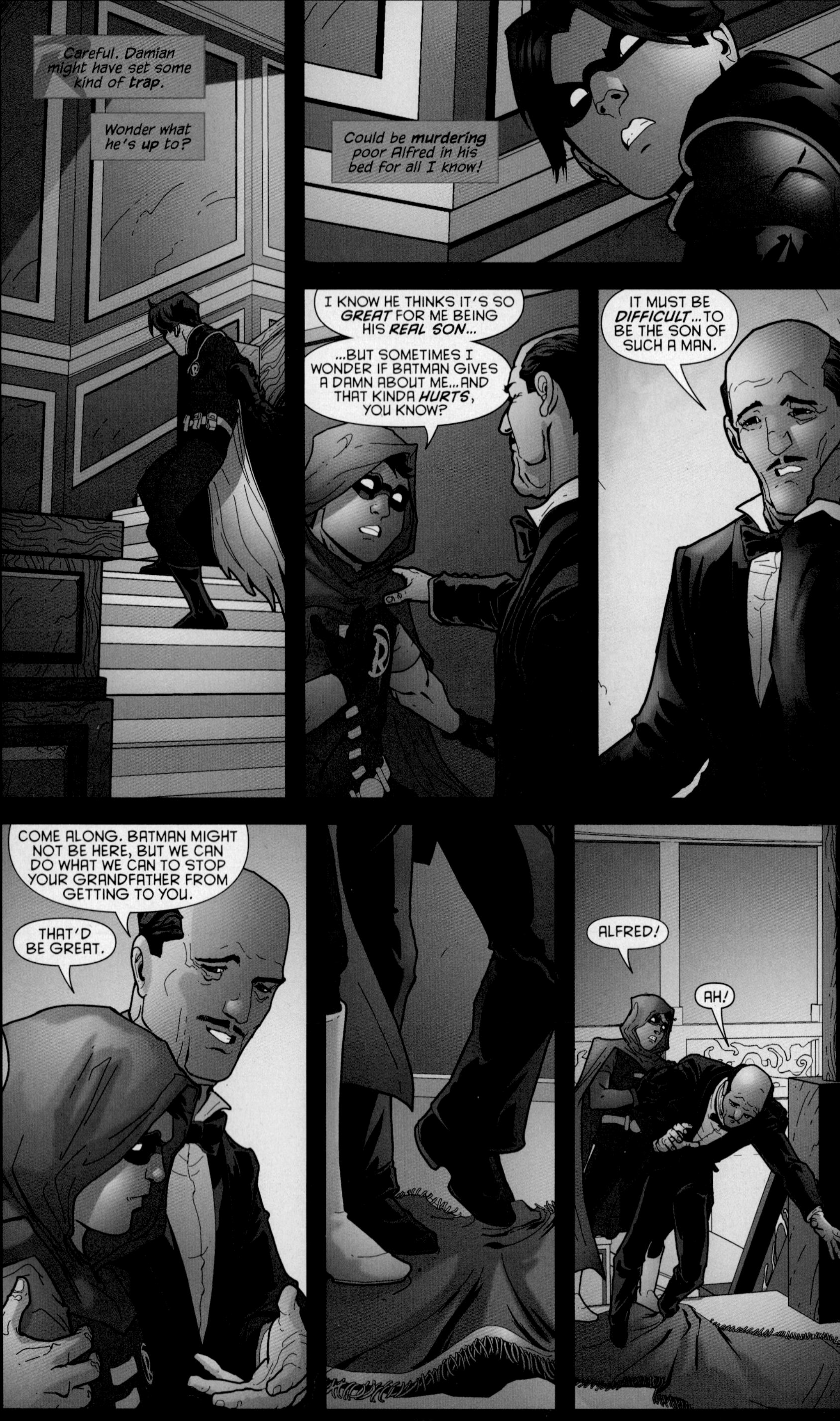

Careful. Damian might have set some kind of trap.
Wonder what he's up to?
Could be murdering poor Alfred in his bed for all I know!
I KNOW HE THINKS IT'S SO GREAT FOR ME BEING HIS REAL SON...
...BUT SOMETIMES I WONDER IF BATMAN GIVES A DAMN ABOUT ME...AND THAT KINDA HURTS, YOU KNOW?
IT MUST BE DIFFICULT...TO BE THE SON OF SUCH A MAN.
COME ALONG. BATMAN MIGHT NOT BE HERE, BUT WE CAN DO WHAT WE CAN TO STOP YOUR GRANDFATHER FROM GETTING TO YOU.
THAT'D BE GREAT.
ALFRED!
AH!

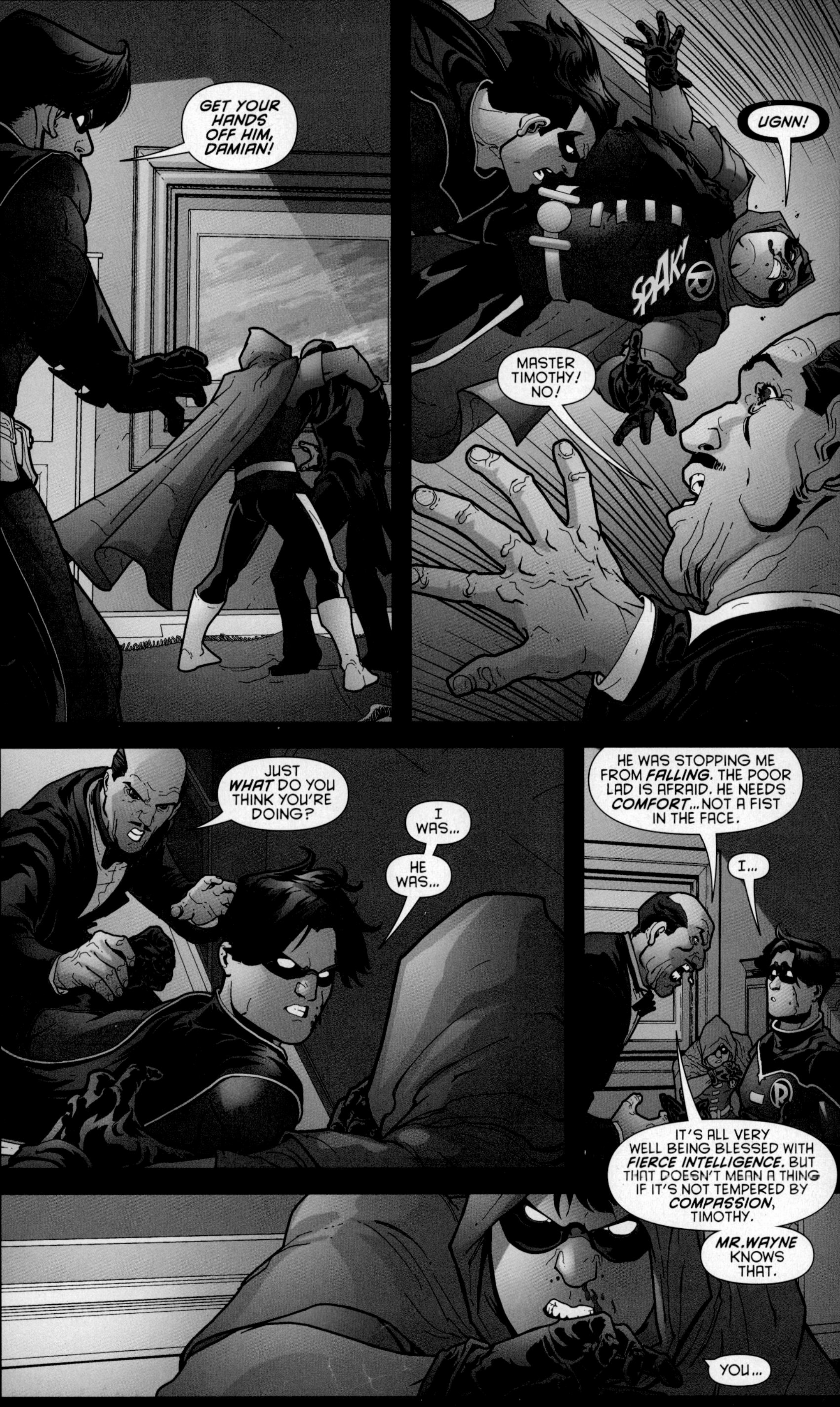

GET YOUR HANDS OFF HIM, DAMIAN!
UGNN!
SPAK!
MASTER TIMOTHY! NO!
JUST WHAT DO YOU THINK YOU'RE DOING?
I WAS...
HE WAS...
HE WAS STOPPING ME FROM FALLING. THE POOR LAD IS AFRAID. HE NEEDS COMFORT... NOT A FIST IN THE FACE.
I...
IT'S ALL VERY WELL BEING BLESSED WITH FIERCE INTELLIGENCE. BUT THAT DOESN'T MEAN A THING IF IT'S NOT TEMPERED BY COMPASSION, TIMOTHY.
MR.WAYNE KNOWS THAT.
YOU...

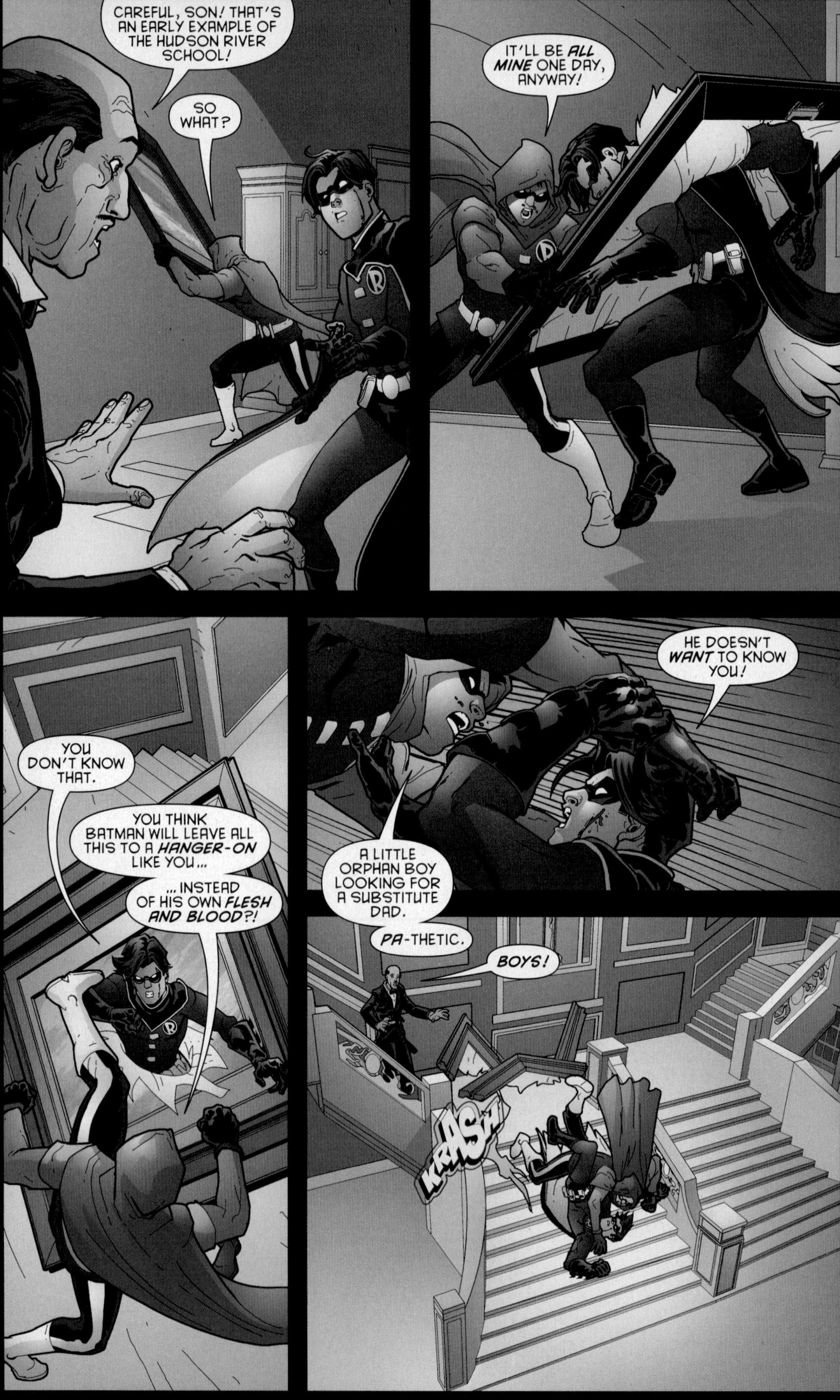
CAREFUL, SON! THAT'S AN EARLY EXAMPLE OF THE HUDSON RIVER SCHOOL!
SO WHAT?
IT'LL BE ALL MINE ONE DAY, ANYWAY!
HE DOESN'T WANT TO KNOW YOU!
YOU DON'T KNOW THAT.
YOU THINK BATMAN WILL LEAVE ALL THIS TO A HANGER-ON LIKE YOU...
...INSTEAD OF HIS OWN FLESH AND BLOOD?!
A LITTLE ORPHAN BOY LOOKING FOR A SUBSTITUTE DAD.
PA-THETIC.
BOYS!
KRASH

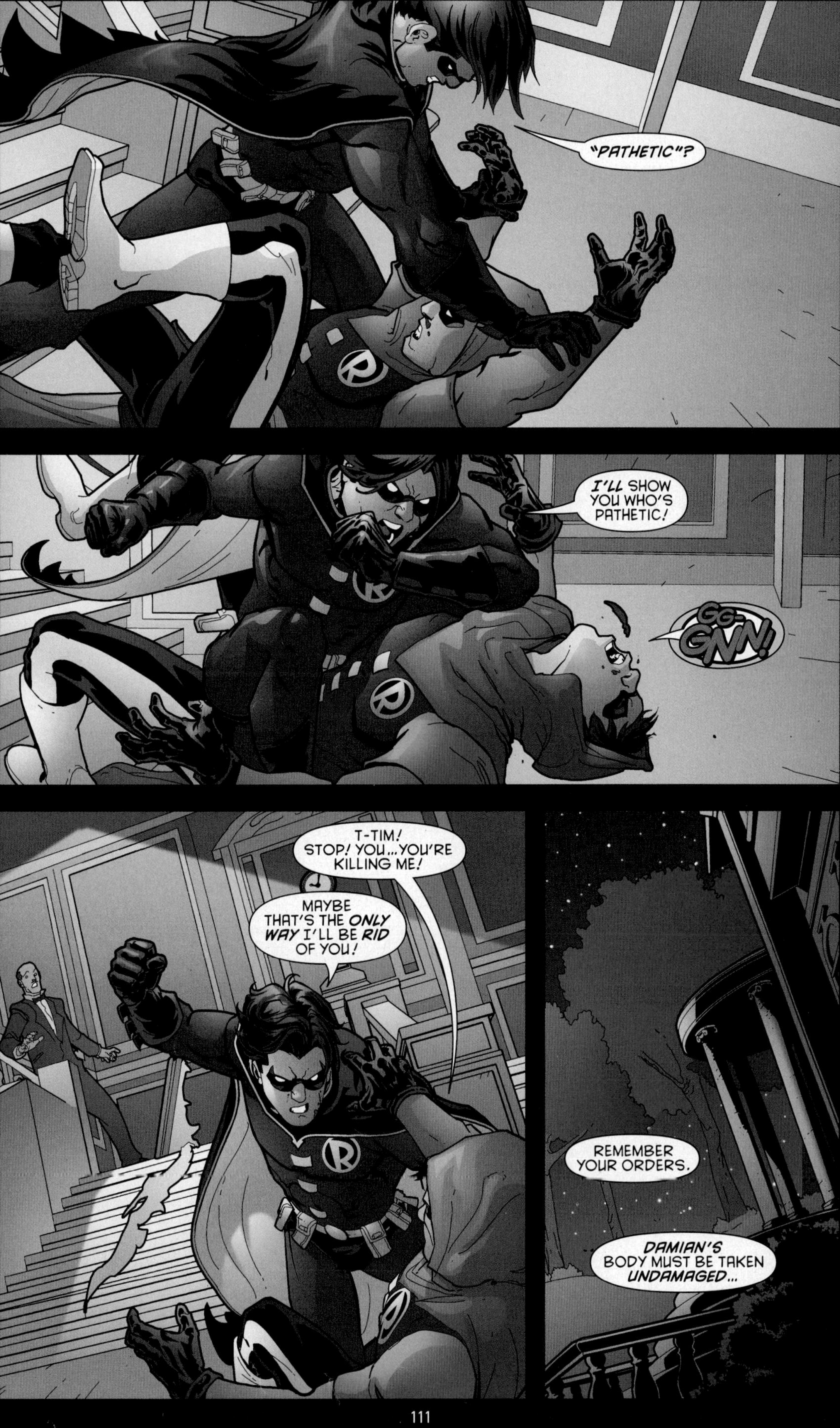
"PATHETIC"?
I'LL SHOW YOU WHO'S PATHETIC!
GG-GNN!
T-TIM! STOP! YOU...YOU'RE KILLING ME!
MAYBE THAT'S THE ONLY WAY I'LL BE RID OF YOU!
REMEMBER YOUR ORDERS.
DAMIAN'S BODY MUST BE TAKEN UNDAMAGED...

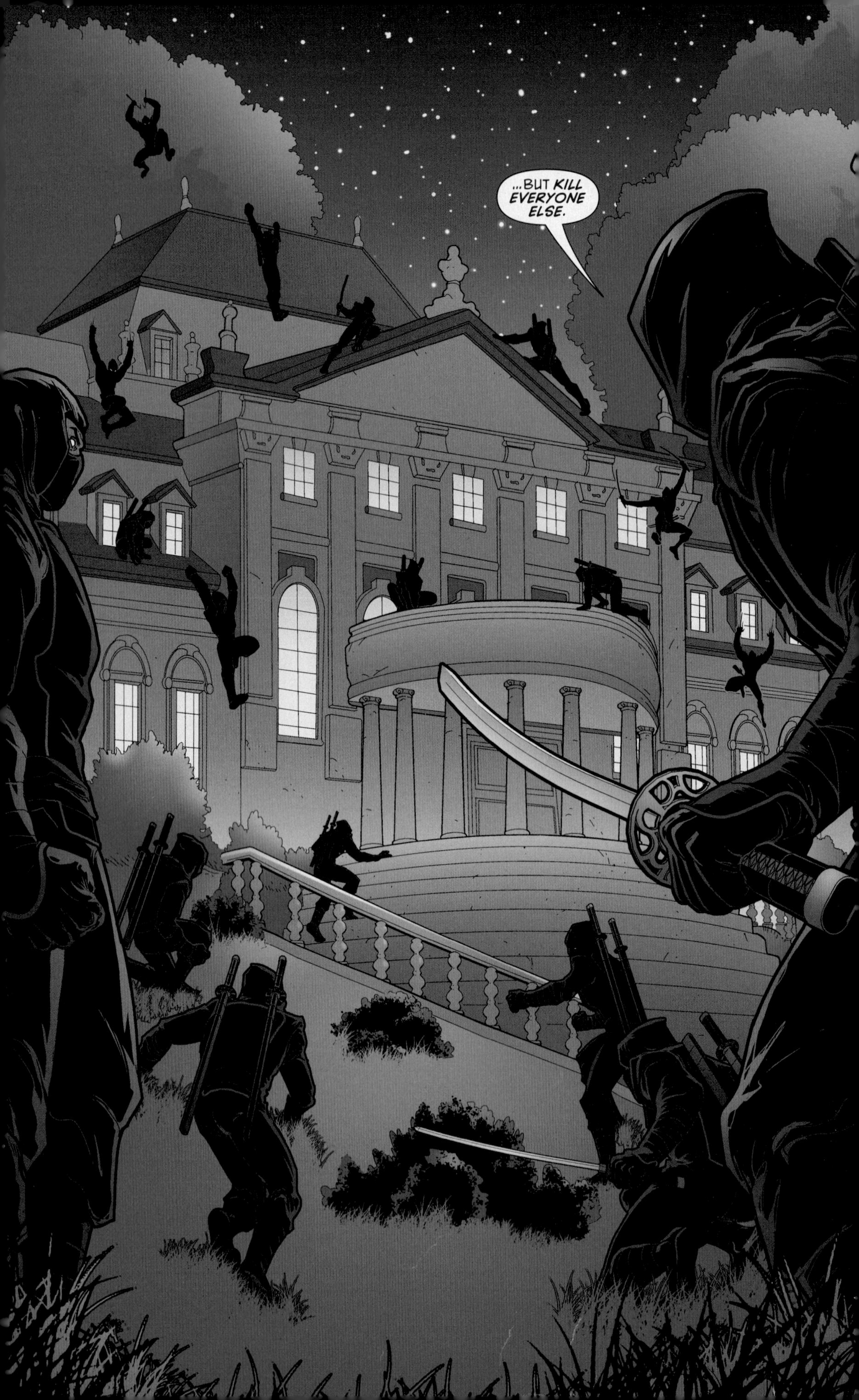
...BUT KILL EVERYONE ELSE.

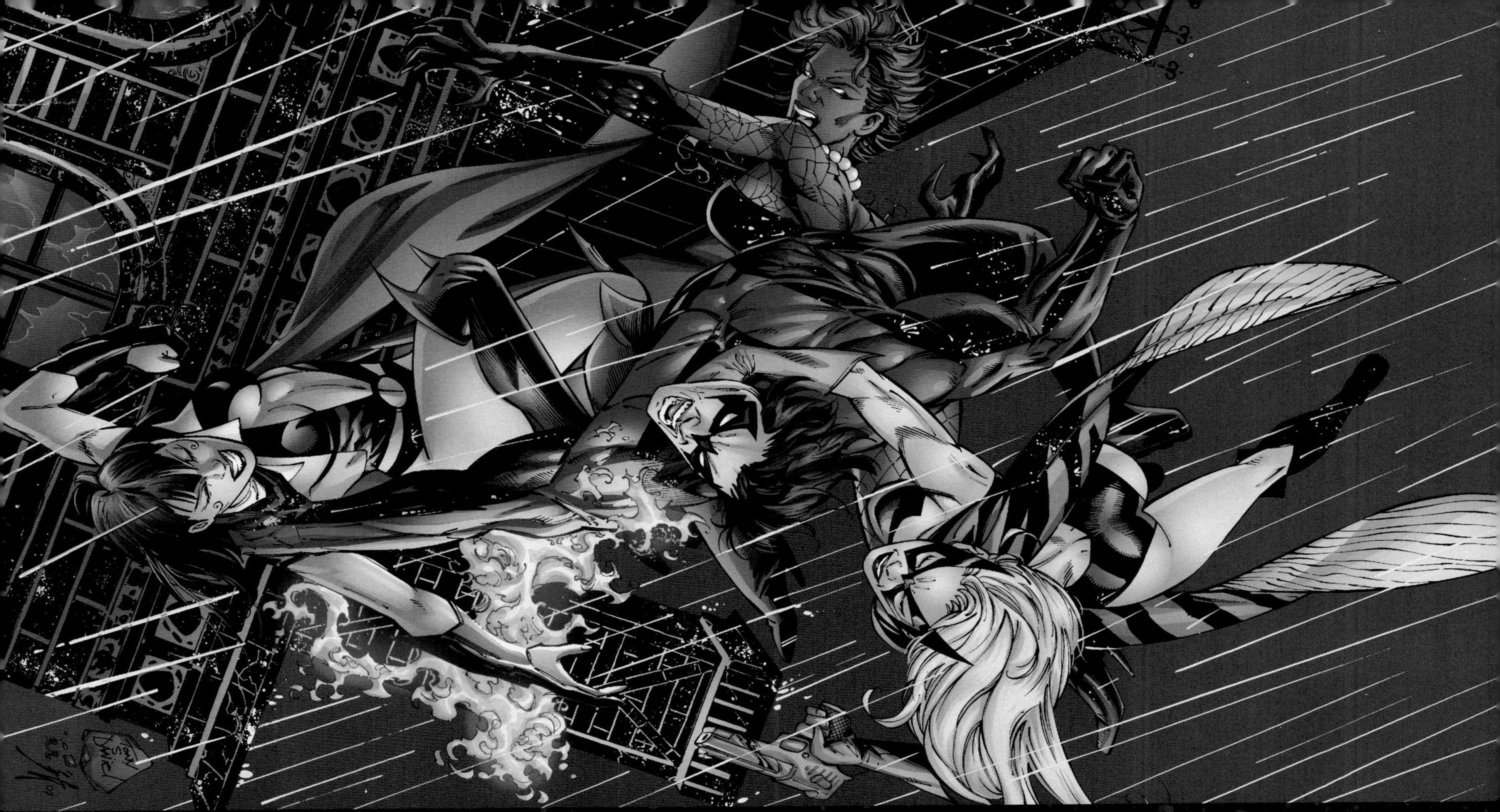

CHAPTER TWO THE LESSER OF TWO EVILS

Cover art by Tony S. Daniel and Jonathan Glapion | Chapter written by Fabian Nicieza | Chapter pencilled by Don Kramer | Chapter inked by Wayne Faucher

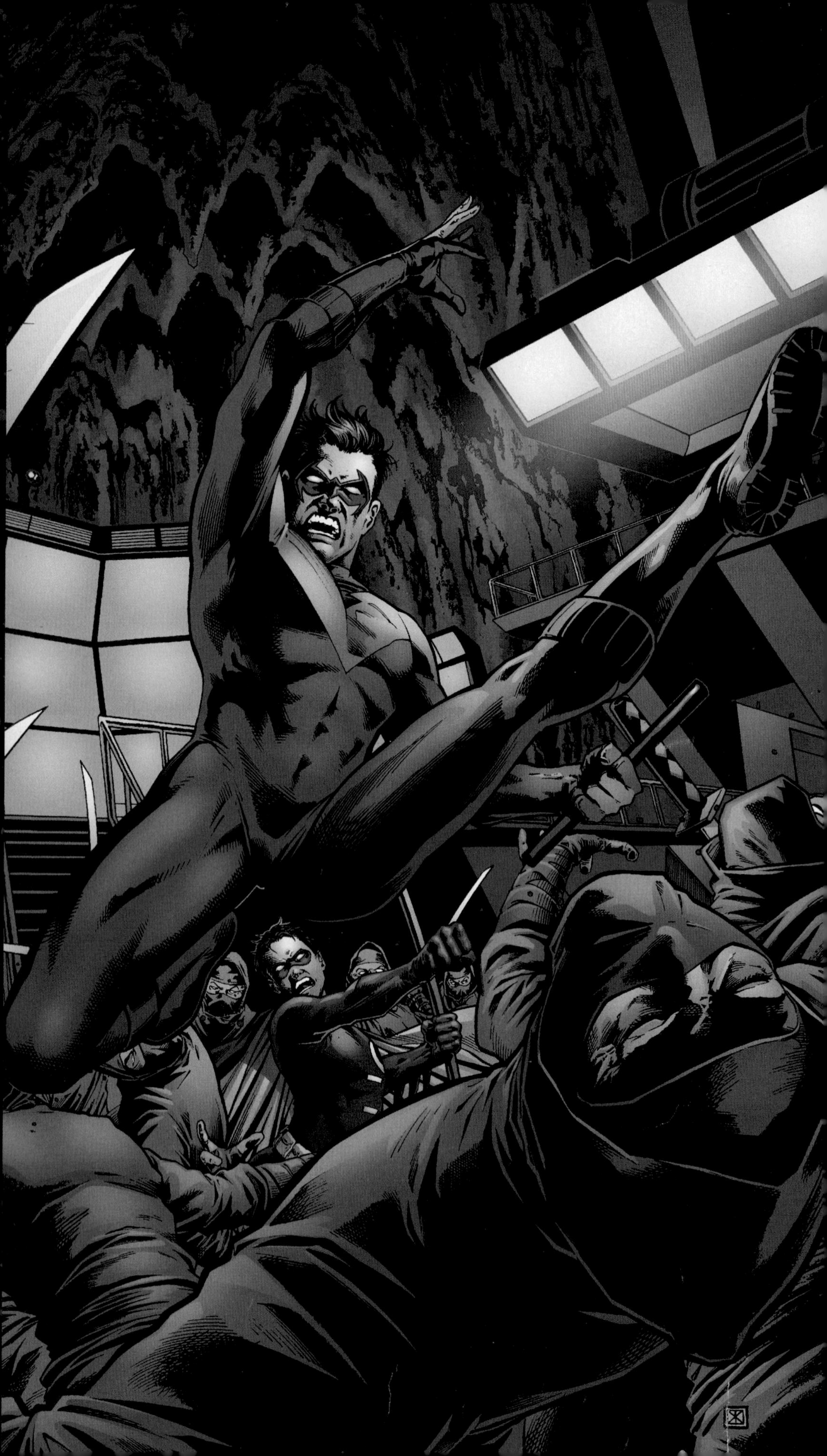

Variant cover by Don Kramer

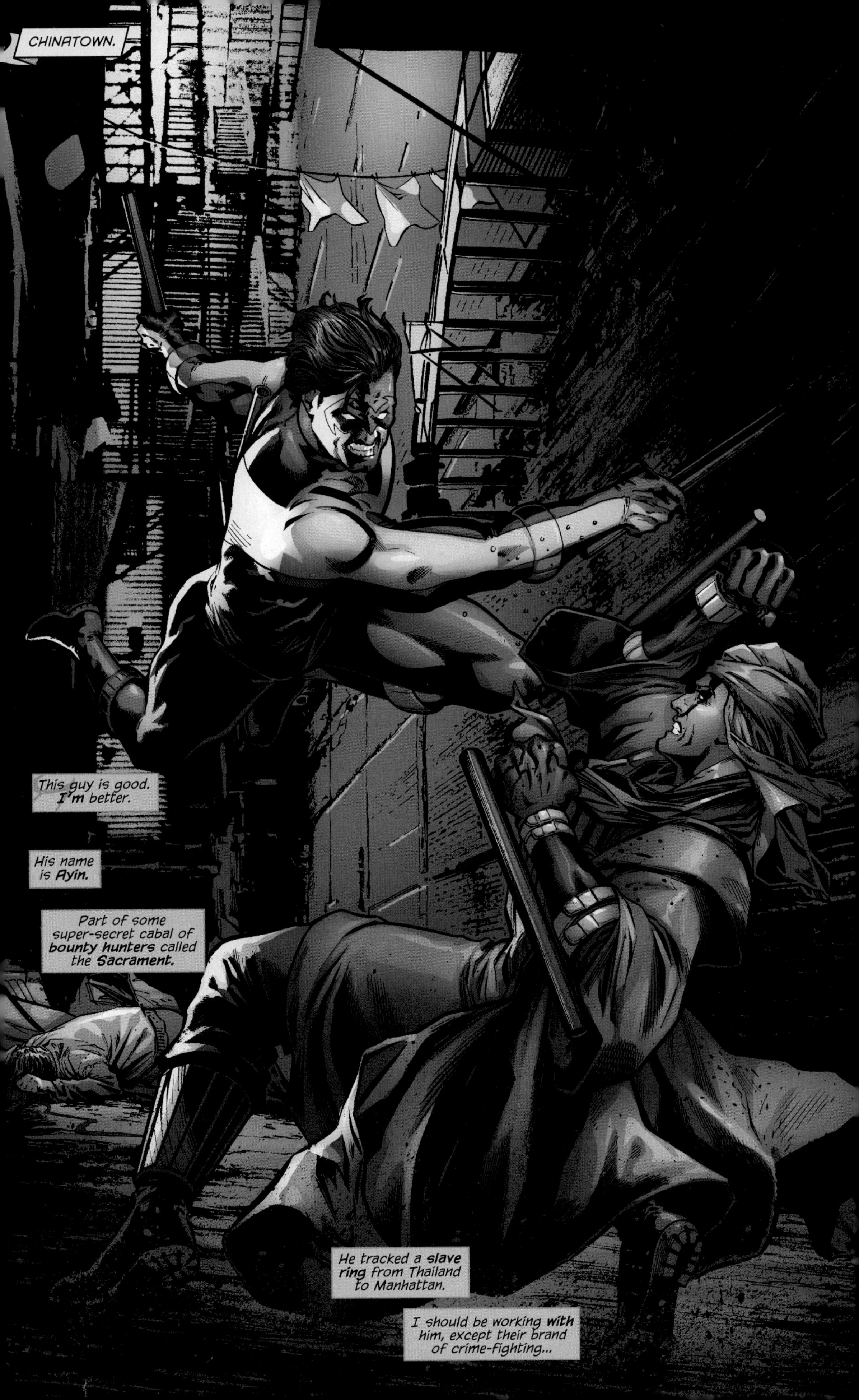
CHINATOWN.
This guy is good. **I'm** better.
His name is **Ayin.**
Part of some super-secret cabal of **bounty hunters** called the **Sacrament.**
He tracked a **slave ring** from Thailand to Manhattan.
I should be working **with** him, except their brand of crime-fighting...

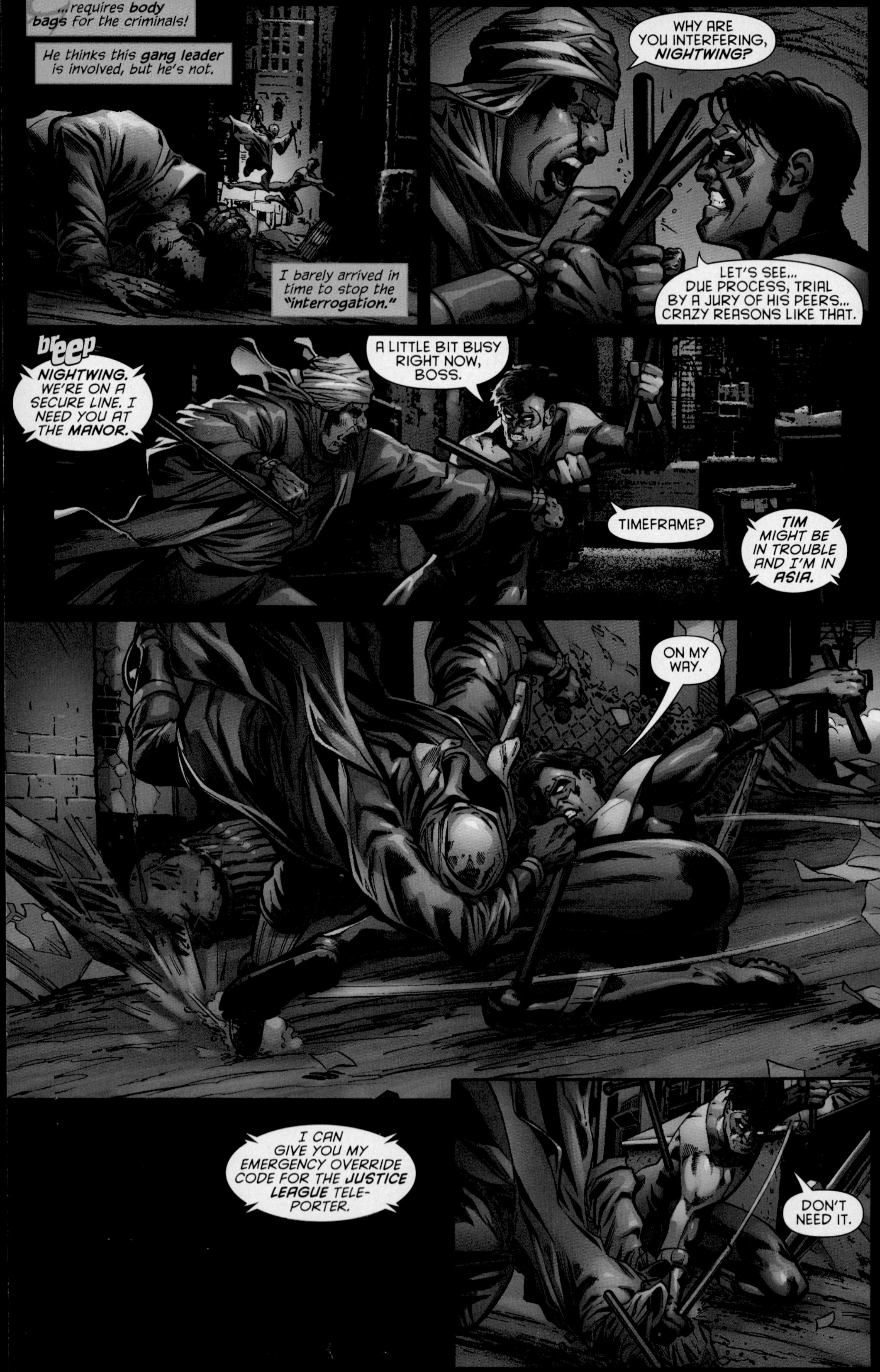

...requires **body bags** for the criminals!
He thinks this **gang leader** is involved, but he's not.
I barely arrived in time to stop the **"interrogation."**
WHY ARE YOU INTERFERING, ***NIGHTWING?***
LET'S SEE... DUE PROCESS, TRIAL BY A JURY OF HIS PEERS... CRAZY REASONS LIKE THAT.
breep
NIGHTWING. WE'RE ON A SECURE LINE. I NEED YOU AT THE **MANOR.**
A LITTLE BIT BUSY RIGHT NOW, BOSS.
TIMEFRAME?
TIM MIGHT BE IN TROUBLE AND I'M IN ***ASIA.***
ON MY WAY.
I CAN GIVE YOU MY EMERGENCY OVERRIDE CODE FOR THE ***JUSTICE LEAGUE*** TELE-PORTER.
DON'T NEED IT.

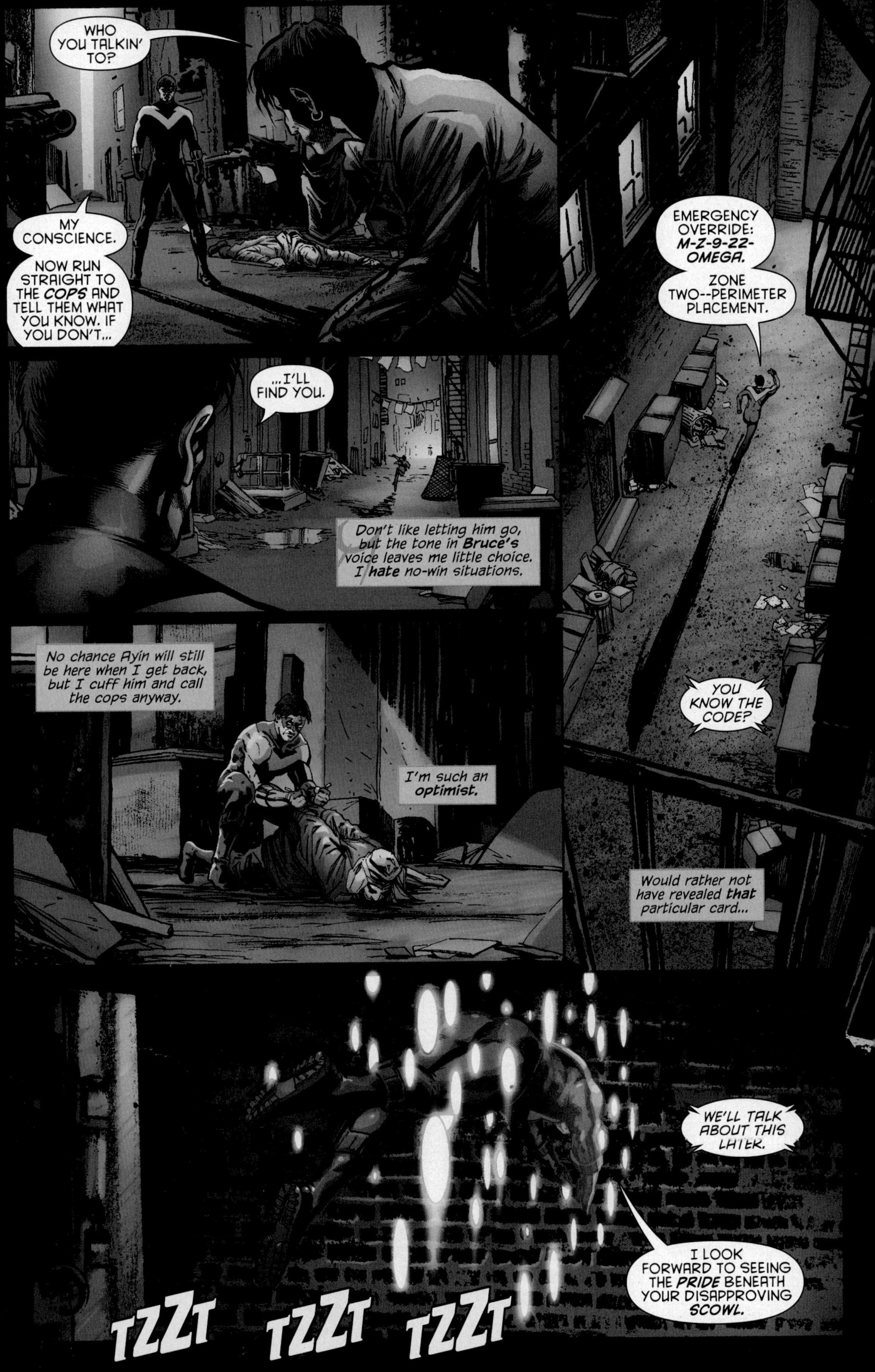

WHO YOU TALKIN' TO?
MY CONSCIENCE.
NOW RUN STRAIGHT TO THE COPS AND TELL THEM WHAT YOU KNOW. IF YOU DON'T...
...I'LL FIND YOU.
Don't like letting him go, but the tone in Bruce's voice leaves me little choice. I hate no-win situations.
No chance Ayin will still be here when I get back, but I cuff him and call the cops anyway.
I'm such an optimist.
EMERGENCY OVERRIDE: M-Z-9-22-OMEGA.
ZONE TWO--PERIMETER PLACEMENT.
YOU KNOW THE CODE?
Would rather not have revealed that particular card...
WE'LL TALK ABOUT THIS LATER.
I LOOK FORWARD TO SEEING THE PRIDE BENEATH YOUR DISAPPROVING SCOWL.
TZZT TZZT TZZT

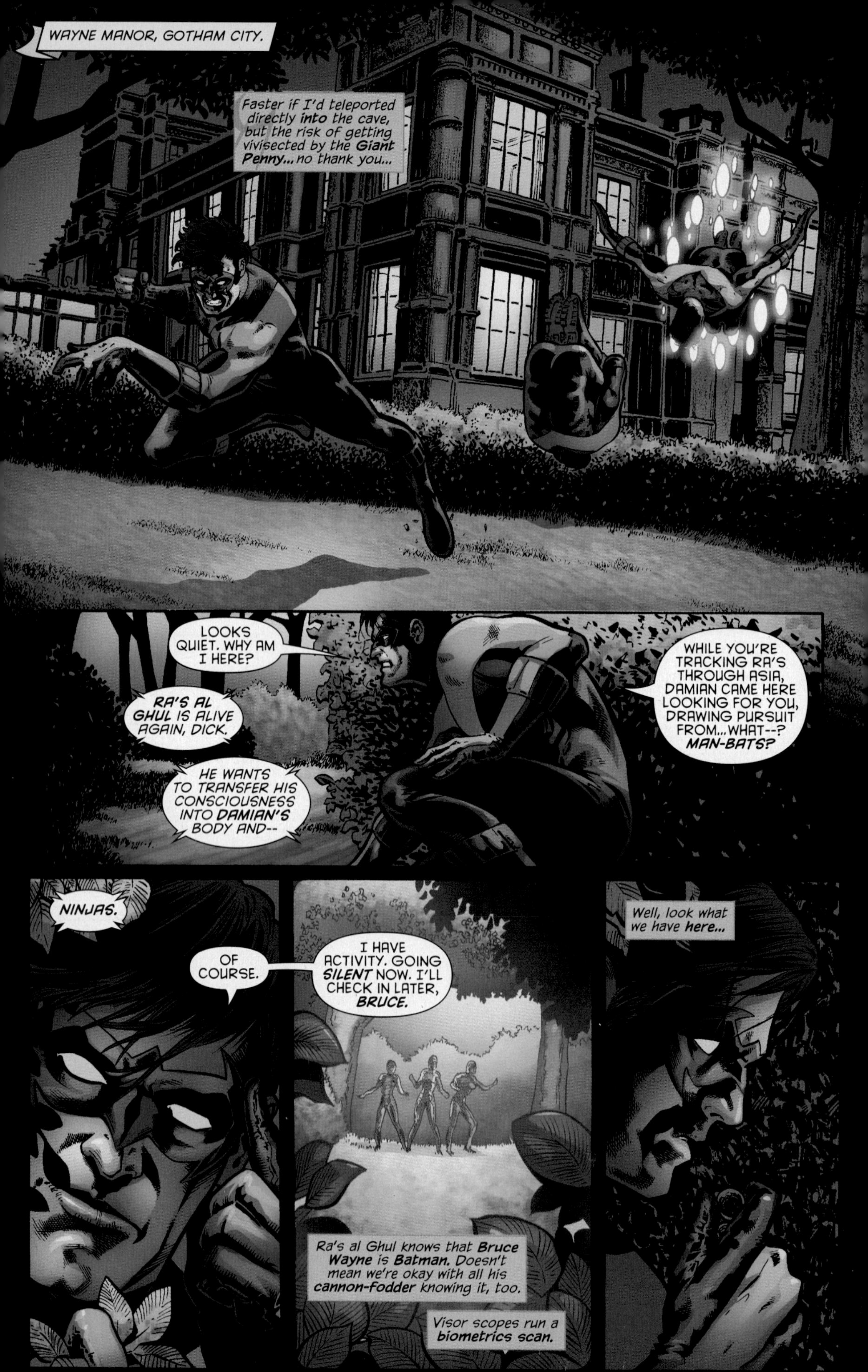
WAYNE MANOR, GOTHAM CITY.
Faster if I'd teleported directly into the cave, but the risk of getting vivisected by the Giant Penny... no thank you...
LOOKS QUIET. WHY AM I HERE?
RA'S AL GHUL IS ALIVE AGAIN, DICK.
HE WANTS TO TRANSFER HIS CONSCIOUSNESS INTO DAMIAN'S BODY AND--
WHILE YOU'RE TRACKING RA'S THROUGH ASIA, DAMIAN CAME HERE LOOKING FOR YOU, DRAWING PURSUIT FROM...WHAT--? MAN-BATS?
NINJAS.
OF COURSE.
I HAVE ACTIVITY. GOING SILENT NOW. I'LL CHECK IN LATER, BRUCE.
Ra's al Ghul knows that Bruce Wayne is Batman. Doesn't mean we're okay with all his cannon-fodder knowing it, too.
Visor scopes run a biometrics scan.
Well, look what we have here...

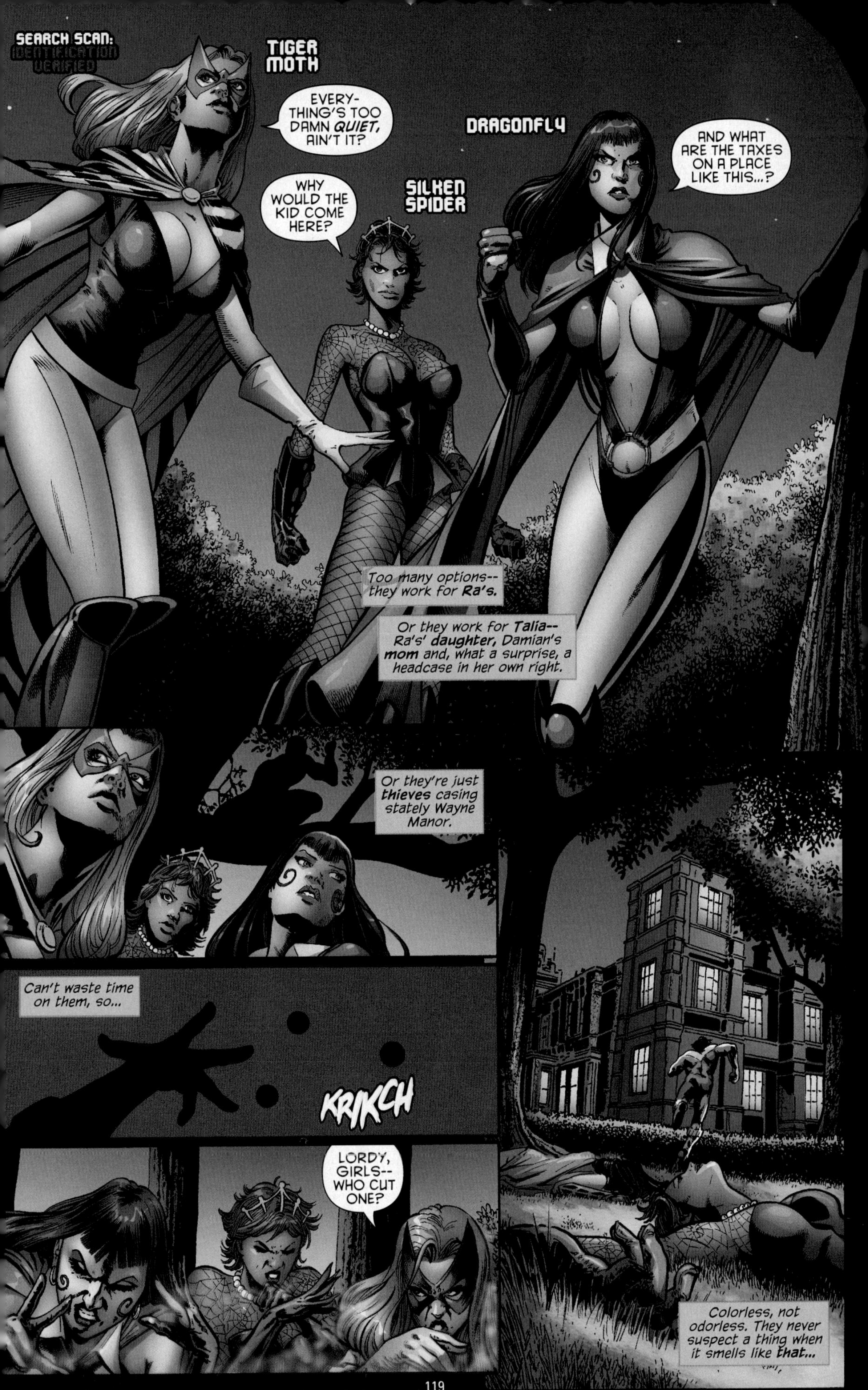
SEARCH SCAN:
IDENTIFICATION VERIFIED
TIGER MOTH
EVERY-THING'S TOO DAMN *QUIET*, AIN'T IT?
DRAGONFLY
AND WHAT ARE THE TAXES ON A PLACE LIKE THIS...?
WHY WOULD THE KID COME HERE?
SILKEN SPIDER
Too many options-- they work for **Ra's.**
Or they work for **Talia--** Ra's' **daughter,** Damian's **mom** and, what a surprise, a headcase in her own right.
Or they're just **thieves** casing stately Wayne Manor.
Can't waste time on them, so...
KRIKCH
LORDY, GIRLS-- WHO CUT ONE?
Colorless, not odorless. They never suspect a thing when it smells like **that...**

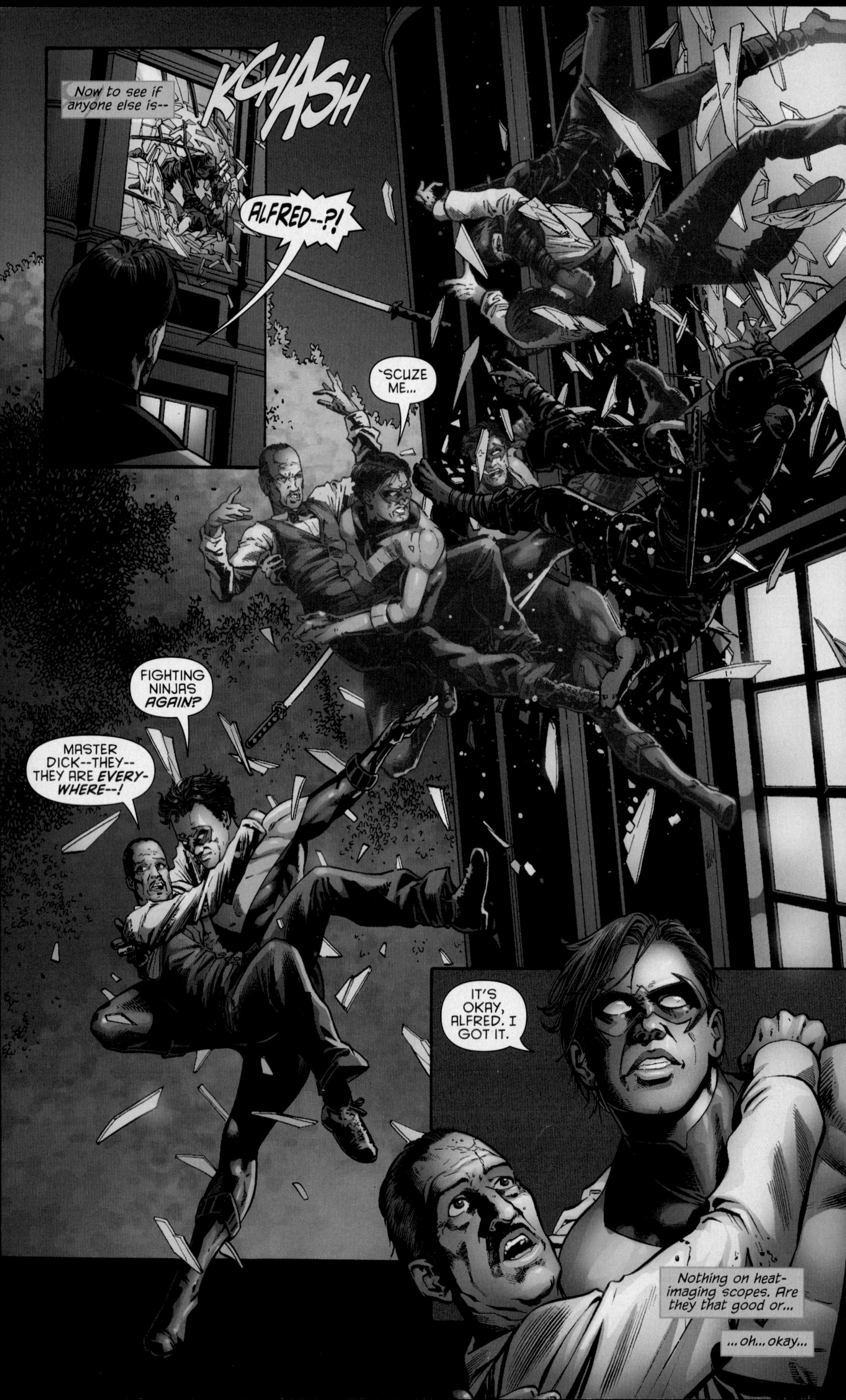
Now to see if anyone else is--
K'CHASH
ALFRED--?!
`SCUZE ME...
FIGHTING NINJAS AGAIN?
MASTER DICK--THEY--THEY ARE EVERY-WHERE--!
IT'S OKAY, ALFRED. I GOT IT.
Nothing on heat-imaging scopes. Are they that good or...
...oh...okay...

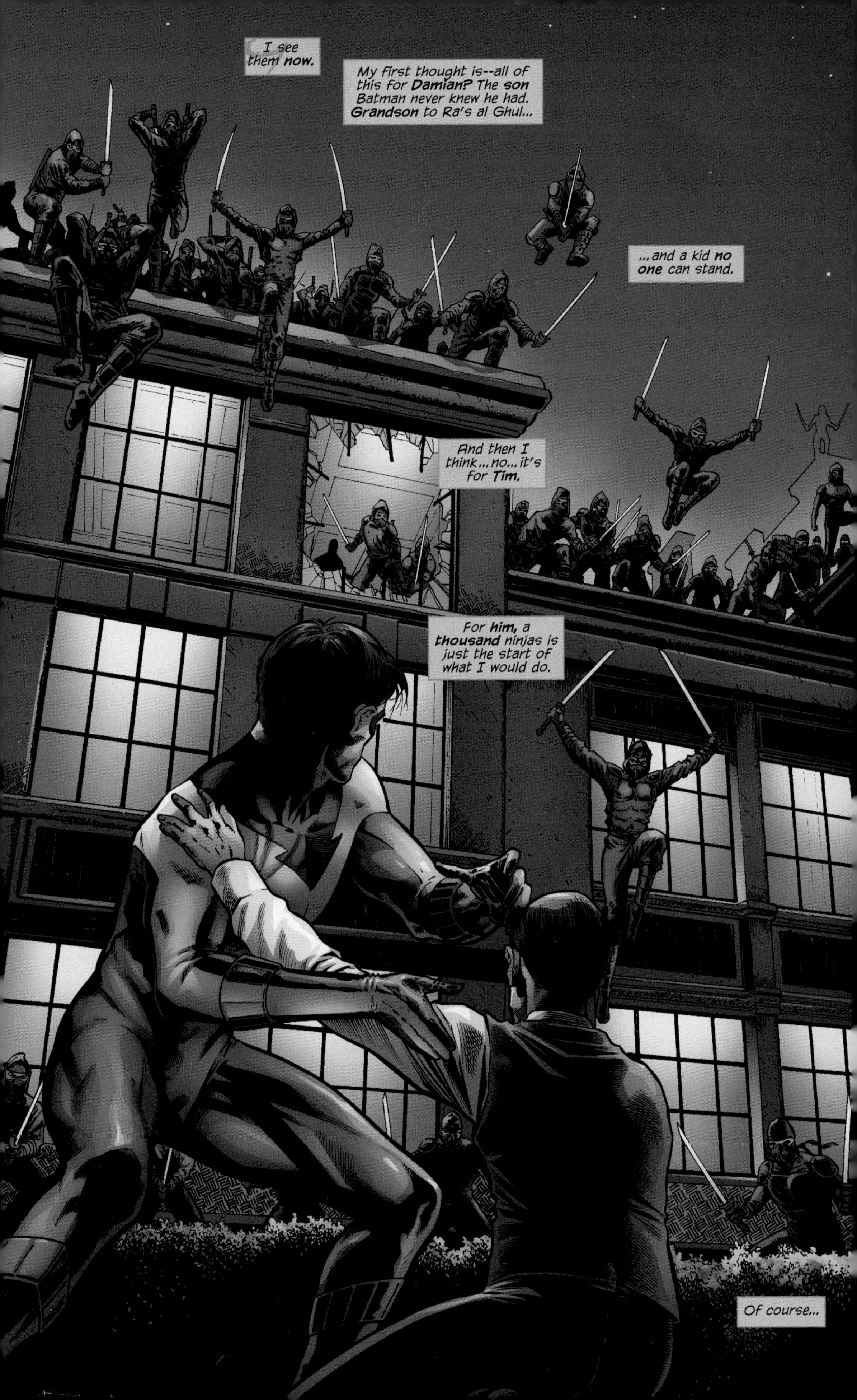
I see them now.
My first thought is--all of this for Damian? The son Batman never knew he had. Grandson to Ra's al Ghul...
...and a kid no one can stand.
And then I think...no...it's for Tim.
For him, a thousand ninjas is just the start of what I would do.
Of course...

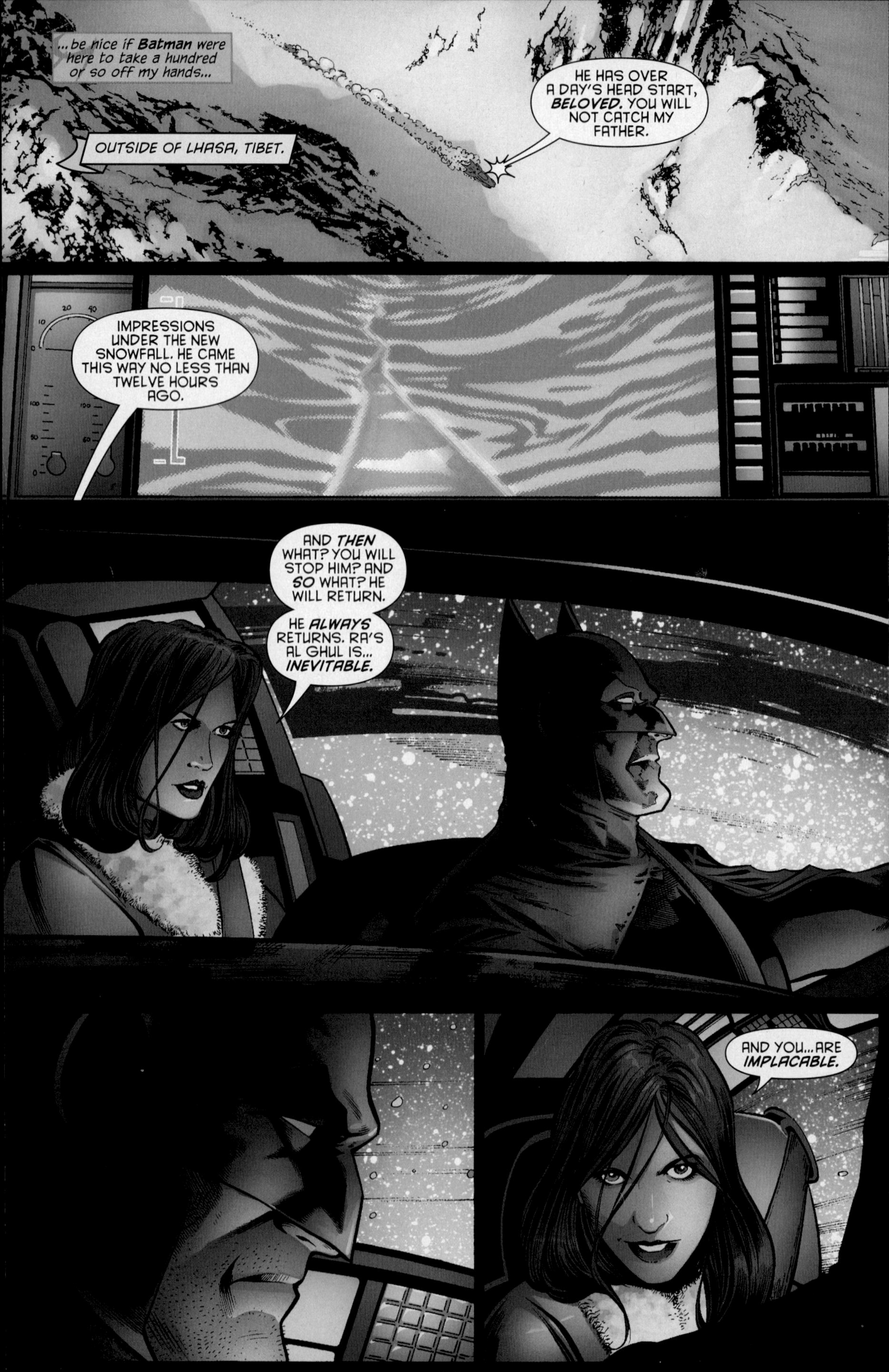

...be nice if Batman were here to take a hundred or so off my hands...
OUTSIDE OF LHASA, TIBET.
HE HAS OVER A DAY'S HEAD START, BELOVED. YOU WILL NOT CATCH MY FATHER.
IMPRESSIONS UNDER THE NEW SNOWFALL. HE CAME THIS WAY NO LESS THAN TWELVE HOURS AGO.
AND THEN WHAT? YOU WILL STOP HIM? AND SO WHAT? HE WILL RETURN.
HE ALWAYS RETURNS. RA'S AL GHUL IS... INEVITABLE.
AND YOU...ARE IMPLACABLE.

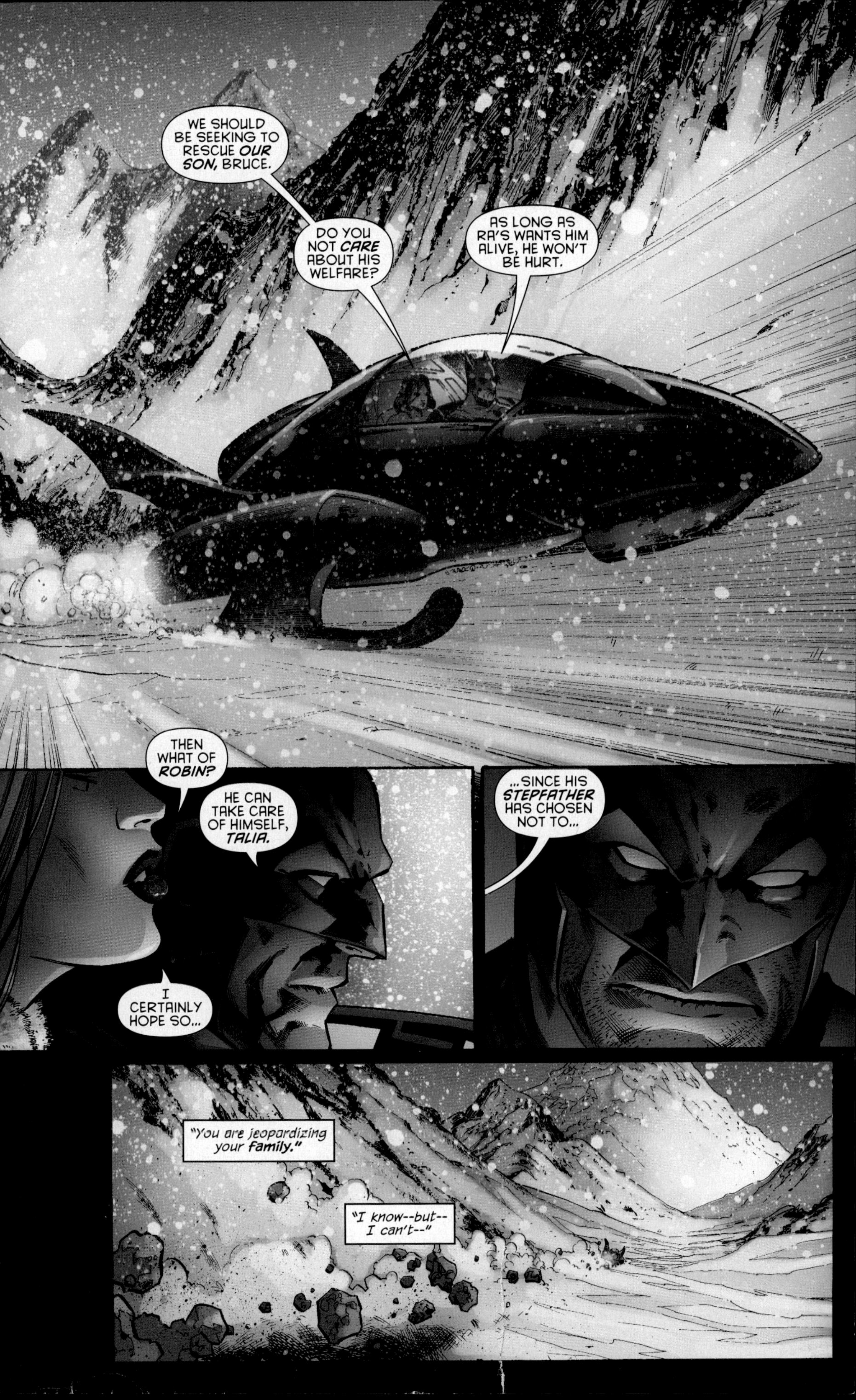
WE SHOULD BE SEEKING TO RESCUE OUR SON, BRUCE.
DO YOU NOT CARE ABOUT HIS WELFARE?
AS LONG AS RA'S WANTS HIM ALIVE, HE WON'T BE HURT.
THEN WHAT OF ROBIN?
HE CAN TAKE CARE OF HIMSELF, TALIA.
I CERTAINLY HOPE SO...
...SINCE HIS STEPFATHER HAS CHOSEN NOT TO...
"You are jeopardizing your family."
"I know--but-- I can't--"

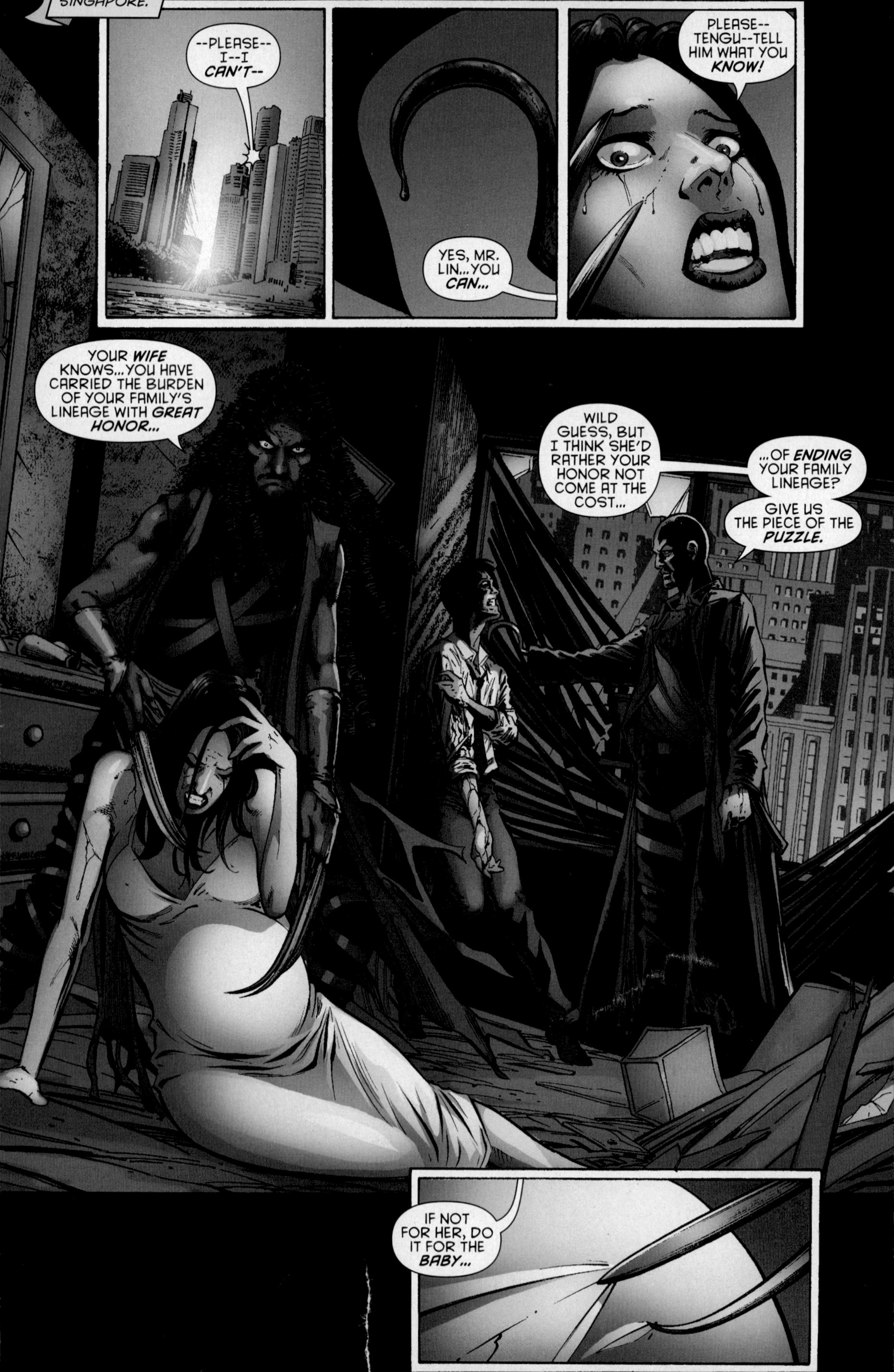
SINGAPORE.
--PLEASE-- I--I CAN'T--
YES, MR. LIN...YOU CAN...
PLEASE-- TENGU--TELL HIM WHAT YOU KNOW!
YOUR WIFE KNOWS...YOU HAVE CARRIED THE BURDEN OF YOUR FAMILY'S LINEAGE WITH GREAT HONOR...
WILD GUESS, BUT I THINK SHE'D RATHER YOUR HONOR NOT COME AT THE COST...
...OF ENDING YOUR FAMILY LINEAGE?
GIVE US THE PIECE OF THE PUZZLE.
IF NOT FOR HER, DO IT FOR THE BABY...

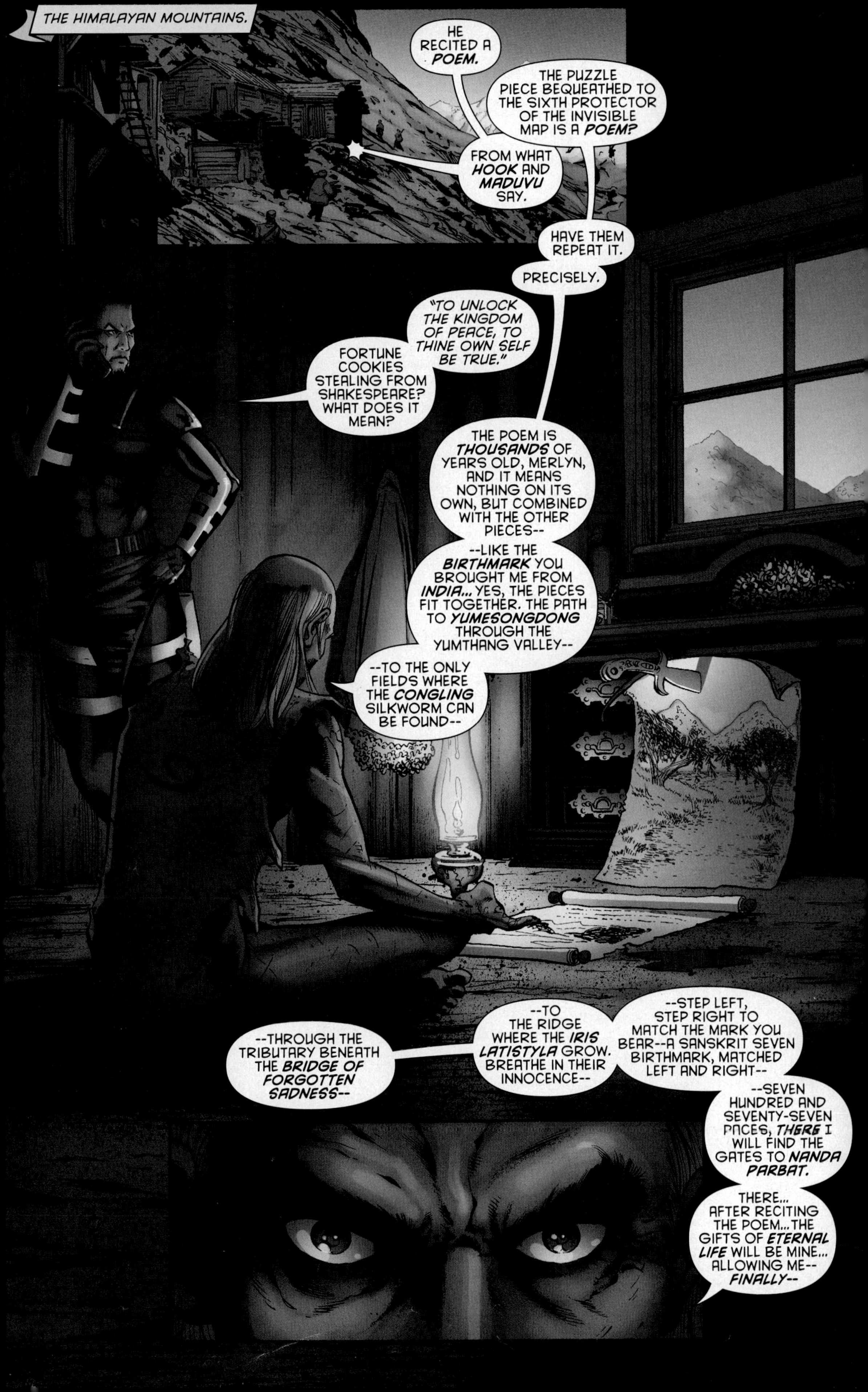
THE HIMALAYAN MOUNTAINS.
HE RECITED A POEM.
THE PUZZLE PIECE BEQUEATHED TO THE SIXTH PROTECTOR OF THE INVISIBLE MAP IS A POEM?
FROM WHAT HOOK AND MADUVU SAY.
HAVE THEM REPEAT IT.
PRECISELY.
"TO UNLOCK THE KINGDOM OF PEACE, TO THINE OWN SELF BE TRUE."
FORTUNE COOKIES STEALING FROM SHAKESPEARE? WHAT DOES IT MEAN?
THE POEM IS THOUSANDS OF YEARS OLD, MERLYN, AND IT MEANS NOTHING ON ITS OWN, BUT COMBINED WITH THE OTHER PIECES--
--LIKE THE BIRTHMARK YOU BROUGHT ME FROM INDIA... YES, THE PIECES FIT TOGETHER. THE PATH TO YUMESONGDONG THROUGH THE YUMTHANG VALLEY--
--TO THE ONLY FIELDS WHERE THE CONGLING SILKWORM CAN BE FOUND--
--THROUGH THE TRIBUTARY BENEATH THE BRIDGE OF FORGOTTEN SADNESS--
--TO THE RIDGE WHERE THE IRIS LATISTYLA GROW. BREATHE IN THEIR INNOCENCE--
--STEP LEFT, STEP RIGHT TO MATCH THE MARK YOU BEAR--A SANSKRIT SEVEN BIRTHMARK, MATCHED LEFT AND RIGHT--
--SEVEN HUNDRED AND SEVENTY-SEVEN PACES, THERE I WILL FIND THE GATES TO NANDA PARBAT.
THERE... AFTER RECITING THE POEM... THE GIFTS OF ETERNAL LIFE WILL BE MINE... ALLOWING ME--FINALLY--

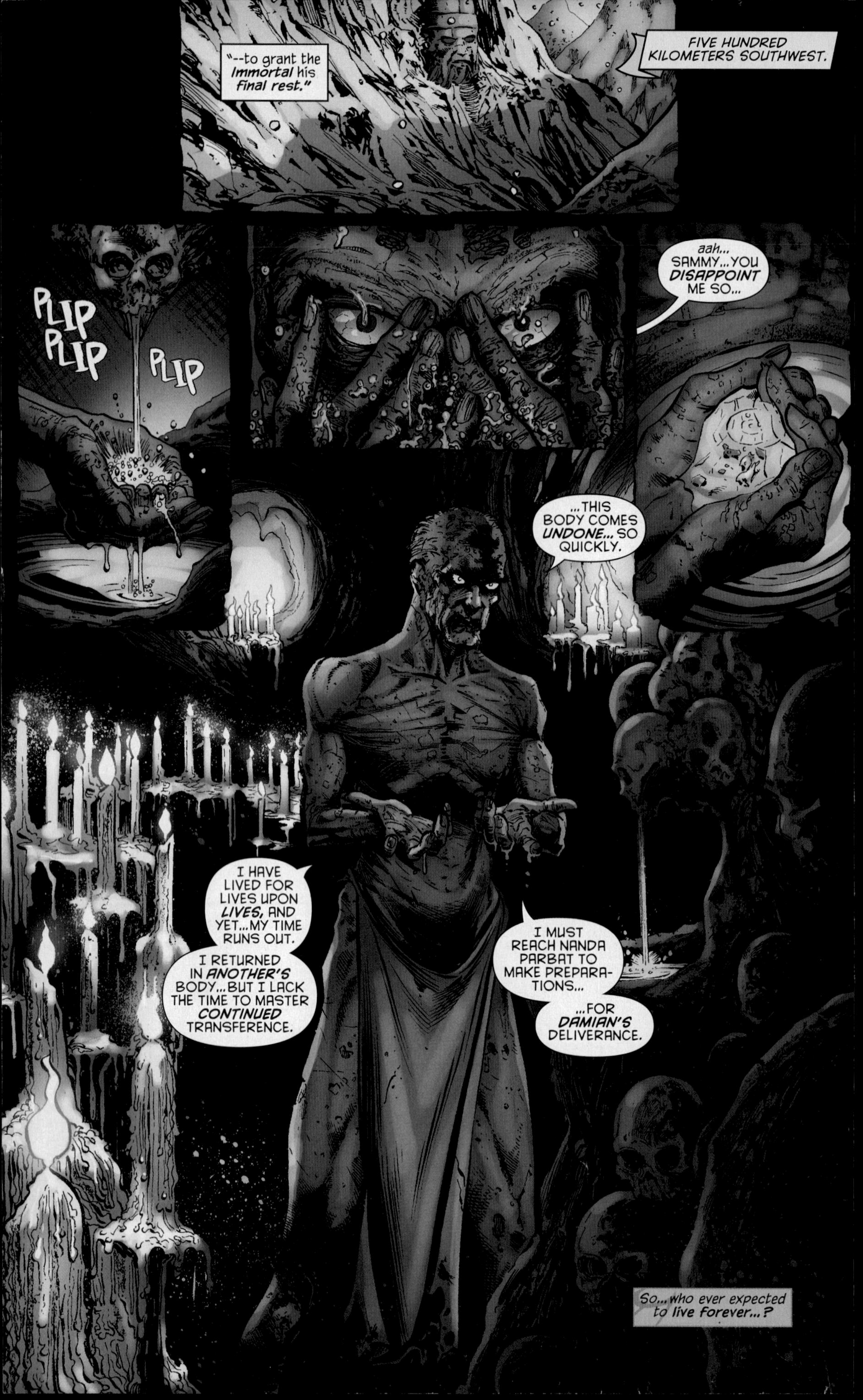
"--to grant the Immortal his final rest."
FIVE HUNDRED KILOMETERS SOUTHWEST.
PLIP PLIP
PLIP
aah... SAMMY...YOU DISAPPOINT ME SO...
...THIS BODY COMES UNDONE... SO QUICKLY.
I HAVE LIVED FOR LIVES UPON LIVES, AND YET...MY TIME RUNS OUT.
I RETURNED IN ANOTHER'S BODY...BUT I LACK THE TIME TO MASTER CONTINUED TRANSFERENCE.
I MUST REACH NANDA PARBAT TO MAKE PREPARATIONS...
...FOR DAMIAN'S DELIVERANCE.
So...who ever expected to live forever...?

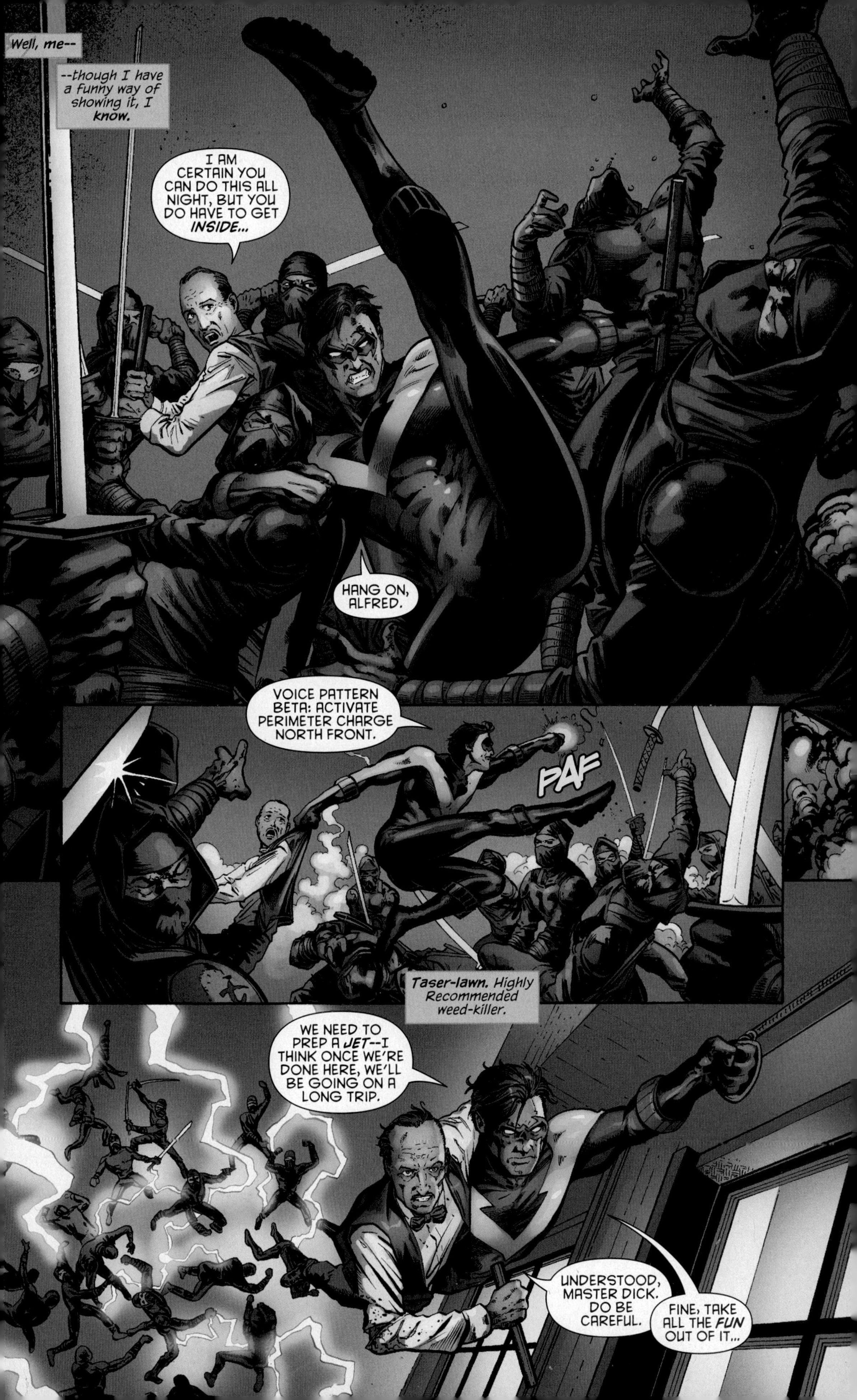
Well, me--
--though I have a funny way of showing it, I know.
I AM CERTAIN YOU CAN DO THIS ALL NIGHT, BUT YOU DO HAVE TO GET INSIDE...
HANG ON, ALFRED.
VOICE PATTERN BETA: ACTIVATE PERIMETER CHARGE NORTH FRONT.
PAF
Taser-lawn. Highly Recommended weed-killer.
WE NEED TO PREP A JET--I THINK ONCE WE'RE DONE HERE, WE'LL BE GOING ON A LONG TRIP.
UNDERSTOOD, MASTER DICK. DO BE CAREFUL.
FINE, TAKE ALL THE FUN OUT OF IT...

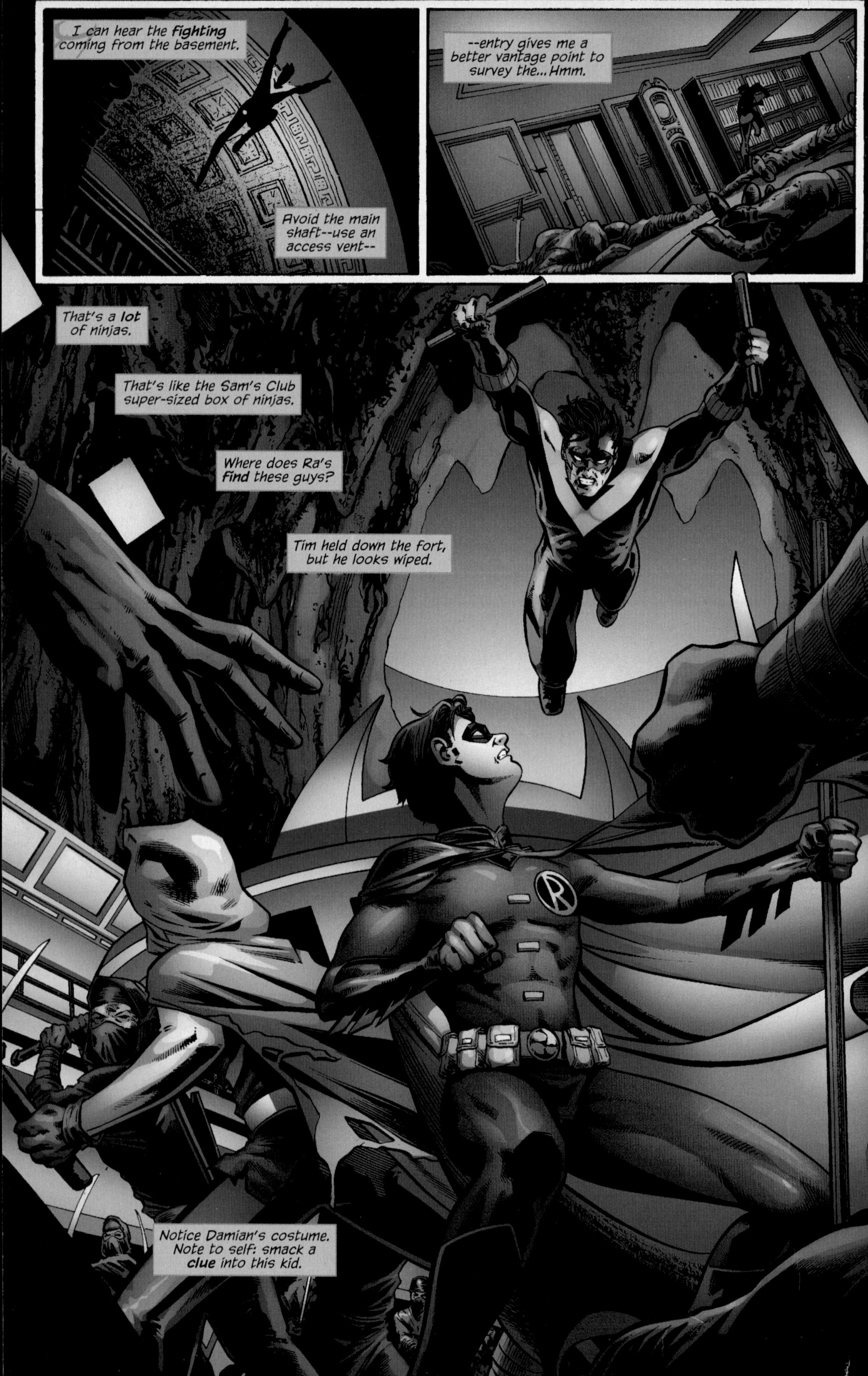

I can hear the **fighting** coming from the basement.
Avoid the main shaft--use an access vent--
--entry gives me a better vantage point to survey the... Hmm.
That's a **lot** of ninjas.
That's like the Sam's Club super-sized box of ninjas.
Where does Ra's **find** these guys?
Tim held down the fort, but he looks wiped.
Notice Damian's costume. Note to self: smack a **clue** into this kid.

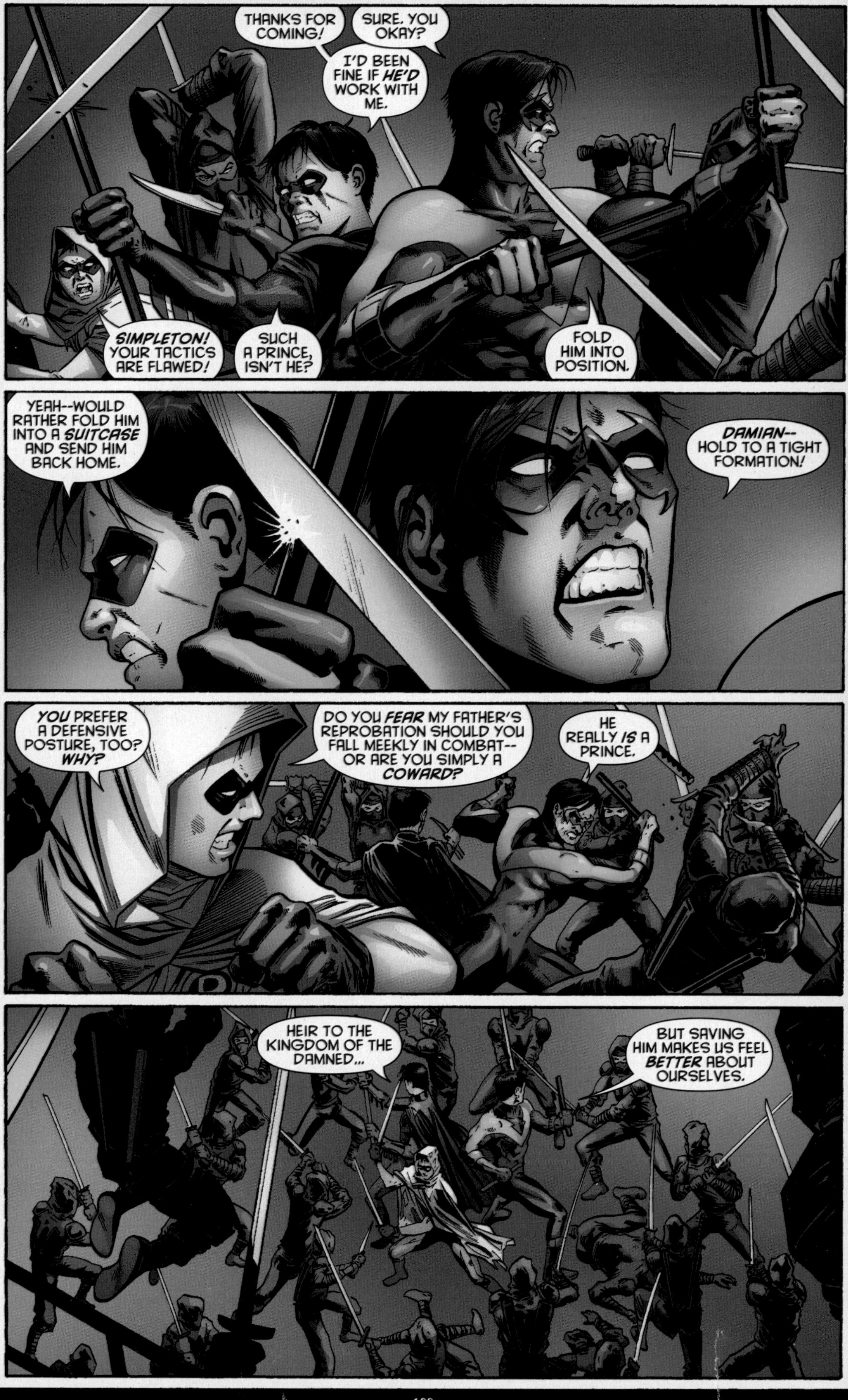
THANKS FOR COMING!
SURE. YOU OKAY?
I'D BEEN FINE IF HE'D WORK WITH ME.
SIMPLETON! YOUR TACTICS ARE FLAWED!
SUCH A PRINCE, ISN'T HE?
FOLD HIM INTO POSITION.
YEAH--WOULD RATHER FOLD HIM INTO A SUITCASE AND SEND HIM BACK HOME.
DAMIAN-- HOLD TO A TIGHT FORMATION!
YOU PREFER A DEFENSIVE POSTURE, TOO? WHY?
DO YOU FEAR MY FATHER'S REPROBATION SHOULD YOU FALL MEEKLY IN COMBAT-- OR ARE YOU SIMPLY A COWARD?
HE REALLY IS A PRINCE.
HEIR TO THE KINGDOM OF THE DAMNED...
BUT SAVING HIM MAKES US FEEL BETTER ABOUT OURSELVES.

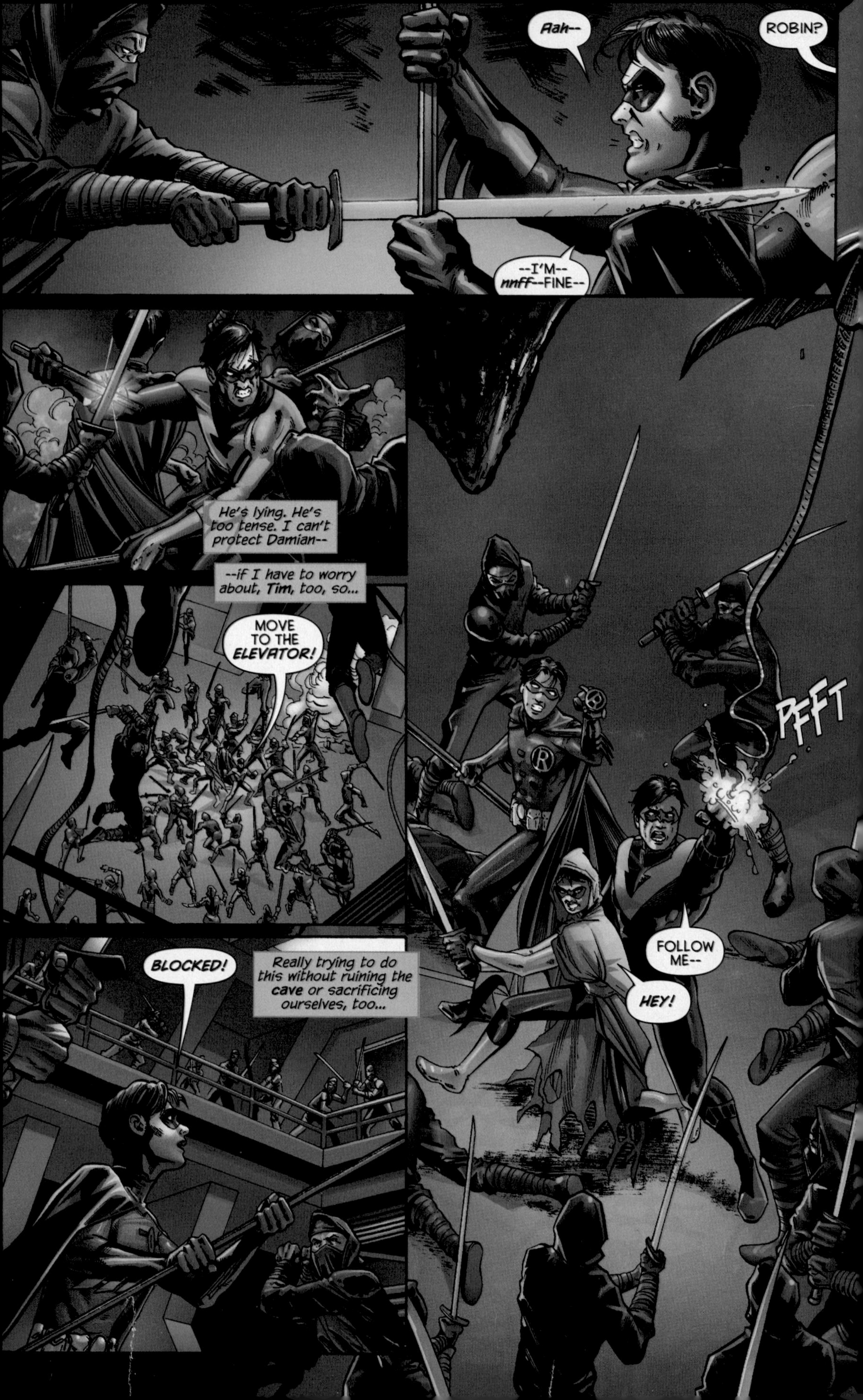
Aah--
ROBIN?
--I'M-- nnff--FINE--
He's lying. He's too tense. I can't protect Damian--
--if I have to worry about, Tim, too, so...
MOVE TO THE ELEVATOR!
BLOCKED!
Really trying to do this without ruining the cave or sacrificing ourselves, too...
PFFT
FOLLOW ME--
HEY!

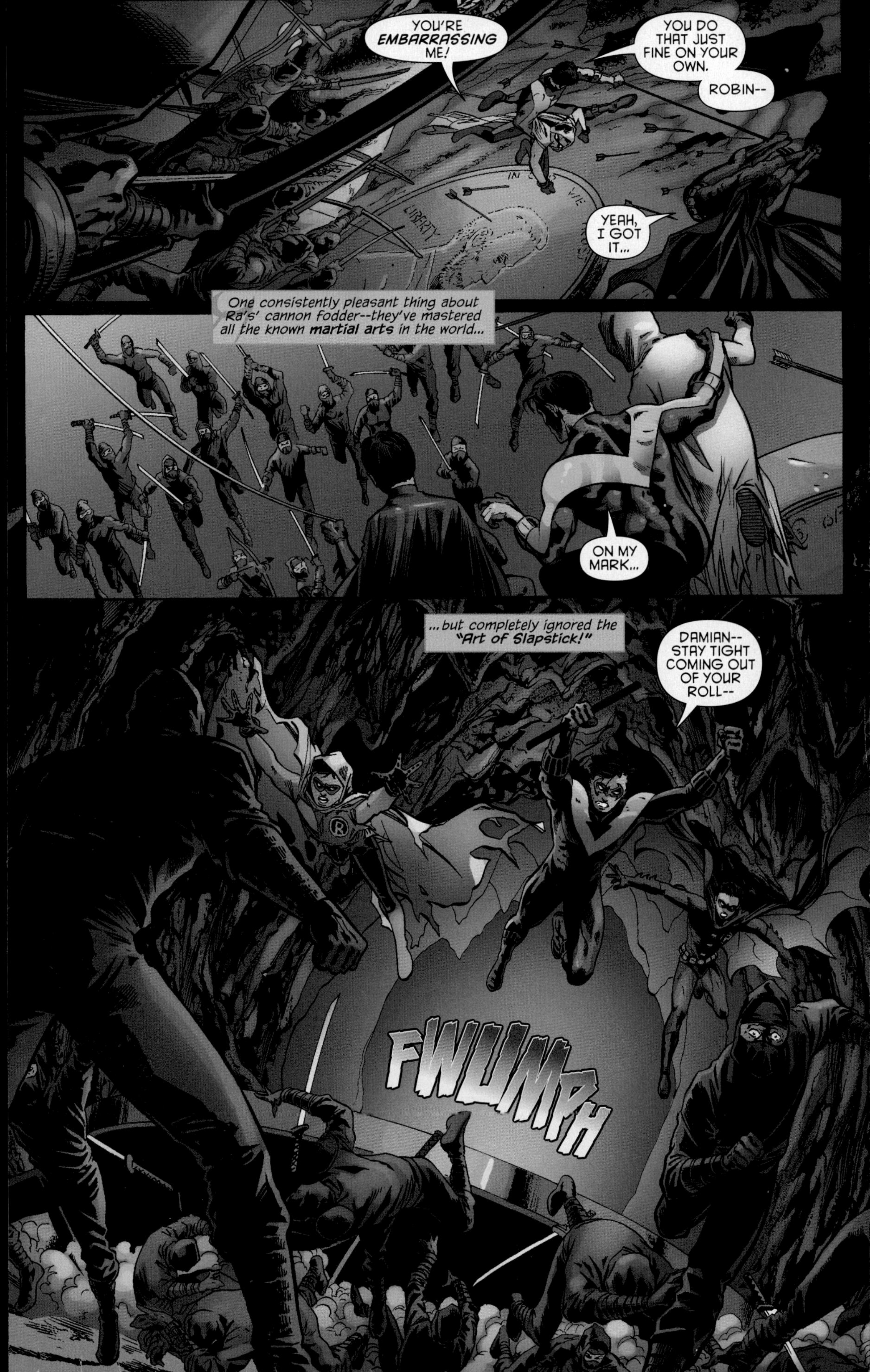

YOU'RE EMBARRASSING ME!
YOU DO THAT JUST FINE ON YOUR OWN.
ROBIN--
YEAH, I GOT IT...
One consistently pleasant thing about Ra's' cannon fodder--they've mastered all the known martial arts in the world...
ON MY MARK...
...but completely ignored the "Art of Slapstick!"
DAMIAN--STAY TIGHT COMING OUT OF YOUR ROLL--
FWUMPH

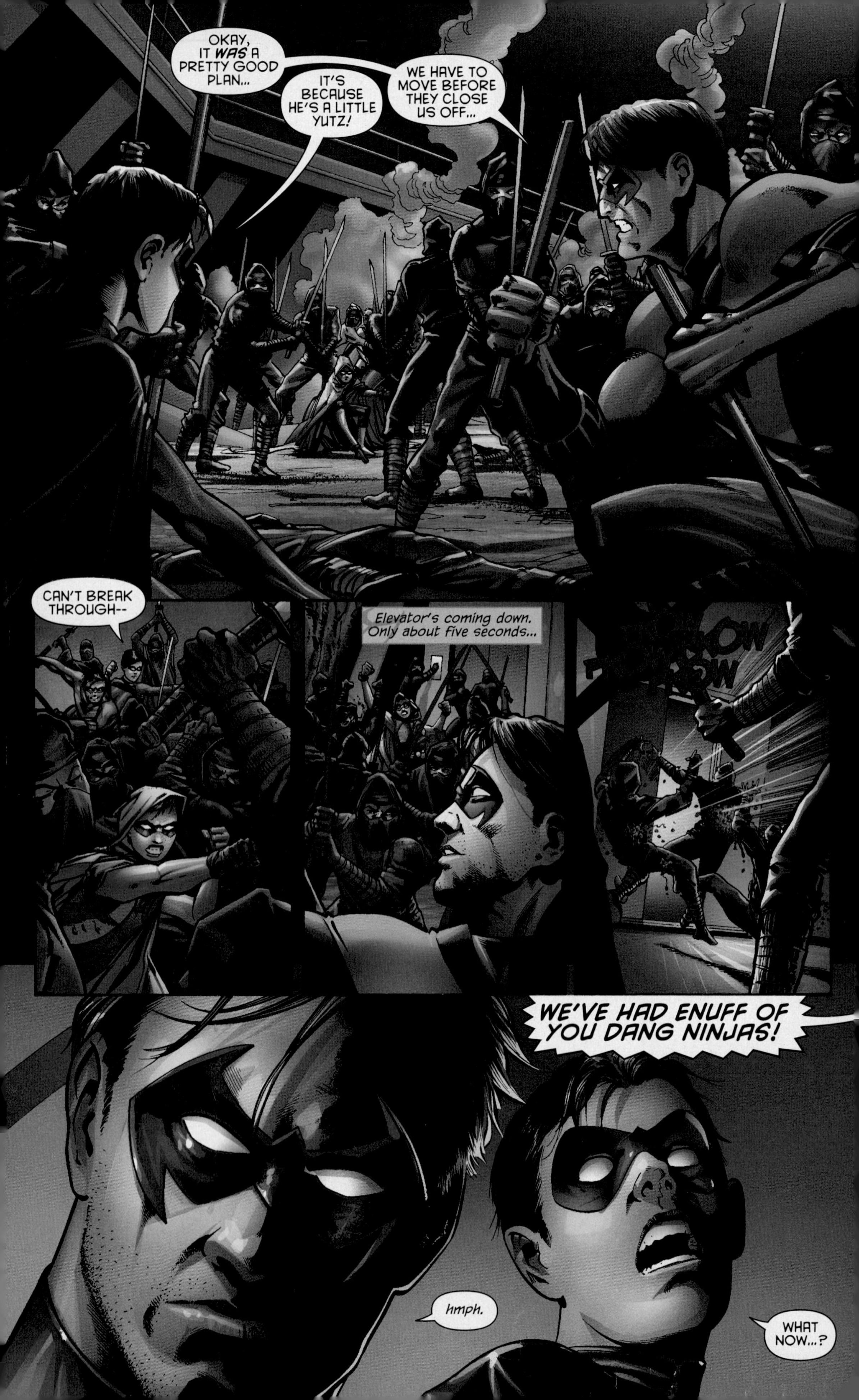
OKAY, IT WAS A PRETTY GOOD PLAN...
IT'S BECAUSE HE'S A LITTLE YUTZ!
WE HAVE TO MOVE BEFORE THEY CLOSE US OFF...
CAN'T BREAK THROUGH--
Elevator's coming down. Only about five seconds...
WE'VE HAD ENUFF OF YOU DANG NINJAS!
hmph.
WHAT NOW...?

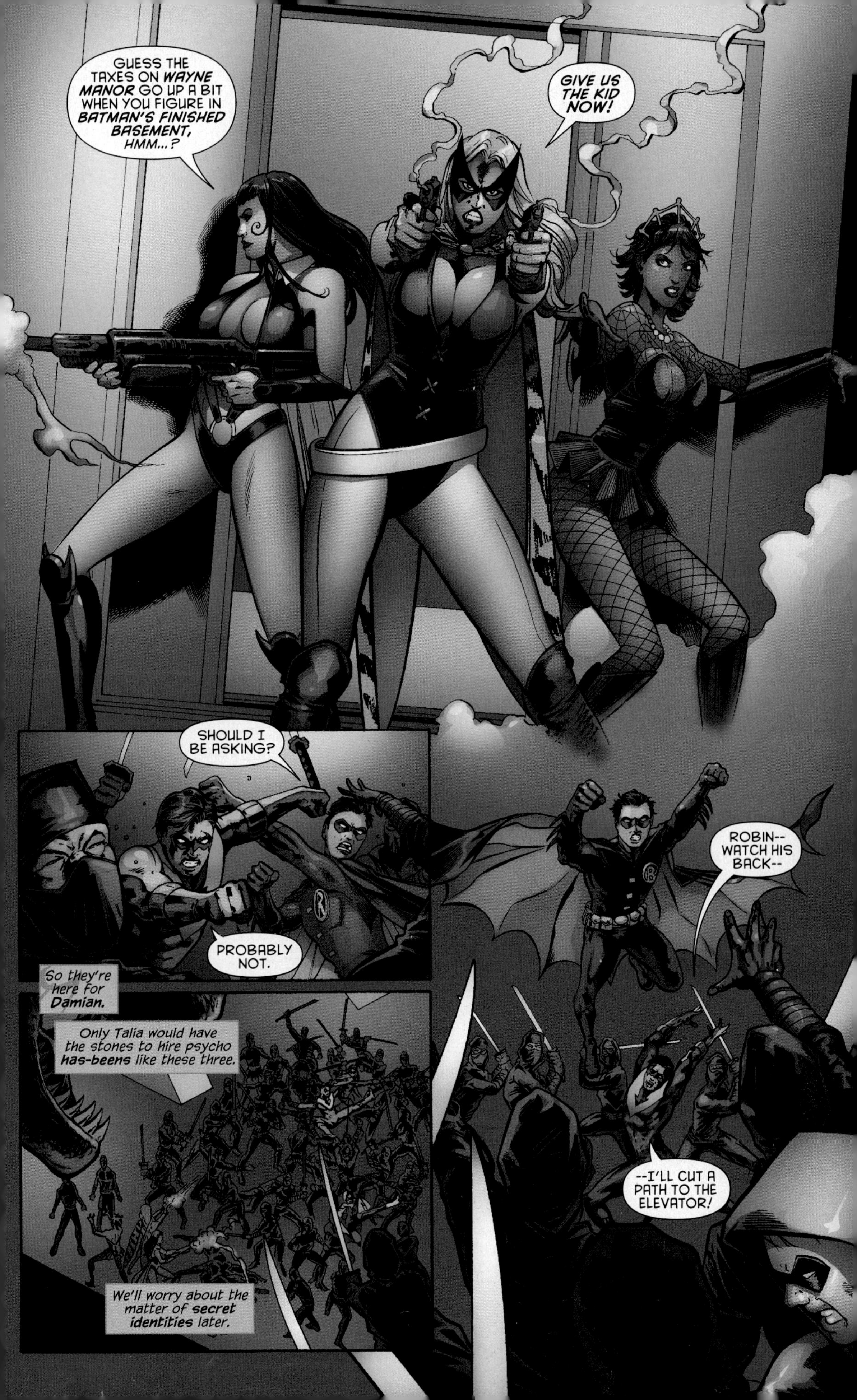
GUESS THE TAXES ON WAYNE MANOR GO UP A BIT WHEN YOU FIGURE IN BATMAN'S FINISHED BASEMENT, HMM...?
GIVE US THE KID NOW!
SHOULD I BE ASKING?
PROBABLY NOT.
ROBIN-- WATCH HIS BACK--
So they're here for Damian.
Only Talia would have the stones to hire psycho has-beens like these three.
--I'LL CUT A PATH TO THE ELEVATOR!
We'll worry about the matter of secret identities later.

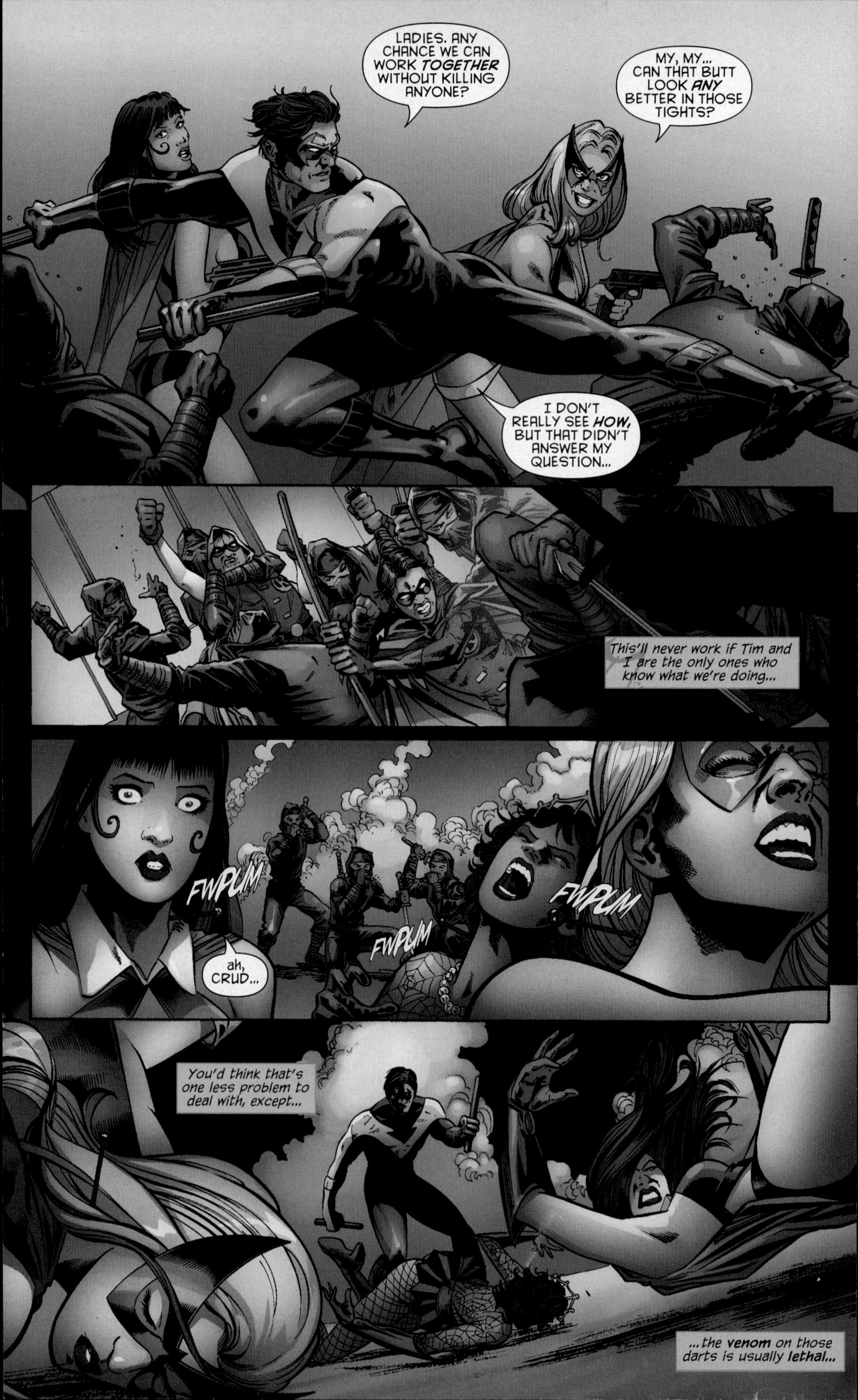
LADIES. ANY CHANCE WE CAN WORK TOGETHER WITHOUT KILLING ANYONE?
MY, MY... CAN THAT BUTT LOOK ANY BETTER IN THOSE TIGHTS?
I DON'T REALLY SEE HOW, BUT THAT DIDN'T ANSWER MY QUESTION...
This'll never work if Tim and I are the only ones who know what we're doing...
FWPUM
ah, CRUD...
FWPUM
FWPUM
You'd think that's one less problem to deal with, except...
...the venom on those darts is usually lethal...

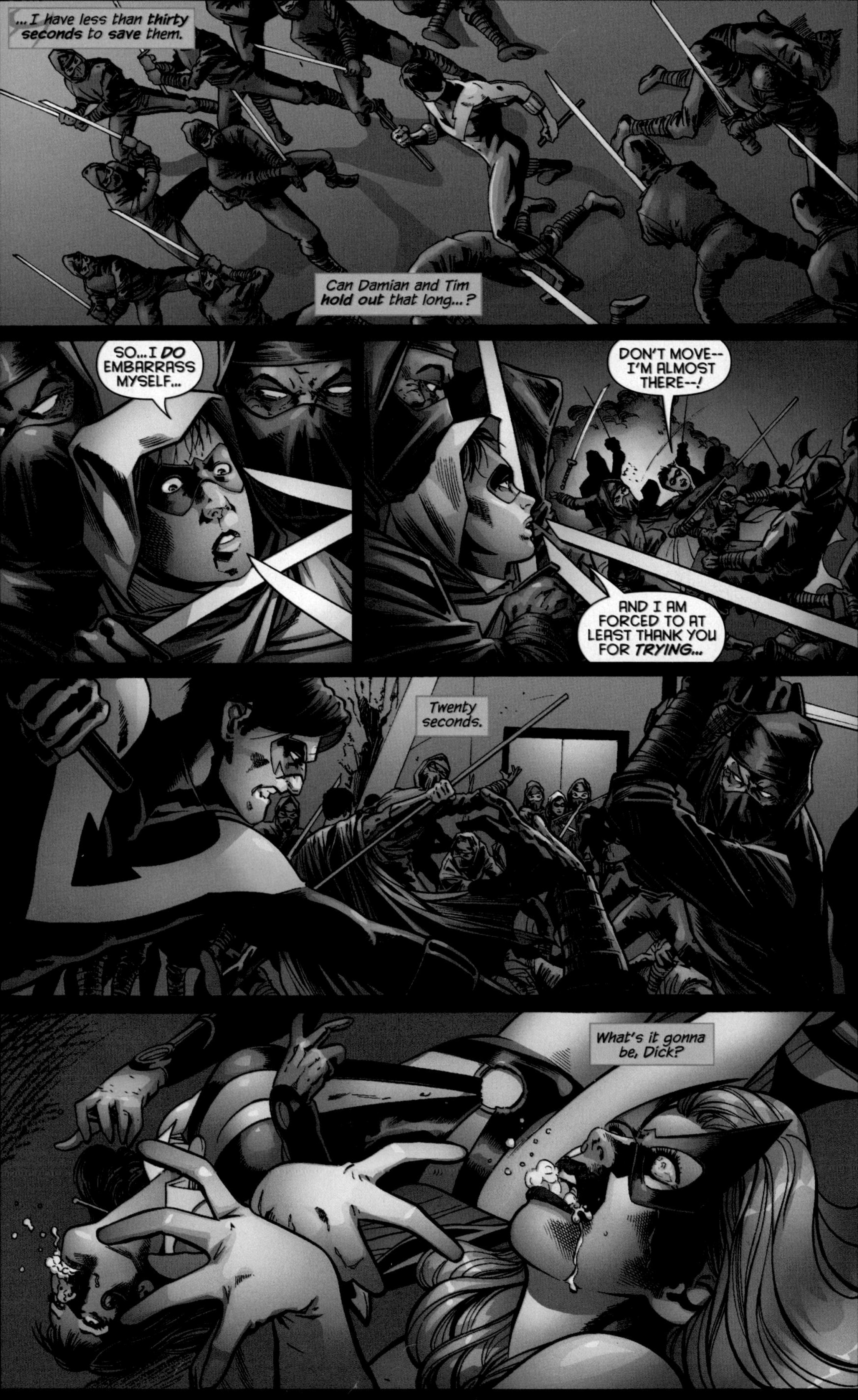
...I have less than thirty seconds to save them.
Can Damian and Tim hold out that long...?
SO...I DO EMBARRASS MYSELF...
DON'T MOVE-- I'M ALMOST THERE--!
AND I AM FORCED TO AT LEAST THANK YOU FOR TRYING...
Twenty seconds.
What's it gonna be, Dick?

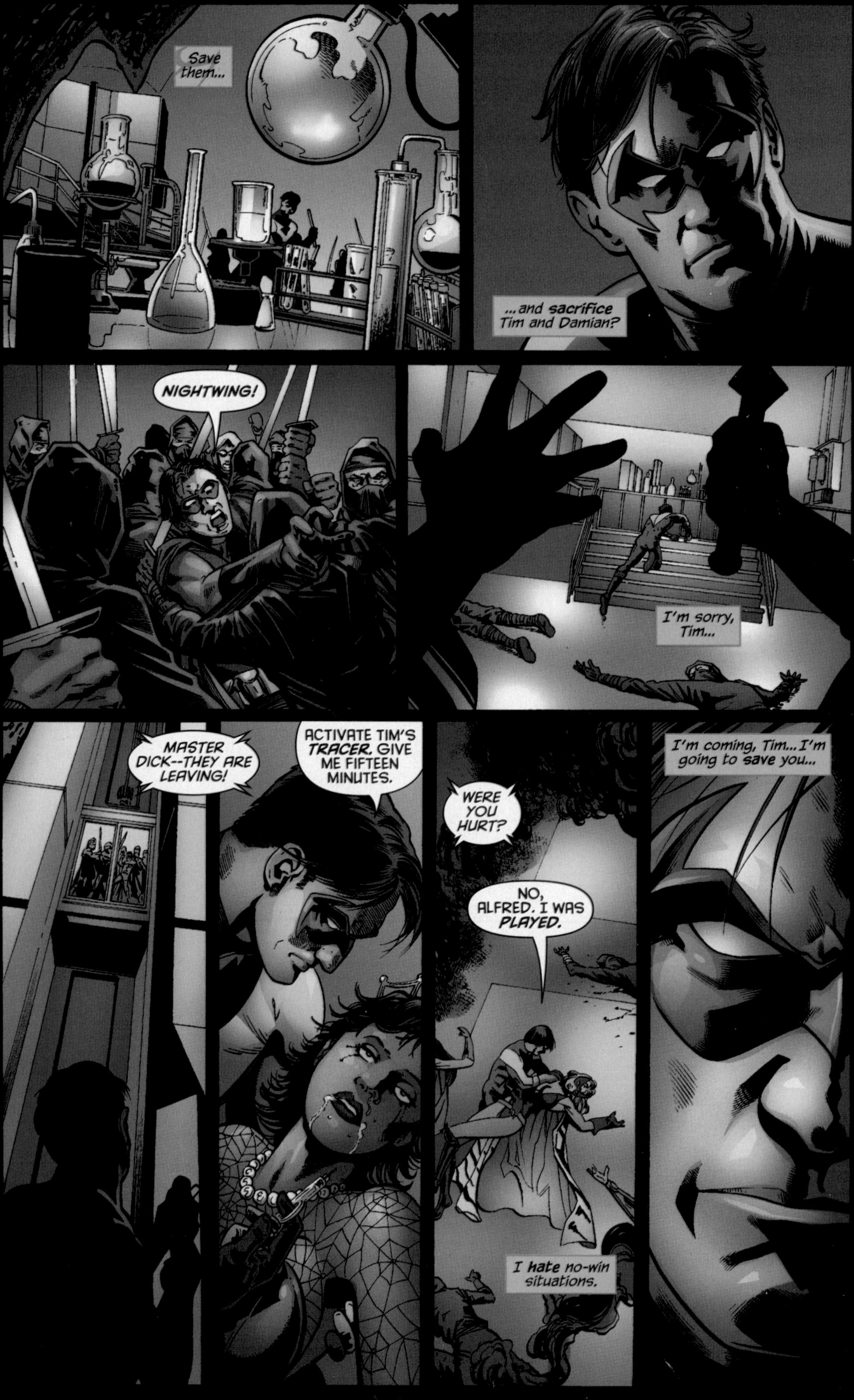
Save them...
...and sacrifice Tim and Damian?
NIGHTWING!
I'm sorry, Tim...
MASTER DICK--THEY ARE LEAVING!
ACTIVATE TIM'S TRACER. GIVE ME FIFTEEN MINUTES.
WERE YOU HURT?
NO, ALFRED. I WAS PLAYED.
I hate no-win situations.
I'm coming, Tim... I'm going to save you...

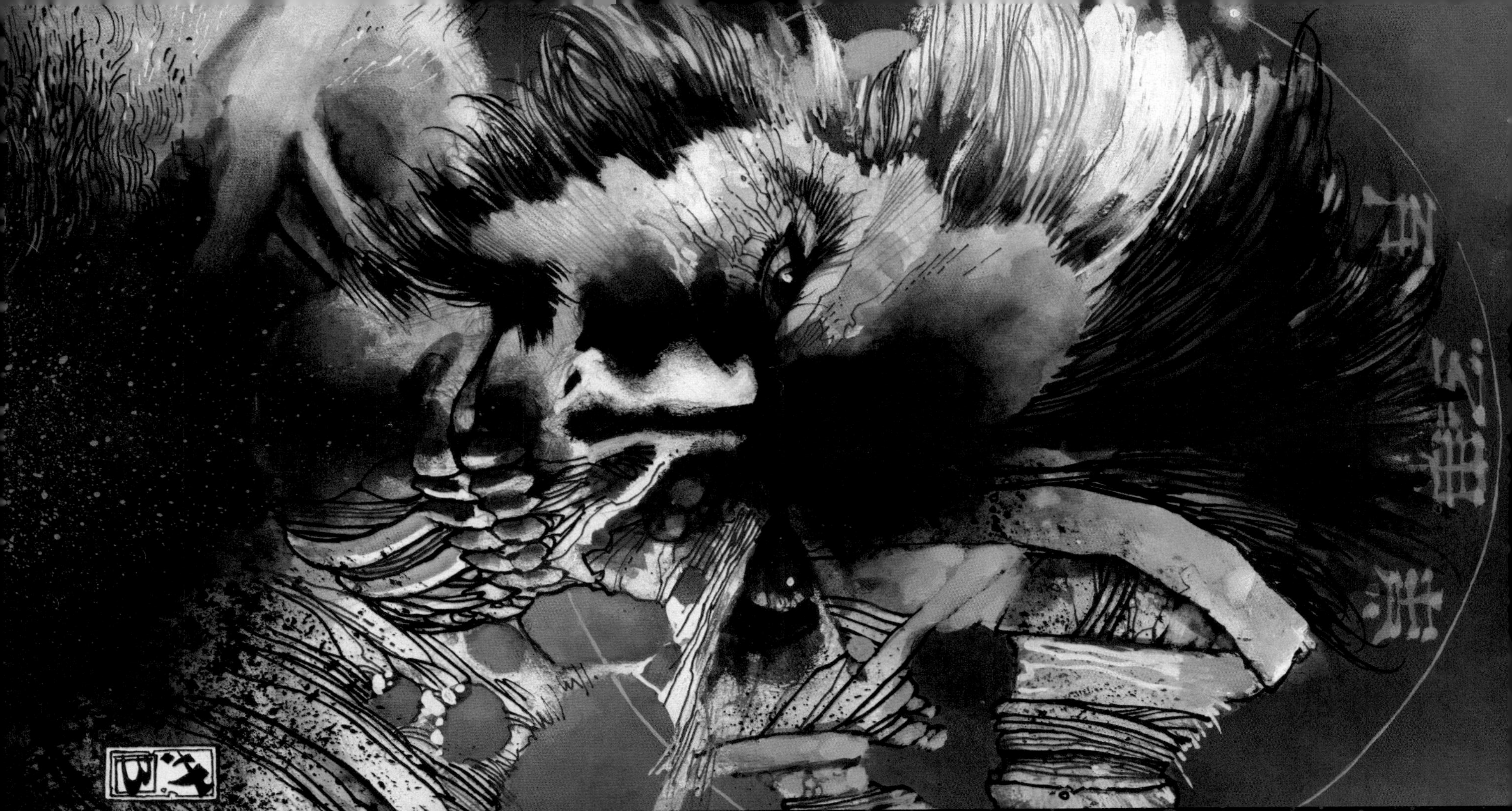

CHAPTER THREE SINS OF THE FATHERS

Cover art by Simone Bianchi | Chapter written by Paul Dini | Chapter pencilled by Ryan Benjamin | Chapter inked by Saleem Crawford

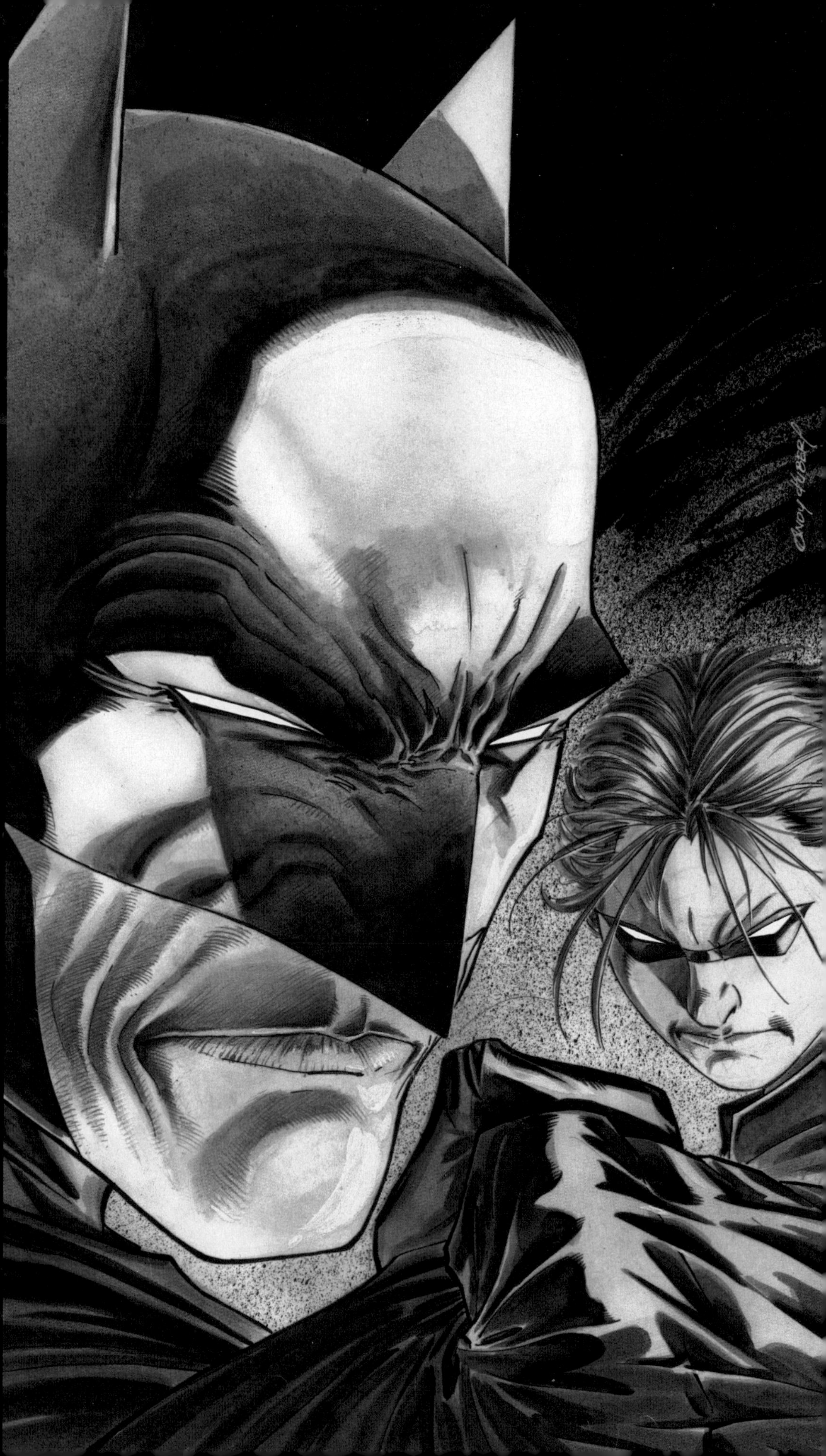

Variant cover by Andy Kubert

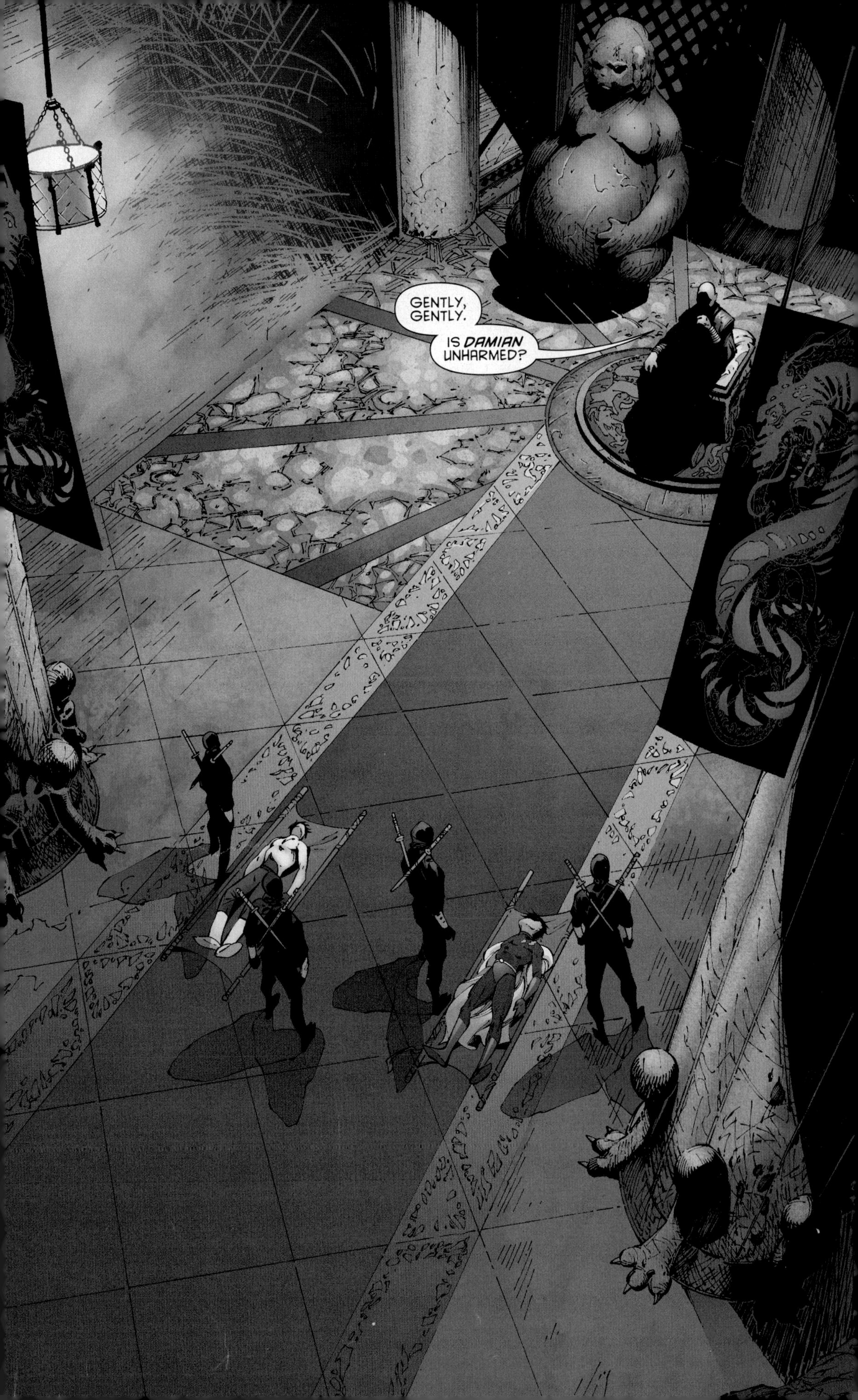
GENTLY, GENTLY.
IS DAMIAN UNHARMED?

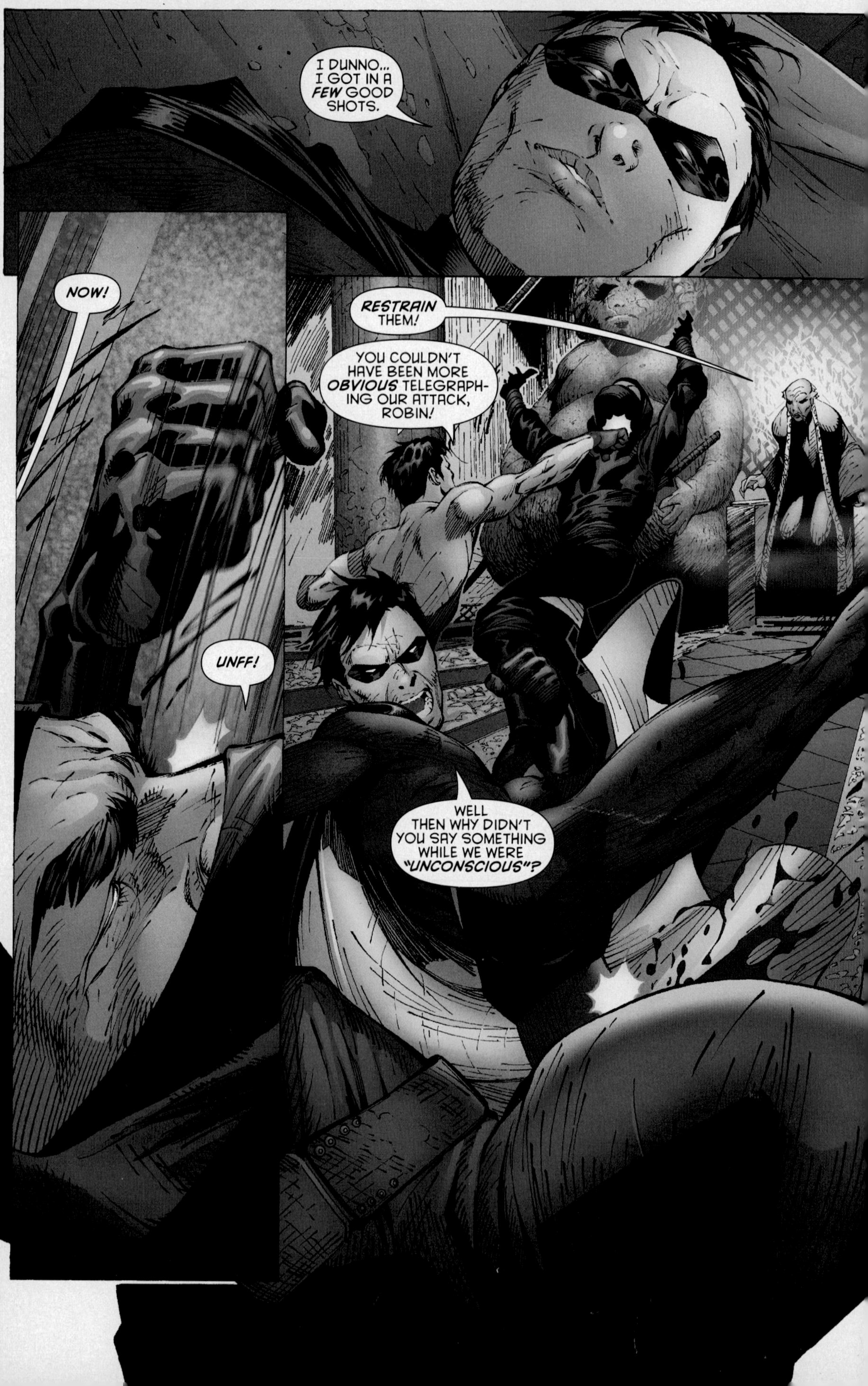
I DUNNO... I GOT IN A FEW GOOD SHOTS.
NOW!
RESTRAIN THEM!
YOU COULDN'T HAVE BEEN MORE OBVIOUS TELEGRAPHING OUR ATTACK, ROBIN!
UNFF!
WELL THEN WHY DIDN'T YOU SAY SOMETHING WHILE WE WERE "UNCONSCIOUS"?

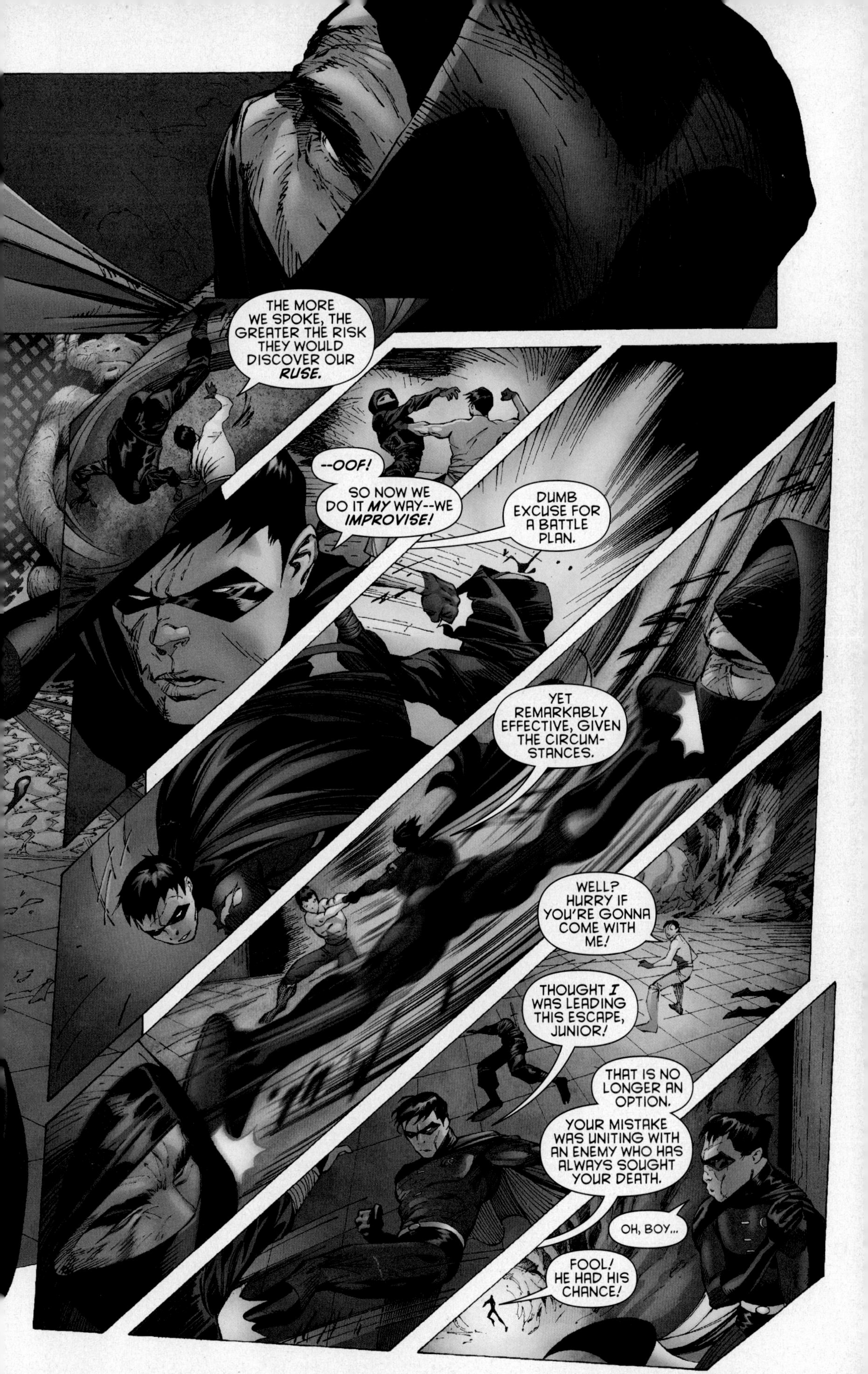
THE MORE WE SPOKE, THE GREATER THE RISK THEY WOULD DISCOVER OUR RUSE.
--OOF!
SO NOW WE DO IT MY WAY--WE IMPROVISE!
DUMB EXCUSE FOR A BATTLE PLAN.
YET REMARKABLY EFFECTIVE, GIVEN THE CIRCUM-STANCES.
WELL? HURRY IF YOU'RE GONNA COME WITH ME!
THOUGHT I WAS LEADING THIS ESCAPE, JUNIOR!
THAT IS NO LONGER AN OPTION.
YOUR MISTAKE WAS UNITING WITH AN ENEMY WHO HAS ALWAYS SOUGHT YOUR DEATH.
OH, BOY...
FOOL! HE HAD HIS CHANCE!

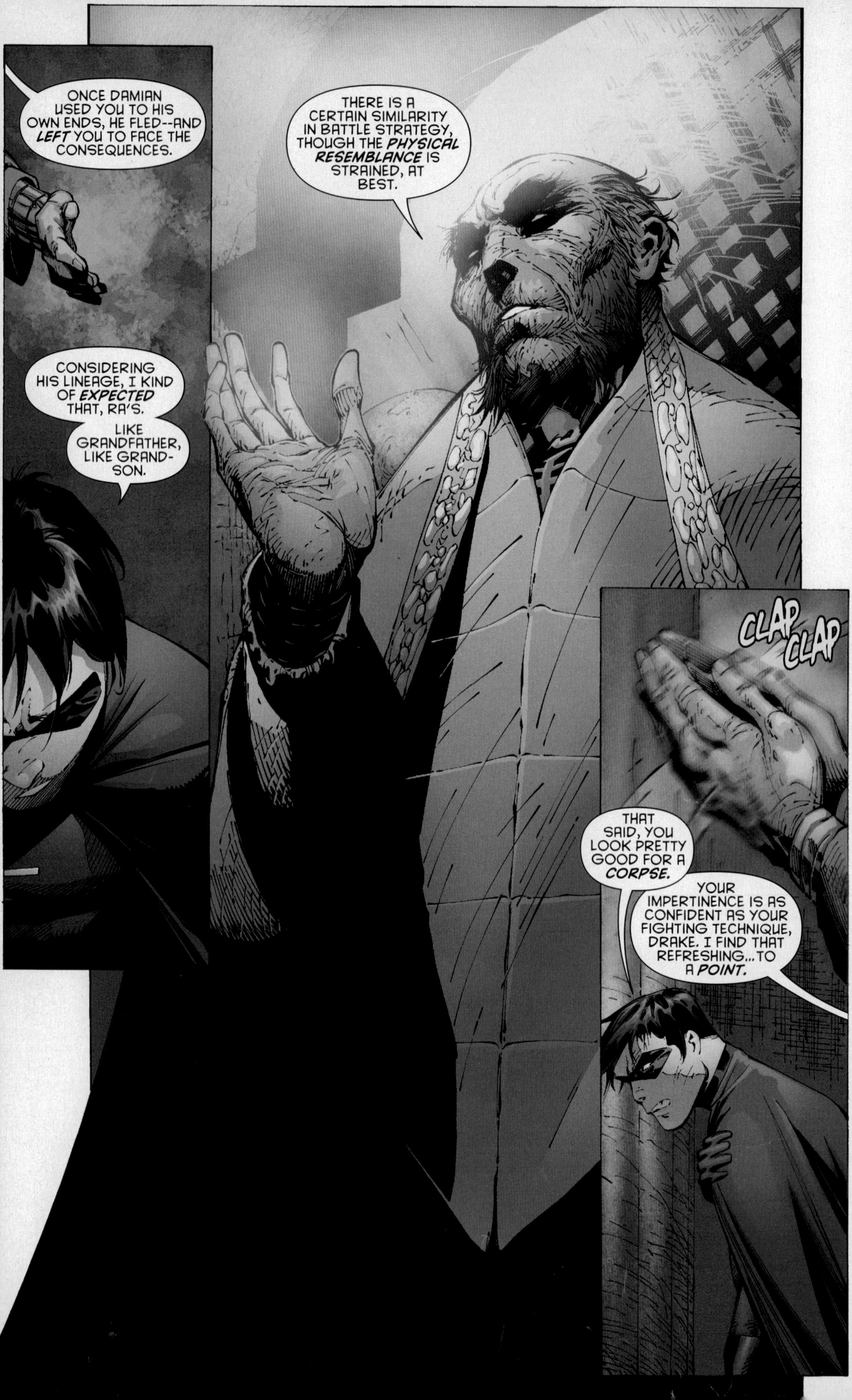
ONCE DAMIAN USED YOU TO HIS OWN ENDS, HE FLED--AND *LEFT* YOU TO FACE THE CONSEQUENCES.
THERE IS A CERTAIN SIMILARITY IN BATTLE STRATEGY, THOUGH THE *PHYSICAL RESEMBLANCE* IS STRAINED, AT BEST.
CONSIDERING HIS LINEAGE, I KIND OF *EXPECTED* THAT, RA'S.
LIKE GRANDFATHER, LIKE GRAND-SON.
CLAP CLAP
THAT SAID, YOU LOOK PRETTY GOOD FOR A *CORPSE.*
YOUR IMPERTINENCE IS AS CONFIDENT AS YOUR FIGHTING TECHNIQUE, DRAKE. I FIND THAT REFRESHING...TO A *POINT.*

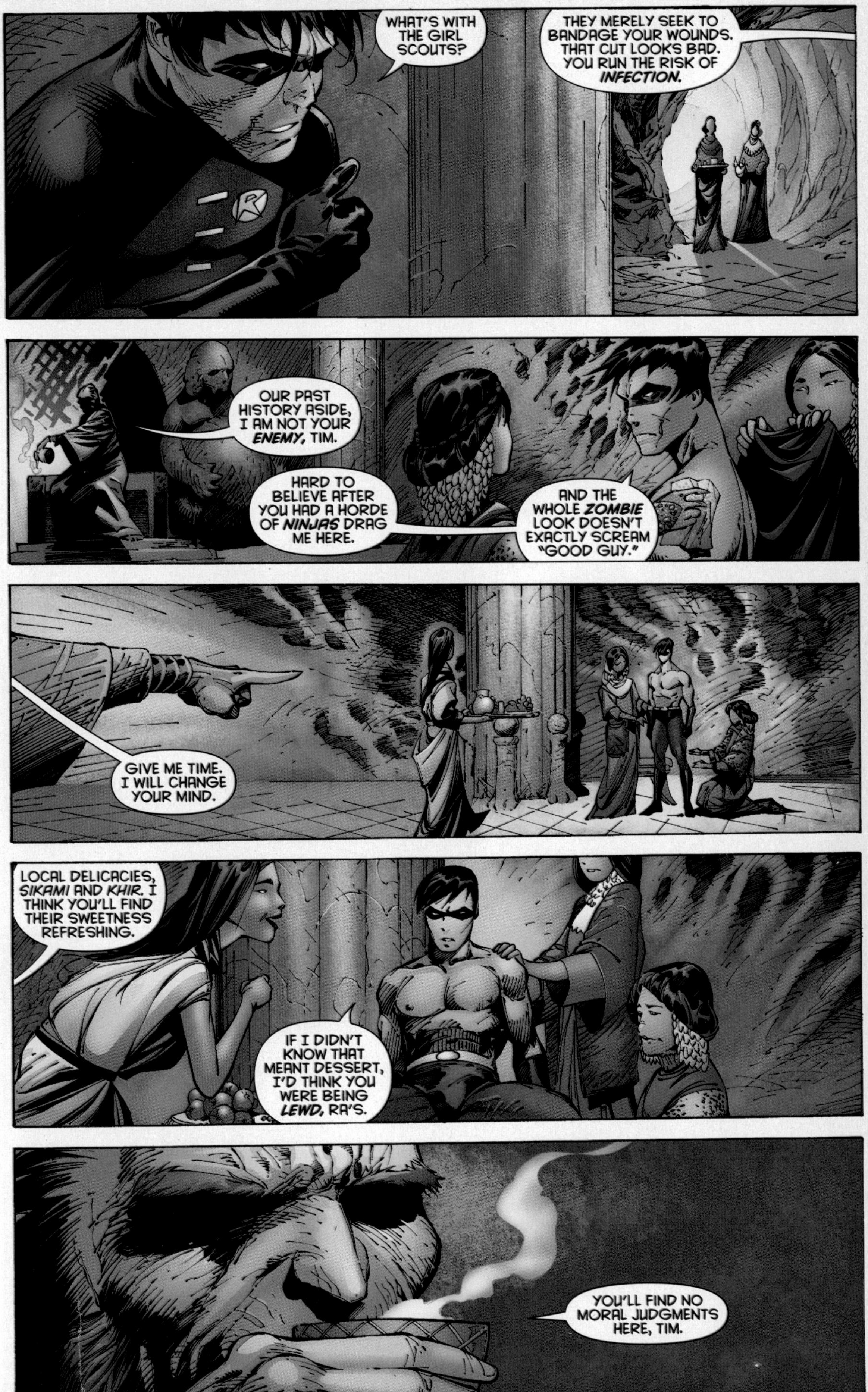
WHAT'S WITH THE GIRL SCOUTS?
THEY MERELY SEEK TO BANDAGE YOUR WOUNDS. THAT CUT LOOKS BAD. YOU RUN THE RISK OF INFECTION.
OUR PAST HISTORY ASIDE, I AM NOT YOUR ENEMY, TIM.
HARD TO BELIEVE AFTER YOU HAD A HORDE OF NINJAS DRAG ME HERE.
AND THE WHOLE ZOMBIE LOOK DOESN'T EXACTLY SCREAM "GOOD GUY."
GIVE ME TIME. I WILL CHANGE YOUR MIND.
LOCAL DELICACIES, SIKAMI AND KHIR. I THINK YOU'LL FIND THEIR SWEETNESS REFRESHING.
IF I DIDN'T KNOW THAT MEANT DESSERT, I'D THINK YOU WERE BEING LEWD, RA'S.
YOU'LL FIND NO MORAL JUDGMENTS HERE, TIM.

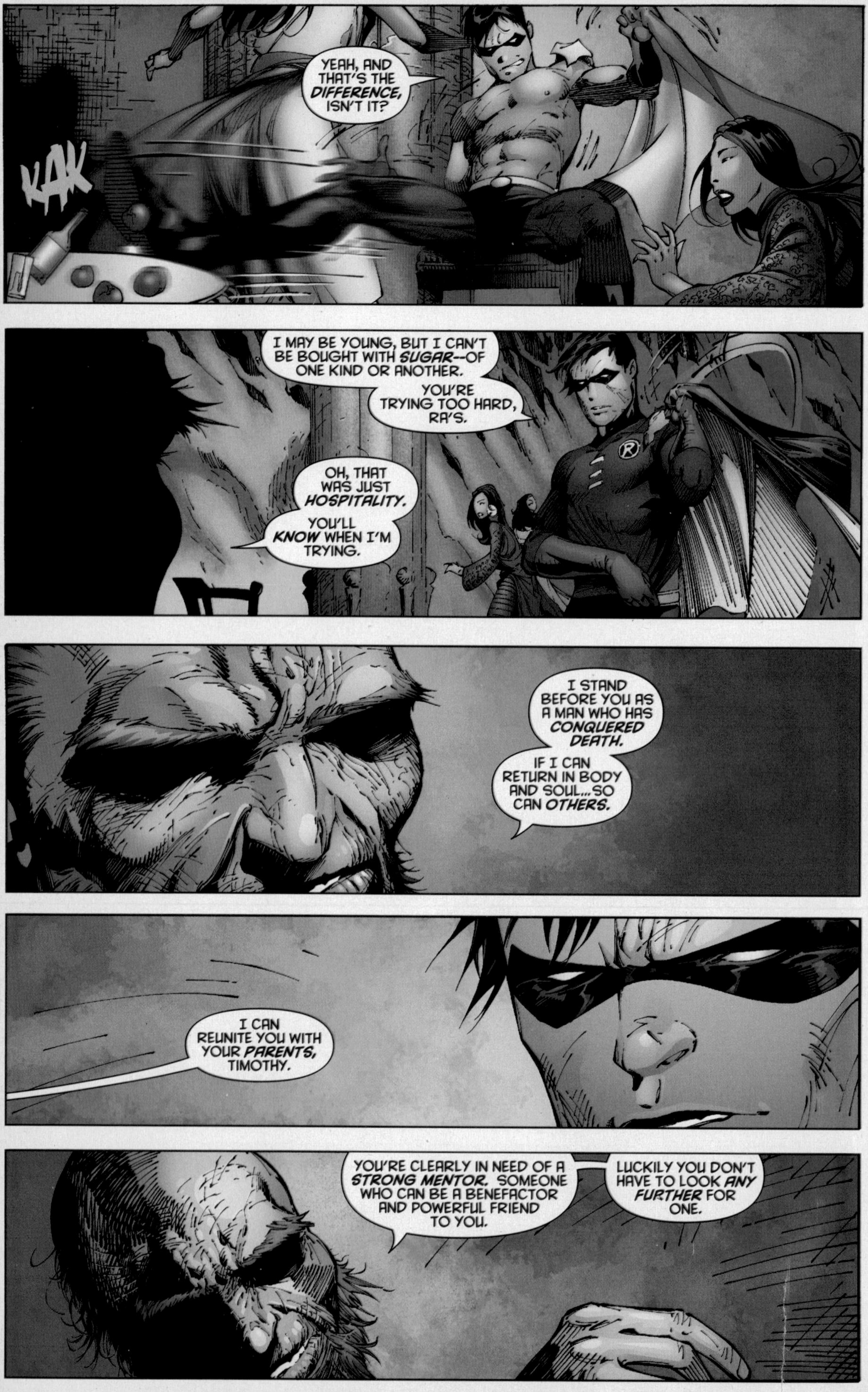
YEAH, AND THAT'S THE *DIFFERENCE,* ISN'T IT?
KAK
I MAY BE YOUNG, BUT I CAN'T BE BOUGHT WITH *SUGAR*--OF ONE KIND OR ANOTHER.
YOU'RE TRYING TOO HARD, RA'S.
OH, THAT WAS JUST *HOSPITALITY.*
YOU'LL *KNOW* WHEN I'M TRYING.
I STAND BEFORE YOU AS A MAN WHO HAS *CONQUERED DEATH.*
IF I CAN RETURN IN BODY AND SOUL...SO CAN *OTHERS.*
I CAN REUNITE YOU WITH YOUR *PARENTS,* TIMOTHY.
YOU'RE CLEARLY IN NEED OF A *STRONG MENTOR.* SOMEONE WHO CAN BE A BENEFACTOR AND POWERFUL FRIEND TO YOU.
LUCKILY YOU DON'T HAVE TO LOOK *ANY FURTHER* FOR ONE.

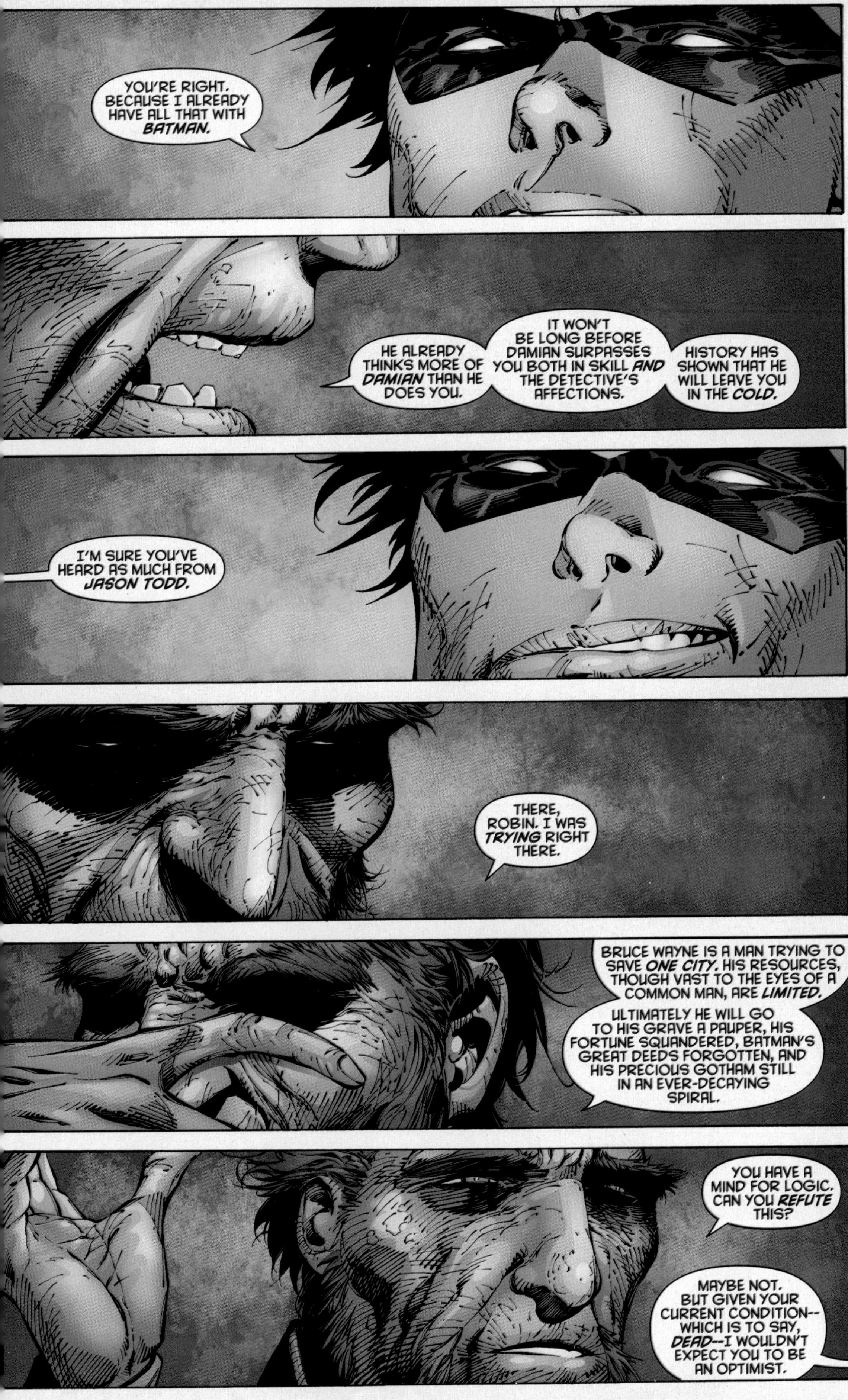
YOU'RE RIGHT. BECAUSE I ALREADY HAVE ALL THAT WITH BATMAN.
HE ALREADY THINKS MORE OF DAMIAN THAN HE DOES YOU.
IT WON'T BE LONG BEFORE DAMIAN SURPASSES YOU BOTH IN SKILL AND THE DETECTIVE'S AFFECTIONS.
HISTORY HAS SHOWN THAT HE WILL LEAVE YOU IN THE COLD.
I'M SURE YOU'VE HEARD AS MUCH FROM JASON TODD.
THERE, ROBIN. I WAS TRYING RIGHT THERE.
BRUCE WAYNE IS A MAN TRYING TO SAVE ONE CITY. HIS RESOURCES, THOUGH VAST TO THE EYES OF A COMMON MAN, ARE LIMITED.
ULTIMATELY HE WILL GO TO HIS GRAVE A PAUPER, HIS FORTUNE SQUANDERED, BATMAN'S GREAT DEEDS FORGOTTEN, AND HIS PRECIOUS GOTHAM STILL IN AN EVER-DECAYING SPIRAL.
YOU HAVE A MIND FOR LOGIC. CAN YOU REFUTE THIS?
MAYBE NOT. BUT GIVEN YOUR CURRENT CONDITION-- WHICH IS TO SAY, DEAD--I WOULDN'T EXPECT YOU TO BE AN OPTIMIST.

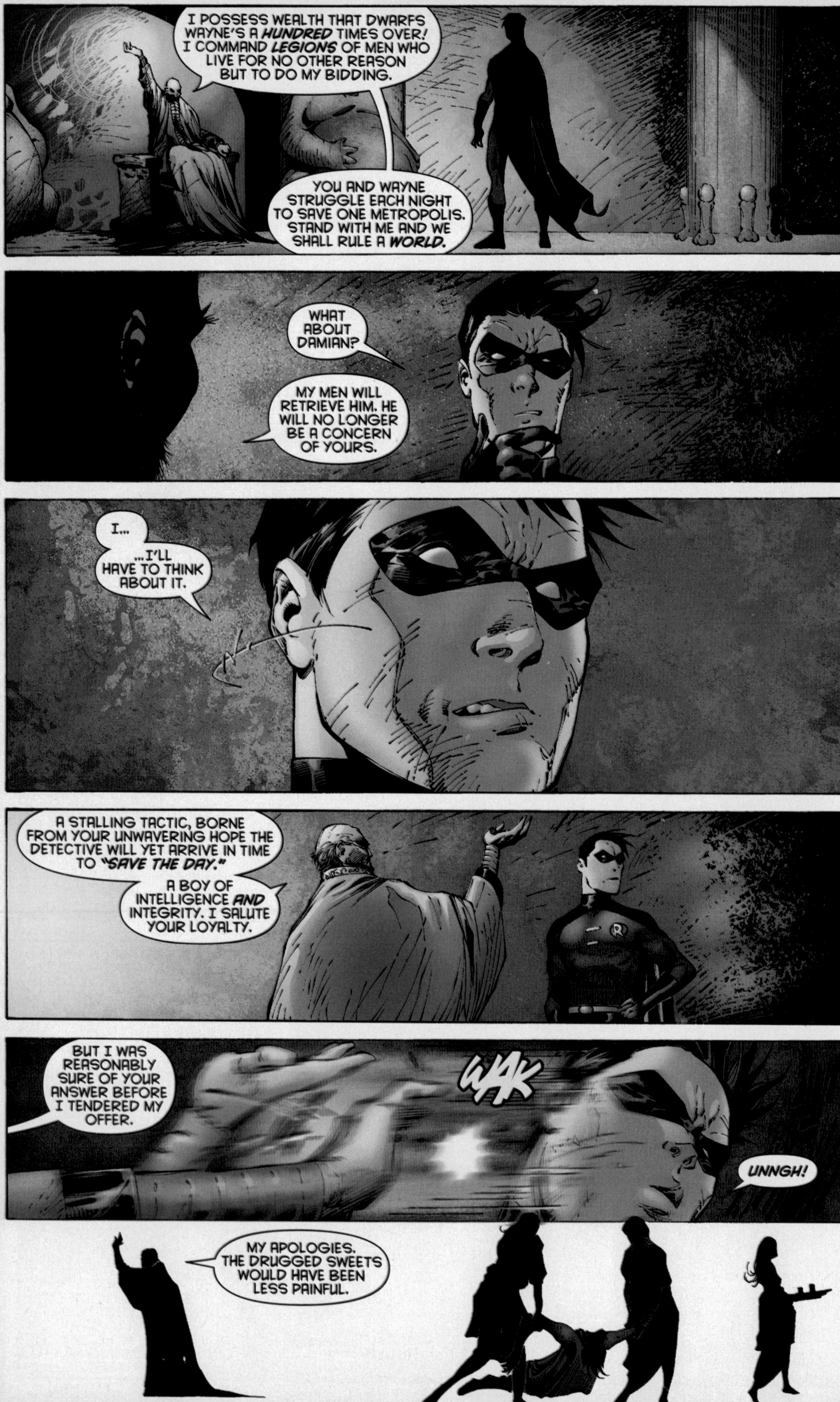
I POSSESS WEALTH THAT DWARFS WAYNE'S A HUNDRED TIMES OVER! I COMMAND LEGIONS OF MEN WHO LIVE FOR NO OTHER REASON BUT TO DO MY BIDDING.
YOU AND WAYNE STRUGGLE EACH NIGHT TO SAVE ONE METROPOLIS. STAND WITH ME AND WE SHALL RULE A WORLD.
WHAT ABOUT DAMIAN?
MY MEN WILL RETRIEVE HIM. HE WILL NO LONGER BE A CONCERN OF YOURS.
I...
...I'LL HAVE TO THINK ABOUT IT.
A STALLING TACTIC, BORNE FROM YOUR UNWAVERING HOPE THE DETECTIVE WILL YET ARRIVE IN TIME TO "SAVE THE DAY."
A BOY OF INTELLIGENCE AND INTEGRITY. I SALUTE YOUR LOYALTY.
BUT I WAS REASONABLY SURE OF YOUR ANSWER BEFORE I TENDERED MY OFFER.
WAK
UNNGH!
MY APOLOGIES. THE DRUGGED SWEETS WOULD HAVE BEEN LESS PAINFUL.

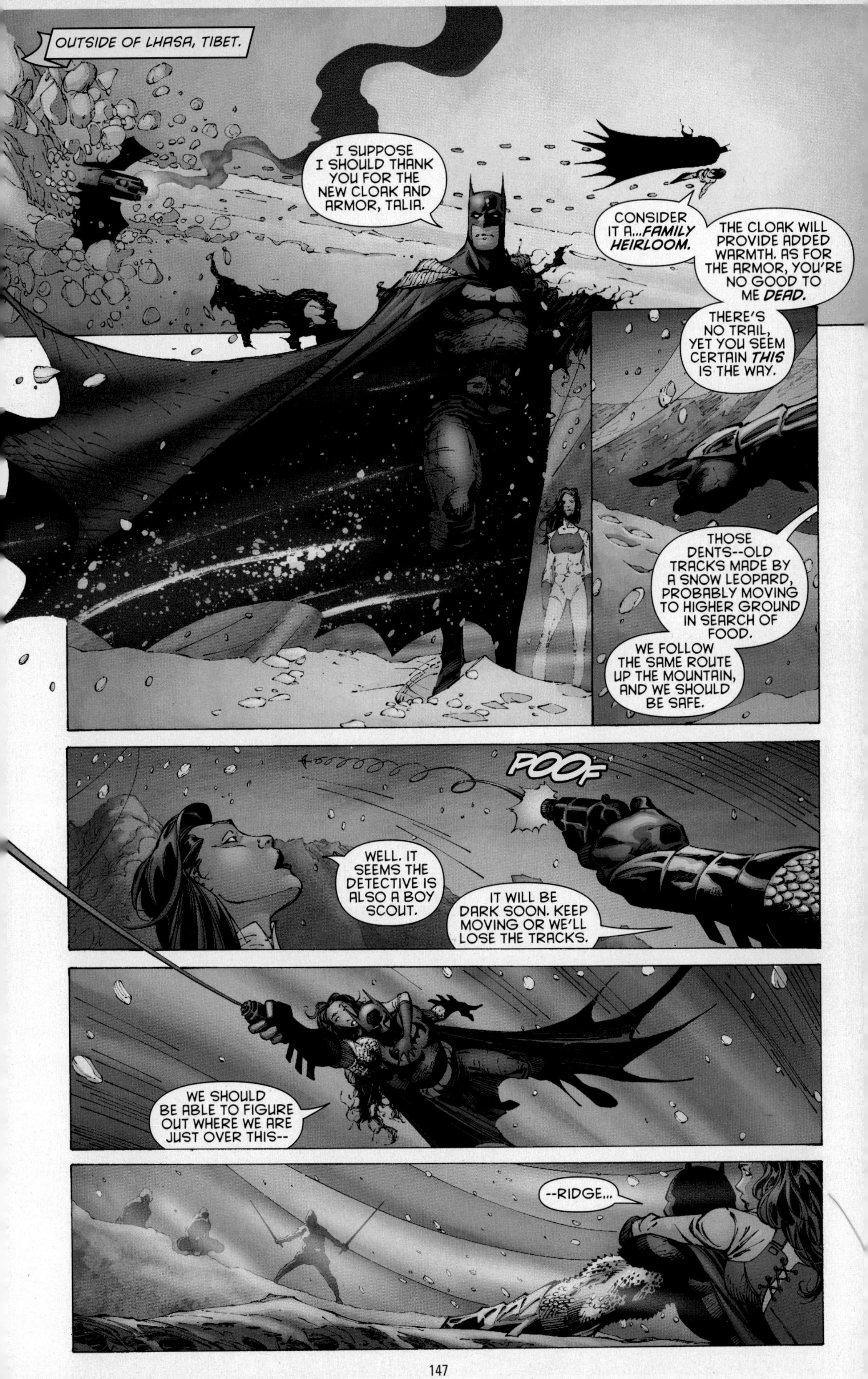
OUTSIDE OF LHASA, TIBET.
I SUPPOSE I SHOULD THANK YOU FOR THE NEW CLOAK AND ARMOR, TALIA.
CONSIDER IT A...FAMILY HEIRLOOM.
THE CLOAK WILL PROVIDE ADDED WARMTH. AS FOR THE ARMOR, YOU'RE NO GOOD TO ME DEAD.
THERE'S NO TRAIL, YET YOU SEEM CERTAIN THIS IS THE WAY.
THOSE DENTS--OLD TRACKS MADE BY A SNOW LEOPARD, PROBABLY MOVING TO HIGHER GROUND IN SEARCH OF FOOD.
WE FOLLOW THE SAME ROUTE UP THE MOUNTAIN, AND WE SHOULD BE SAFE.
POOF
WELL. IT SEEMS THE DETECTIVE IS ALSO A BOY SCOUT.
IT WILL BE DARK SOON. KEEP MOVING OR WE'LL LOSE THE TRACKS.
WE SHOULD BE ABLE TO FIGURE OUT WHERE WE ARE JUST OVER THIS--
--RIDGE...

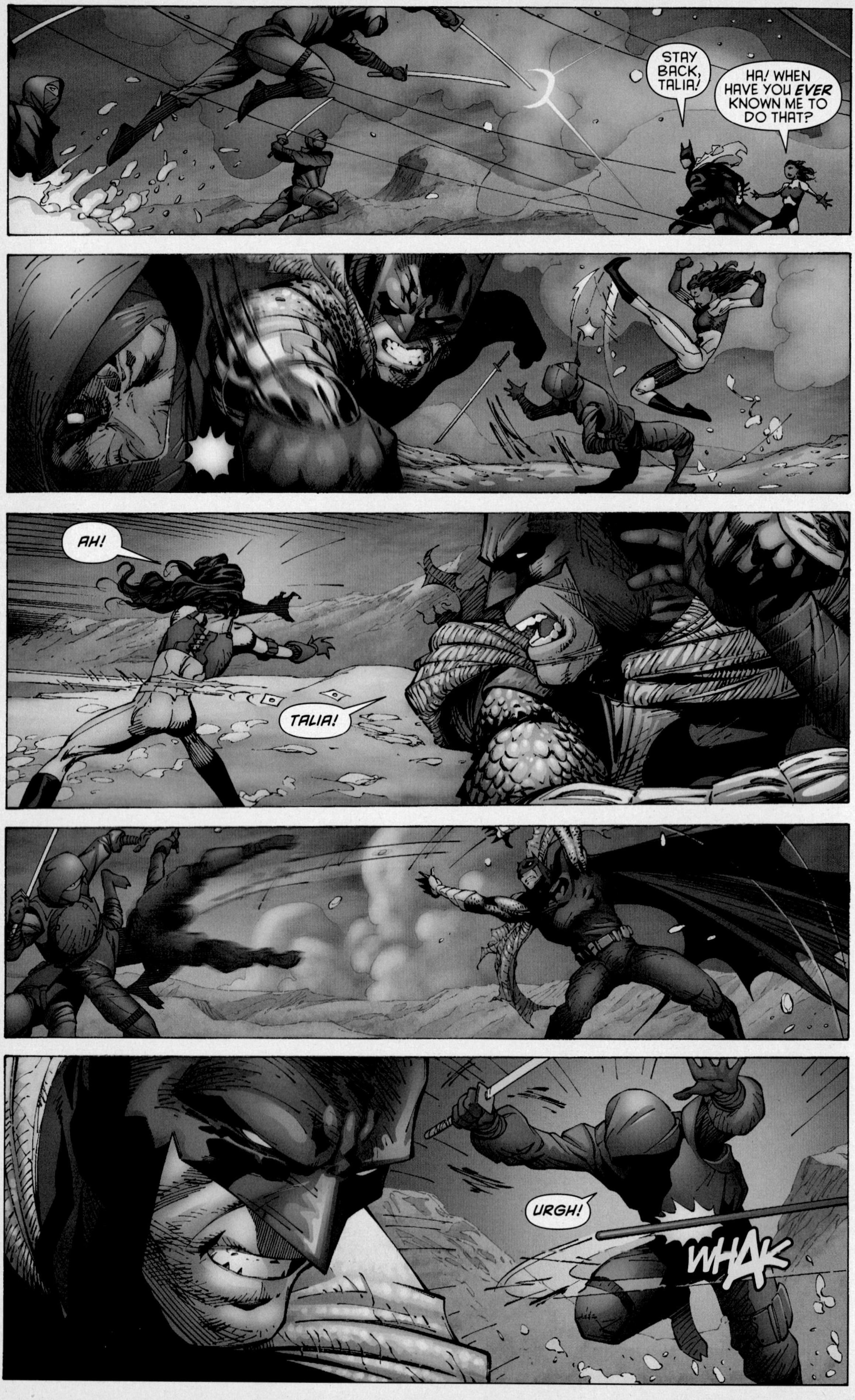
STAY BACK, TALIA!
HA! WHEN HAVE YOU EVER KNOWN ME TO DO THAT?
AH!
TALIA!
URGH!
WHAK

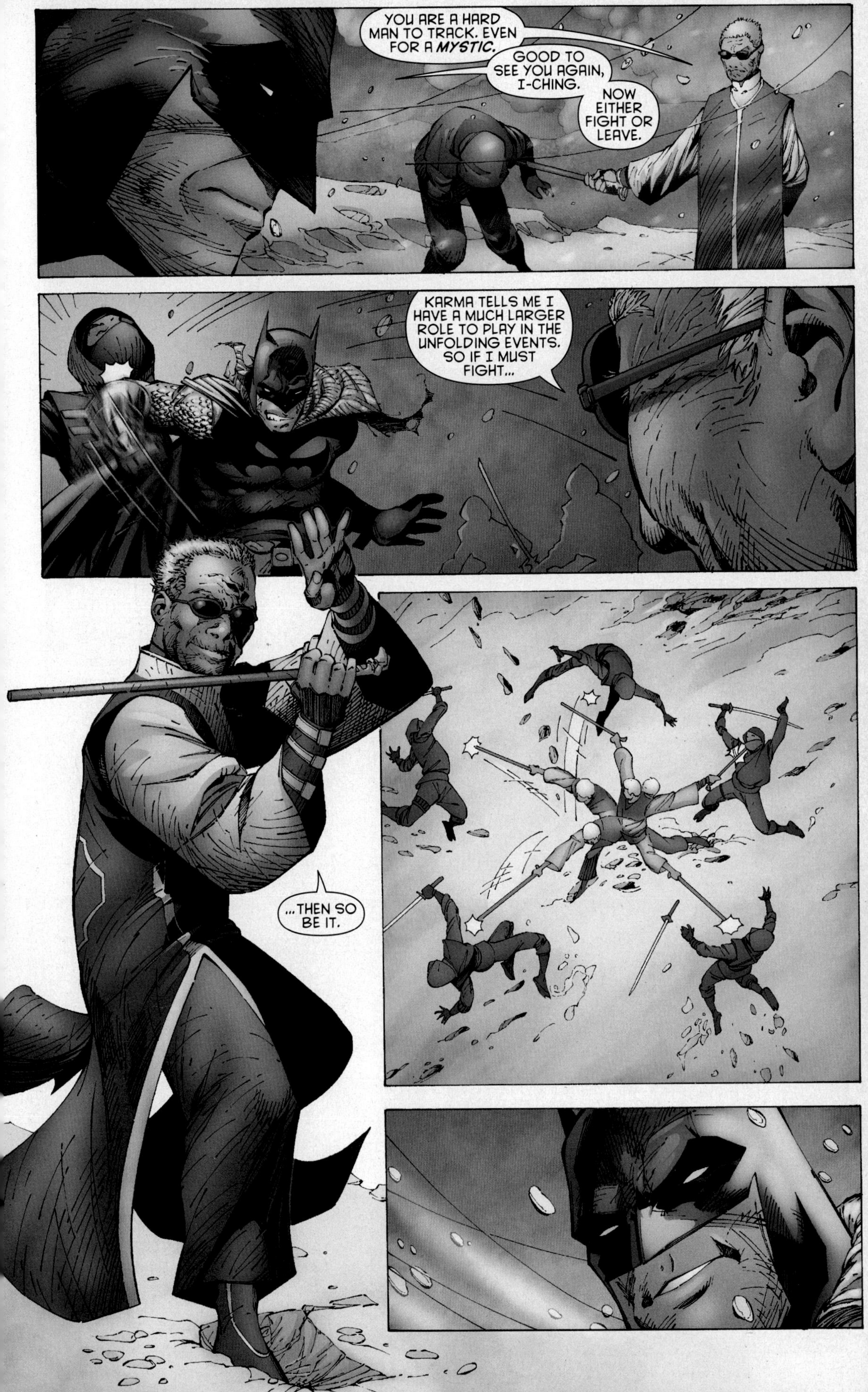
YOU ARE A HARD MAN TO TRACK. EVEN FOR A *MYSTIC.*
GOOD TO SEE YOU AGAIN, I-CHING.
NOW EITHER FIGHT OR LEAVE.
KARMA TELLS ME I HAVE A MUCH LARGER ROLE TO PLAY IN THE UNFOLDING EVENTS. SO IF I MUST FIGHT...
...THEN SO BE IT.

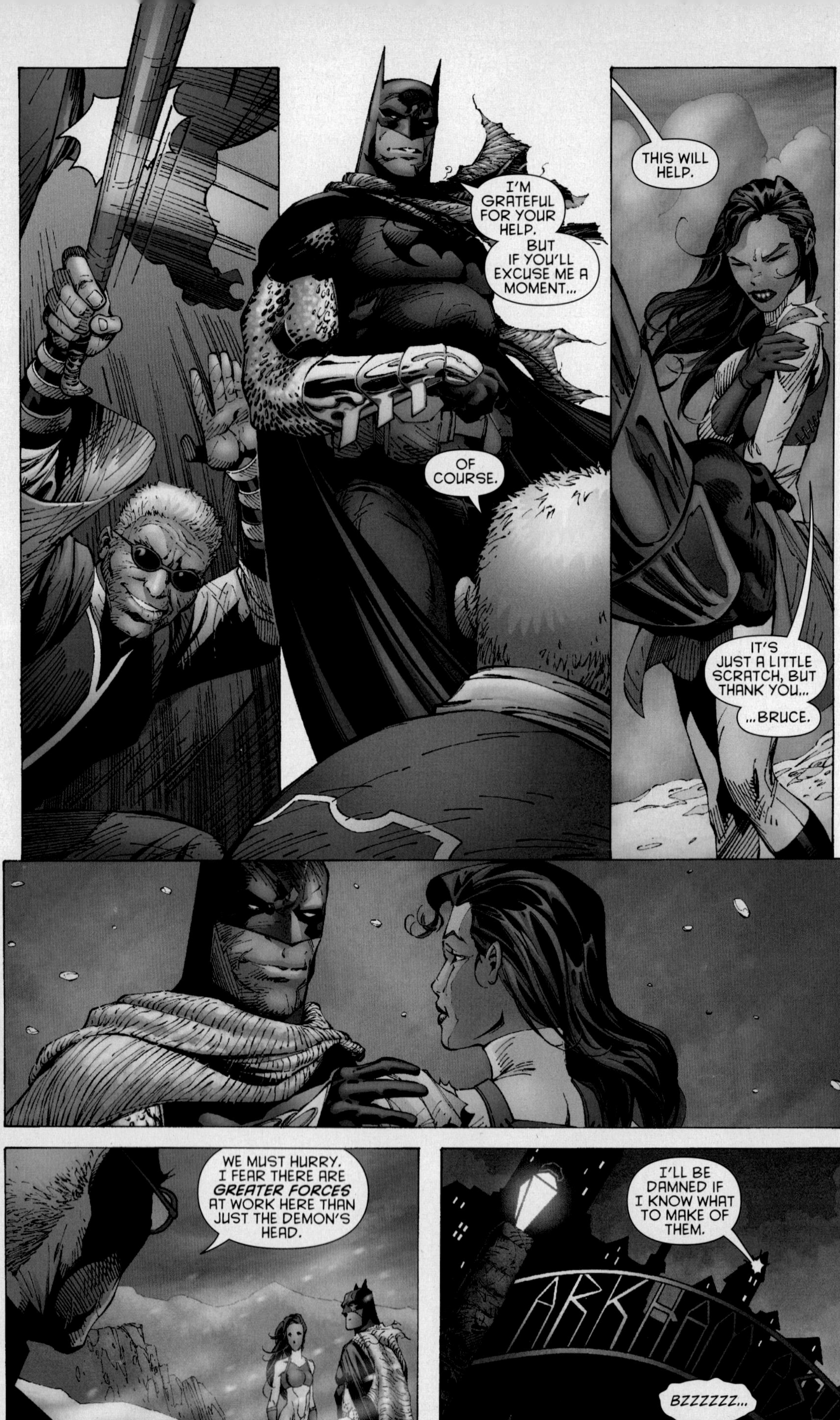
I'M GRATEFUL FOR YOUR HELP.
BUT IF YOU'LL EXCUSE ME A MOMENT...
OF COURSE.
THIS WILL HELP.
IT'S JUST A LITTLE SCRATCH, BUT THANK YOU...
...BRUCE.
WE MUST HURRY. I FEAR THERE ARE GREATER FORCES AT WORK HERE THAN JUST THE DEMON'S HEAD.
I'LL BE DAMNED IF I KNOW WHAT TO MAKE OF THEM.
ARKHAM
BZZZZZZ...

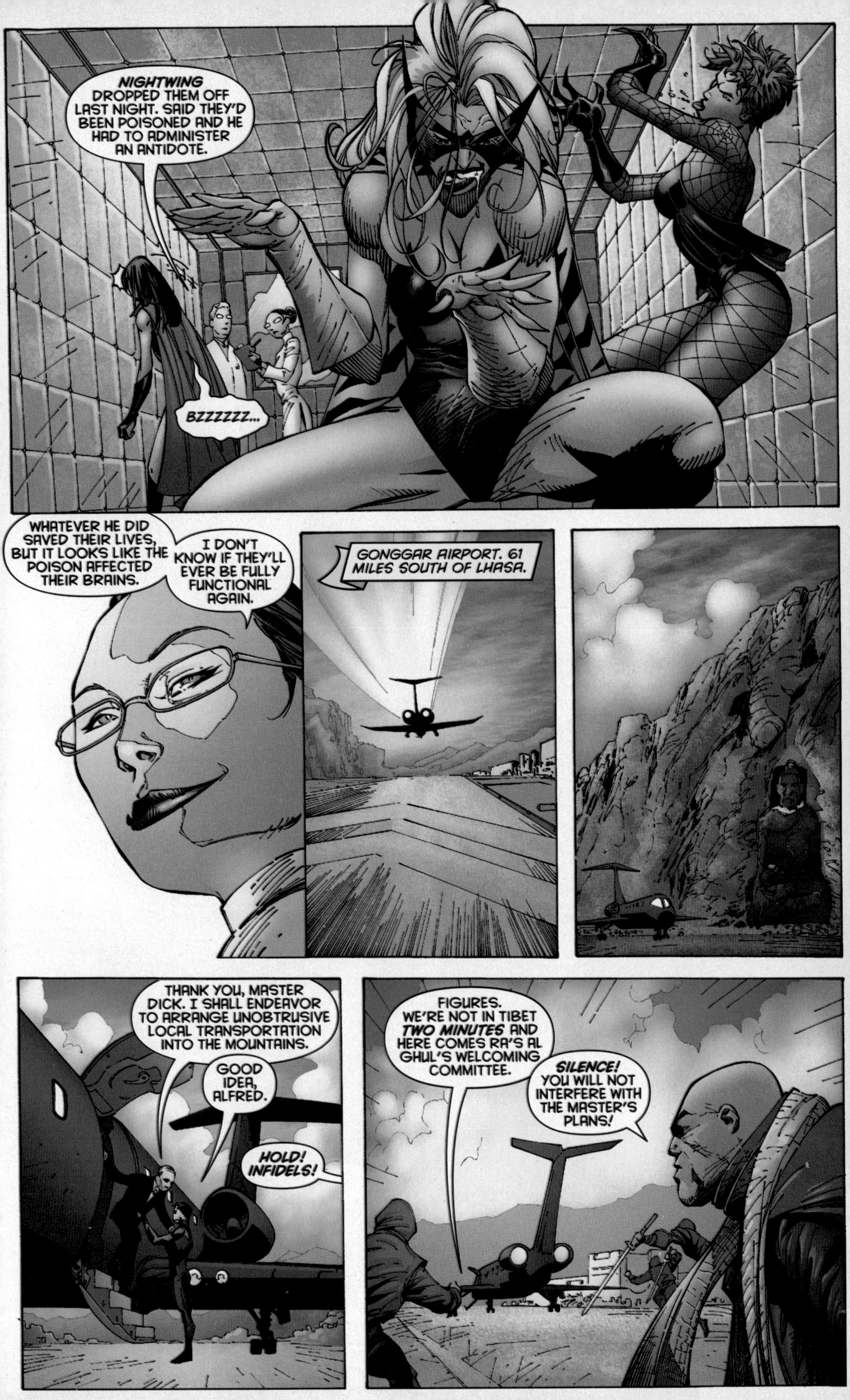
NIGHTWING DROPPED THEM OFF LAST NIGHT. SAID THEY'D BEEN POISONED AND HE HAD TO ADMINISTER AN ANTIDOTE.
BZZZZZZ...
WHATEVER HE DID SAVED THEIR LIVES, BUT IT LOOKS LIKE THE POISON AFFECTED THEIR BRAINS.
I DON'T KNOW IF THEY'LL EVER BE FULLY FUNCTIONAL AGAIN.
GONGGAR AIRPORT. 61 MILES SOUTH OF LHASA.
THANK YOU, MASTER DICK. I SHALL ENDEAVOR TO ARRANGE UNOBTRUSIVE LOCAL TRANSPORTATION INTO THE MOUNTAINS.
GOOD IDEA, ALFRED.
HOLD! INFIDELS!
FIGURES. WE'RE NOT IN TIBET TWO MINUTES AND HERE COMES RA'S AL GHUL'S WELCOMING COMMITTEE.
SILENCE! YOU WILL NOT INTERFERE WITH THE MASTER'S PLANS!

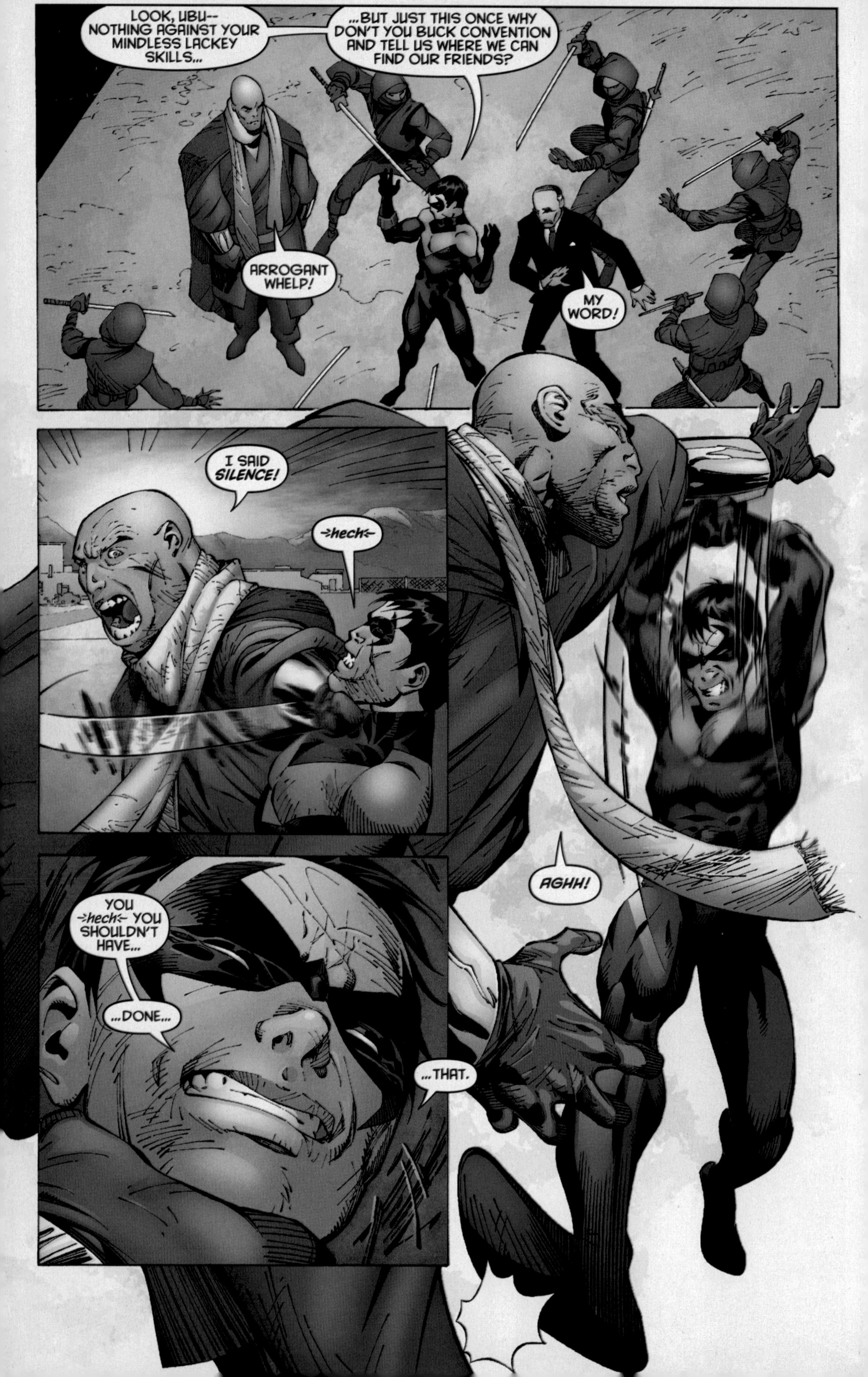

LOOK, UBU--
NOTHING AGAINST YOUR MINDLESS LACKEY SKILLS...
...BUT JUST THIS ONCE WHY DON'T YOU BUCK CONVENTION AND TELL US WHERE WE CAN FIND OUR FRIENDS?
ARROGANT WHELP!
MY WORD!
I SAID SILENCE!
-hech-
AGHH!
YOU -hech- YOU SHOULDN'T HAVE...
...DONE...
...THAT.

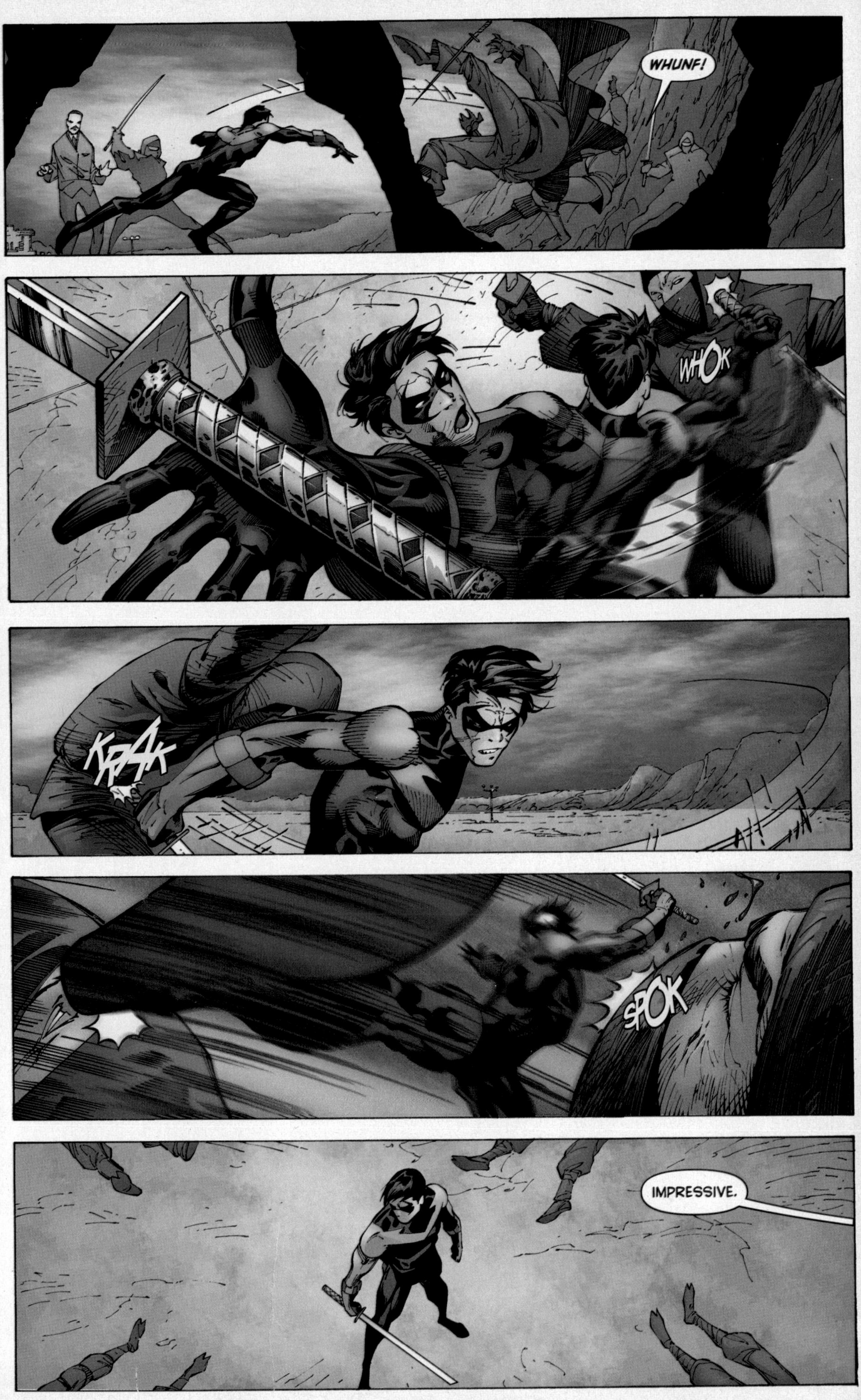
WHUNF!
WHOK
KRAK
SPOK
IMPRESSIVE.

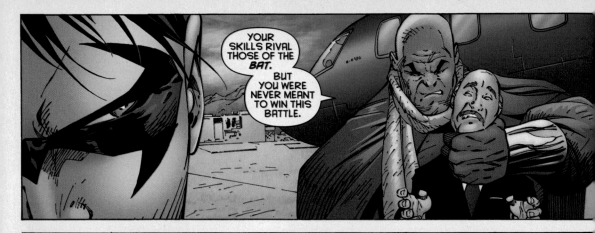

YOUR SKILLS RIVAL THOSE OF THE *BAT*.

BUT YOU WERE NEVER MEANT TO WIN THIS BATTLE.

I AM FIRST AMONG ACOLYTES TO THE GREAT RA'S AL GHUL AND *CANNOT* FAIL HIM. LEAVE TIBET OR I SNAP THIS SERVANT'S NECK.

DESPITE MY CURRENT PREDICAMENT, I MUST SAY IT IS A PLEASURE TO MEET A KINDRED SOUL.

REALLY, MENIAL? WHAT *KINSHIP* COULD YOU CLAIM TO ME?

UUFF!

YOU SEE, I AM EVERY BIT AS LOYAL TO BATMAN AS YOU ARE TO RA'S, AND I TOO CANNOT FAIL *HIM*.

WELL DONE, FAITHFUL ACOLYTE.

ALL PART OF THE SERVICE, SIR.

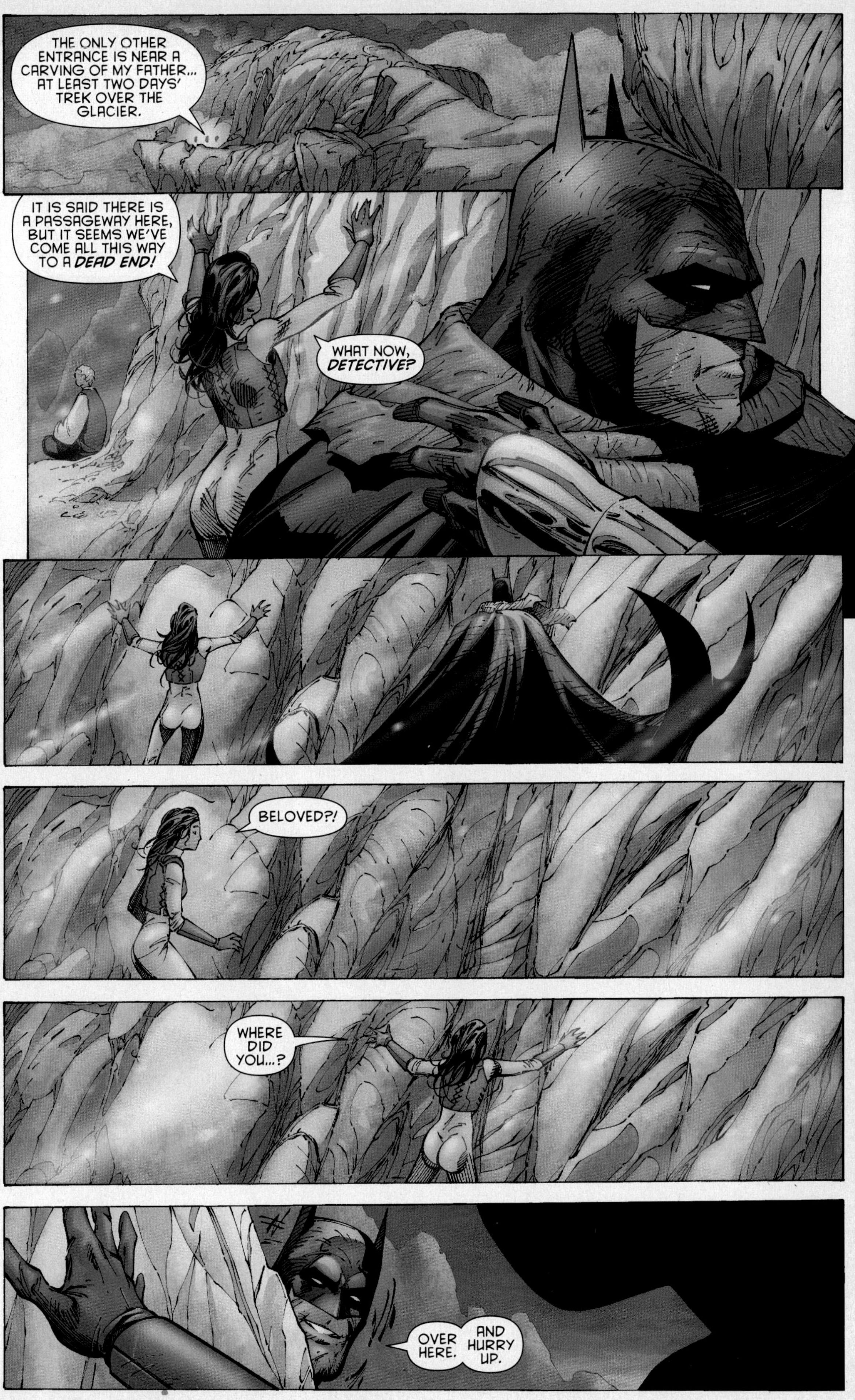
THE ONLY OTHER ENTRANCE IS NEAR A CARVING OF MY FATHER... AT LEAST TWO DAYS' TREK OVER THE GLACIER.
IT IS SAID THERE IS A PASSAGEWAY HERE, BUT IT SEEMS WE'VE COME ALL THIS WAY TO A *DEAD END!*
WHAT NOW, *DETECTIVE?*
BELOVED?!
WHERE DID YOU...?
OVER HERE.
AND HURRY UP.

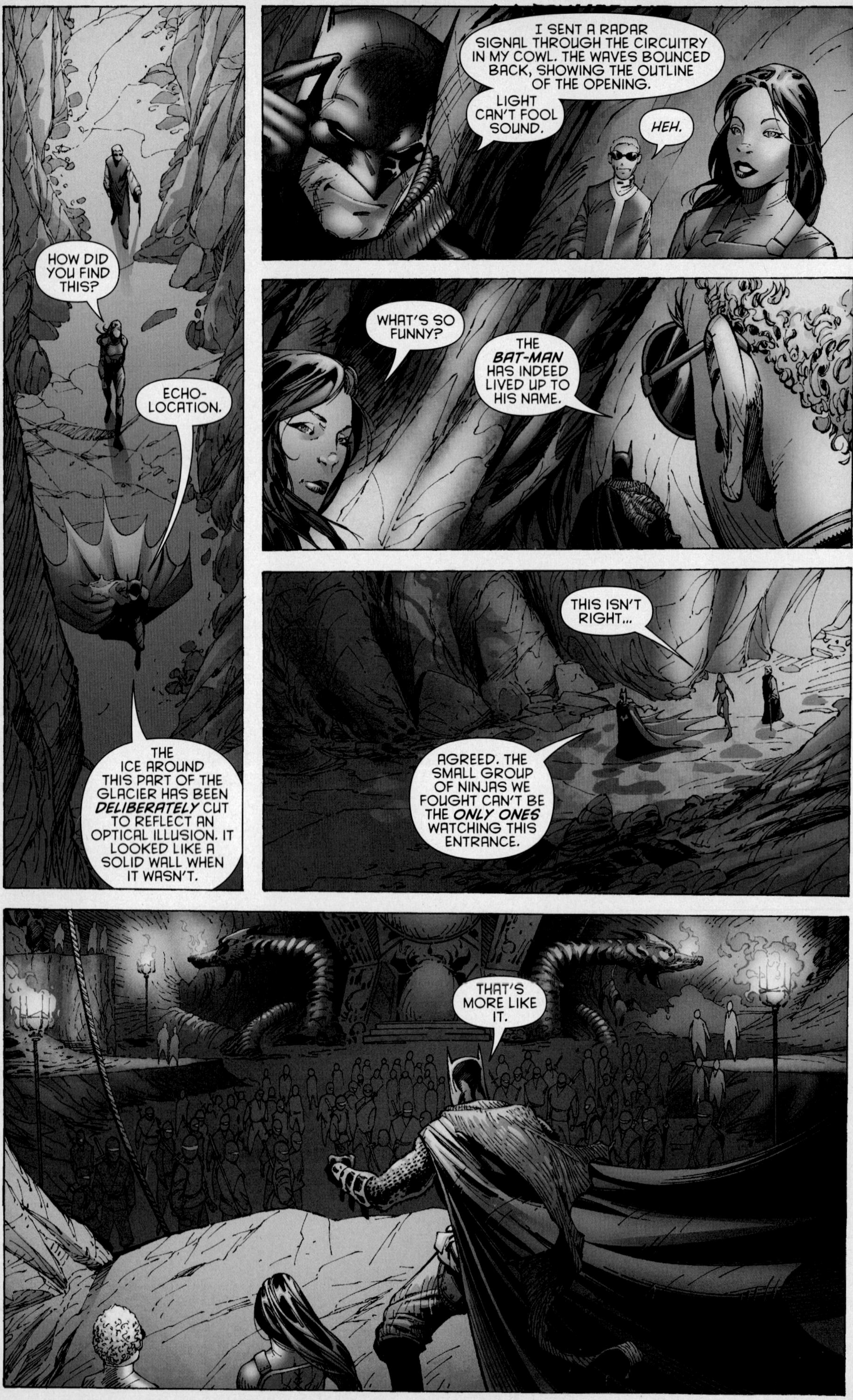
HOW DID YOU FIND THIS?
ECHO-LOCATION.
THE ICE AROUND THIS PART OF THE GLACIER HAS BEEN DELIBERATELY CUT TO REFLECT AN OPTICAL ILLUSION. IT LOOKED LIKE A SOLID WALL WHEN IT WASN'T.
I SENT A RADAR SIGNAL THROUGH THE CIRCUITRY IN MY COWL. THE WAVES BOUNCED BACK, SHOWING THE OUTLINE OF THE OPENING.
LIGHT CAN'T FOOL SOUND.
HEH.
WHAT'S SO FUNNY?
THE BAT-MAN HAS INDEED LIVED UP TO HIS NAME.
THIS ISN'T RIGHT...
AGREED. THE SMALL GROUP OF NINJAS WE FOUGHT CAN'T BE THE ONLY ONES WATCHING THIS ENTRANCE.
THAT'S MORE LIKE IT.

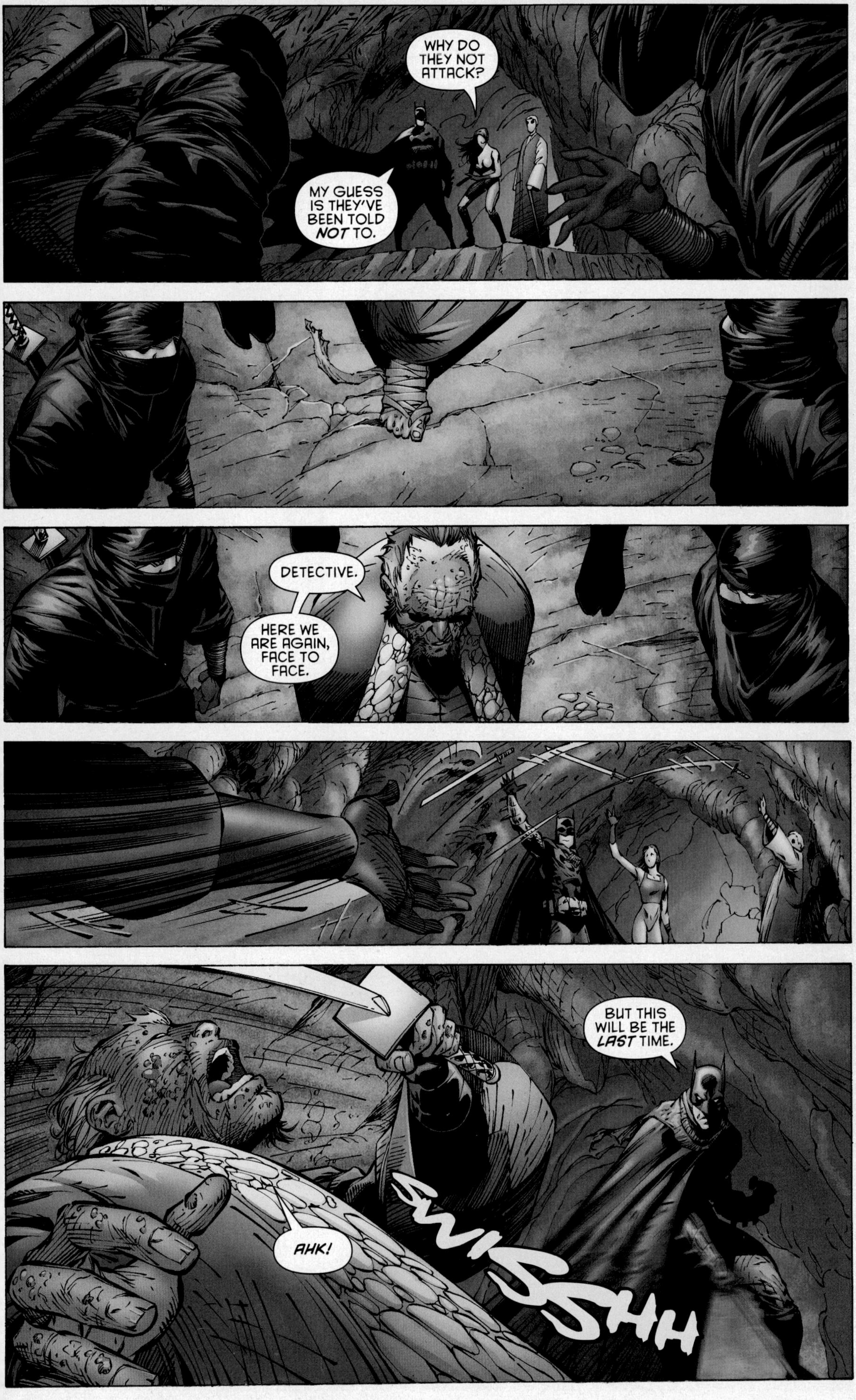
WHY DO THEY NOT ATTACK?
MY GUESS IS THEY'VE BEEN TOLD *NOT* TO.
DETECTIVE.
HERE WE ARE AGAIN, FACE TO FACE.
BUT THIS WILL BE THE *LAST* TIME.
SWISSHH
AHK!

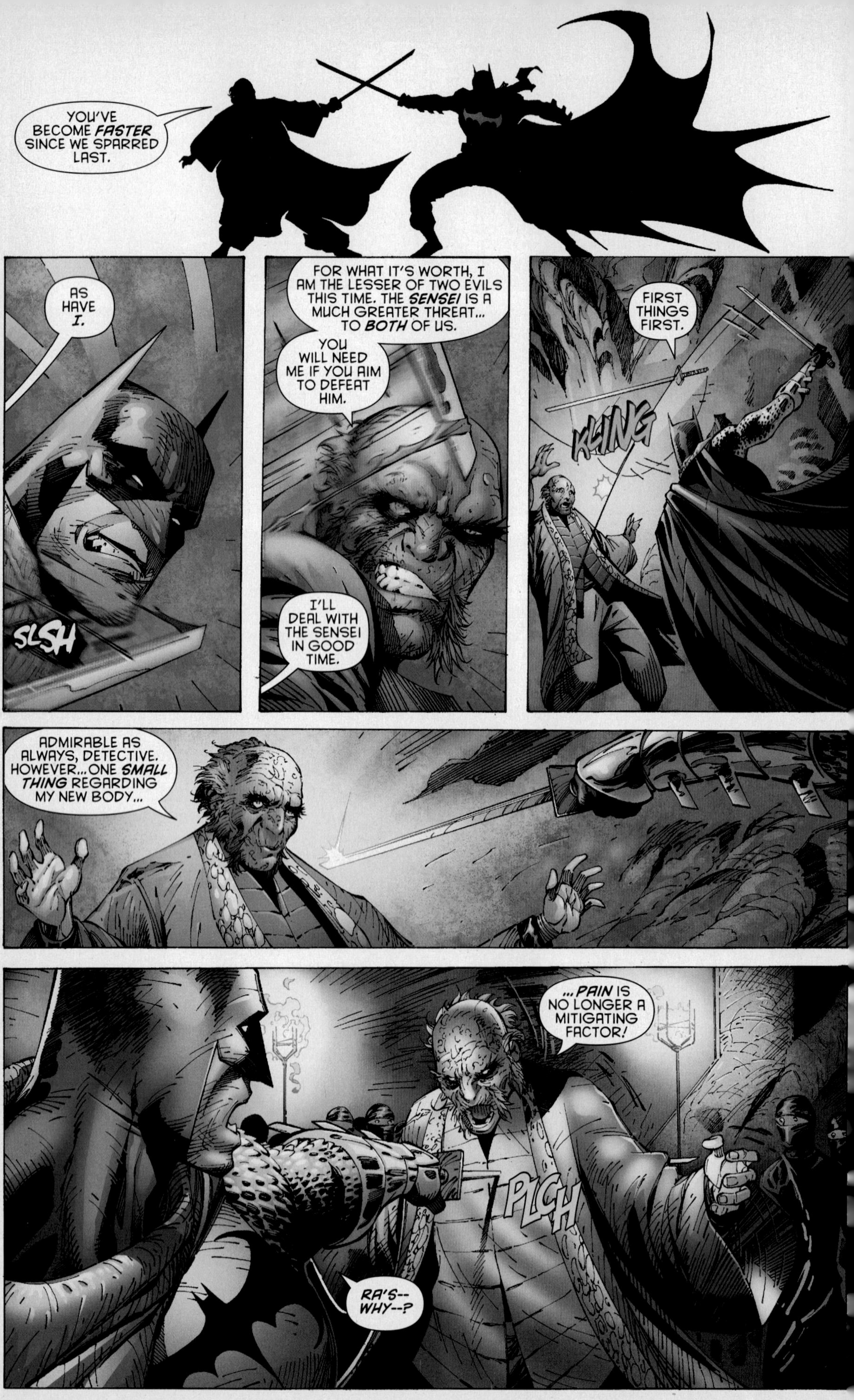
YOU'VE BECOME FASTER SINCE WE SPARRED LAST.
AS HAVE I.
SLSH
FOR WHAT IT'S WORTH, I AM THE LESSER OF TWO EVILS THIS TIME. THE SENSEI IS A MUCH GREATER THREAT... TO BOTH OF US.
YOU WILL NEED ME IF YOU AIM TO DEFEAT HIM.
I'LL DEAL WITH THE SENSEI IN GOOD TIME.
FIRST THINGS FIRST.
KLING
ADMIRABLE AS ALWAYS, DETECTIVE. HOWEVER...ONE SMALL THING REGARDING MY NEW BODY...
...PAIN IS NO LONGER A MITIGATING FACTOR!
PLCH
RA'S-- WHY--?

THAT'S THE NICE THING ABOUT COMING BACK IN A *CORPSE*.

THERE ARE DOWNSIDES, OF COURSE.

FOR INSTANCE, MY STATE OF *DECAY* IS INCREASING *EXPONENTIALLY*.

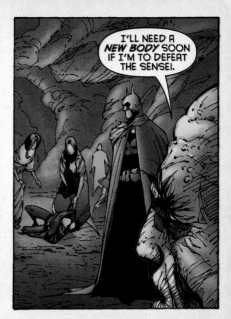

I'LL NEED A *NEW BODY* SOON IF I'M TO DEFEAT THE SENSEI.

ROBIN!

DO NOT WORRY... I MAY NOT USE *HIS* BODY.

THERE IS *ANOTHER* OPTION...

DAMIAN!

YOU BOTH SHOULD BE *PROUD*... IT TOOK A SQUAD OF MY BEST TO TRACK DAMIAN DOWN.

LET THEM *GO*, RA'S. YOU NEED A HOST BODY, TAKE *MINE*.

NO, BRUCE!

CLICHÉD, DETECTIVE. EVEN FOR YOU. NO, I CRAVE *YOUTH*.

MONSTER! YOU CANNOT...!

SUPPRESS THE OLD FAKER.

UGHH!

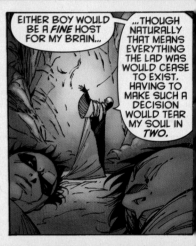

EITHER BOY WOULD BE A *FINE* HOST FOR MY BRAIN...

...THOUGH NATURALLY THAT MEANS EVERYTHING THE LAD WAS WOULD CEASE TO EXIST. HAVING TO MAKE SUCH A DECISION WOULD TEAR MY SOUL IN *TWO*.

WHICH IS WHY I'M GOING TO MAKE *YOU* DO IT.

WHICH WILL IT BE, DETECTIVE?

WHICH ONE OF YOUR BOYS LIVES...

...AND WHICH ONE *DIES?*

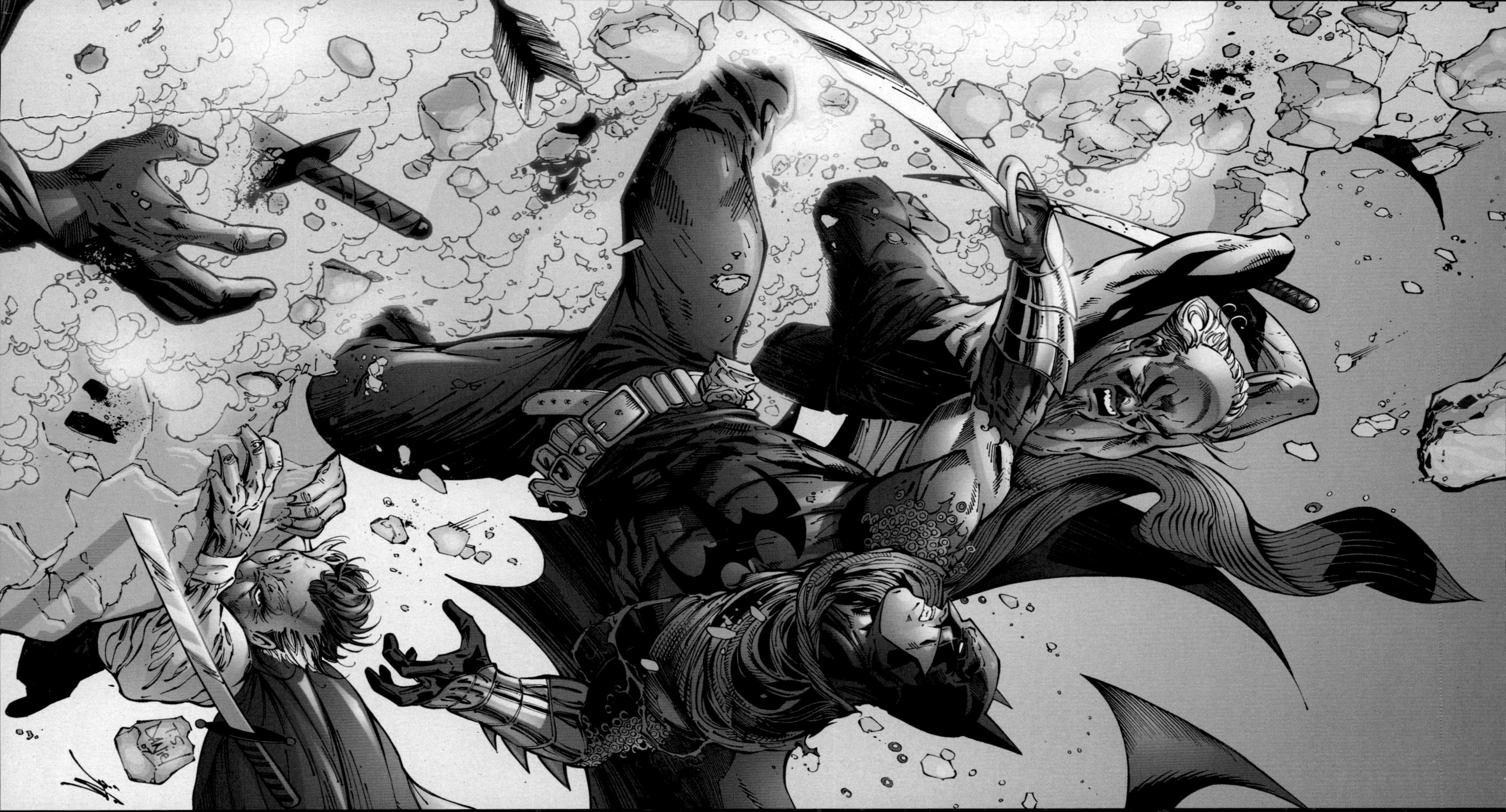

CHAPTER FOUR HE WHO IS MASTER

Cover art by Tony S. Daniel and Jonathan Glapion | Chapter written by Grant Morrison | Chapter pencilled by Tony S. Daniel | Chapter inked by Jonathan Glapion

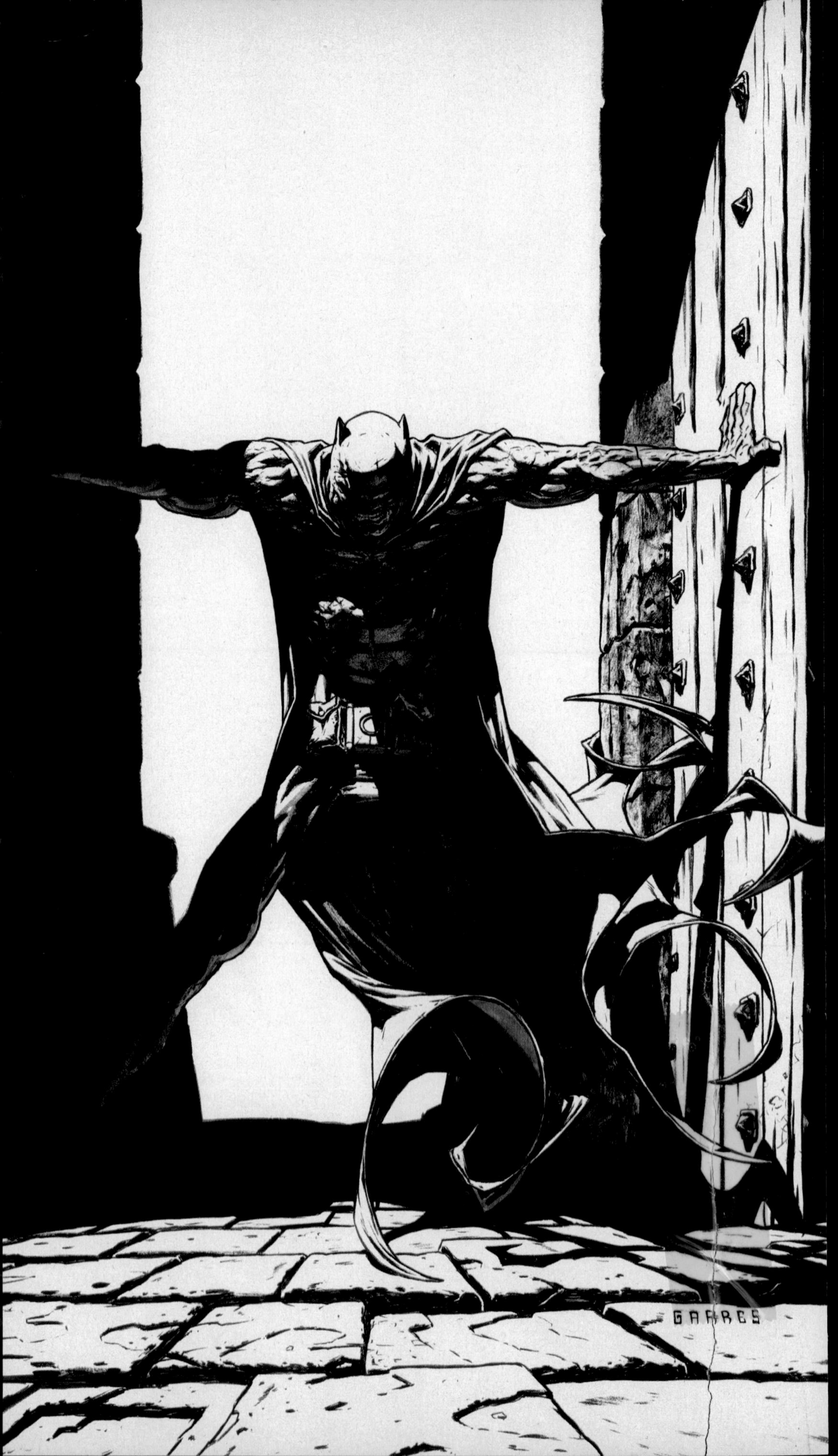

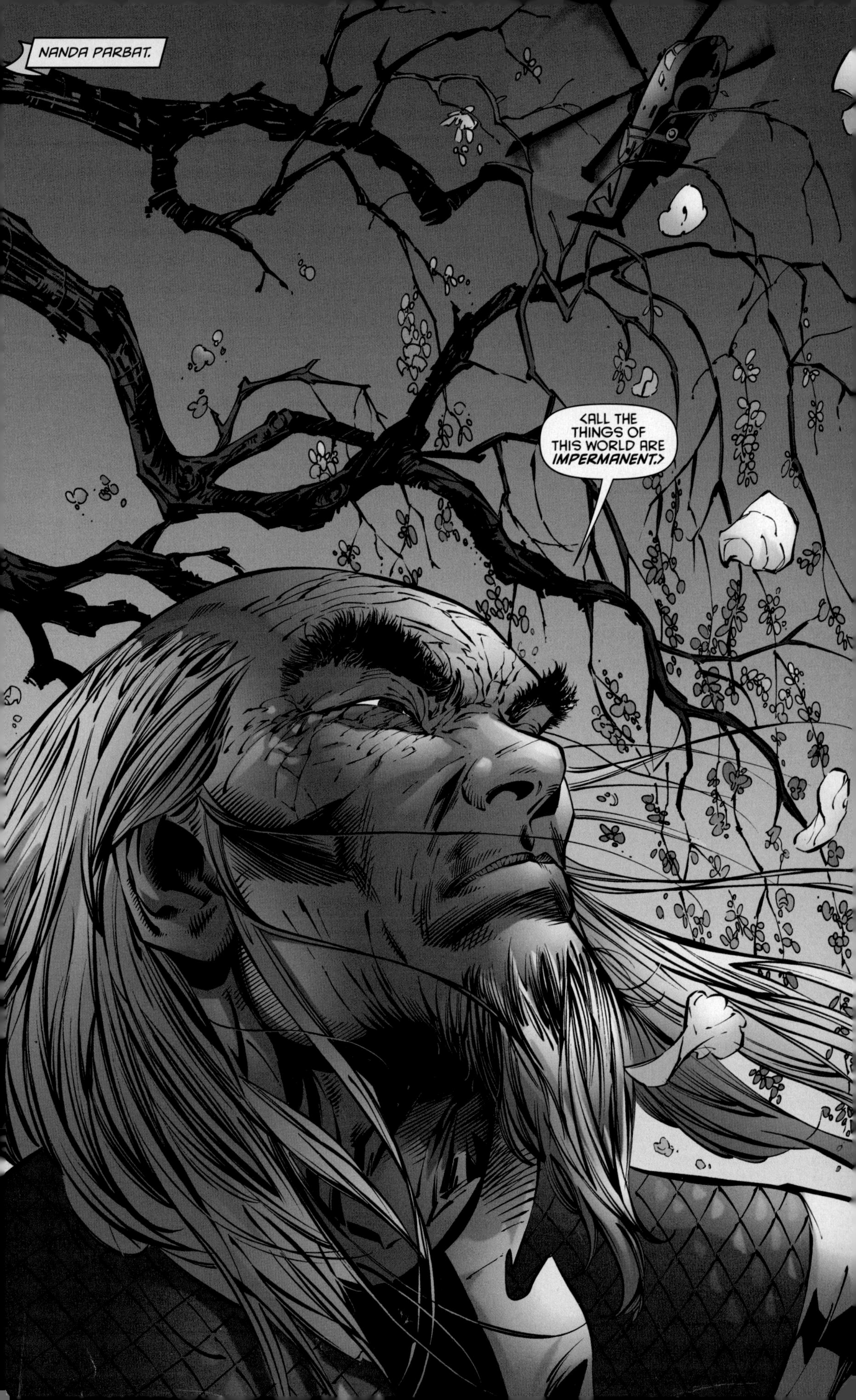
NANDA PARBAT.
<ALL THE THINGS OF THIS WORLD ARE *IMPERMANENT.*>

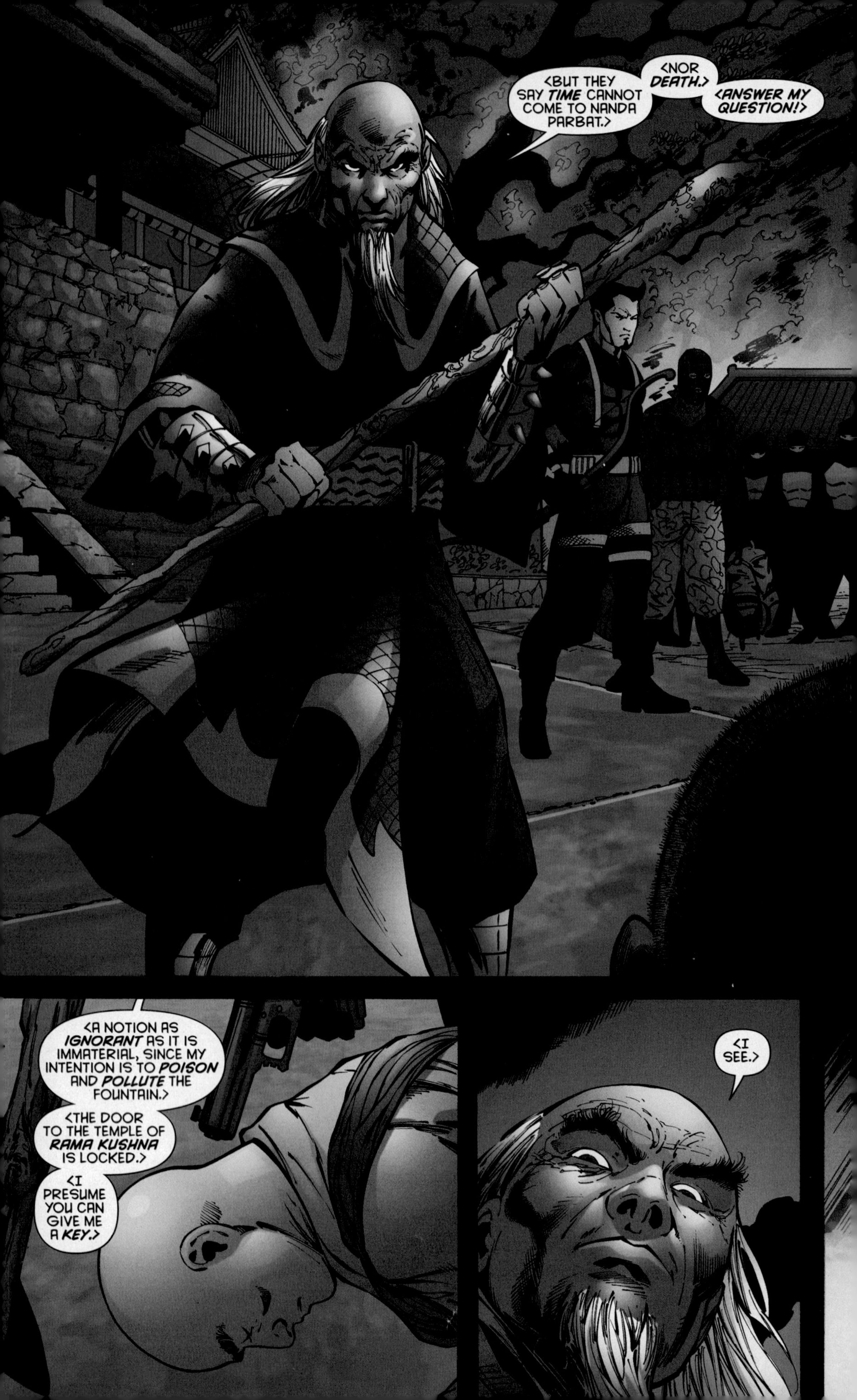

<BUT THEY SAY *TIME* CANNOT COME TO NANDA PARBAT.>
<NOR *DEATH.*>
<*ANSWER MY QUESTION!*>
<A NOTION AS *IGNORANT* AS IT IS IMMATERIAL, SINCE MY INTENTION IS TO *POISON* AND *POLLUTE* THE FOUNTAIN.>
<THE DOOR TO THE TEMPLE OF *RAMA KUSHNA* IS LOCKED.>
<I PRESUME YOU CAN GIVE ME A *KEY.*>
<I SEE.>

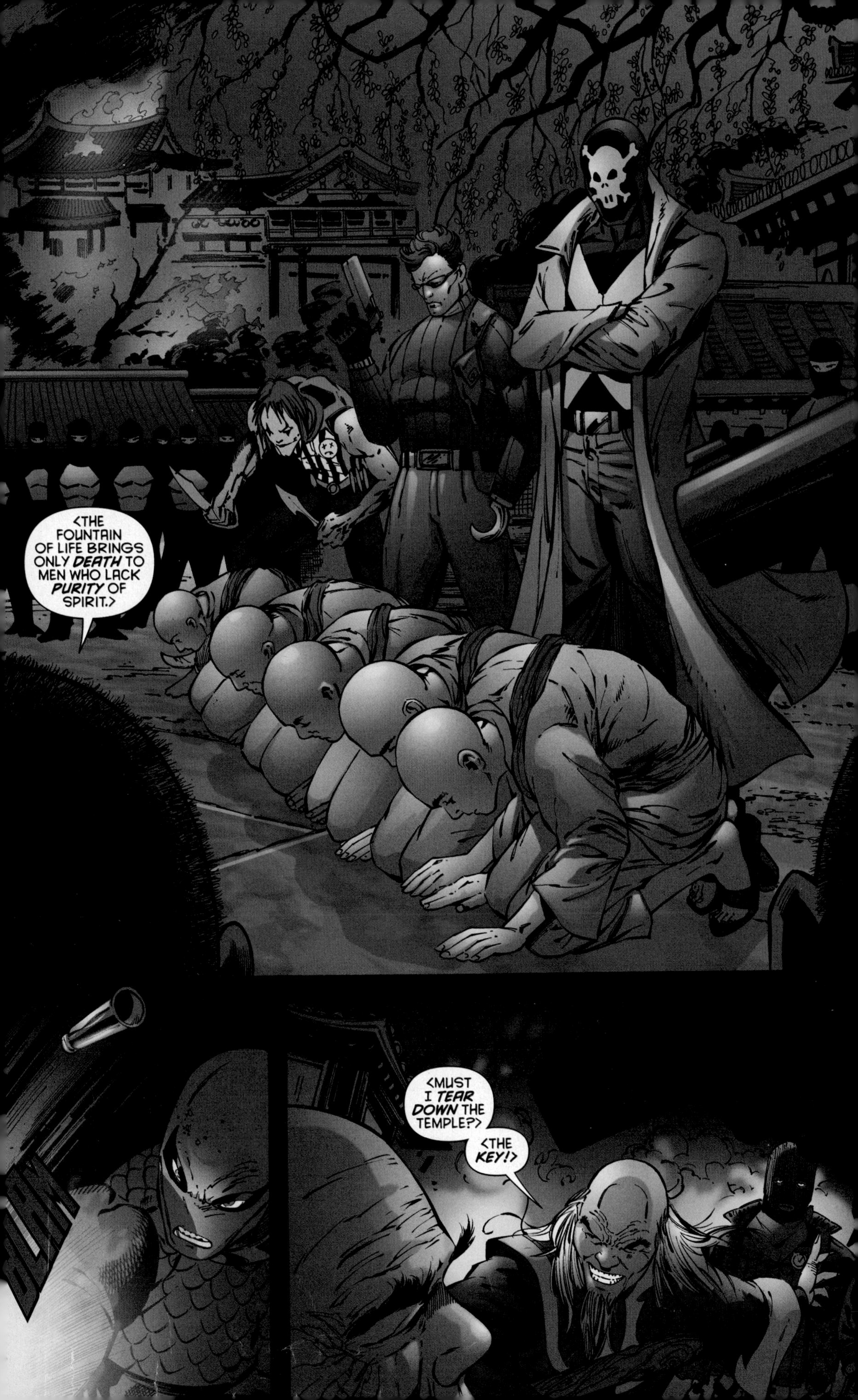

<THE FOUNTAIN OF LIFE BRINGS ONLY DEATH TO MEN WHO LACK PURITY OF SPIRIT.>
<MUST I TEAR DOWN THE TEMPLE?>
<THE KEY!>

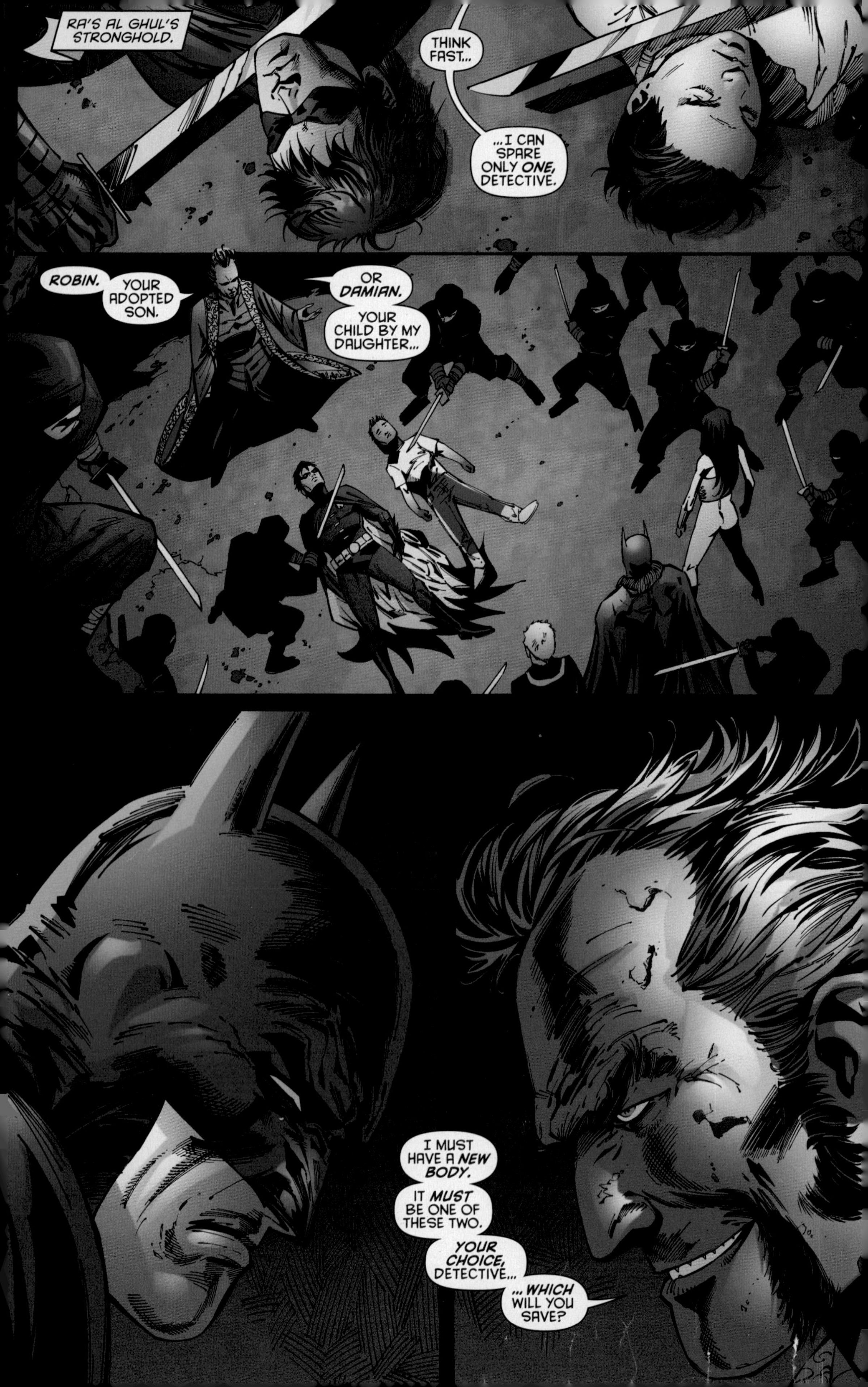
RA'S AL GHUL'S STRONGHOLD.
THINK FAST...
...I CAN SPARE ONLY *ONE,* DETECTIVE.
ROBIN.
YOUR ADOPTED SON.
OR ***DAMIAN.***
YOUR CHILD BY MY DAUGHTER...
I MUST HAVE A ***NEW BODY.***
IT ***MUST*** BE ONE OF THESE TWO.
YOUR CHOICE, DETECTIVE...
...***WHICH*** WILL YOU SAVE?

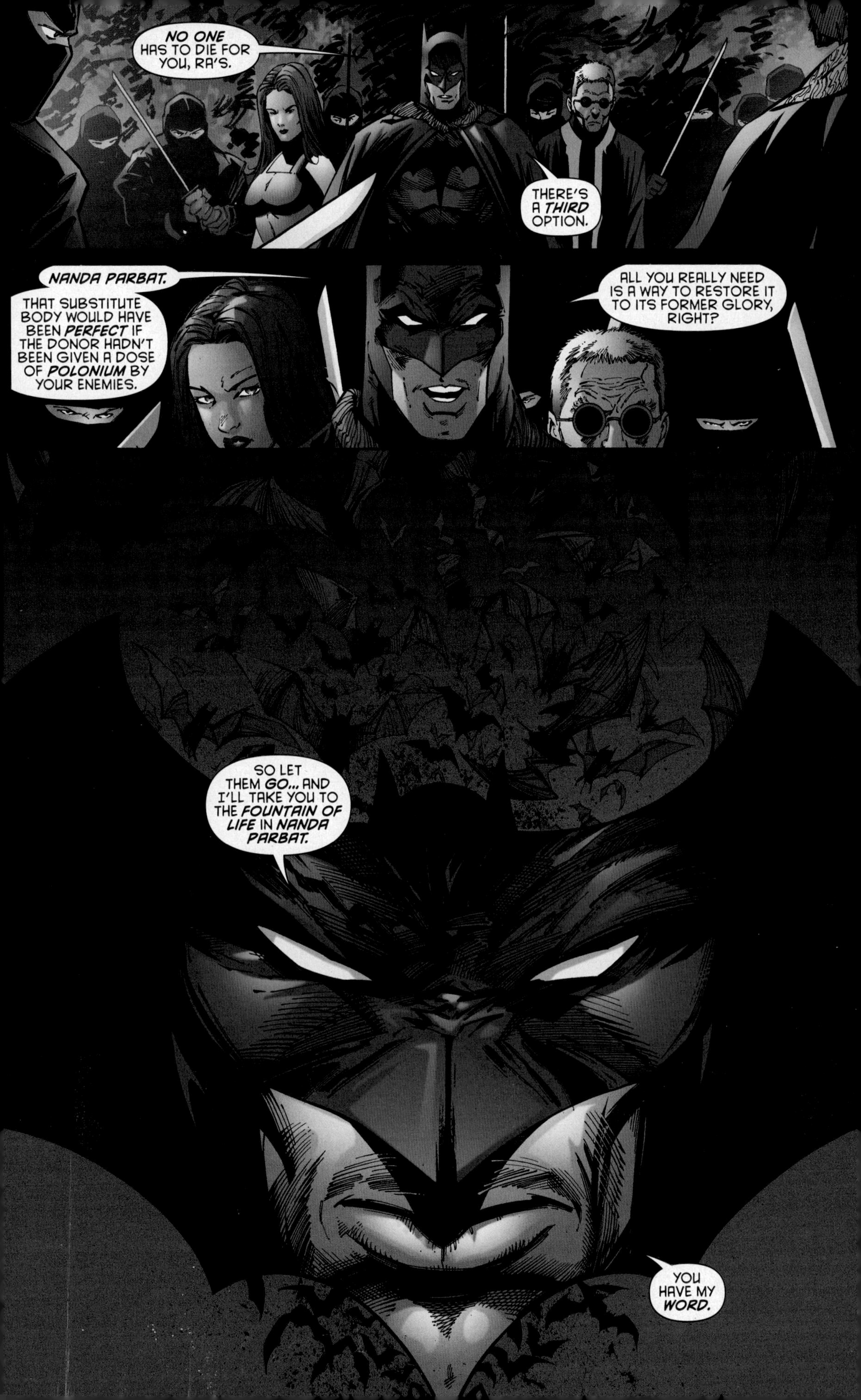
NO ONE HAS TO DIE FOR YOU, RA'S.
THERE'S A THIRD OPTION.
NANDA PARBAT.
THAT SUBSTITUTE BODY WOULD HAVE BEEN PERFECT IF THE DONOR HADN'T BEEN GIVEN A DOSE OF POLONIUM BY YOUR ENEMIES.
ALL YOU REALLY NEED IS A WAY TO RESTORE IT TO ITS FORMER GLORY, RIGHT?
SO LET THEM GO... AND I'LL TAKE YOU TO THE FOUNTAIN OF LIFE IN NANDA PARBAT.
YOU HAVE MY WORD.

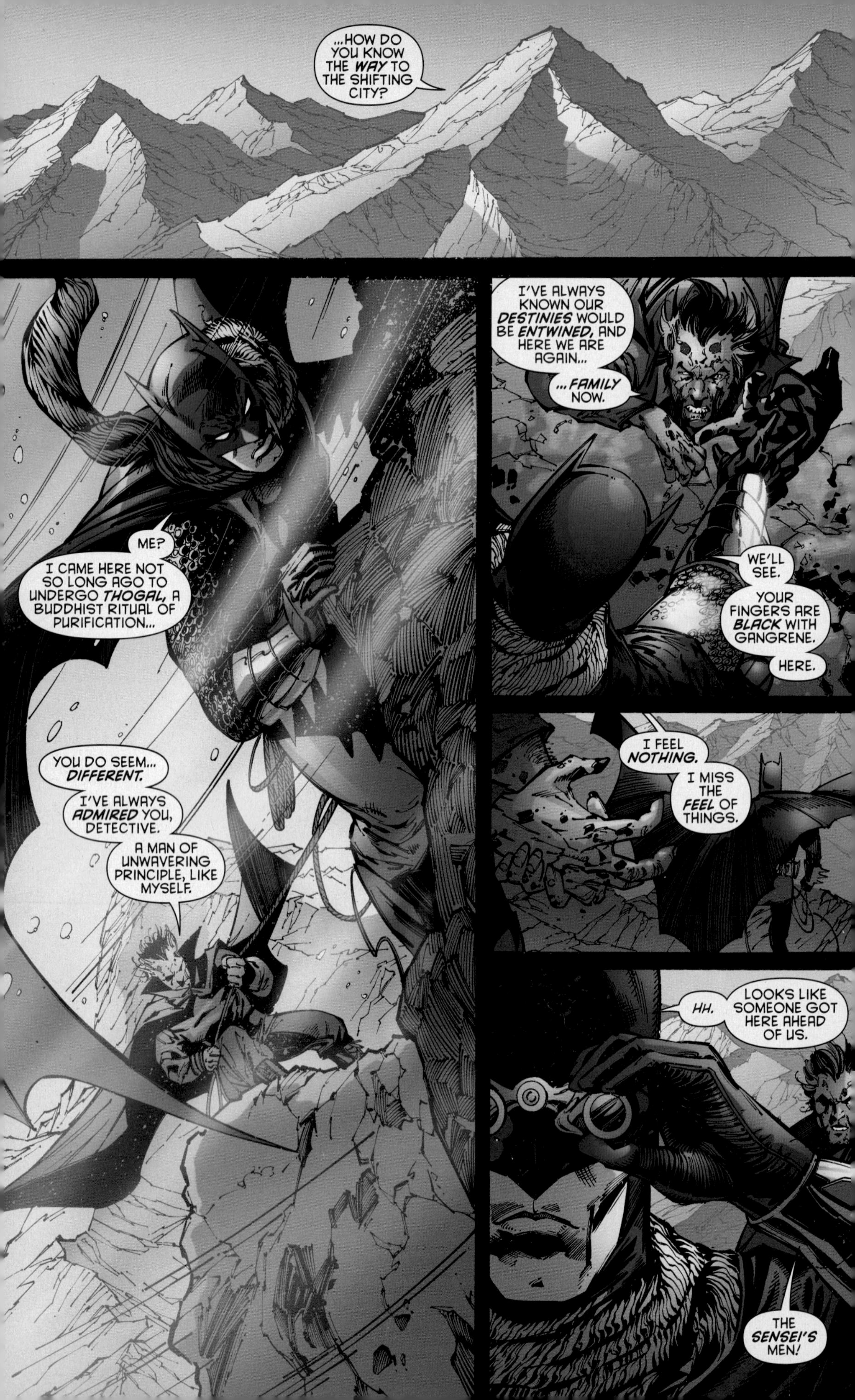
...HOW DO YOU KNOW THE WAY TO THE SHIFTING CITY?
ME?
I CAME HERE NOT SO LONG AGO TO UNDERGO THOGAL, A BUDDHIST RITUAL OF PURIFICATION...
YOU DO SEEM... DIFFERENT.
I'VE ALWAYS ADMIRED YOU, DETECTIVE.
A MAN OF UNWAVERING PRINCIPLE, LIKE MYSELF.
I'VE ALWAYS KNOWN OUR DESTINIES WOULD BE ENTWINED, AND HERE WE ARE AGAIN...
...FAMILY NOW.
WE'LL SEE.
YOUR FINGERS ARE BLACK WITH GANGRENE.
HERE.
I FEEL NOTHING.
I MISS THE FEEL OF THINGS.
HH.
LOOKS LIKE SOMEONE GOT HERE AHEAD OF US.
THE SENSEI'S MEN!

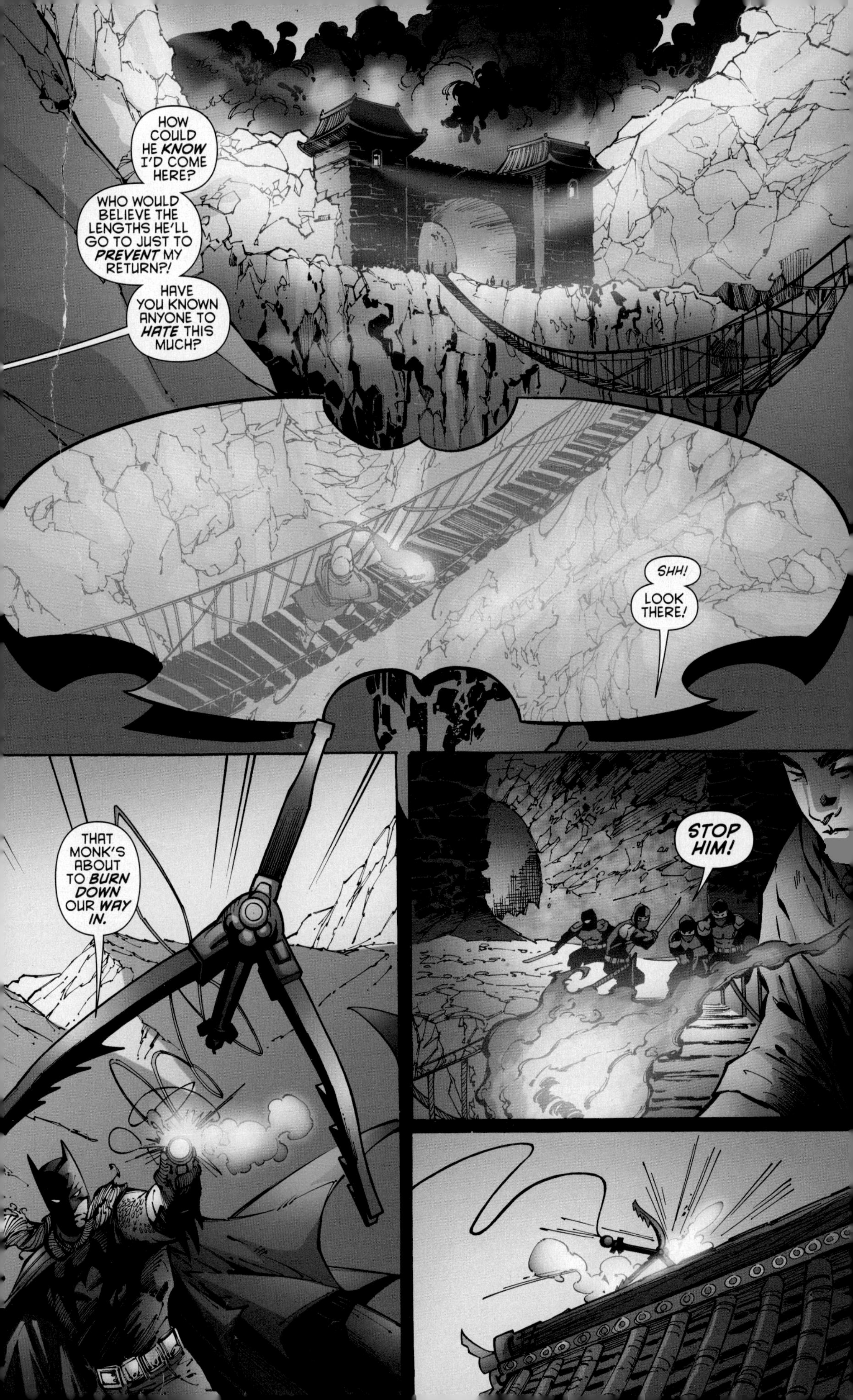
HOW COULD HE KNOW I'D COME HERE?
WHO WOULD BELIEVE THE LENGTHS HE'LL GO TO JUST TO PREVENT MY RETURN?!
HAVE YOU KNOWN ANYONE TO HATE THIS MUCH?
SHH!
LOOK THERE!
THAT MONK'S ABOUT TO BURN DOWN OUR WAY IN.
STOP HIM!

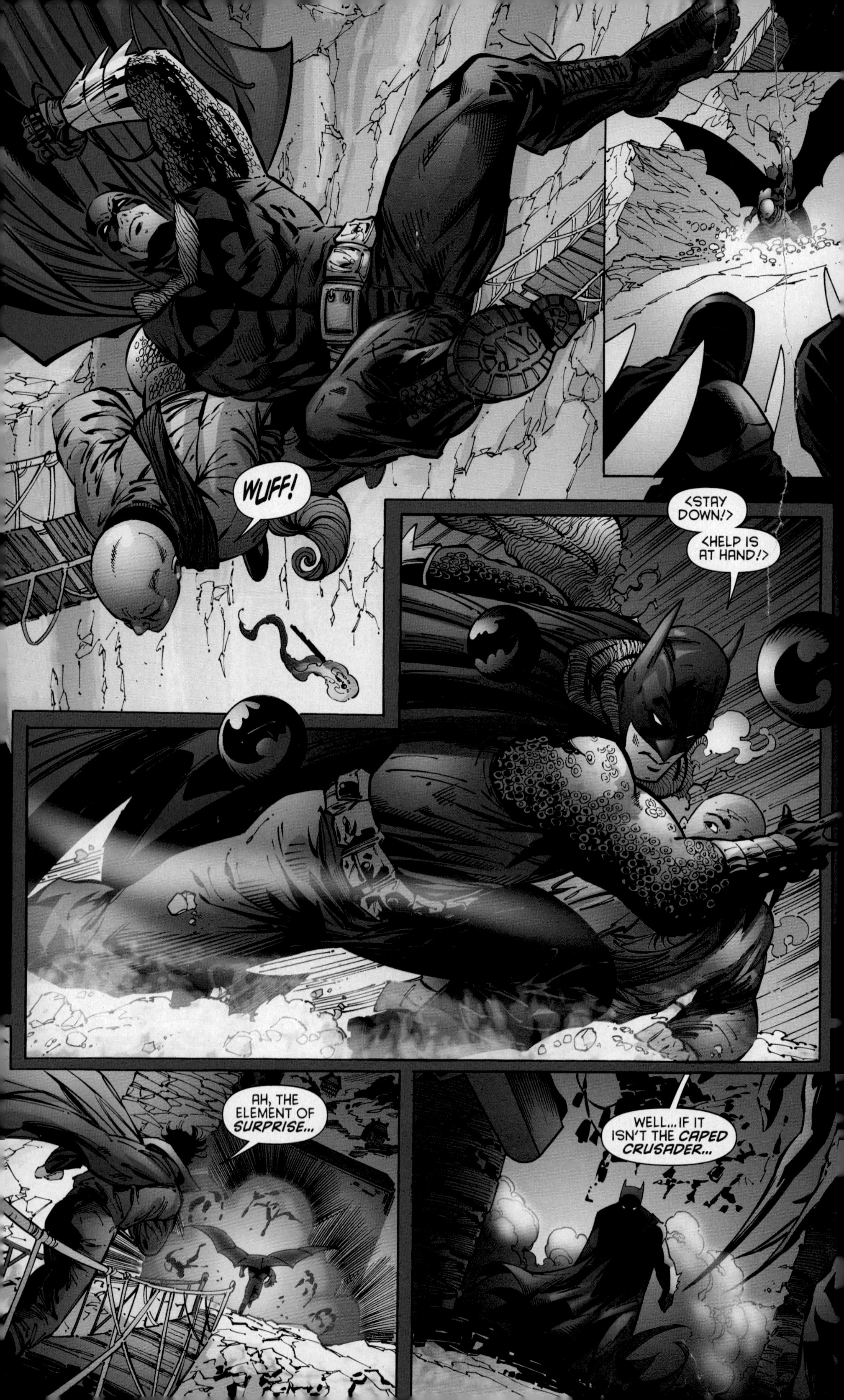
WUFF!
<STAY DOWN!>
<HELP IS AT HAND!>
AH, THE ELEMENT OF SURPRISE...
WELL... IF IT ISN'T THE CAPED CRUSADER...

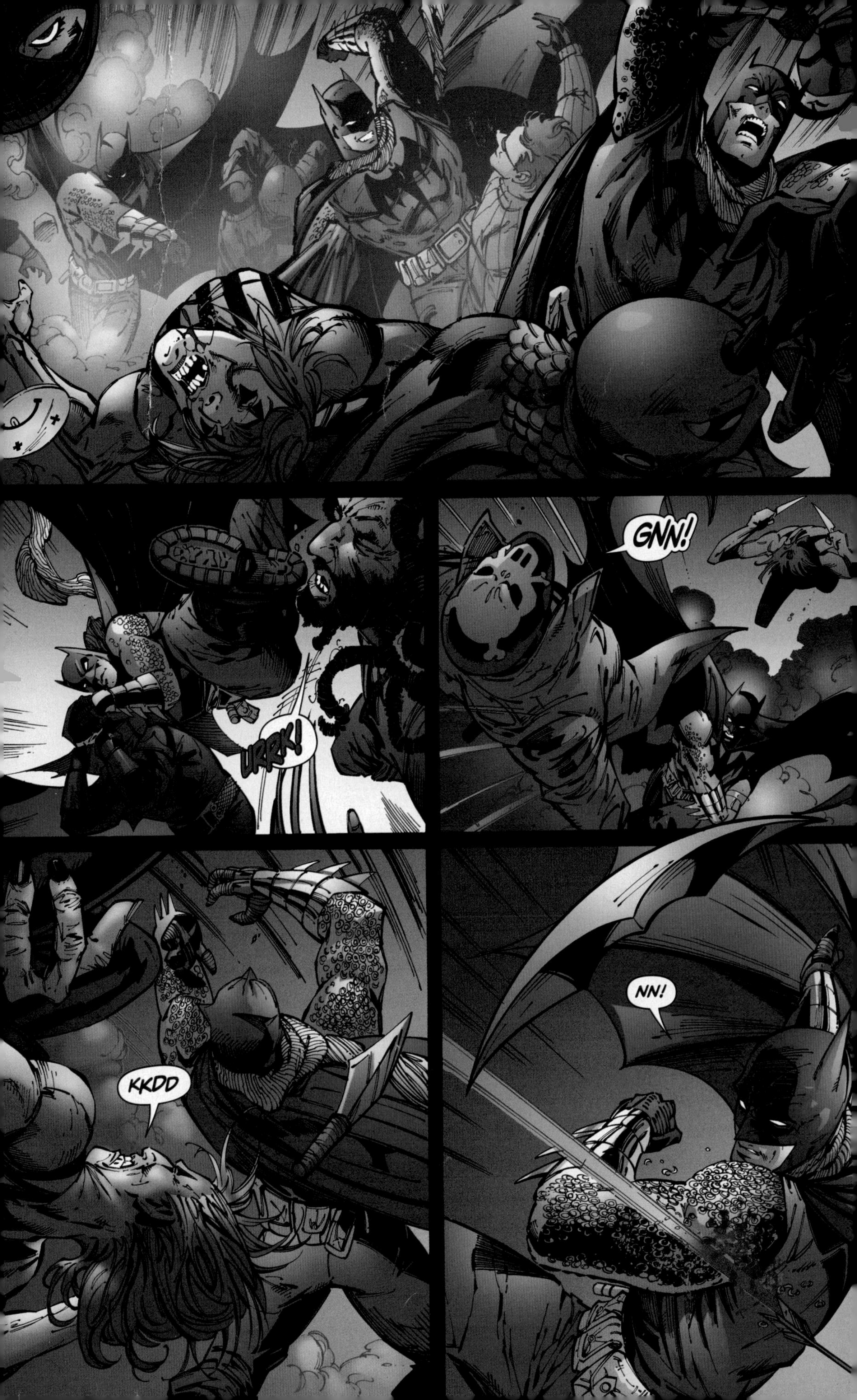
URRK!
GNN!
KKDD
NN!

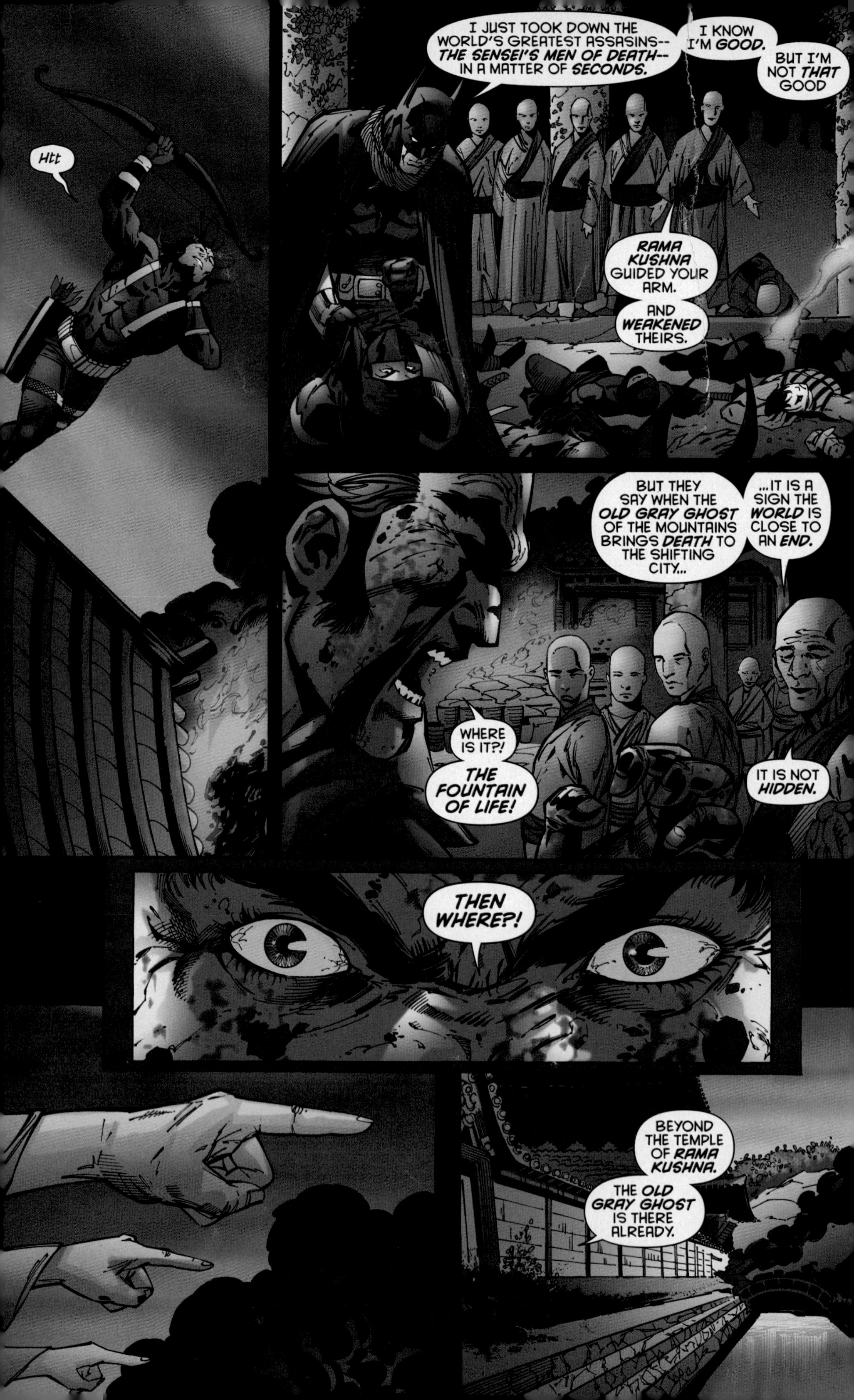
Htt
I JUST TOOK DOWN THE WORLD'S GREATEST ASSASINS-- THE SENSEI'S MEN OF DEATH-- IN A MATTER OF SECONDS.
I KNOW I'M GOOD.
BUT I'M NOT THAT GOOD
RAMA KUSHNA GUIDED YOUR ARM.
AND WEAKENED THEIRS.
BUT THEY SAY WHEN THE OLD GRAY GHOST OF THE MOUNTAINS BRINGS DEATH TO THE SHIFTING CITY...
...IT IS A SIGN THE WORLD IS CLOSE TO AN END.
WHERE IS IT?!
THE FOUNTAIN OF LIFE!
IT IS NOT HIDDEN.
THEN WHERE?!
BEYOND THE TEMPLE OF RAMA KUSHNA.
THE OLD GRAY GHOST IS THERE ALREADY.

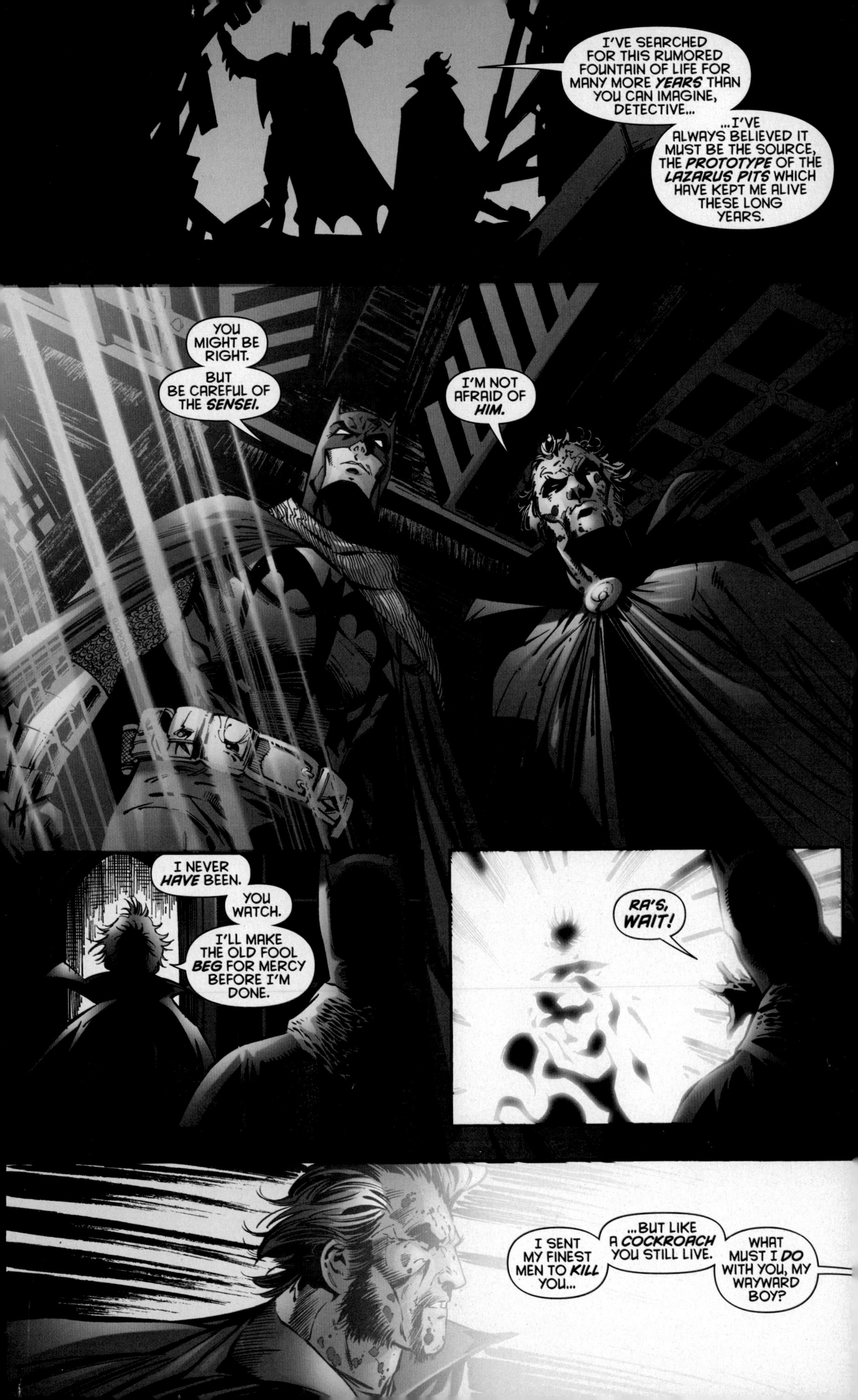
I'VE SEARCHED FOR THIS RUMORED FOUNTAIN OF LIFE FOR MANY MORE YEARS THAN YOU CAN IMAGINE, DETECTIVE...
...I'VE ALWAYS BELIEVED IT MUST BE THE SOURCE, THE PROTOTYPE OF THE LAZARUS PITS WHICH HAVE KEPT ME ALIVE THESE LONG YEARS.
YOU MIGHT BE RIGHT.
BUT BE CAREFUL OF THE SENSEI.
I'M NOT AFRAID OF HIM.
I NEVER HAVE BEEN.
YOU WATCH.
I'LL MAKE THE OLD FOOL BEG FOR MERCY BEFORE I'M DONE.
RA'S, WAIT!
I SENT MY FINEST MEN TO KILL YOU...
...BUT LIKE A COCKROACH YOU STILL LIVE.
WHAT MUST I DO WITH YOU, MY WAYWARD BOY?

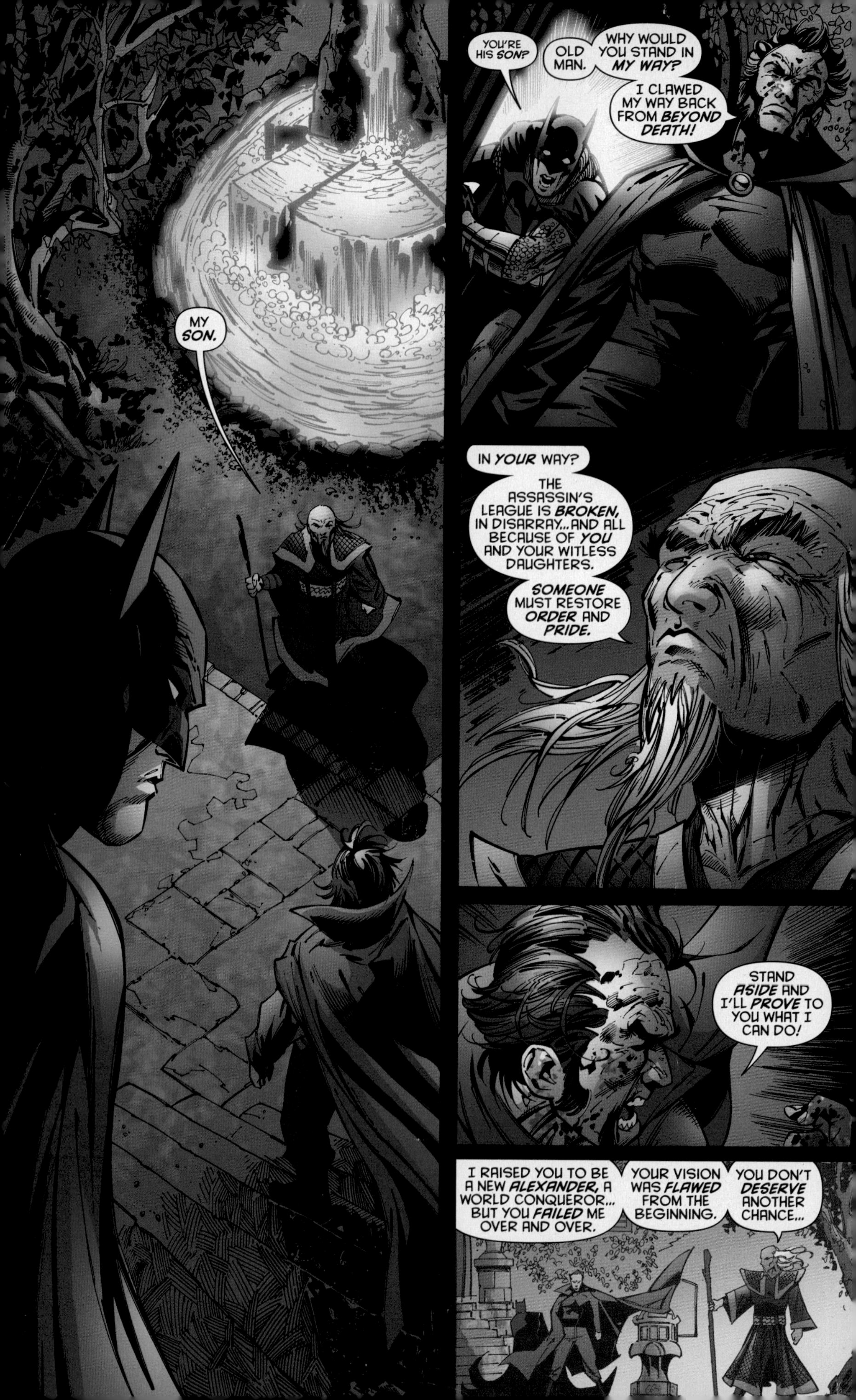
MY SON.
YOU'RE HIS SON?
OLD MAN.
WHY WOULD YOU STAND IN MY WAY?
I CLAWED MY WAY BACK FROM BEYOND DEATH!
IN YOUR WAY?
THE ASSASSIN'S LEAGUE IS BROKEN, IN DISARRAY...AND ALL BECAUSE OF YOU AND YOUR WITLESS DAUGHTERS.
SOMEONE MUST RESTORE ORDER AND PRIDE.
STAND ASIDE AND I'LL PROVE TO YOU WHAT I CAN DO!
I RAISED YOU TO BE A NEW ALEXANDER, A WORLD CONQUEROR... BUT YOU FAILED ME OVER AND OVER.
YOUR VISION WAS FLAWED FROM THE BEGINNING.
YOU DON'T DESERVE ANOTHER CHANCE...

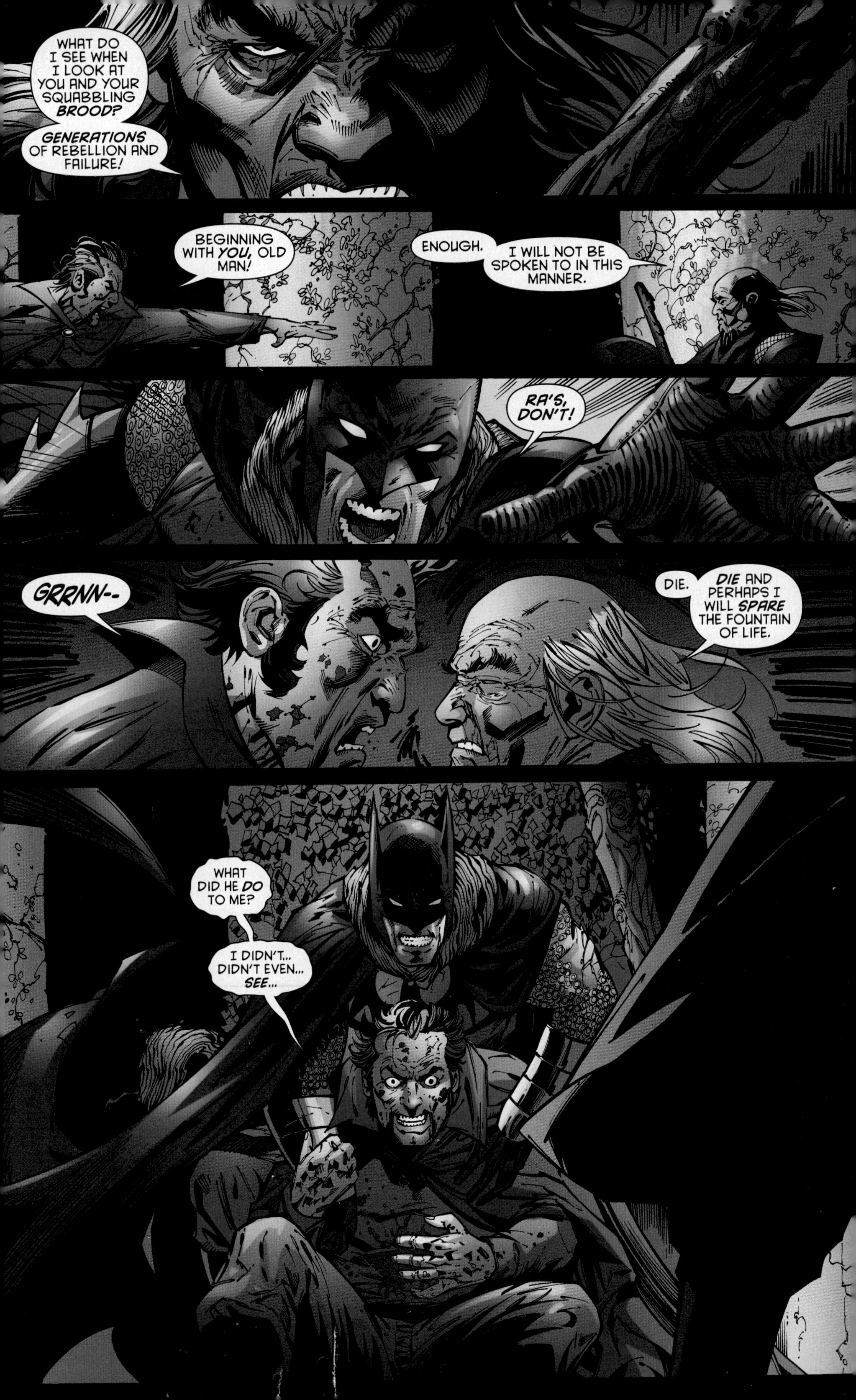
WHAT DO I SEE WHEN I LOOK AT YOU AND YOUR SQUABBLING BROOD?
GENERATIONS OF REBELLION AND FAILURE!
BEGINNING WITH YOU, OLD MAN!
ENOUGH.
I WILL NOT BE SPOKEN TO IN THIS MANNER.
RA'S, DON'T!
GRRNN--
DIE.
DIE AND PERHAPS I WILL SPARE THE FOUNTAIN OF LIFE.
WHAT DID HE DO TO ME?
I DIDN'T... DIDN'T EVEN... SEE...

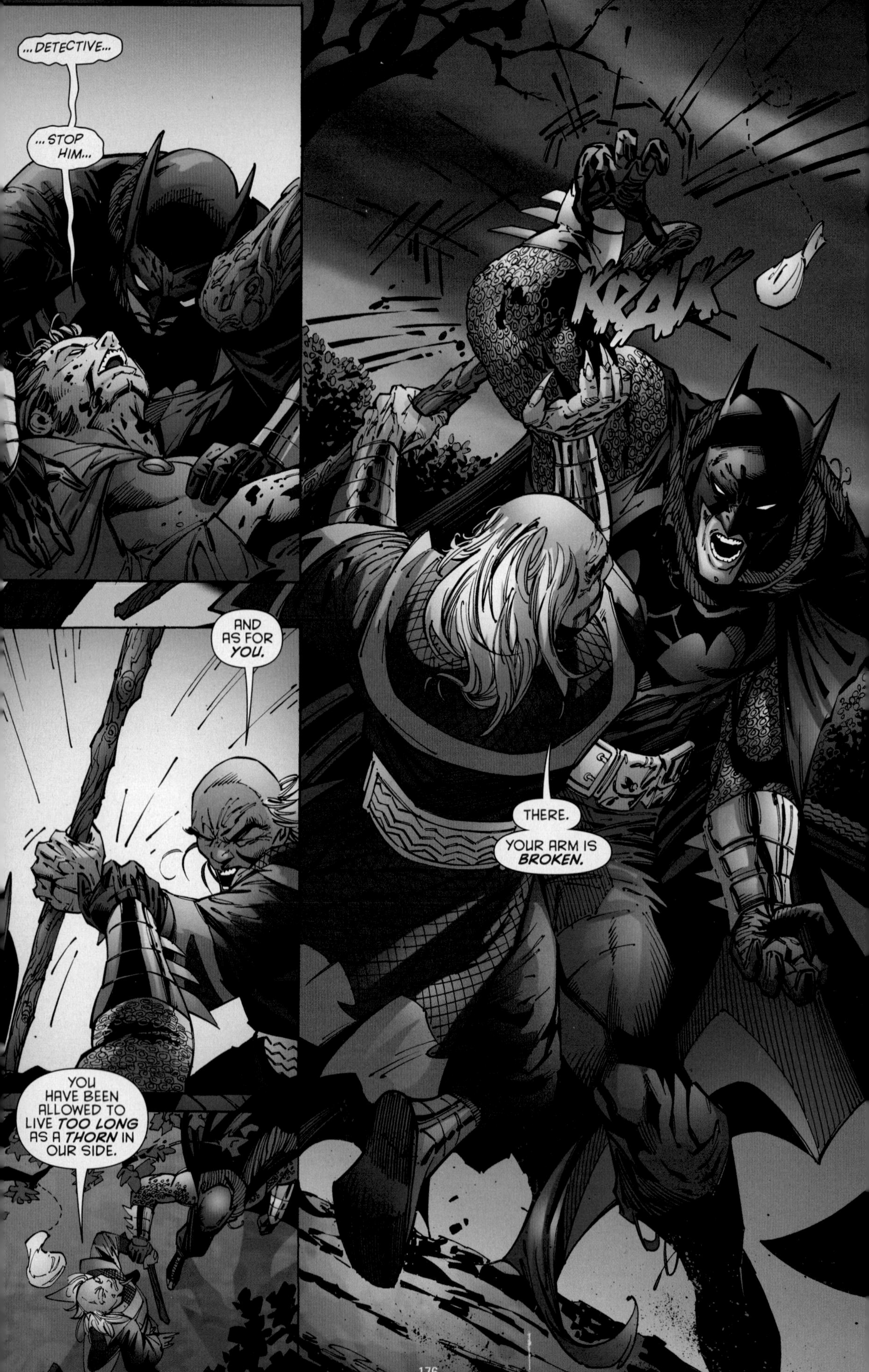
...DETECTIVE...
...STOP HIM...
AND AS FOR YOU.
YOU HAVE BEEN ALLOWED TO LIVE TOO LONG AS A THORN IN OUR SIDE.
KRAK
THERE.
YOUR ARM IS BROKEN.

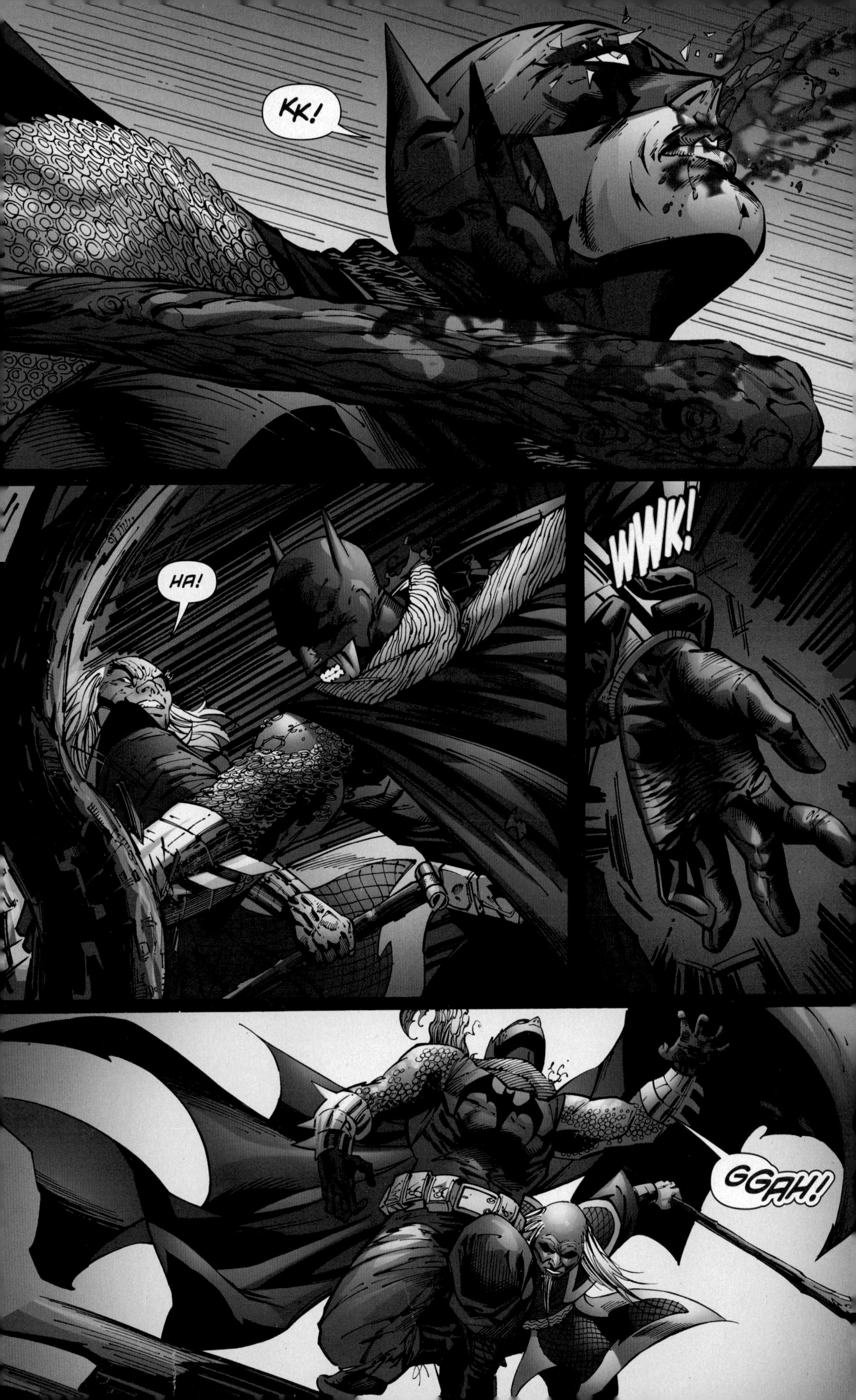
KK!
HA!
WWK!
GGAH!

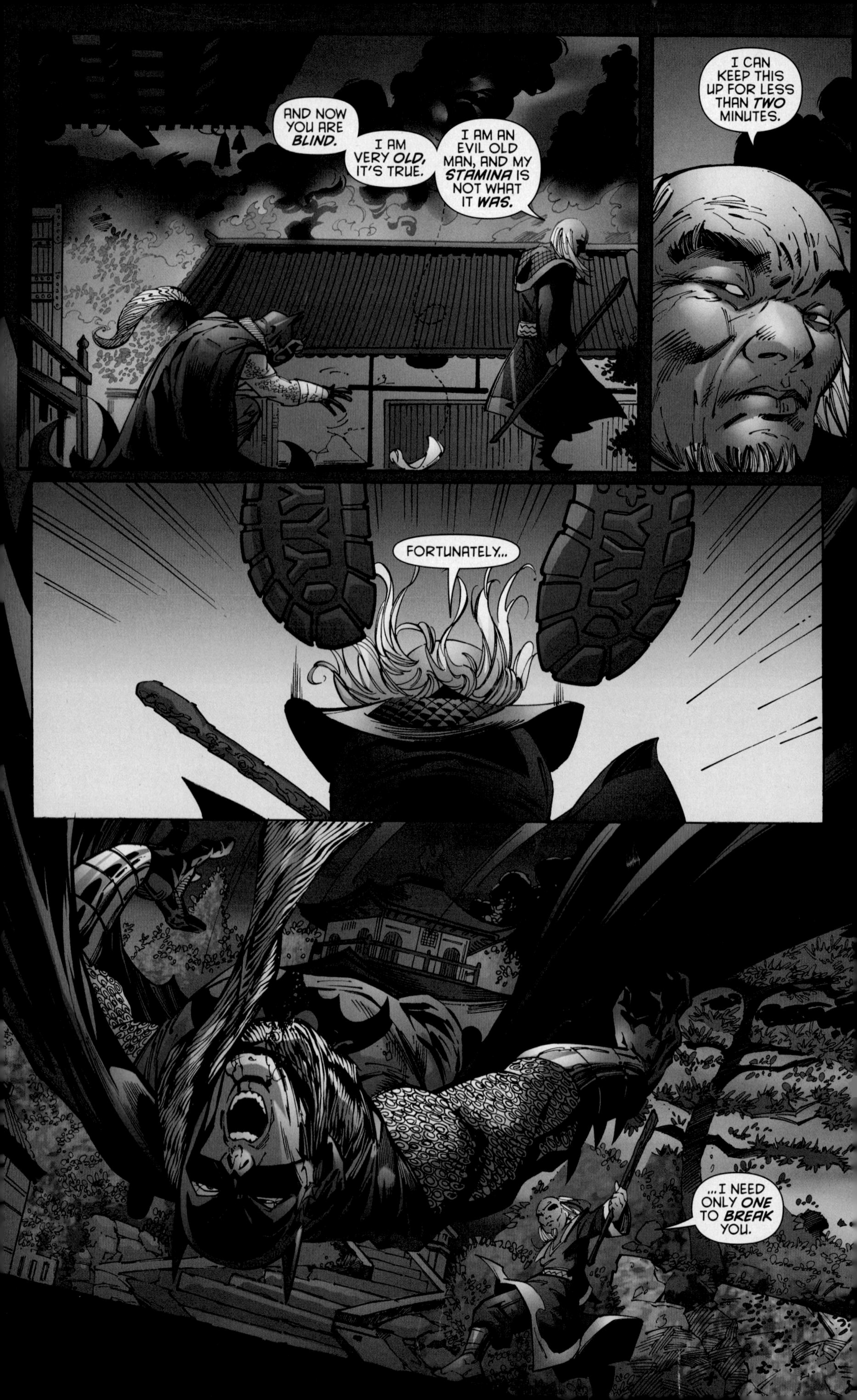
AND NOW YOU ARE BLIND.
I AM VERY OLD, IT'S TRUE.
I AM AN EVIL OLD MAN, AND MY STAMINA IS NOT WHAT IT WAS.
I CAN KEEP THIS UP FOR LESS THAN TWO MINUTES.
FORTUNATELY...
...I NEED ONLY ONE TO BREAK YOU.

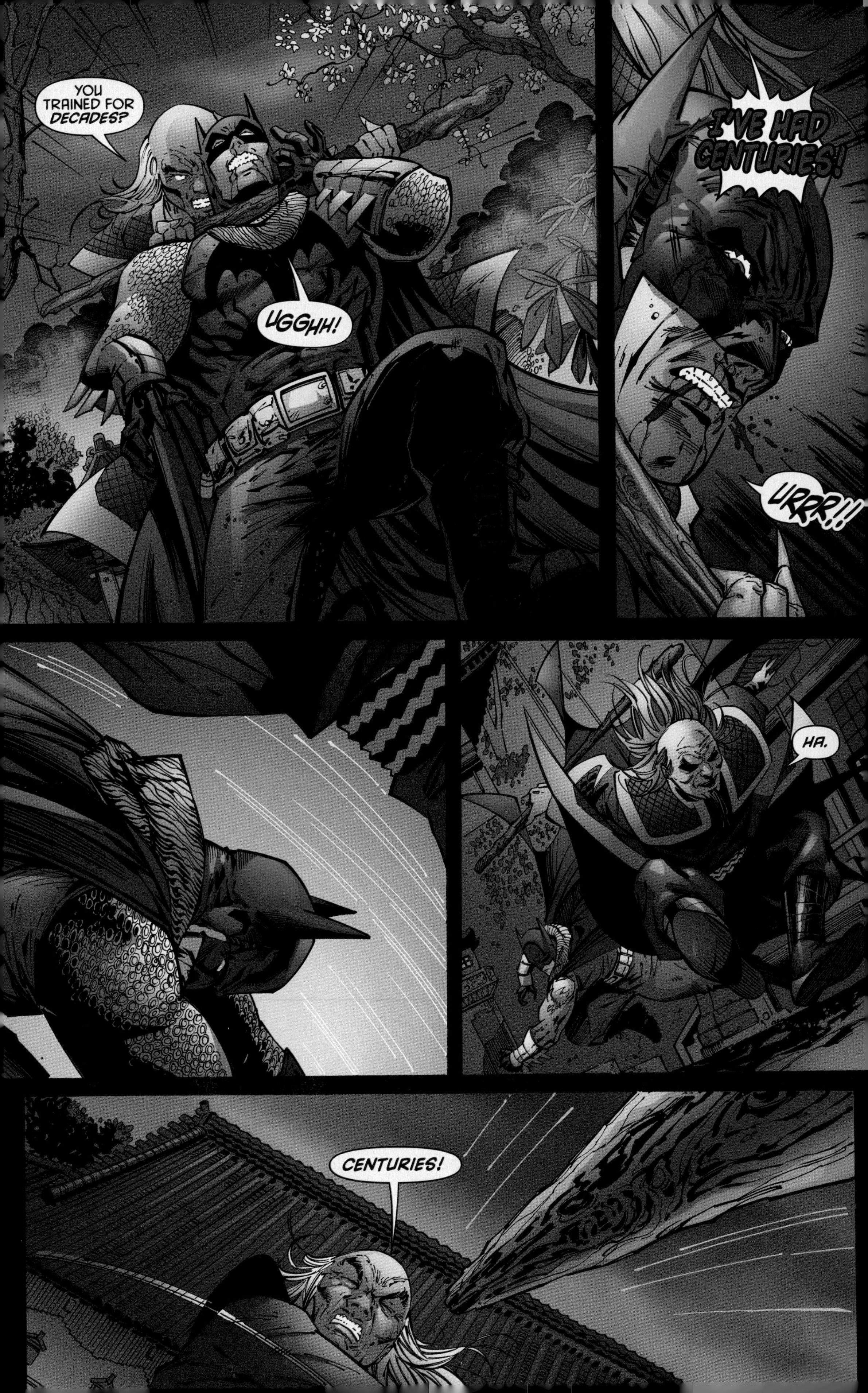
YOU TRAINED FOR DECADES?
UGGHH!
I'VE HAD CENTURIES!
URRR!!
HA.
CENTURIES!

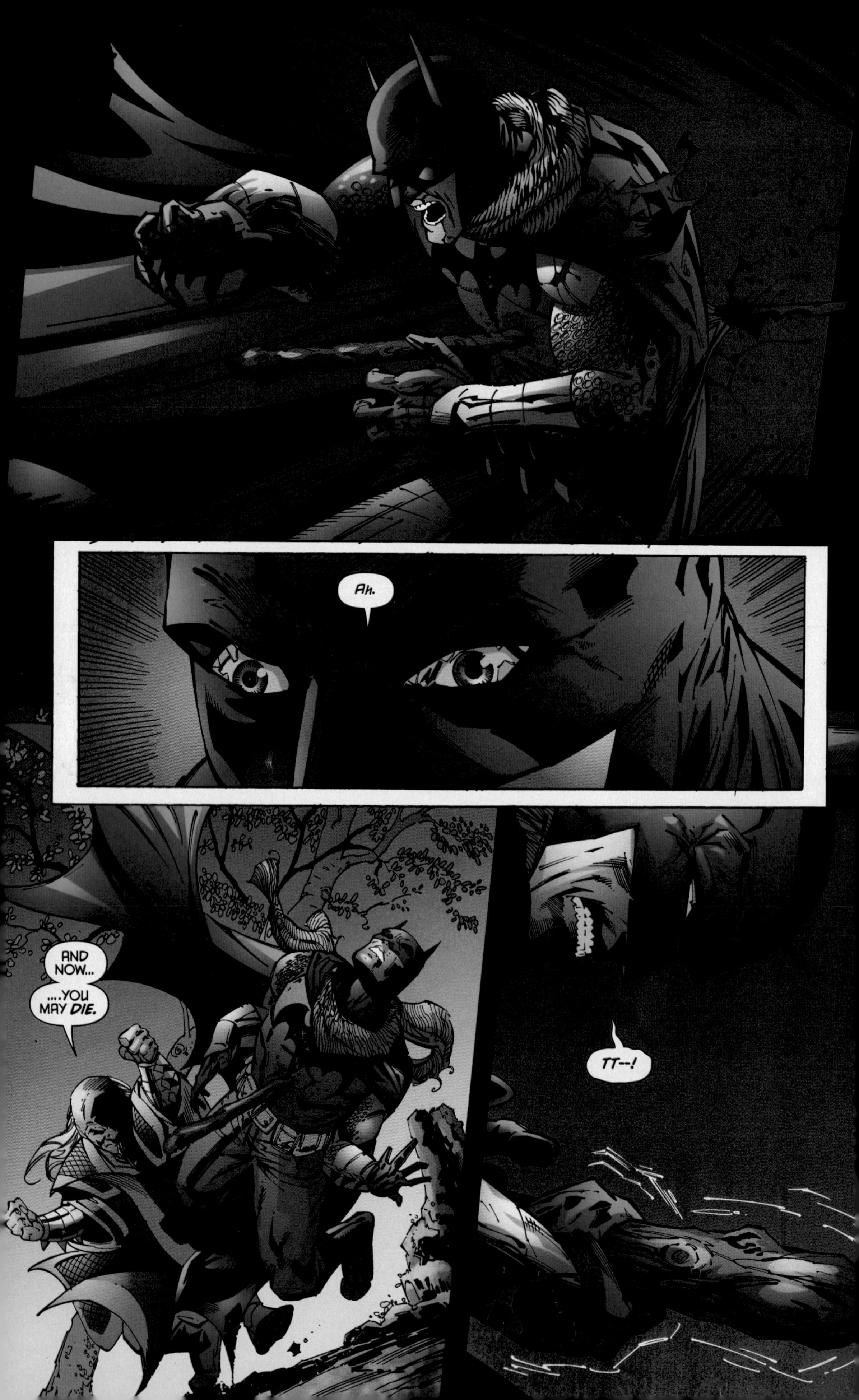
Ah.
AND NOW...
...YOU MAY DIE.
TT--!

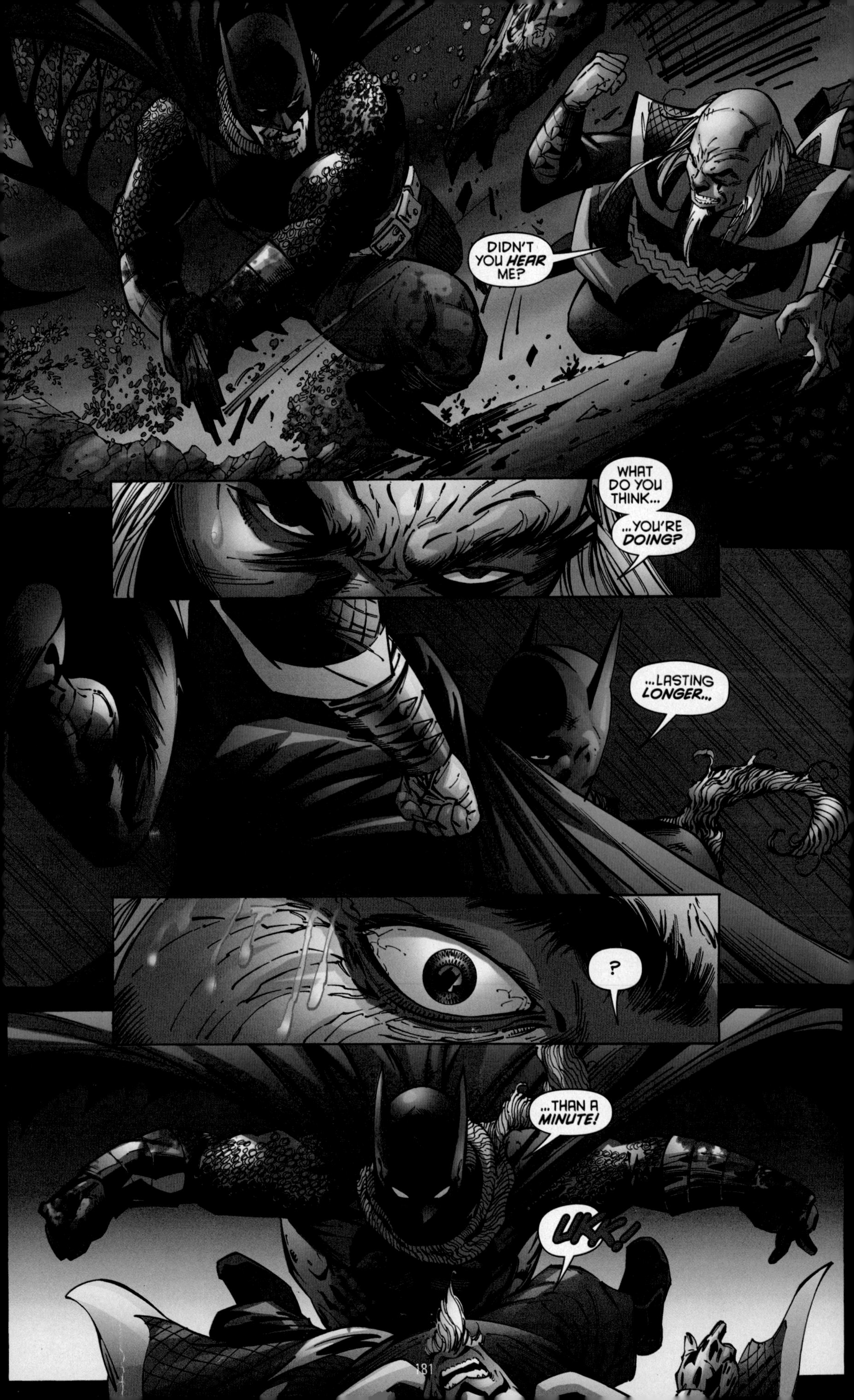
DIDN'T YOU HEAR ME?
WHAT DO YOU THINK...
...YOU'RE DOING?
...LASTING LONGER...
?
...THAN A MINUTE!
UKK!

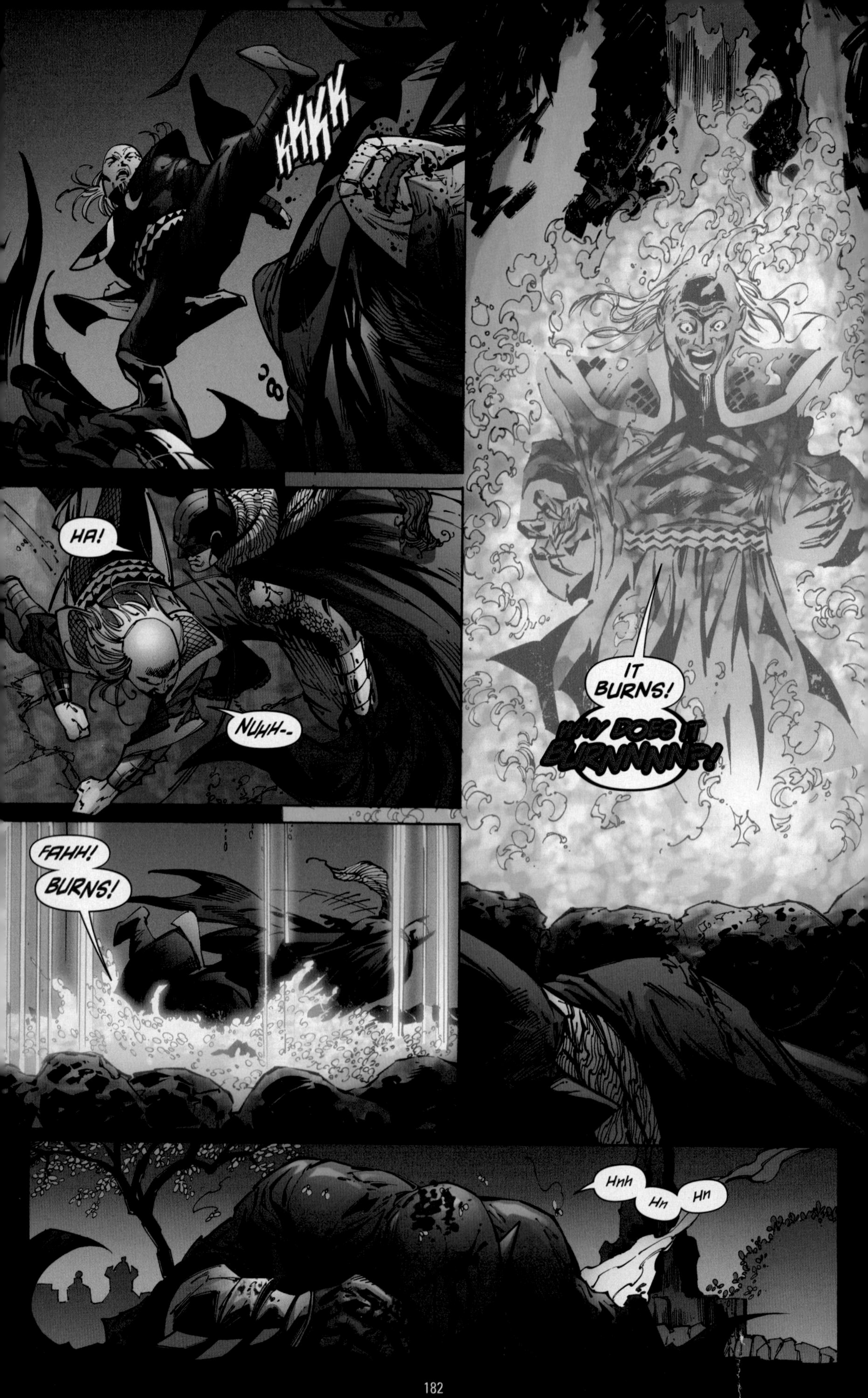
KKKK
HA!
NUHH--
FAHH! BURNS!
IT BURNS!
WHY DOES IT BURNNNNN?!
Hnh
Hn
Hn

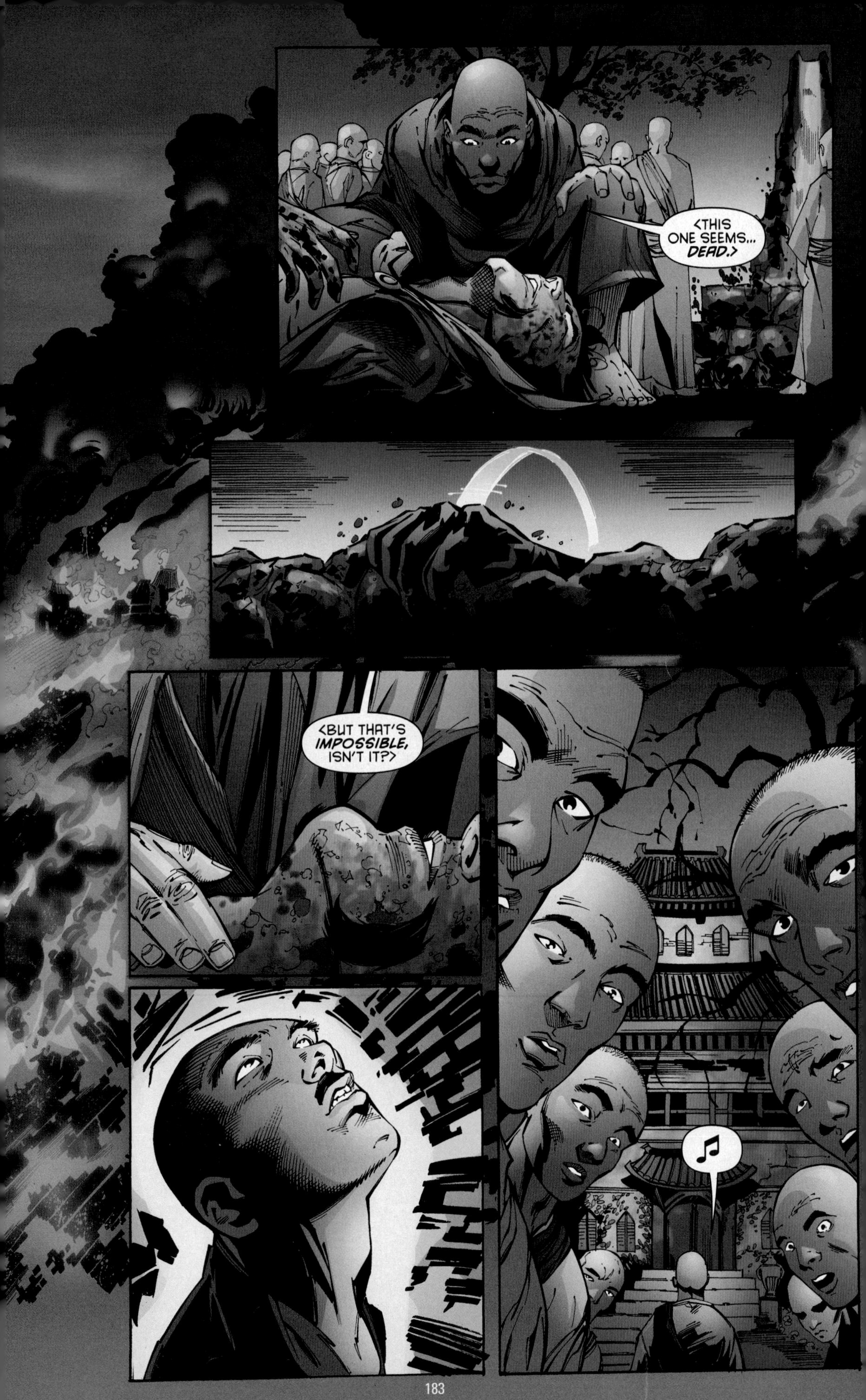
<THIS ONE SEEMS... DEAD.>
<BUT THAT'S IMPOSSIBLE, ISN'T IT?>
♫

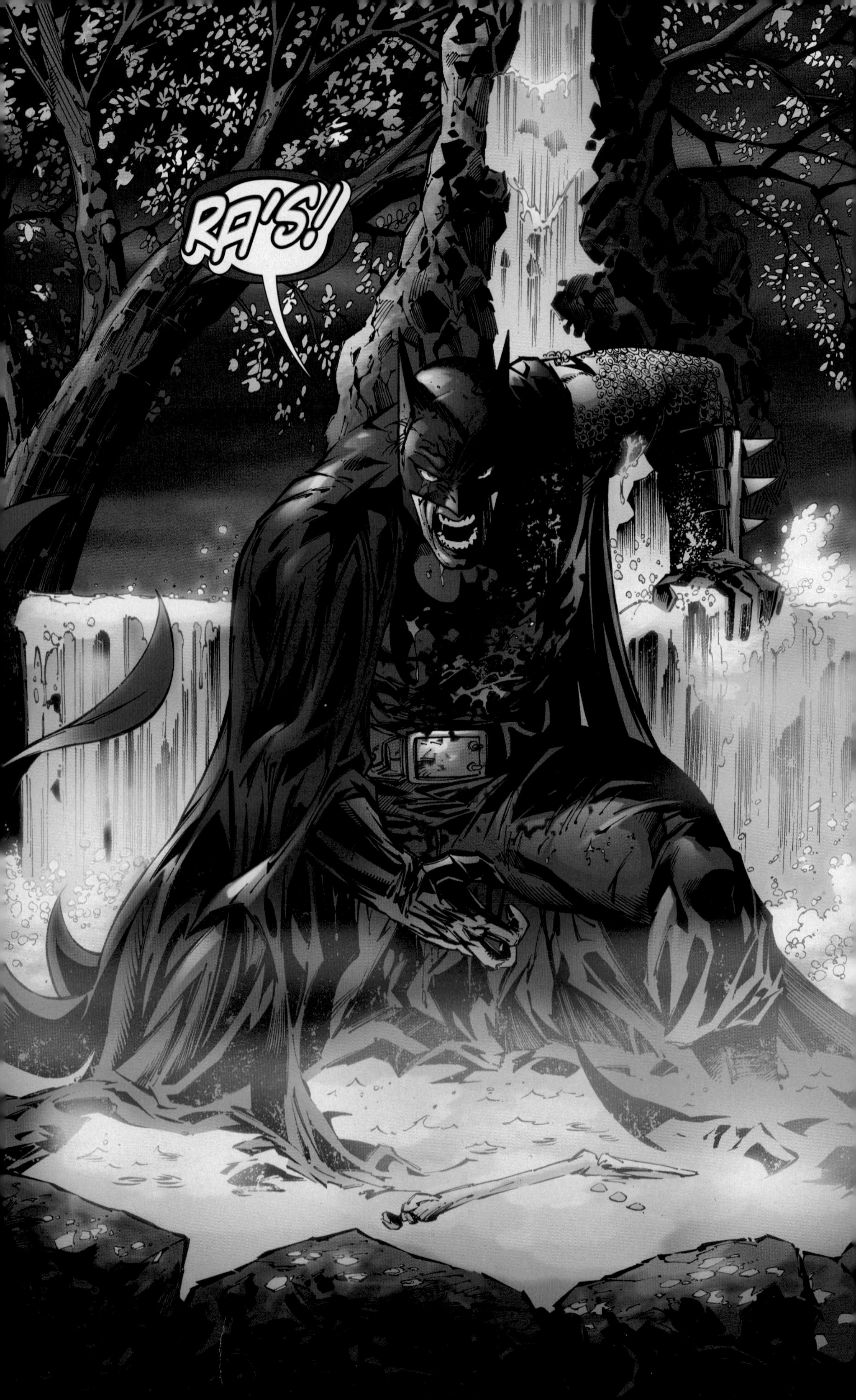
RA'S!!

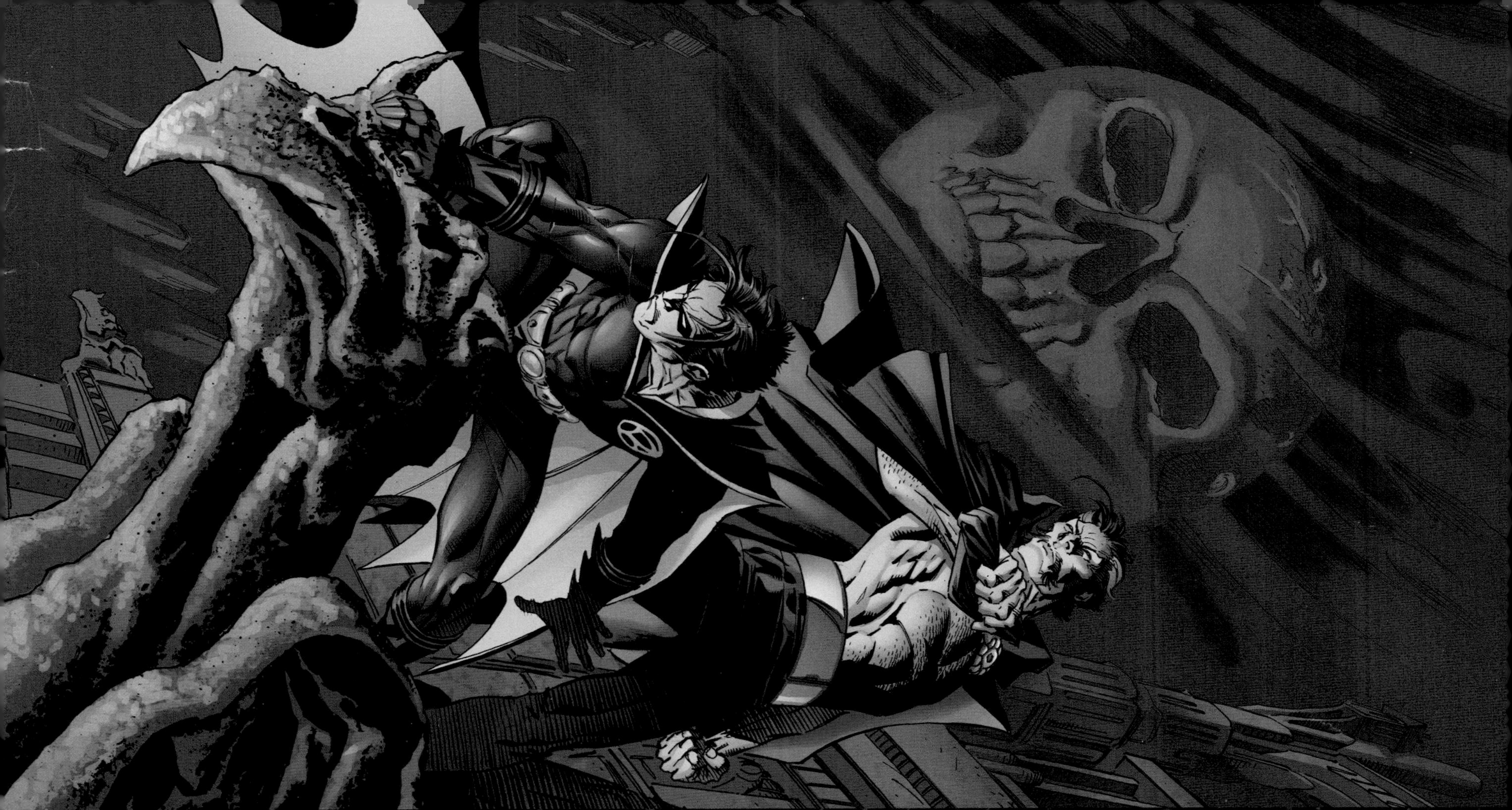

CHAPTER FIVE TEMPTATION

Cover art by Andy Kubert | Chapter written by Peter Milligan | Chapter pencilled by David Baldeón | Chapter inked by Steve Bird

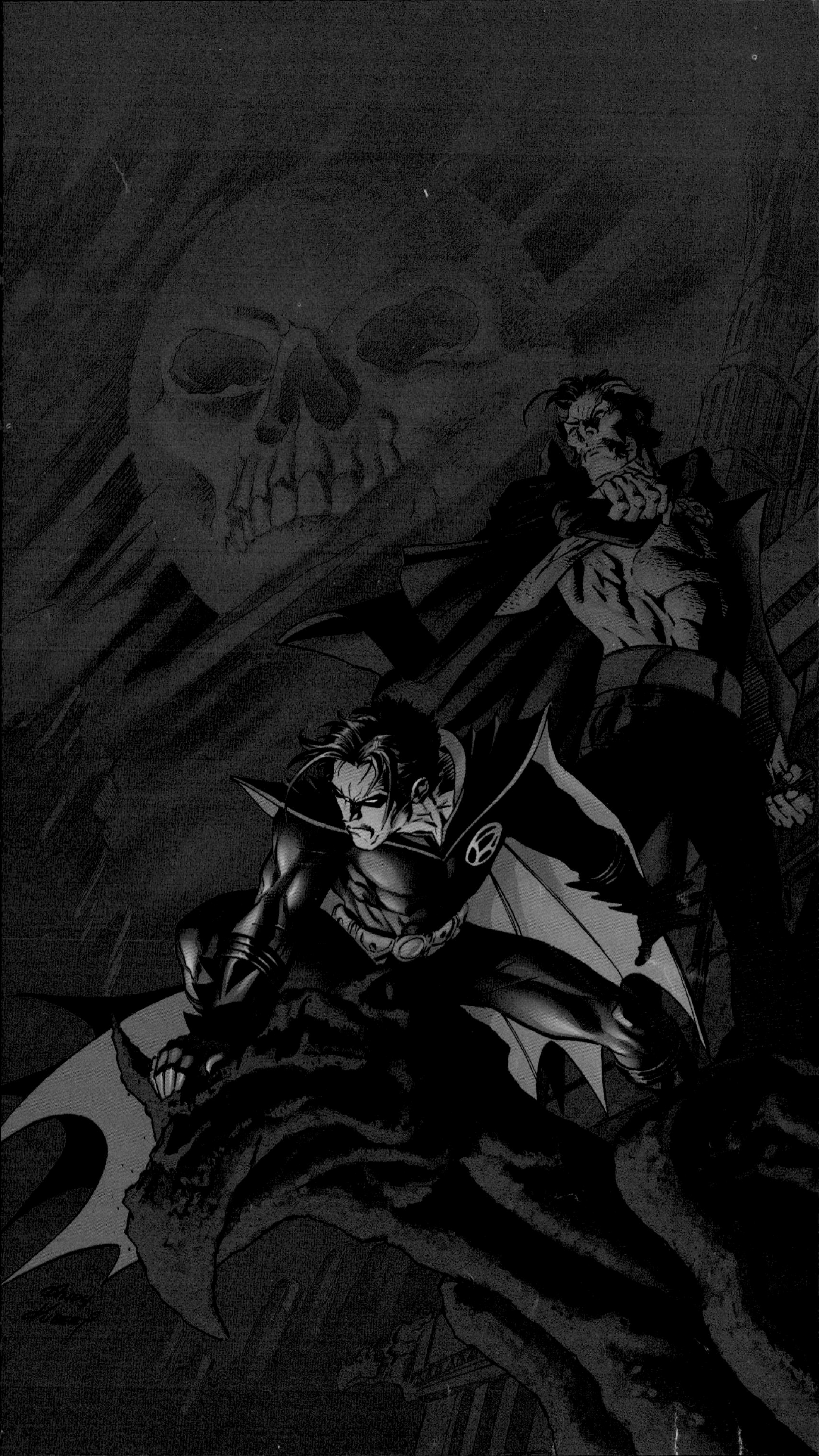

Variant cover by Andy Kubert

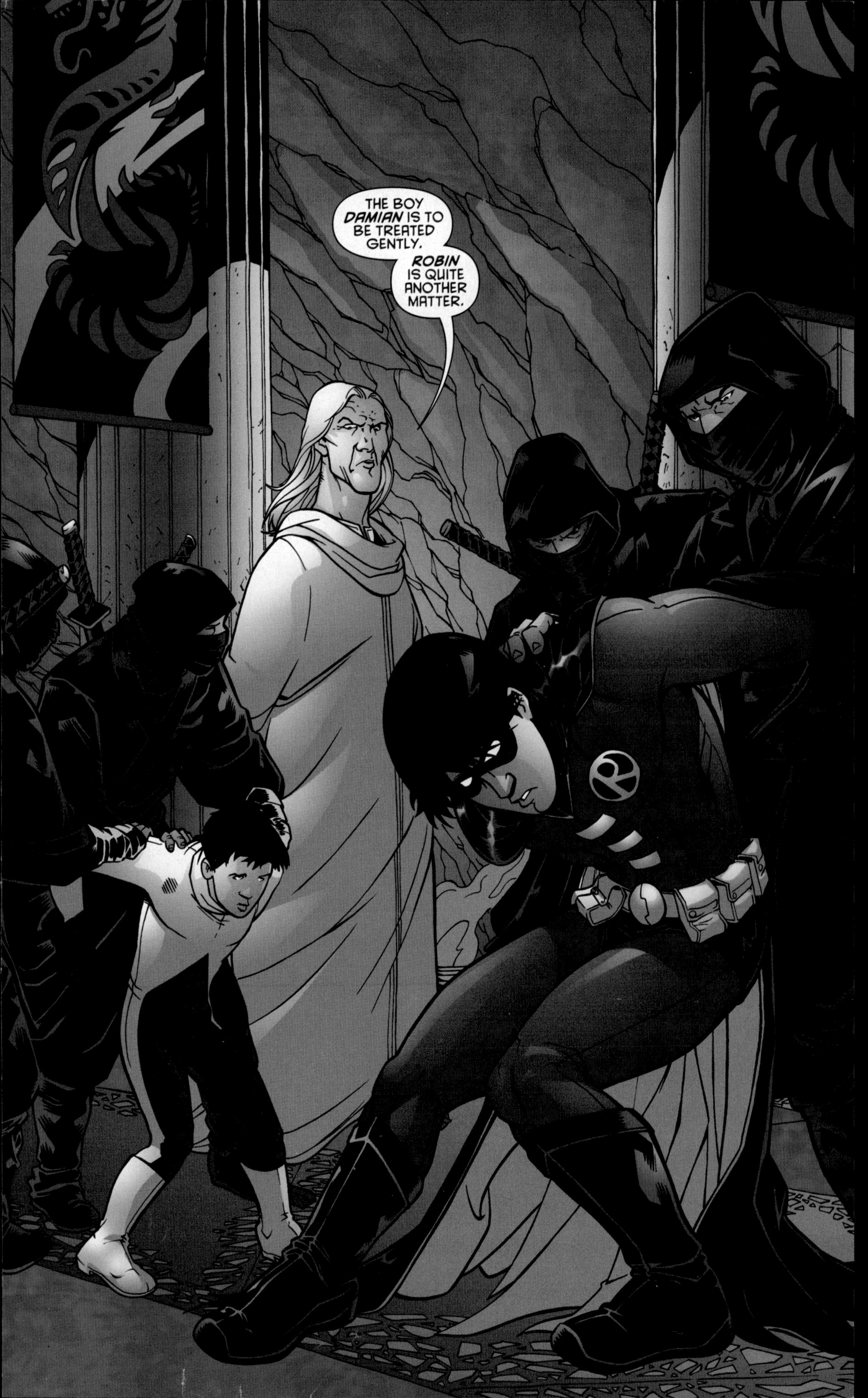
THE BOY *DAMIAN* IS TO BE TREATED GENTLY.
ROBIN IS QUITE ANOTHER MATTER.

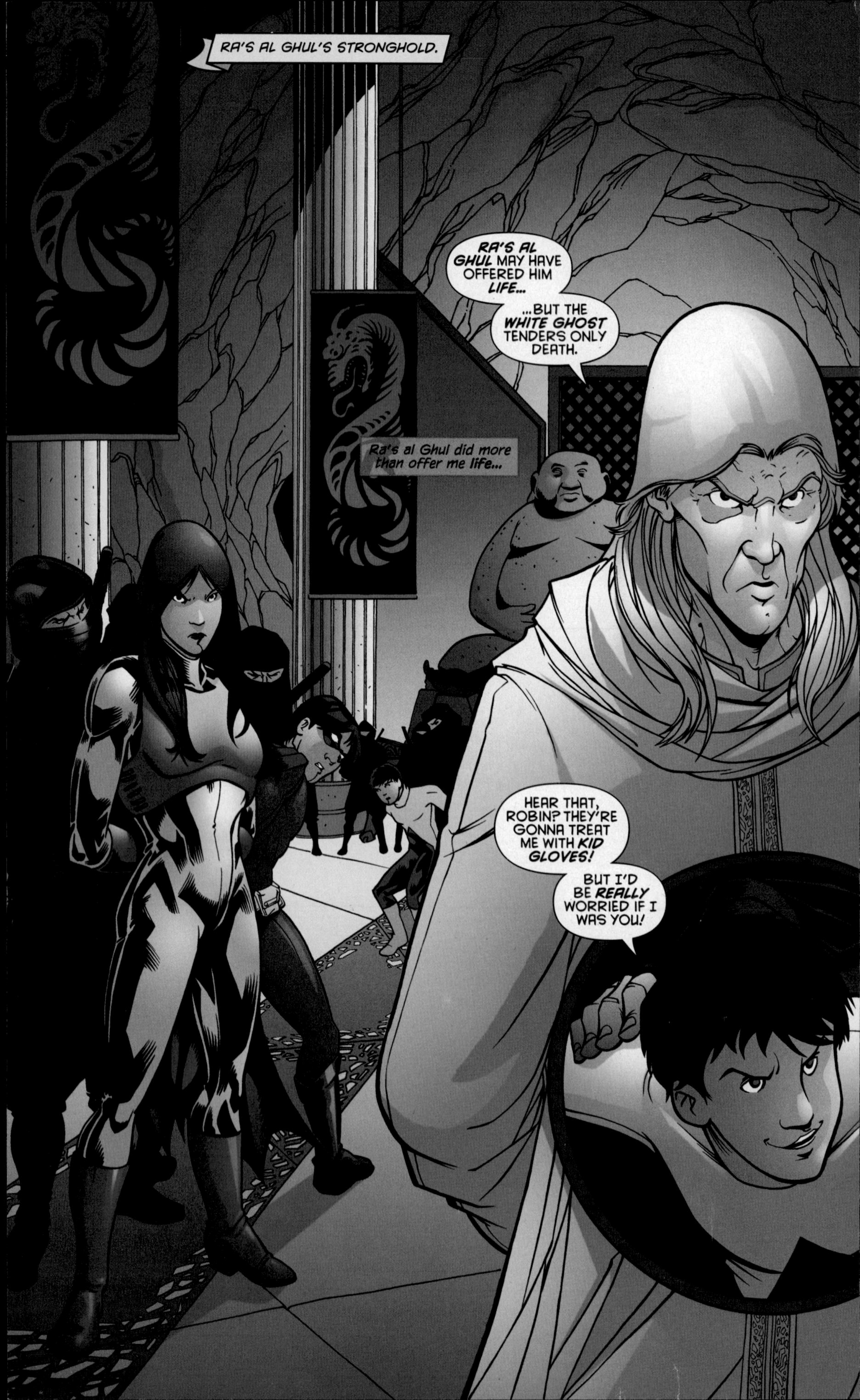
RA'S AL GHUL'S STRONGHOLD.
RA'S AL GHUL MAY HAVE OFFERED HIM LIFE...
...BUT THE WHITE GHOST TENDERS ONLY DEATH.
Ra's al Ghul did more than offer me life...
HEAR THAT, ROBIN? THEY'RE GONNA TREAT ME WITH KID GLOVES!
BUT I'D BE REALLY WORRIED IF I WAS YOU!

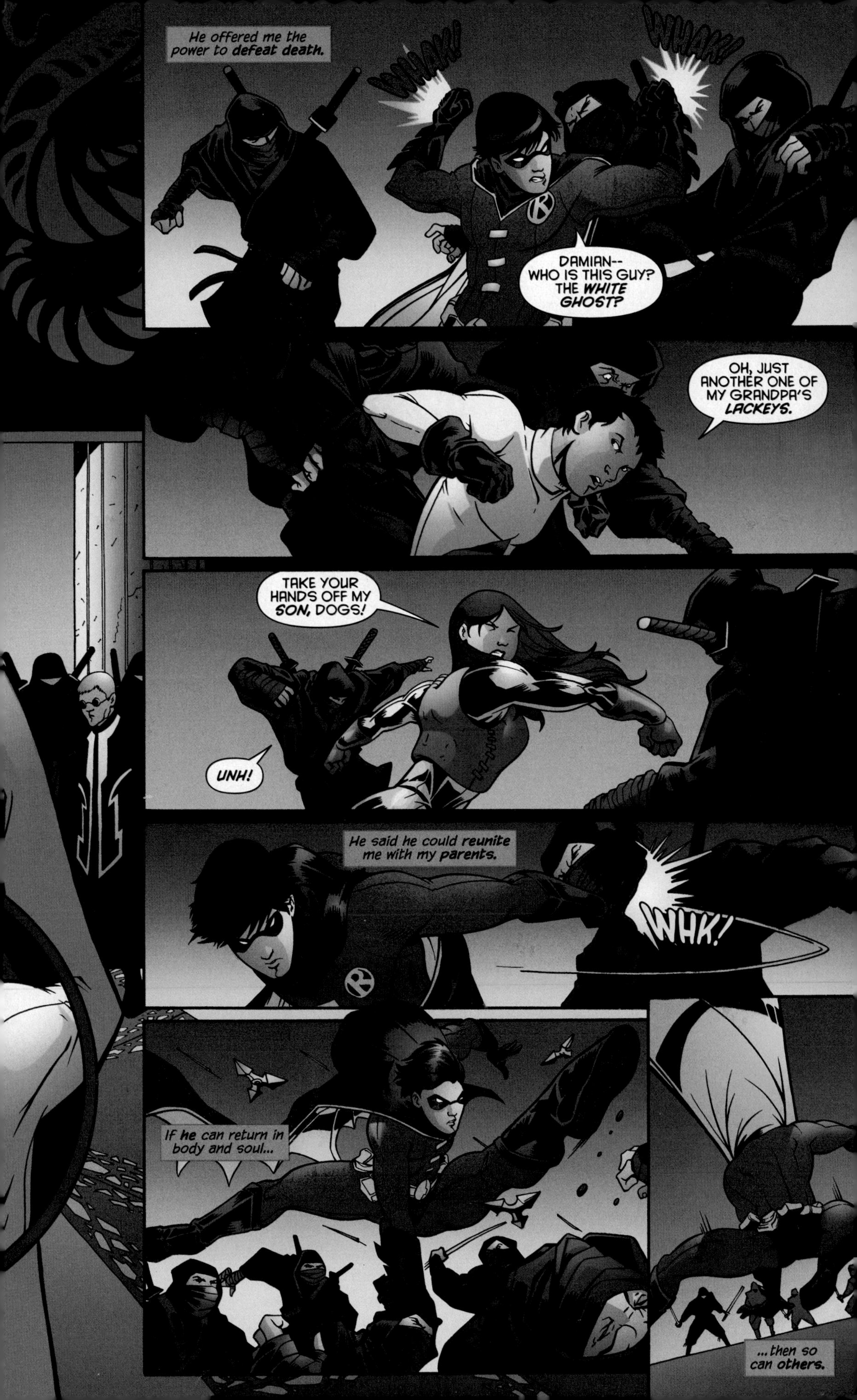
He offered me the power to defeat death.
WHAAK!
WHAK!!
DAMIAN-- WHO IS THIS GUY? THE WHITE GHOST?
OH, JUST ANOTHER ONE OF MY GRANDPA'S LACKEYS.
TAKE YOUR HANDS OFF MY SON, DOGS!
UNH!
He said he could reunite me with my parents.
WHK!
If he can return in body and soul...
...then so can others.

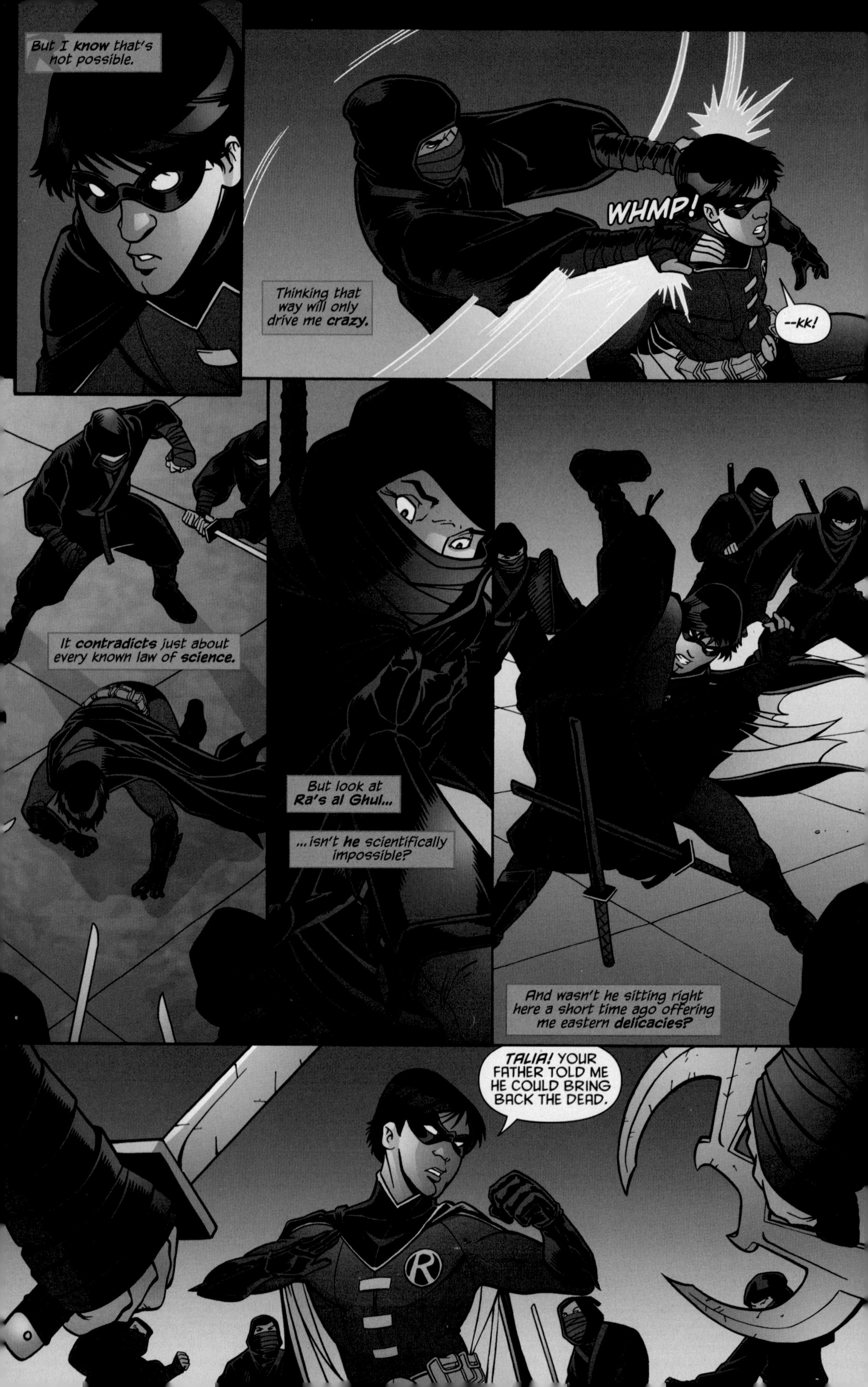

But I know that's not possible.
Thinking that way will only drive me crazy.
WHMP!
--kk!
It contradicts just about every known law of science.
But look at Ra's al Ghul...
...isn't he scientifically impossible?
And wasn't he sitting right here a short time ago offering me eastern delicacies?
TALIA! YOUR FATHER TOLD ME HE COULD BRING BACK THE DEAD.

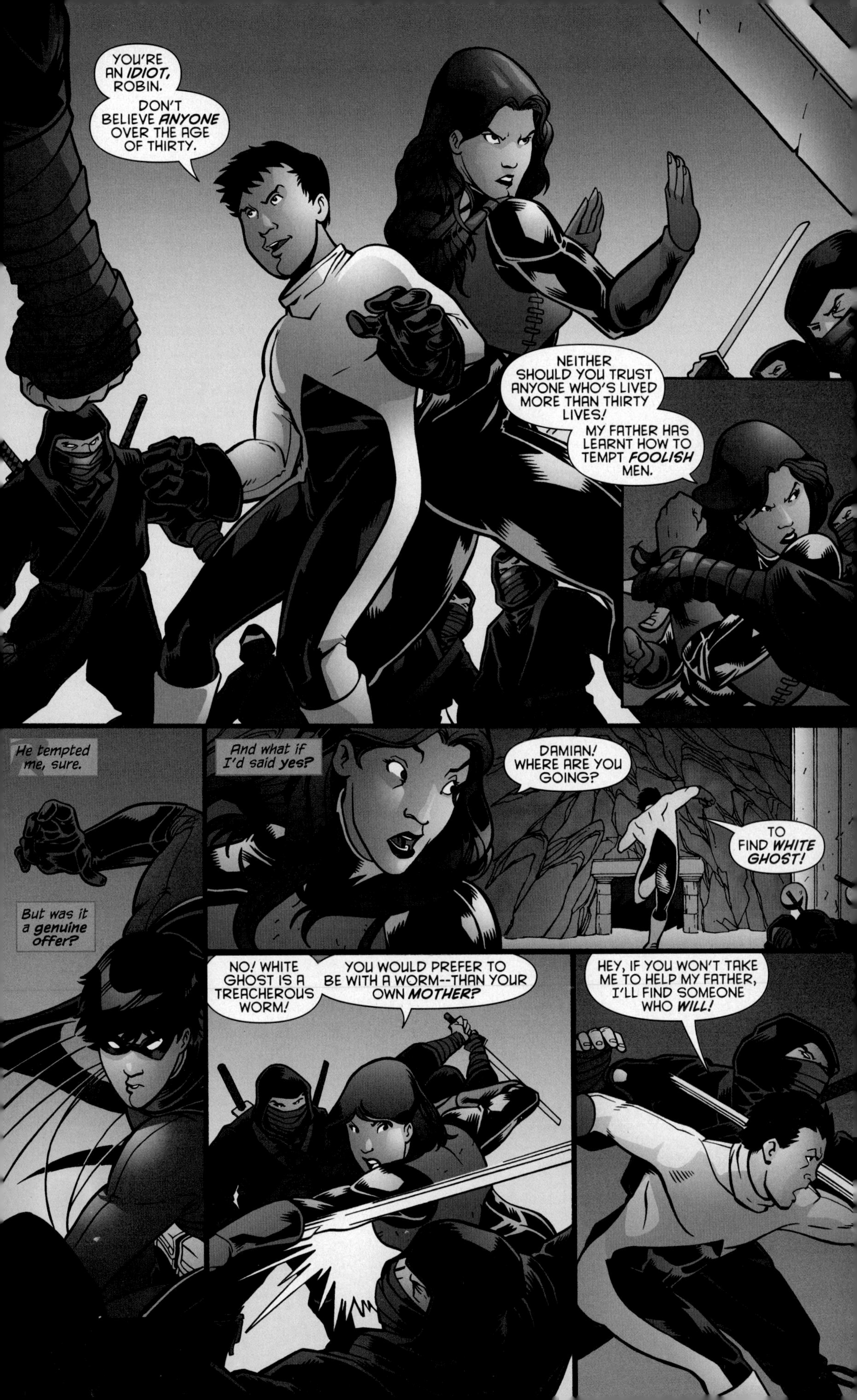
YOU'RE AN *IDIOT*, ROBIN.
DON'T BELIEVE *ANYONE* OVER THE AGE OF THIRTY.
NEITHER SHOULD YOU TRUST ANYONE WHO'S LIVED MORE THAN THIRTY LIVES!
MY FATHER HAS LEARNT HOW TO TEMPT *FOOLISH* MEN.
He tempted me, sure.
But was it a *genuine* offer?
And what if I'd said *yes?*
DAMIAN! WHERE ARE YOU GOING?
TO FIND *WHITE GHOST!*
NO! WHITE GHOST IS A TREACHEROUS WORM!
YOU WOULD PREFER TO BE WITH A WORM--THAN YOUR OWN *MOTHER?*
HEY, IF YOU WON'T TAKE ME TO HELP MY FATHER, I'LL FIND SOMEONE WHO *WILL!*

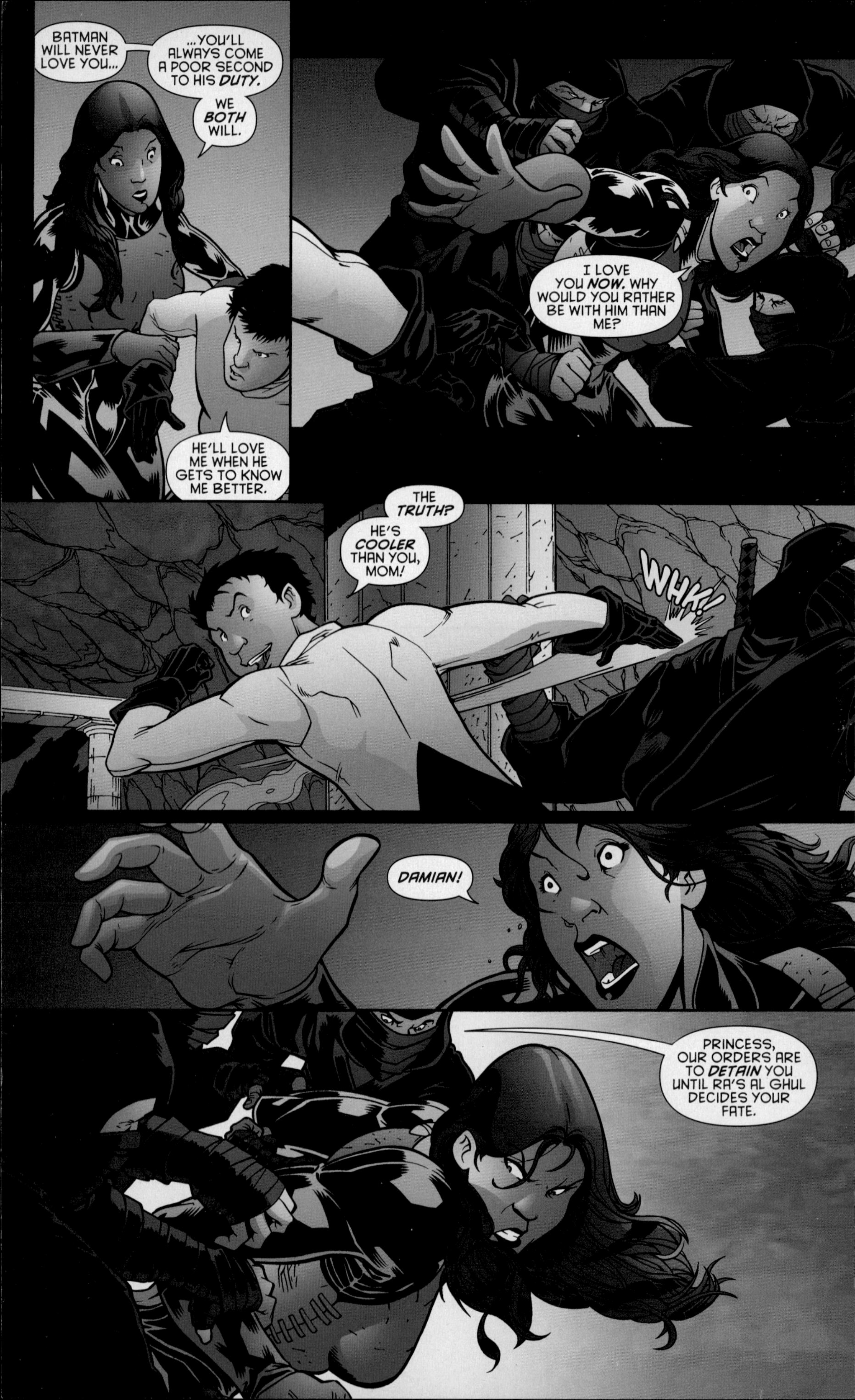
BATMAN WILL NEVER LOVE YOU...
...YOU'LL ALWAYS COME A POOR SECOND TO HIS *DUTY.*
WE *BOTH* WILL.
HE'LL LOVE ME WHEN HE GETS TO KNOW ME BETTER.
I LOVE YOU *NOW.* WHY WOULD YOU RATHER BE WITH HIM THAN ME?
THE *TRUTH?*
HE'S *COOLER* THAN YOU, MOM!
WHK!
DAMIAN!
PRINCESS, OUR ORDERS ARE TO *DETAIN* YOU UNTIL RA'S AL GHUL DECIDES YOUR FATE.

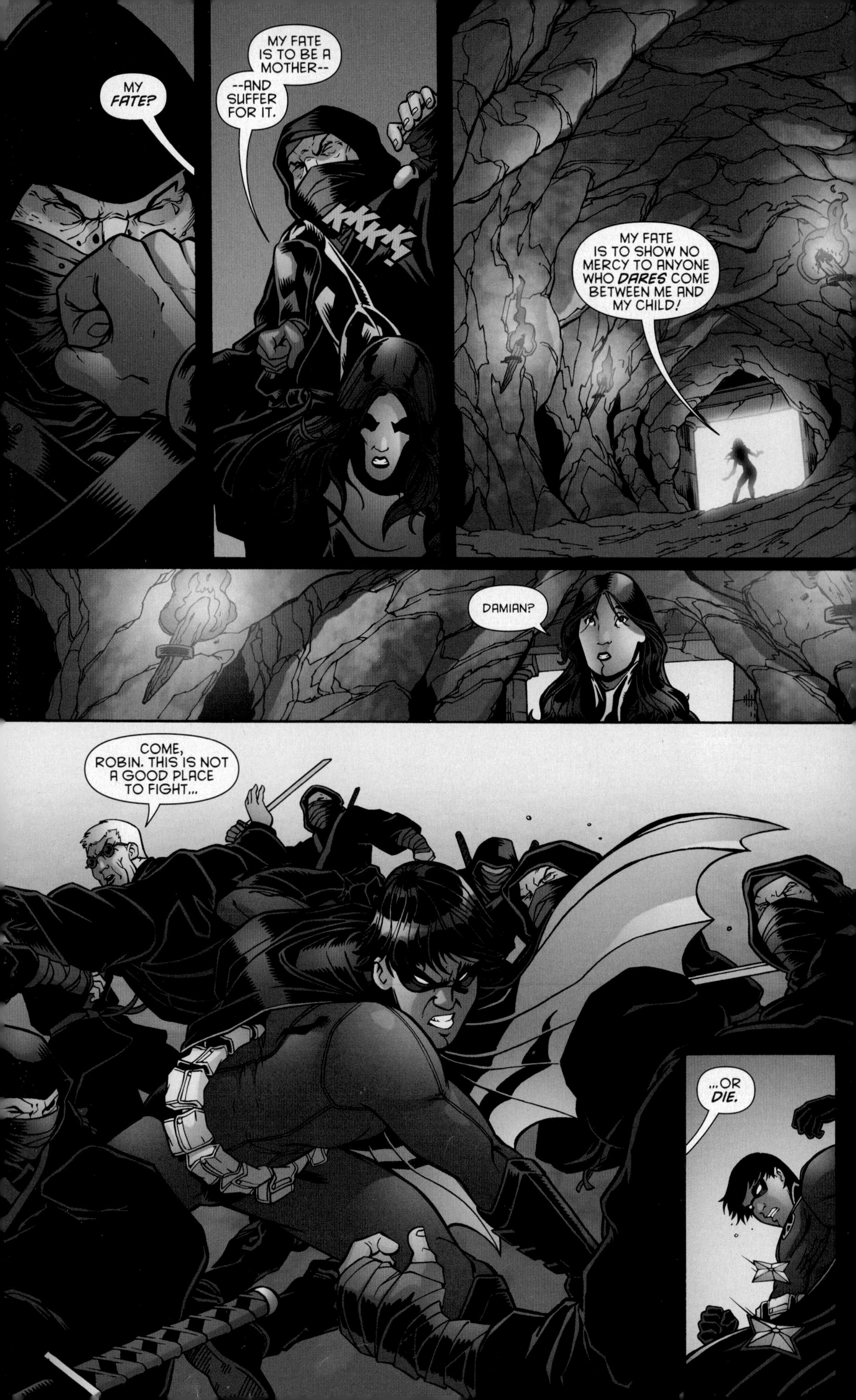
MY FATE?
MY FATE IS TO BE A MOTHER--
--AND SUFFER FOR IT.
KKKK!
MY FATE IS TO SHOW NO MERCY TO ANYONE WHO DARES COME BETWEEN ME AND MY CHILD!
DAMIAN?
COME, ROBIN. THIS IS NOT A GOOD PLACE TO FIGHT...
...OR DIE.

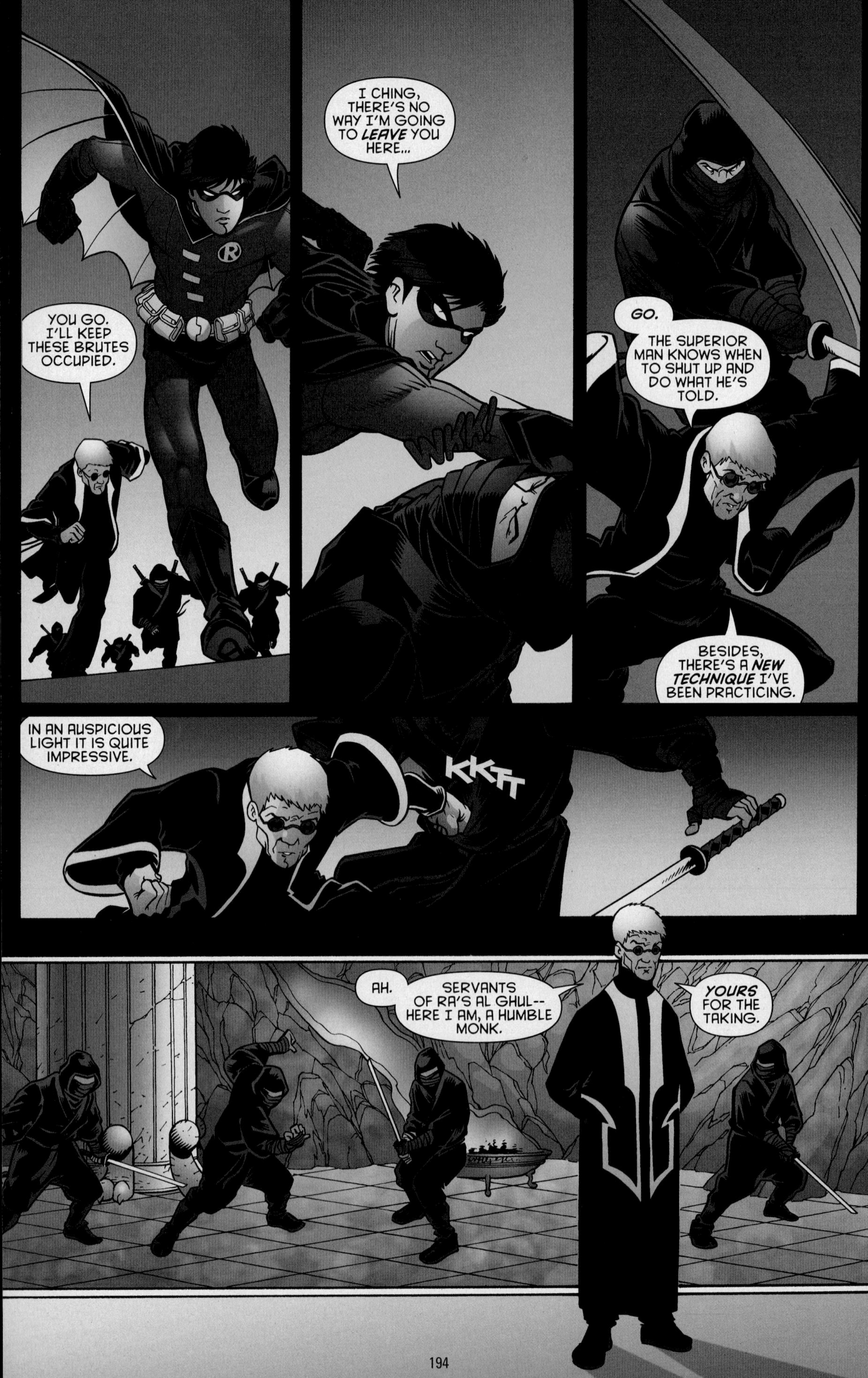
YOU GO. I'LL KEEP THESE BRUTES OCCUPIED.
I CHING, THERE'S NO WAY I'M GOING TO LEAVE YOU HERE...
WKK!
GO.
THE SUPERIOR MAN KNOWS WHEN TO SHUT UP AND DO WHAT HE'S TOLD.
BESIDES, THERE'S A NEW TECHNIQUE I'VE BEEN PRACTICING.
IN AN AUSPICIOUS LIGHT IT IS QUITE IMPRESSIVE.
KKFT
AH.
SERVANTS OF RA'S AL GHUL-- HERE I AM, A HUMBLE MONK.
YOURS FOR THE TAKING.

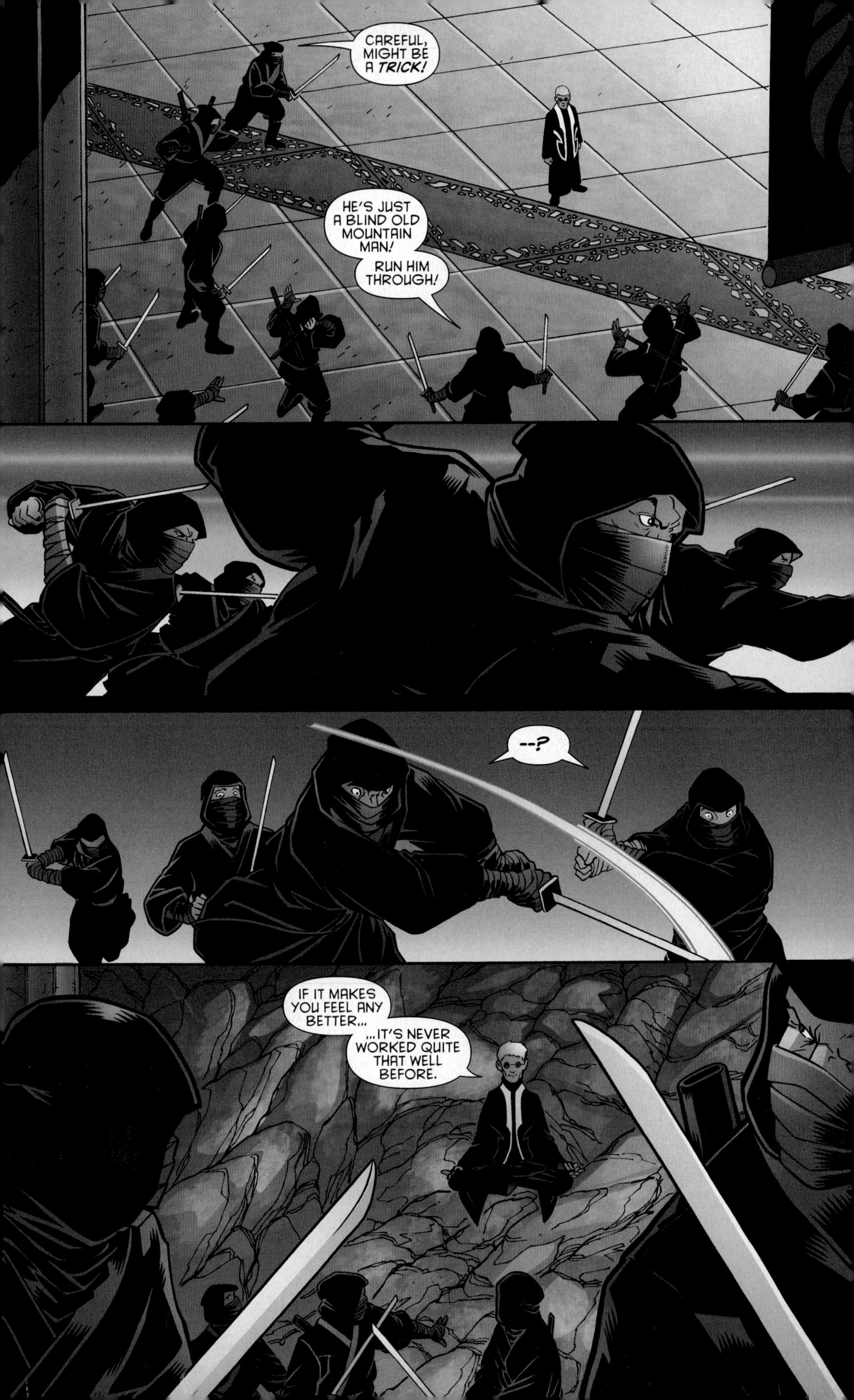
CAREFUL, MIGHT BE A TRICK!
HE'S JUST A BLIND OLD MOUNTAIN MAN!
RUN HIM THROUGH!
--?
IF IT MAKES YOU FEEL ANY BETTER...
...IT'S NEVER WORKED QUITE THAT WELL BEFORE.

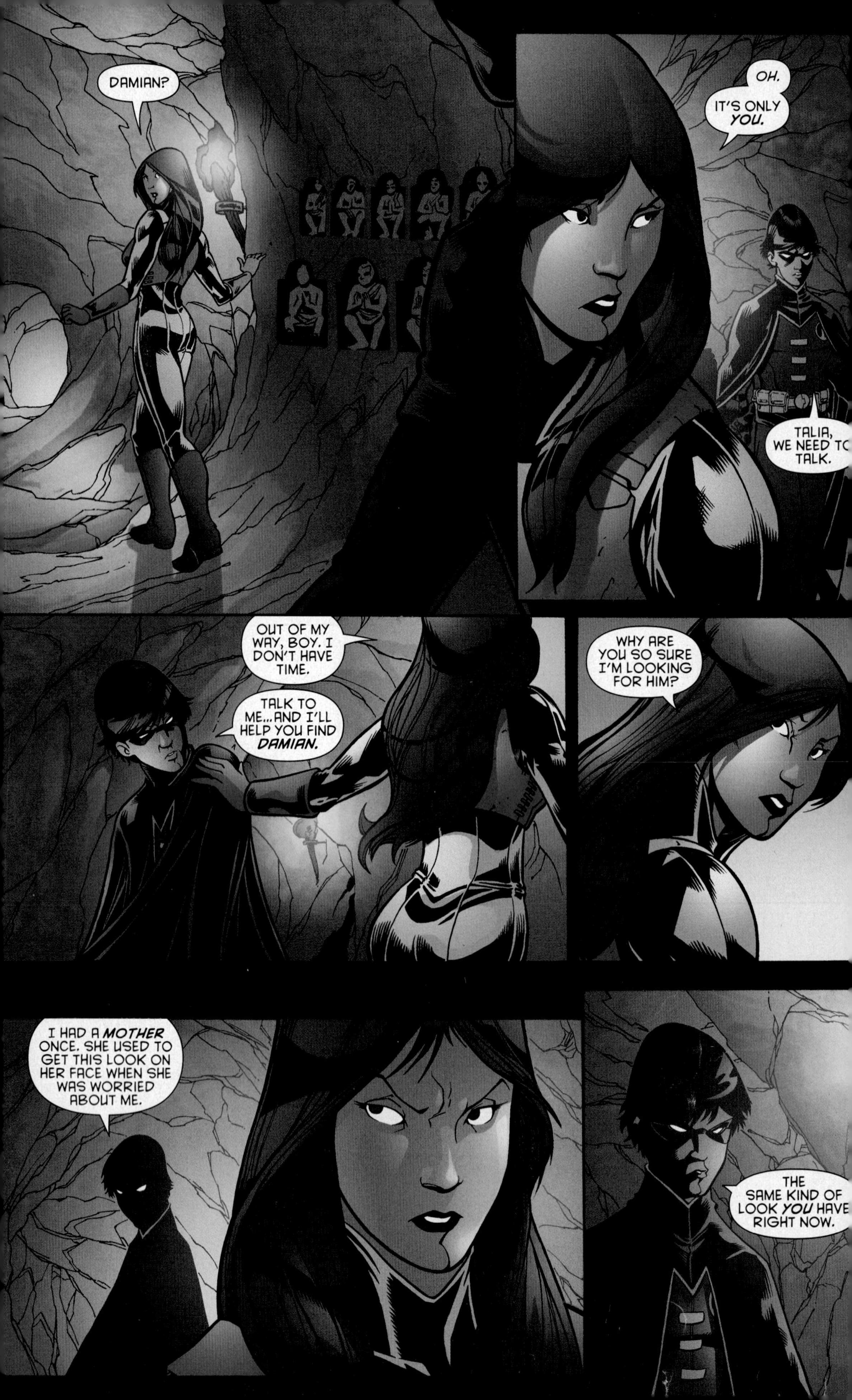
DAMIAN?
OH.
IT'S ONLY YOU.
TALIA, WE NEED TO TALK.
OUT OF MY WAY, BOY. I DON'T HAVE TIME.
TALK TO ME...AND I'LL HELP YOU FIND DAMIAN.
WHY ARE YOU SO SURE I'M LOOKING FOR HIM?
I HAD A MOTHER ONCE. SHE USED TO GET THIS LOOK ON HER FACE WHEN SHE WAS WORRIED ABOUT ME.
THE SAME KIND OF LOOK YOU HAVE RIGHT NOW.

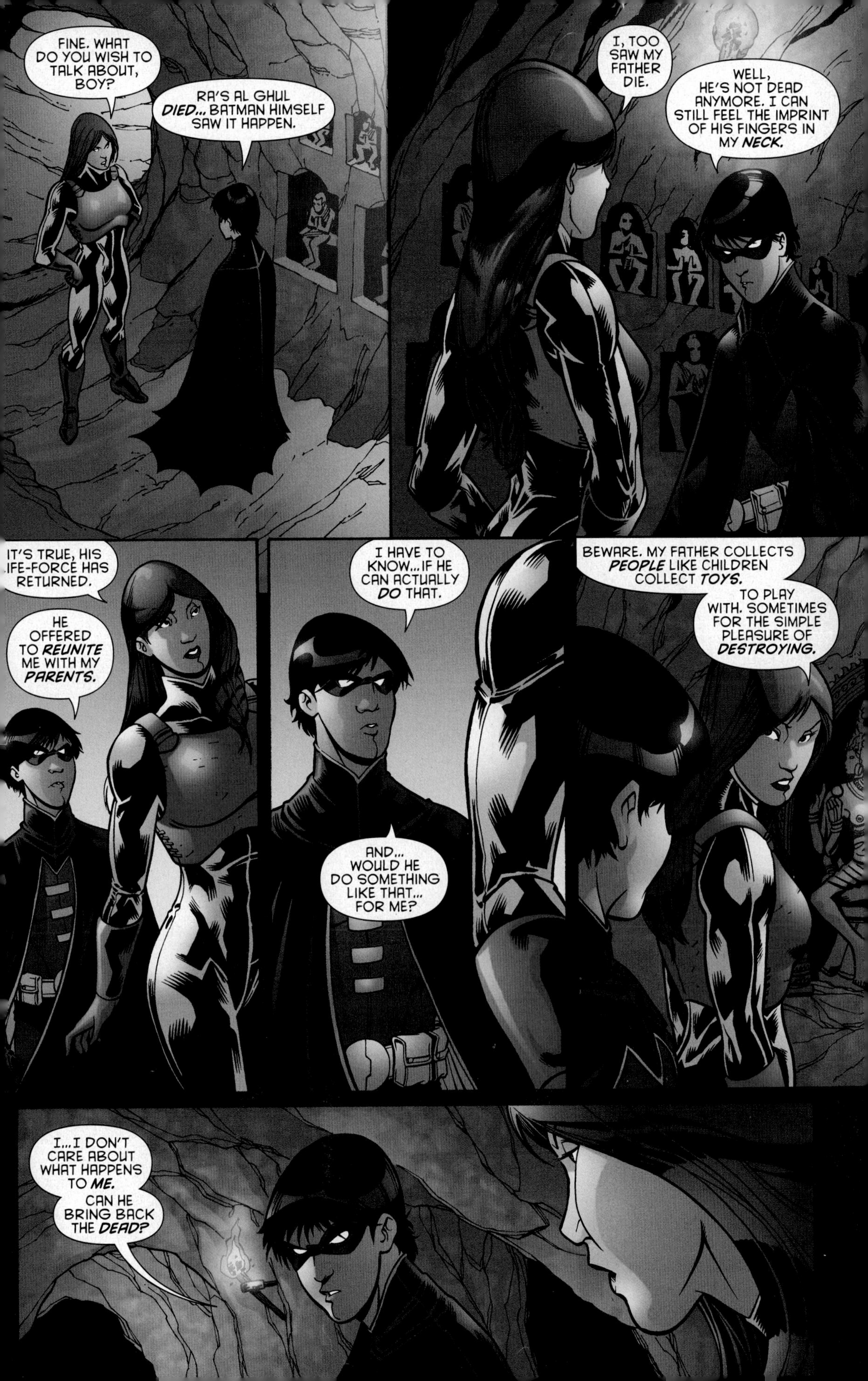

FINE. WHAT DO YOU WISH TO TALK ABOUT, BOY?
RA'S AL GHUL *DIED*... BATMAN HIMSELF SAW IT HAPPEN.
I, TOO SAW MY FATHER DIE.
WELL, HE'S NOT DEAD ANYMORE. I CAN STILL FEEL THE IMPRINT OF HIS FINGERS IN MY *NECK.*
IT'S TRUE, HIS IFE-FORCE HAS RETURNED.
HE OFFERED TO *REUNITE* ME WITH MY *PARENTS.*
I HAVE TO KNOW... IF HE CAN ACTUALLY *DO* THAT.
AND... WOULD HE DO SOMETHING LIKE THAT... FOR ME?
BEWARE. MY FATHER COLLECTS *PEOPLE* LIKE CHILDREN COLLECT *TOYS.*
TO PLAY WITH. SOMETIMES FOR THE SIMPLE PLEASURE OF *DESTROYING.*
I... I DON'T CARE ABOUT WHAT HAPPENS TO *ME.*
CAN HE BRING BACK THE *DEAD?*

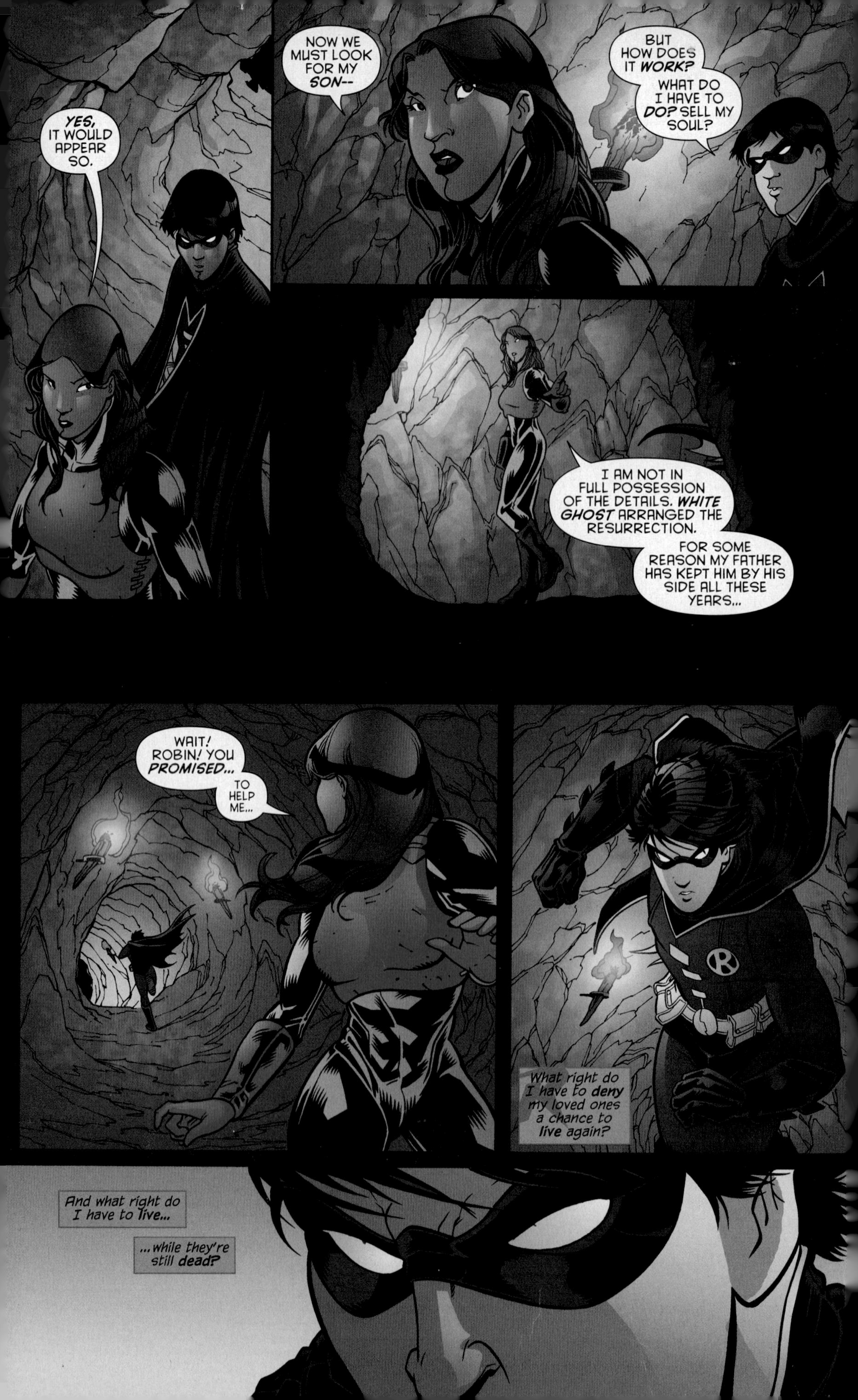
YES, IT WOULD APPEAR SO.
NOW WE MUST LOOK FOR MY SON--
BUT HOW DOES IT WORK?
WHAT DO I HAVE TO DO? SELL MY SOUL?
I AM NOT IN FULL POSSESSION OF THE DETAILS. WHITE GHOST ARRANGED THE RESURRECTION.
FOR SOME REASON MY FATHER HAS KEPT HIM BY HIS SIDE ALL THESE YEARS...
WAIT! ROBIN! YOU PROMISED...
TO HELP ME...
What right do I have to deny my loved ones a chance to live again?
And what right do I have to live...
...while they're still dead?

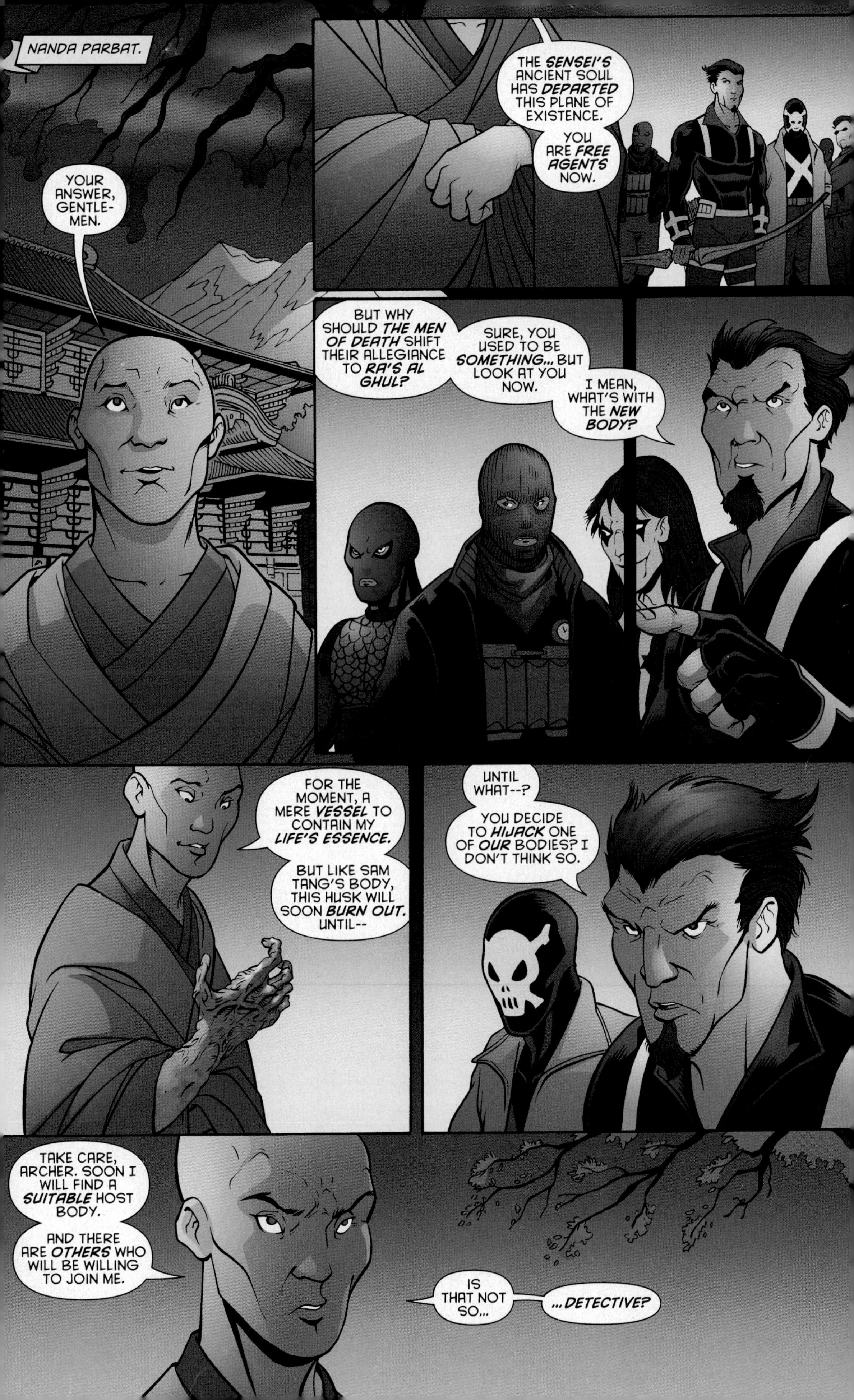
NANDA PARBAT.
YOUR ANSWER, GENTLEMEN.
THE SENSEI'S ANCIENT SOUL HAS DEPARTED THIS PLANE OF EXISTENCE.
YOU ARE FREE AGENTS NOW.
BUT WHY SHOULD THE MEN OF DEATH SHIFT THEIR ALLEGIANCE TO RA'S AL GHUL?
SURE, YOU USED TO BE SOMETHING... BUT LOOK AT YOU NOW.
I MEAN, WHAT'S WITH THE NEW BODY?
FOR THE MOMENT, A MERE VESSEL TO CONTAIN MY LIFE'S ESSENCE.
BUT LIKE SAM TANG'S BODY, THIS HUSK WILL SOON BURN OUT. UNTIL--
UNTIL WHAT--?
YOU DECIDE TO HIJACK ONE OF OUR BODIES? I DON'T THINK SO.
TAKE CARE, ARCHER. SOON I WILL FIND A SUITABLE HOST BODY.
AND THERE ARE OTHERS WHO WILL BE WILLING TO JOIN ME.
IS THAT NOT SO...
...DETECTIVE?

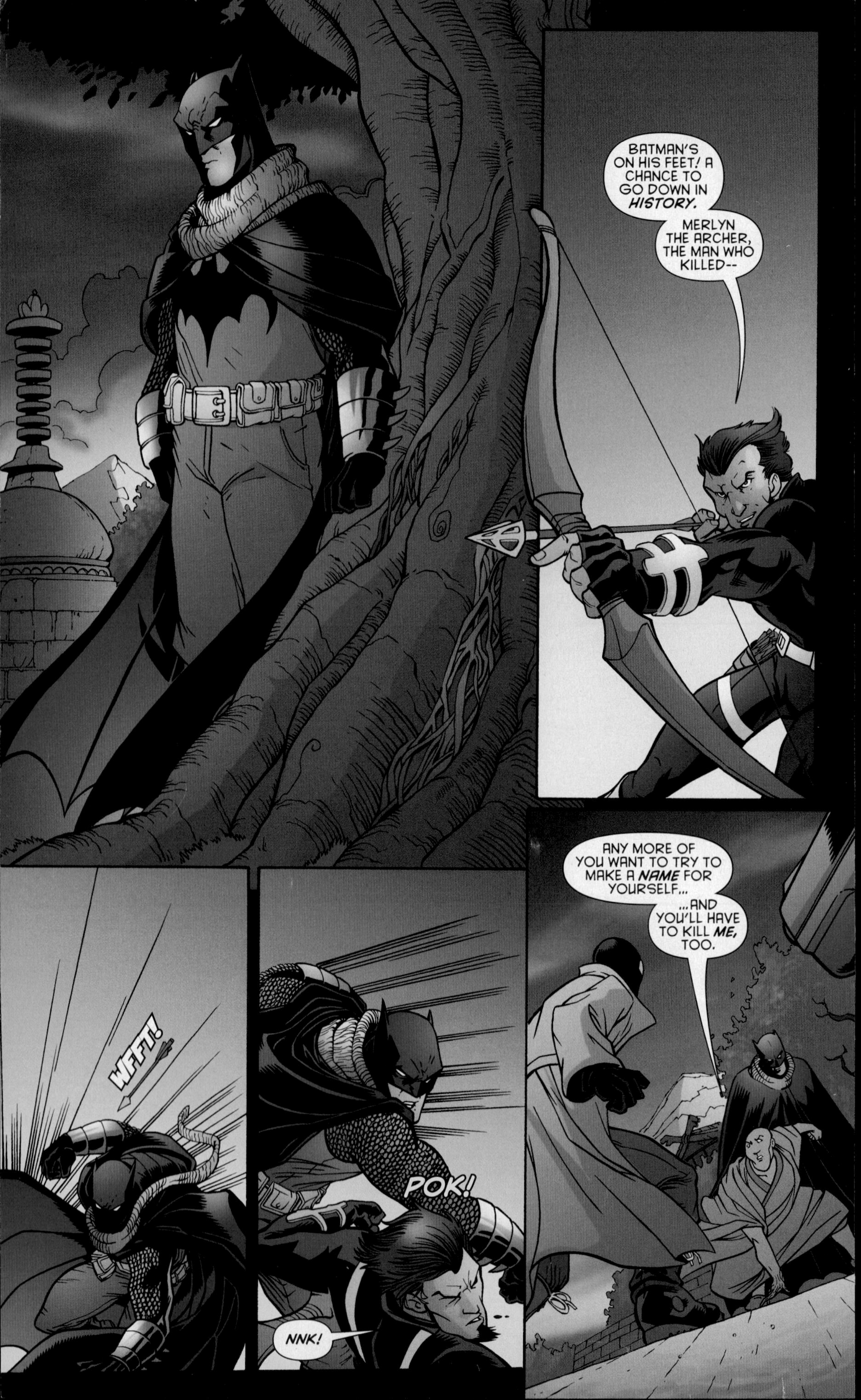
BATMAN'S ON HIS FEET! A CHANCE TO GO DOWN IN *HISTORY.*
MERLYN THE ARCHER, THE MAN WHO KILLED--
WFFT!
POK!
NNK!
ANY MORE OF YOU WANT TO TRY TO MAKE A *NAME* FOR YOURSELF...
...AND YOU'LL HAVE TO KILL *ME,* TOO.

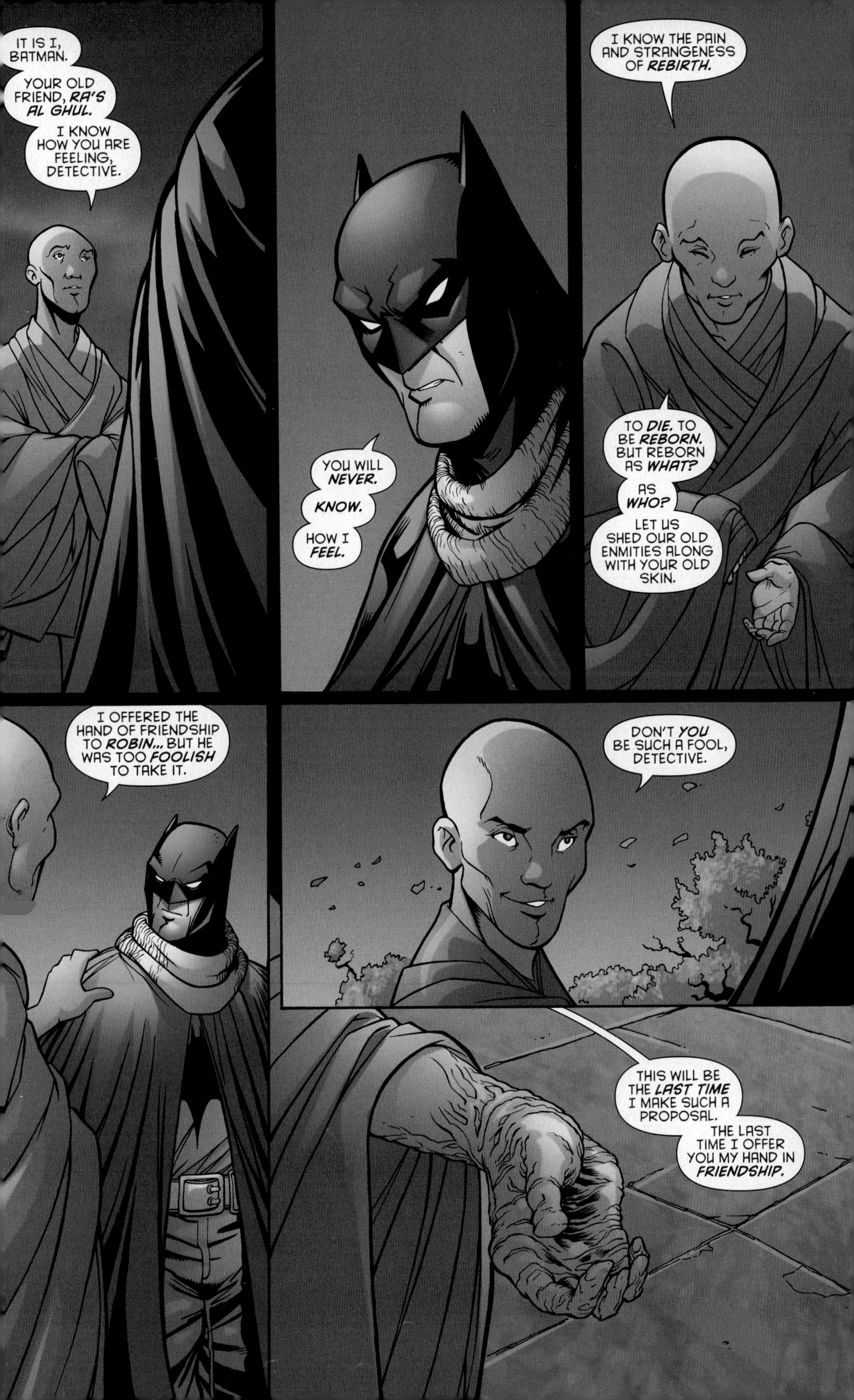
IT IS I, BATMAN.
YOUR OLD FRIEND, RA'S AL GHUL.
I KNOW HOW YOU ARE FEELING, DETECTIVE.
YOU WILL NEVER.
KNOW.
HOW I FEEL.
I KNOW THE PAIN AND STRANGENESS OF REBIRTH.
TO DIE. TO BE REBORN. BUT REBORN AS WHAT?
AS WHO?
LET US SHED OUR OLD ENMITIES ALONG WITH YOUR OLD SKIN.
I OFFERED THE HAND OF FRIENDSHIP TO ROBIN... BUT HE WAS TOO FOOLISH TO TAKE IT.
DON'T YOU BE SUCH A FOOL, DETECTIVE.
THIS WILL BE THE LAST TIME I MAKE SUCH A PROPOSAL.
THE LAST TIME I OFFER YOU MY HAND IN FRIENDSHIP.

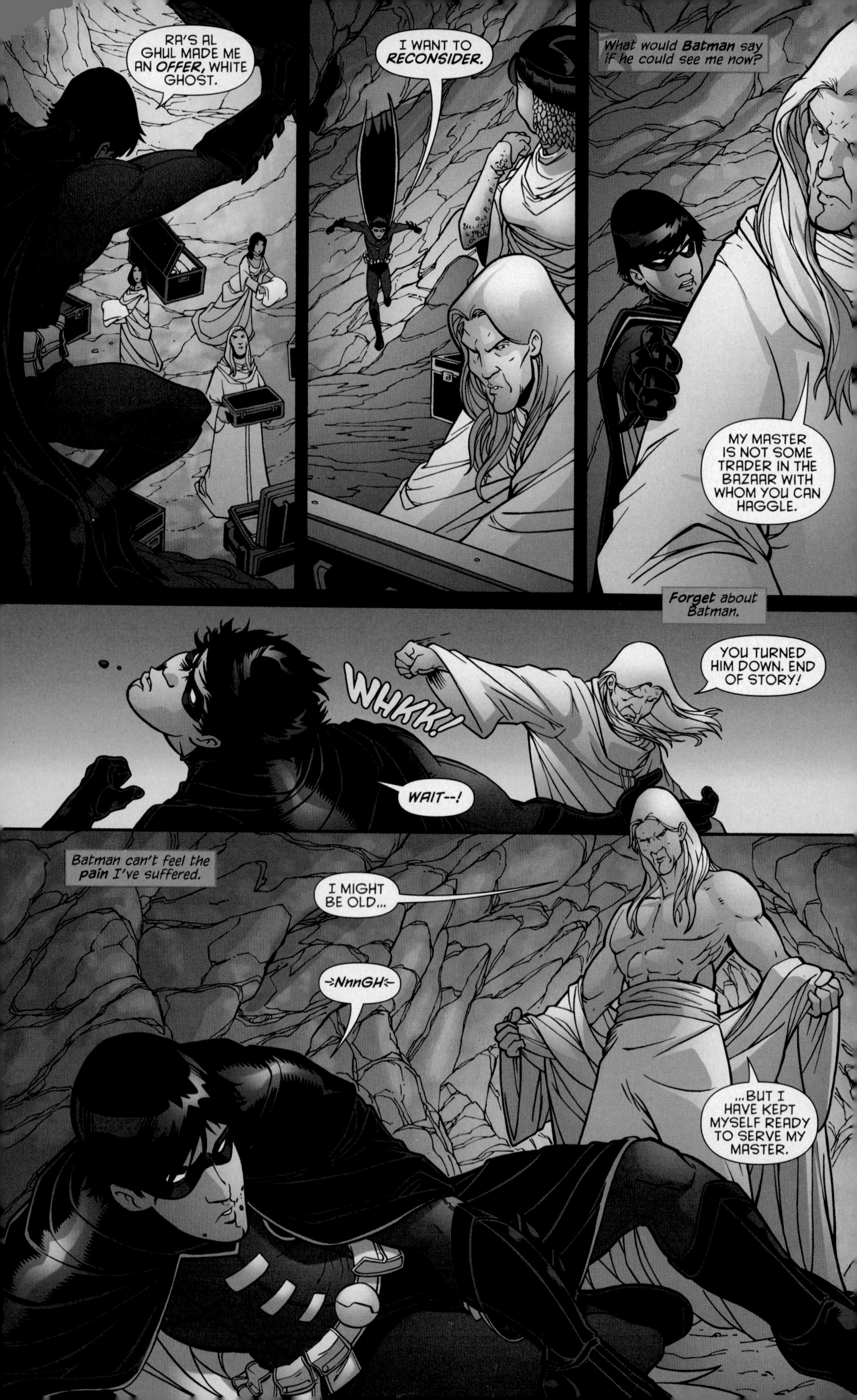
RA'S AL GHUL MADE ME AN OFFER, WHITE GHOST.
I WANT TO RECONSIDER.
What would Batman say if he could see me now?
MY MASTER IS NOT SOME TRADER IN THE BAZAAR WITH WHOM YOU CAN HAGGLE.
Forget about Batman.
YOU TURNED HIM DOWN. END OF STORY!
WHKK!
WAIT--!
Batman can't feel the pain I've suffered.
I MIGHT BE OLD...
NnnGH
...BUT I HAVE KEPT MYSELF READY TO SERVE MY MASTER.

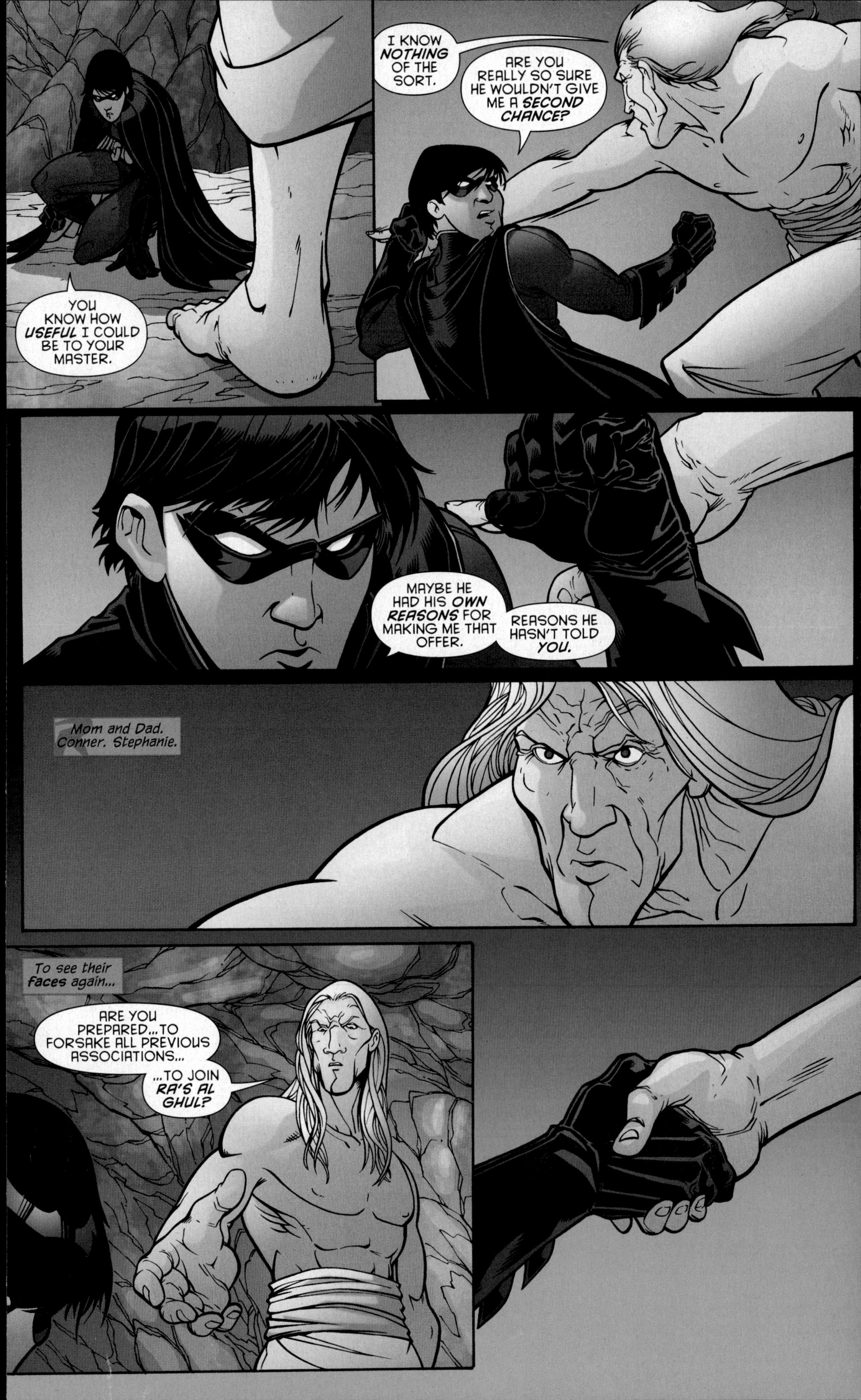
YOU KNOW HOW USEFUL I COULD BE TO YOUR MASTER.
I KNOW NOTHING OF THE SORT.
ARE YOU REALLY SO SURE HE WOULDN'T GIVE ME A SECOND CHANCE?
MAYBE HE HAD HIS OWN REASONS FOR MAKING ME THAT OFFER.
REASONS HE HASN'T TOLD YOU.
Mom and Dad. Conner. Stephanie.
To see their faces again...
ARE YOU PREPARED...TO FORSAKE ALL PREVIOUS ASSOCIATIONS...
...TO JOIN RA'S AL GHUL?

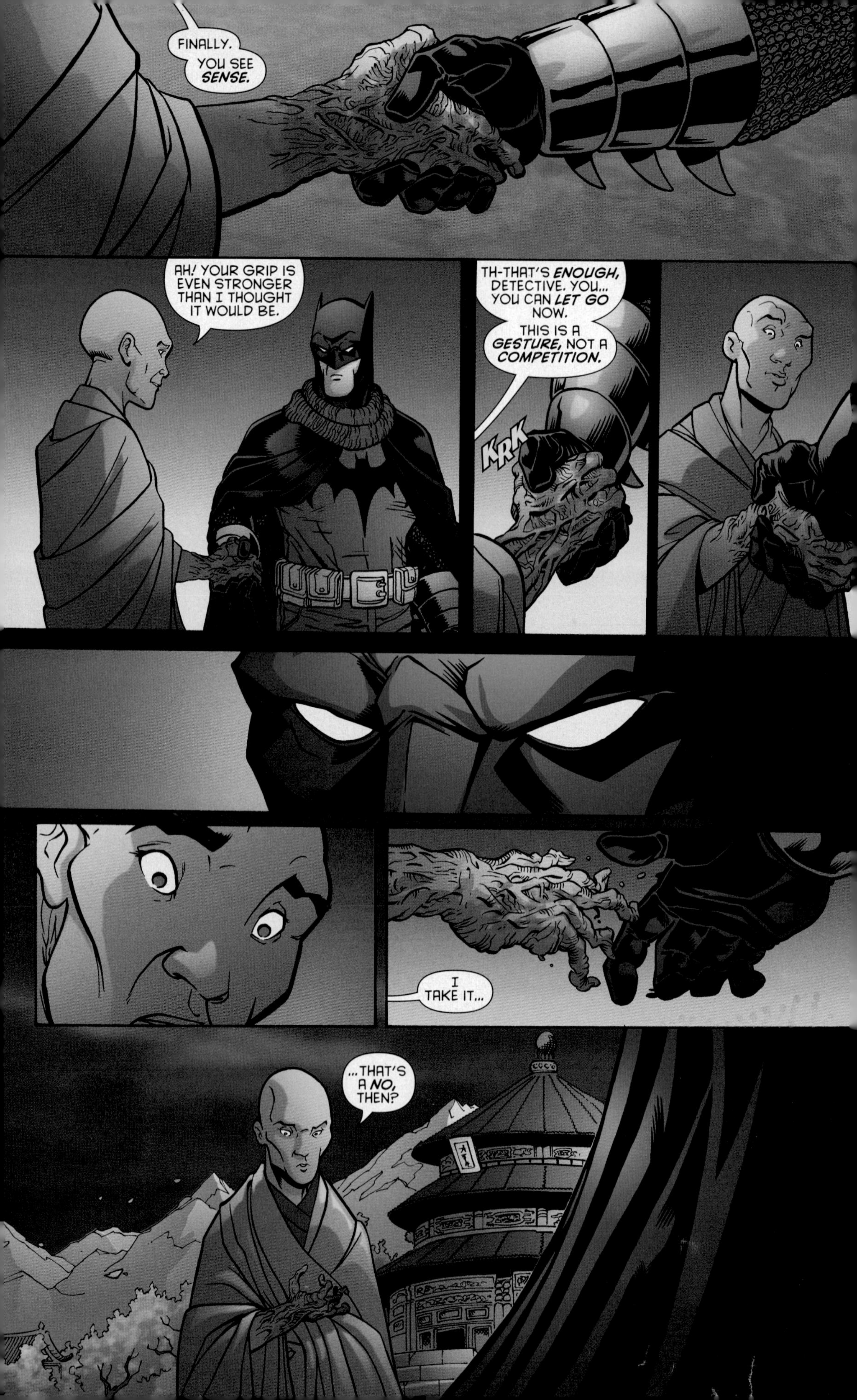
FINALLY. YOU SEE SENSE.
AH! YOUR GRIP IS EVEN STRONGER THAN I THOUGHT IT WOULD BE.
TH-THAT'S ENOUGH, DETECTIVE. YOU... YOU CAN LET GO NOW.
THIS IS A GESTURE, NOT A COMPETITION.
KRK
I TAKE IT...
...THAT'S A NO, THEN?

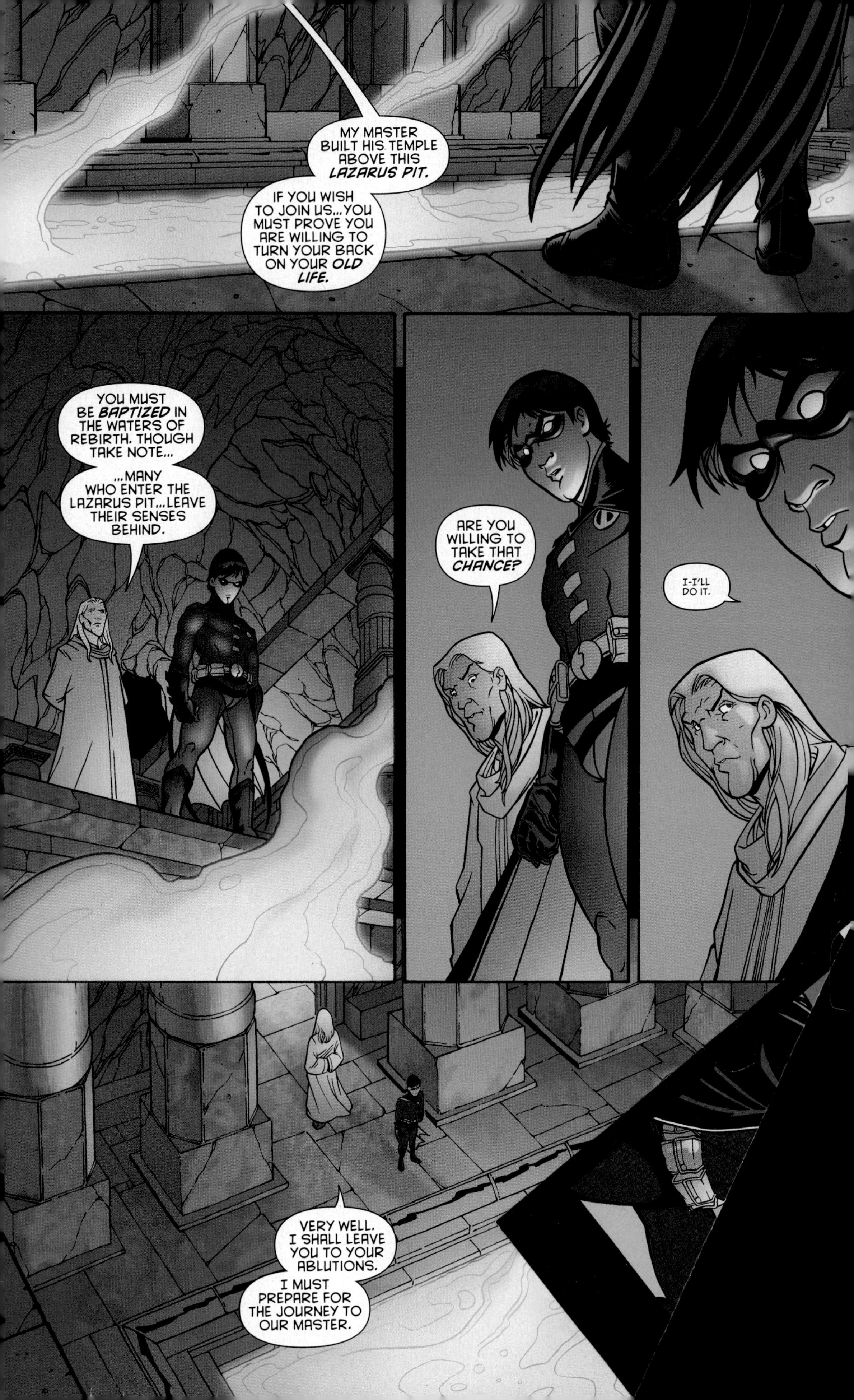
MY MASTER BUILT HIS TEMPLE ABOVE THIS LAZARUS PIT.
IF YOU WISH TO JOIN US...YOU MUST PROVE YOU ARE WILLING TO TURN YOUR BACK ON YOUR OLD LIFE.
YOU MUST BE BAPTIZED IN THE WATERS OF REBIRTH. THOUGH TAKE NOTE...
...MANY WHO ENTER THE LAZARUS PIT...LEAVE THEIR SENSES BEHIND.
ARE YOU WILLING TO TAKE THAT CHANCE?
I-I'LL DO IT.
VERY WELL. I SHALL LEAVE YOU TO YOUR ABLUTIONS.
I MUST PREPARE FOR THE JOURNEY TO OUR MASTER.

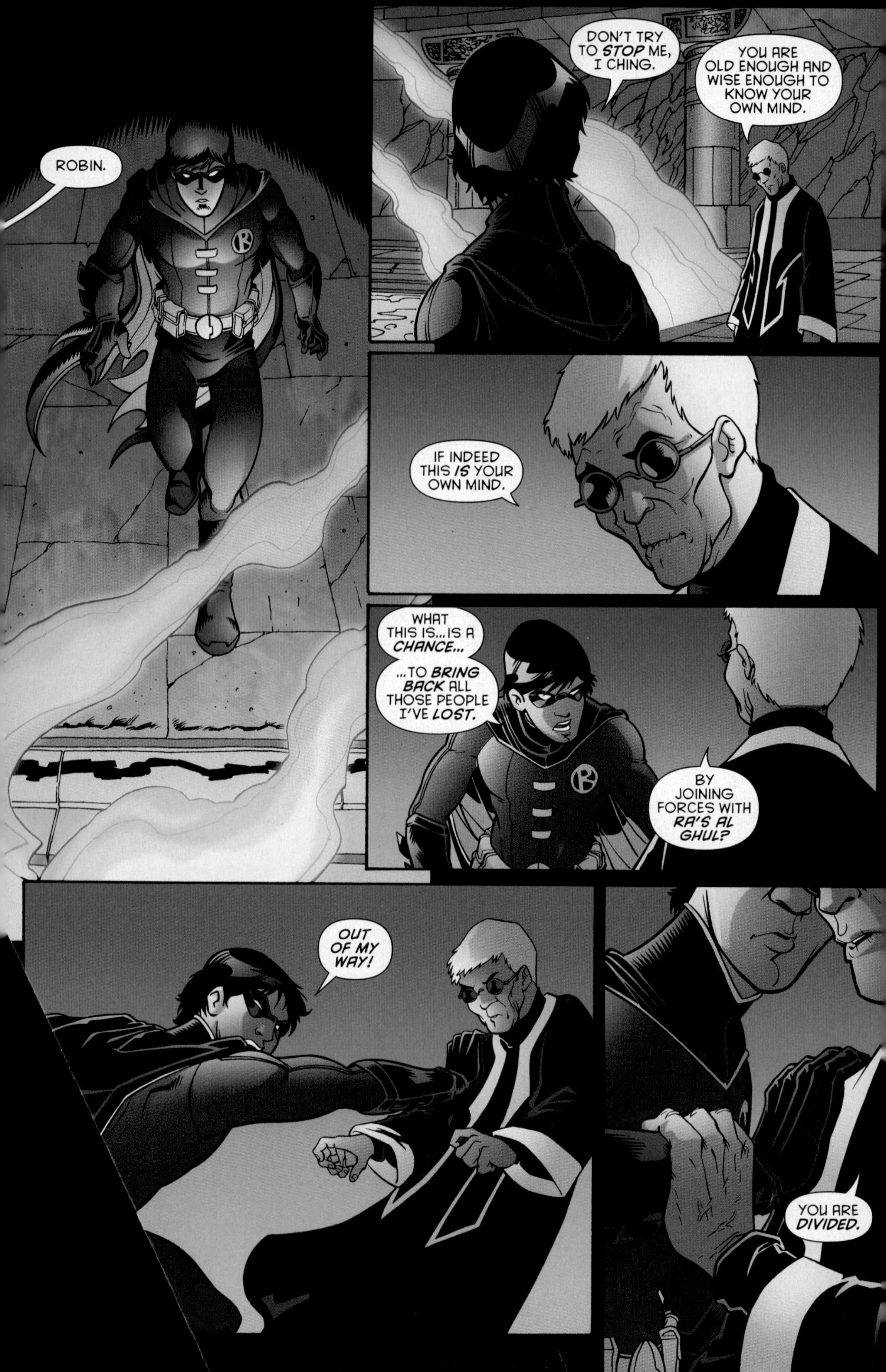

ROBIN.
DON'T TRY TO STOP ME, I CHING.
YOU ARE OLD ENOUGH AND WISE ENOUGH TO KNOW YOUR OWN MIND.
IF INDEED THIS IS YOUR OWN MIND.
WHAT THIS IS...IS A CHANCE...
...TO BRING BACK ALL THOSE PEOPLE I'VE LOST.
BY JOINING FORCES WITH RA'S AL GHUL?
OUT OF MY WAY!
YOU ARE DIVIDED.

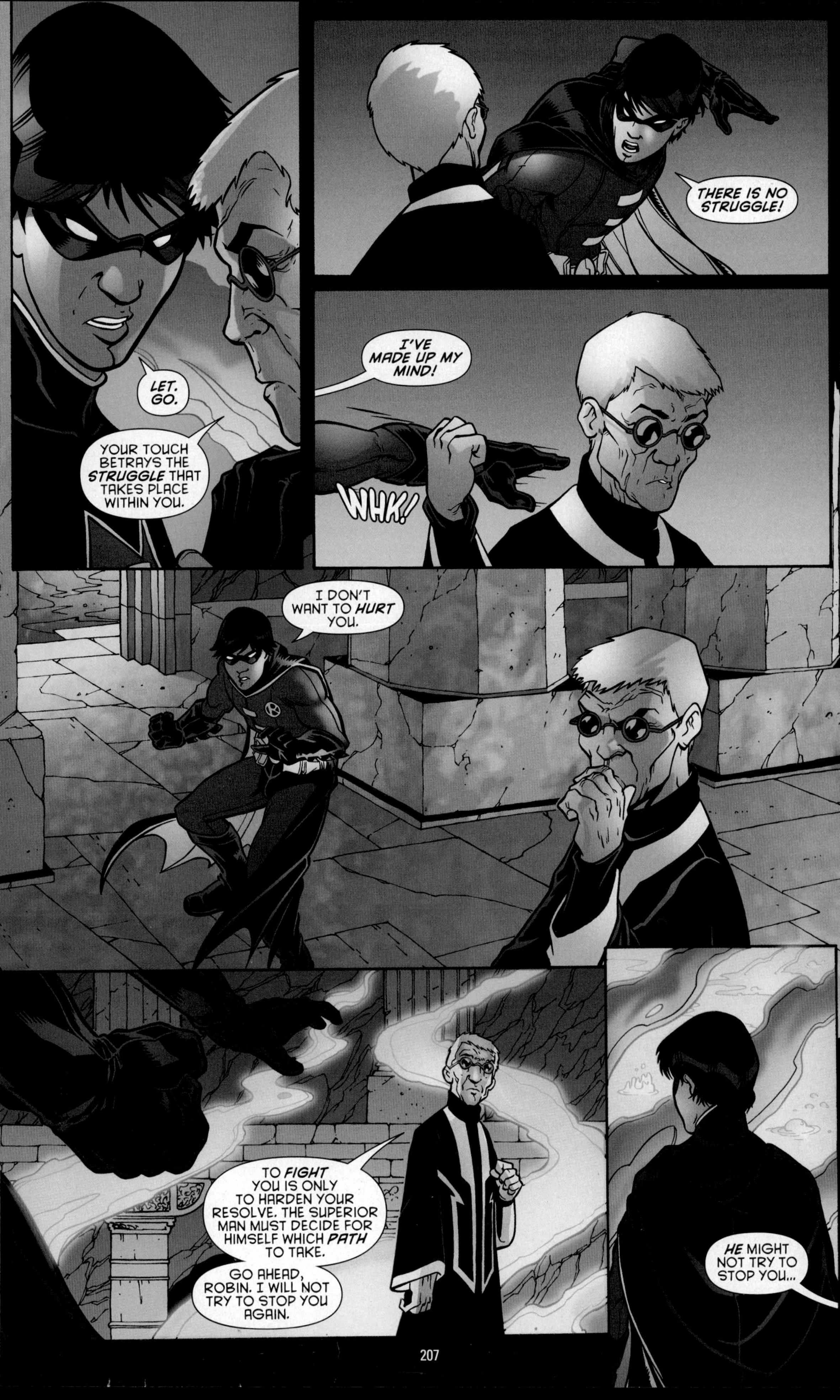
LET. GO.
YOUR TOUCH BETRAYS THE STRUGGLE THAT TAKES PLACE WITHIN YOU.
THERE IS NO STRUGGLE!
I'VE MADE UP MY MIND!
WHK!
I DON'T WANT TO HURT YOU.
TO FIGHT YOU IS ONLY TO HARDEN YOUR RESOLVE. THE SUPERIOR MAN MUST DECIDE FOR HIMSELF WHICH PATH TO TAKE.
GO AHEAD, ROBIN. I WILL NOT TRY TO STOP YOU AGAIN.
HE MIGHT NOT TRY TO STOP YOU...

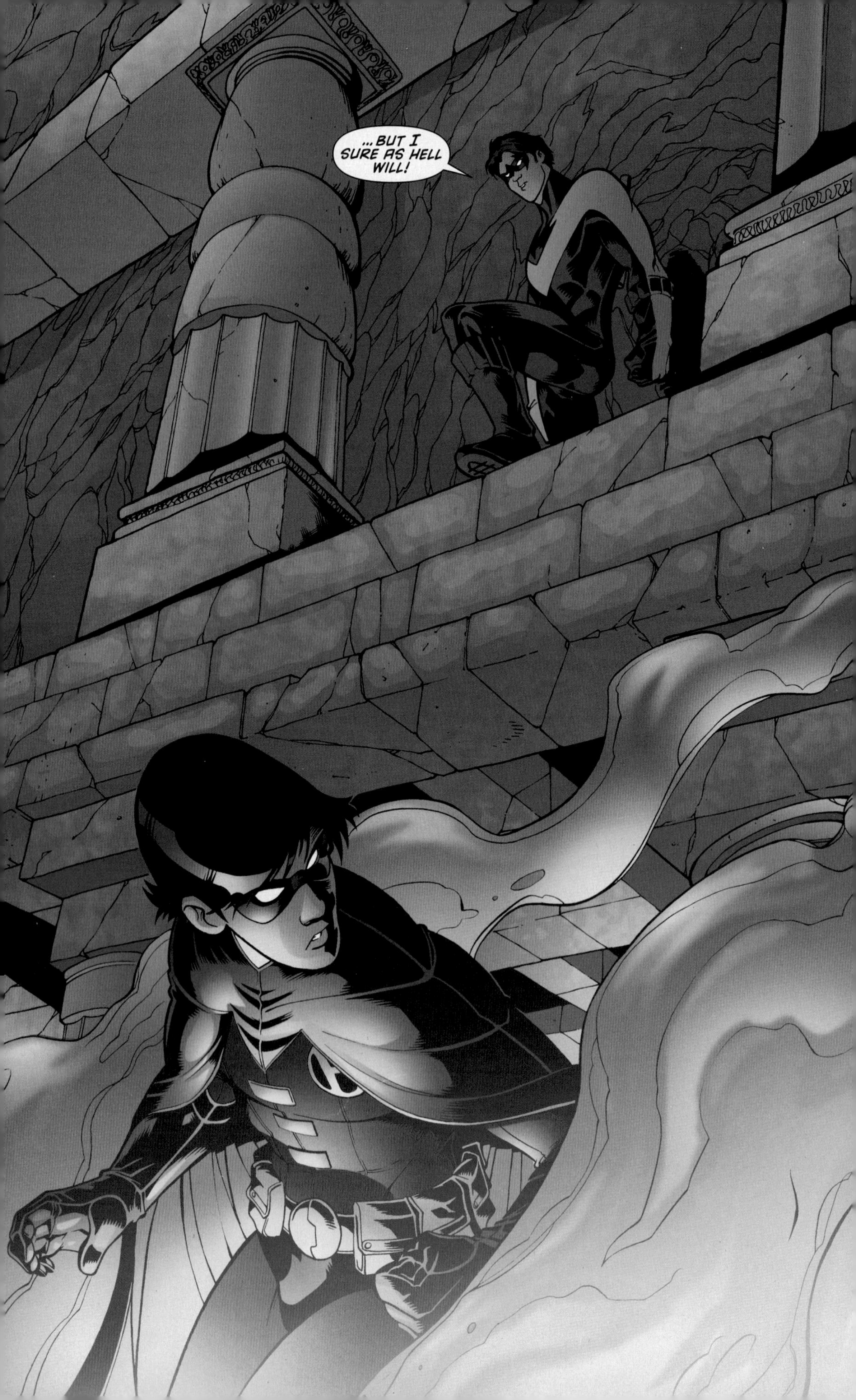
...BUT I SURE AS HELL WILL!

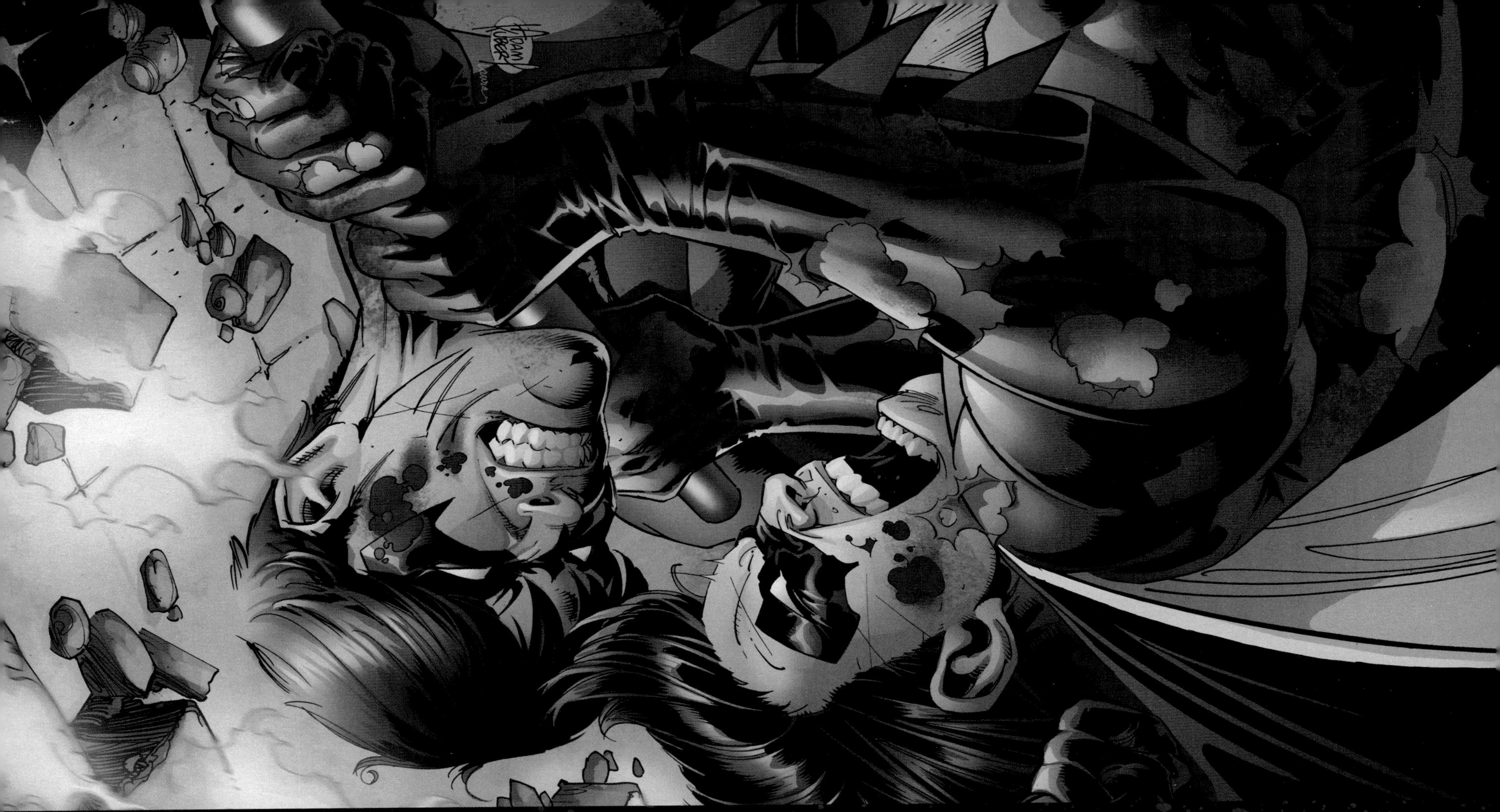
ADAM KUBERT

CHAPTER SIX LIVING PROOF

Cover art by Adam Kubert Chapter written by Fabian Nicieza Chapter pencilled by Don Kramer with Carlos Rodriguez Chapter inked by Wayne Faucher with Bit

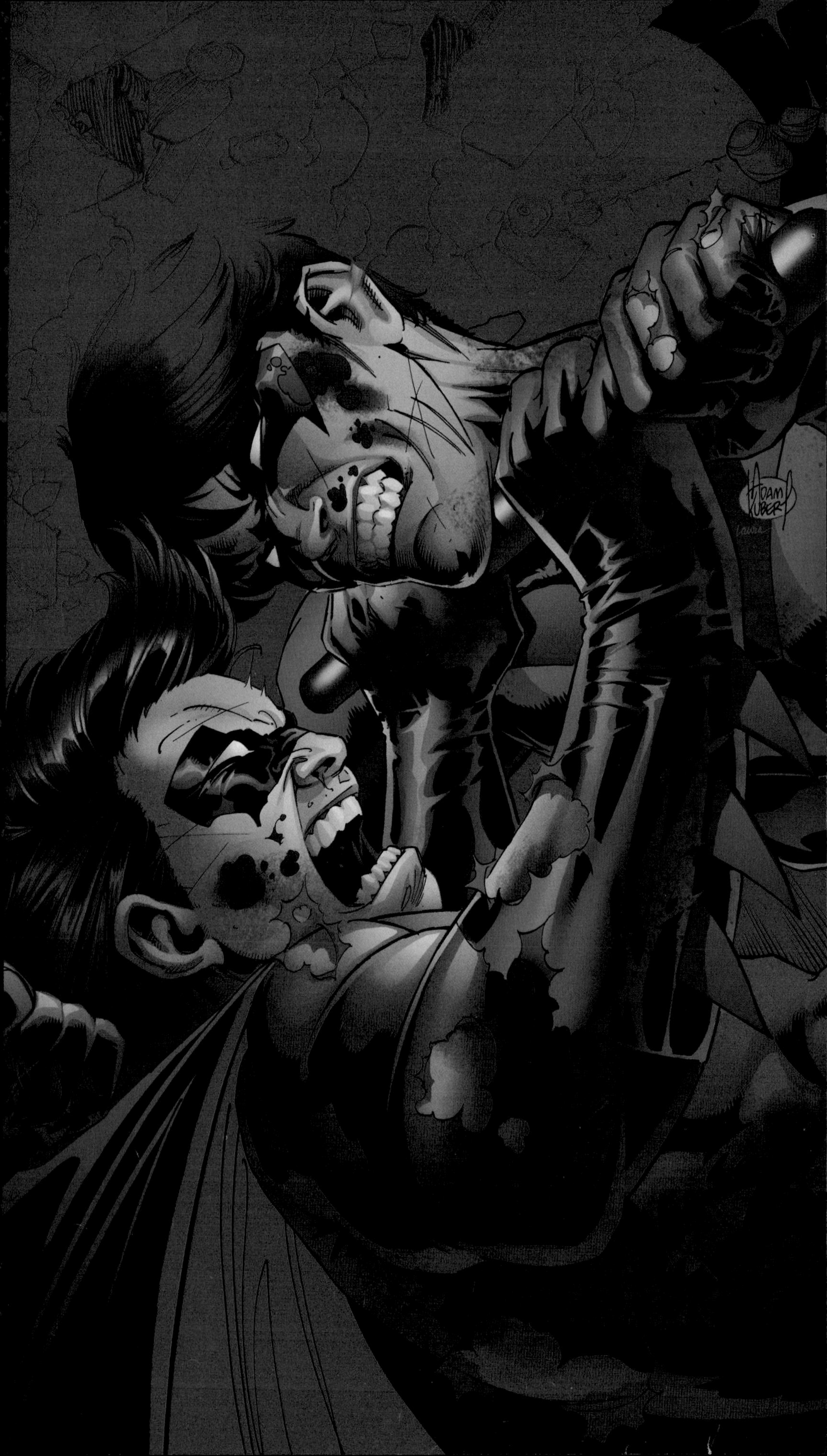
ADAM KUBERT
Variant cover by Adam Kubert

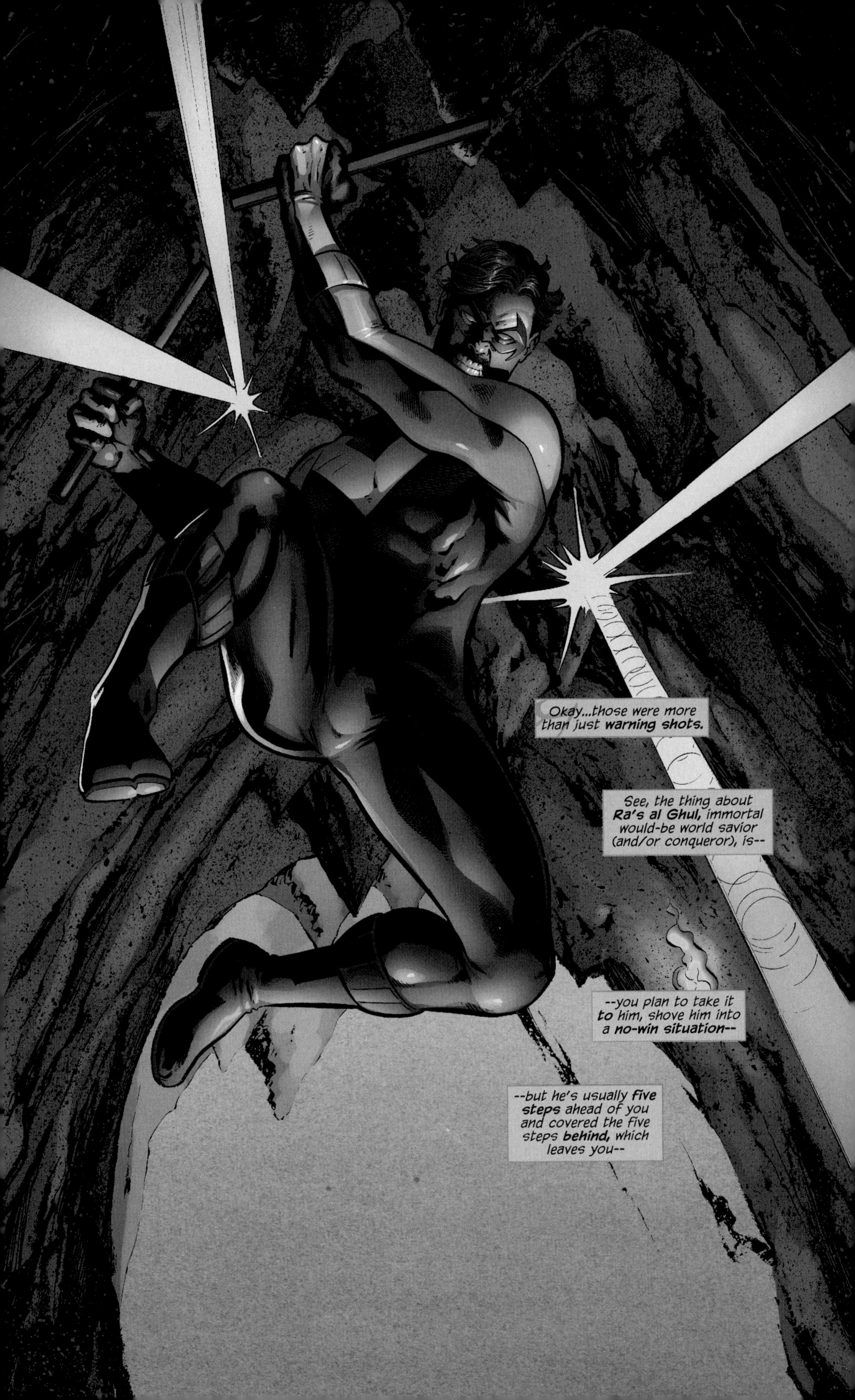

Okay...those were more than just warning shots.
See, the thing about Ra's al Ghul, immortal would-be world savior (and/or conqueror), is--
--you plan to take it to him, shove him into a no-win situation--
--but he's usually five steps ahead of you and covered the five steps behind, which leaves you--

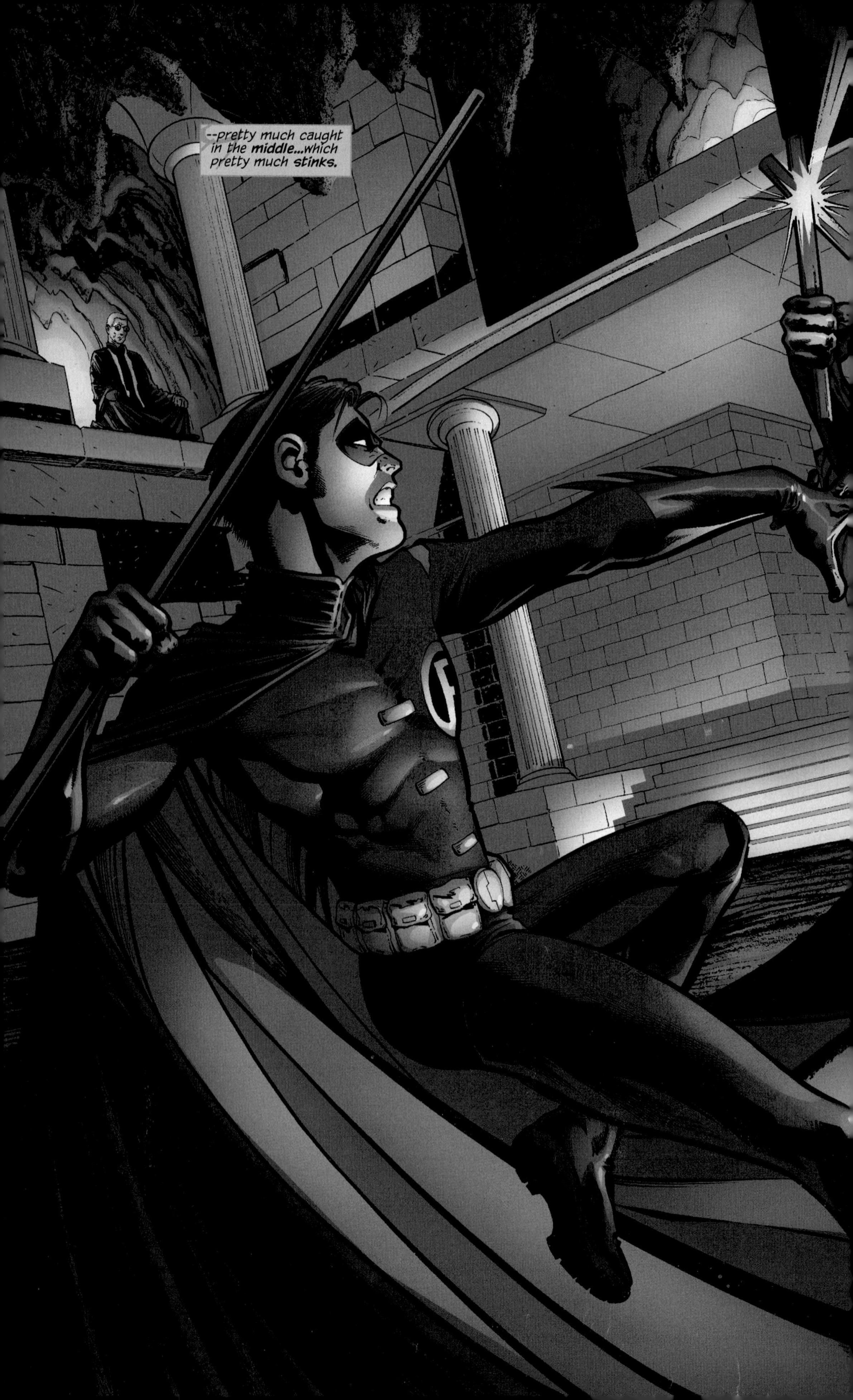
--pretty much caught in the **middle**...which pretty much **stinks.**

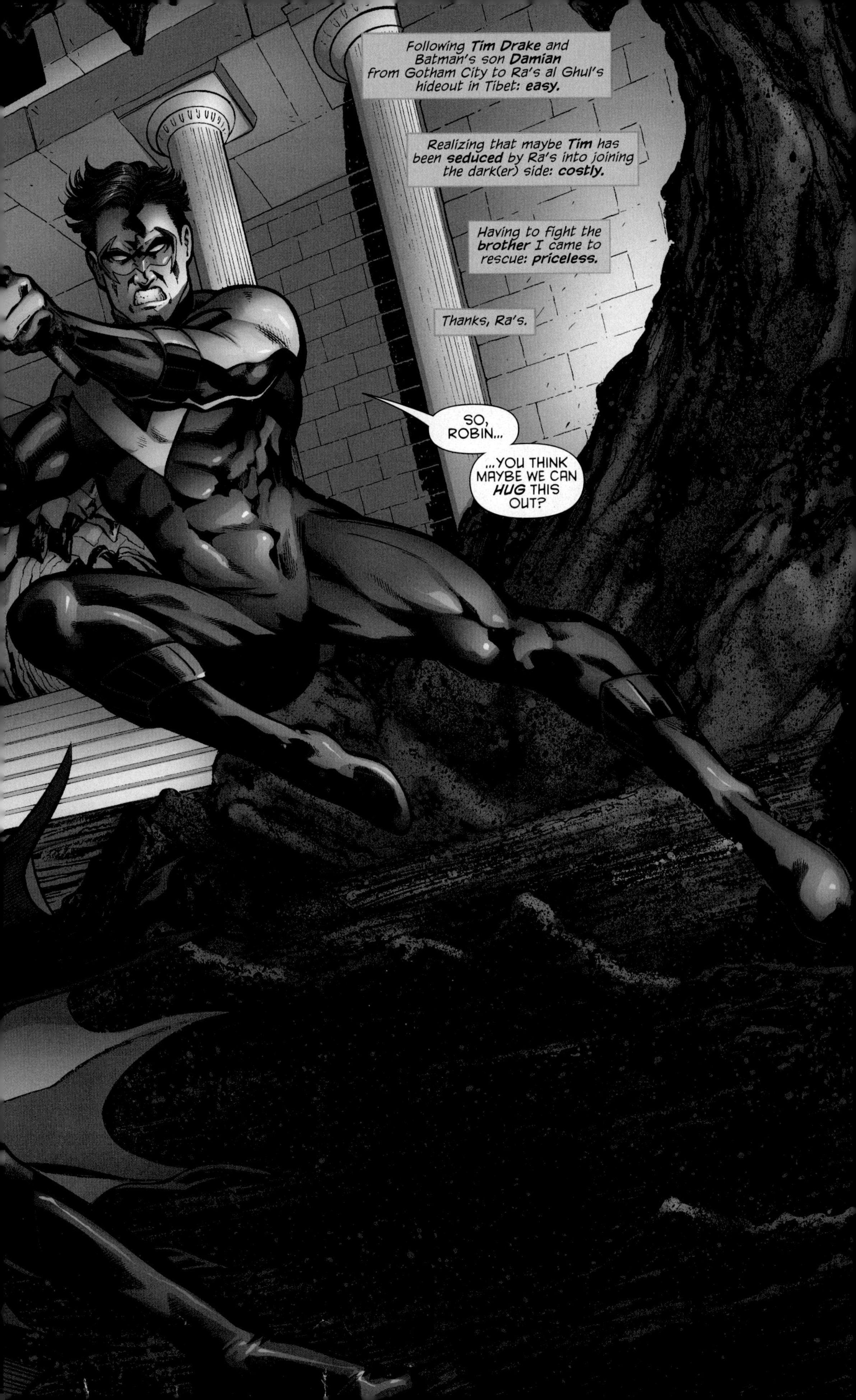

Following Tim Drake and Batman's son Damian from Gotham City to Ra's al Ghul's hideout in Tibet: easy.
Realizing that maybe Tim has been seduced by Ra's into joining the dark(er) side: costly.
Having to fight the brother I came to rescue: priceless.
Thanks, Ra's.
SO, ROBIN...
...YOU THINK MAYBE WE CAN HUG THIS OUT?

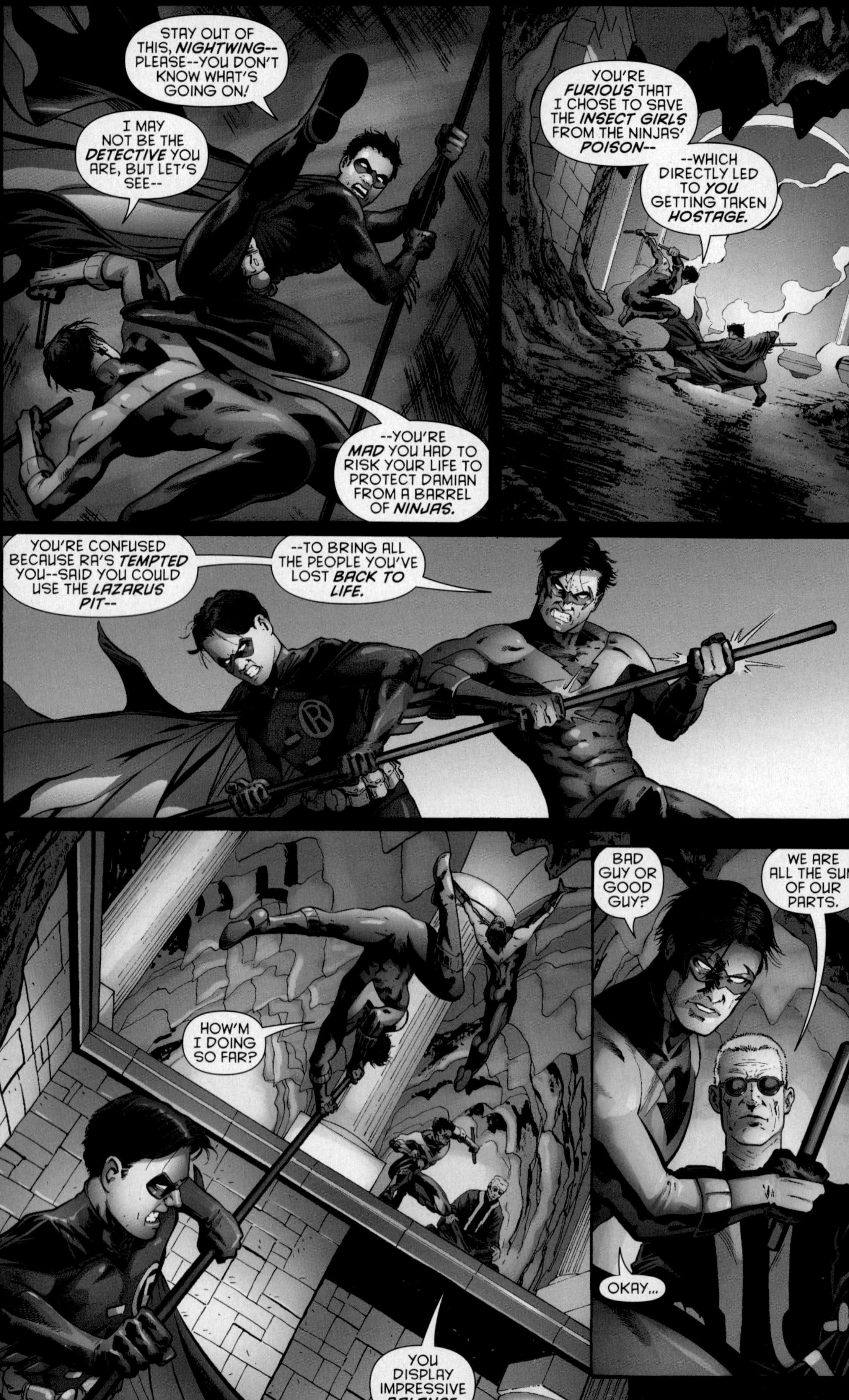
STAY OUT OF THIS, NIGHTWING-- PLEASE--YOU DON'T KNOW WHAT'S GOING ON!
I MAY NOT BE THE DETECTIVE YOU ARE, BUT LET'S SEE--
--YOU'RE MAD YOU HAD TO RISK YOUR LIFE TO PROTECT DAMIAN FROM A BARREL OF NINJAS.
YOU'RE FURIOUS THAT I CHOSE TO SAVE THE INSECT GIRLS FROM THE NINJAS' POISON--
--WHICH DIRECTLY LED TO YOU GETTING TAKEN HOSTAGE.
YOU'RE CONFUSED BECAUSE RA'S TEMPTED YOU--SAID YOU COULD USE THE LAZARUS PIT--
--TO BRING ALL THE PEOPLE YOU'VE LOST BACK TO LIFE.
HOW'M I DOING SO FAR?
YOU DISPLAY IMPRESSIVE BALANCE.
BAD GUY OR GOOD GUY?
WE ARE ALL THE SUM OF OUR PARTS.
OKAY...

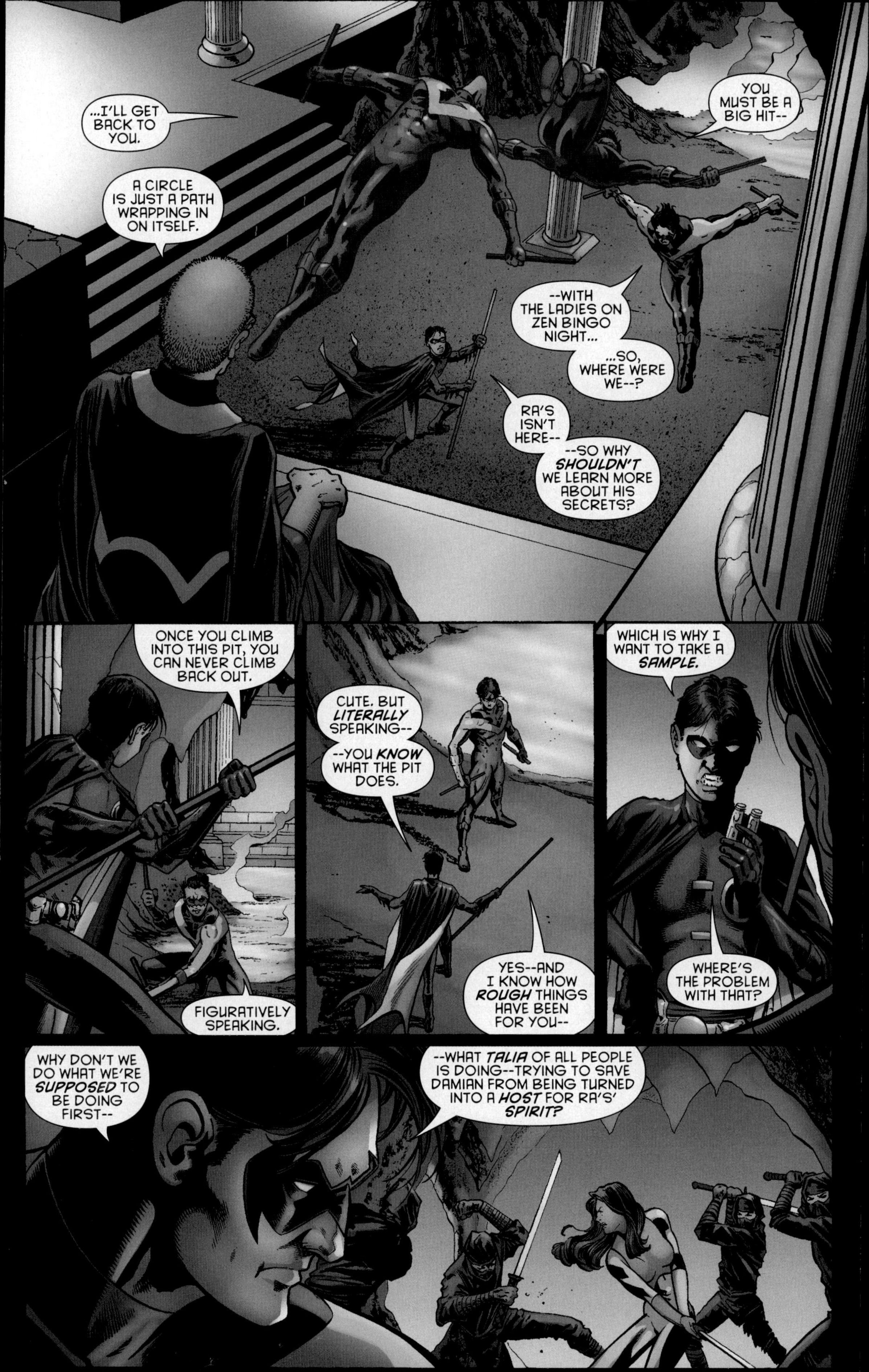
...I'LL GET BACK TO YOU.
YOU MUST BE A BIG HIT--
A CIRCLE IS JUST A PATH WRAPPING IN ON ITSELF.
--WITH THE LADIES ON ZEN BINGO NIGHT...
...SO, WHERE WERE WE--?
RA'S ISN'T HERE--
--SO WHY SHOULDN'T WE LEARN MORE ABOUT HIS SECRETS?
ONCE YOU CLIMB INTO THIS PIT, YOU CAN NEVER CLIMB BACK OUT.
FIGURATIVELY SPEAKING.
CUTE. BUT LITERALLY SPEAKING--
--YOU KNOW WHAT THE PIT DOES.
YES--AND I KNOW HOW ROUGH THINGS HAVE BEEN FOR YOU--
WHICH IS WHY I WANT TO TAKE A SAMPLE.
WHERE'S THE PROBLEM WITH THAT?
WHY DON'T WE DO WHAT WE'RE SUPPOSED TO BE DOING FIRST--
--WHAT TALIA OF ALL PEOPLE IS DOING--TRYING TO SAVE DAMIAN FROM BEING TURNED INTO A HOST FOR RA'S' SPIRIT?

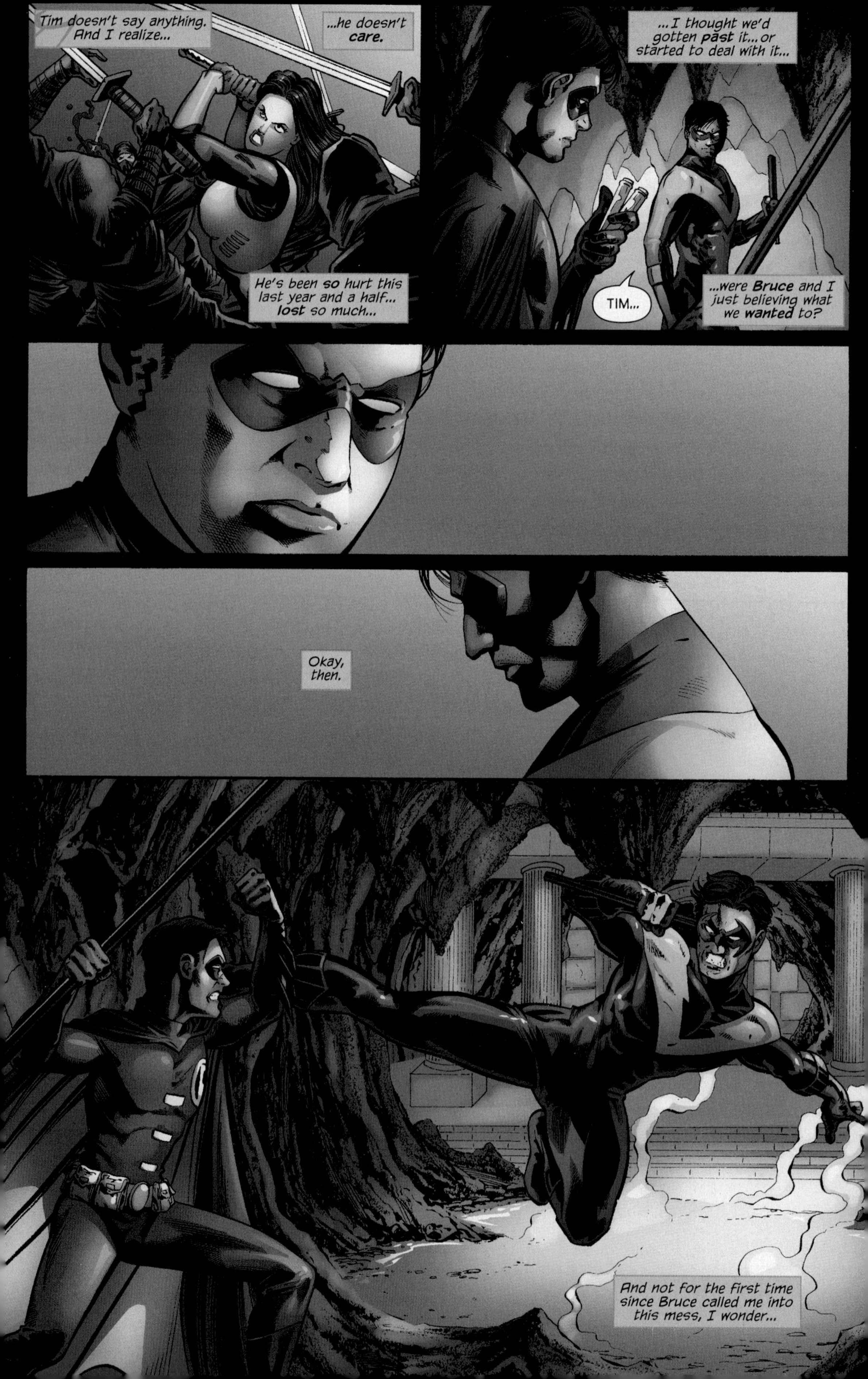
Tim doesn't say anything. And I realize...
...he doesn't care.
He's been so hurt this last year and a half... lost so much...
...I thought we'd gotten past it...or started to deal with it...
TIM...
...were Bruce and I just believing what we wanted to?
Okay, then.
And not for the first time since Bruce called me into this mess, I wonder...

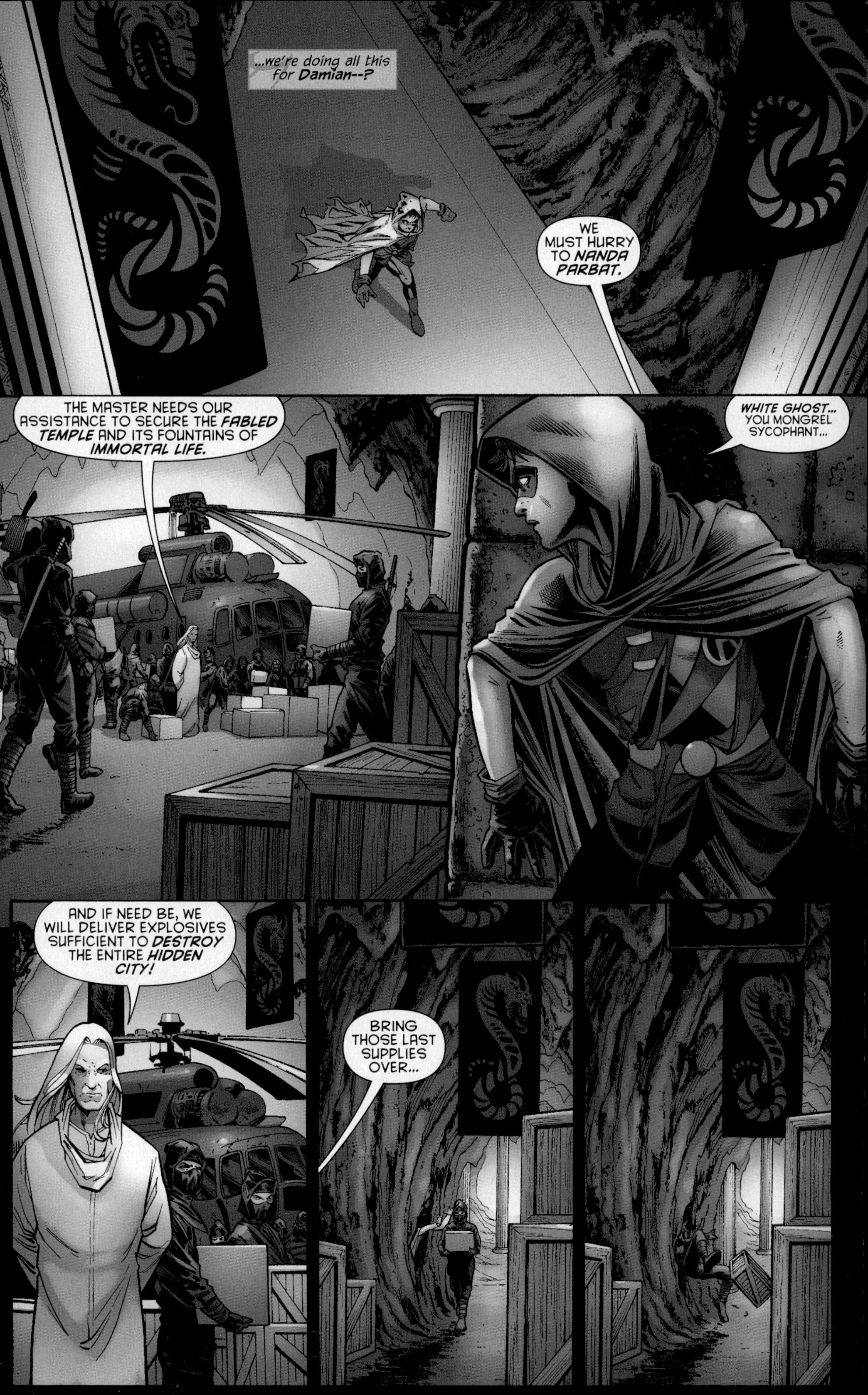

...we're doing all this for Damian--?
WE MUST HURRY TO NANDA PARBAT.
THE MASTER NEEDS OUR ASSISTANCE TO SECURE THE FABLED TEMPLE AND ITS FOUNTAINS OF IMMORTAL LIFE.
WHITE GHOST... YOU MONGREL SYCOPHANT...
AND IF NEED BE, WE WILL DELIVER EXPLOSIVES SUFFICIENT TO DESTROY THE ENTIRE HIDDEN CITY!
BRING THOSE LAST SUPPLIES OVER...

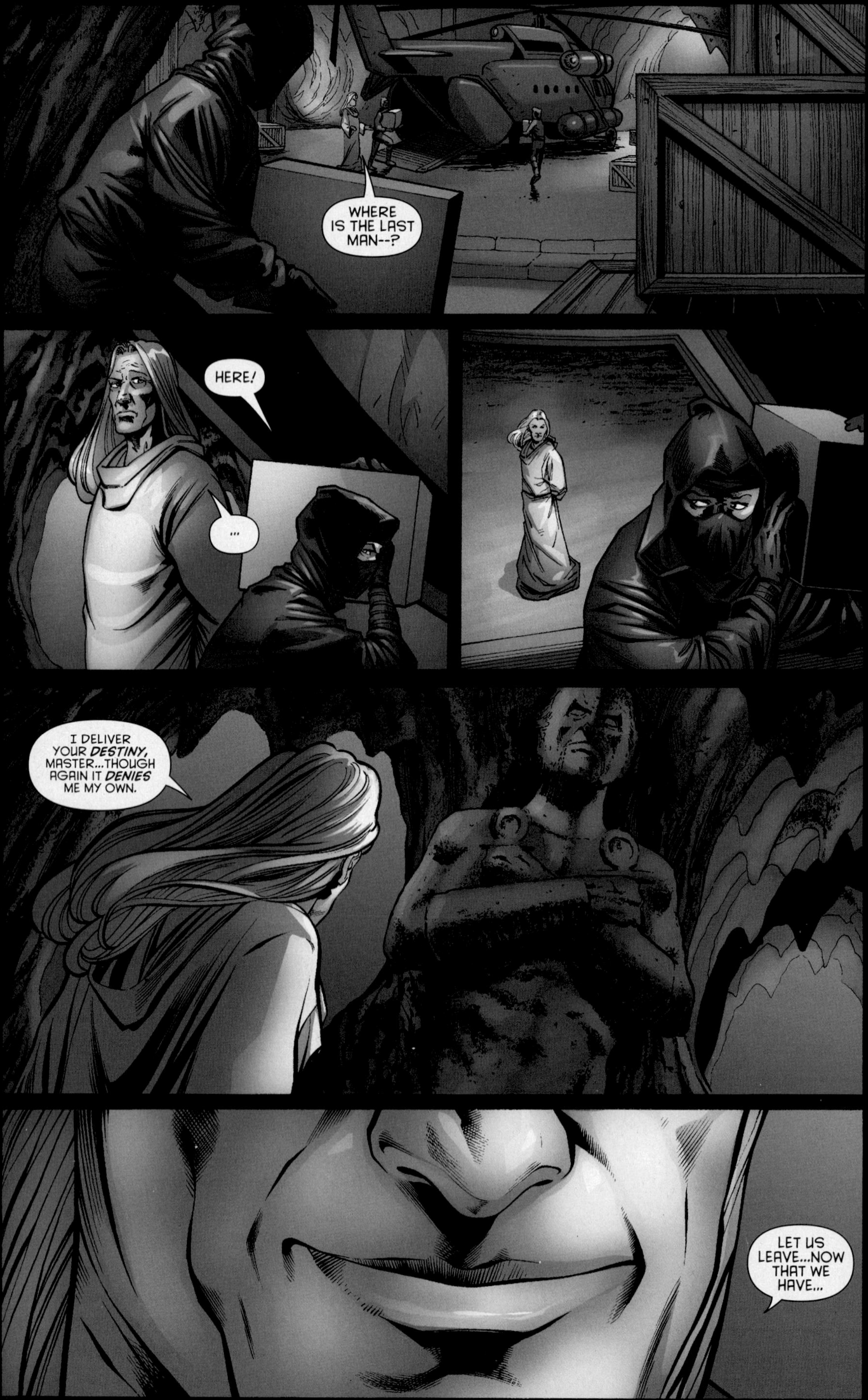
WHERE IS THE LAST MAN--?
HERE!
...
I DELIVER YOUR *DESTINY*, MASTER...THOUGH AGAIN IT *DENIES* ME MY OWN.
LET US LEAVE...NOW THAT WE HAVE...

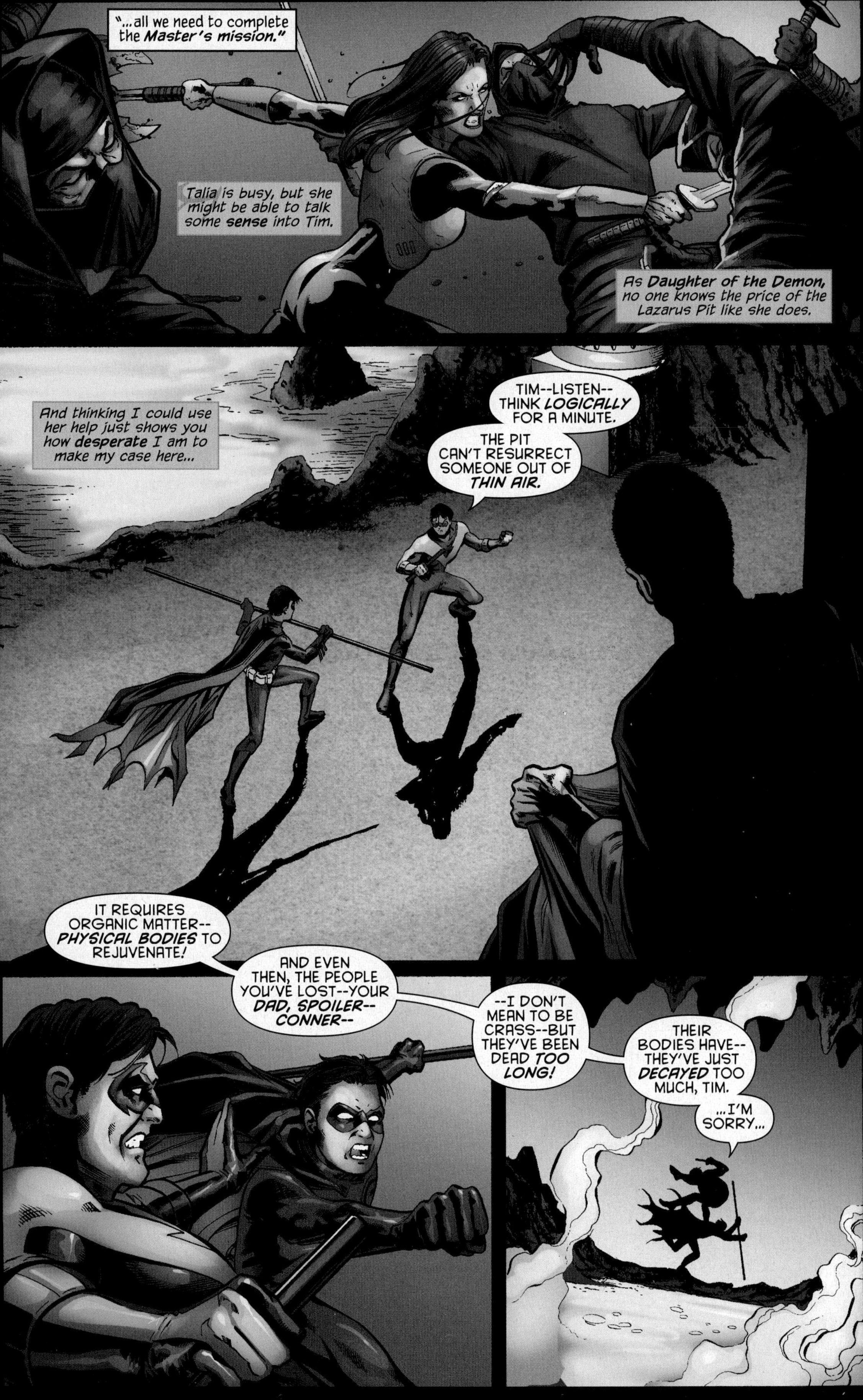
"...all we need to complete the Master's mission."
Talia is busy, but she might be able to talk some sense into Tim.
As Daughter of the Demon, no one knows the price of the Lazarus Pit like she does.
And thinking I could use her help just shows you how desperate I am to make my case here...
TIM--LISTEN--THINK LOGICALLY FOR A MINUTE.
THE PIT CAN'T RESURRECT SOMEONE OUT OF THIN AIR.
IT REQUIRES ORGANIC MATTER--PHYSICAL BODIES TO REJUVENATE!
AND EVEN THEN, THE PEOPLE YOU'VE LOST--YOUR DAD, SPOILER--CONNER--
--I DON'T MEAN TO BE CRASS--BUT THEY'VE BEEN DEAD TOO LONG!
THEIR BODIES HAVE--THEY'VE JUST DECAYED TOO MUCH, TIM.
...I'M SORRY...

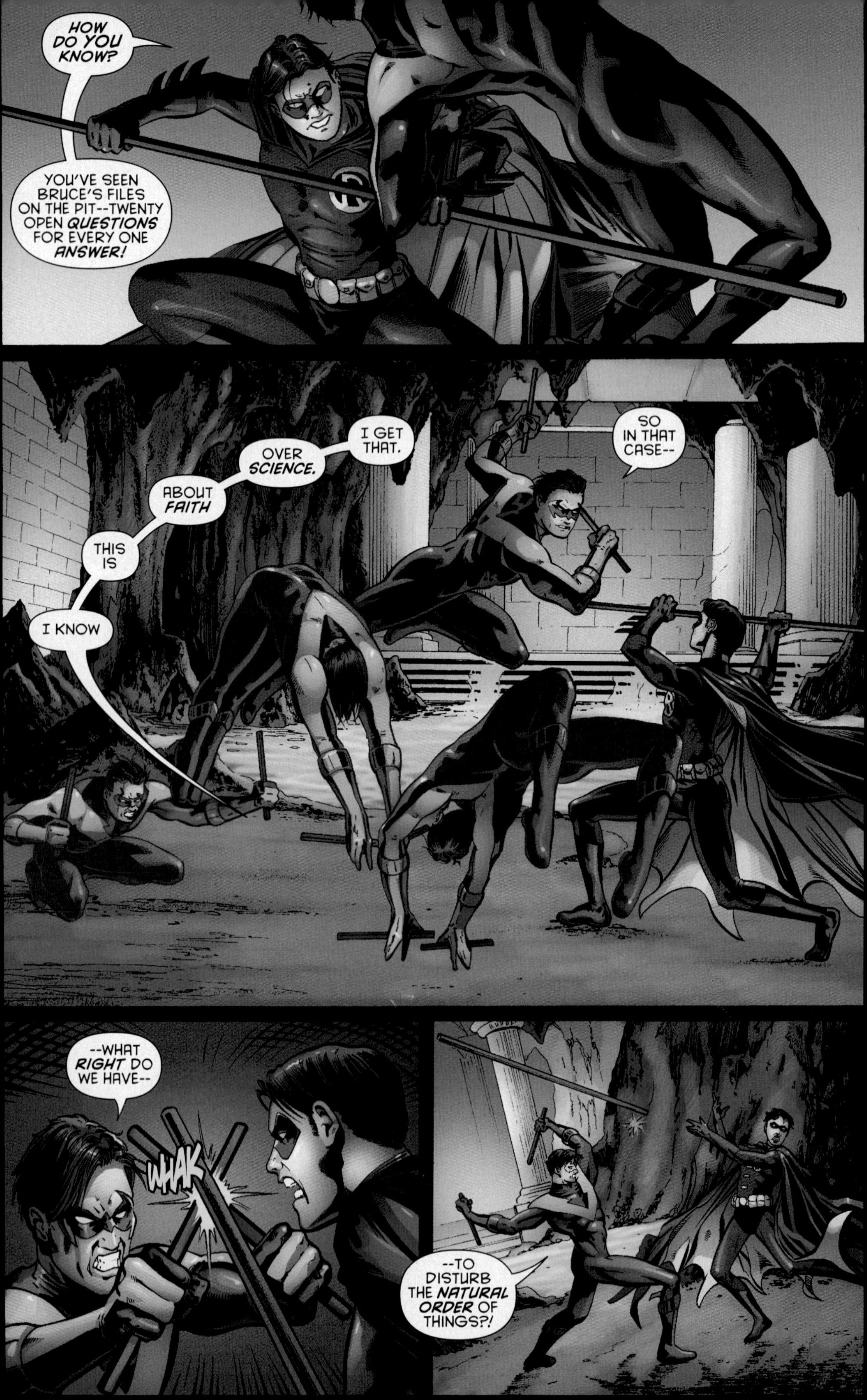
HOW DO YOU KNOW?
YOU'VE SEEN BRUCE'S FILES ON THE PIT--TWENTY OPEN QUESTIONS FOR EVERY ONE ANSWER!
I KNOW
THIS IS
ABOUT FAITH
OVER SCIENCE.
I GET THAT.
SO IN THAT CASE--
--WHAT RIGHT DO WE HAVE--
WHAK
--TO DISTURB THE NATURAL ORDER OF THINGS?!

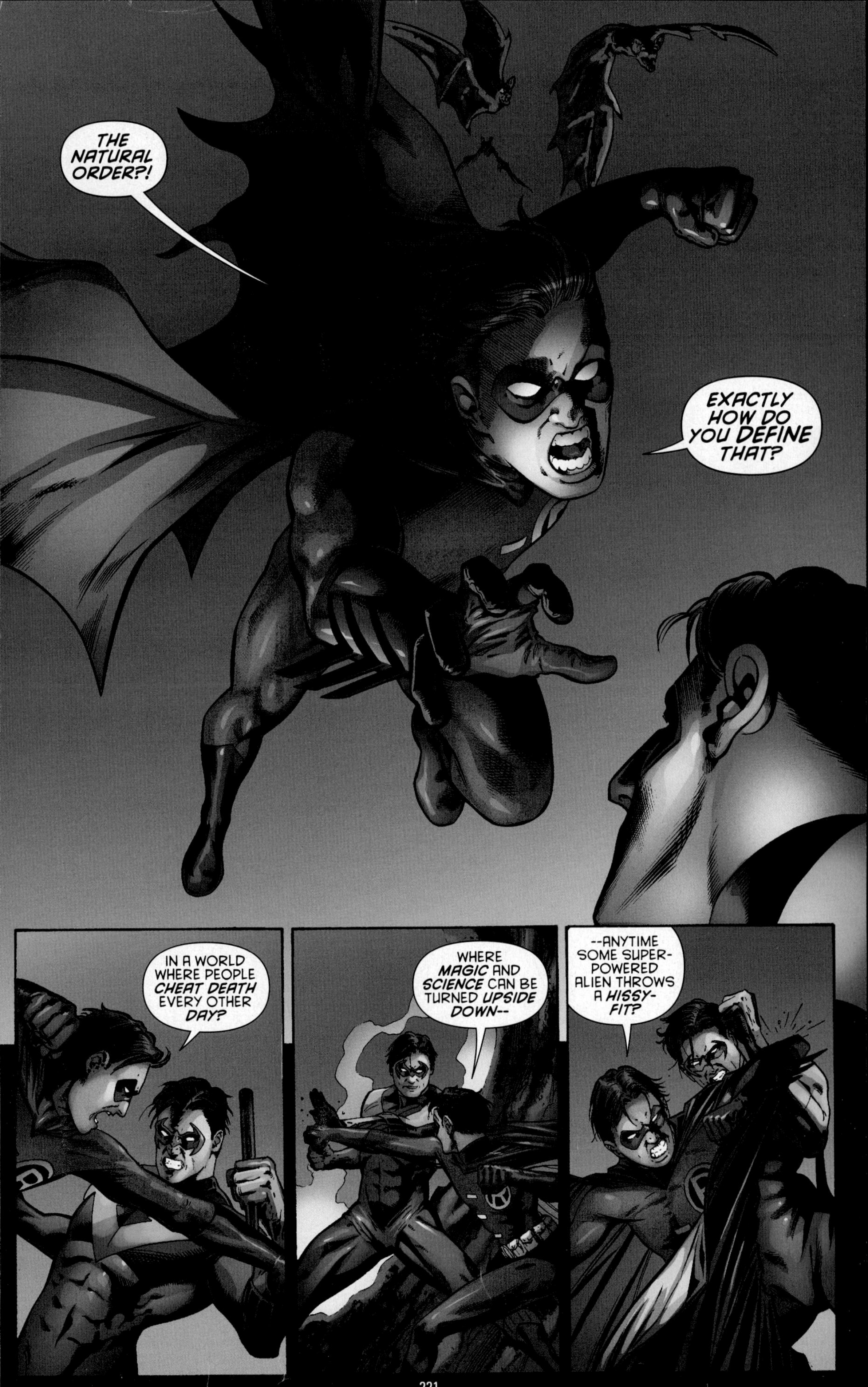
THE NATURAL ORDER?!
EXACTLY HOW DO YOU DEFINE THAT?
IN A WORLD WHERE PEOPLE CHEAT DEATH EVERY OTHER DAY?
WHERE MAGIC AND SCIENCE CAN BE TURNED UPSIDE DOWN--
--ANYTIME SOME SUPER-POWERED ALIEN THROWS A HISSY-FIT?

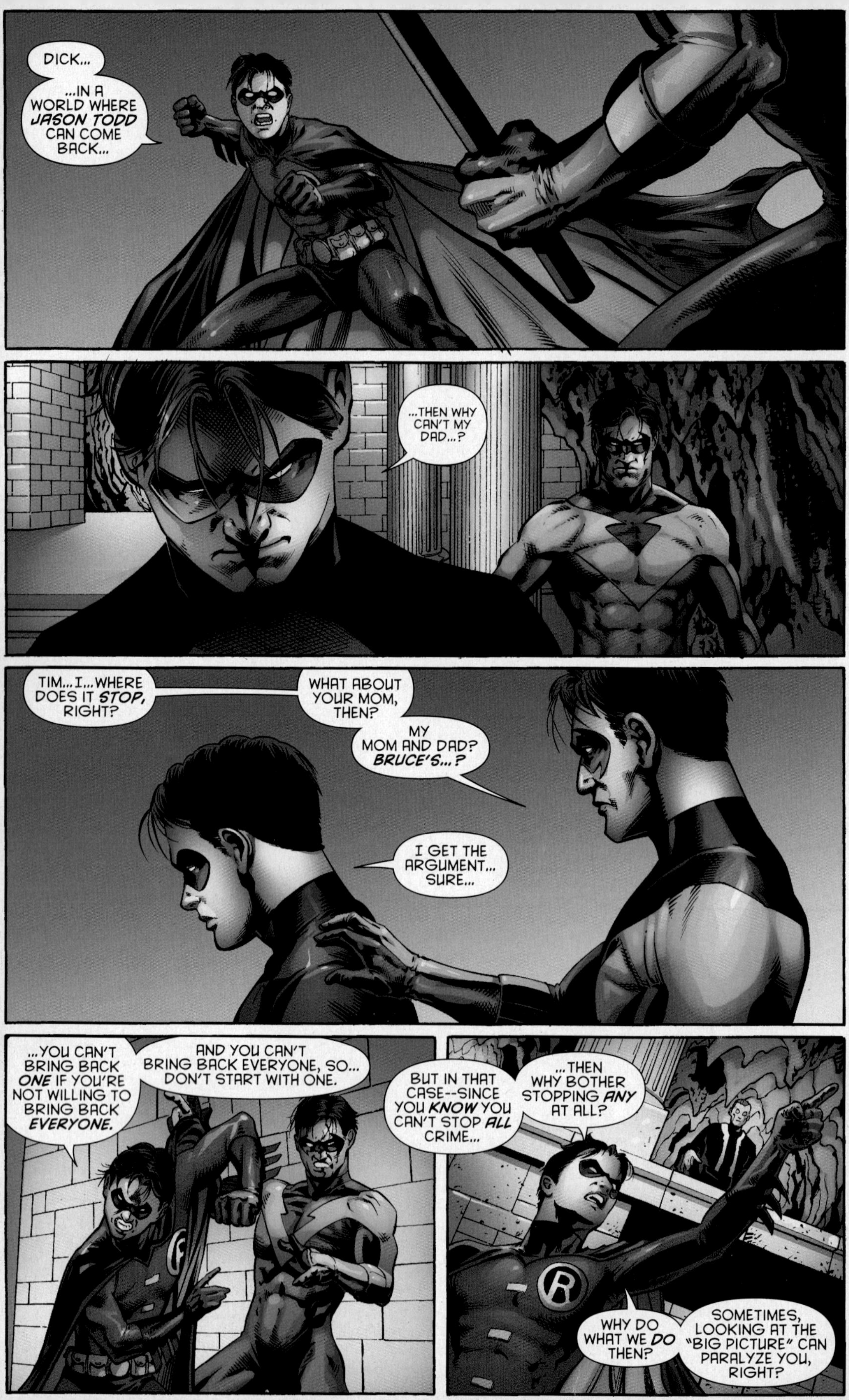
DICK...
...IN A WORLD WHERE JASON TODD CAN COME BACK...
...THEN WHY CAN'T MY DAD...?
TIM... I... WHERE DOES IT STOP, RIGHT?
WHAT ABOUT YOUR MOM, THEN?
MY MOM AND DAD? BRUCE'S...?
I GET THE ARGUMENT... SURE...
...YOU CAN'T BRING BACK ONE IF YOU'RE NOT WILLING TO BRING BACK EVERYONE.
AND YOU CAN'T BRING BACK EVERYONE, SO... DON'T START WITH ONE.
BUT IN THAT CASE--SINCE YOU KNOW YOU CAN'T STOP ALL CRIME...
...THEN WHY BOTHER STOPPING ANY AT ALL?
WHY DO WHAT WE DO THEN?
SOMETIMES, LOOKING AT THE "BIG PICTURE" CAN PARALYZE YOU, RIGHT?

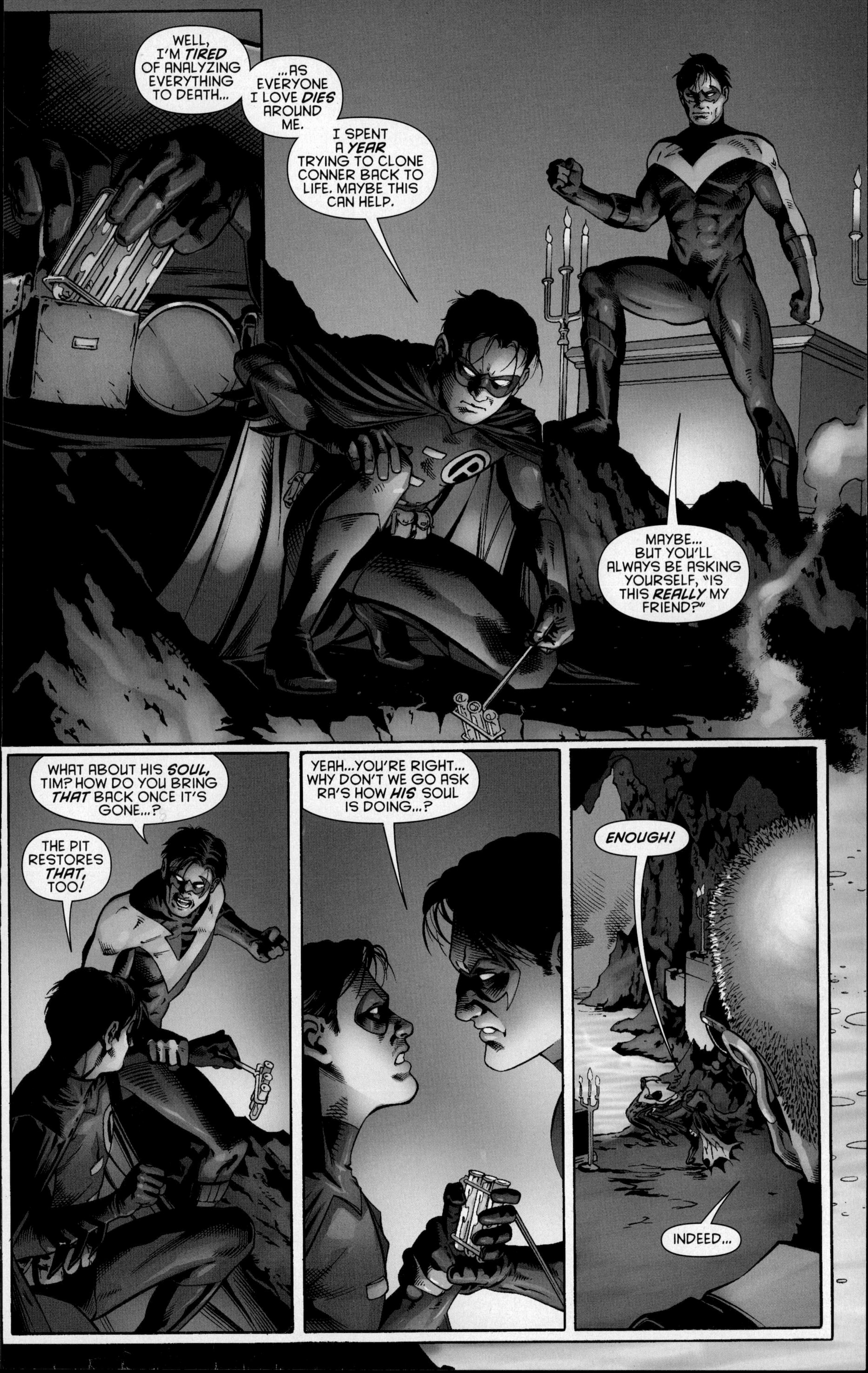
WELL, I'M *TIRED* OF ANALYZING EVERYTHING TO DEATH...
...AS EVERYONE I LOVE *DIES* AROUND ME.
I SPENT A *YEAR* TRYING TO CLONE CONNER BACK TO LIFE. MAYBE THIS CAN HELP.
MAYBE... BUT YOU'LL ALWAYS BE ASKING YOURSELF, "IS THIS *REALLY* MY FRIEND?"
WHAT ABOUT HIS *SOUL,* TIM? HOW DO YOU BRING *THAT* BACK ONCE IT'S GONE...?
THE PIT RESTORES *THAT,* TOO!
YEAH...YOU'RE RIGHT... WHY DON'T WE GO ASK RA'S HOW *HIS* SOUL IS DOING...?
ENOUGH!
INDEED...

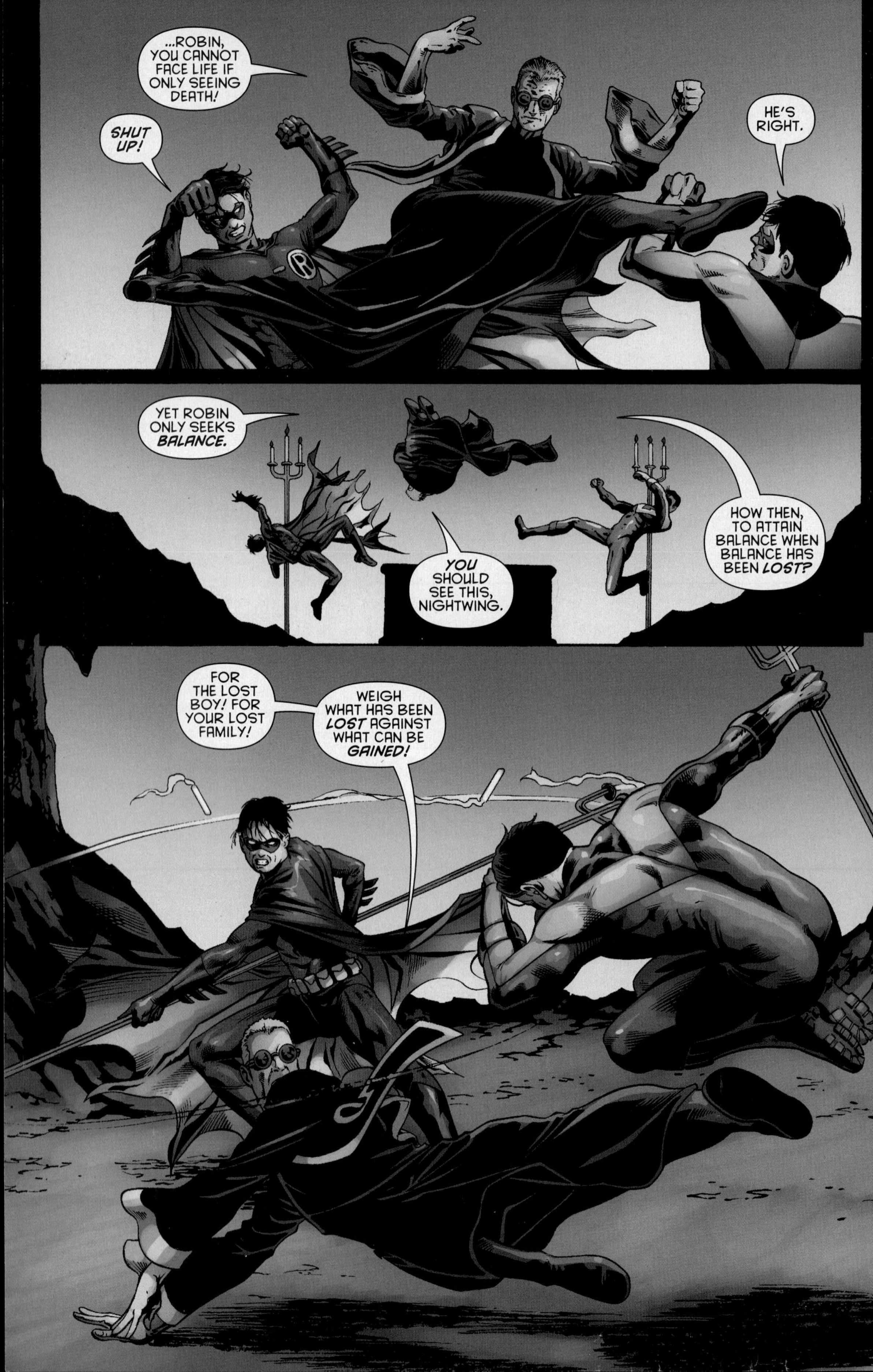
...ROBIN, YOU CANNOT FACE LIFE IF ONLY SEEING DEATH!
SHUT UP!
HE'S RIGHT.
YET ROBIN ONLY SEEKS BALANCE.
YOU SHOULD SEE THIS, NIGHTWING.
HOW THEN, TO ATTAIN BALANCE WHEN BALANCE HAS BEEN LOST?
FOR THE LOST BOY! FOR YOUR LOST FAMILY!
WEIGH WHAT HAS BEEN LOST AGAINST WHAT CAN BE GAINED!

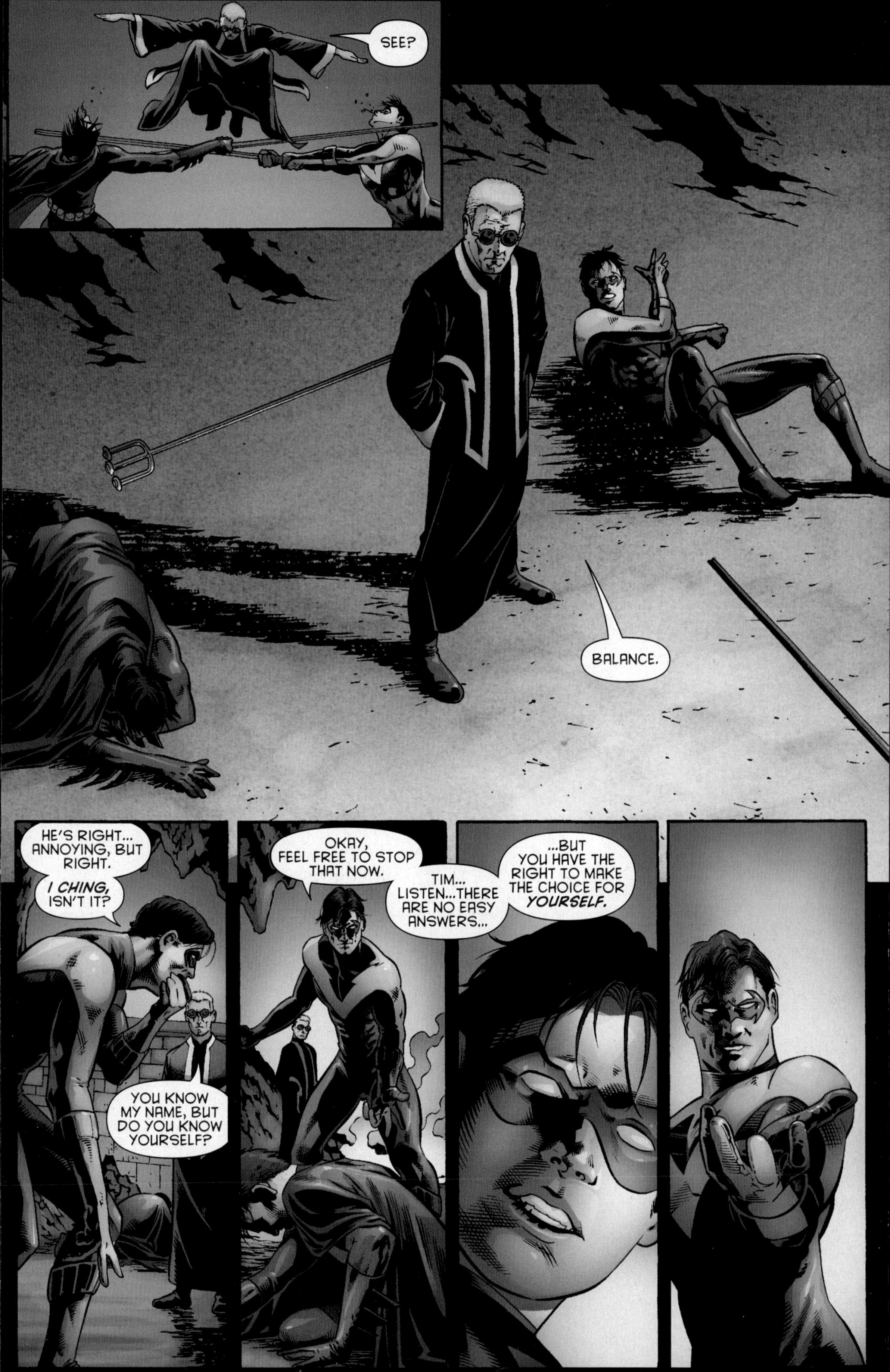

SEE?
BALANCE.
HE'S RIGHT... ANNOYING, BUT RIGHT.
I CHING, ISN'T IT?
YOU KNOW MY NAME, BUT DO YOU KNOW YOURSELF?
OKAY, FEEL FREE TO STOP THAT NOW.
TIM... LISTEN...THERE ARE NO EASY ANSWERS...
...BUT YOU HAVE THE RIGHT TO MAKE THE CHOICE FOR *YOURSELF.*

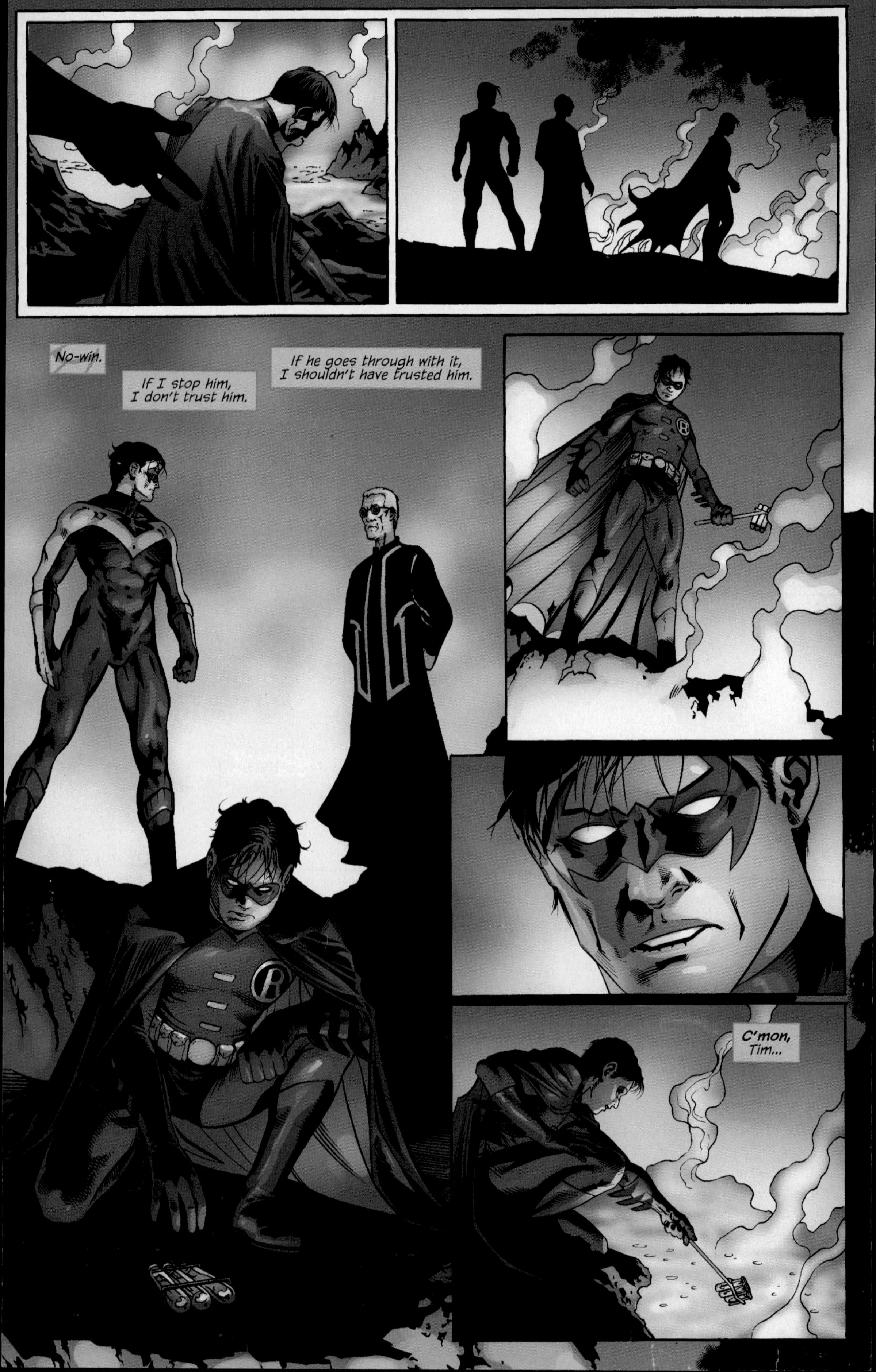
No-win.
If I stop him, I don't trust him.
If he goes through with it, I shouldn't have trusted him.
C'mon, Tim...

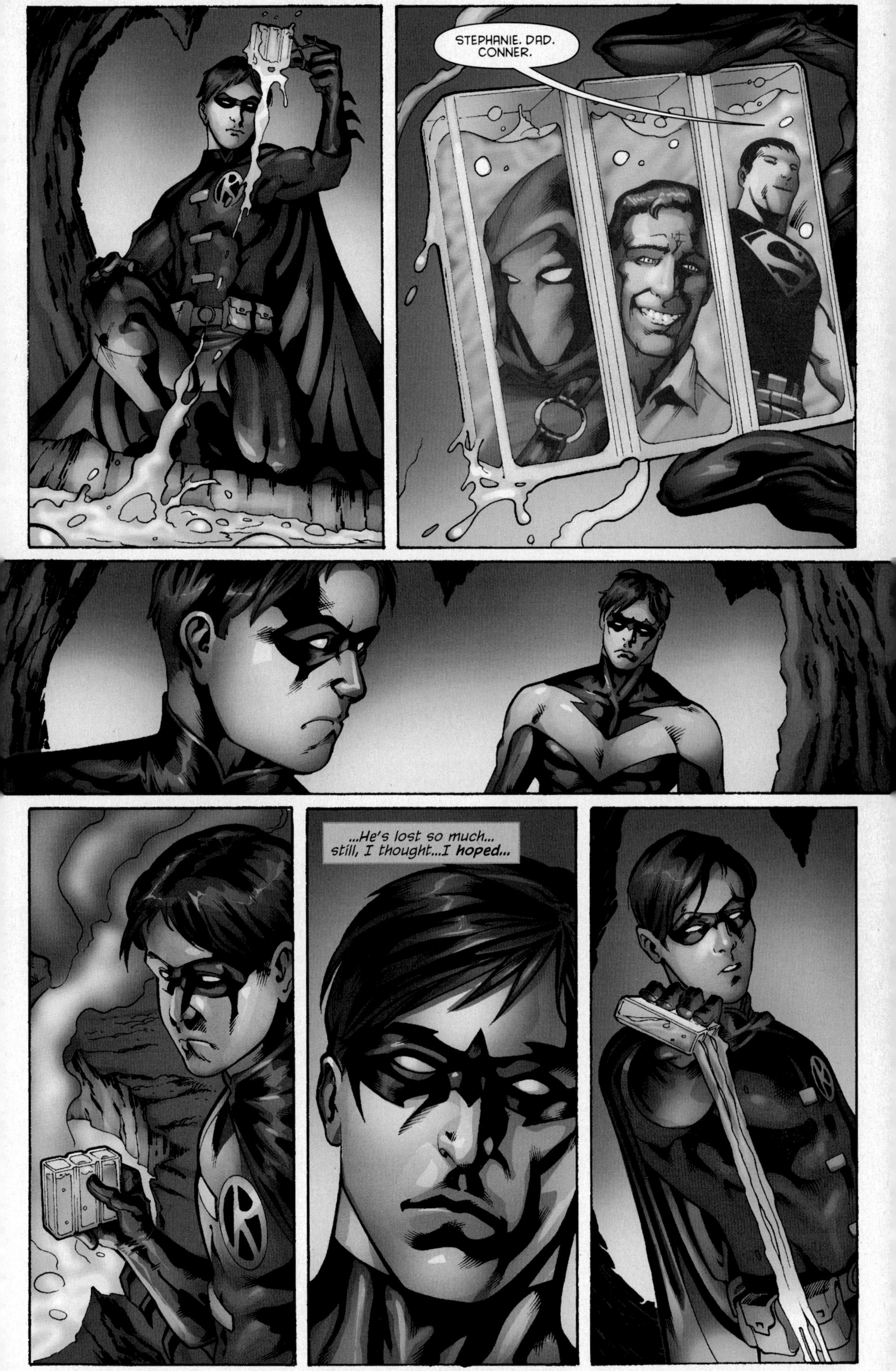
STEPHANIE. DAD. CONNER.
...He's lost so much... still, I thought...I hoped...

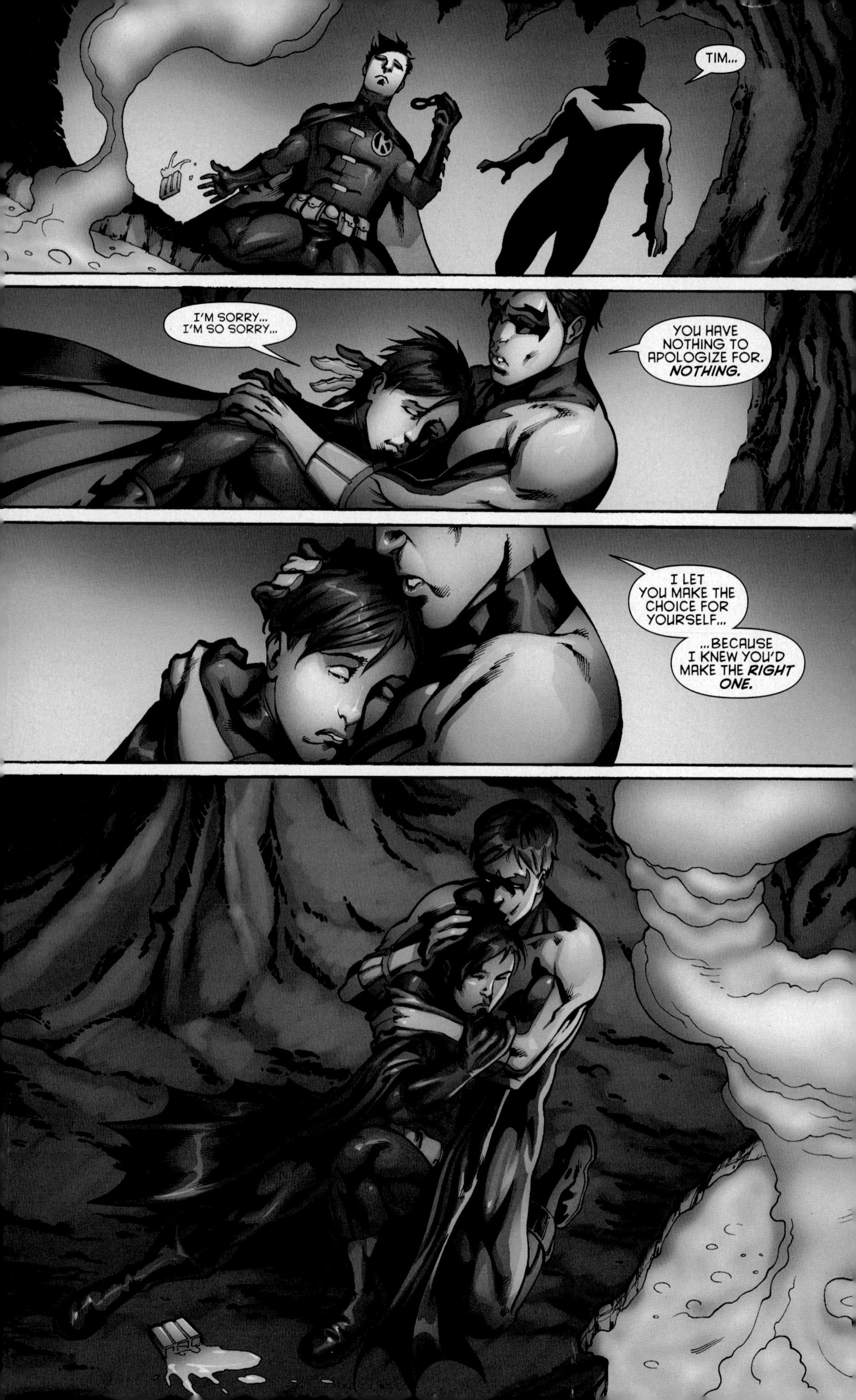
TIM...
I'M SORRY... I'M SO SORRY...
YOU HAVE NOTHING TO APOLOGIZE FOR. ***NOTHING.***
I LET YOU MAKE THE CHOICE FOR YOURSELF...
...BECAUSE I KNEW YOU'D MAKE THE ***RIGHT ONE.***

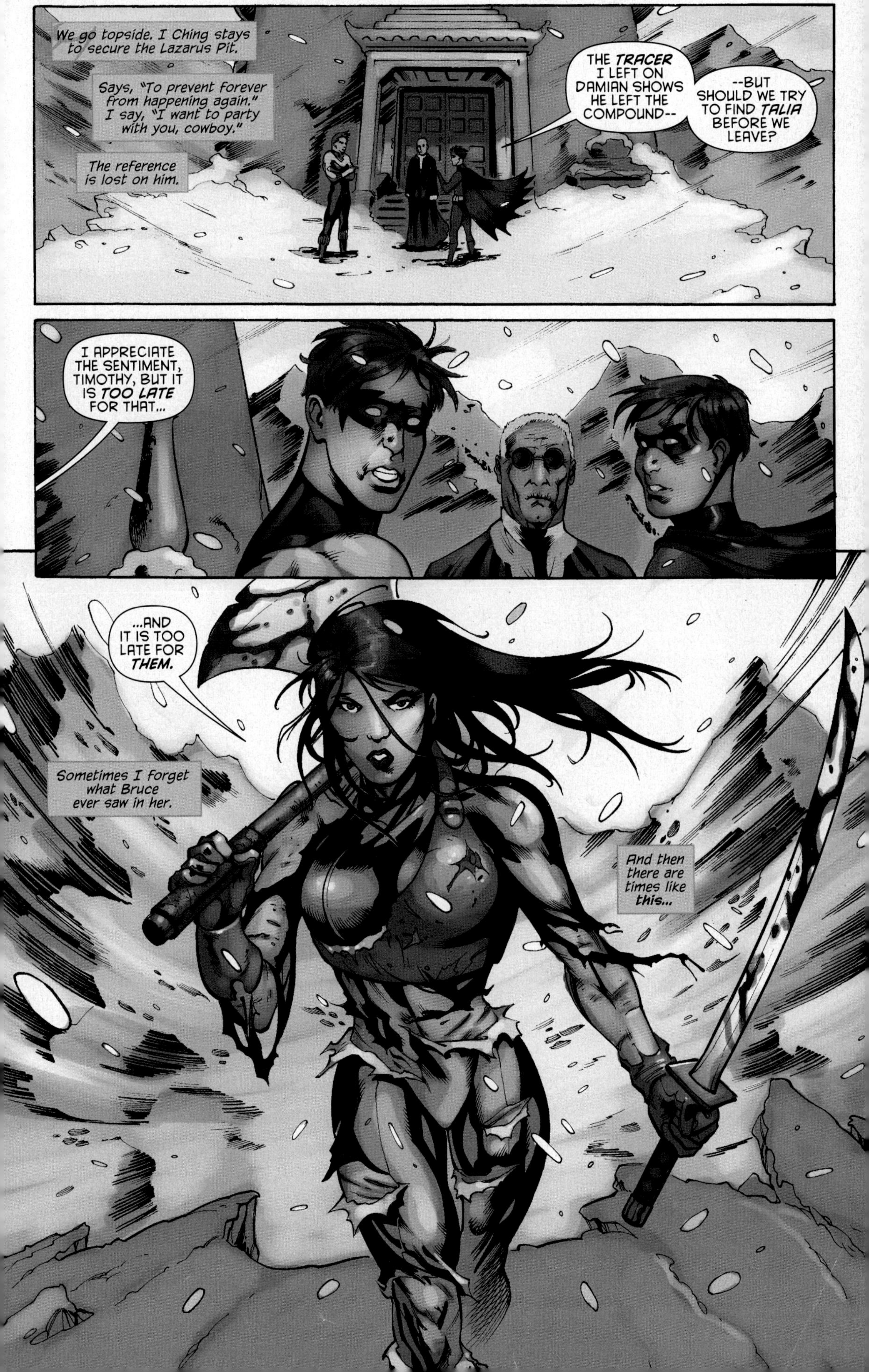

We go topside. I Ching stays to secure the Lazarus Pit.
Says, "To prevent forever from happening again." I say, "I want to party with you, cowboy."
The reference is lost on him.
THE TRACER I LEFT ON DAMIAN SHOWS HE LEFT THE COMPOUND--
--BUT SHOULD WE TRY TO FIND TALIA BEFORE WE LEAVE?
I APPRECIATE THE SENTIMENT, TIMOTHY, BUT IT IS TOO LATE FOR THAT...
...AND IT IS TOO LATE FOR THEM.
Sometimes I forget what Bruce ever saw in her.
And then there are times like this...

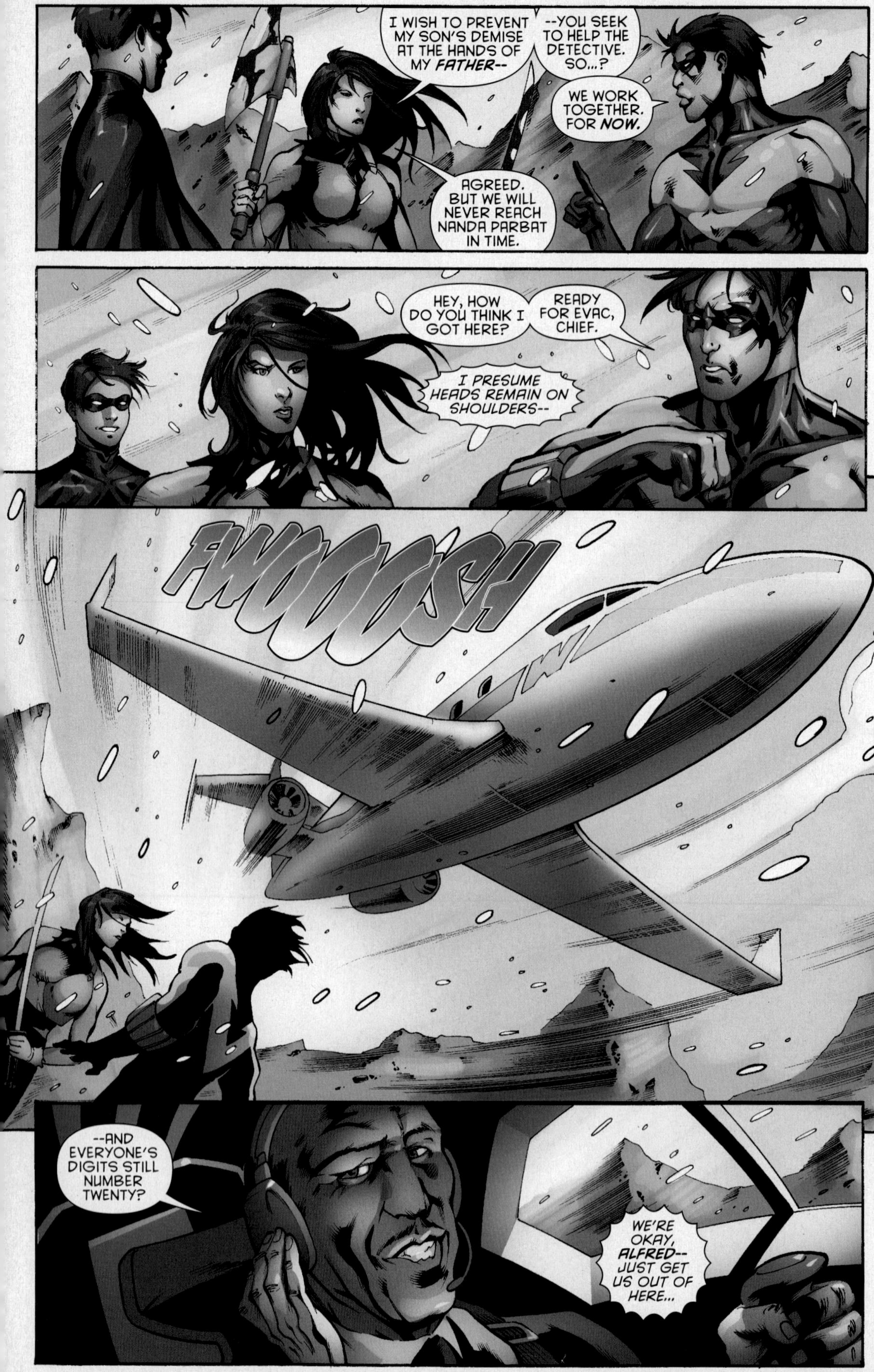
I WISH TO PREVENT MY SON'S DEMISE AT THE HANDS OF MY FATHER--
--YOU SEEK TO HELP THE DETECTIVE. SO...?
WE WORK TOGETHER. FOR NOW.
AGREED. BUT WE WILL NEVER REACH NANDA PARBAT IN TIME.
HEY, HOW DO YOU THINK I GOT HERE?
READY FOR EVAC, CHIEF.
I PRESUME HEADS REMAIN ON SHOULDERS--
FWOOOSH
--AND EVERYONE'S DIGITS STILL NUMBER TWENTY?
WE'RE OKAY, ALFRED-- JUST GET US OUT OF HERE...

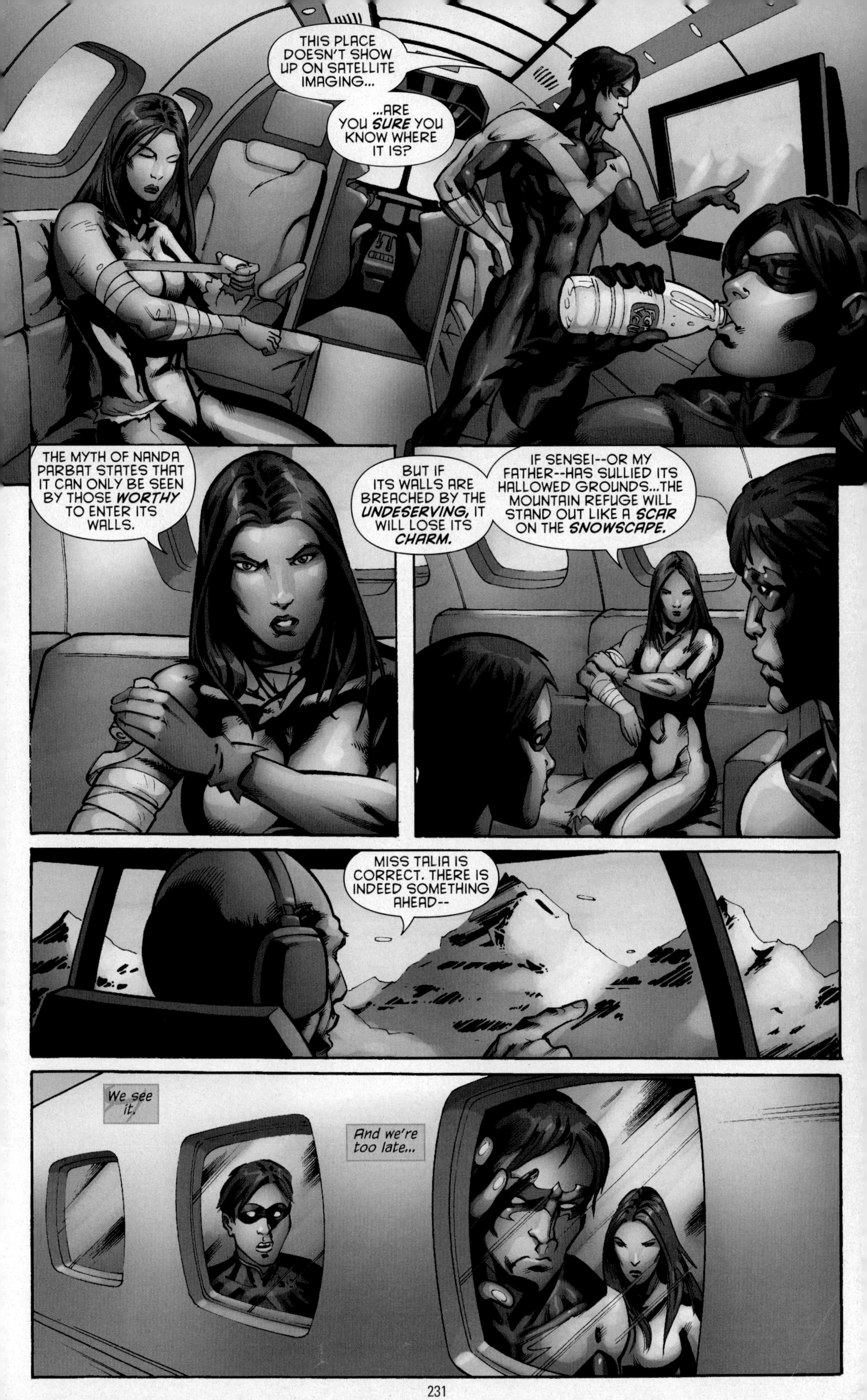
THIS PLACE DOESN'T SHOW UP ON SATELLITE IMAGING...
...ARE YOU SURE YOU KNOW WHERE IT IS?
THE MYTH OF NANDA PARBAT STATES THAT IT CAN ONLY BE SEEN BY THOSE WORTHY TO ENTER ITS WALLS.
BUT IF ITS WALLS ARE BREACHED BY THE UNDESERVING, IT WILL LOSE ITS CHARM.
IF SENSEI--OR MY FATHER--HAS SULLIED ITS HALLOWED GROUNDS...THE MOUNTAIN REFUGE WILL STAND OUT LIKE A SCAR ON THE SNOWSCAPE.
MISS TALIA IS CORRECT. THERE IS INDEED SOMETHING AHEAD--
We see it.
And we're too late...

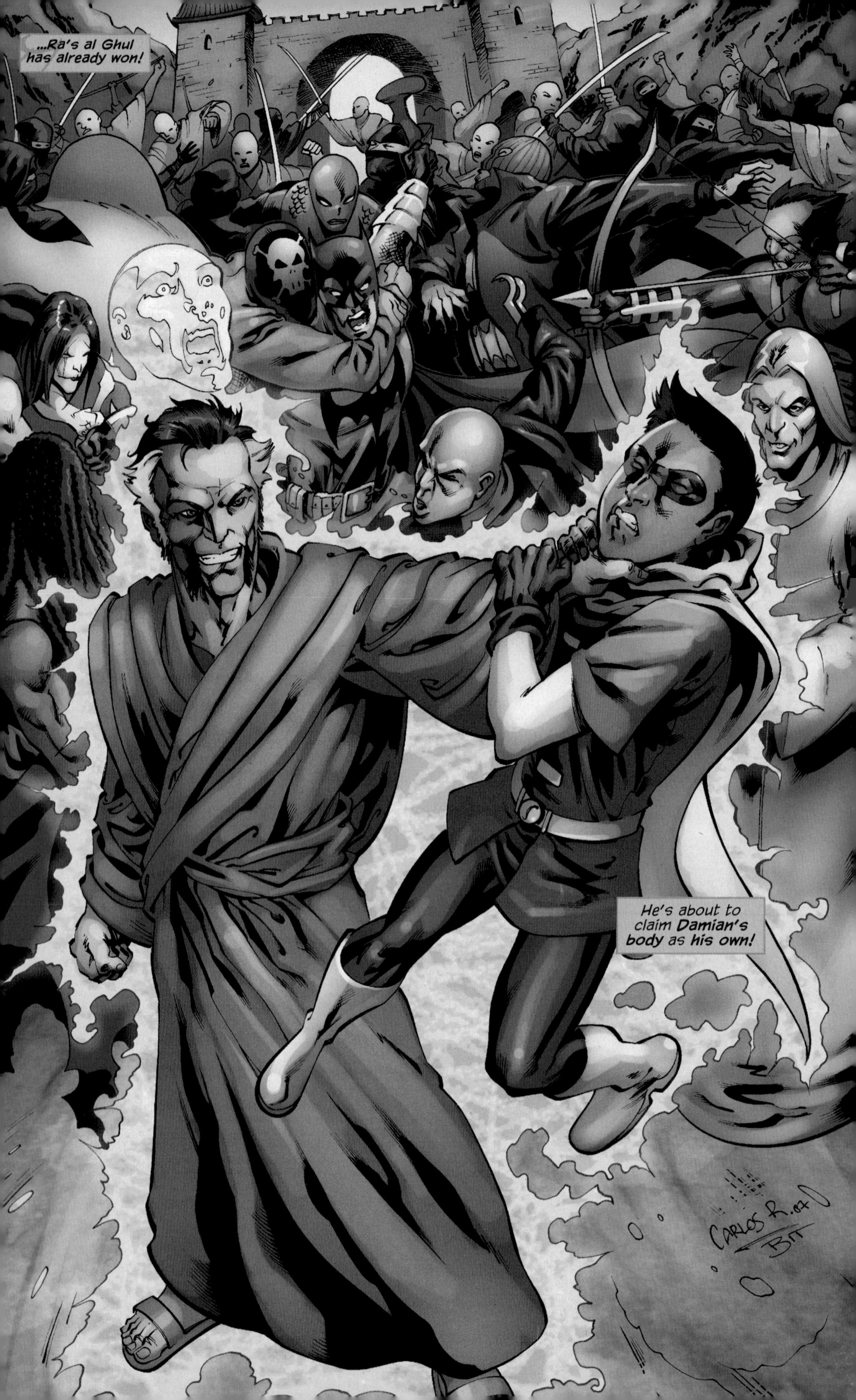
...Ra's al Ghul has already won!
He's about to claim Damian's body as his own!
CARLOS R. 07

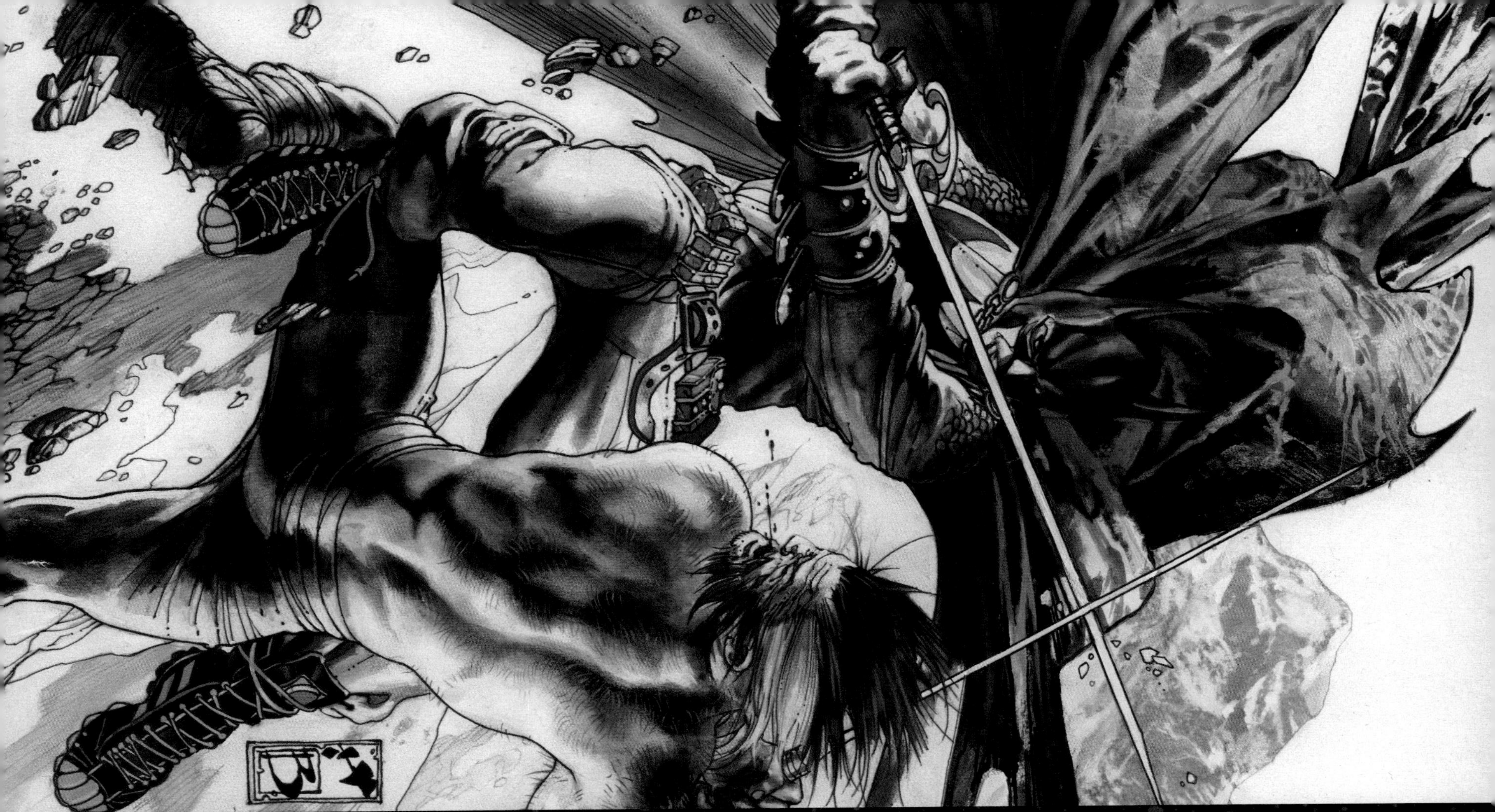

CHAPTER SEVEN ENTITLEMENT

Cover art by Simone Bianchi   Chapter written by Paul Dini   Chapter pencilled by Ryan Benjamin with Don Kramer   Chapter inked by Saleem Crawford with Wayne Faucher

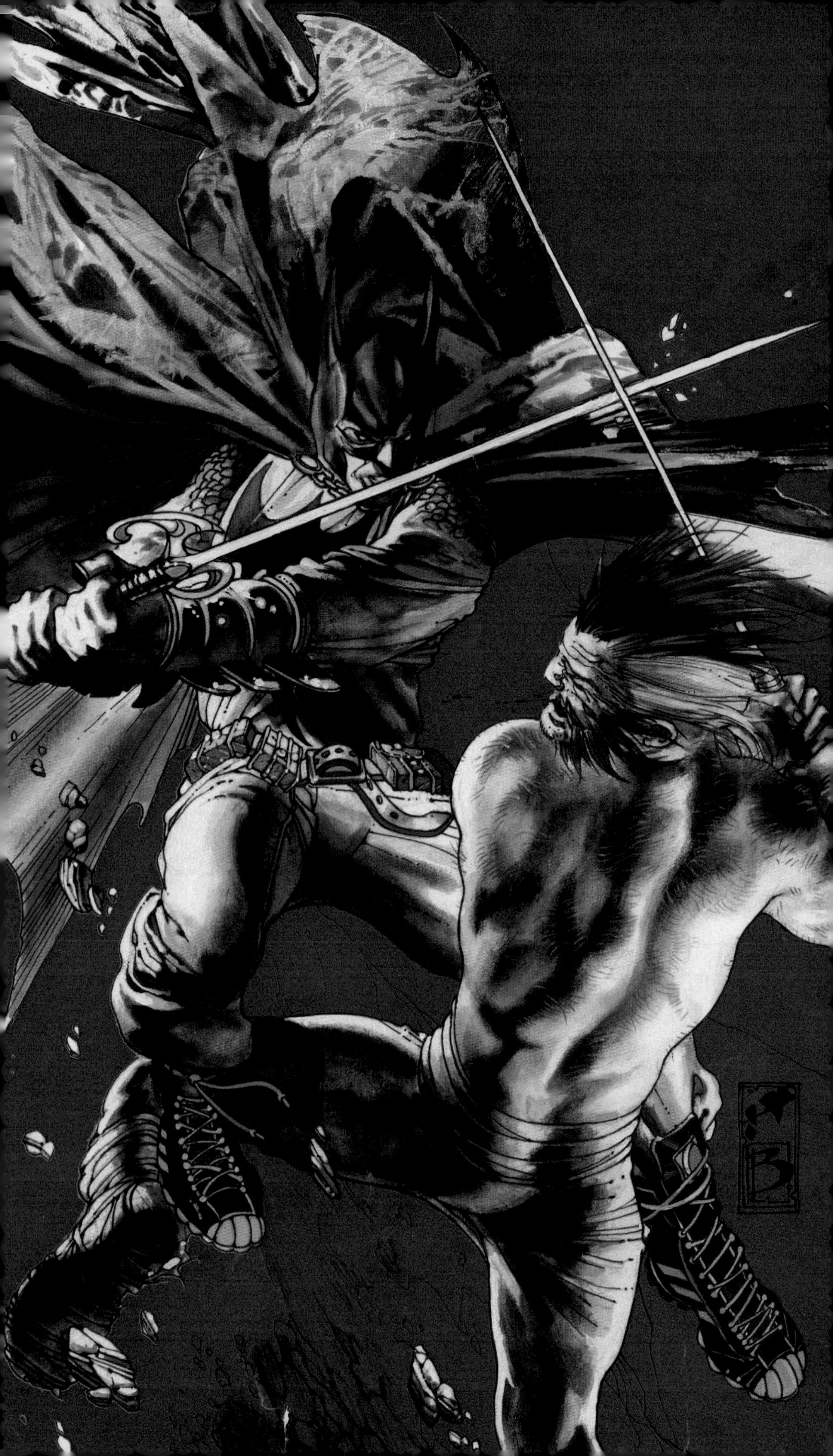

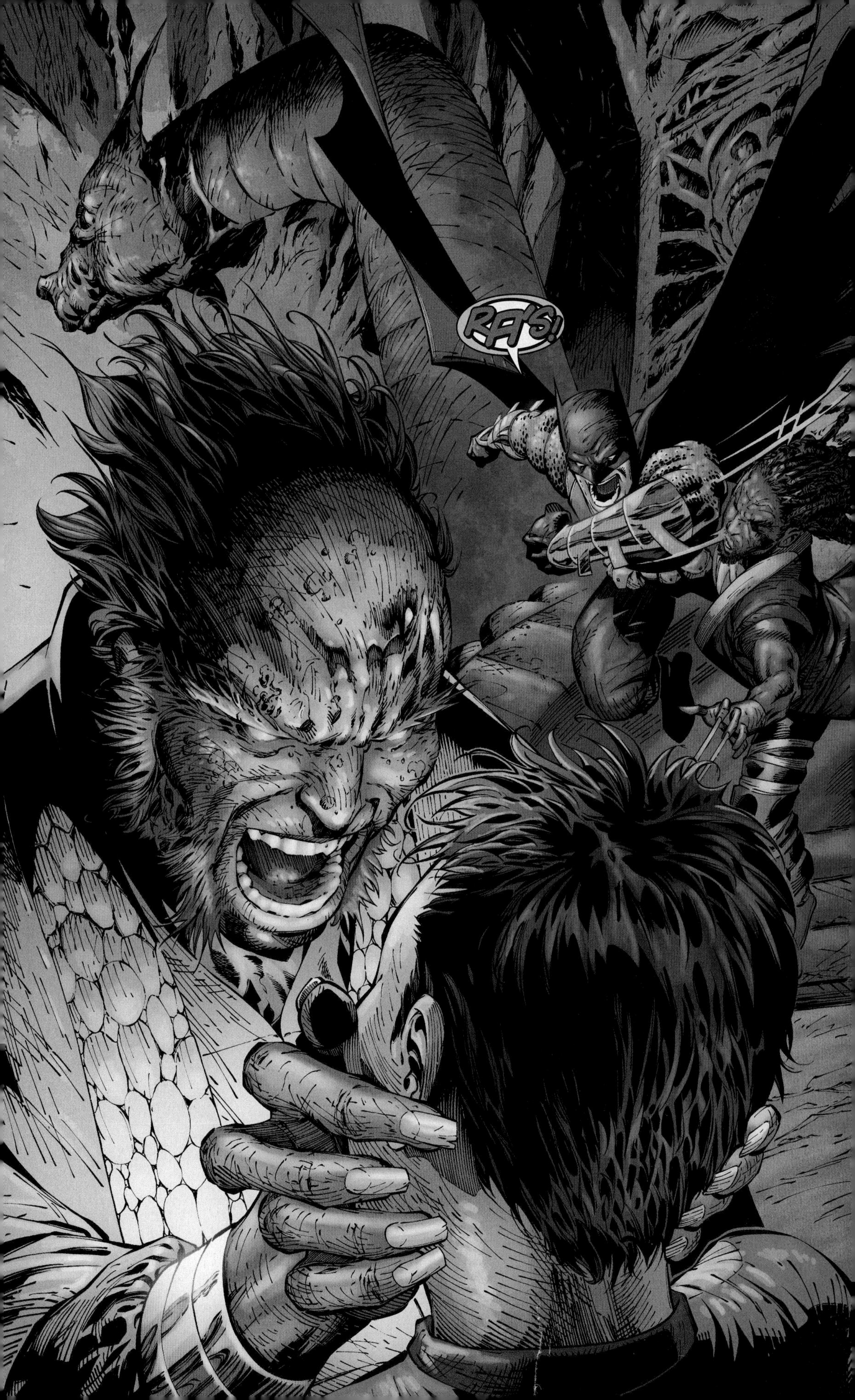
RA'S!

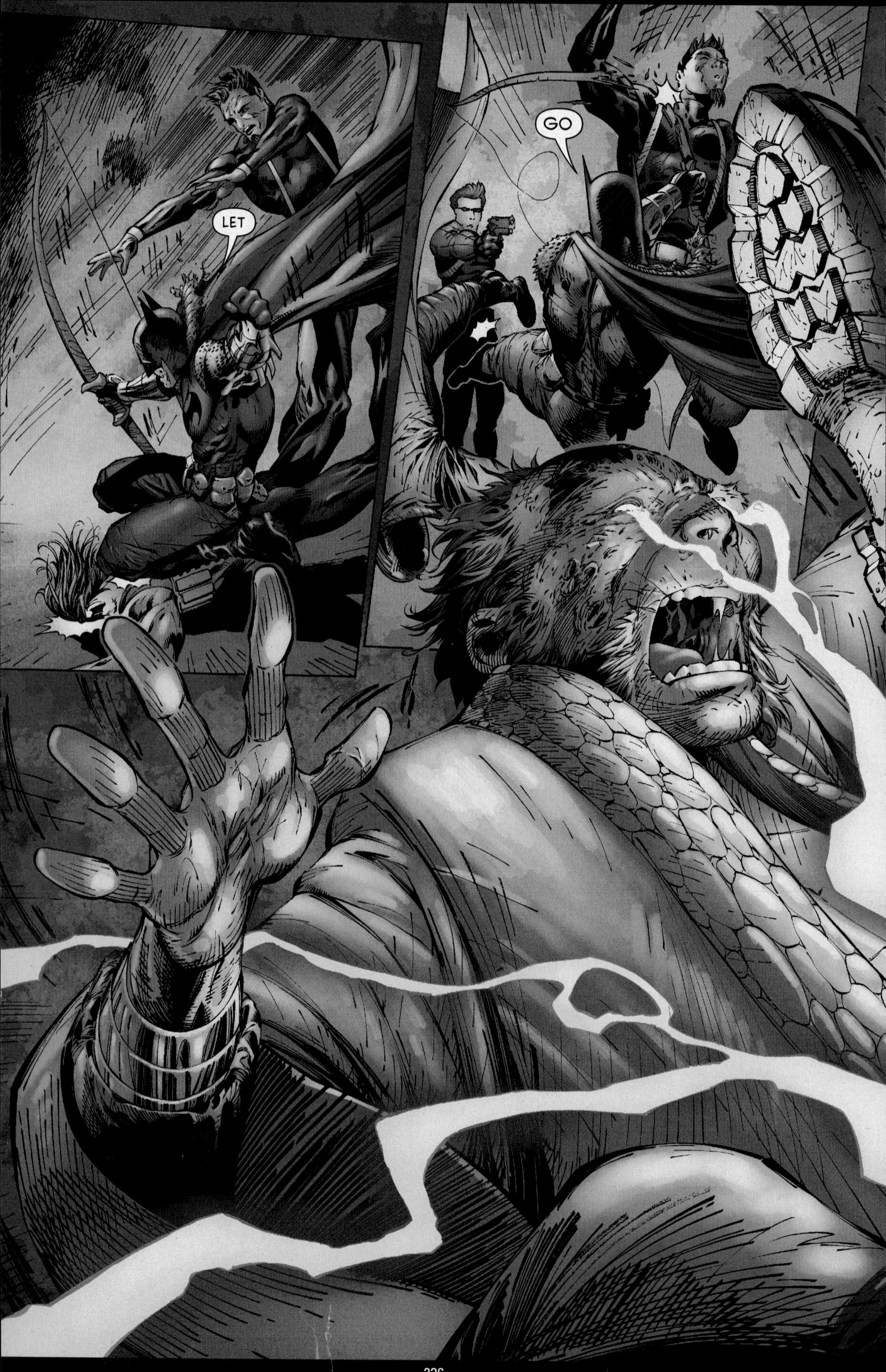
LET
GO

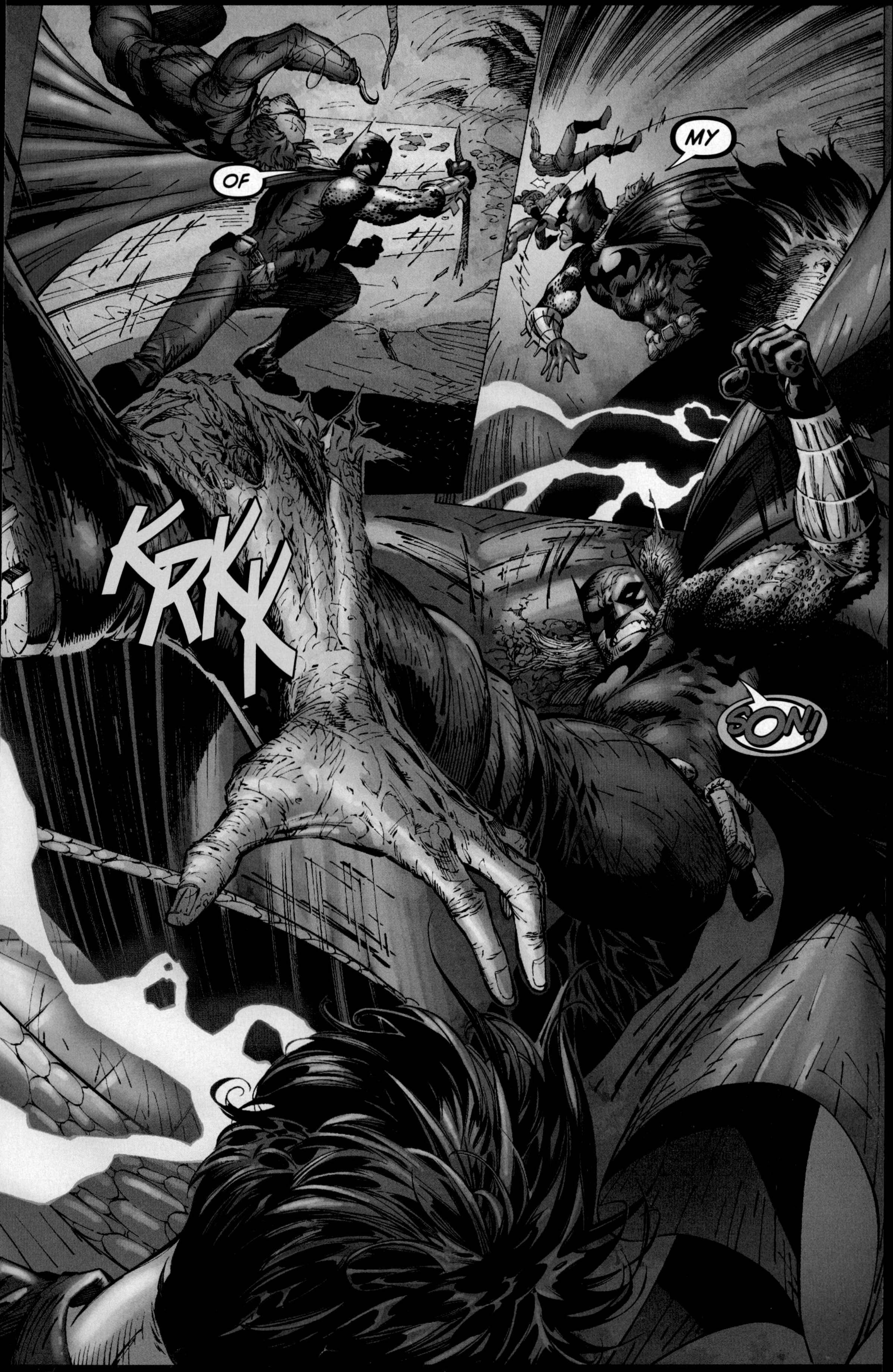
OF
MY
KRKK
SON!!

UNH!

BY THE GODS...!

KRKK

WH-WHAT--

WHAK

BMPP

--ARE YOU DOING?!

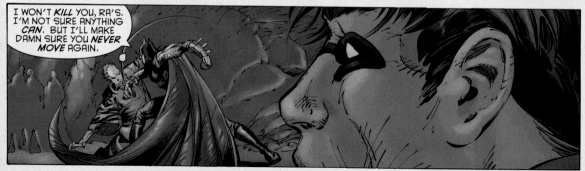

I WON'T KILL YOU, RA'S. I'M NOT SURE ANYTHING CAN. BUT I'LL MAKE DAMN SURE YOU NEVER MOVE AGAIN.

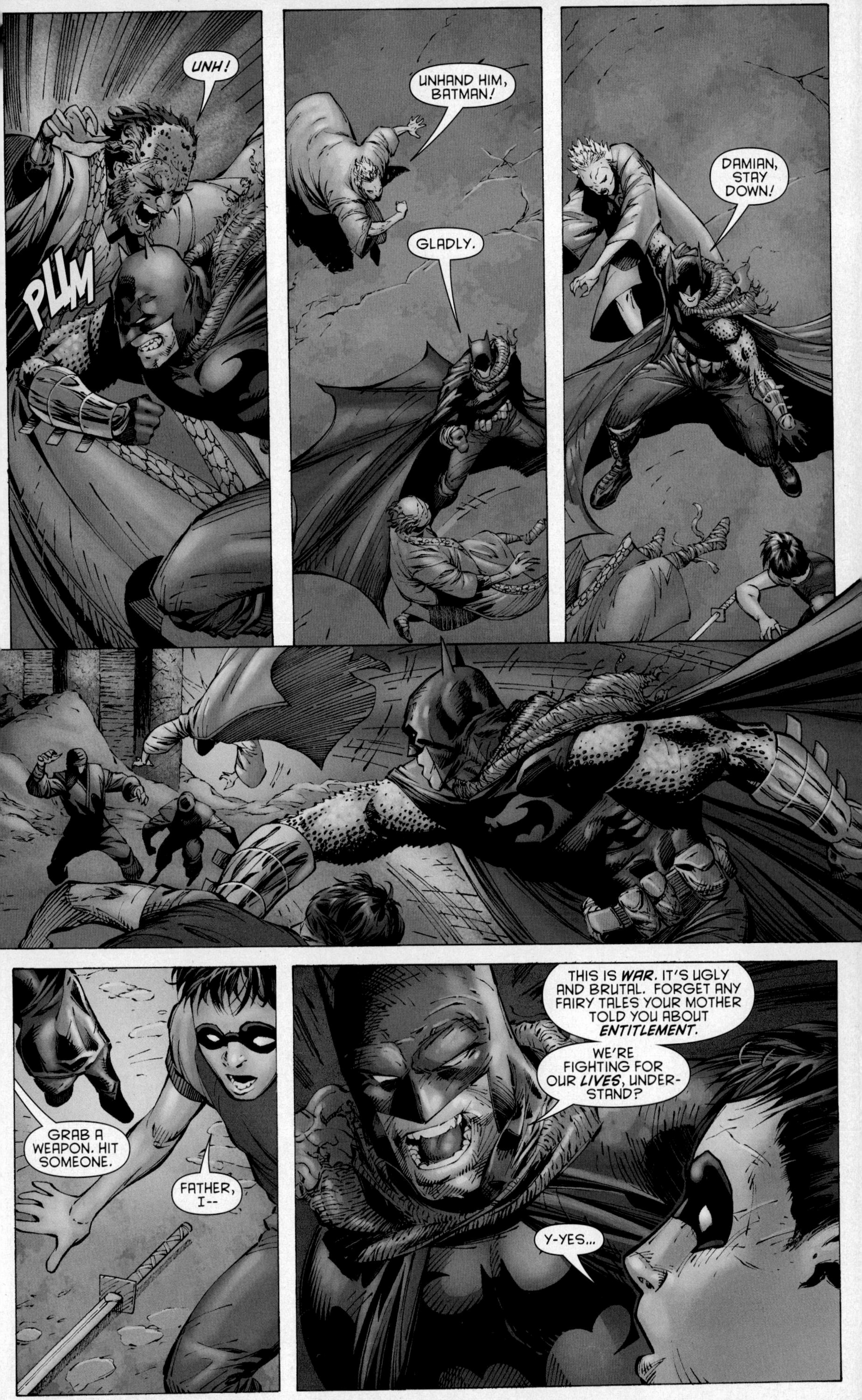
UNH!
PUM
UNHAND HIM, BATMAN!
GLADLY.
DAMIAN, STAY DOWN!
GRAB A WEAPON. HIT SOMEONE.
FATHER, I--
THIS IS WAR. IT'S UGLY AND BRUTAL. FORGET ANY FAIRY TALES YOUR MOTHER TOLD YOU ABOUT ENTITLEMENT.
WE'RE FIGHTING FOR OUR LIVES, UNDER-STAND?
Y-YES...

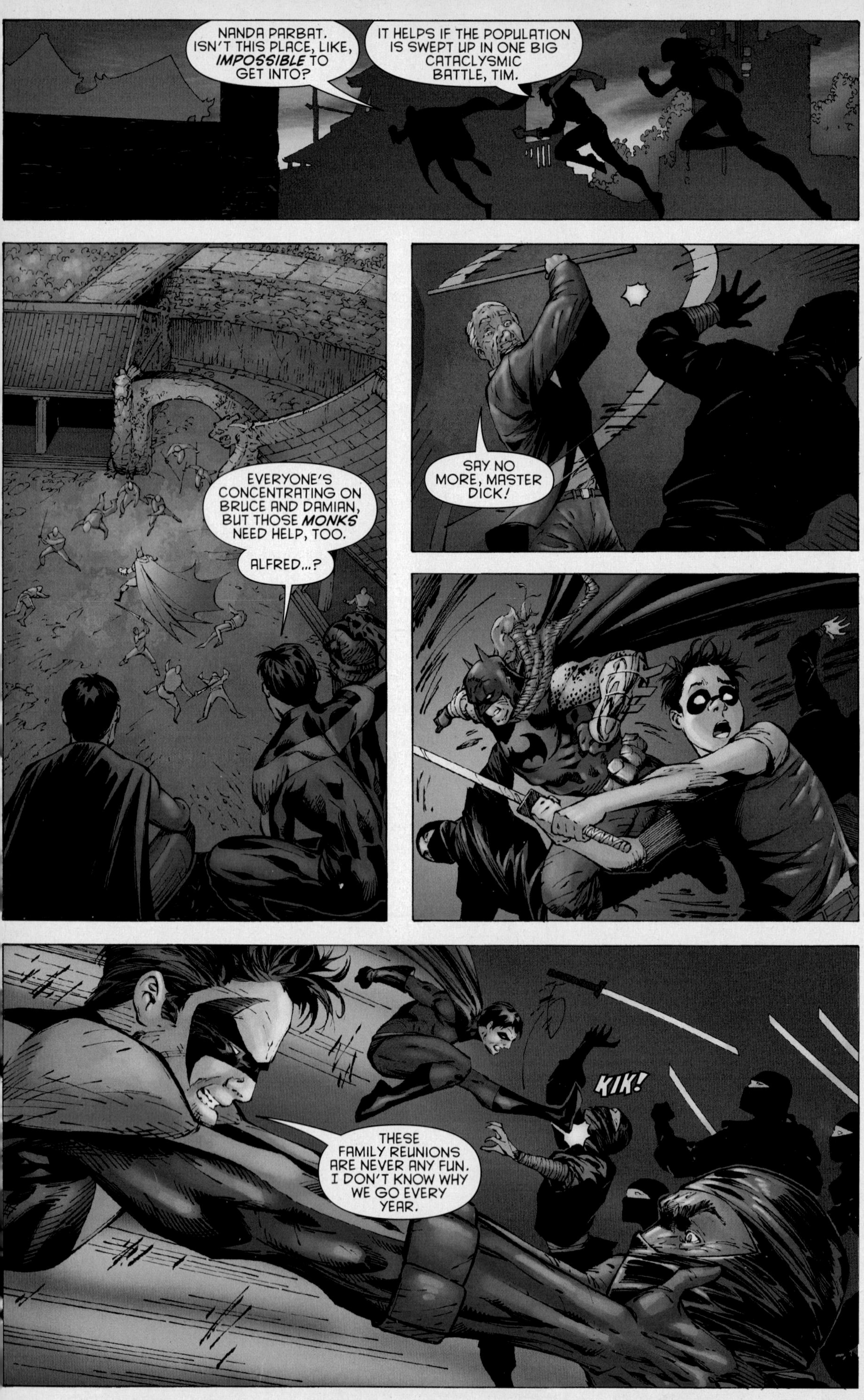
NANDA PARBAT. ISN'T THIS PLACE, LIKE, ***IMPOSSIBLE*** TO GET INTO?
IT HELPS IF THE POPULATION IS SWEPT UP IN ONE BIG CATACLYSMIC BATTLE, TIM.
EVERYONE'S CONCENTRATING ON BRUCE AND DAMIAN, BUT THOSE ***MONKS*** NEED HELP, TOO.
ALFRED...?
SAY NO MORE, MASTER DICK!
KIK!
THESE FAMILY REUNIONS ARE NEVER ANY FUN. I DON'T KNOW WHY WE GO EVERY YEAR.

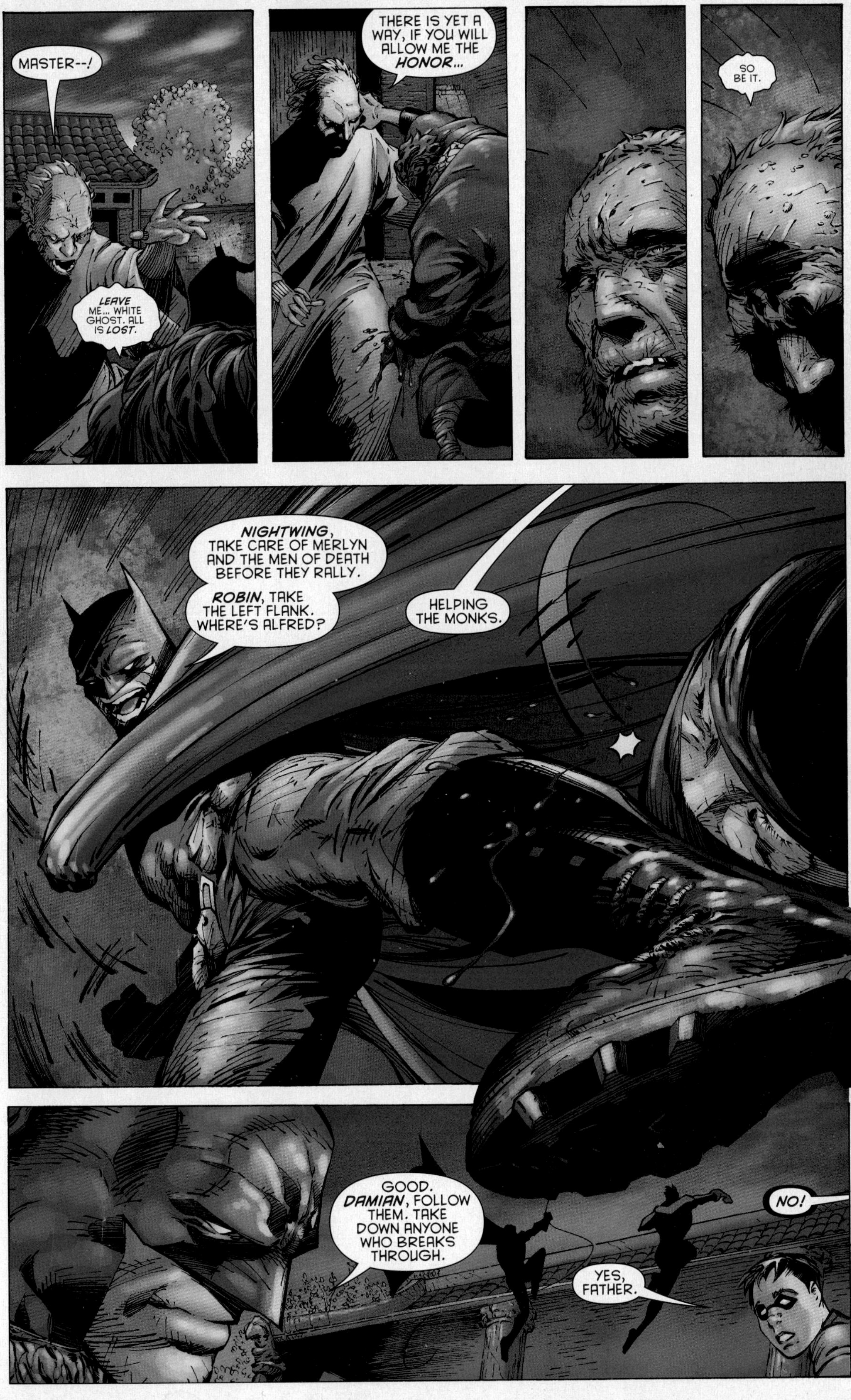
MASTER--!
LEAVE ME... WHITE GHOST. ALL IS LOST.
THERE IS YET A WAY, IF YOU WILL ALLOW ME THE HONOR...
SO BE IT.
NIGHTWING, TAKE CARE OF MERLYN AND THE MEN OF DEATH BEFORE THEY RALLY.
ROBIN, TAKE THE LEFT FLANK. WHERE'S ALFRED?
HELPING THE MONKS.
GOOD. DAMIAN, FOLLOW THEM. TAKE DOWN ANYONE WHO BREAKS THROUGH.
NO!
YES, FATHER.

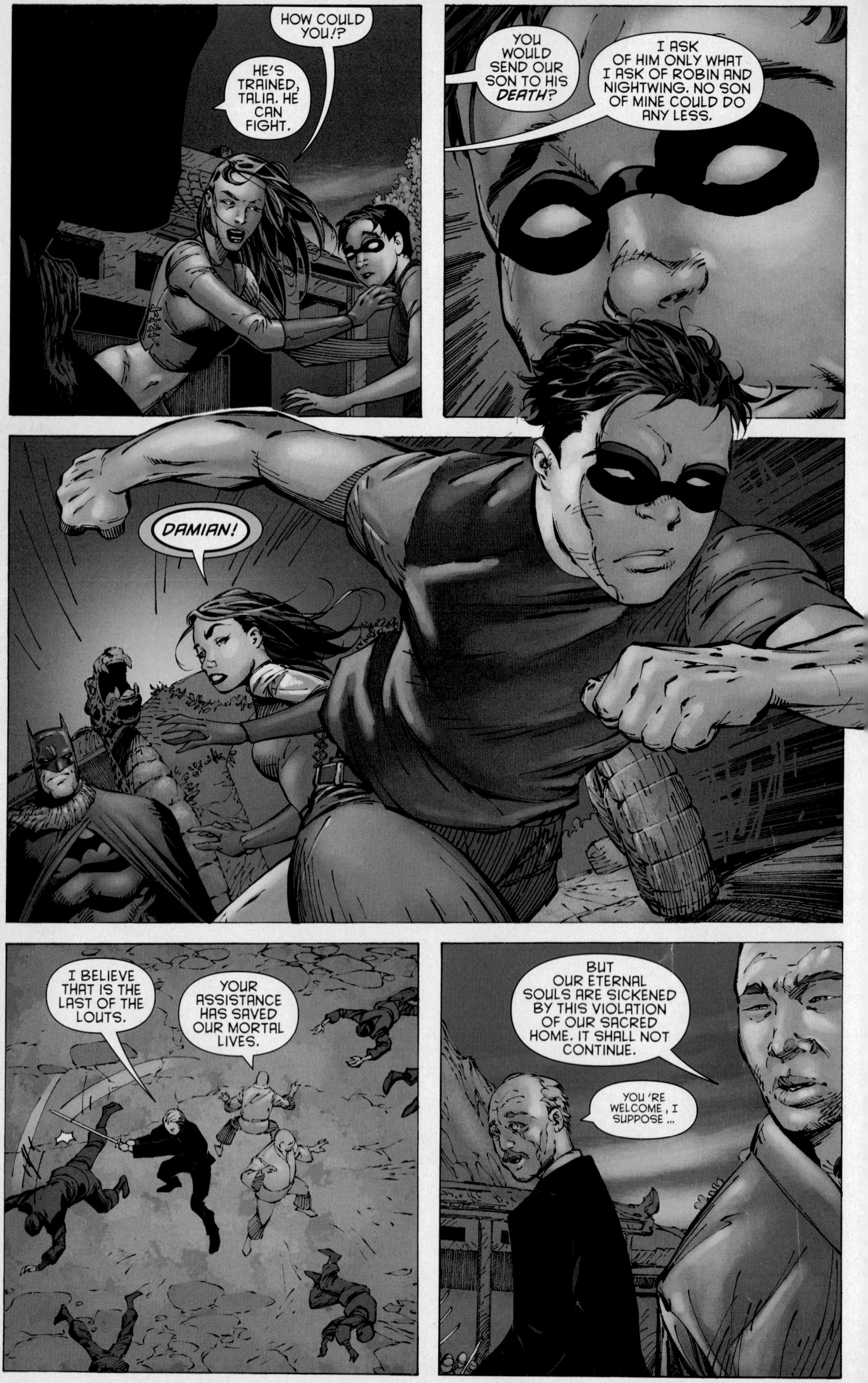
HOW COULD YOU!?
HE'S TRAINED, TALIA. HE CAN FIGHT.
YOU WOULD SEND OUR SON TO HIS DEATH?
I ASK OF HIM ONLY WHAT I ASK OF ROBIN AND NIGHTWING. NO SON OF MINE COULD DO ANY LESS.
DAMIAN!
I BELIEVE THAT IS THE LAST OF THE LOUTS.
YOUR ASSISTANCE HAS SAVED OUR MORTAL LIVES.
BUT OUR ETERNAL SOULS ARE SICKENED BY THIS VIOLATION OF OUR SACRED HOME. IT SHALL NOT CONTINUE.
YOU'RE WELCOME, I SUPPOSE...

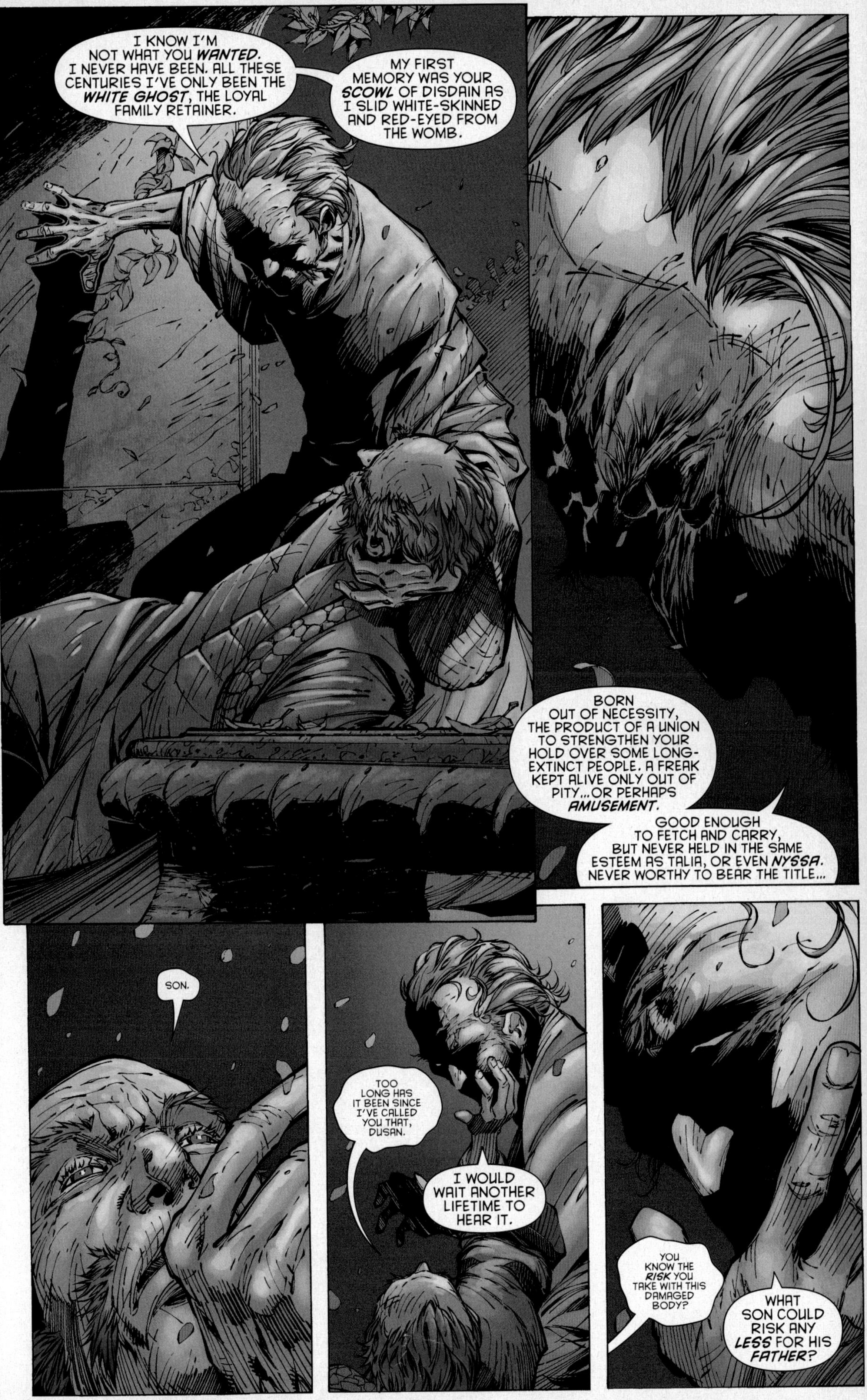
I KNOW I'M NOT WHAT YOU WANTED. I NEVER HAVE BEEN. ALL THESE CENTURIES I'VE ONLY BEEN THE WHITE GHOST, THE LOYAL FAMILY RETAINER.
MY FIRST MEMORY WAS YOUR SCOWL OF DISDAIN AS I SLID WHITE-SKINNED AND RED-EYED FROM THE WOMB.
BORN OUT OF NECESSITY, THE PRODUCT OF A UNION TO STRENGTHEN YOUR HOLD OVER SOME LONG-EXTINCT PEOPLE. A FREAK KEPT ALIVE ONLY OUT OF PITY...OR PERHAPS AMUSEMENT.
GOOD ENOUGH TO FETCH AND CARRY, BUT NEVER HELD IN THE SAME ESTEEM AS TALIA, OR EVEN NYSSA. NEVER WORTHY TO BEAR THE TITLE...
SON.
TOO LONG HAS IT BEEN SINCE I'VE CALLED YOU THAT, DUSAN.
I WOULD WAIT ANOTHER LIFETIME TO HEAR IT.
YOU KNOW THE RISK YOU TAKE WITH THIS DAMAGED BODY?
WHAT SON COULD RISK ANY LESS FOR HIS FATHER?

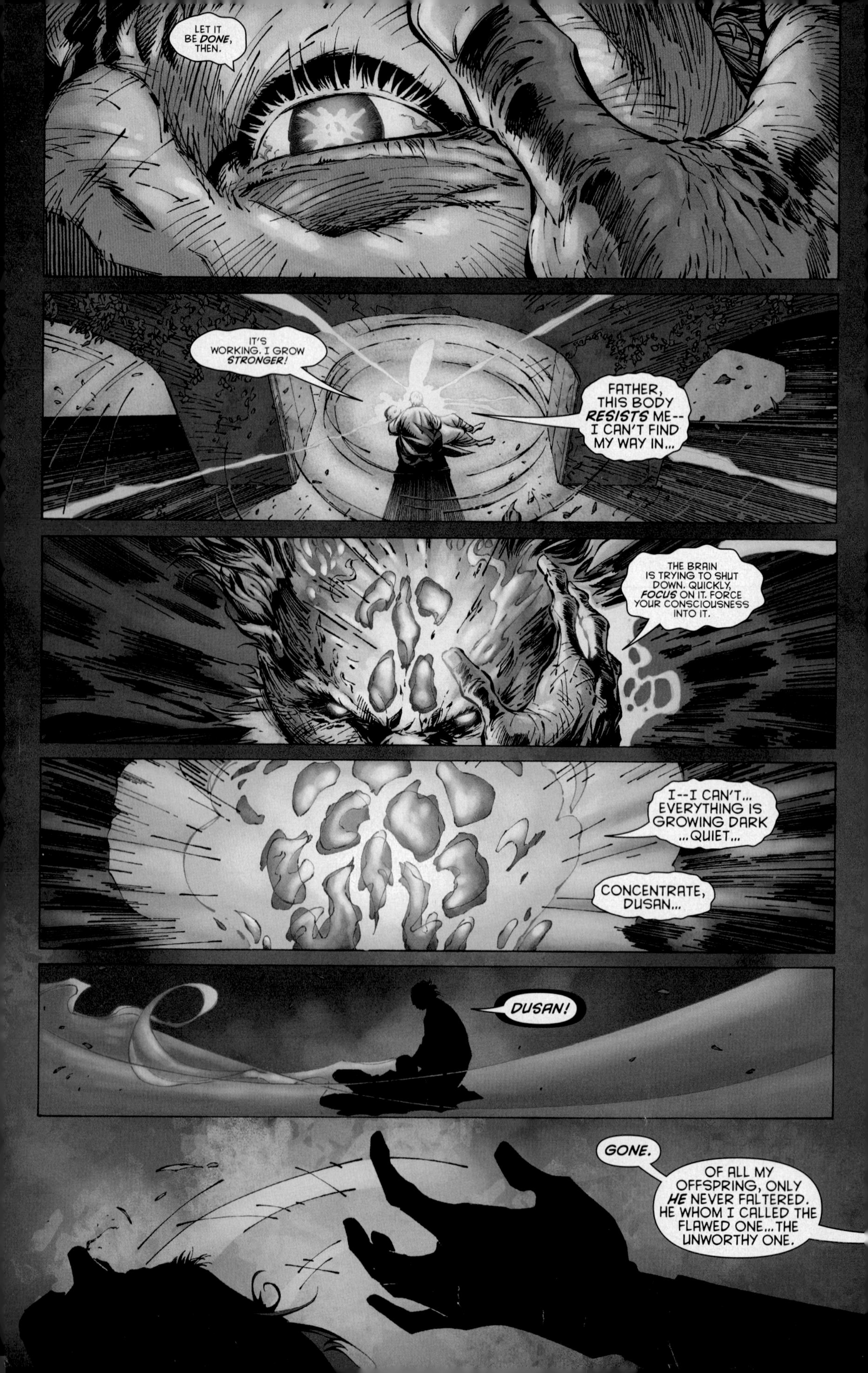
LET IT BE *DONE*, THEN.
IT'S WORKING. I GROW *STRONGER!*
FATHER, THIS BODY *RESISTS* ME-- I CAN'T FIND MY WAY IN...
THE BRAIN IS TRYING TO SHUT DOWN. QUICKLY, *FOCUS* ON IT. FORCE YOUR CONSCIOUSNESS INTO IT.
I--I CAN'T... EVERYTHING IS GROWING DARK ...QUIET...
CONCENTRATE, DUSAN...
DUSAN!
GONE.
OF ALL MY OFFSPRING, ONLY *HE* NEVER FALTERED. HE WHOM I CALLED THE FLAWED ONE... THE UNWORTHY ONE.

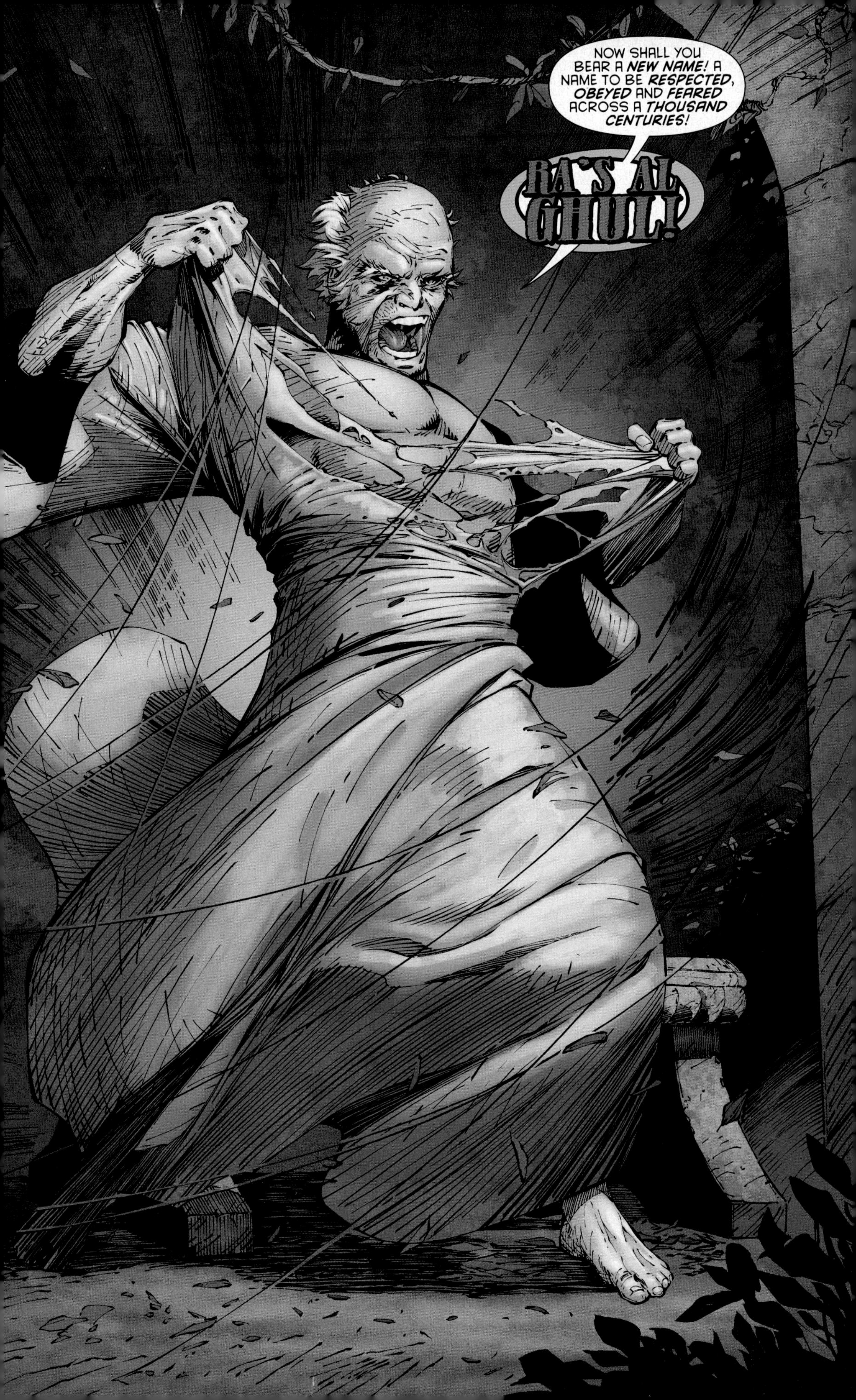
NOW SHALL YOU BEAR A *NEW NAME!* A NAME TO BE *RESPECTED, OBEYED* AND *FEARED* ACROSS A *THOUSAND CENTURIES!*
RA'S AL GHUL!

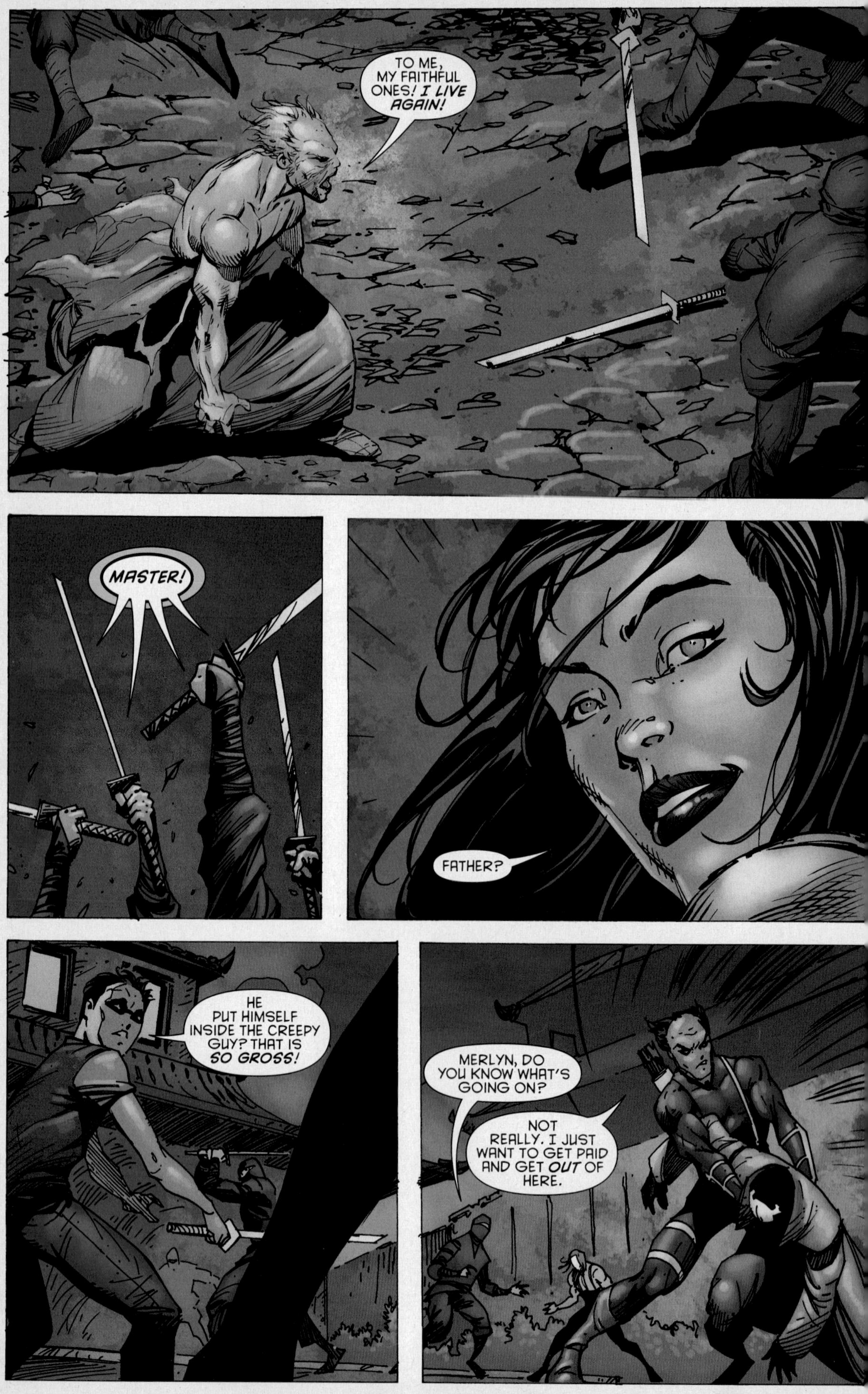
TO ME, MY FAITHFUL ONES! I LIVE AGAIN!
MASTER!
FATHER?
HE PUT HIMSELF INSIDE THE CREEPY GUY? THAT IS SO GROSS!
MERLYN, DO YOU KNOW WHAT'S GOING ON?
NOT REALLY. I JUST WANT TO GET PAID AND GET OUT OF HERE.

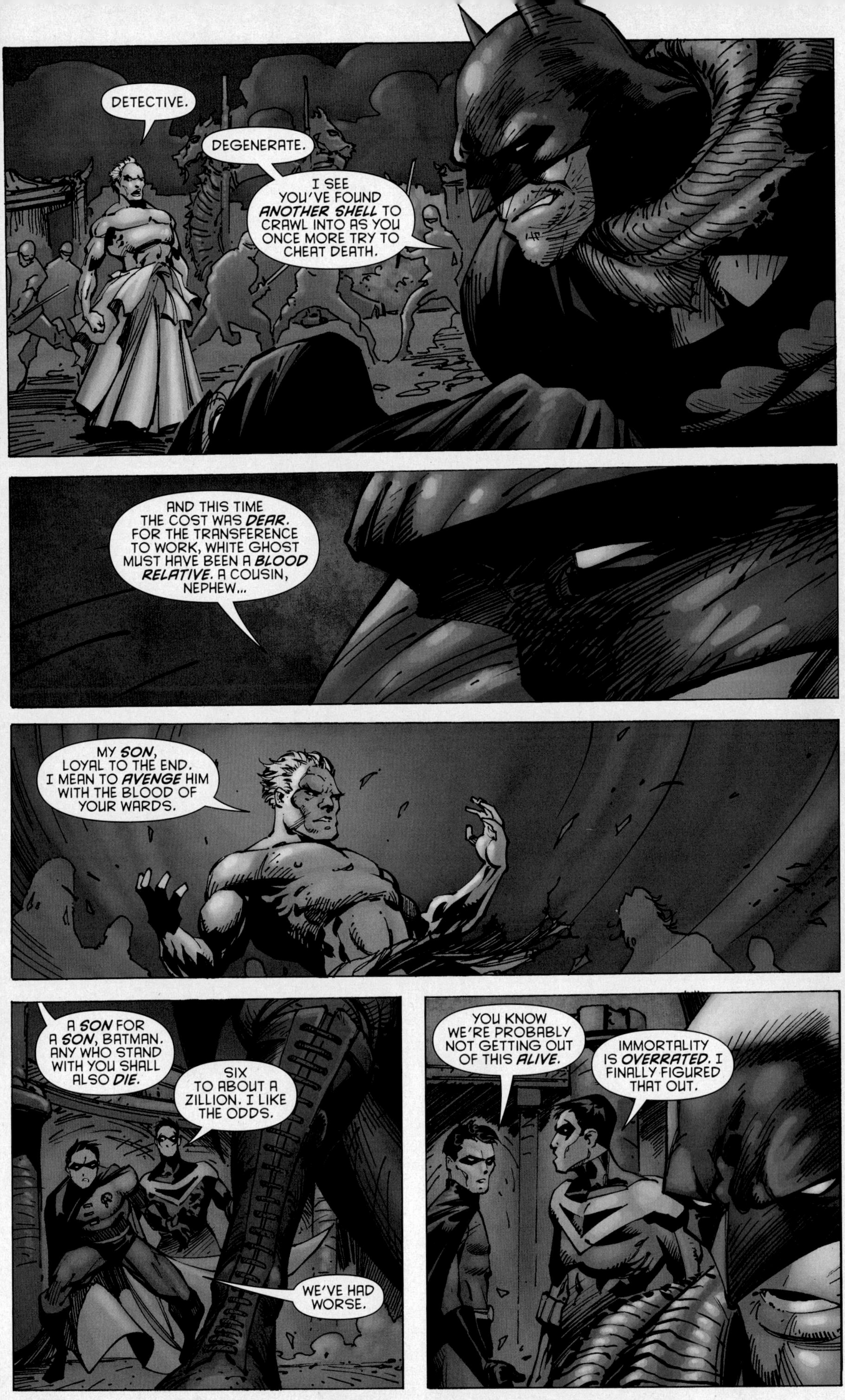
DETECTIVE.
DEGENERATE.
I SEE YOU'VE FOUND ANOTHER SHELL TO CRAWL INTO AS YOU ONCE MORE TRY TO CHEAT DEATH.
AND THIS TIME THE COST WAS DEAR. FOR THE TRANSFERENCE TO WORK, WHITE GHOST MUST HAVE BEEN A BLOOD RELATIVE. A COUSIN, NEPHEW...
MY SON, LOYAL TO THE END. I MEAN TO AVENGE HIM WITH THE BLOOD OF YOUR WARDS.
A SON FOR A SON, BATMAN. ANY WHO STAND WITH YOU SHALL ALSO DIE.
SIX TO ABOUT A ZILLION. I LIKE THE ODDS.
WE'VE HAD WORSE.
YOU KNOW WE'RE PROBABLY NOT GETTING OUT OF THIS ALIVE.
IMMORTALITY IS OVERRATED. I FINALLY FIGURED THAT OUT.

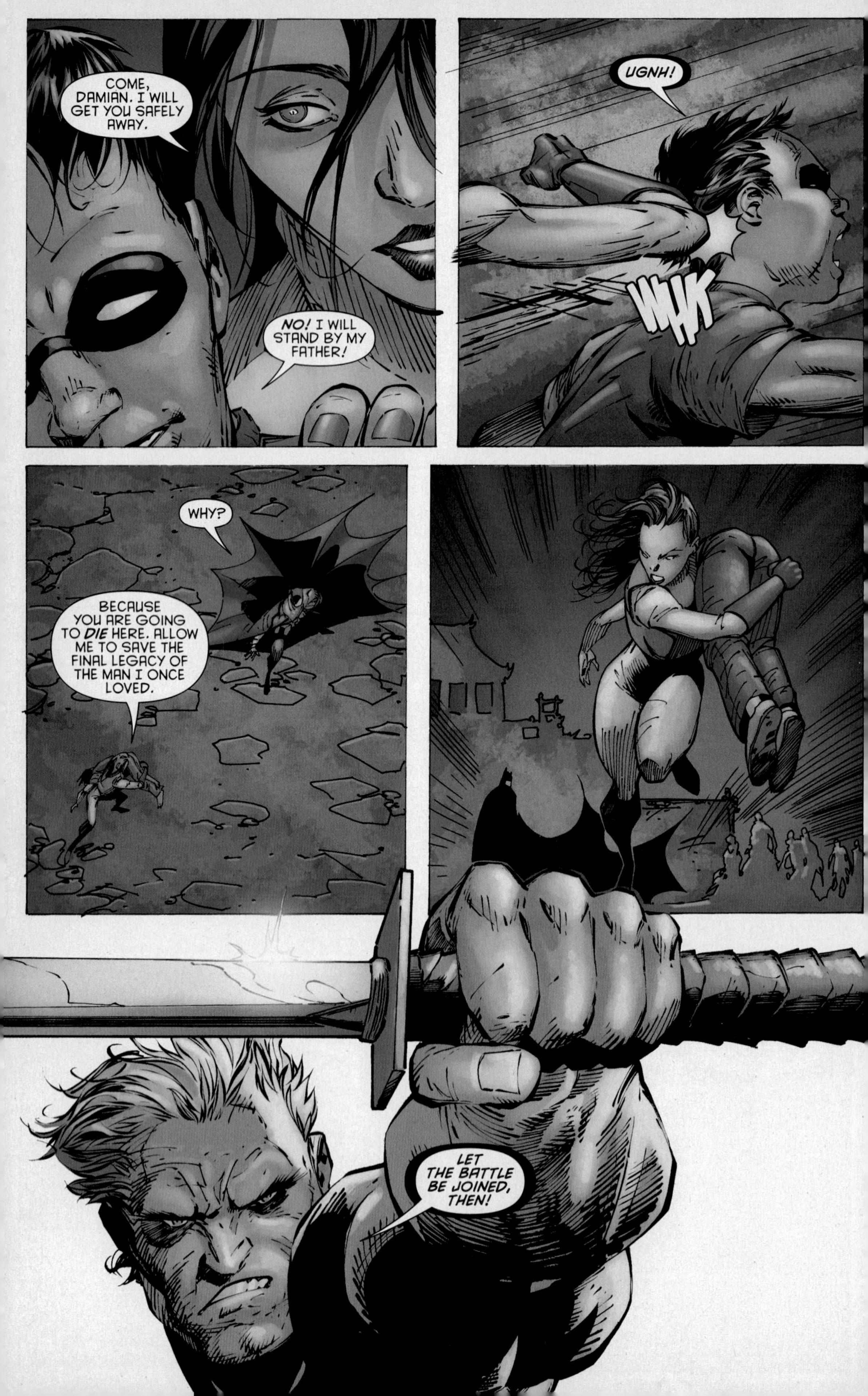
COME, DAMIAN. I WILL GET YOU SAFELY AWAY.
NO! I WILL STAND BY MY FATHER!
UGNH!
WHK
WHY?
BECAUSE YOU ARE GOING TO DIE HERE. ALLOW ME TO SAVE THE FINAL LEGACY OF THE MAN I ONCE LOVED.
LET THE BATTLE BE JOINED, THEN!

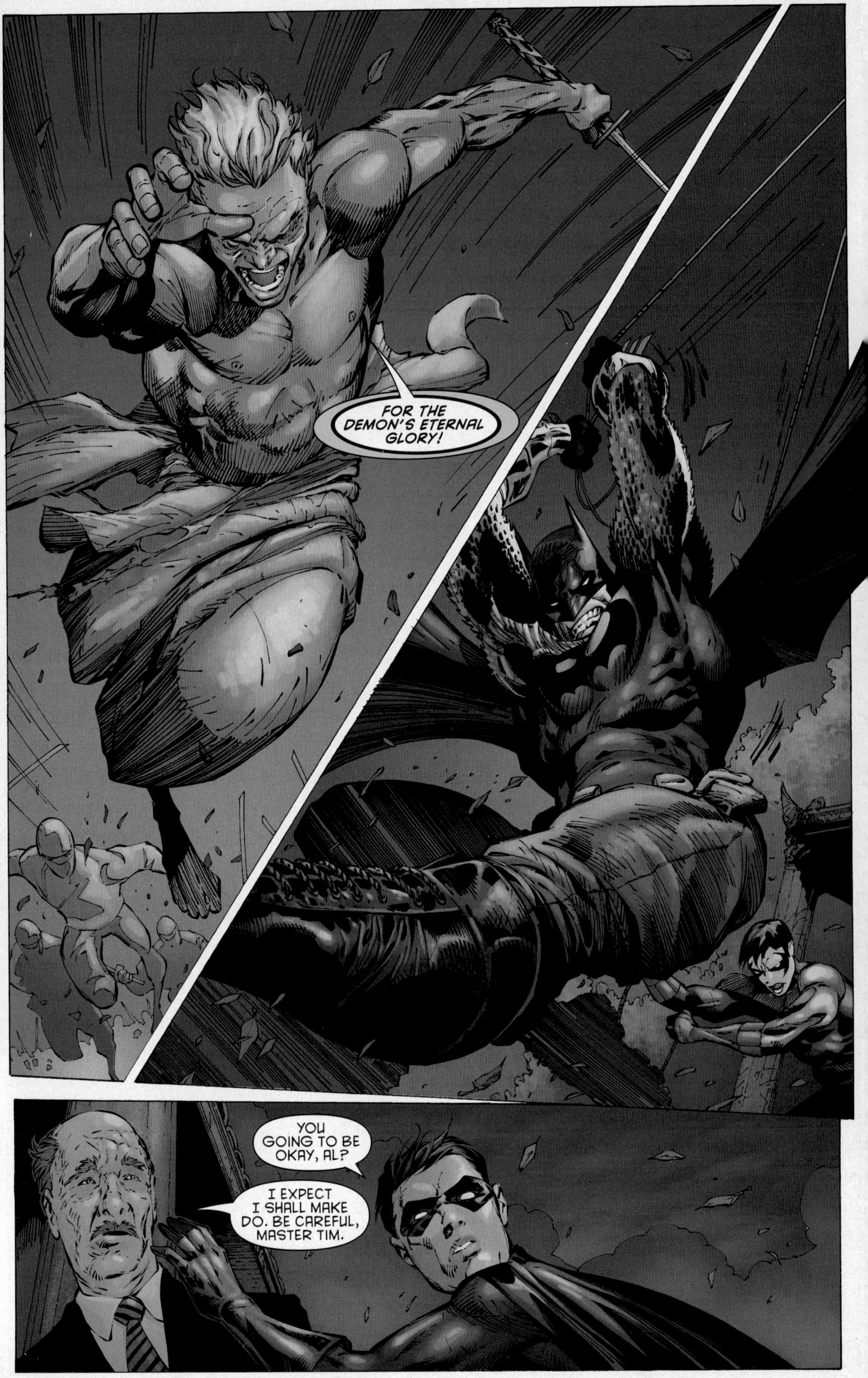
FOR THE DEMON'S ETERNAL GLORY!
YOU GOING TO BE OKAY, AL?
I EXPECT I SHALL MAKE DO. BE CAREFUL, MASTER TIM.

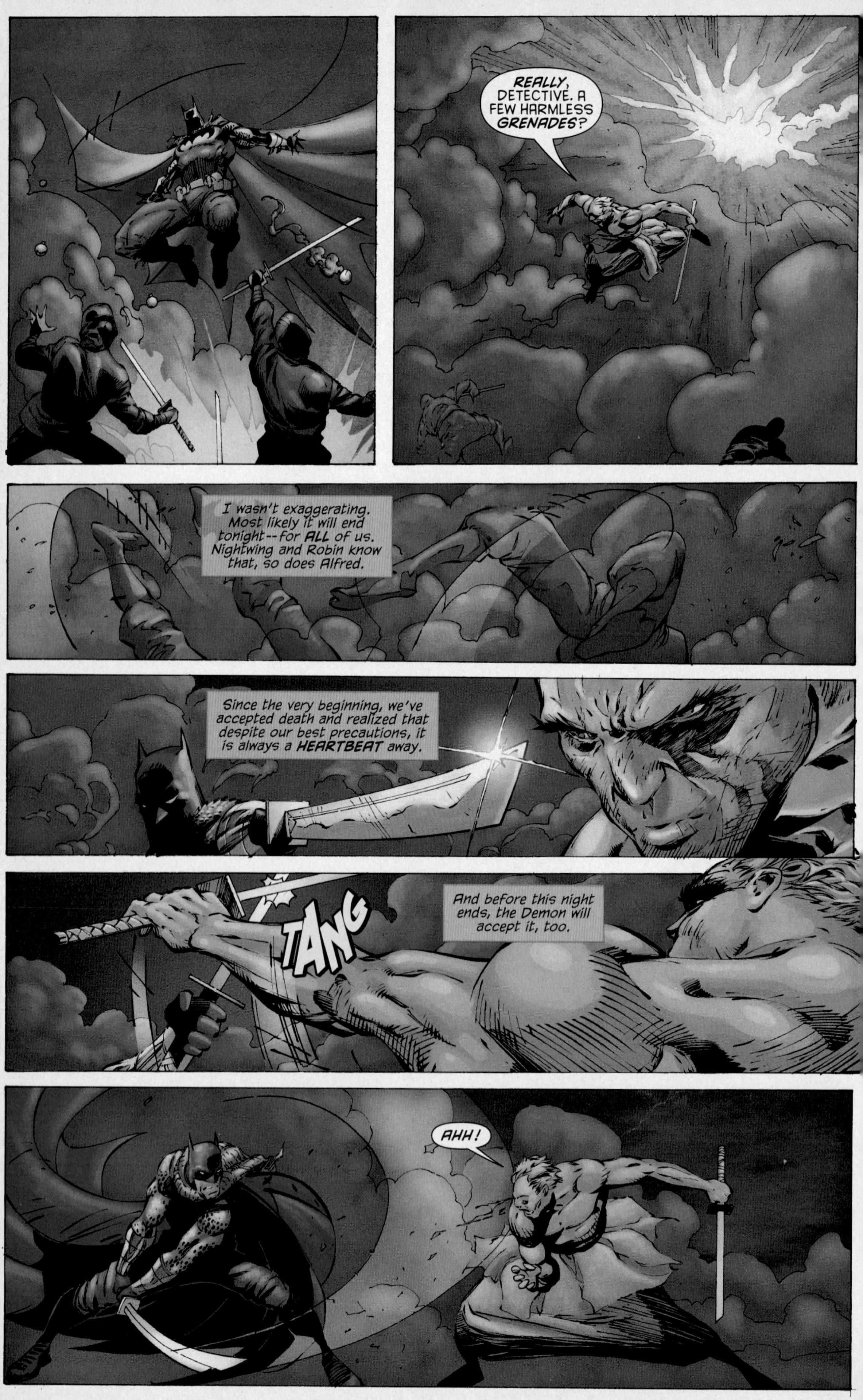
REALLY, DETECTIVE. A FEW HARMLESS GRENADES?
I wasn't exaggerating. Most likely it will end tonight--for ALL of us. Nightwing and Robin know that, so does Alfred.
Since the very beginning, we've accepted death and realized that despite our best precautions, it is always a HEARTBEAT away.
TANG
And before this night ends, the Demon will accept it, too.
AHH!

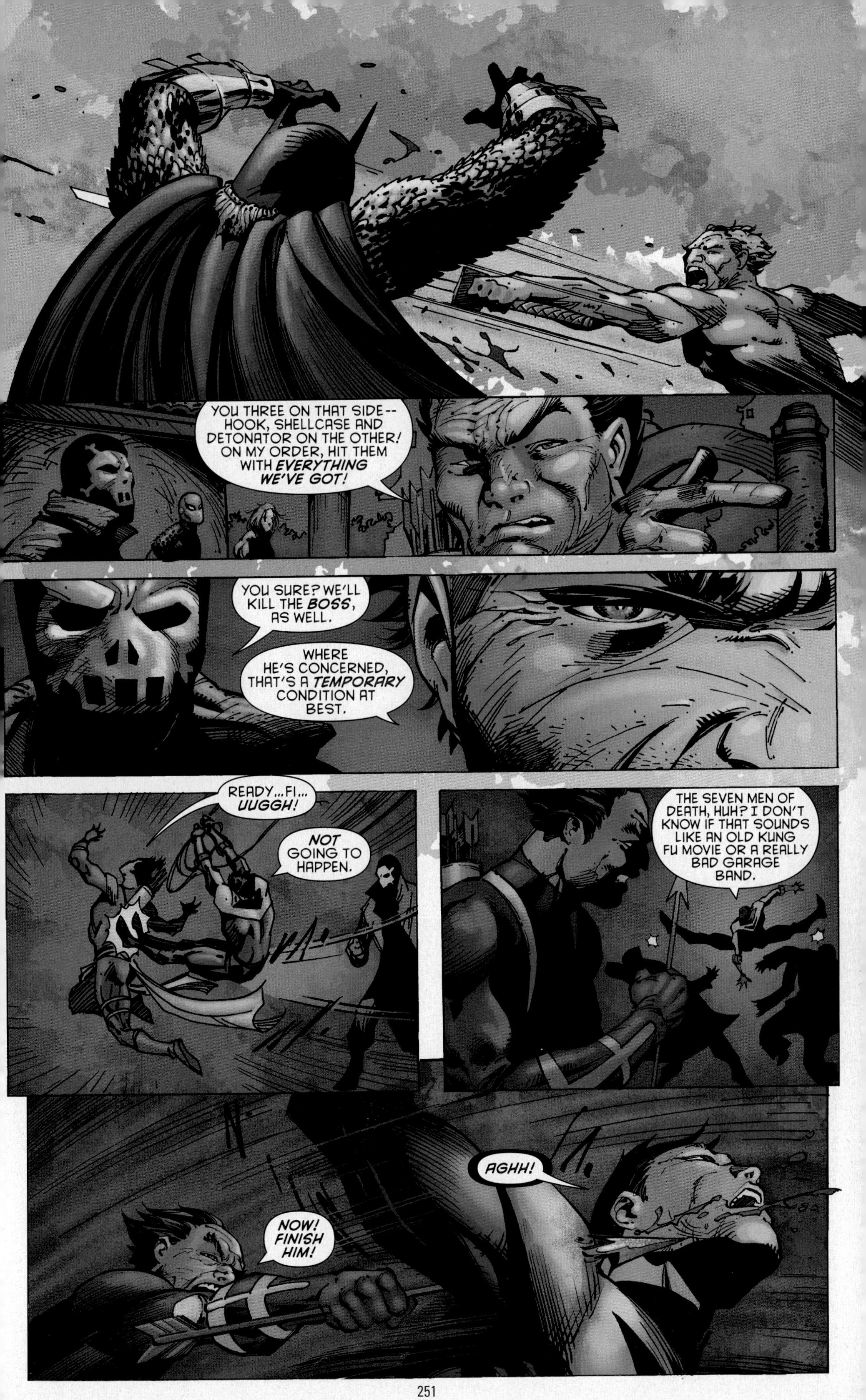
YOU THREE ON THAT SIDE--HOOK, SHELLCASE AND DETONATOR ON THE OTHER! ON MY ORDER, HIT THEM WITH EVERYTHING WE'VE GOT!
YOU SURE? WE'LL KILL THE BOSS, AS WELL.
WHERE HE'S CONCERNED, THAT'S A TEMPORARY CONDITION AT BEST.
READY...FI... UUGGH!
NOT GOING TO HAPPEN.
THE SEVEN MEN OF DEATH, HUH? I DON'T KNOW IF THAT SOUNDS LIKE AN OLD KUNG FU MOVIE OR A REALLY BAD GARAGE BAND.
AGHH!
NOW! FINISH HIM!

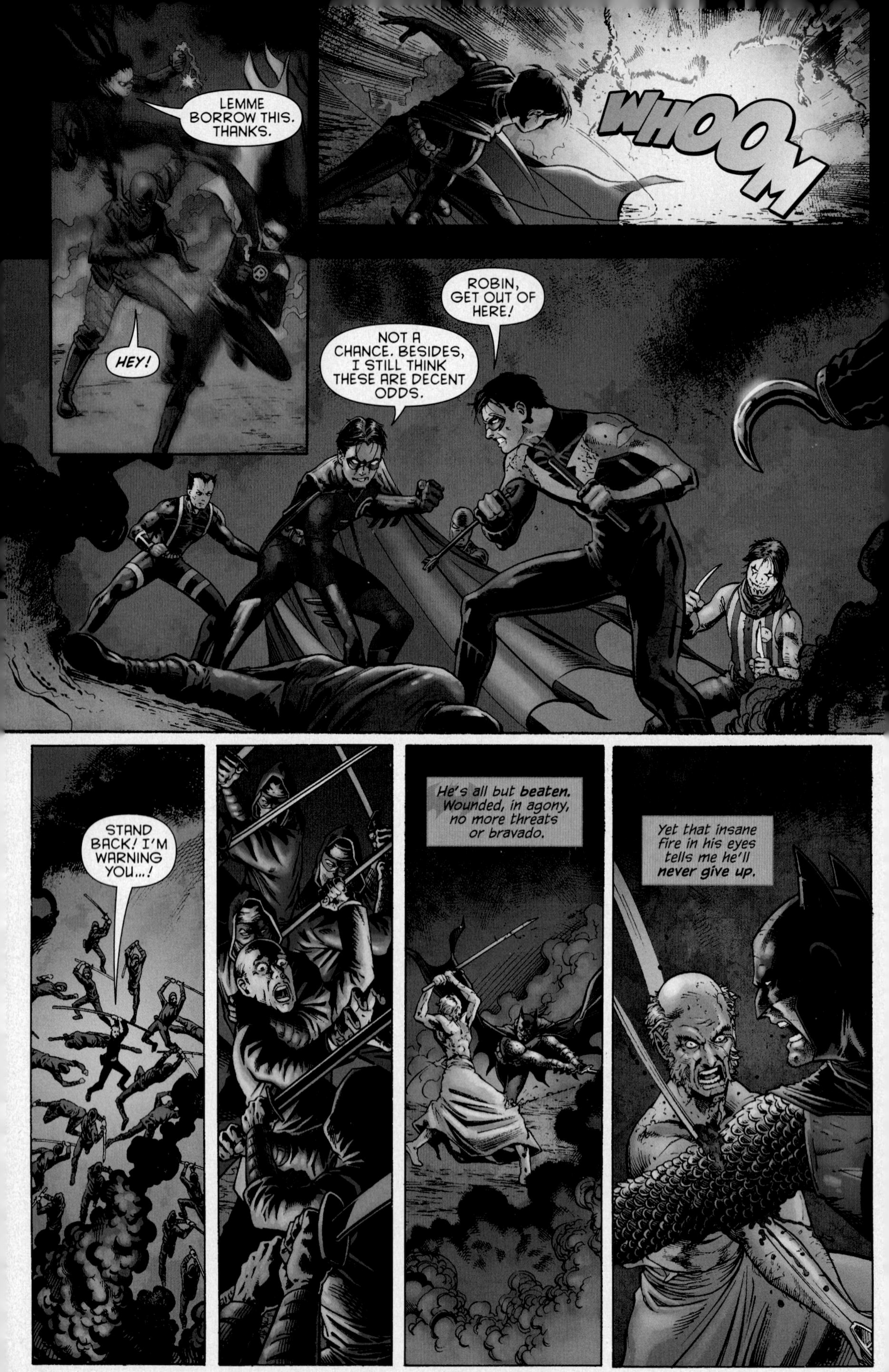
LEMME BORROW THIS. THANKS.
WHOOOM
HEY!
ROBIN, GET OUT OF HERE!
NOT A CHANCE. BESIDES, I STILL THINK THESE ARE DECENT ODDS.
STAND BACK! I'M WARNING YOU...!
He's all but beaten. Wounded, in agony, no more threats or bravado.
Yet that insane fire in his eyes tells me he'll never give up.

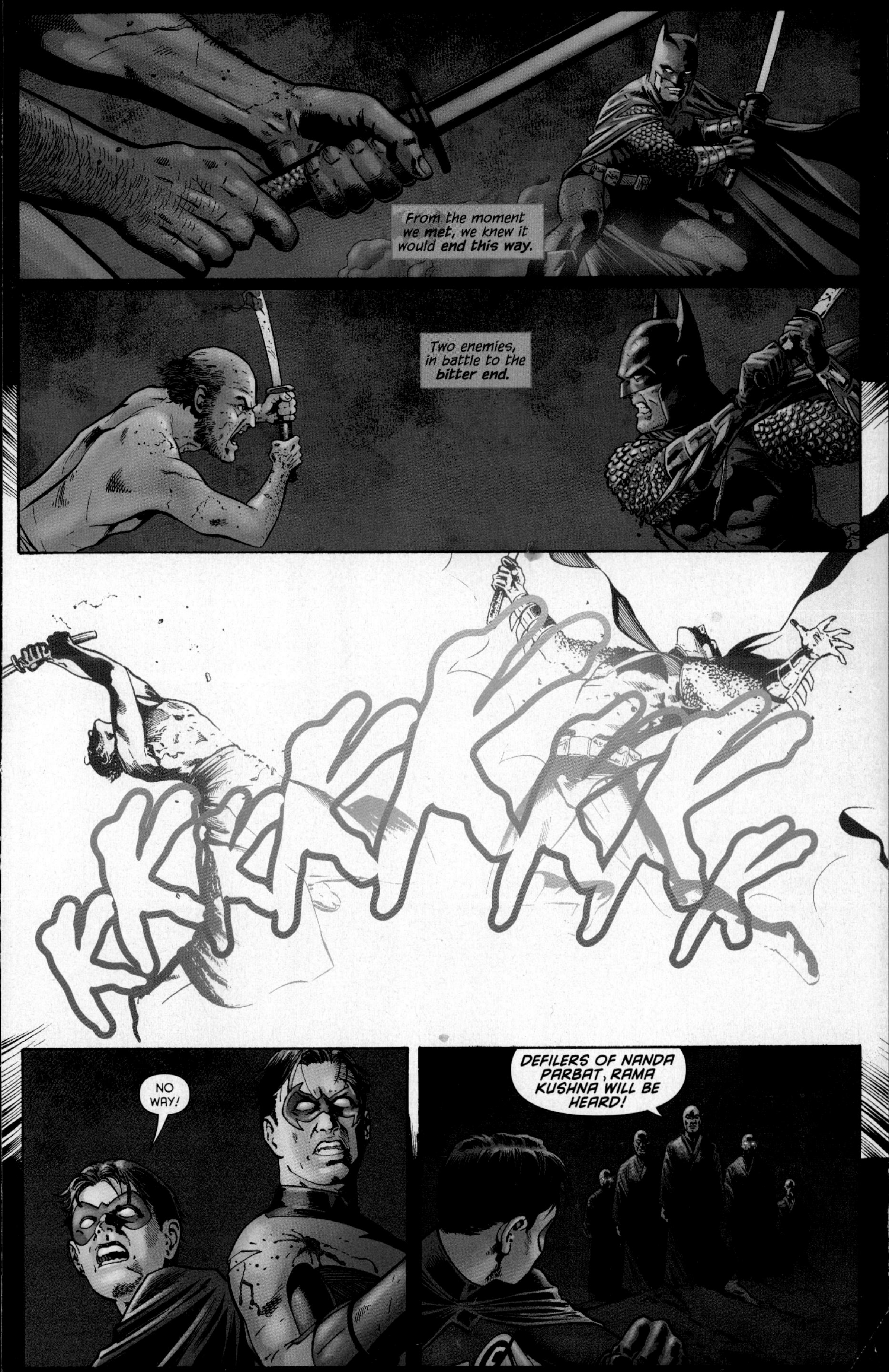
From the moment we met, we knew it would end this way.
Two enemies, in battle to the bitter end.
KKRAANNKK
NO WAY!
DEFILERS OF NANDA PARBAT, RAMA KUSHNA WILL BE HEARD!

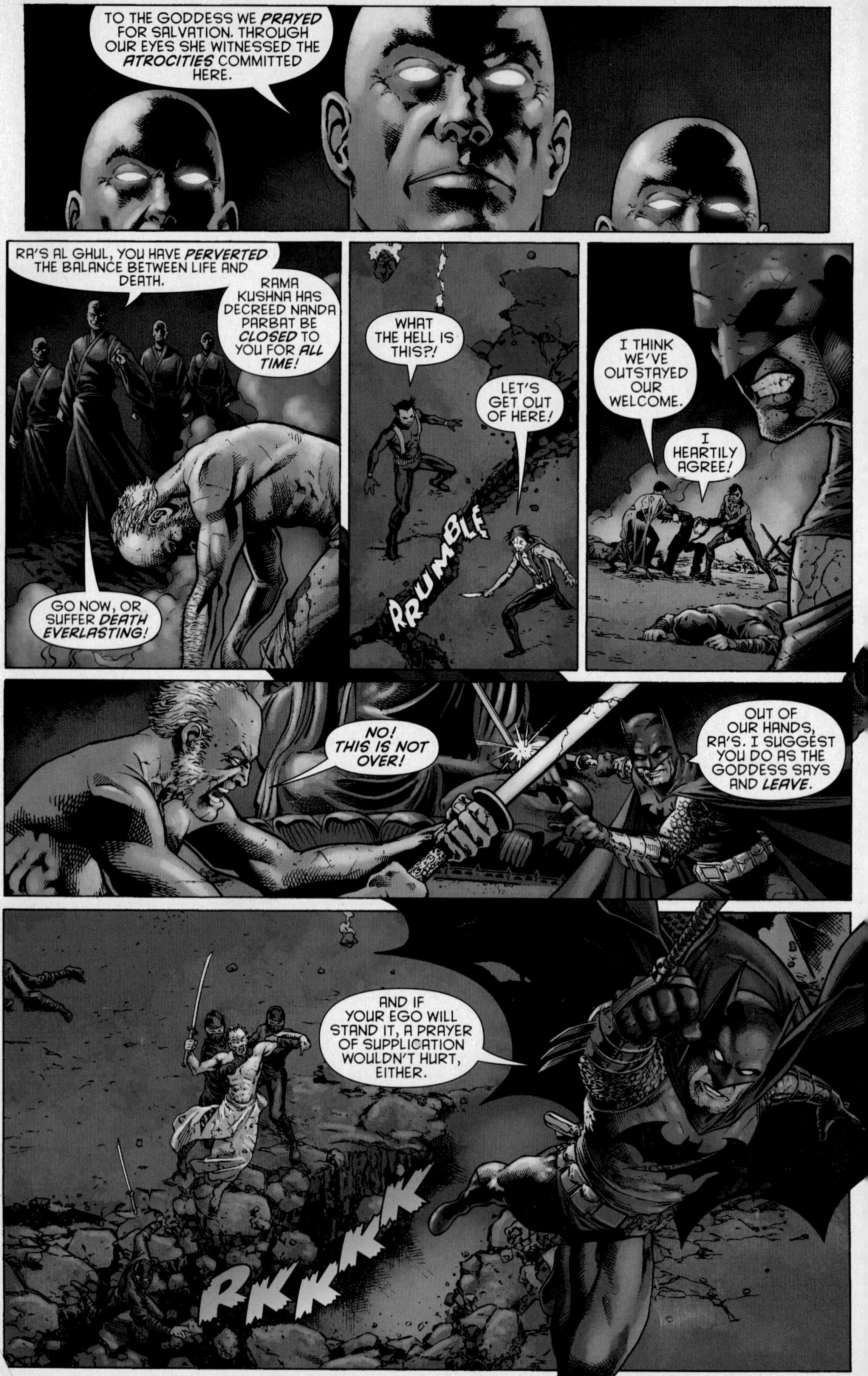
TO THE GODDESS WE PRAYED FOR SALVATION. THROUGH OUR EYES SHE WITNESSED THE ATROCITIES COMMITTED HERE.
RA'S AL GHUL, YOU HAVE PERVERTED THE BALANCE BETWEEN LIFE AND DEATH.
RAMA KUSHNA HAS DECREED NANDA PARBAT BE CLOSED TO YOU FOR ALL TIME!
GO NOW, OR SUFFER DEATH EVERLASTING!
WHAT THE HELL IS THIS?!
LET'S GET OUT OF HERE!
RRUMBLE
I THINK WE'VE OUTSTAYED OUR WELCOME.
I HEARTILY AGREE!
NO! THIS IS NOT OVER!
OUT OF OUR HANDS, RA'S. I SUGGEST YOU DO AS THE GODDESS SAYS AND LEAVE.
AND IF YOUR EGO WILL STAND IT, A PRAYER OF SUPPLICATION WOULDN'T HURT, EITHER.
RKKKK

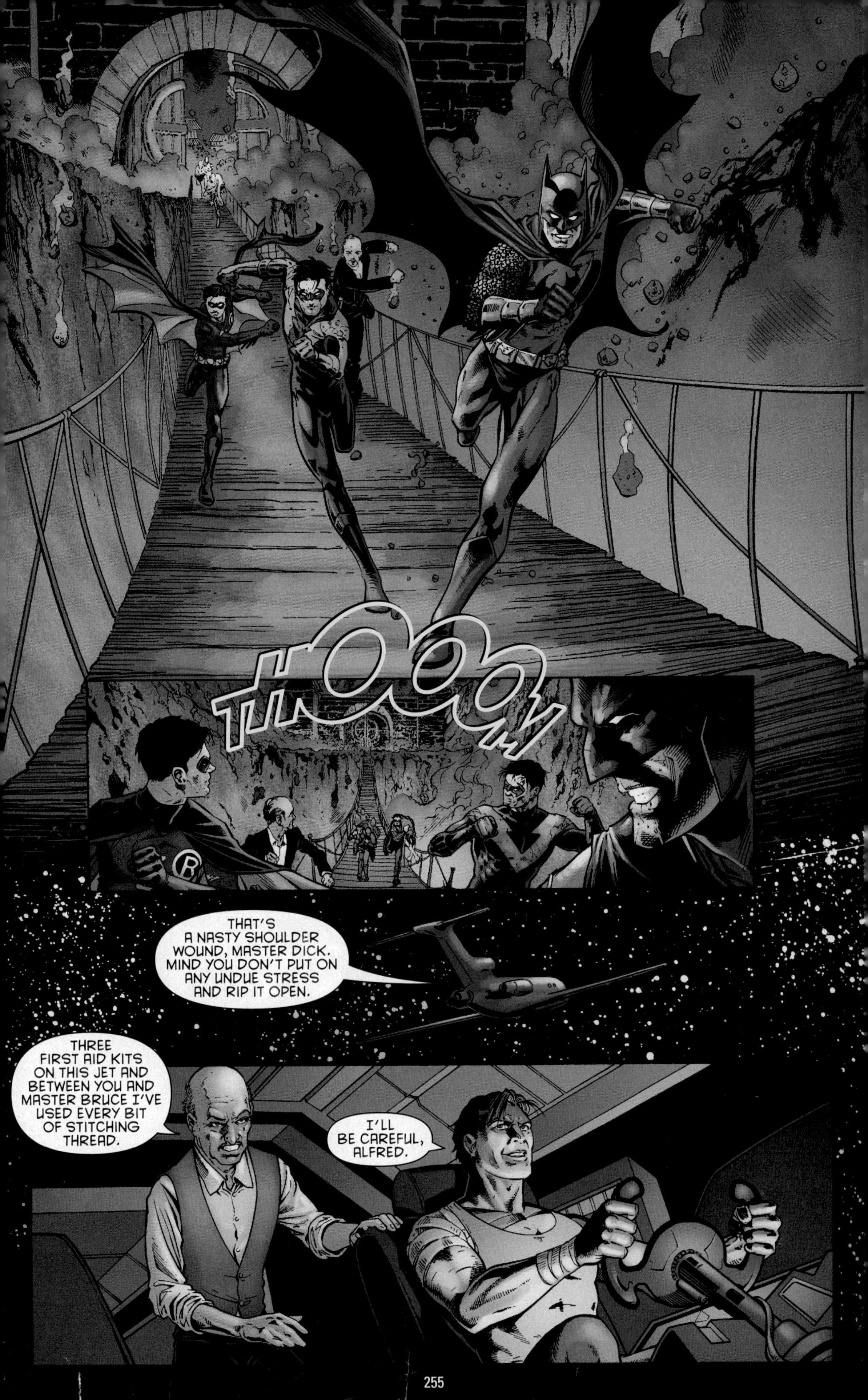
THOOOM
THAT'S A NASTY SHOULDER WOUND, MASTER DICK. MIND YOU DON'T PUT ON ANY UNDUE STRESS AND RIP IT OPEN.
THREE FIRST AID KITS ON THIS JET AND BETWEEN YOU AND MASTER BRUCE I'VE USED EVERY BIT OF STITCHING THREAD.
I'LL BE CAREFUL, ALFRED.

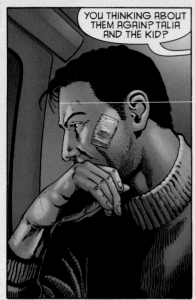

YOU THINKING ABOUT THEM AGAIN? TALIA AND THE KID?

I WAS HOPING THEY'RE SAFE. AND HOPING TALIA TAKES HIM SOMEPLACE FAR AWAY FROM THE LIFE THEY'VE KNOWN.

EVEN IF THAT LIFE DOESN'T INCLUDE *YOU*?

IF DAMIAN WANTS THAT LIFE, HE'LL CHOOSE IT... JUST AS YOU AND DICK DID.

FOR NOW HE DESERVES A LIFE *FREE* FROM DESTINY... MINE OR ANYONE ELSE'S.

A VERY NICE SENTIMENT, MASTER BRUCE, AND MOST APPROPRIATE FOR THE SEASON.

THE SEASON, ALFRED?

IT'S *CHRISTMAS*, SIR. DON'T TELL ME YOU HAD FORGOTTEN?

WELL, BETTER LATE THAN NEVER, I SUPPOSE.

TO *FAMILY*.

FAMILY, SIR.

THE END